E V E R Y M A N, I will go with thee,

and be thy guide,

In thy most need to go by thy side

EDWARD GIBBON

Born on 27 April 1737 at Putney. Educated at Westminster School, Oxford, and privately at Lausanne. Toured Italy, 1764–5, and conceived the plan of his 'History'. Settled in London in 1772 and sat in Parliament from 1774 to 1783. Lived in Luasanne, 1784–93, and died in London on 16 January 1794.

EDWARD GIBBON

Decline and Fall of the Roman Empire

IN SIX VOLUMES   VOLUME FIVE

Introduction by
Christopher Dawson

Dent: London and Melbourne
EVERYMAN'S LIBRARY

This edition was first published in
Everyman's Library 1910
Last reprinted 1987

No. 475 Hardback ISBN 0 460 00475 1

CONTENTS

THE

HISTORY OF THE DECLINE AND FALL

OF THE

ROMAN EMPIRE

CHAPTER XLVII

Theological History of the Doctrine of the Incarnation—The Human and Divine Nature of Christ—Enmity of the Patriarchs of Alexandria and Constantinople—St. Cyril and Nestorius—Third General Council of Ephesus—Heresy of Eutyches—Fourth General Council of Chalcedon—Civil and Ecclesiastical Discord—Intolerance of Justinian —The Three Chapters—The Monothelite Controversy—State of the Oriental Sects—I. The Nestorians—II. The Jacobites—III. The Maronites—IV. The Armenians—V. The Copts and Abyssinians

AFTER the extinction of paganism, the Christians in peace and piety might have enjoyed their solitary triumph. But the principle of discord was alive in their bosom, and they were more solicitous to explore the nature, than to practise the laws, of their founder. I have already observed that the disputes of the TRINITY were succeeded by those of the INCARNATION; alike scandalous to the church, alike pernicious to the state, still more minute in their origin, still more durable in their effects. It is my design to comprise in the present chapter a religious war of two hundred and fifty years, to represent the ecclesiastical and political schism of the Oriental sects, and to introduce their clamorous or sanguinary contests by a modest inquiry into the doctrines of the primitive church.[1]

[1] By what means shall I authenticate this previous inquiry, which I have studied to circumscribe and compress?—If I persist in supporting each fact or reflection by its proper and special evidence, every line would demand a string of testimonies, and every note would swell to a critical dissertation. But the numberless passages of antiquity which I have seen with my own eyes are compiled, digested, and illustrated by *Petavius* and *Le Clerc*, by *Beausobre* and *Mosheim*. I shall be content to fortify my narrative by the names and characters of these respectable guides; and in the contemplation of a minute or remote object, I am not ashamed to borrow the aid of the strongest glasses:—1. The *Dogmata Theologica* of Petavius are a work of incredible labour and compass; the volumes which relate solely to the Incarnation (two folios, fifth and sixth, of 837 pages)

I. A laudable regard for the honour of the first proselytes has countenanced the belief, the hope, the wish, that the Ebionites, or at least the Nazarenes, were distinguished only by their obstinate perseverance in the practice of the Mosaic rites. Their churches have disappeared, their books are obliterated: their obscure freedom might allow a latitude of faith, and the softness of their infant creed would be variously moulded by the zeal or prudence of three hundred years. Yet the most charitable criticism must refuse these sectaries any knowledge of the pure and proper divinity of Christ. Educated in the school of Jewish prophecy and prejudice, they had never been taught to elevate their hopes above a human and temporal Messiah.[1] If they had courage to hail their king when he appeared in a plebeian garb, their grosser apprehensions were incapable of discerning their God, who had studiously disguised his celestial character under the name and person of a mortal.[2] The familiar companions of

are divided into sixteen books—the first of history, the remainder of controversy and doctrine. The Jesuit's learning is copious and correct; his Latinity is pure, his method clear, his argument profound and well connected; but he is the slave of the fathers, the scourge of heretics, and the enemy of truth and candour, as often as *they* are inimical to the Catholic cause. 2. The Arminian Le Clerc, who has composed in a quarto volume (Amsterdam, 1716) the ecclesiastical history of the two first centuries, was free both in his temper and situation; his sense is clear, but his thoughts are narrow; he reduces the reason or folly of ages to the standard of his private judgment, and his impartiality is sometimes quickened, and sometimes tainted, by his opposition to the fathers. See the heretics (Cerinthians, lxxx.; Ebionites, ciii.; Carpocratians, cxx.; Valentinians, cxxi.; Basilidians, cxxiii.; Marcionites, cxli., etc.) under their proper dates. 3. The Histoire Critique du Manichéisme (Amsterdam, 1734, 1739, in two vols. in 4to, with a posthumous dissertation sur les Nazarènes, Lausanne, 1745) of M. de Beausobre, is a treasure of ancient philosophy and theology. The learned historian spins with incomparable art the systematic thread of opinion, and transforms himself by turns into the person of a saint, a sage, or an heretic. Yet his refinement is sometimes excessive: he betrays an amiable partiality in favour of the weaker side, and, while he guards against calumny, he does not allow sufficient scope for superstition and fanaticism. A copious table of contents will direct the reader to any point that he wishes to examine. 4. Less profound than Petavius, less independent than Le Clerc, less ingenious than Beausobre, the historian Mosheim is full, rational, correct, and moderate. In his learned work, De Rebus Christianis ante Constantinum (Helmstadt, 1753, in 4to), see the *Nazarenes* and *Ebionites*, p. 172-179, 328-332; the Gnostics in general, p. 179, etc.; *Cerinthus*, p. 196-202; Basilides, p. 352-361; Carpocrates, p. 363-367; Valentinus, p. 371-389; Marcion, p. 404-410; the Manichæans, p. 829-837, etc.

[1] Καὶ γὰρ πάντες ἡμεῖς τὸν Χριστὸν ἄνθρωπον ἐξ ἀνθρώπων προσδοκῶμεν γενήσεσθαι, says the Jew Tryphon (Justin. Dialog. p. 207 [p. 142, ed. Jebb]), in the name of his countrymen; and the modern Jews, the few who divert their thoughts from money to religion, still hold the same language, and allege the literal sense of the prophets.

[2] Chrysostom (Basnage, Hist. des Juifs, tom. v. c. 9, p. 183) and Athana-

Jesus of Nazareth conversed with their friend and countryman, who, in all the actions of rational and animal life, appeared of the same species with themselves. His progress from infancy to youth and manhood was marked by a regular increase in stature and wisdom; and after a painful agony of mind and body, he expired on the cross. He lived and died for the service of mankind: but the life and death of Socrates had likewise been devoted to the cause of religion and justice; and although the stoic or the hero may disdain the humble virtues of Jesus, the tears which he shed over his friends and country may be esteemed the purest evidence of his humanity. The miracles of the gospel could not astonish a people who held with intrepid faith the more splendid prodigies of the Mosaic law. The prophets of ancient days had cured diseases, raised the dead, divided the sea, stopped the sun, and ascended to heaven in a fiery chariot. And the metaphorical style of the Hebrews might ascribe to a saint and martyr the adoptive title of Son of God.

Yet in the insufficient creed of the Nazarenes and the Ebionites a distinction is faintly noticed between the heretics, who confounded the generation of Christ in the common order of nature, and the less guilty schismatics, who revered the virginity of his mother and excluded the aid of an earthly father. The incredulity of the former was countenanced by the visible circumstances of his birth, the legal marriage of his reputed parents, Joseph and Mary, and his lineal claim to the kingdom of David and the inheritance of Judah. But the secret and authentic history has been recorded in several copies of the Gospel according to St. Matthew,[1] which these sectaries long preserved in the original Hebrew,[2] as the sole evidence of their faith. The natural suspicions of the husband, conscious of his own chastity,

---

sius (Petav. Dogmat. Theolog. tom. v. l. i. c. 2, p. 3) are obliged to confess that the divinity of Christ is rarely mentioned by himself or his apostles.

[1] The two first chapters of St. Matthew did not exist in the Ebionite copies (Epiphan. Hæres. xxx. 13); and the miraculous conception is one of the last articles which Dr. Priestley has curtailed from his scanty creed.

[2] It is probable enough that the first of the gospels for the use of the Jewish converts was composed in the Hebrew or Syriac idiom: the fact is attested by a chain of fathers—Papias, Irenæus, Origen, Jerom, etc. It is devoutly believed by the Catholics, and admitted by Casaubon, Grotius, and Isaac Vossius, among the Protestant critics. But this Hebrew Gospel of St. Matthew is most unaccountably lost; and we may accuse the diligence or fidelity of the primitive churches, who have preferred the unauthorised version of some nameless Greek. Erasmus and his followers, who respect our Greek text as the original gospel, deprive themselves of the evidence which declares it to be the work of an apostle. See Simon, Hist. Critique, etc., tom. iii. c. 5-9, p. 47-101, and the Prolegomena of Mill and Wetstein to the New Testament.

were dispelled by the assurance (in a dream) that his wife was pregnant of the Holy Ghost: and as this distant and domestic prodigy could not fall under the personal observation of the historian, he must have listened to the same voice which dictated to Isaiah the future conception of a virgin. The son of a virgin, generated by the ineffable operation of the Holy Spirit, was a creature without example or resemblance, superior in every attribute of mind and body to the children of Adam. Since the introduction of the Greek or Chaldean philosophy,[1] the Jews[2] were persuaded of the pre-existence, transmigration, and immortality of souls; and Providence was justified by a supposition that they were confined in their earthly prisons to expiate the stains which they had contracted in a former state.[3] But the degrees of purity and corruption are almost immeasurable. It might be fairly presumed that the most sublime and virtuous of human spirits was infused into the offspring of Mary and the Holy Ghost;[4] that his abasement was the result of his voluntary choice; and that the object of his mission was to purify, not his own, but the sins of the world. On his return to his native skies he received the immense reward of his obedience: the everlasting kingdom of the Messiah, which had been darkly foretold by the prophets, under the carnal images of peace, of conquest, and of dominion. Omnipotence could enlarge the human faculties of Christ to the extent of his celestial office. In the language of antiquity, the title of God has not been severely confined to the first parent; and his incomparable minister, his only begotten

---

[1] The metaphysics of the soul are disengaged by Cicero (Tusculan. l. i.) and Maximus of Tyre (Dissertat. xvi.) from the intricacies of dialogue, which sometimes amuse, and often perplex, the readers of the *Phædrus*, the *Phædon*, and the *Laws* of Plato.

[2] The disciples of Jesus were persuaded that a man might have sinned before he was born (John ix. 2), and the Pharisees held the transmigration of virtuous souls (Joseph. de Bell. Judaico, l. ii. c. 7 [c. 8, § 14]); and a modern Rabbi is modestly assured that Hermes, Pythagoras, Plato, etc., derived their metaphysics from his illustrious countrymen.

[3] Four different opinions have been entertained concerning the origin of human souls. 1. That they are eternal and divine. 2. That they were created, in a separate state of existence, before their union with the body. 3. That they have been propagated from the original stock of Adam, who contained in himself the mental as well as the corporeal seed of his posterity. 4. That each soul is occasionally created and embodied in the moment of conception.—The last of these sentiments appears to have prevailed among the moderns; and our spiritual history is grown less sublime, without becoming more intelligible.

[4] Ὅτι ἡ τοῦ Σωτῆρος ψυχὴ, ἡ τοῦ Ἀδὰμ ἦν, was one of the fifteen heresies imputed to Origen, and denied by his apologist (Photius, Bibliothec. cod. cxvii. p. 296 [p. 92, ed. Bekk.]). Some of the Rabbis attribute one and the same soul to the persons of Adam, David, and the Messiah.

Son, might claim, without presumption, the religious, though secondary, worship of a subject world.

II. The seeds of the faith, which had slowly arisen in the rocky and ungrateful soil of Judea, were transplanted, in full maturity, to the happier climes of the Gentiles; and the strangers of Rome or Asia, who never beheld the manhood, were the more readily disposed to embrace the divinity, of Christ. The polytheist and the philosopher, the Greek and the barbarian, were alike accustomed to conceive a long succession, an infinite chain of angels, or demons, or deities, or æons, or emanations, issuing from the throne of light. Nor could it seem strange or incredible that the first of these æons, the *Logos*, or Word of God, of the same substance with the Father, should descend upon earth, to deliver the human race from vice and error, and to conduct them in the paths of life and immortality. But the prevailing doctrine of the eternity and inherent pravity of matter infected the primitive churches of the East. Many among the Gentile proselytes refused to believe that a celestial spirit, an undivided portion of the first essence, had been personally united with a mass of impure and contaminated flesh; and, in their zeal for the divinity, they piously abjured the humanity, of Christ. While his blood was still recent on Mount Calvary,[1] the *Docetes*, a numerous and learned sect of Asiatics, invented the *phantastic* system which was afterwards propagated by the Marcionites, the Manichæans, and the various names of the Gnostic heresy.[2] They denied the truth and authenticity of the gospels, as far as they relate the conception of Mary, the birth of Christ, and the thirty years that preceded the exercise of his ministry. He first appeared on the banks of the Jordan in the form of perfect manhood; but it was a form only, and not a substance; a human figure created by the hand of Omnipotence to imitate the faculties and actions of a man, and to impose a perpetual illusion on the senses of his friends and enemies. Articulate sounds vibrated on the ears of the disciples; but the image which was impressed on their optic nerve eluded

---

[1] Apostolis adhuc in seculo superstitibus, apud Judæam Christi sanguine recente, PHANTASMA domini corpus asserebatur. Hieronym. advers. Lucifer. c. 8. The epistle of Ignatius to the Smyrnæans, and even the Gospel according to St. John, are levelled against the growing error of the Docetes, who had obtained too much credit in the world (1 John iv. 1-5).

[2] About the year 200 of the Christian era, Irenæus and Hippolytus refuted the thirty-two sects, τῆς ψευδωνύμου γνωσέως, which had multiplied to fourscore in the time of Epiphanius (Phot. Biblioth. cod. cxx, cxxi, cxxii). The five books of Irenæus exist only in barbarous **Latin**; but the original might perhaps be found in some monastery of Greece.

the more stubborn evidence of the touch; and they enjoyed the spiritual, not the corporeal, presence of the Son of God. The rage of the Jews was idly wasted against an impassive phantom; and the mystic scenes of the passion and death, the resurrection and ascension of Christ, were represented on the theatre of Jerusalem for the benefit of mankind. If it were urged that such ideal mimicry, such incessant deception, was unworthy of the God of truth, the Docetes agreed with too many of their orthodox brethren in the justification of pious falsehood. In the system of the Gnostics the Jehovah of Israel, the Creator of this lower world, was a rebellious, or at least an ignorant, spirit. The Son of God descended upon earth to abolish his temple and his law; and, for the accomplishment of this salutary end, he dexterously transferred to his own person the hope and pre-diction of a temporal Messiah.

One of the most subtle disputants of the Manichæan school has pressed the danger and indecency of supposing that the God of the Christians, in the state of a human fœtus, emerged at the end of nine months from a female womb. The pious horror of his antagonists provoked them to disclaim all sensual circum-stances of conception and delivery; to maintain that the divinity passed through Mary like a sunbeam through a plate of glass; and to assert that the seal of her virginity remained unbroken even at the moment when she became the mother of Christ. But the rashness of these concessions has encouraged a milder sentiment of those Docetes who taught, not that Christ was a phantom, but that he was clothed with an impassible and incorruptible body. Such, indeed, in the more orthodox system, he has acquired since his resurrection, and such he must have always possessed, if it were capable of pervading, without resistance or injury, the density of intermediate matter. Devoid of its most essential properties, it might be exempt from the attributes and infirmities of the flesh. A fœtus that could increase from an invisible point to its full maturity; a child that could attain the stature of perfect manhood, without deriving any nourishment from the ordinary sources, might continue to exist without repairing a daily waste by a daily supply of external matter. Jesus might share the repasts of his disciples without being subject to the calls of thirst or hunger; and his virgin purity was never sullied by the involuntary stains of sensual concupiscence. Of a body thus singularly constituted, a question would arise, by what means and of what materials it was originally framed; and our sounder theology is startled by an answer which was not peculiar to the Gnostics, that both the form and the substance proceeded from the divine essence. The idea of pure and absolute spirit is a refinement of modern philosophy: the incorporeal essence, ascribed by the ancients to human souls, celestial beings, and even the Deity himself, does not exclude the notion of extended space; and their imagination was satisfied with a subtle nature of air, or fire, or ether, incomparably more perfect than the grossness of the material world. If we define the place, we must describe the figure, of the Deity. Our experience, perhaps our vanity, represents the powers of reason and virtue under a human form. The Anthropomorphites, who swarmed among the monks of Egypt and the Catholics of Africa, could produce the express declaration of Scripture, that man was made after the image of his Creator.[1] The venerable Serapion, one of the saints of the Nitrian desert, relinquished, with many a tear, his darling prejudice; and bewailed, like an infant, his unlucky conversion, which had stolen away his God, and left his mind without any visible object of faith or devotion.[2]

III. Such were the fleeting shadows of the Docetes. A more substantial, though less simple hypothesis, was contrived by Cerinthus of Asia,[3] who dared to oppose the last of the apostles. Placed on the confines of the Jewish and Gentile world, he laboured to reconcile the Gnostic with the Ebionite, by con-

---

[1] The pilgrim Cassian, who visited Egypt in the beginning of the fifth century, observes and laments the reign of anthropomorphism among the monks, who were not conscious that they embraced the system of Epicurus (Cicero, de Nat. Deorum, i. 18, 49). Ab universo propemodum genere monachorum, qui per totam provinciam Egypti morabantur, pro simplicitatis errore susceptum est, ut e contrario memoratum pontificem (*Theophilus*) velut hæresi gravissimâ depravatum, pars maxima seniorum ab universo fraternitatis corpore decerneret detestandum (Cassian, Collation. x. 1). As long as St. Augustin remained a Manichæan, he was scandalised by the anthropomorphism of the vulgar Catholics.

[2] Ita est in oratione senex mente confusus, eo quod illam ἀνθρωπόμορφον imaginem Deitatis, quam proponere sibi in oratione consueverat, aboleri de suo corde sentiret, ut in amarissimos fletus, crebrosque singultus repente prorumpens, in terram prostratus, cum ejulatû validissimo proclamaret; "Heu me miserum! tulerunt a me Deum meum, et quem nunc teneam non habeo, vel quem adorem, aut interpellam jam nescio." Cassian, Collat. x. 2.

[3] St. John and Cerinthus (A.D. 80, Cleric. Hist. Eccles. p. 493) accidentally met in the public bath of Ephesus; but the apostle fled from the heretic lest the building should tumble on their heads. This foolish story, reprobated by Dr. Middleton (Miscellaneous Works, vol. ii.), is related however by Irenæus (iii. 3), on the evidence of Polycarp, and was probably suited to the time and residence of Cerinthus. The obsolete, yet probably the true, reading of 1 John iv. 3—ὁ λύει τὸν Ἰησοῦν—alludes to the double nature of that primitive heretic.

fessing in the same Messiah the supernatural union of a man and a God; and this mystic doctrine was adopted with many fanciful improvements by Carpocrates, Basilides, and Valentine,[1] the heretics of the Egyptian school. In their eyes JESUS of Nazareth was a mere mortal, the legitimate son of Joseph and Mary: but he was the best and wisest of the human race, selected as the worthy instrument to restore upon earth the worship of the true and supreme Deity. When he was baptised in the Jordan, the CHRIST, the first of the æons, the Son of God himself, descended on Jesus in the form of a dove, to inhabit his mind and direct his actions during the allotted period of his ministry. When the Messiah was delivered into the hands of the Jews, the Christ, an immortal and impassible being, forsook his earthly tabernacle, flew back to the *pleroma* or world of spirits, and left the solitary Jesus to suffer, to complain, and to expire. But the justice and generosity of such a desertion are strongly questionable; and the fate of an innocent martyr, at first impelled, and at length abandoned, by his divine companion, might provoke the pity and indignation of the profane. Their murmurs were variously silenced by the sectaries who espoused and modified the double system of Cerinthus. It was alleged that, when Jesus was nailed to the cross, he was endowed with a miraculous apathy of mind and body, which rendered him insensible of his apparent sufferings. It was affirmed that these momentary, though real pangs, would be abundantly repaid by the temporal reign of a thousand years reserved for the Messiah in his kingdom of the new Jerusalem. It was insinuated that if he suffered, he deserved to suffer; that human nature is never absolutely perfect; and that the cross and passion might serve to expiate the venial transgressions of the son of Joseph, before his mysterious union with the Son of God.[2]

IV. All those who believe the immateriality of the soul, a

[1] The Valentinians embraced a complex and almost incoherent system. 1. Both Christ and Jesus were æons, though of different degrees; the one acting as the rational soul, the other as the divine spirit of the Saviour. 2. At the time of the passion they both retired, and left only a sensitive soul and a human body. 3. Even that body was ethereal, and perhaps apparent.—Such are the laborious conclusions of Mosheim. But I much doubt whether the Latin translator understood Irenæus, and whether Irenæus and the Valentinians understood themselves.

[2] The heretics abused the passionate exclamations of "My God, my God, why hast thou *forsaken* me?" Rousseau, who has drawn an eloquent but indecent parallel between Christ and Socrates, forgets that not a word of impatience or despair escaped from the mouth of the dying philosopher. In the Messiah such sentiments could be only apparent; and such ill-sounding words are properly explained as the application of a psalm and prophecy.

specious and noble tenet, must confess, from their present experience, the incomprehensible union of mind and matter. A similar union is not inconsistent with a much higher, or even with the highest, degree of mental faculties; and the incarnation of an æon or archangel, the most perfect of created spirits, does not involve any positive contradiction or absurdity. In the age of religious freedom, which was determined by the council of Nice, the dignity of Christ was measured by private judgment according to the indefinite rule of Scripture, or reason, or tradition. But when his pure and proper divinity had been established on the ruins of Arianism, the faith of the Catholics trembled on the edge of a precipice where it was impossible to recede, dangerous to stand, dreadful to fall; and the manifold inconveniences of their creed were aggravated by the sublime character of their theology. They hesitated to pronounce— *that* God himself, the second person of an equal and consubstantial trinity, was manifested in the flesh;[1] *that* a being who pervades the universe had been confined in the womb of Mary; *that* his eternal duration had been marked by the days, and months, and years of human existence; *that* the Almighty had been scourged and crucified; *that* his impassible essence had felt pain and anguish; *that* his omniscience was not exempt from ignorance; and *that* the source of life and immortality expired on Mount Calvary. These alarming consequences were affirmed with unblushing simplicity by Apollinaris,[2] bishop of Laodicea, and one of the luminaries of the church. The son of a learned grammarian, he was skilled in all the sciences of Greece; eloquence, erudition, and philosophy, conspicuous in the volumes of Apollinaris, were humbly devoted to the service of religion.

---

[1] This strong expression might be justified by the language of St. Paul (1 Tim. iii. 16); but we are deceived by our modern Bibles. The word ὃ (*which*) was altered to θεὸς (*God*) at Constantinople in the beginning of the sixth century: the true reading, which is visible in the Latin and Syriac versions, still exists in the reasoning of the Greek as well as of the Latin fathers; and this fraud, with that of the *three witnesses of St. John*, is admirably detected by Sir Isaac Newton. (See his two letters translated by M. de Missy, in the Journal Britannique, tom. xv. p. 148-190, 351-390.) I have weighed the arguments, and may yield to the authority of the first of philosophers, who was deeply skilled in critical and theological studies.

[2] For Apollinaris and his sect, see Socrates, l. ii. c. 46, l. iii. c. 16; Sozomen, l. v. c. 18, l. vi. c. 25, 27; Theodoret, l. v. 3, 10, 11; Tillemont, Mémoires Ecclésiastiques, tom. vii. p. 602-638; Not., p. 789-794, in 4to, Venise, 1732. The contemporary saints always mention the bishop of Laodicea as a friend and brother. The style of the more recent historians is harsh and hostile; yet Philostorgius compares him (l. viii. c. 11-15) to Basil and Gregory.

The worthy friend of Athanasius, the worthy antagonist of Julian, he bravely wrestled with the Arians and Polytheists, and, though he affected the rigour of geometrical demonstration, his commentaries revealed the literal and allegorical sense of the Scriptures. A mystery which had long floated in the looseness of popular belief was defined by his perverse diligence in a technical form; and he first proclaimed the memorable words, "One incarnate nature of Christ," which are still re-echoed with hostile clamours in the churches of Asia, Egypt, and Æthiopia. He taught that the Godhead was united or mingled with the body of a man; and that the *Logos,* the eternal wisdom, supplied in the flesh the place and office of a human soul. Yet, as the profound doctor had been terrified at his own rashness, Apollinaris was heard to mutter some faint accents of excuse and explanation. He acquiesced in the old distinction of the Greek philosophers between the rational and sensitive soul of man; that he might reserve the *Logos* for intellectual functions, and employ the subordinate human principle in the meaner actions of animal life. With the moderate Docetes he revered Mary as the spiritual, rather than as the carnal, mother of Christ, whose body either came from heaven, impassible and incorruptible, or was absorbed, and as it were transformed, into the essence of the Deity. The system of Apollinaris was strenuously encountered by the Asiatic and Syrian divines, whose schools are honoured by the names of Basil, Gregory, and Chrysostom, and tainted by those of Diodorus, Theodore, and Nestorius. But the person of the aged bishop of Laodicea, his character and dignity, remained inviolate; and his rivals, since we may not suspect them of the weakness of toleration, were astonished, perhaps, by the novelty of the argument, and diffident of the final sentence of the Catholic church. Her judgment at length inclined in their favour; the heresy of Apollinaris was condemned, and the separate congregations of his disciples were proscribed by the Imperial laws. But his principles were secretly entertained in the monasteries of Egypt, and his enemies felt the hatred of Theophilus and Cyril, the successive patriarchs of Alexandria.

V. The grovelling Ebionite and the fantastic Docetes were rejected and forgotten: the recent zeal against the errors of Apollinaris reduced the Catholics to a seeming agreement with the double nature of Cerinthus. But instead of a temporary and occasional alliance, *they* established, and *we* still embrace, the substantial, indissoluble, and everlasting union of a perfect God with a perfect man, of the second person of the trinity with a reasonable soul and human flesh. In the beginning of the fifth century the *unity* of the *two natures* was the prevailing doctrine of the church. On all sides it was confessed that the mode of their co-existence could neither be represented by our ideas nor expressed by our language. Yet a secret and incurable discord was cherished between those who were most apprehensive of confounding, and those who were most fearful of separating, the divinity and the humanity of Christ. Impelled by religious frenzy, they fled with adverse haste from the error which they mutually deemed most destructive of truth and salvation. On either hand they were anxious to guard, they were jealous to defend, the union and the distinction of the two natures, and to invent such forms of speech, such symbols of doctrine, as were least susceptible of doubt or ambiguity. The poverty of ideas and language tempted them to ransack art and nature for every possible comparison, and each comparison misled their fancy in the explanation of an incomparable mystery. In the polemic microscope an atom is enlarged to a monster, and each party was skilful to exaggerate the absurd or impious conclusions that might be extorted from the principles of their adversaries. To escape from each other they wandered through many a dark and devious thicket, till they were astonished by the horrid phantoms of Cerinthus and Apollinaris, who guarded the opposite issues of the theological labyrinth. As soon as they beheld the twilight of sense and heresy, they started, measured back their steps, and were again involved in the gloom of impenetrable orthodoxy. To purge themselves from the guilt or reproach of damnable error, they disavowed their consequences, explained their principles, excused their indiscretions, and unanimously pronounced the sounds of concord and faith. Yet a latent and almost invisible spark still lurked among the embers of controversy: by the breath of prejudice and passion it was quickly kindled to a mighty flame, and the verbal disputes [1] of the Oriental sects have shaken the pillars of the church and state.

The name of CYRIL of Alexandria is famous in controversial

---

[1] I appeal to the confession of two Oriental prelates, Gregory Abulpharagius the Jacobite primate of the East, and Elias the Nestorian metropolitan of Damascus (see Asseman, Bibliothec. Oriental. tom. ii. p. 291; tom. iii. p. 514, etc.), that the Melchites, Jacobites, Nestorians, etc., agree in the *doctrine*, and differ only in the *expression*. Our most learned and rational divines—Basnage, Le Clerc, Beausobre, La Croze, Mosheim, Jablonski—are inclined to favour this charitable judgment; but the zeal of Petavius is loud and angry, and the moderation of Dupin is conveyed in a whisper.

story, and the title of *saint* is a mark that his opinions and his party have finally prevailed. In the house of his uncle, the archbishop Theophilus, he imbibed the orthodox lessons of zeal and dominion, and five years of his youth were profitably spent in the adjacent monasteries of Nitria. Under the tuition of the abbot Serapion, he applied himself to ecclesiastical studies with such indefatigable ardour, that in the course of *one* sleepless night he has perused the four gospels, the catholic epistles, and the epistle to the Romans. Origen he detested; but the writings of Clemens and Dionysius, of Athanasius and Basil, were continually in his hands: by the theory and practice of dispute, his faith was confirmed and his wit was sharpened; he extended round his cell the cobwebs of scholastic theology, and meditated the works of allegory and metaphysics, whose remains, in seven verbose folios, now peaceably slumber by the side of their rivals.[1] Cyril prayed and fasted in the desert, but his thoughts (it is the reproach of a friend [2]) were still fixed on the world; and the call of Theophilus, who summoned him to the tumult of cities and synods, was too readily obeyed by the aspiring hermit. With the approbation of his uncle he assumed the office and acquired the fame of a popular preacher. His comely person adorned the pulpit; the harmony of his voice resounded in the cathedral; his friends were stationed to lead or second the applause of the congregation;[3] and the hasty notes of the scribes preserved his discourses, which, in their effect, though not in their composition, might be compared with those of the Athenian orators. The death of Theophilus expanded and realised the hopes of his nephew. The clergy of Alexandria was divided; the soldiers and their general supported the claims of the archdeacon; but a resistless multitude, with voices and with hands, asserted the cause of their favourite; and after a period of thirty-nine years Cyril was seated on the throne of Athanasius.[4]

---

[1] La Croze (Hist. du Christianisme des Indes, tom. i. p. 24) avows his contempt for the genius and writings of Cyril—De tous les ouvrages des anciens, il y en a peu qu'on lise avec moins d'utilité: and Dupin (Bibliothèque Ecclésiastique, tom. iv. p. 42-52), in words of respect, teaches us to despise them.

[2] Of Isidore of Pelusium (l. i. Epist. 25, p. 8). As the letter is not of the most creditable sort, Tillemont, less sincere than the Bollandists, affects a doubt whether *this* Cyril is the nephew of Theophilus (Mém. Ecclés. tom. xiv. p. 268).

[3] A grammarian is named by Socrates (l. vii. c. 13) διάπυρος δὲ ἀκροατὴς τοῦ ἐπισκόπου Κυρίλλου καθεστὼς, καὶ περὶ τὸ κρότους ἐν ταῖς διδασκαλίαις αὐτοῦ ἐγείρειν ἦν σπουδαιότατος.

[4] See the youth and promotion of Cyril, in Socrates (l. vii. c. 7) and

The prize was not unworthy of his ambition. At a distance from the court, and at the head of an immense capital, the patriarch, as he was now styled, of Alexandria had gradually usurped the state and authority of a civil magistrate. The public and private charities of the city were managed by his discretion; his voice inflamed or appeased the passions of the multitude; his commands were blindly obeyed by his numerous and fanatic *parabolani*,[1] familiarised in their daily office with scenes of death; and the præfects of Egypt were awed or provoked by the temporal power of these Christian pontiffs. Ardent in the prosecution of heresy, Cyril auspiciously opened his reign by oppressing the Novatians, the most innocent and harmless of the sectaries. The interdiction of their religious worship appeared in his eyes a just and meritorious act; and he confiscated their holy vessels, without apprehending the guilt of sacrilege. The toleration, and even the privileges of the Jews, who had multiplied to the number of forty thousand, were secured by the laws of the Cæsars and Ptolemies, and a long prescription of seven hundred years since the foundation of Alexandria. Without any legal sentence, without any royal mandate, the patriarch, at the dawn of day, led a seditious multitude to the attack of the synagogues. Unarmed and unprepared, the Jews were incapable of resistance; their houses of prayer were levelled with the ground, and the episcopal warrior, after rewarding his troops with the plunder of their goods, expelled from the city the remnant of the unbelieving nation. Perhaps he might plead the insolence of their prosperity, and their deadly hatred of the Christians, whose blood they had recently shed in a malicious or accidental tumult. Such crimes would have deserved the animadversion of the magistrate; but in this promiscuous outrage the innocent were confounded with the guilty, and Alexandria was impoverished by the loss of a wealthy and industrious colony. The zeal of Cyril exposed him to the penalties of the Julian law; but in a feeble government

Renaudot (Hist. Patriarch. Alexandrin. p. 106, 108). The Abbé Renaudot drew his materials from the Arabic history of Severus, bishop of Hermopolis Magna, or Ashmunein, in the tenth century, who can never be trusted, unless our assent is extorted by the internal evidence of facts.

[1] The *Parabolani* of Alexandria were a charitable corporation, instituted during the plague of Gallienus, to visit the sick and to bury the dead. They gradually enlarged, abused, and sold the privileges of their order. Their outrageous conduct during the reign of Cyril provoked the emperor to deprive the patriarch of their nomination, and to restrain their number to five or six hundred. But these restraints were transient and ineffectual. See the Theodosian Code, l. xvi. tit. ii. [leg. 42], and Tillemont, Mém. Ecclés. tom. xiv. p. 276-278.

and a superstitious age he was secure of impunity, and even of praise. Orestes complained; but his just complaints were too quickly forgotten by the ministers of Theodosius, and too deeply remembered by a priest who affected to pardon, and continued to hate, the præfect of Egypt. As he passed through the streets his chariot was assaulted by a band of five hundred of the Nitrian monks; his guards fled from the wild beasts of the desert; his protestations that he was a Christian and a Catholic were answered by a volley of stones, and the face of Orestes was covered with blood. The loyal citizens of Alexandria hastened to his rescue; he instantly satisfied his justice and revenge against the monk by whose hand he had been wounded, and Ammonius expired under the rod of the lictor. At the command of Cyril his body was raised from the ground, and transported in solemn procession to the cathedral; the name of Ammonius was changed to that of Thaumasius, the *wonderful*; his tomb was decorated with the trophies of martyrdom; and the patriarch ascended the pulpit to celebrate the magnanimity of an assassin and a rebel. Such honours might incite the faithful to combat and die under the banners of the saint; and he soon prompted, or accepted, the sacrifice of a virgin, who professed the religion of the Greeks, and cultivated the friendship of Orestes. Hypatia, the daughter of Theon the mathematician,[1] was initiated in her father's studies; her learned comments have elucidated the geometry of Apollonius and Diophantus; and she publicly taught, both at Athens and Alexandria, the philosophy of Plato and Aristotle. In the bloom of beauty, and in the maturity of wisdom, the modest maid refused her lovers and instructed her disciples; the persons most illustrious for their rank or merit were impatient to visit the female philosopher; and Cyril beheld with a jealous eye the gorgeous train of horses and slaves who crowded the door of her academy. A rumour was spread among the Christians that the daughter of Theon was the only obstacle to the reconciliation of the præfect and the archbishop; and that obstacle was speedily removed. On a fatal day, in the holy season of Lent, Hypatia was torn from her chariot, stripped naked, dragged to the church, and inhumanly

---

[1] For Theon and his daughter Hypatia, see Fabricius, Bibliothec. tom. viii. p. 210, 211. Her article in the Lexicon of Suidas is curious and original. Hesychius (Meursii Opera, tom. vii. p. 295, 296) observes that she was persecuted διὰ τὴν ὑπερβάλλουσαν σοφίαν; and an epigram in the Greek Anthology (l. i. c. 76, p. 159, edit. Brodæi) celebrates her knowledge and eloquence. She is honourably mentioned (Epist. 10, 15, 16, 33-80, 124, 135, 153) by her friend and disciple the philosophic bishop Synesius.

butchered by the hands of Peter the reader and a troop of savage and merciless fanatics: her flesh was scraped from her bones with sharp oyster-shells,[1] and her quivering limbs were delivered to the flames. The just progress of inquiry and punishment was stopped by seasonable gifts; but the murder of Hypatia has imprinted an indelible stain on the character and religion of Cyril of Alexandria.[2]

Superstition, perhaps, would more gently expiate the blood of a virgin than the banishment of a saint; and Cyril had accompanied his uncle to the iniquitous synod of the Oak. When the memory of Chrysostom was restored and consecrated, the nephew of Theophilus, at the head of a dying faction, still maintained the justice of his sentence; nor was it till after a tedious delay and an obstinate resistance that he yielded to the consent of the Catholic world.[3] His enmity to the Byzantine pontiffs [4] was a sense of interest, not a sally of passion: he envied their fortunate station in the sunshine of the Imperial court; and he dreaded their upstart ambition, which oppressed the metropolitans of Europe and Asia, invaded the provinces of Antioch and Alexandria, and measured their diocese by the limits of the empire. The long moderation of Atticus, the mild usurper of the throne of Chrysostom, suspended the animosities of the Eastern patriarchs; but Cyril was at length awakened by the exaltation of a rival more worthy of his esteem and hatred. After the short and troubled reign of Sisinnius, bishop of Constantinople, the factions of the clergy and people were appeased by the choice of the emperor, who, on this occasion, consulted the voice of fame, and invited the merit of a stranger.

---

[1] Ὀστράκοις ἀνεῖλον, καὶ μεληδὸν διασπάσαντες, etc. Oyster-shells were plentifully strewed on the sea-beach before the Cæsareum. I may therefore prefer the literal sense without rejecting the metaphorical version of *tegulæ*, tiles, which is used by M. de Valois. I am ignorant, and the assassins were probably regardless, whether their victim was yet alive.

[2] These exploits of St. Cyril are recorded by Socrates (l. vii. c. 13, 14, 15); and the most reluctant bigotry is compelled to copy an historian who coolly styles the murderers of Hypatia ἄνδρες τὸ φρόνημα ἔνθερμοι. At the mention of that injured name, I am pleased to observe a blush even on the cheek of Baronius (A.D. 415, No. 48).

[3] He was deaf to the entreaties of Atticus of Constantinople, and of Isidore of Pelusium, and yielded only (if we may believe Nicephorus, l. xiv. c. 18) to the personal intercession of the Virgin. Yet in his last years he still muttered that John Chrysostom had been justly condemned (Tillemont, Mém. Ecclés. tom. xiv. p. 278-282; Baronius, Annal. Eccles. A.D. 412, No. 46-64.

[4] See their characters in the history of Socrates (l. vii. c. 25-28); their power and pretensions in the huge compilation of Thomassin (Discipline de l'Eglise, tom. i. p. 80-91).

Nestorius,[1] a native of Germanicia and a monk of Antioch, was recommended by the austerity of his life and the eloquence of his sermons; but the first homily which he preached before the devout Theodosius betrayed the acrimony and impatience of his zeal. " Give me, O Cæsar! " he exclaimed, " give me the earth purged of heretics, and I will give you in exchange the kingdom of heaven. Exterminate with me the heretics, and with you I will exterminate the Persians." On the fifth day, as if the treaty had been already signed, the patriarch of Constantinople discovered, surprised, and attacked a secret conventicle of the Arians; they preferred death to submission: the flames that were kindled by their despair soon spread to the neighbouring houses, and the triumph of Nestorius was clouded by the name of *incendiary*. On either side of the Hellespont his episcopal vigour imposed a rigid formulary of faith and discipline— a chronological error concerning the festival of Easter was punished as an offence against the church and state. Lydia and Caria, Sardes and Miletus, were purified with the blood of the obstinate Quartodecimans; and the edict of the emperor, or rather of the patriarch, enumerates three-and-twenty degrees and denominations in the guilt and punishment of heresy.[2] But the sword of persecution which Nestorius so furiously wielded was soon turned against his own breast. Religion was the pretence; but, in the judgment of a contemporary saint, ambition was the genuine motive of episcopal warfare.[3]

In the Syrian school Nestorius had been taught to abhor the confusion of the two natures, and nicely to discriminate the humanity of his *master* Christ from the divinity of the *Lord* Jesus.[4] The Blessed Virgin he revered as the mother of Christ, but his ears were offended with the rash and recent title of

[1] His elevation and conduct are described by Socrates (l. vii. c. 29, 31); and Marcellinus seems to have applied the eloquentiæ **satis**, sapientiæ parum, of Sallust.

[2] Cod. Theodos. l. xvi. tit. v. leg. 65; with the illustrations of Baronius (A.D. 428, No. 25, etc.), Godefroy (ad locum), and Pagi Critica, tom. ii. p. 208.

[3] Isidore of Pelusium (l. iv. Epist. 57). His words are strong and scandalous—τί θαυμάζεις, εἰ καὶ νῦν περὶ πρᾶγμα θεῖον καὶ λόγου κρεῖττον διαφωνεῖν προσποιοῦνται ὑπὸ φιλαρχίας ἐκβακχευόμενοι. Isidore is a saint, but he never became a bishop; and I half suspect that the pride of Diogenes trampled on the pride of Plato.

[4] La Croze (Christianisme des Indes, tom. i. p. 44-53; Thesaurus Epistolicus La Crozianus, tom. iii. p. 276-280) has detected the use of ὁ δεσπότης and ὁ κύριος Ἰησοῦς, which, in the fourth, fifth, and sixth centuries, discriminates the school of Diodorus of Tarsus and his Nestorian disciples.

mother of God,[1] which had been insensibly adopted since the origin of the Arian controversy. From the pulpit of Constantinople, a friend of the patriarch, and afterwards the patriarch himself, repeatedly preached against the use, or the abuse, of a word [2] unknown to the apostles, unauthorised by the church, and which could only tend to alarm the timorous, to mislead the simple, to amuse the profane, and to justify, by a seeming resemblance, the old genealogy of Olympus.[3] In his calmer moments Nestorius confessed that it might be tolerated or excused by the union of the two natures, and the communication of their *idioms* : [4] but he was exasperated by contradiction to disclaim the worship of a new-born, an infant Deity, to draw his inadequate similes from the conjugal or civil partnerships of life, and to describe the manhood of Christ as the robe, the instrument, the tabernacle of his Godhead. At these blasphemous sounds the pillars of the sanctuary were shaken. The unsuccessful competitors of Nestorius indulged their pious or personal resentment, the Byzantine clergy was secretly displeased with the intrusion of a stranger: whatever is superstitious or absurd might claim the protection of the monks; and the people was interested in the glory of their virgin patroness.[5] The sermons of the archbishop, and the service of the altar, were disturbed by seditious clamour; his authority and doctrine were renounced by separate congregations; every

---

[1] Θεοτόκος—*Deipara* : as in zoology we familiarly speak of oviparous and viviparous animals. It is not easy to fix the invention of this word, which La Croze (Christianisme des Indes, tom. i. p. 16) ascribes to Eusebius of Cæsarea and the Arians. The orthodox testimonies are produced by Cyril and Petavius (Dogmat. Theolog. tom. v. l. v. c. 15, p. 254, etc.); but the veracity of the saint is questionable, and the epithet of Θεοτόκος so easily slides from the margin to the text of a Catholic MS.

[2] Basnage, in his Histoire de l'Eglise, a work of controversy (tom. i. p. 505), justifies the mother, by the blood, of God (Acts xx. 28, with Mill's various readings). But the Greek MSS. are far from unanimous; and the primitive style of the blood of Christ is preserved in the Syriac version, even in those copies which were used by the Christians of St. Thomas on the coast of Malabar (La Croze, Christianisme des Indes, tom. i. p. 347). The jealousy of the Nestorians and Monophysites has guarded the purity of their text.

[3] The pagans of Egypt already laughed at the new Cybele of the Christians (Isidor. l. i. Epist. 54); a letter was forged in the name of Hypatia, to ridicule the theology of her assassin (Synodicon, c. 216, in iv. tom. Concil. p. 484). In the article of NESTORIUS, Bayle has scattered some loose philosophy on the worship of the Virgin Mary.

[4] The ἀντίδοσις of the Greeks, a mutual loan or transfer of the idioms or properties of each nature to the other—of infinity to man, possibility to God, etc. Twelve rules on this nicest of subjects compose the Theological Grammar of Petavius (Dogmata Theolog. tom. v. l. iv. c. 14, 15, p. 209, etc.).

[5] See Ducange, C. P. Christiana, l. i. p. 30, etc.

wind scattered round the empire the leaves of controversy; and
the voice of the combatants on a sonorous theatre re-echoed in
the cells of Palestine and Egypt. It was the duty of Cyril to
enlighten the zeal and ignorance of his innumerable monks: in
the school of Alexandria he had imbibed and professed the
incarnation of one nature; and the successor of Athanasius
consulted his pride and ambition when he rose in arms against
another Arius, more formidable and more guilty, on the second
throne of the hierarchy. After a short correspondence, in which
the rival prelates disguised their hatred in the hollow language
of respect and charity, the patriarch of Alexandria denounced
to the prince and people, to the East and to the West, the
damnable errors of the Byzantine pontiff. From the East, more
especially from Antioch, he obtained the ambiguous counsels of
toleration and silence, which were addressed to both parties
while they favoured the cause of Nestorius. But the Vatican
received with open arms the messengers of Egypt. The vanity
of Celestine was flattered by the appeal; and the partial version
of a monk decided the faith of the pope, who, with his Latin
clergy, was ignorant of the language, the arts, and the theology
of the Greeks. At the head of an Italian synod, Celestine
weighed the merits of the cause, approved the creed of Cyril,
condemned the sentiments and person of Nestorius, degraded
the heretic from his episcopal dignity, allowed a respite of ten
days for recantation and penance, and delegated to his enemy
the execution of this rash and illegal sentence. But the patriarch
of Alexandria, whilst he darted the thunders of a god, exposed
the errors and passions of a mortal; and his twelve anathemas [1]
still torture the orthodox slaves who adore the memory of a saint
without forfeiting their allegiance to the synod of Chalcedon.
These bold assertions are indelibly tinged with the colours of
the Apollinarian heresy; but the serious, and perhaps the sincere,
professions of Nestorius have satisfied the wiser and less partial
theologians of the present times. [2]

[1] Concil. tom. iii. p. 943. They have never been *directly* approved by
the church (Tillemont. Mém. Ecclés. tom. xiv. p. 368-372). I almost pity
the agony of rage and sophistry with which Petavius seems to be agitated
in the sixth book of his Dogmata Theologica.

[2] Such as the rational Basnage (ad tom. i.; Variar. Lection. Canisii in
Præfat. c. 2, p. 11-23) and La Croze, the universal scholar (Christianisme
des Indes, tom. i. p. 16-20; De l'Éthiopie, p. 26, 27; Thesaur. Epist.
p. 176, etc., 283, 285). His free sentence is confirmed by that of his friends
Jablonski (Thesaur. Epist. tom. i. p. 193-201) and Mosheim (idem, p. 304:
Nestorium crimine caruisse est et mea sententia); and three more respectable judges will not easily be found. Asseman, a learned and modest
slave, can *hardly* discern (Bibliothec. Orient. tom. iv. p. 190-224) the
guilt and error of the Nestorians.

Yet neither the emperor nor the primate of the East were disposed to obey the mandate of an Italian priest; and a synod of the Catholic, or rather of the Greek, church was unanimously demanded as the sole remedy that could appease or decide this ecclesiastical quarrel.[1] Ephesus, on all sides accessible by sea and land, was chosen for the place, the festival of Pentecost for the day, of the meeting; a writ of summons was despatched to each metropolitan, and a guard was stationed to protect and confine the fathers till they should settle the mysteries of heaven and the faith of the earth. Nestorius appeared not as a criminal, but as a judge; he depended on the weight rather than the number of his prelates, and his sturdy slaves from the baths of Zeuxippus were armed for every service of injury or defence. But his adversary Cyril was more powerful in the weapons both of the flesh and of the spirit. Disobedient to the letter, or at least to the meaning, of the royal summons, he was attended by fifty Egyptian bishops, who expected from their patriarch's nod the inspiration of the Holy Ghost. He had contracted an intimate alliance with Memnon bishop of Ephesus. The despotic primate of Asia disposed of the ready succours of thirty or forty episcopal votes: a crowd of peasants, the slaves of the church, was poured into the city to support with blows and clamours a metaphysical argument; and the people zealously asserted the honour of the Virgin, whose body reposed within the walls of Ephesus.[2] The fleet which had transported Cyril from Alexandria was laden with the riches of Egypt; and he disembarked a numerous body of mariners, slaves, and fanatics, enlisted with blind obedience under the banner of St. Mark and the mother of God. The fathers, and even the guards, of the council were awed by this martial array; the adversaries of Cyril and Mary were insulted in the streets or threatened in their houses; his eloquence and liberality made a daily increase in the number of his adherents; and the Egyptian soon computed that he might

---

[1] The origin and progress of the Nestorian controversy, till the synod of Ephesus, may be found in Socrates (l. vii. c. 32), Evagrius (l. i. c. 1, 2), Liberatus (Brev. c. 1-4), the original Acts (Concil. tom. iii. p. 551-991. edit. Venice, 1728), the Annals of Baronius and Pagi, and the faithful collections of Tillemont (Mém. Ecclés. tom. xiv. p. 283-377).

[2] The Christians of the four first centuries were ignorant of the death and burial of Mary. The tradition of Ephesus is affirmed by the synod (ἔνθα ὁ θεολόγος Ἰωάννης, καὶ ἡ θεοτόκος παρθένος ἡ ἁγία Μαρία—Concil. tom. iii. p. 1102); yet it has been superseded by the claim of Jerusalem; and her *empty* sepulchre, as it was shown to the pilgrims, produced the fable of her resurrection and assumption, in which the Greek and Latin churches have piously acquiesced. See Baronius (Annal. Ecclés. A.D. 48, No. 6, etc.) and Tillemont (Mém. Ecclés. tom. i. p. 467-477).

command the attendance and the voices of two hundred bishops.[1]
But the author of the twelve anathemas foresaw and dreaded
the opposition of John of Antioch, who, with a small though
respectable train of metropolitans and divines, was advancing by slow journeys from the distant capital of the East.
Impatient of a delay which he stigmatised as voluntary and
culpable,[2] Cyril announced the opening of the synod sixteen
days after the festival of Pentecost. Nestorius, who depended
on the near approach of his Eastern friends, persisted, like his
predecessor Chrysostom, to disclaim the jurisdiction, and to
disobey the summons, of his enemies: they hastened his trial,
and his accuser presided in the seat of judgment. Sixty-eight
bishops, twenty-two of metropolitan rank, defended his cause
by a modest and temperate protest: they were excluded from
the councils of their brethren. Candidian, in the emperor's
name, requested a delay of four days; the profane magistrate
was driven with outrage and insult from the assembly of the
saints. The whole of this momentous transaction was crowded
into the compass of a summer's day: the bishops delivered
their separate opinions; but the uniformity of style reveals the
influence or the hand of a master, who has been accused of corrupting the public evidence of their acts and subscriptions.[3]
Without a dissenting voice they recognised in the epistles of
Cyril the Nicene creed and the doctrine of the fathers: but the
partial extracts from the letters and homilies of Nestorius were
interrupted by curses and anathemas; and the heretic was
degraded from his episcopal and ecclesiastical dignity. The
sentence, maliciously inscribed to the new Judas, was affixed
and proclaimed in the streets of Ephesus: the weary prelates,
as they issued from the church of the mother of God, were

---

[1] The Acts of Chalcedon (Concil. tom. iv. p. 1405, 1408) exhibit a lively
picture of the blind, obstinate servitude of the bishops of Egypt to their
patriarch.

[2] Civil or ecclesiastical business detained the bishops at Antioch till the
18th of May. Ephesus was at the distance of thirty days' journey; and
ten days more may be fairly allowed for accidents and repose. The march
of Xenophon over the same ground enumerates above 260 parasangs or
leagues; and this measure might be illustrated from ancient and modern
itineraries, if I knew how to compare the speed of an army, a synod, and
a caravan. John of Antioch is reluctantly acquitted by Tillemont himself
(Mém. Ecclés. tom. xiv. p. 386-389).

[3] Μεμφόμενον μὴ κατὰ τὸ δέον τὰ ἐν Ἐφέσῳ συντεθῆναι ὑπομνήματα,
πανουργίᾳ δὲ καί τινι ἀθέσμῳ καινοτομίᾳ Κυρίλλου τεχνάζοντος. Evagrius,
l. i. c. 7. The same imputation was urged by Count Irenæus (tom. iii. p.
1249); and the orthodox critics do not find it an easy task to defend the
purity of the Greek or Latin copies of the Acts.

saluted as her champions; and her victory was celebrated by the illuminations, the songs, and the tumult of the night.

On the fifth day the triumph was clouded by the arrival and indignation of the Eastern bishops. In a chamber of the inn, before he had wiped the dust from his shoes, John of Antioch gave audience to Candidian the Imperial minister, who related his ineffectual efforts to prevent or to annul the hasty violence of the Egyptian. With equal haste and violence the Oriental synod of fifty bishops degraded Cyril and Memnon from their episcopal honours; condemned, in the twelve anathemas, the purest venom of the Apollinarian heresy; and described the Alexandrian primate as a monster, born and educated for the destruction of the church.[1] *His* throne was distant and inaccessible; but they instantly resolved to bestow on the flock of Ephesus the blessing of a faithful shepherd. By the vigilance of Memnon the churches were shut against them, and a strong garrison was thrown into the cathedral. The troops, under the command of Candidian, advanced to the assault; the outguards were routed and put to the sword, but the place was impregnable: the besiegers retired; their retreat was pursued by a vigorous sally; they lost their horses, and many of the soldiers were dangerously wounded with clubs and stones. Ephesus, the city of the Virgin, was defiled with rage and clamour, with sedition and blood; the rival synods darted anathemas and excommunications from their spiritual engines; and the court of Theodosius was perplexed by the adverse and contradictory narratives of the Syrian and Egyptian factions. During a busy period of three months the emperor tried every method, except the most effectual means of indifference and contempt, to reconcile this theological quarrel. He attempted to remove or intimidate the leaders by a common sentence of acquittal or condemnation; he invested his representatives at Ephesus with ample power and military force; he summoned from either party eight chosen deputies to a free and candid conference in the neighbourhood of the capital, far from the contagion of popular frenzy. But the Orientals refused to yield, and the Catholics, proud of their numbers and of their Latin allies, rejected all terms of union or toleration. The patience of the meek Theodosius was provoked, and he dissolved in anger this

---

[1] Ὁ δὲ ἐπ' ὀλέθρῳ τῶν ἐκκλησιῶν τεχθείς καὶ τραφείς. After the coalition of John and Cyril these invectives were mutually forgotten. The style of declamation must never be confounded with the genuine sense which respectable enemies entertain of each other's merit (Concil. tom. iii. p. 1244).

episcopal tumult, which at the distance of thirteen centuries assumes the venerable aspect of the third œcumenical council.[1] " God is my witness," said the pious prince, " that I am not the author of this confusion. His providence will discern and punish the guilty. Return to your provinces, and may your private virtues repair the mischief and scandal of your meeting." They returned to their provinces; but the same passions which had distracted the synod of Ephesus were diffused over the Eastern world. After three obstinate and equal campaigns, John of Antioch and Cyril of Alexandria condescended to explain and embrace: but their seeming re-union must be imputed rather to prudence than to reason, to the mutual lassitude rather than to the Christian charity of the patriarchs.

The Byzantine pontiff had instilled into the royal ear a baleful prejudice against the character and conduct of his Egyptian rival. An epistle of menace and invective,[2] which accompanied the summons, accused him as a busy, insolent, and envious priest, who perplexed the simplicity of the faith, violated the peace of the church and state, and, by his artful and separate addresses to the wife and sister of Theodosius, presumed to suppose, or to scatter, the seeds of discord in the Imperial family. At the stern command of his sovereign, Cyril had repaired to Ephesus, where he was resisted, threatened, and confined, by the magistrates in the interest of Nestorius and the Orientals, who assembled the troops of Lydia and Ionia to suppress the fanatic and disorderly train of the patriarch. Without expecting the royal licence, he escaped from his guards, precipitately embarked, deserted the imperfect synod, and retired to his episcopal fortress of safety and independence. But his artful emissaries, both in the court and city, successfully laboured to appease the resentment, and to conciliate the favour, of the emperor. The feeble son of Arcadius was alternately swayed by his wife and sister,

---

[1] See the Acts of the Synod of Ephesus in the original Greek, and a Latin version almost contemporary (Concil. tom. iii. p. 991-1339), with the Synodicon adversus Tragœdiam Irenæi, tom. iv. p. 235-497), the Ecclesiastical Histories of Socrates (l. vii. c. 34) and Evagrius (l. i. c. 3, 4, 5), and the Breviary of Liberatus (in Concil. tom. vi. p. 419-459, c. 5, 6), and the Mémoires Ecclés. of Tillemont (tom. xiv. p. 377-487).

[2] Ταραχὴν (says the emperor in pointed language) τό γε ἐπὶ σαυτῷ καὶ χωρισμὸν ταῖς ἐκκλησίαις ἐμβέβληκας . . . . ὡς θρασυτέρας ὁρμῆς πρεπούσης μᾶλλον ἢ ἀκριβείας . . . . καὶ ποικιλίας μᾶλλον τούτων ἡμῖν ἀρκούσης ἥπερ ἁπλότητος . . . . παντὸς μᾶλλον ἢ ἱέρεως . . . . τά τε τῶν ἐκκλησιῶν, τά τε τῶν βασιλέων μέλλειν χωρίζειν βούλεσθαι, ὡς οὐκ οὔσης ἀφορμῆς ἑτέρας εὐδοκιμήσεως. I should be curious to know how much Nestorius paid for these expressions, so mortifying to his rival.

by the eunuchs and women of the palace: superstition and avarice were their ruling passions; and the orthodox chiefs were assiduous in their endeavours to alarm the former and to gratify the latter. Constantinople and the suburbs were sanctified with frequent monasteries, and the holy abbots, Dalmatius and Eutyches,[1] had devoted their zeal and fidelity to the cause of Cyril, the worship of Mary, and the unity of Christ. From the first moment of their monastic life they had never mingled with the world, or trod the profane ground of the city. But in this awful moment of the danger of the church, their vow was superseded by a more sublime and indispensable duty. At the head of a long order of monks and hermits, who carried burning tapers in their hands, and chanted litanies to the mother of God, they proceeded from their monasteries to the palace. The people was edified and inflamed by this extraordinary spectacle, and the trembling monarch listened to the prayers and adjurations of the saints, who boldly pronounced that none could hope for salvation unless they embraced the person and the creed of the orthodox successor of Athanasius. At the same time every avenue of the throne was assaulted with gold. Under the decent names of *eulogies* and *benedictions,* the courtiers of both sexes were bribed according to the measure of their power and rapaciousness. But their incessant demands despoiled the sanctuaries of Constantinople and Alexandria; and the authority of the patriarch was unable to silence the just murmur of his clergy, that a debt of sixty thousand pounds had already been contracted to support the expense of this scandalous corruption.[2] Pulcheria, who relieved her brother from the weight of an empire, was the firmest pillar of orthodoxy; and so intimate was the alliance between the thunders of the synod and the whispers of the court, that Cyril was assured of success if he could displace one eunuch, and substitute another in the favour of Theodosius.

[1] Eutyches, the heresiarch Eutyches, is honourably named by Cyril as a friend, a saint, and the strenuous defender of the faith. His brother, the abbot Dalmatius, is likewise employed to bind the emperor and all his chamberlains *terribili conjuratione.* Synodicon, c. 203, in Concil. tom. iv. p. 467.

[2] Clerici qui hic sunt contristantur, quod ecclesia Alexandrina nudata sit hujus causâ turbelæ: et debet præter illa quæ hinc transmissa sint *auri libras mille quingentas.* Et nunc ei scriptum est ut præstet; sed de tuâ ecclesiâ præsta avaritiæ quorum nosti, etc. This curious and original letter, from Cyril's archdeacon to his creature the new bishop of Constantinople, has been unaccountably preserved in an old Latin version (Synodicon, c. 203, Concil. tom. iv. p. 465-468). The mask is almost dropped, and the saints speak the honest language of interest and confederacy.

Yet the Egyptian could not boast of a glorious or decisive victory. The emperor, with unaccustomed firmness, adhered to his promise of protecting the innocence of the Oriental bishops; and Cyril softened his anathemas, and confessed, with ambiguity and reluctance, a twofold nature of Christ, before he was permitted to satiate his revenge against the unfortunate Nestorius.[1]

The rash and obstinate Nestorius, before the end of the synod, was oppressed by Cyril, betrayed by the court, and faintly supported by his Eastern friends. A sentiment of fear or indignation prompted him, while it was yet time, to affect the glory of a voluntary abdication:[2] his wish, or at least request, was readily granted; he was conducted with honour from Ephesus to his old monastery of Antioch; and, after a short pause, his successors, Maximian and Proclus, were acknowledged as the lawful bishops of Constantinople. But in the silence of his cell the degraded patriarch could no longer resume the innocence and security of a private monk. The past he regretted, he was discontented with the present, and the future he had reason to dread: the Oriental bishops successively disengaged their cause from his unpopular name, and each day decreased the number of the schismatics who revered Nestorius as the confessor of the faith. After a residence at Antioch of four years, the hand of Theodosius subscribed an edict[3] which ranked him with Simon the magician, proscribed his opinions and followers, condemned his writings to the flames, and banished his person first to Petra in Arabia, and at length to Oasis, one of the *islands* of the Libyan desert.[4] Secluded from the church and from the world, the

---

[1] The tedious negotiations that succeeded the synod of Ephesus are diffusely related in the original Acts (Concil. tom. iii. p. 1339-1771) ad fin. vol. and the Synodicon, in tom. iv.), Socrates (l. vii. c. 28, 35, 40, 41), Evagrius (l. i. c. 6, 7, 8, 12), Liberatus (c. 7-10), Tillemont (Mém. Ecclés. tom. xiv. p. 487-676). The most patient reader will thank me for compressing so much nonsense and falsehood in a few lines.

[2] Αὐτοῦ τε αὖ δεηθέντος, ἐπετράπη κατὰ τὸ οἰκεῖον ἐπαναζεῦξαι μοναστήριον. Evagrius, l. i. c. 7. The original letters in the Synodicon (c. 15, 24, 25, 26) justify the *appearance* of a voluntary resignation, which is asserted by Ebed-Jesu, a Nestorian writer, apud Asseman. Biblioth. Oriental. tom. iii. p. 299, 302.

[3] See the Imperial letters in the Acts of the Synod of Ephesus (Concil. tom. iii. p. 1730-1735). The odious name of *Simonians*, which was affixed to the disciples of this τερατώδους διδασκαλίας, was designed ὡς ἂν ὀνείδεσι προβληθέντες αἰώνιον ὑπομένοιεν τιμωρίαν τῶν ἁμαρτημάτων, καὶ μήτε ζῶντας τιμωρίας, μήτε θανόντας ἀτιμίας ἐκτὸς ὑπάρχειν. Yet these were Christians! who differed only in names and in shadows.

[4] The metaphor of islands is applied by the grave civilians (Pandect. l. xlviii. tit. 22, leg. 7 [§ 5]) to those happy spots which are discriminated by water and verdure from the Libyan sands. Three of these under the common name of Oasis, or Alvahat: 1. The temple of Jupiter Ammon.

exile was still pursued by the rage of bigotry and war. A wandering tribe of the Blemmyes or Nubians invaded his solitary prison: in their retreat they dismissed a crowd of useless captives; but no sooner had Nestorius reached the banks of the Nile, than he would gladly have escaped from a Roman and orthodox city to the milder servitude of the savages. His flight was punished as a new crime: the soul of the patriarch inspired the civil and ecclesiastical powers of Egypt; the magistrates, the soldiers, the monks, devoutly tortured the enemy of Christ and St. Cyril; and, as far as the confines of Æthiopia, the heretic was alternately dragged and recalled, till his aged body was broken by the hardships and accidents of these reiterated journeys. Yet his mind was still independent and erect; the president of Thebais was awed by his pastoral letters; he survived the Catholic tyrant of Alexandria, and, after sixteen years' banishment, the synod of Chalcedon would perhaps have restored him to the honours, or at least to the communion, of the church. The death of Nestorius prevented his obedience to their welcome summons;[1] and his disease might afford some colour to the scandalous report, that his tongue, the organ of blasphemy, had been eaten by the worms. He was buried in a city of Upper Egypt, known by the names of Chemnis, or Panopolis, or Akmim;[2] but the immortal malice of the Jacobites has persevered for ages to cast stones against his sepulchre, and to propagate the foolish tradition that it was never watered by the rain of heaven, which equally descends on the righteous and the ungodly.[3] Humanity may drop a tear on the fate of Nestorius;

---

2. The middle Oasis, three days' journey to the west of Lycopolis. 3. The southern, where Nestorius was banished, in the first climate, and only three days' journey from the confines of Nubia. See a learned Note of Michaelis (ad Descript. Ægypt. Abulfedæ, p. 21-34).

[1] The invitation of Nestorius to the synod of Chalcedon is related by Zacharias, bishop of Melitene (Evagrius, l. ii. c. 2; Asseman. Biblioth. Orient. tom. ii. p. 55), and the famous Xenaias or Philoxenus, bishop of Hierapolis (Asseman. Biblioth. Orient. tom. ii. p. 40, etc.), denied by Evagrius and Asseman, and stoutly maintained by La Croze (Thesaur. Epistol. tom. iii. p. 181, etc). The fact is not improbable; yet it was the interest of the Monophysites to spread the invidious report; and Eutychius (tom. ii. p. 12) affirms that Nestorius died after an exile of seven years, and consequently ten years before the synod of Chalcedon.

[2] Consult D'Anville (Mémoire sur l'Egypt. p. 191), Pocock (Description of the East, vol. i. p. 76), Abulfeda (Descript. Ægypt. p. 14), and his commentator Michaelis (Not. p. 78-83), and the Nubian Geographer (p. 42), who mentions, in the twelfth century, the ruins and the sugar-canes of Akmim.

[3] Eutychius (Annal. tom. ii. p. 12) and Gregory Bar-Hebræus, or Abulpharagius (Asseman. tom. ii. p. 316), represent the credulity of the tenth and thirteenth centuries.

yet justice must observe that he suffered the persecution which he had approved and inflicted.[1]

The death of the Alexandrian primate, after a reign of thirty-two years, abandoned the Catholics to the intemperance of zeal and the abuse of victory.[2] The *monophysite* doctrine (one incarnate nature) was rigorously preached in the churches of Egypt and the monasteries of the East; the primitive creed of Apollinaris was protected by the sanctity of Cyril; and the name of EUTYCHES, his venerable friend, has been applied to the sect most adverse to the Syrian heresy of Nestorius. His rival Eutyches was the abbot, or archimandrite, or superior of three hundred monks; but the opinions of a simple and illiterate recluse might have expired in the cell where he had slept above seventy years if the resentment or indiscretion of Flavian, the Byzantine pontiff, had not exposed the scandal to the eyes of the Christian world. His domestic synod was instantly convened, their proceedings were sullied with clamour and artifice, and the aged heretic was surprised into a seeming confession that Christ had not derived his body from the substance of the Virgin Mary. From their partial decree Eutyches appealed to a general council; and his cause was vigorously asserted by his godson Chrysaphius, the reigning eunuch of the palace, and his accomplice Dioscorus, who had succeeded to the throne, the creed, the talents, and the vices of the nephew of Theophilus. By the special summons of Theodosius, the second synod of Ephesus was judiciously composed of ten metropolitans and ten bishops from each of the six dioceses of the Eastern empire: some exceptions of favour or merit enlarged the number to one hundred and thirty-five; and the Syrian Barsumas, as the chief and representative of the monks, was invited to sit and vote with the successors of the apostles. But the despotism of the Alexandrian patriarch again oppressed the freedom of debate: the same spiritual and carnal weapons were again drawn from the arsenals of Egypt; the Asiatic veterans, a band of archers,

---

[1] We are obliged to Evagrius (l. i. c. 7) for some extracts from the letters of Nestorius; but the lively picture of his sufferings is treated with insult by the hard and stupid fanatic.

[2] Dixi Cyrillum dum viveret, auctoritate suâ effecisse, ne Eutychianismus et Monophysitarum error in nervum erumperet: idque verum puto . . . aliquo . . . honesto modo παλινῳδίαν cecinerat. The learned but cautious Jablonski did not always speak the whole truth. Cum Cyrillo lenius omnino egi, quam si tecum aut cum aliis rei hujus probe gnaris et æquis rerum æstimatoribus sermones privatos conferrum (Thesaur. Epistol. La Crozian. tom. i. p. 197, 198); an excellent key to his dissertations on the Nestorian controversy!

served under the orders of Dioscorus; and the more formidable monks, whose minds were inaccessible to reason or mercy, besieged the doors of the cathedral. The general and, as it should seem, the unconstrained voice of the fathers accepted the faith and even the anathemas of Cyril; and the heresy of the two natures was formally condemned in the persons and writings of the most learned Orientals. " May those who divide Christ be divided with the sword, may they be hewn in pieces, may they be burned alive! " were the charitable wishes of a Christian synod.[1] The innocence and sanctity of Eutyches were acknowledged without hesitation; but the prelates, more especially those of Thrace and Asia, were unwilling to depose their patriarch for the use or even the abuse of his lawful jurisdiction. They embraced the knees of Dioscorus, as he stood with a threatening aspect on the footstool of his throne, and conjured him to forgive the offences and to respect the dignity of his brother. " Do you mean to raise a sedition? " exclaimed the relentless tyrant. " Where are the officers? " At these words a furious multitude of monks and soldiers, with stakes, and swords, and chains, burst into the church: the trembling bishops hid themselves behind the altar or under the benches; and as they were not inspired with the zeal of martyrdom, they successively subscribed a blank paper, which was afterwards filled with the condemnation of the Byzantine pontiff. Flavian was instantly delivered to the wild beasts of this spiritual amphitheatre: the monks were stimulated by the voice and example of Barsumas to avenge the injuries of Christ: it is said that the patriarch of Alexandria reviled, and buffeted, and kicked, and trampled his brother of Constantinople:[2] it is certain that the victim, before he could reach the place of his exile, expired on the third day of the wounds and bruises which he had received

---

[1] Ἡ ἀγία σύνοδος εἶπεν, ἆρον, καῦσον Εὐσέβιον, οὗτος ζῶν καῇ, οὗτος εἰς δύο γένηται, ὡς ἐμέρισε, μερισθῇ . . . . εἴ τις λέγει δύο, ἀνάθεμα. At the request of Dioscorus, those who were not able to roar (βοῆσαι), stretched out their hands. At Chalcedon, the Orientals disclaimed these exclamations: but the Egyptians more consistently declared ταῦτα καὶ τότε εἴπομεν καὶ νῦν λέγομεν. (Concil. tom. iv. p. 1012.)

[2] Ἔλεγε δὲ (Eusebius, bishop of Dorylæum) τὸν Φλαβιανόν τε δειλαίως ἀναιρεθῆναι πρὸς Διοσκόρου ὠθούμενόν τε καὶ λακτιζόμενον: and this testimony of Evagrius (l. ii. c. 2) is amplified by the historian Zonaras (tom. ii. l. xiii. [c. 23] p. 44), who affirms that Dioscorus kicked like a wild ass. But the language of Liberatus (Brev. c. 12, in Concil. tom. vi. p. 438) is more cautious; and the Acts of Chalcedon, which lavish the names of homicide, Cain, etc., do not justify so pointed a charge. The monk Barsumas is more particularly accused—ἔσφαξε τὸν μακάριον Φλανιανόν· αὐτὸς ἔστηκε καὶ ἔλεγε, σφάξον. (Concil. tom. iv. p. 1413).

at Ephesus. This second synod has been justly branded as a gang of robbers and assassins; yet the accusers of Dioscorus would magnify his violence, to alleviate the cowardice and inconstancy of their own behaviour.

The faith of Egypt had prevailed: but the vanquished party was supported by the same pope who encountered without fear the hostile rage of Attila and Genseric. The theology of Leo, his famous *tome* or epistle on the mystery of the incarnation, had been disregarded by the synod of Ephesus: his authority, and that of the Latin church, was insulted in his legates, who escaped from slavery and death to relate the melancholy tale of the tyranny of Dioscorus and the martyrdom of Flavian. His provincial synod annulled the irregular proceedings of Ephesus; but as this step was itself irregular, he solicited the convocation of a general council in the free and orthodox provinces of Italy. From his independent throne the Roman bishop spoke and acted without danger as the head of the Christians, and his dictates were obsequiously transcribed by Placidia and her son Valentinian, who addressed their Eastern colleague to restore the peace and unity of the church. But the pageant of Oriental royalty was moved with equal dexterity by the hand of the eunuch; and Theodosius could pronounce, without hesitation, that the church was already peaceful and triumphant, and that the recent flame had been extinguished by the just punishment of the Nestorians. Perhaps the Greeks would be still involved in the heresy of the Monophysites, if the emperor's horse had not fortunately stumbled; Theodosius expired; his orthodox sister, Pulcheria, with a nominal husband, succeeded to the throne; Chrysaphius was burnt, Dioscorus was disgraced, the exiles were recalled, and the *tome* of Leo was subscribed by the Oriental bishops. Yet the pope was disappointed in his favourite project of a Latin council: he disdained to preside in the Greek synod which was speedily assembled at Nice in Bithynia; his legates required in a peremptory tone the presence of the emperor; and the weary fathers were transported to Chalcedon under the immediate eye of Marcian and the senate of Constantinople. A quarter of a mile from the Thracian Bosphorus the church of St. Euphemia was built on the summit of a gentle though lofty ascent: the triple structure was celebrated as a prodigy of art, and the boundless prospect of the land and sea might have raised the mind of a sectary to the contemplation of the God of the universe. Six hundred and thirty bishops were ranged in order in the nave of the church; but the patriarchs of the East were preceded by the legates, of whom the third was a simple priest; and the place of honour was reserved for twenty laymen of consular or senatorian rank. The gospel was ostentatiously displayed in the centre, but the rule of faith was defined by the papal and imperial ministers, who moderated the thirteen sessions of the council of Chalcedon.[1] Their partial interposition silenced the intemperate shouts and execrations which degraded the episcopal gravity; but, on the formal accusation of the legates, Dioscorus was compelled to descend from his throne to the rank of a criminal, already condemned in the opinion of his judges. The Orientals, less adverse to Nestorius than to Cyril, accepted the Romans as their deliverers: Thrace, and Pontus, and Asia, were exasperated against the murderer of Flavian, and the new patriarchs of Constantinople and Antioch secured their places by the sacrifice of their benefactor. The bishops of Palestine, Macedonia, and Greece were attached to the faith of Cyril; but in the face of the synod, in the heat of the battle, the leaders, with their obsequious train, passed from the right to the left wing, and decided the victory by this seasonable desertion. Of the seventeen suffragans who sailed from Alexandria, four were tempted from their allegiance, and the thirteen, falling prostrate on the ground, implored the mercy of the council, with sighs and tears, and a pathetic declaration, that, if they yielded, they should be massacred, on their return to Egypt, by the indignant people. A tardy repentance was allowed to expiate the guilt or error of the accomplices of Dioscorus: but their sins were accumulated on his head; he neither asked nor hoped for pardon, and the moderation of those who pleaded for a general amnesty was drowned in the prevailing cry of victory and revenge. To save the reputation of his late adherents, some *personal* offences were skilfully detected; his rash and illegal excommunication of the pope, and his contumacious refusal (while he was detained a prisoner) to attend the summons of the synod. Witnesses were introduced to prove the special facts of his pride, avarice, and cruelty; and the fathers heard with abhorrence that the alms of

---

[1] The acts of the Council of Chalcedon (Concil. tom. iv. p. 761-2071) comprehend those of Ephesus (p. 890-1189), which again comprise the synod of Constantinople under Flavian (p. 930-1072); and it requires some attention to disengage this double involution. The whole business of Eutyches, Flavian, and Dioscorus, is related by Evagrius (l. i. c. 9-12, and l. ii. c. 1, 2, 3, 4) and Liberatus (Brev. c. 11, 12, 13, 14). Once more, and almost for the last time, I appeal to the diligence of Tillemont (Mém. Ecclés. tom. xv. p. 479-719). The annals of Baronius and Pagi will accompany me much further on my long and laborious journey.

the church were lavished on the female dancers, that his palace, and even his bath, was open to the prostitutes of Alexandria, and that the infamous Pansophia, or Irene, was publicly entertained as the concubine of the patriarch.[1]

For these scandalous offences Dioscorus was deposed by the synod and banished by the emperor; but the purity of his faith was declared in the presence, and with the tacit approbation, of the fathers. Their prudence supposed rather than pronounced the heresy of Eutyches, who was never summoned before their tribunal; and they sat silent and abashed when a bold Monophysite, casting at their feet a volume of Cyril, challenged them to anathematise in his person the doctrine of the saint. If we fairly peruse the acts of Chalcedon as they are recorded by the orthodox party,[2] we shall find that a great majority of the bishops embraced the simple unity of Christ; and the ambiguous concession that he was formed OF or FROM two natures might imply either their previous existence, or their subsequent confusion, or some dangerous interval between the conception of the man and the assumption of the God. The Roman theology, more positive and precise, adopted the term most offensive to the ears of the Egyptians, that Christ existed IN two natures; and this momentous particle[3] (which the memory, rather than the

---

[1] Μάλιστα ἡ περιβόητος Πανσοφία, ἡ καλουμένη Ὀρεινὴ (perhaps Εἰρήνη), περὶ ἧς καὶ ὁ πολυάνθρωπος τῆς Ἀλεξανδρέων δῆμος ἀφῆκε φωνήν, αὐτῆς τε καὶ τοῦ ἐραστοῦ μεμνημένος (Concil. tom. iv. p. 1276). A specimen of the wit and malice of the people is preserved in the Greek Anthology (l. ii. c. 5, p. 188, edit. Wechel), although the application was unknown to the editor Brodæus. The nameless epigrammatist raises a tolerable pun, by confounding the episcopal salutation of " Peace be to all! " with the genuine or corrupted name of the bishop's concubine:—

Εἰρήνη πάντεσσιν, ἐπίσκοπος εἶπεν ἐπελθών.
Πῶς δύναται πᾶσιν, ἣν μόνος ἔνδον ἔχει ;

I am ignorant whether the patriarch, who seems to have been a jealous lover, is the Cimon of a preceding epigram, whose πεὸς ἑστηκός was viewed with envy and wonder by Priapus himself.

[2] Those who reverence the infallibility of synods may try to ascertain their sense. The leading bishops were attended by partial or careless scribes, who dispersed their copies round the world. Our Greek MSS. are sullied with the false and proscribed reading of ἐκ τῶν φυσέων (Concil. tom. iii. p. 1460): the authentic translation of pope Leo I. does not seem to have been executed, and the old Latin versions materially differ from the present Vulgate, which was revised (A.D. 550) by Rusticus, a Roman priest, from the best MSS. of the Ἀκοίμητοι at Constantinople (Ducange, C.P. Christiana, l. iv. p. 151), a famous monastery of Latins, Greeks, and Syrians. See Concil. tom. iv. p. 1959-2049, and Pagi, Critica, tom. ii. p. 326, etc.

[3] It is darkly represented in the microscope of Petavius (tom. v. l. iii. c. 5); yet the subtle theologian is himself afraid—ne quis fortasse super-

understanding, must retain) had almost produced a schism among the Catholic bishops. The *tome* of Leo had been respectfully, perhaps sincerely, subscribed; but they protested, in two successive debates, that it was neither expedient nor lawful to transgress the sacred landmarks which had been fixed at Nice, Constantinople, and Ephesus, according to the rule of Scripture and tradition. At length they yielded to the importunities of their masters, but their infallible decree, after it had been ratified with deliberate votes and vehement acclamations, was overturned in the next session by the opposition of the legates and their Oriental friends. It was in vain that a multitude of episcopal voices repeated in chorus, " The definition of the fathers is orthodox and immutable! The heretics are now discovered! Anathema to the Nestorians! Let them depart from the synod! Let them repair to Rome." [1] The legates threatened, the emperor was absolute, and a committee of eighteen bishops prepared a new decree, which was imposed on the reluctant assembly. In the name of the fourth general council, the Christ in one person, but *in* two natures, was announced to the Catholic world: an invisible line was drawn between the heresy of Apollinaris and the faith of St. Cyril; and the road to paradise, 'a bridge as sharp as a razor, was suspended over the abyss by the master-hand of the theological artist. During ten centuries of blindness and servitude Europe received her religious opinions from the oracle of the Vatican; and the same doctrine, already varnished with the rust of antiquity, was admitted without dispute into the creed of the reformers, who disclaimed the supremacy of the Roman pontiff. The synod of Chalcedon still triumphs in the Protestant churches; but the ferment of controversy has subsided, and the most pious Christians of the present day are ignorant, or careless, of their own belief concerning the mystery of the incarnation.

Far different was the temper of the Greeks and Egyptians under the orthodox reigns of Leo and Marcian. Those pious emperors enforced with arms and edicts the symbol of their faith; [2] and it was declared by the conscience or honour of five

vacaneam, et nimis anxiam putet hujusmodi vocularum inquisitionem, et ab instituti theologici gravitate alienam (p. 124).

[1] Ἐβόησαν, ἢ ὁ ὅρος κρατείτω, ἢ ἀπερχόμεθα . . . . οἱ ἀντιλέγοντες φανεροὶ γένωνται, οἱ ἀντιλέγοντες Νεστοριανοί εἰσιν, οἱ ἀντιλέγοντες εἰς Ῥώμην ἀπέλθωσιν (Concil. tom. iv. p. 1449). Evagrius and Liberatus present only the placid face of the synod, and discreetly slide over these embers, suppositos cineri doloso.

[2] See, in the Appendix to the Acts of Chalcedon, the confirmation of the synod by Marcian (Concil. tom. iv. p. 1781, 1783); his letters to the monks

hundred bishops, that the decrees of the synod of Chalcedon
might be lawfully supported, even with blood. The Catholics
observed with satisfaction that the same synod was odious both
to the Nestorians and the Monophysites;[1] but the Nestorians
were less angry, or less powerful, and the East was distracted
by the obstinate and sanguinary zeal of the Monophysites.
Jerusalem was occupied by an army of monks; in the name
of the one incarnate nature, they pillaged, they burnt, they
murdered; the sepulchre of Christ was defiled with blood; and
the gates of the city were guarded in tumultuous rebellion
against the troops of the emperor. After the disgrace and exile
of Dioscorus, the Egyptians still regretted their spiritual father,
and detested the usurpation of his successor, who was introduced by the fathers of Chalcedon. The throne of Proterius
was supported by a guard of two thousand soldiers; he waged
a five years' war against the people of Alexandria; and on the
first intelligence of the death of Marcian, he became the victim
of their zeal. On the third day before the festival of Easter the
patriarch was besieged in the cathedral, and murdered in the
baptistery. The remains of his mangled corpse were delivered
to the flames, and his ashes to the wind: and the deed was inspired by the vision of a pretended angel; an ambitious monk
who, under the name of Timothy the Cat,[2] succeeded to the place
and opinions of Dioscorus. This deadly superstition was inflamed on either side by the principle and the practice of retaliation: in the pursuit of a metaphysical quarrel many thousands[3]
were slain, and the Christians of every degree were deprived of
the substantial enjoyments of social life, and of the invisible

of Alexandria (p. 1791), of Mount Sinai (p. 1793), of Jerusalem and Palestine
(p. 1798); his laws against the Eutychians (p. 1809, 1811, 1831); the
correspondence of Leo with the provincial synods on the revolution of
Alexandria (p. 1835-1930).

[1] Photius (or rather Eulogius of Alexandria) confesses, in a fine passage,
the specious colour of this double charge against pope Leo and his synod
of Chalcedon (Biblioth. cod. ccxxv. p. 768 [p. 243, ed. Bekk.]). He waged
a double war against the enemies of the church, and wounded either foe
with the darts of his adversary—καταλλήλοις βέλεσι τοὺς ἀντιπάλους
ἐτίτρωσκε. Against Nestorius he seemed to introduce the σύγχυσις of
the Monophysites; against Eutyches he appeared to countenance the
ὑποστασέων διάφορα of the Nestorians. The apologist claims a charitable
interpretation for the saints: if the same had been extended to the heretics,
the sound of the controversy would have been lost in the air.

[2] Αἴλουρος, from his nocturnal expeditions. In darkness and disguise
he crept round the cells of the monastery, and whispered the revelation to
his slumbering brethren (Theodor. Lector. l. i. [c. 8]).

[3] Φόνους τε τολμηθῆναι μυρίους, [καὶ] αἱμάτων πλήθει μολυνθῆναι μὴ μόνον
τὴν γῆν ἀλλὰ καὶ αὐτὸν τὸν ἀέρα. Such is the hyperbolic language of the
Henoticon.

gifts of baptism and the holy communion. Perhaps an extravagant fable of the times may conceal an allegorical picture
of these fanatics, who tortured each other and themselves.
"Under the consulship of Venantius and Celer," says a grave
bishop, "the people of Alexandria, and all Egypt, were seized
with a strange and diabolical frenzy: great and small, slaves
and freedmen, monks and clergy, the natives of the land, who
opposed the synod of Chalcedon, lost their speech and reason,
barked like dogs, and tore, with their own teeth, the flesh from
their hands and arms." [1]

The disorders of thirty years at length produced the famous
HENOTICON [2] of the emperor Zeno, which in his reign, and in
that of Anastasius, was signed by all the bishops of the East,
under the penalty of degradation and exile if they rejected or
infringed this salutary and fundamental law. The clergy may
smile or groan at the presumption of a layman who defines the
articles of faith; yet, if he stoops to the humiliating task, his
mind is less infected by prejudice or interest, and the authority
of the magistrate can only be maintained by the concord of the
people. It is in ecclesiastical story that Zeno appears least contemptible; and I am not able to discern any Manichæan or
Eutychian guilt in the generous saying of Anastasius, That it
was unworthy of an emperor to persecute the worshippers of
Christ and the citizens of Rome. The Henoticon was most
pleasing to the Egyptians; yet the smallest blemish has not been
descried by the jealous and even jaundiced eyes of our orthodox
schoolmen, and it accurately represents the Catholic faith of the
incarnation, without adopting or disclaiming the peculiar terms
or tenets of the hostile sects. A solemn anathema is pronounced
against Nestorius and Eutyches; against all heretics by whom
Christ is divided, or confounded, or reduced to a phantom.
Without defining the number or the article of the word *nature*,
the pure system of St. Cyril, the faith of Nice, Constantinople,
and Ephesus, is respectfully confirmed; but, instead of bowing
at the name of the fourth council, the subject is dismissed by
the censure of all contrary doctrines, *if* any such have been
taught either elsewhere or at Chalcedon. Under this ambiguous

[1] See the Chronicle of Victor Tunnunensis, in the Lectiones Antiquæ of
Canisius, republished by Basnage, tom. i. p. 326.
[2] The Henoticon is transcribed by Evagrius (l. iii. c. 13 [14]), and translated by Liberatus (Brev. c. 18). Pagi (Critica, tom. ii. p. 411) and
Asseman (Biblioth. Orient. tom. i. p. 343) are satisfied that it is free from
heresy; but Petavius (Dogmat. Theolog. tom. v. l. i. c. 13, p. 40) most
unaccountably affirms Chalcedonensem ascivit. An adversary would
prove that he had never read the Henoticon.

expression the friends and the enemies of the last synod might
unite in a silent embrace. The most reasonable Christians
acquiesced in this mode of toleration; but their reason was
feeble and inconstant, and their obedience was despised as timid
and servile by the vehement spirit of their brethren. On a subject which engrossed the thoughts and discourses of men, it was
difficult to preserve an exact neutrality; a book, a sermon, a
prayer, rekindled the flame of controversy; and the bonds of
communion were alternately broken and renewed by the private
animosity of the bishops. The space between Nestorius and
Eutyches was filled by a thousand shades of language and
opinion; the *acephali* [1] of Egypt, and the Roman pontiffs, of
equal valour, though of unequal strength, may be found at the
two extremities of the theological scale. The acephali, without a king or a bishop, were separated above three hundred
years from the patriarchs of Alexandria, who had accepted the
communion of Constantinople, without exacting a formal condemnation of the synod of Chalcedon. For accepting the
communion of Alexandria, without a formal approbation of
the same synod, the patriarchs of Constantinople were anathematised by the popes. Their inflexible despotism involved the
most orthodox of the Greek churches in this spiritual contagion,
denied or doubted the validity of their sacraments, [2] and
fomented, thirty-five years, the schism of the East and West,
till they finally abolished the memory of four Byzantine pontiffs
who had dared to oppose the supremacy of St. Peter. [3] Before
that period the precarious truce of Constantinople and Egypt
had been violated by the zeal of the rival prelates. Macedonius,
who was suspected of the Nestorian heresy, asserted, in disgrace

[1] See Renaudot (Hist. Patriarch. Alex. p. 123, 131, 145, 195, 247). They
were reconciled by the care of Mark I. (A.D. 799-819): he promoted their
chiefs to the bishoprics of Athribis and Talba (perhaps Tava: see D'Anville,
p. 82), and supplied the sacraments, which had failed for want of an
episcopal ordination.

[2] De his quos baptizavit, quos ordinavit Acacius, majorum traditione
confectam et veram, præcipue religiosæ solicitudini congruam præbemus
sine difficultate medicinam (Gelasius, in Epist. i. ad Euphemium, Concil.
tom. v. p. 286). The offer of a medicine proves the disease, and numbers
must have perished before the arrival of the Roman physician. Tillemont himself (Mém. Ecclés. tom. xvi. p. 372, 642, etc.) is shocked at the
proud, uncharitable temper of the popes: they are now glad, says he, to
invoke St. Flavian of Antioch, St. Elias of Jerusalem, etc., to whom they
refused communion whilst upon earth. But Cardinal Baronius is firm and
hard as the rock of St. Peter.

[3] Their names were erased from the diptych of the church: ex venerabili
diptycho, in quo piæ memoriæ transitum ad cœlum habentium episco-
porum vocabula continentur (Concil. tom. iv. p. 1846). This ecclesiastical
record was therefore equivalent to the book of life.

and exile, the synod of Chalcedon, while the successor of Cyril would have purchased its overthrow with a bribe of two thousand pounds of gold.

In the fever of the times the sense, or rather the sound of a syllable, was sufficient to disturb the peace of an empire. The TRISAGION [1] (thrice holy), " Holy, holy, holy, Lord God of Hosts!" is supposed by the Greeks to be the identical hymn which the angels and cherubim eternally repeat before the throne of God, and which, about the middle of the fifth century, was miraculously revealed to the church of Constantinople. The devotion of Antioch soon added, " who was crucified for us!" and this grateful address, either to Christ alone, or to the whole Trinity, may be justified by the rules of theology, and has been gradually adopted by the Catholics of the East and West. But it had been imagined by a Monophysite bishop; [2] the gift of an enemy was at first rejected as a dire and dangerous blasphemy, and the rash innovation had nearly cost the emperor Anastasius his throne and his life. [3] The people of Constantinople was devoid of any rational principles of freedom; but they held, as a lawful cause of rebellion, the colour of a livery in the races, or the colour of a mystery in the schools. The Trisagion, with and without this obnoxious addition, was chanted in the cathedral by two adverse choirs, and, when their lungs were exhausted, they had recourse to the more solid arguments of sticks and stones; the aggressors were punished by the emperor, and defended by the patriarch; and the crown and mitre were staked on the event of this momentous quarrel. The streets were instantly crowded with innumerable swarms of men, women, and children; the legions of monks, in regular array, marched, and shouted, and fought at their head. " Christians! this is the day of martyrdom: let us not desert our spiritual father; anathema to the Manichæan tyrant! he is unworthy to reign." Such was

---

[1] Petavius (Dogmat. Theolog. tom. v. l. v. c. 2, 3, 4, p. 217-225) and Tillemont (Mém. Ecclés. tom. xiv. p. 713, etc., 799) represent the history and doctrine of the Trisagion. In the twelve centuries between Isaiah and St. Proclus's boy, who was taken up into heaven before the bishop and people of Constantinople, the song was considerably improved. The boy heard the angels sing, " Holy God! Holy strong! Holy immortal!"

[2] Peter Gnapheus, the *fuller* (a trade which he had exercised in his monastery), patriarch of Antioch. His tedious story is discussed in the Annals of Pagi (A.D. 477-490) and a dissertation of M. de Valois at the end of his Evagrius.

[3] The troubles under the reign of Anastasius must be gathered from the Chronicles of Victor, Marcellinus, and Theophanes. As the last was not published in the time of Baronius, his critic Pagi is more copious, as well as more correct.

the Catholic cry; and the galleys of Anastasius lay upon their oars before the palace, till the patriarch had pardoned his penitent, and hushed the waves of the troubled multitude. The triumph of Macedonius was checked by a speedy exile; but the zeal of his flock was again exasperated by the same question, " Whether one of the Trinity had been crucified? " On this momentous occasion the blue and green factions of Constantinople suspended their discord, and the civil and military powers were annihilated in their presence. The keys of the city, and the standards of the guards, were deposited in the forum of Constantine, the principal station and camp of the faithful. Day and night they were incessantly busied either in singing hymns to the honour of their God, or in pillaging and murdering the servants of their prince. The head of his favourite monk, the friend, as they styled him, of the enemy of the Holy Trinity, was borne aloft on a spear; and the fire-brands, which had been darted against heretical structures, diffused the undistinguishing flames over the most orthodox buildings. The statues of the emperor were broken, and his person was concealed in a suburb, till, at the end of three days, he dared to implore the mercy of his subjects. Without his diadem, and in the posture of a suppliant, Anastasius appeared on the throne of the circus. The Catholics, before his face, rehearsed their genuine Trisagion; they exulted in the offer which he proclaimed by the voice of a herald of abdicating the purple; they listened to the admonition, that, since *all* could not reign, they should previously agree in the choice of a sovereign: and they accepted the blood of two unpopular ministers, whom their master without hesitation condemned to the lions. These furious but transient seditions were encouraged by the success of Vitalian, who, with an army of Huns and Bulgarians, for the most part idolaters, declared himself the champion of the Catholic faith. In this pious rebellion he depopulated Thrace, besieged Constantinople, exterminated sixty-five thousand of his fellow-Christians, till he obtained the recall of the bishops, the satisfaction of the pope, and the establishment of the council of Chalcedon, an orthodox treaty, reluctantly signed by the dying Anastasius, and more faithfully performed by the uncle of Justinian. And such was the event of the *first* of the religious wars which have been waged in the name and by the disciples of the God of Peace.[1]

[1] The general history, from the council of Chalcedon to the death of Anastasius, may be found in the Breviary of Liberatus (c. 14-19), the second and third books of Evagrius, the Abstract of the two books of Theodore

Justinian has been already seen in the various lights of a prince, a conqueror, and a lawgiver: the theologian [1] still remains, and it affords an unfavourable prejudice that his theology should form a very prominent feature of his portrait. The sovereign sympathised with his subjects in their superstitious reverence for living and departed saints: his Code, and more especially his Novels, confirm and enlarge the privileges of the clergy; and in every dispute between a monk and a layman, the partial judge was inclined to pronounce that truth and innocence and justice were always on the side of the church. In his public and private devotions the emperor was assiduous and exemplary; his prayers, vigils, and fasts displayed the austere penance of a monk; his fancy was amused by the hope or belief of personal inspiration; he had secured the patronage of the Virgin and St. Michael the archangel; and his recovery from a dangerous disease was ascribed to the miraculous succour of the holy martyrs Cosmas and Damian. The capital and the provinces of the East were decorated with the monuments of his religion; [2] and though the far greater part of these costly structures may be attributed to his taste or ostentation, the zeal of the royal architect was probably quickened by a genuine sense of love and gratitude towards his invisible benefactors. Among the titles of Imperial greatness the name of *Pious* was most pleasing to his ear; to promote the temporal and spiritual interest of the church was the serious business of his life; and the duty of father of his country was often sacrificed to that of defender of the faith. The controversies of the times were congenial to his temper and understanding; and the theological professors must inwardly deride the diligence of a stranger who cultivated their art and neglected his own. " What can ye fear," said a bold conspirator to his associates, " from your bigoted tyrant? Sleepless and

the Reader, the Acts of the Synods, and the Epistles of the Popes (Concil. tom. v.). The series is continued with some disorder in the fifteenth and sixteenth tomes of the Mémoires Ecclésiastiques of Tillemont. And here I must take leave for ever of that incomparable guide, whose bigotry is overbalanced by the merits of erudition, diligence, veracity, and scrupulous minuteness. He was prevented by death from completing, as he designed, the sixth century of the church and empire.

[1] The strain of the Anecdotes of Procopius (c. 11, 13, 18, 27, 28) with the learned remarks of Alemannus is confirmed, rather than contradicted, by the Acts of the Councils, the fourth book of Evagrius, and the complaints of the African Facundus, in his twelfth book—de tribus capitulis, " cum videri doctus appetit importune . . . spontaneis quæstionibus ecclesiam turbat." See Procop. de Bell. Goth. l. iii. c. 35 [tom. ii. p. 429, ed. Bonn].

[2] Procop. de Ædificiis, l. i. c. 6, 7, etc., passim.

unarmed he sits whole nights in his closet debating with reverend greybeards, and turning over the pages of ecclesiastical volumes." [1] The fruits of these lucubrations were displayed in many a conference, where Justinian might shine as the loudest and most subtle of the disputants; in many a sermon, which, under the name of edicts and epistles, proclaimed to the empire the theology of their master. While the barbarians invaded the provinces, while the victorious legions marched under the banners of Belisarius and Narses, the successor of Trajan, unknown to the camp, was content to vanquish at the head of a synod. Had he invited to these synods a disinterested and rational spectator, Justinian might have learned " *that* religious controversy is the offspring of arrogance and folly; *that* true piety is most laudably expressed by silence and submission; *that* man, ignorant of his own nature, should not presume to scrutinise the nature of his God; and *that* it is sufficient for us to know that power and benevolence are the perfect attributes of the Deity." [2]

Toleration was not the virtue of the times, and indulgence to rebels has seldom been the virtue of princes. But when the prince descends to the narrow and peevish character of a disputant, he is easily provoked to supply the defect of argument by the plenitude of power, and to chastise without mercy the perverse blindness of those who wilfully shut their eyes against the light of demonstration. The reign of Justinian was a uniform yet various scene of persecution; and he appears to have surpassed his indolent predecessors, both in the contrivance of his laws and the rigour of their execution. The insufficient term of three months was assigned for the conversion or exile of all heretics; [3] and if he still connived at their precarious stay,

---

[1] Ὃς δὴ κάθηται ἀφύλακτος ἐς ἀεὶ ἐπὶ λέσχης τινὸς ἀωρὶ νυκτῶν, ὁμοῦ τοῖς τῶν ἱερέων ἔσχατον γέρουσιν [ἐσχατογέρουσιν] ἀνακυκλεῖν τὰ Χριστιανῶν λόγια σπουδὴν ἔχων. Procop. de Bell. Goth. l. iii. c. 32 [tom. ii. p. 409, ed. Bonn]. In the Life of St. Eutychius (apud Aleman. ad Procop. Arcan. c. 18 [tom. iii. p. 439, ed. Bonn]) the same character is given with a design to praise Justinian

[2] For these wise and moderate sentiments Procopius (de Bell. Goth. l. i. c. 3) is scourged in the preface of Alemannus, who ranks him among the *political* Christians—sed longe verius hæresium omnium sentinas, prorsusque Atheos—abominable Atheists, who preached the imitation of God's mercy to man (ad Hist. Arcan. c. 13).

[3] This alternative, a precious circumstance, is preserved by John Malala (tom. ii. p. 63, edit. Venet. 1733 [p. 449, ed Bonn]), who deserves more credit as he draws towards his end. After numbering the heretics, Nestorians, Eutychians, etc., ne expectent, says Justinian, ut digni veniâ judicentur: jubemus enim ut . . . convicti et aperti hæretici justæ et idoneæ animadversioni subjiciantur. Baronius copies and applauds this edict of the Code (A.D. 527, No. 39, 40)

they were deprived, under his iron yoke, not only of the benefits of society, but of the common birthright of men and Christians.

At the end of four hundred years the Montanists of Phrygia [1] still breathed the wild enthusiasm of perfection and prophecy which they had imbibed from their male and female apostles, the special organs of the Paraclete. On the approach of the Catholic priests and soldiers, they grasped with alacrity the crown of martyrdom; the conventicle and the congregation perished in the flames, but these primitive fanatics were not extinguished three hundred years after the death of their tyrant. Under the protection of the Gothic confederates, the church of the Arians at Constantinople had braved the severity of the laws: their clergy equalled the wealth and magnificence of the senate; and the gold and silver which were seized by the rapacious hand of Justinian might perhaps be claimed as the spoils of the provinces and the trophies of the barbarians. A secret remnant of pagans, who still lurked in the most refined and most rustic conditions of mankind, excited the indignation of the Christians, who were perhaps unwilling that any strangers should be the witnesses of their intestine quarrels. A bishop was named as the inquisitor of the faith, and his diligence soon discovered, in the court and city, the magistrates, lawyers, physicians, and sophists, who still cherished the superstition of the Greeks. They were sternly informed that they must choose without delay between the displeasure of Jupiter or Justinian, and that their aversion to the gospel could no longer be disguised under the scandalous mask of indifference or impiety. The patrician Photius perhaps alone was resolved to live and to die like his ancestors: he enfranchised himself with the stroke of a dagger, and left his tyrant the poor consolation of exposing with ignominy the lifeless corpse of the fugitive. His weaker brethren submitted to their earthly monarch, underwent the ceremony of baptism, and laboured, by their extraordinary zeal, to erase the suspicion, or to expiate the guilt, of idolatry. The native country of Homer, and the theatre of the Trojan war, still retained the last sparks of his mythology: by the care of the same bishop, seventy thousand pagans were detected and converted in Asia, Phrygia, Lydia, and Caria; ninety-six churches were built for the new proselytes; and linen vestments, bibles and liturgies, and vases of gold and silver, were supplied by the pious

[1] See the character and principles of the Montanists, in Mosheim, de Rebus Christ. ante Constantinum, p. 410-424.

munificence of Justinian.[1] The Jews, who had been gradually stripped of their immunities, were oppressed by a vexatious law, which compelled them to observe the festival of Easter the same day on which it was celebrated by the Christians.[2] And they might complain with the more reason, since the Catholics themselves did not agree with the astronomical calculations of their sovereign: the people of Constantinople delayed the beginning of their Lent a whole week after it had been ordained by authority; and they had the pleasure of fasting seven days, while meat was exposed for sale by the command of the emperor. The Samaritans of Palestine [3] were a motley race, an ambiguous sect, rejected as Jews by the pagans, by the Jews as schismatics, and by the Christians as idolators. The abomination of the cross had already been planted on their holy mount of Garizim,[4] but the persecution of Justinian offered only the alternative of baptism or rebellion. They chose the latter: under the standard of a desperate leader they rose in arms, and retaliated their wrongs on the lives, the property, and the temples of a defenceless people. The Samaritans were finally subdued by the regular forces of the East: twenty thousand were slain, twenty thousand were sold by the Arabs to the infidels of Persia and India, and the remains of that unhappy nation atoned for the crime of treason by the sin of hypocrisy. It has been computed that one hundred thousand Roman subjects were extirpated in the Samaritan war,[5] which converted the once fruitful province into a desolate

---

[1] Theophan. Chron. p. 153 [tom. i. p. 276, ed. Bonn]. John, the Monophysite bishop of Asia, is a more authentic witness of this transaction, in which he was himself employed by the emperor (Asseman. Bib. Orient. tom. ii. p. 85).

[2] Compare Procopius (Hist. Arcan. c. 28 [tom. iii. p. 156, ed. Bonn] and Aleman's Notes) with Theophanes (Chron. p. 190 [tom. i. p. 340, ed. Bonn]). The council of Nice has intrusted the patriarch, or rather the astronomers, of Alexandria, with the annual proclamation of Easter; and we still read, or rather we do not read, many of the Paschal epistles of St. Cyril. Since the reign of Monophytism in Egypt, the Catholics were perplexed by such a foolish prejudice as that which so long opposed, among the Protestants, the reception of the Gregorian style.

[3] For the religion and history of the Samaritans, consult Basnage, Histoire des Juifs, a learned and impartial work.

[4] Sichem, Neapolis, Naplous, the ancient and modern seat of the Samaritans, is situate in a valley between the barren Ebal, the mountain of cursing to the north, and the fruitful *Garizim*, or mountain of cursing to the south, ten or eleven hours' travel from Jerusalem. See Maundrell, Journey from Aleppo, etc., p. 59-63.

[5] Procop. Anecdot. c. 11 [p. 75, ed. Bonn]; Theophan. Chron. p. 122 [vol. i. p. 274, ed. Bonn]; John Malala, Chron. tom. ii. p. 62 [p. 447, ed. Bonn]. I remember an observation, half philosophical, half superstitious, that the province which had been ruined by the bigotry of Justinian was the same through which the Mohammedans penetrated into the empire.

and smoking wilderness. But in the creed of Justinian the guilt of murder could not be applied to the slaughter of unbelievers; and he piously laboured to establish with fire and sword the unity of the Christian faith.[1]

With these sentiments, it was incumbent on him, at least, to be always in the right. In the first years of his administration he signalised his zeal as the disciple and patron of orthodoxy: the reconciliation of the Greeks and Latins established the *tome* of St. Leo as the creed of the emperor and the empire; the Nestorians and Eutychians were exposed, on either side, to the double edge of persecution; and the four synods, of Nice, Constantinople, Ephesus, and *Chalcedon*, were ratified by the code of a Catholic law-giver.[2] But while Justinian strove to maintain the uniformity of faith and worship, his wife Theodora, whose vices were not incompatible with devotion, had listened to the Monophysite teachers; and the open or clandestine enemies of the church revived and multiplied at the smile of their gracious patroness. The capital, the palace, the nuptial bed, were torn by spiritual discord; yet so doubtful was the sincerity of the royal consorts, that their seeming disagreement was imputed by many to a secret and mischievous confederacy against the religion and happiness of their people.[3] The famous dispute of the THREE CHAPTERS,[4] which has filled more volumes than it deserves lines, is deeply marked with this subtle and disingenuous spirit. It was now three hundred years since the

---

[1] The expression of Procopius is remarkable: οὐ γὰρ οἱ ἐδόκει φόνος ἀνθρώπων εἶναι, ἤν γε μὴ τῆς αὑτοῦ δόξης οἱ τελευτῶντες τύχοιεν ὄντες. Anecdot. c. 13 [p. 84, ed. Bonn].

[2] See the Chronicle of Victor, p. 328, and the original evidence of the laws of Justinian. During the first years of his reign, Baronius himself is in extreme good humour with the emperor, who courted the popes, till he got them into his power.

[3] Procopius, Anecdot. c. 13; Evagrius, l. iv. c. 10. If the ecclesiastical never read the secret historian, their common suspicion proves at least the general hatred.

[4] On the subject of the three chapters, the original acts of the fifth general council of Constantinople supply much useless though authentic knowledge (Concil. tom. vi. p. 1-419). The *Greek* Evagrius is less copious and correct (l. iv. c. 38) than the three zealous *Africans*, Facundus (in his twelve books, de tribus capitulis, which are most correctly published by Sirmond), Liberatus (in his Breviarium, c. 22, 23, 24), and Victor Tununensis in his Chronicle (in tom. i. Antiq. Lect. Canisii, p. 330-334). The Liber Pontificalis, or Anastasius (in Vigilio, Pelagio, etc.), is original *Italian* evidence. The modern reader will derive some information from Dupin (Biblioth. Ecclés. tom. v. p. 189-207) and Basnage (Hist. de l'Eglise, tom. i. p. 519-541); yet the latter is too firmly resolved to depreciate the authority and character of the popes.

body of Origen [1] had been eaten by the worms: his soul, of which he held the pre-existence, was in the hands of its Creator; but his writings were eagerly perused by the monks of Palestine. In these writings the piercing eye of Justinian descried more than ten metaphysical errors; and the primitive doctor, in the company of Pythagoras and Plato, was devoted by the clergy to the *eternity* of hell-fire, which he had presumed to deny. Under the cover of this precedent a treacherous blow was aimed at the council of Chalcedon. The fathers had listened without impatience to the praise of Theodore of Mopsuestia; [2] and their justice or indulgence had restored both Theodoret of Cyrrhus and Ibas of Edessa to the communion of the church. But the characters of these Oriental bishops were tainted with the reproach of heresy; the first had been the master, the two others were the friends, of Nestorius: their most suspicious passages were accused under the title of the *three chapters ;* and the condemnation of their memory must involve the honour of a synod whose name was pronounced with sincere or affected reverence by the Catholic world. If these bishops, whether innocent or guilty, were annihilated in the sleep of death, they would not probably be awakened by the clamour which, after a hundred years, was raised over their grave. If they were already in the fangs of the demon, their torments could neither be aggravated nor assuaged by human industry. If in the company of saints and angels they enjoyed the rewards of piety, they must have smiled at the idle fury of the theological insects who still crawled on the surface of the earth. The foremost of these insects, the emperor of the Romans, darted his sting, and distilled his venom, perhaps without discerning the true motives of Theodora and her ecclesiastical faction. The victims were no longer subject to his power, and the vehement style of his edicts could only proclaim their damnation, and invite the clergy of the East to join in a full chorus of curses and anathemas. The East, with some hesitation, consented to the voice of her sovereign: the fifth general council, of three patriarchs and one hundred and

---

[1] Origen had indeed too great a propensity to imitate the πλάνη and δυσσέβεια of the old philosophers (Justinian, ad Mennam, in Concil. tom. vi. p. 356). His moderate opinions were too repugnant to the zeal of the church, and he was found guilty of the heresy of reason.

[2] Basnage (Præfat. p. 11-14, ad tom. i. Antiq. Lect. Canis.) has fairly weighed the guilt and innocence of Theodore of Mopsuestia. If he composed 10,000 volumes, as many errors would be a charitable allowance. In all the subsequent catalogues of heresiarchs, he alone, without his two brethren, is included; and it is the duty of Asseman (Biblioth. Orient. tom. iv. p. 203-207) to justify the sentence.

sixty-five bishops, was held at Constantinople; and the authors, as well as the defenders of the three chapters, were separated from the communion of the saints, and solemnly delivered to the prince of darkness. But the Latin churches were more jealous of the honour of Leo and the synod of Chalcedon; and if they had fought as they usually did under the standard of Rome, they might have prevailed in the cause of reason and humanity. But their chief was a prisoner in the hands of the enemy; the throne of St. Peter, which had been disgraced by the simony, was betrayed by the cowardice, of Vigilius, who yielded, after a long and inconsistent struggle, to the despotism of Justinian and the sophistry of the Greeks. His apostacy provoked the indignation of the Latins, and no more than two bishops could be found who would impose their hands on his deacon and successor Pelagius. Yet the perseverance of the popes insensibly transferred to their adversaries the appellation of schismatics; the Illyrian, African, and Italian churches were oppressed by the civil and ecclesiastical powers, not without some effort of military force; [1] the distant barbarians transcribed the creed of the Vatican, and, in the period of a century, the schism of the three chapters expired in an obscure angle of the Venetian province. [2] But the religious discontent of the Italians had already promoted the conquests of the Lombards, and the Romans themselves were accustomed to suspect the faith, and to detest the government, of their Byzantine tyrant.

Justinian was neither steady nor consistent in the nice process of fixing his volatile opinions and those of his subjects. In his youth he was offended by the slightest deviation from the orthodox line; in his old age he transgressed the measure of temperate heresy, and the Jacobites, not less than the Catholics, were scandalised by his declaration that the body of Christ was incorruptible, and that his manhood was never subject to any wants and infirmities, the inheritance of our mortal flesh. This

---

[1] See the complaints of Liberatus and Victor, and the exhortations of pope Pelagius to the conqueror and exarch of Italy. Schisma . . . per potestates publicas opprimatur, etc. (Concil. tom. vi. p. 467, etc.). An army was detained to suppress the sedition of an Illyrian city. See Procopius (de Bell. Goth. l. iv. c. 25 [tom. iii. p. 594, ed. Bonn]): ὧνπερ ἕνεκα σφίσιν αὐτοῖς οἱ Χριστιανοὶ διαμάχονται. He seems to promise an ecclesiastical history. It would have been curious and impartial.

[2] The bishops of the patriarchate of Aquileia were reconciled by pope Honorius A.D. 638 (Muratori, Annali d'Italia, tom. v. p. 376); but they again relapsed, and the schism was not finally extinguished till 698. Fourteen years before, the church of Spain had overlooked the fifth general council with contemptuous silence (xiii. Concil. Toletan. in Concil. tom. vii. p. 487-494).

fantastic opinion was announced in the last edicts of Justinian; and at the moment of his seasonable departure, the clergy had refused to subscribe, the prince was prepared to persecute, and the people were resolved to suffer or resist. A bishop of Trèves, secure beyond the limits of his power, addressed the monarch of the East in the language of authority and affection. " Most gracious Justinian, remember your baptism and your creed. Let not your grey hairs be defiled with heresy. Recall your fathers from exile, and your followers from perdition. You cannot be ignorant that Italy and Gaul, Spain and Africa, already deplore your fall and anathematise your name. Unless, without delay, you destroy what you have taught; unless you exclaim with a loud voice, I have erred, I have sinned, anathema to Nestorius, anathema to Eutyches, you deliver your soul to the same flames in which *they* will eternally burn." He died and made no sign.[1] His death restored in some degree the peace of the church, and the reigns of his four successors, Justin, Tiberius, Maurice, and Phocas, are distinguished by a rare, though fortunate, vacancy in the ecclesiastical history of the East.[2]

The faculties of sense and reason are least capable of acting on themselves; the eye is most inaccessible to the sight, the soul to the thought; yet we think, and even feel, that *one will*, a sole principle of action, is essential to a rational and conscious being. When Heraclius returned from the Persian war, the orthodox hero consulted his bishops whether the Christ whom he adored, of one person but of two natures, was actuated by a single or a double will. They replied in the singular, and the emperor was encouraged to hope that the Jacobites of Egypt and Syria might be reconciled by the profession of a doctrine most certainly harmless and most probably true, since it was taught even by the Nestorians themselves.[3] The experiment was tried without

---

[1] Nicetius, bishop of Trèves (Concil. tom. vi. p. 511-513): he himself, like most of the Gallican prelates (Gregor. Epist. l. vii. Ep. 5, in Concil. tom. vi. p. 1007), was separated from the communion of the four patriarchs by his refusal to condemn the three chapters. Baronius almost pronounces the damnation of Justinian (A.D. 565, No. 6).

[2] After relating the last heresy of Justinian (l. iv. c. 39, 40, 41) and the edict of his successor (l. v. c. 3 [4]), the remainder of the history of Evagrius is filled with civil, instead of ecclesiastical, events.

[3] This extraordinary, and perhaps inconsistent, doctrine of the Nestorians, had been observed by La Croze (Christianisme des Indes, tom. i. p. 19, 20), and is more fully exposed by Abulpharagius (Biblioth. Orient. tom. ii. p. 292; Hist. Dynast. p. 91, vers. Latin. Pocock), and Asseman himself (tom. iv. p. 218). They seem ignorant that they might allege the positive authority of the ecthesis. Ὁ μίαρος Νεστόριος καίπερ διαιρῶν

effect, and the timid or vehement Catholics condemned even the semblance of a retreat in the presence of a subtle and audacious enemy. The orthodox (the prevailing) party devised new modes of speech, and argument, and interpretation: to either nature of Christ they speciously applied a proper and distinct energy; but the difference was no longer visible when they allowed that the human and the divine will were invariably the same.[1] The disease was attended with the customary symptoms; but the Greek clergy, as if satiate with the endless controversy of the incarnation, instilled a healing counsel into the ear of the prince and people. They declared themselves MONOTHE-LITES (asserters of the unity of will), but they treated the words as new, the questions as superfluous; and recommended a religious silence as the most agreeable to the prudence and charity of the gospel. This law of silence was successively imposed by the *ecthesis* or exposition of Heraclius, the *type* or model of his grandson Constans;[2] and the Imperial edicts were subscribed with alacrity or reluctance by the four patriarchs of Rome, Constantinople, Alexandria, and Antioch. But the bishop and monks of Jerusalem sounded the alarm: in the language, or even in the silence, of the Greeks, the Latin churches detected a latent heresy; and the obedience of pope Honorius to the commands of his sovereign was retracted and censured by the bolder ignorance of his successors. They condemned the execrable and abominable heresy of the Monothelites, who revived the errors of Manes, Apollinaris, Eutyches, etc.; they signed the sentence of excommunication on the tomb of St. Peter; the ink was mingled with the sacramental wine, the blood of Christ; and no ceremony was omitted that could fill the superstitious mind with horror and affright. As the representative of the Western church, pope Martin and his Lateran synod anathematised the perfidious and guilty silence of the

τὴν θείαν τοῦ Κυρίου ἐνανθρώπησιν, καὶ δύο εἰσάγων υἱοὺς (the common reproach of the Monophysites), δύο θελήματα τούτων εἴπειν οὐκ ἐτόλμησε, τουνάντιον δὲ τοῦτο βουλίαν τῶν . . . . δύο πρόσωπων ἐδόξασε (Concil. tom. vii. p. 205).

[1] See the orthodox faith in Petavius (Dogmata Theolog. tom. v. l. ix. c. 6-10, p. 433-447): all the depths of this controversy are sounded in the Greek dialogue between Maximus and Pyrrhus (ad calcem, tom. viii. Annal. Baron. p. 755-794), which relates a real conference, and produced as a short-lived conversion.

[2] Impiissimam ecthesim . . . scelerosum typum (Concil. tom. vii. p. 366) diabolicæ operationis genimina (fors. *germina*, or else the Greek γενήματα, in the original—Concil. p. 363, 364) are the expressions of the eighteenth anathema. The epistle of pope Martin to Amandus, a Gallican bishop, stigmatises the Monothelites and their heresy with equal virulence (p. 392).

Greeks: one hundred and five bishops of Italy, for the most part the subjects of Constans, presumed to reprobate his wicked *type* and the impious *ecthesis* of his grandfather; and to confound the authors and their adherents with the twenty-one notorious heretics, the apostates from the church and the organs of the devil. Such an insult under the tamest reign could not pass with impunity. Pope Martin ended his days on the inhospitable shore of the Tauric Chersonesus, and his oracle, the abbot Maximus, was inhumanly chastised by the amputation of his tongue and his right hand.[1] But the same invincible spirit survived in their successors; and the triumph of the Latins avenged their recent defeat and obliterated the disgrace of the three chapters. The synods of Rome were confirmed by the sixth general council of Constantinople, in the palace and the presence of a new Constantine, a descendant of Heraclius. The royal convert converted the Byzantine pontiff and a majority of the bishops;[2] the dissenters, with their chief, Macarius of Antioch, were condemned to the spiritual and temporal pains of heresy; the East condescended to accept the lessons of the West; and the creed was finally settled which teaches the Catholics of every age that two wills or energies are harmonised in the person of Christ. The majesty of the pope and the Roman synod was represented by two priests, one deacon, and three bishops; but these obscure Latins had neither arms to compel, nor treasures to bribe, nor language to persuade; and I am ignorant by what arts they could determine the lofty emperor of the Greeks to abjure the catechism of his infancy, and to persecute the religion of his fathers. Perhaps the monks and people of Constantinople[3] were favourable to the Lateran creed, which is indeed the least reasonable of the two: and the suspicion is coun-

---

[1] The sufferings of Martin and Maximus are described with pathetic simplicity in their original letters and acts (Concil. tom. vii. p. 63-78; Baron. Annal. Eccles. A.D. 656, No. 2, et annos subsequent.). Yet the chastisement of their disobedience, ἐξόρια and σώματος αἰκισμος, had been previously announced in the Type of Constans (Concil. tom. vii. p. 240).

[2] Eutychius (Annal. tom. ii. p. 348) most erroneously supposes that the 124 bishops of the Roman synod transported themselves to Constantinople; and by adding them to the 168 Greeks, thus composes the sixth council of 292 fathers.

[3] The Monothelite Constans was hated by all, διὰ τοι ταῦτα (says Theophanes, Chron p. 292 [ed. Par.; tom. i. p. 538, ed. Bonn]) ἐμισήθη σφόδρως παρὰ πάντων. When the Monothelite monk failed in his miracle, the people shouted, ὁ λαὸς ἀνεβόησε (Concil. tom. vii. p. 1032). But this was a natural and transient emotion; and I much fear that the latter is an anticipation of orthodoxy in the good people of Constantinople.

tenanced by the unnatural moderation of the Greek clergy, who appear in this quarrel to be conscious of their weakness. While the synod debated, a fanatic proposed a more summary decision, by raising a dead man to life: the prelates assisted at the trial; but the acknowledged failure may serve to indicate that the passions and prejudices of the multitude were not enlisted on the side of the Monothelites. In the next generation, when the son of Constantine was deposed and slain by the disciple of Macarius, they tasted the feast of revenge and dominion; the image or monument of the sixth council was defaced, and the original acts were committed to the flames. But in the second year their patron was cast headlong from the throne, the bishops of the East were released from their occasional conformity, the Roman faith was more firmly replanted by the orthodox successors of Bardanes, and the fine problems of the incarnation were forgotten in the more popular and visible quarrel of the worship of images.[1]

Before the end of the seventh century the creed of the incarnation, which had been defined at Rome and Constantinople, was uniformly preached in the remote islands of Britain and Ireland;[2] the same ideas were entertained, or rather the same words were repeated, by all the Christians whose liturgy was performed in the Greek or the Latin tongue. Their numbers and visible splendour bestowed an imperfect claim to the appellation of Catholics: but in the East they were marked with the

---

[1] The history of Monothelitism may be found in the Acts of the Synods of Rome (tom. vii. p. 77-395, 601-608) and Constantinople (p. 609-1429). Baronius extracted some original documents from the Vatican library; and his chronology is rectified by the diligence of Pagi. Even Dupin (Bibliothèque Ecclés. tom. vi. p. 57-71) and Basnage (Hist. de l'Eglise, tom. i. p. 541-555) afford a tolerable abridgment.

[2] In the Lateran synod of 679, Wilfrid, an Anglo-Saxon bishop, subscribed pro omni Aquilonari parte Britanniæ et Hiberniæ, quæ ab Anglorum et Brittonum, necnon Scotorum et Pictorum gentibus colebantur (Eddius, in Vit. St. Wilfrid, c. 31, apud Pagi, Critica, tom. iii. p. 88). Theodore (magnæ insulæ Britanniæ archiepiscopus et philosophus) was long expected at Rome (Concil. tom. vii. p. 714), but he contented himself with holding (A.D. 680) his provincial synod of Hatfield, in which he received the decrees of pope Martin and the first Lateran council against the Monothelites (Concil. tom. vii. p. 597, etc.). Theodore, a monk of Tarsus in Cilicia, had been named to the primacy of Britain by pope Vitalian (A.D. 668, see Baronius and Pagi), whose esteem for his learning and piety was tainted by some distrust of his national character—ne quid contrarium veritati fidei, Græcorum more, in ecclesiam cui præesset introduceret. The Cilican was sent from Rome to Canterbury under the tuition of an African guide (Bedæ Hist. Eccles. Anglorum, l. iv. c. 1). He adhered to the Roman doctrine; and the same creed of the incarnation has been uniformly transmitted from Theodore to the modern primates, whose sound understanding is perhaps seldom engaged with that abstruse mystery.

less honourable name of *Melchites*, or Royalists; [1] of men whose faith, instead of resting on the basis of Scripture, reason, or tradition, had been established, and was still maintained, by the arbitrary power of a temporal monarch. Their adversaries might allege the words of the fathers of Constantinople, who profess themselves the slaves of the king; and they might relate, with malicious joy, how the decrees of Chalcedon had been inspired and reformed by the emperor Marcian and his virgin bride. The prevailing faction will naturally inculcate the duty of submission, nor is it less natural that dissenters should feel and assert the principles of freedom. Under the rod of persecution the Nestorians and Monophysites degenerated into rebels and fugitives; and the most ancient and useful allies of Rome were taught to consider the emperor not as the chief but as the enemy of the Christians. Language, the leading principle which unites or separates the tribes of mankind, soon discriminated the sectaries of the East by a peculiar and perpetual badge which abolished the means of intercourse and the hope of reconciliation. The long dominion of the Greeks, their colonies, and above all their eloquence, had propagated a language doubtless the most perfect that has been contrived by the art of man. Yet the body of the people, both in Syria and Egypt, still persevered in the use of their national idioms; with this difference, however, that the Coptic was confined to the rude and illiterate peasants of the Nile, while the Syriac,[2] from the mountains of Assyria to the Red Sea, was adapted to the higher topics of poetry and argument. Armenia and Abyssinia were infected by the speech or learning of the Greeks; and their barbaric tongues, which have been revived in the studies of modern Europe, were unintelligible to the inhabitants of the Roman empire. The Syriac and the Coptic, the Armenian and the Æthiopic, are consecrated in the service of their respective

---

[1] This name, unknown till the tenth century, appears to be of Syriac origin. It was invented by the Jacobites, and eagerly adopted by the Nestorians and Mahometans; but it was accepted without shame by the Catholics, and is frequently used in the Annals of Eutychius (Asseman. Biblioth. Orient. tom. ii. p. 507, etc., tom. iii. p. 355; Renaudot, Hist. Patriarch. Alexandrin. p. 119). Ἡμεῖς δοῦλοι τοῦ Βασιλέως, was the acclamation of the fathers of Constantinople (Concil. tom. vii. p. 765).

[2] The Syriac, which the natives revere as the primitive language, was divided into three dialects. 1. The *Aramæan*, as it was refined at Edessa and the cities of Mesopotamia; 2. The *Palestine*, which was used in Jerusalem, Damascus, and the rest of Syria; 3. The *Nabathæan*, the rustic idiom of the mountains of Assyria and the villages of Irak (Gregor. Abulpharag. Hist. Dynast. p. 11). On the Syriac, see Ebed-Jesu (Asseman. tom. iii. p. 326, etc.), whose prejudice alone could prefer it to the Arabic.

churches; and their theology is enriched by domestic versions [1] both of the scriptures and of the most popular fathers. After a period of thirteen hundred and sixty years, the spark of controversy, first kindled by a sermon of Nestorius, still burns in the bosom of the East, and the hostile communions still maintain the faith and discipline of their founders. In the most abject state of ignorance, poverty, and servitude, the Nestorians and Monophysites reject the spiritual supremacy of Rome, and cherish the toleration of their Turkish masters, which allows them to anathematise, on one hand, St. Cyril and the synod of Ephesus; on the other, pope Leo and the council of Chalcedon. The weight which they cast into the downfall of the Eastern empire demands our notice, and the reader may be amused with the various prospect of, I. The Nestorians; II. The Jacobites; [2] III. The Maronites; IV. The Armenians; V. The Copts; and VI. The Abyssinians. To the three former the Syriac is common; but of the latter, each is discriminated by the use of a national idiom. Yet the modern natives of Armenia and Abyssinia would be incapable of conversing with their ancestors; and the Christians of Egypt and Syria, who reject the religion, have adopted the language, of the Arabians. The lapse of time has seconded the sacerdotal arts; and in the East as well as in the West the Deity is addressed in an obsolete tongue unknown to the majority of the congregation.

I. Both in his native and his episcopal province the heresy of the unfortunate Nestorius was speedily obliterated. The Oriental bishops, who at Ephesus had resisted to his face the arrogance of Cyril, were mollified by his tardy concessions. The same prelates, or their successors, subscribed, not without a murmur, the decrees of Chalcedon; the power of the Monophysites reconciled them with the Catholics in the conformity of passion, of interest, and, insensibly, of belief; and their last

[1] I shall not enrich my ignorance with the spoils of Simon, Walton, Mill, Wetstein, Assemannus, Ludolphus, La Croze, whom I have consulted with some care. It appears, 1. *That*, of all the versions which are celebrated by the fathers, it is doubtful whether any are now extant in their pristine integrity. 2. *That* the Syriac has the best claim, and that the consent of the Oriental sects is a proof that it is more ancient than their schism.

[2] In the account of the Monophysites and Nestorians I am deeply indebted to the Bibliotheca Orientalis Clementino-Vaticana of Joseph Simon Assemannus. That learned Maronite was despatched in the year 1715 by pope Clement XI. to visit the monasteries of Egypt and Syria, in search of MSS. His four folio volumes, published at Rome 1719-1728, contain a part only, though perhaps the most valuable, of his extensive project. As a native and as a scholar, he possessed the Syriac literature; and, though a dependent of Rome, he wishes to be moderate and candid.

reluctant sigh was breathed in the defence of the three chapters.
Their dissenting brethren, less moderate or more sincere, were
crushed by the penal laws; and, as early as the reign of
Justinian, it became difficult to find a church of Nestorians
within the limits of the Roman empire. Beyond those limits
they had discovered a new world in which they might hope for
liberty and aspire to conquest. In Persia, notwithstanding the
resistance of the Magi, Christianity had struck a deep root, and
the nations of the East reposed under its salutary shade. The
catholic, or primate, resided in the capital: in *his* synods, and in
their dioceses, his metropolitans, bishops, and clergy represented
the pomp and order of a regular hierarchy: they rejoiced in the
increase of proselytes, who were converted from the Zendavesta
to the Gospel, from the secular to the monastic life; and their
zeal was stimulated by the presence of an artful and formidable
enemy. The Persian church had been founded by the missionaries of Syria; and their language, discipline, and doctrine were
closely interwoven with its original frame. The *catholics* were
elected and ordained by their own suffragans; but their filial
dependence on the patriarchs of Antioch is attested by the
canons of the Oriental church.[1] In the Persian school of Edessa[2]
the rising generations of the faithful imbibed their theological
idiom: they studied in the Syriac version the ten thousand
volumes of Theodore of Mopsuestia; and they revered the
apostolic faith and holy martyrdom of his disciple Nestorius,
whose person and language were equally unknown to the
nations beyond the Tigris. The first indelible lesson of Ibas,
bishop of Edessa, taught them to execrate the *Egyptians*, who,
in the synod of Ephesus, had impiously confounded the two
natures of Christ. The flight of the masters and scholars, who
were twice expelled from the Athens of Syria, dispersed a crowd

[1] See the Arabic canons of Nice in the translation of Abraham Ecche-
lensis, No. 37, 38, 39, 40. Concil. tom. ii. p. 335, 336, edit. Venet. These
vulgar titles, *Nicene* and *Arabic*, are both apocryphal. The council of Nice
enacted no more than twenty canons (Theodoret, Hist. Eccles. l. i. c. 8);
and the remainder, seventy or eighty, were collected from the synods of
the Greek church. The Syriac edition of Maruthas is no longer extant
(Asseman. Biblioth. Oriental. tom. i. p. 195, tom. iii. p. 74), and the
Arabic version is marked with many recent interpolations. Yet this Code
contains many curious relics of ecclesiastical discipline; and since it is
equally revered by all the Eastern communions, it was probably finished
before the schism of the Nestorians and Jacobites (Fabric. Biblioth.
Græc. tom. xi. p. 363-367).
[2] Theodore the Reader (l. ii. c. 5, 49, ad calcem Hist. Eccles.) has noticed
this Persian school of Edessa. Its ancient splendour and the two eras of
its downfall (A.D. 431 and 489) are clearly discussed by Assemanni (Biblioth.
Orient. tom. ii. p. 402, iii. p. 376, 378, iv. p. 70, 924).

of missionaries inflamed by the double zeal of religion and revenge. And the rigid unity of the Monophysites, who, under the reigns of Zeno and Anastasius, had invaded the thrones of the East, provoked their antagonists in a land of freedom to avow a moral, rather than a physical, union of the two persons of Christ. Since the first preaching of the gospel the Sassanian kings beheld with an eye of suspicion a race of aliens and apostates who had embraced the religion, and who might favour the cause, of the hereditary foes of their country. The royal edicts had often prohibited their dangerous correspondence with the Syrian clergy: the progress of the schism was grateful to the jealous pride of Perozes, and he listened to the eloquence of an artful prelate, who painted Nestorius as the friend of Persia, and urged him to secure the fidelity of his Christian subjects by granting a just preference to the victims and enemies of the Roman tyrant. The Nestorians composed a large majority of the clergy and people: they were encouraged by the smile, and armed with the sword, of despotism; yet many of their weaker brethren were startled at the thought of breaking loose from the communion of the Christian world, and the blood of seven thousand seven hundred Monophysites or Catholics confirmed the uniformity of faith and discipline in the churches of Persia.[1] Their ecclesiastical institutions are distinguished by a liberal principle of reason, or at least of policy: the austerity of the cloister was relaxed and gradually forgotten: houses of charity were endowed for the education of orphans and foundlings; the law of celibacy, so forcibly recommended to the Greeks and Latins, was disregarded by the Persian clergy; and the number of the elect was multiplied by the public and reiterated nuptials of the priests, the bishops, and even the patriarch himself. To this standard of natural and religious freedom myriads of fugitives resorted from all the provinces of the Eastern empire; the narrow bigotry of Justinian was punished by the emigration of his most industrious subjects; they transported into Persia the arts both of peace and war: and those who deserved the favour were promoted in the service of a discerning monarch. The arms of Nushirvan, and his fiercer grandson, were assisted with advice, and money, and troops, by the desperate sectaries who

[1] A dissertation on the state of the Nestorians has swelled in the hands of Assemanni to a folio volume of 950 pages, and his learned researches are digested in the most lucid order. Besides this fourth volume of the *Bibliotheca Orientalis*, the extracts in the three preceding tomes (tom. i. p. 203, ii. p. 321-463, iii. 64-70, 378-395, etc., 403-408, 580-589) may be usefully consulted.

still lurked in their native cities of the East: their zeal was rewarded with the gift of the Catholic churches; but when those cities and churches were recovered by Heraclius, their open profession of treason and heresy compelled them to seek a refuge in the realm of their foreign ally. But the seeming tranquillity of the Nestorians was often endangered and sometimes overthrown. They were involved in the common evils of Oriental despotism: their enmity to Rome could not always atone for their attachment to the gospel: and a colony of three hundred thousand Jacobites, the captives of Apamea and Antioch, was permitted to erect a hostile altar in the face of the *catholic* and in the sunshine of the court. In his last treaty Justinian introduced some conditions which tended to enlarge and fortify the toleration of Christianity in Persia. The emperor, ignorant of the rights of conscience, was incapable of pity or esteem for the heretics who denied the authority of the holy synods: but he flattered himself that they would gradually perceive the temporal benefits of union with the empire and the Church of Rome; and if he failed in exciting their gratitude, he might hope to provoke the jealousy of their sovereign. In a later age the Lutherans have been burnt at Paris and protected in Germany, by the superstition and policy of the most Christian king.

The desire of gaining souls for God and subjects for the church has excited in every age the diligence of the Christian priests. From the conquest of Persia, they carried their spiritual arms to the north, the east, and the south; and the simplicity of the gospel was fashioned and painted with the colours of the Syriac theology. In the sixth century, according to the report of a Nestorian traveller,[1] Christianity was successfully preached to the Bactrians, the Huns, the Persians, the Indians, the Persarmenians, the Medes, and the Elamites: the barbaric churches,

---

[1] See the Topographia Christiana of Cosmas, surnamed Indicopleustes, or the Indian navigator, l. iii. p. 178, 179; l. xi. p. 337. The entire work, of which some curious extracts may be found in Photius (cod. xxxvi. p. 9, 10, edit. Hoeschel), Thevenot (in the 1st part of his Relation des Voyages, etc.), and Fabricius (Biblioth. Græc. l. iii. c. 25, tom. ii. p. 603-617), has been published by Father Montfaucon at Paris, 1707, in the Nova Collectio Patrum (tom. ii. p. 113-346). It was the design of the author to confute the impious heresy of those who maintained that the earth is a globe, and not a flat oblong table, as it is represented in the Scriptures (l. ii. p. 138 [125, *sq.*]). But the nonsense of the monk is mingled with the practical knowledge of the traveller, who performed his voyage, A.D. 522, and published his book at Alexandria, A.D. 547 (l. ii. p. 140, 141; Montfaucon, Præfat. c. 1). The Nestorianism of Cosmas, unknown to his learned editor, was detected by La Croze (Christianisme des Indes, tom. i. p. 40-55), and is confirmed by Assemanni (Biblioth. Orient. tom. iv. p. 605, 606).

from the Gulf of Persia to the Caspian Sea, were almost infinite; and their recent faith was conspicuous in the number and sanctity of their monks and martyrs. The pepper coast of Malabar and the isles of the ocean, Socotora and Ceylon, were peopled with an increasing multitude of Christians; and the bishops and clergy of those sequestered regions derived their ordination from the catholic of Babylon. In a subsequent age the zeal of the Nestorians overleaped the limits which had confined the ambition and curiosity both of the Greeks and Persians. The missionaries of Balch and Samarcand pursued without fear the footsteps of the roving Tartar, and insinuated themselves into the camps of the valleys of Imaus and the banks of the Selinga. They exposed a metaphysical creed to those illiterate shepherds: to those sanguinary warriors they recommended humanity and repose. Yet a khan, whose power they vainly magnified, is said to have received at their hands the rites of baptism and even of ordination; and the fame of *Prester* or *Presbyter* John [1] has long amused the credulity of Europe. The royal convert was indulged in the use of a portable altar; but he despatched an embassy to the patriarch to inquire how, in the season of Lent, he should abstain from animal food, and how he might celebrate the Eucharist in a desert that produced neither corn nor wine. In their progress by sea and land the Nestorians entered China by the port of Canton and the northern residence of Sigan. Unlike the senators of Rome, who assumed with a smile the characters of priests and augurs, the mandarins, who affect in public the reason of philosophers, are devoted in private to every mode of popular superstition. They cherished and they confounded the gods of Palestine and of India; but the propagation of Christianity awakened the jealousy of the state, and, after a short vicissitude of favour and persecution, the foreign sect expired in ignorance and oblivion. [2] Under the reign

---

[1] In its long progress to Mosul, Jerusalem, Rome, etc., the story of Prester John evaporated in a monstrous fable, of which some features have been borrowed from the Lama of Thibet (Hist. Généalogique des Tatares, P. ii. p. 42; Hist. de Gengiscan, p. 31, etc.), and were ignorantly transferred by the Portuguese to the emperor of Abyssinia (Ludolph. Hist. Æthiop. Comment. l. ii. c. 1). Yet it is probable that in the eleventh and twelfth centuries Nestorian Christianity was professed in the horde of the Keraites (D'Herbelot, p. 256, 915, 959; Assemanni, tom. iv. p. 468-504).

[2] The Christianity of China, between the seventh and the thirteenth century, is invincibly proved by the consent of Chinese, Arabian, Syriac, and Latin evidence (Assemanni. Biblioth. Orient. tom. iv. p. 502-552; Mém. de l'Académie des Inscript. tom. xxx. p. 802-819). The inscription of Siganfu, which describes the fortunes of the Nestorian church, from the first mission, A.D. 636, to the current year 781, is accused of forgery by La

of the caliphs the Nestorian church was diffused from China to Jerusalem and Cyprus; and their numbers, with those of the Jacobites, were computed to surpass the Greek and Latin communions.[1] Twenty-five metropolitans or archbishops composed their hierarchy; but several of these were dispensed, by the distance and danger of the way, from the duty of personal attendance, on the easy condition that every six years they should testify their faith and obedience to the *catholic* or patriarch of Babylon, a vague appellation which has been successively applied to the royal seats of Seleucia, Ctesiphon, and Bagdad. These remote branches are long since withered; and the old patriarchal trunk [2] is now divided by the *Elijahs* of Mosul, the representatives almost in lineal descent of the genuine and primitive succession; the *Josephs* of Amida, who are reconciled to the church of Rome; [3] and the *Simeons* of Van or Ormia, whose revolt, at the head of forty thousand families, was promoted in the sixteenth century by the Sophis of Persia. The number of three hundred thousand is allowed for the whole body of the Nestorians, who, under the name of Chaldæans or Assyrians, are confounded with the most learned or the most powerful nation of Eastern antiquity.

According to the legend of antiquity, the gospel was preached in India by St. Thomas.[4] At the end of the ninth century his shrine, perhaps in the neighbourhood of Madras, was devoutly

Croze, Voltaire, etc., who become the dupes of their own cunning, while they are afraid of a Jesuitical fraud.

[The inscription of Siganfu, which is Nestorian in character, was stigmatised as a forgery by Voltaire, Julian, Renan, and others, but competent specialists, both European and Chinese, now recognise it as a genuine document of the eighth century. It was discovered by a Jesuit missionary, Alvarez Semedo, at Singanfu, the old capital of the Tang dynasty, in 1623. It was raised by Iezdbouzid, priest and chorepiscopus of Chumdan, that is the capital of the Chinese empire. Cf. St. Martin, vol. i. p. 69.—O. S.]

[1] Jacobitæ et Nestorianæ plures quam Græci et Latini. Jacob a Vitriaco, Hist. Hierosol. l. ii. c. 76, p. 1093, in the Gesta Dei per Francos. The numbers are given by Thomassin, Discipline de l'Eglise, tom. i. p. 172.

[2] The division of the patriarchate may be traced in the Bibliotheca Orient. of Assemanni, tom. i. p. 523-549, tom. ii. p. 457, etc., tom. iii. p. 603, 621-623, tom. iv. p. 164-169, 423, 622-629, etc.

[3] The pompous language of Rome, on the submission of a Nestorian patriarch, is elegantly represented in the seventh book of Fra-Paolo, Babylon, Nineveh, Arbela, and the trophies of Alexander, Tauris and Ecbatana, the Tigris and Indus.

[4] The Indian missionary, St. Thomas, an apostle, a Manichæan, or an Armenian merchant (La Croze, Christianisme des Indes, tom. i. p. 57-70), was famous, however, as early as the time of Jerom (ad Marcellam, Epist. 148 [Ep. 59, p. 328, ed., Vallars.]). Marco Polo was informed on the spot that he suffered martyrdom in the city of Maabar, or Meliapour, a league only from Madras (D'Anville, Eclaircissemens sur l'Inde, p. 125), where the

visited by the ambassadors of Alfred; and their return with a cargo of pearls and spices rewarded the zeal of the English monarch, who entertained the largest projects of trade and discovery.[1] When the Portuguese first opened the navigation of India, the Christians of St. Thomas had been seated for ages on the coast of Malabar, and the difference of their character and colour attested the mixture of a foreign race. In arms, in arts, and possibly in virtue, they excelled the natives of Hindostan; the husbandmen cultivated the palm tree, the merchants were enriched by the pepper trade, the soldiers preceded the *nairs* or nobles of Malabar, and their hereditary privileges were respected by the gratitude or the fear of the king of Cochin and the Zamorin himself. They acknowledged a Gentoo sovereign, but they were governed, even in temporal concerns, by the bishop of Angamala. He still asserted his ancient title of metropolitan of India, but his real jurisdiction was exercised in fourteen hundred churches, and he was intrusted with the care of two hundred thousand souls. Their religion would have rendered them the firmest and most cordial allies of the Portuguese; but the inquisitors soon discerned in the Christians of St. Thomas the unpardonable guilt of heresy and schism. Instead of owning themselves the subjects of the Roman pontiff, the spiritual and temporal monarch of the globe, they adhered, like their ancestors, to the communion of the Nestorian patriarch; and the bishops whom he ordained at Mosul traversed the dangers of the sea and land to reach their diocese on the coast of Malabar. In their Syriac liturgy the names of Theodore and Nestorius were piously commemorated: they united their adoration of the two persons of Christ; the title of Mother of God was offensive to their ear; and they measured with scrupulous avarice the honours of the Virgin Mary, whom the superstition of the Latins had *almost* exalted to the rank of a goddess. When her image was first presented to the disciples of St. Thomas they indignantly exclaimed, " We are Christians, not idolaters! " and their simple devotion was

Portuguese founded an episcopal church under the name of St. Thomé, and where the saint performed an annual miracle, till he was silenced by the profane neighbourhood of the English (La Croze, tom. ii. p. 7-16).

[1] Neither the author of the Saxon Chronicle (A.D. 883) nor William of Malmesbury (de Gestis Regum Angliæ, l. ii. c. 4, p. 44) were capable, in the twelfth century, of inventing this extraordinary fact; they are incapable of explaining the motives and measures of Alfred, and their hasty notice serves only to provoke our curiosity. William of Malmesbury feels the difficulties of the enterprise, quod quivis in hoc sæculo miretur; and I almost suspect that the English ambassadors collected their cargo and legend in Egypt. The royal author has not enriched his Orosius (see Barrington's Miscellanies) with an Indian as well as a Scandinavian voyage.

content with the veneration of the cross.   Their separation from
the Western world had left them in ignorance of the improvements or corruptions of a thousand years; and their conformity
with the faith and practice of the fifth century would equally
disappoint the prejudices of a Papist or a Protestant.   It was
the first care of the ministers of Rome to intercept all correspondence with the Nestorian patriarch, and several of his bishops
expired in the prisons of the holy office.   The flock, without a
shepherd, was assaulted by the power of the Portuguese, the arts
of the Jesuits, and the zeal of Alexis de Menezes, archbishop of
Goa, in his personal visitation of the coast of Malabar.   The
synod of Diamper, at which he presided, consummated the pious
work of the re-union, and rigorously imposed the doctrine and
discipline of the Roman church, without forgetting auricular
confession, the strongest engine of ecclesiastical torture.   The
memory of Theodore and Nestorius was condemned, and
Malabar was reduced under the dominion of the pope, of the
primate, and of the Jesuits who invaded the see of Angamala
or Cranganor.   Sixty years of servitude and hypocrisy were
patiently endured; but as soon as the Portuguese empire was
shaken by the courage and industry of the Dutch, the Nestorians
asserted with vigour and effect the religion of their fathers.   The
Jesuits were incapable of defending the power which they had
abused; the arms of forty thousand Christians were pointed
against their falling tyrants; and the Indian archdeacon
assumed the character of bishop till a fresh supply of episcopal
gifts and Syriac missionaries could be obtained from the patriarch
of Babylon.   Since the expulsion of the Portuguese the Nestorian
creed is freely professed on the coast of Malabar.   The trading
companies of Holland and England are the friends of toleration;
but if oppression be less mortifying than contempt, the Christians
of St. Thomas have reason to complain of the cold and silent
indifference of their brethren of Europe.[1]

II. The history of the Monophysites is less copious and interesting than that of the Nestorians.   Under the reigns of Zeno
and Anastasius their artful leaders surprised the ear of the prince,
usurped the thrones of the East, and crushed on its native soil
the school of the Syrians.   The rule of the Monophysite faith

---

[1] Concerning the Christians of St. Thomas, see Assemann. Biblioth.
Orient. tom. iv. p. 391-407, 435-451; Geddes's Church History of Malabar;
and, above all, La Croze, Histoire du Christianisme des Indes, in two vols.
12mo, La Haye, 1758—a learned and agreeable work.   They have drawn
from the same source the Portuguese and Italian narratives; and the prejudices of the Jesuits are sufficiently corrected by those of the Protestants.

was defined with exquisite discretion by Severus, patriarch of Antioch; he condemned, in the style of the Henoticon, the adverse heresies of Nestorius and Eutyches; maintained against the latter the reality of the body of Christ; and constrained the Greeks to allow that he was a liar who spoke truth.[1]   But the approximation of ideas could not abate the vehemence of passion; each party was the more astonished that their blind antagonist could dispute on so trifling a difference; the tyrant of Syria enforced the belief of his creed, and his reign was polluted with the blood of three hundred and fifty monks, who were slain, not perhaps without provocation or resistance, under the walls of Apamea.[2]   The successor of Anastasius replanted the orthodox standard in the East; Severus fled into Egypt; and his friend, the eloquent Xenaias,[3] who had escaped from the Nestorians of Persia, was suffocated in his exile by the Melchites of Paphlagonia.   Fifty-four bishops were swept from their thrones, eight hundred ecclesiastics were cast into prison,[4] and, notwithstanding the ambiguous favour of Theodora, the Oriental flocks, deprived of their shepherds, must insensibly have been either famished or poisoned.   In this spiritual distress the expiring faction was revived, and united, and perpetuated by the labours of a monk; and the name of James Baradæus [5] has been preserved in the appellation of *Jacobites*, a familiar sound which

[1] Οἶον εἰπεῖν ψευδαλήθης is the expression of Theodore, in his Treatise of the Incarnation, p. 245, 247, as he is quoted by La Croze (Hist. du Christianisme d'Ethiopie et d'Arménie, p. 35), who exclaims, perhaps too hastily, " Quel pitoyable raisonnement! " Renaudot has touched (Hist. Patriarch. Alex. p. 127-138) the Oriental accounts of Severus; and his authentic creed may be found in the epistle of John the Jacobite patriarch of Antioch, in the tenth century, to his brother Mennas of Alexandria (Asseman. Biblioth. Orient. tom. ii. p. 132-141).

[2] Epist. Archimandritarum et Monachorum Syriæ Secundæ ad Papam Hormisdam, Concil. tom. v. p. 598-602.   The courage of St. Sabas, ut leo animosus, will justify the suspicion that the arms of these monks were not always spiritual or defensive (Baronius, A.D. 513, No. 7, etc.).

[3] Assemanni (Biblioth. Orient. tom. ii. p. 10-46) and La Croze (Christianisme d'Ethiopie, p. 36-40) will supply the history of Xenaias, or Philoxenus, bishop of Mabug, or Hierapolis, in Syria.   He was a perfect master of the Syriac language, and the author or editor of a version of the New Testament.

[4] The names and titles of fifty-four bishops who were exiled by Justin are preserved in the Chronicle of Dionysius (apud Asseman. tom. ii. p. 54). Severus was personally summoned to Constantinople—for his trial, says Liberatus (Brev. c. 19)—that his tongue might be cut out, says Evagrius (l. iv. c. 4).   The prudent patriarch did not stay to examine the difference. This ecclesiastical revolution is fixed by Pagi to the month of September of the year 518 (Critica, tom. ii. p. 506).

[5] The obscure history of James, or Jacobus Baradæus, or Zanzalus, may be gathered from Eutychius (Annal. tom. ii. p. 144, 147), Renaudot (Hist. Patriarch. Alex. p. 133), and Assemannus (Biblioth. Orient. tom. i. p. 424;

may startle the ear of an English reader. From the holy confessors in their prison of Constantinople he received the powers of bishop of Edessa and apostle of the East, and the ordination of fourscore thousand bishops, priests, and deacons, is derived from the same inexhaustible source. The speed of the zealous missionary was promoted by the fleetest dromedaries of a devout chief of the Arabs; the doctrine and discipline of the Jacobites were secretly established in the dominions of Justinian; and each Jacobite was compelled to violate the laws and to hate the Roman legislator. The successors of Severus, while they lurked in convents or villages, while they sheltered their proscribed heads in the caverns of hermits or the tents of the Saracens, still asserted, as they now assert, their indefeasible right to the title, the rank, and the prerogatives of patriarch of Antioch: under the milder yoke of the infidels they reside about a league from Merdin, in the pleasant monastery of Zapharan, which they have embellished with cells, aqueducts, and plantations. The secondary, though honourable, place is filled by the *maphrian*, who, in his station at Mosul itself, defies the Nestorian *catholic* with whom he contests the primacy of the East. Under the patriarch and the maphrian one hundred and fifty archbishops and bishops have been counted in the different ages of the Jacobite church; but the order of the hierarchy is relaxed or dissolved, and the greater part of their dioceses is confined to the neighbourhood of the Euphrates and the Tigris. The cities of Aleppo and Amida, which are often visited by the patriarch, contain some wealthy merchants and industrious mechanics, but the multitude derive their scanty sustenance from their daily labour: and poverty, as well as superstition, may impose their excessive fasts—five annual lents, during which both the clergy and laity abstain not only from flesh or eggs, but even from the taste of wine, of oil, and of fish. Their present numbers are esteemed from fifty to fourscore thousand souls, the remnant of a populous church, which has gradually decreased under the oppression of twelve centuries. Yet in that long period some strangers of merit have been converted to the Monophysite faith, and a Jew was the father of Abulpharagius,[1] primate of the East,

tom. ii. p. 62-69, 324-332, 414; tom. iii. p. 385-388). He seems to be unknown to the Greeks. The Jacobites themselves had rather deduce their name and pedigree from St. James the apostle.

[1] The account of his person and writings is perhaps the most curious article in the Bibliotheca of Assemannus (tom. ii. p. 244-321, under the name of *Gregorius Bar-Hebræus*). La Croze (Christianisme d'Ethiopie, p. 53-63) ridicules the prejudice of the Spaniards against the Jewish blood which secretly defiles their church and state.

so truly eminent both in his life and death. In his life he was an elegant writer of the Syriac and Arabic tongues, a poet, physician, and historian, a subtle philosopher, and a moderate divine. In his death his funeral was attended by his rival the Nestorian patriarch, with a train of Greeks and Armenians, who forgot their disputes, and mingled their tears over the grave of an enemy. The sect which was honoured by the virtues of Abulpharagius appears, however, to sink below the level of their Nestorian brethren. The superstition of the Jacobites is more abject, their fasts more rigid,[1] their intestine divisions are more numerous, and their doctors (as far as I can measure the degrees of nonsense) are more remote from the precincts of reason. Something may possibly be allowed for the rigour of the Monophysite theology, much more for the superior influence of the monastic order. In Syria, in Egypt, in Æthiopia, the Jacobite monks have ever been distinguished by the austerity of their penance and the absurdity of their legends. Alive or dead, they are worshipped as the favourites of the Deity; the crosier of bishop and patriarch is reserved for their venerable hands; and they assume the government of men while they are yet reeking with the habits and prejudices of the cloister.[2]

III. In the style of the Oriental Christians, the Monothelites of every age are described under the appellation of *Maronites*,[3] a name which has been insensibly transferred from a hermit to a monastery, from a monastery to a nation. Maron, a saint or savage of the fifth century, displayed his religious madness in Syria; the rival cities of Apamea and Emesa disputed his relics, a stately church was erected on his tomb, and six hundred of his disciples united their solitary cells on the banks of the Orontes. In the controversies of the incarnation they nicely threaded the orthodox line between the sects of Nestorius and Eutyches; but the unfortunate question of *one will* or operation in the two natures of Christ was generated by their curious leisure. Their

---

[1] This *excessive* abstinence is censured by La Croze (p. 352), and even by the Syrian Assemannus (tom. i. p. 226; tom. ii. p. 304, 305).
[2] The state of the Monophysites is excellently illustrated in a dissertation at the beginning of the second volume of Assemannus, which contains 142 pages. The Syriac Chronicle of Gregory Bar-Hebræus, or Abulpharagius (Biblioth. Orient. tom. ii. p. 321-463), pursues the double series of the Nestorian *Catholics* and the *Maphrians* of the Jacobites.
[3] The synonymous use of the two words may be proved from Eutychius (Annal. tom. ii. p. 191, 267, 332), and many similar passages which may be found in the methodical table of Pocock. He was not actuated by any prejudice against the Maronites of the tenth century; and we may believe a Melchite, whose testimony is confirmed by the Jacobites and Latins.

proselyte, the emperor Heraclius, was rejected as a Maronite from the walls of Emesa; he found a refuge in the monastery of his brethren; and their theological lessons were repaid with the gift of a spacious and wealthy domain. The name and doctrine of this venerable school were propagated among the Greeks and Syrians, and their zeal is expressed by Macarius, patriarch of Antioch, who declared before the synod of Constantinople, that sooner than subscribe the *two wills* of Christ, he would submit to be hewn piecemeal and cast into the sea.[1] A similar or a less cruel mode of persecution soon converted the unresisting subjects of the plain, while the glorious title of *Mardaites*,[2] or rebels, was bravely maintained by the hardy natives of Mount Libanus. John Maron, one of the most learned and popular of the monks, assumed the character of patriarch of Antioch; his nephew, Abraham, at the head of the Maronites, defended their civil and religious freedom against the tyrants of the East. The son of the orthodox Constantine pursued with pious hatred a people of soldiers, who might have stood the bulwark of his empire against the common foes of Christ and of Rome. An army of Greeks invaded Syria; the monastery of St. Maron was destroyed with fire; the bravest chieftains were betrayed and murdered, and twelve thousand of their followers were transplanted to the distant frontiers of Armenia and Thrace. Yet the humble nation of the Maronites has survived the empire of Constantinople, and they still enjoy, under their Turkish masters, a free religion and a mitigated servitude. Their domestic governors are chosen among the ancient nobility: the patriarch, in his monastery of Canobin, still fancies himself on the throne of Antioch; nine bishops compose his synod, and one hundred and fifty priests, who retain the liberty of marriage, are intrusted with the care of one hundred thousand souls. Their country extends from the ridge of Mount Libanus to the shores of Tripoli; and the gradual descent affords, in a narrow space, each variety of soil and climate, from the Holy Cedars, erect under the weight of snow,[3]

---

[1] Concil. tom. vii. p. 780. The Monothelite cause was supported with firmness and subtlety by Constantine, a *Syrian* priest of Apamea (p. 1040, etc.).

[2] Theophanes (Chron. p. 295, 296, 300, 302, 306 [tom. i. p. 542 *sq.*, 552, 555, 561, ed. Bonn]) and Cedrenus (p. 437, 440 [ed. Par.; tom. i. p. 765 *sqq.*, ed. Bonn]) relate the exploits of the Mardaites: the name (*Mard*, in Syriac *rebellavit*) is explained by La Roque (Voyage de la Syrie, tom. ii. p. 53); the dates are fixed by Pagi (A.D. 676, No. 4-14; A.D. 685, No. 3, 4); and even the obscure story of the patriarch John Maron (Asseman. Biblioth. Orient. tom. i. p. 496-520) illustrates, from the year 686 to 707, the troubles of Mount Libanus.

[3] In the last century twenty large cedars still remained (Voyage de La

to the vine, the mulberry, and the olive trees of the fruitful valley. In the twelfth century the Maronites, abjuring the Monothelite error, were reconciled to the Latin churches of Antioch and Rome,[1] and the same alliance has been frequently renewed by the ambition of the popes and the distress of the Syrians. But it may reasonably be questioned whether their union has ever been perfect or sincere; and the learned Maronites of the college of Rome have vainly laboured to absolve their ancestors from the guilt of heresy and schism.[2]

IV. Since the age of Constantine, the ARMENIANS [3] had signalised their attachment to the religion and empire of the Christians. The disorders of their country, and their ignorance of the Greek tongue, prevented their clergy from assisting at the synod of Chalcedon, and they floated eighty-four years [4] in a state of indifference or suspense, till their vacant faith was finally occupied by the missionaries of Julian of Halicarnassus,[5] who in

Roque, tom. i. p. 68-76); at present they are reduced to four or five (Volney, tom. i. p. 264). These trees, so famous in Scripture, were guarded by excommunication: the wood was sparingly borrowed for small crosses, etc.; an annual mass was chanted under their shade; and they were endowed by the Syrians with a sensitive power of erecting their branches to repel the snow, to which Mount Libanus is less faithful than it is painted by Tacitus: inter ardores opacum fidumque nivibus—a daring metaphor (Hist. v. 6).

[1] The evidence of William of Tyre (Hist. in Gestis Dei per Francos, l. xxii. c. 8, p. 1022 [fol. Hanov. 1611]) is copied or confirmed by Jacques de Vitra (Hist. Hierosolym. l. ii. c. 77, p. 1093, 1094). But this unnatural league expired with the power of the Franks; and Abulpharagius (who died in 1286) considers the Maronites as a sect of Monothelites (Biblioth. Orient. tom. ii. p. 292).

[2] I find a description and history of the Maronites in the Voyage de la Syrie et du Mont Liban par La Roque (2 vols. in 12mo, Amsterdam, 1723; particularly tom. i. p. 42-47, 174-184, tom. ii. p. 10-120). In the ancient part he copies the prejudices of Nairon and the other Maronites of Rome, which Assemannus is afraid to renounce and ashamed to support. Jablonski (Institut. Hist. Christ. tom. iii. p. 186), Niebuhr (Voyage de l'Arabie, etc., tom. ii. p. 346, 370-381), and, above all, the judicious Volney (Voyage en Egypte et en Syrie, tom. ii. p. 8-31, Paris, 1787), may be consulted.

[3] The religion of the Armenians is briefly described by La Croze (Hist. du Christ. de l'Ethiopie et de l'Arménie, p. 269-402). He refers to the great Armenian History of Galanus (3 vols. in fol. Rome, 1650-1661), and commends the state of Armenia in the third volume of. the Nouveaux Mémoires des Missions du Levant. The work of a Jesuit must have sterling merit when it is praised by La Croze.

[4] The schism of the Armenians is placed eighty-four years after the council of Chalcedon (Pagi, Critica, ad A.D. 535). It was consummated at the end of seventeen years; and it is from the year of Christ 552 that we date the era of the Armenians (L'Art de vérifier les Dates, p. xxxv.).

[5] The sentiments and success of Julian of Halicarnassus may be seen in Liberatus (Brev. c. 19), Renaudot (Hist. Patriarch. Alex. p. 132, 303), and Assemannus (Biblioth. Orient. tom. ii. Dissertat. de Monophysitis, p. viii. p. 286).

Egypt, their common exile, had been vanquished by the arguments or the influence of his rival Severus, the Monophysite
patriarch of Antioch. The Armenians alone are the pure disciples of Eutyches, an unfortunate parent, who has been renounced by the greater part of his spiritual progeny. They
alone persevere in the opinion that the manhood of Christ was
created, or existed without creation, of a divine and incorruptible
substance. Their adversaries reproach them with the adoration
of a phantom; and they retort the accusation, by deriding or
execrating the blasphemy of the Jacobites, who impute to the
Godhead the vile infirmities of the flesh, even the natural effects
of nutrition and digestion. The religion of Armenia could not
derive much glory from the learning or the power of its inhabitants. The royalty expired with the origin of their schism;
and their Christian kings, who arose and fell in the thirteenth
century on the confines of Cilicia, were the clients of the Latins
and the vassals of the Turkish sultan of Iconium. The helpless
nation has seldom been permitted to enjoy the tranquillity of
servitude. From the earliest period to the present hour Armenia
has been the theatre of perpetual war: the lands between Tauris
and Erivan were dispeopled by the cruel policy of the Sophis;
and myriads of Christian families were transplanted, to perish or
to propagate in the distant provinces of Persia. Under the rod
of oppression, the zeal of the Armenians is fervent and intrepid;
they have often preferred the crown of martyrdom to the white
turban of Mohammed; they devoutly hate the error and idolatry
of the Greeks; and their transient union with the Latins is not
less devoid of truth than the thousand bishops whom their
patriarch offered at the feet of the Roman pontiff.[1] The *catholic*,
or patriarch, of the Armenians resides in the monastery of
Ekmiasin, three leagues from Erivan. Forty-seven archbishops,
each of whom may claim the obedience of four or five suffragans,
are consecrated by his hand; but the far greater part are only
titular prelates, who dignify with their presence and service the
simplicity of his court. As soon as they have performed the
liturgy, they cultivate the garden; and our bishops will hear
with surprise that the austerity of their life increases in just
proportion to the elevation of their rank. In the fourscore
thousand towns or villages of his spiritual empire, the patriarch

---

[1] See a remarkable fact of the twelfth century in the History of Nicetas
Choniates (p. 258). Yet three hundred years before, Photius (Epistol. ii.
p. 49, edit. Montacut.) had gloried in the conversion of the Armenians—
λατρεύει σήμερον ὀρθοδόξως [τὴν χριστιάνων λατρείαν].

receives a small and voluntary tax from each person above the age of fifteen; but the annual amount of six hundred thousand crowns is insufficient to supply the incessant demands of charity and tribute. Since the beginning of the last century the Armenians have obtained a large and lucrative share of the commerce of the East: in their return from Europe, the caravan usually halts in the neighbourhood of Erivan, the altars are enriched with the fruits of their patient industry; and the faith of Eutyches is preached in their recent congregations of Barbary and Poland.[1]

V. In the rest of the Roman empire the despotism of the prince might eradicate or silence the sectaries of an obnoxious creed. But the stubborn temper of the Egyptians maintained their opposition to the synod of Chalcedon, and the policy of Justinian condescended to expect and to seize the opportunity of discord. The Monophysite church of Alexandria[2] was torn by the disputes of the *corruptibles* and *incorruptibles*, and on the death of the patriarch the two factions upheld their respective candidates.[3] Gaian was the disciple of Julian, Theodosius had been the pupil of Severus: the claims of the former were supported by the consent of the monks and senators, the city and the province; the latter depended on the priority of his ordination, the favour of the empress Theodora, and the arms of the eunuch Narses, which might have been used in more honourable warfare. The exile of the popular candidate to Carthage and Sardinia inflamed the ferment of Alexandria; and after a schism of one hundred and seventy years, the *Gaianites* still revered the memory and doctrine of their founder. The strength of numbers and of discipline was tried in a desperate and bloody conflict; the streets were filled with the dead bodies of citizens and soldiers; the pious women, ascending the roofs of their houses, showered down every sharp or ponderous utensil on the heads of the enemy; and the final victory of Narses was owing to the flames with which he wasted the third capital of

---

[1] The travelling Armenians are in the way of every traveller, and their mother church is on the high road between Constantinople and Ispahan: for their present state, see Fabricius (Lux Evangelii, etc., c. xxxviii. p. 40-51), Olearius (l. iv. c. 40), Chardin (vol. ii. p. 232), Tournefort (lettre xx.), and, above all, Tavernier (tom. i. p. 28-37, 510-518), that rambling jeweller, who had read nothing, but had seen so much and so well.

[2] The history of the Alexandrian patriarchs, from Dioscorus to Benjamin, is taken from Renaudot (p. 114-164), and the second tome of the Annals of Eutychius.

[3] Liberat. Brev. c. 20, 23; Victor. Chron. p. 329, 330; Procop. Anecdot. c. 26, 27.

the Roman world. But the lieutenant of Justinian had not conquered in the cause of a heretic; Theodosius himself was speedily, though gently, removed; and Paul of Tanis, an orthodox monk, was raised to the throne of Athanasius. The powers of government were strained in his support; he might appoint or displace the dukes and tribunes of Egypt; the allowance of bread, which Diocletian had granted, was suppressed, the churches were shut, and a nation of schismatics was deprived at once of their spiritual and carnal food. In his turn, the tyrant was excommunicated by the zeal and revenge of the people; and none except his servile Melchites would salute him as a man, a Christian, or a bishop. Yet such is the blindness of ambition, that, when Paul was expelled on a charge of murder, he solicited, with a bribe of seven hundred pounds of gold, his restoration to the same station of hatred and ignominy. His successor Apollinaris entered the hostile city in military array, alike qualified for prayer or for battle. His troops, under arms, were distributed through the streets; the gates of the cathedral were guarded, and a chosen band was stationed in the choir to defend the person of their chief. He stood erect on his throne, and, throwing aside the upper garment of a warrior, suddenly appeared before the eyes of the multitude in the robes of patriarch of Alexandria. Astonishment held them mute; but no sooner had Apollinaris begun to read the tome of St. Leo, than a volley of curses, and invectives, and stones assaulted the odious minister of the emperor and the synod. A charge was instantly sounded by the successor of the apostles; the soldiers waded to their knees in blood; and two hundred thousand Christians are said to have fallen by the sword: an incredible account, even if it be extended from the slaughter of a day to the eighteen years of the reign of Apollinaris. Two succeeding patriarchs, Eulogius [1] and John,[2] laboured in the conversion of heretics with arms and arguments more worthy of their evangelical profession. The

---

[1] Eulogius, who had been a monk of Antioch, was more conspicuous for subtlety than eloquence. He proves that the enemies of the faith, the Gaianites and Theodosians, ought not to be reconciled; that the same proposition may be orthodox in the mouth of St. Cyril, heretical in that of Severus; that the opposite assertions of St. Leo are equally true, etc. His writings are no longer extant, except in the Extracts of Photius, who had perused them with care and satisfaction, cod. ccviii., ccxxv., ccxxvi., ccxxvii., ccxxx., cclxxx.

[2] See the Life of John the Eleemosynary by his contemporary Leontius, bishop of Neapolis in Cyprus, whose Greek text, either lost or hidden, is reflected in the Latin version of Baronius (A.D. 610, No. 9, A.D. 620, No. 8). Pagi (Critica, tom. ii. p. 763) and Fabricius (l. v. c. 11, tom. vii. p. 454) have made some critical observations.

theological knowledge of Eulogius was displayed in many a volume, which magnified the errors of Eutyches,and Severus, and attempted to reconcile the ambiguous language of St. Cyril with the orthodox creed of pope Leo and the fathers of Chalcedon. The bounteous alms of John the Eleemosynary were dictated by superstition, or benevolence, or policy. Seven thousand five hundred poor were maintained at his expense; on his accession he found eight thousand pounds of gold in the treasury of the church; he collected ten thousand from the liberality of the faithful; yet the primate could boast in his testament that he left behind him no more than the third part of the smallest of the silver coins, The churches of Alexandria were delivered to the Catholics, the religion of the Monophysites was proscribed in Egypt, and a law was revived which excluded the natives from the honours and emoluments of the state.

A more important conquest still remained, of the patriarch, the oracle and leader of the Egyptian church. Theodosius had resisted the threats and promises of Justinian with the spirit of an apostle or an enthusiast. " Such," replied the patriarch, " were the offers of the tempter when he showed the kingdoms of the earth. But my soul is far dearer to me than life or dominion. The churches are in the hands of a prince who can kill the body; but my conscience is my own; and in exile, poverty, or chains, I will steadfastly adhere to the faith of my holy predecessors, Athanasius, Cyril, and Dioscorus. Anathema to the tome of Leo and the synod of Chalcedon! Anthema to all who embrace their creed! Anathema to them now and for evermore! Naked came I out of my mother's womb, naked shall I descend into the grave. Let those who love God follow me and seek their salvation." After comforting his brethren, he embarked for Constantinople, and sustained, in six successive interviews, the almost irresistible weight of the royal presence. His opinions were favourably entertained in the palace and the city; the influence of Theodora assured him a safe-conduct and honourable dismission; and he ended his days, though not on the throne, yet in the bosom of his native country. On the news of his death, Apollinaris indecently feasted the nobles and the clergy; but his joy was checked by the intelligence of a new election; and while he enjoyed the wealth of Alexandria, his rivals reigned in the monasteries of Thebais, and were maintained by the voluntary oblations of the people. A perpetual succession of patriarchs arose from the ashes of Theodosius; and the Monophysite churches of Syria and Egypt were united

by the name of Jacobites and the communion of the faith. But
the same faith, which has been confined to a narrow sect of the
Syrians, was diffused over the mass of the Egyptian or Coptic
nation, who almost unanimously rejected the decrees of the
synod of Chalcedon. A thousand years were now elapsed since
Egypt had ceased to be a kingdom, since the conquerors of Asia
and Europe had trampled on the ready necks of a people whose
ancient wisdom and power ascends beyond the records of history.
The conflict of zeal and persecution rekindled some sparks of
their national spirit. They abjured, with a foreign heresy, the
manners and language of the Greeks: every Melchite, in their
eyes, was a stranger, every Jacobite a citizen; the alliance of
marriage, the offices of humanity, were condemned as a deadly
sin; the natives renounced all allegiance to the emperor; and
his orders, at a distance from Alexandria, were obeyed only
under the pressure of military force. A generous effort might
have redeemed the religion and liberty of Egypt, and her six
hundred monasteries might have poured forth their myriads of
holy warriors, for whom death should have no terrors, since life
had no comfort or delight. But experience has proved the
distinction of active and passive courage; the fanatic who
endures without a groan the torture of the rack or the stake,
would tremble and fly before the face of an armed enemy. The
pusillanimous temper of the Egyptians could only hope for a
change of masters; the arms of Chosroes depopulated the land,
yet under his reign the Jacobites enjoyed a short and precarious
respite. The victory of Heraclius renewed and aggravated the
persecution, and the patriarch again escaped from Alexandria
to the desert. In his flight, Benjamin was encouraged by a
voice which bade him expect, at the end of ten years, the aid of
a foreign nation, marked like the Egyptians themselves with the
ancient rite of circumcision. The character of these deliverers,
and the nature of the deliverance, will be hereafter explained;
and I shall step over the interval of eleven centuries to observe
the present misery of the Jacobites of Egypt. The populous
city of Cairo affords a residence, or rather a shelter, for their
indigent patriarch and a remnant of ten bishops; forty monasteries have survived the inroads of the Arabs; and the progress of servitude and apostacy has reduced the Coptic nation
to the despicable number of twenty-five or thirty thousand
families;[1] a race of illiterate beggars, whose only consolation is

---

[1] This number is taken from the curious Recherches sur les Egyptiens
et les Chinois (tom. ii. p. 192, 193); and appears more probable than the

derived from the superior wretchedness of the Greek patriarch and his diminutive congregation.[1]

VI. The Coptic patriarch, a rebel to the Cæsars, or a slave to the Caliphs, still gloried in the filial obedience of the kings of Nubia and Æthiopia. He repaid their homage by magnifying their greatness; and it was boldly asserted that they could bring into the field a hundred thousand horse, with an equal number of camels;[2] that their hand could pour or restrain the waters of the Nile;[3] and the peace and plenty of Egypt was obtained, even in this world, by the intercession of the patriarch. In exile at Constantinople, Theodosius recommended to his patroness the conversion of the black nations of Nubia, from the tropic of Cancer to the confines of Abyssinia.[4] Her design was suspected and emulated by the more orthodox emperor. The rival missionaries, a Melchite and a Jacobite, embarked at the same time; but the empress, from a motive of love or fear, was more effectually obeyed; and the Catholic priest was detained by the president of Thebais, while the king of Nubia and his court were hastily baptised in the faith of Dioscorus. The tardy

600,000 ancient or 15,000 modern Copts of Gemelli Carreri. Cyril Lucar, the Protestant patriarch of Constantinople, laments that those heretics were ten times more numerous than his orthodox Greeks, ingeniously applying the πολλαὶ κεν δεκάδες δευοίατο οἰνοχόοιο of Homer (Iliad. ii. 128), the most perfect expression of contempt (Fabric. Lux Evangelii, 740).

[1] The history of the Copts, their religion, manners, etc., may be found in the Abbé Renaudot's motley work, neither a translation nor an original; the Chronicon Orientale of Peter, a Jacobite; in the two versions of Abraham Ecchellensis, Paris, 1651; and John Simon Asseman, Venet. 1729. These annals descend no lower than the thirteenth century. The more recent accounts must be searched for in the travellers into Egypt, and the Nouveaux Mémoires des Missions du Levant. In the last century Joseph Abudacnus, a native of Cairo, published at Oxford, in thirty pages, a slight Historia Jacobitarum, 147, post 150.

[2] About the year 737. See Renaudot, Hist. Patriarch. Alex. p. 221, 222; Elmacin, Hist. Saracen. p. 99.

[3] Ludolph. Hist. Æthiopic. et Comment. l. i. c. 8; Renaudot, Hist. Patriarch. Alex. p. 480, etc. This opinion, introduced into Egypt and Europe by the artifice of the Copts, the pride of the Abyssinians, the fear and ignorance of the Turks and Arabs, has not even the semblance of truth. The rains of Æthiopia do not, in the increase of the Nile, consult the will of the monarch. If the river approaches at Napata within three days' journey of the Red Sea (see D'Anville's Maps), a canal that should divert its course would demand, and most probably surpass, the power of the Cæsars.

[4] The Abyssinians, who still preserve the features and olive complexion of the Arabs, afford a proof that two thousand years are not sufficient to change the colour of the human race. The Nubians, an African race, are pure negroes, as black as those of Senegal or Congo, with flat noses, thick lips, and woolly hair (Buffon, Hist. Naturelle, tom. v. p. 117, 143, 144, 166, 219, edit. in 12mo, Paris, 1769). The ancients beheld, without much attention, the extraordinary phenomenon which has exercised the philosophers and theologians of modern times.

envoy of Justinian was received and dismissed with honour; but when he accused the heresy and treason of the Egyptians, the negro convert was instructed to reply that he would never abandon his brethren, the true believers, to the persecuting ministers of the synod of Chalcedon.[1]   During several ages the bishops of Nubia were named and consecrated by the Jacobite patriarch of Alexandria: as late as the twelfth century Christianity prevailed; and some rites, some ruins, are still visible in the savage towns of Sennaar and Dongola.[2]   But the Nubians at length executed their threats of returning to the worship of idols; the climate required the indulgence of polygamy, and they have finally preferred the triumph of the Koran to the abasement of the Cross.   A metaphysical religion may appear too refined for the capacity of the negro race: yet a black or a parrot might be taught to repeat the *words* of the Chalcedonian or Monophysite creed.

Christianity was more deeply rooted in the Abyssinian empire; and, although the correspondence has been sometimes interrupted above seventy or a hundred years, the mother-church of Alexandria retains her colony in a state of perpetual pupilage. Seven bishops once composed the Æthiopic synod: had their number amounted to ten, they might have elected an independent primate; and one of their kings was ambitious of promoting his brother to the ecclesiastical throne.   But the event was foreseen, the increase was denied; the episcopal office has been gradually confined to the *abuna*,[3] the head and author of the Abyssinian priesthood; the patriarch supplies each vacancy with an Egyptian monk; and the character of a stranger appears more venerable in the eyes of the people, less dangerous in those of the monarch.   In the sixth century, when the schism of Egypt was confirmed, the rival chiefs, with their patrons Justinian and Theodora, strove to outstrip each other in the conquest of a remote and independent province.   The industry of the empress

[1] Asseman. Biblioth. Orient. tom. i. p. 329.

[2] The Christianity of the Nubians, A.D. 1153, is attested by the sheriff al Edrisi, falsely described under the name of the Nubian geographer (p. 18), who represents them as a nation of Jacobites.   The rays of historical light that twinkle in the history of Renaudot (p. 178, 220-224, 281-286, 405, 434, 451, 464), are all previous to this era.   See the modern state in the Lettres Édifiantes (Recueil, iv.) and Busching (tom. ix. p. 152-159, par Berenger).

[3] The abuna is improperly dignified by the Latins with the title of patriarch.   The Abyssinians acknowledge only the four patriarchs, and their chief is no more than a metropolitan or national primate (Ludolph. Hist. Æthiopic. et Comment. l. iii. c. 7).   The seven bishops of Renaudot (p. 511), who existed A.D. 1131, are unknown to the historian.

was again victorious, and the pious Theodora has established in that sequestered church the faith and discipline of the Jacobites.[1] Encompassed on all sides by the enemies of their religion, the Æthiopians slept near a thousand years, forgetful of the world, by whom they were forgotten. They were awakened by the Portuguese, who, turning the southern promontory of Africa, appeared in India and the Red Sea, as if they had descended through the air from a distant planet. In the first moments of their interview, the subjects of Rome and Alexandria observed the resemblance rather than the difference of their faith; and each nation expected the most important benefits from an alliance with their Christian brethren. In their lonely situation the Æthiopians had almost relapsed into the savage life. Their vessels, which had traded to Ceylon, scarcely presumed to navigate the rivers of Africa; the ruins of Axume were deserted, the nation was scattered in villages, and the emperor, a pompous name, was content, both in peace and war, with the immovable residence of a camp. Conscious of their own indigence, the Abyssinians had formed the rational project of importing the arts and ingenuity of Europe;[2] and their ambassadors at Rome and Lisbon were instructed to solicit a colony of smiths, carpenters, tilers, masons, printers, surgeons, and physicians, for the use of their country. But the public danger soon called for the instant and effectual aid of arms and soldiers, to defend an unwarlike people from the barbarians who ravaged the inland country, and the Turks and Arabs who advanced from the seacoast in more formidable array. Æthiopia was saved by four hundred and fifty Portuguese, who displayed in the field the native valour of Europeans, and the artificial powers of the musket and cannon. In a moment of terror the emperor had promised to reconcile himself and his subjects to the Catholic faith; a Latin patriarch represented the supremacy of the pope;[3]

[1] I know not why Assemannus (Biblioth. Orient. tom. ii. p. 384) should call in question these probable missions of Theodora into Nubia and Æthiopia. The slight notices of Abyssinia till the year 1500 are supplied by Renaudot (p. 336-341, 381, 382, 405, 443, etc., 452, 456, 463, 475, 480, 511, 525, 559-564) from the Coptic writers. The mind of Ludolphus was a perfect blank.

[2] Ludolph. Hist. Æthiop. l. iv. c. 5. The most necessary arts are now exercised by the Jews, and the foreign trade is in the hands of the Armenians. What Gregory principally admired and envied was the industry of Europe—artes et opificia.

[3] John Bermudez, whose relation, printed at Lisbon, 1569, was translated into English by Purchas (Pilgrims, l. vii. c. 7, p. 1149, etc.), and from thence into French by La Croze (Christianisme d'Ethiopie, p. 92-265). The piece is curious; but the author may be suspected of deceiving Abyssinia, Rome, and Portugal. His title to the rank of patriarch is dark and doubtful (Ludolph. Comment. No. 101, p. 473).

the empire, enlarged in a tenfold proportion, was supposed to contain more gold than the mines of America; and the wildest hopes of avarice and zeal were built on the willing submission of the Christians of Africa.

But the vows which pain had extorted were forsworn on the return of health. The Abyssinians still adhered with unshaken constancy to the Monophysite faith; their languid belief was inflamed by the exercise of dispute; they branded the Latins with the names of Arians and Nestorians, and imputed the adoration of *four* gods to those who separated the two natures of Christ. Fremona, a place of worship, or rather of exile, was assigned to the Jesuit missionaries. Their skill in the liberal and mechanic arts, their theological learning, and the decency of their manners, inspired a barren esteem; but they were not endowed with the gift of miracles,[1] and they vainly solicited a reinforcement of European troops. The patience and dexterity of forty years at length obtained a more favourable audience, and two emperors of Abyssinia were persuaded that Rome could insure the temporal and everlasting happiness of her votaries. The first of these royal converts lost his crown and his life; and the rebel army was sanctified by the *abuna*, who hurled an anathema at the apostate and absolved his subjects from their oath of fidelity. The fate of Zadenghel was revenged by the courage and fortune of Susneus, who ascended the throne under the name of Segued, and more vigorously prosecuted the pious enterprise of his kinsman. After the amusement of some unequal combats between the Jesuits and his illiterate priests, the emperor declared himself a proselyte to the synod of Chalcedon, presuming that his clergy and people would embrace without delay the religion of their prince. The liberty of choice was succeeded by a law which imposed, under pain of death, the belief of the two natures of Christ: the Abyssinians were enjoined to work and to play on the Sabbath; and Segued, in the face of Europe and Africa, renounced his connection with the Alexandrian church. A Jesuit, Alphonso Mendez, the Catholic patriarch of Æthiopia, accepted, in the name of Urban VIII., the homage and abjuration of his penitent. " I confess," said the emperor on his knees, " I confess that the pope is the vicar of Christ, the successor of St. Peter, and the sovereign of the world.

---

[1] Religio Romana . . . nec precibus patrum nec miraculis ab ipsis editis suffulciebatur, is the uncontradicted assurance of the devout emperor Susneus to his patriarch Mendez (Ludolph. Comment. No. 126, p. 529); and such assurances should be preciously kept, as an antidote against any marvellous legends.

To him I swear true obedience, and at his feet I offer my person and kingdom." A similar oath was repeated by his son, his brother, the clergy, the nobles, and even the ladies of the court: the Latin patriarch was invested with honours and wealth; and his missionaries erected their churches or citadels in the most convenient stations of the empire. The Jesuits themselves deplore the fatal indiscretion of their chief, who forgot the mildness of the gospel and the policy of his order, to introduce with hasty violence the liturgy of Rome and the inquisition of Portugal. He condemned the ancient practice of circumcision, which health rather than superstition had first invented in the climate of Æthiopia.[1] A new baptism, a new ordination, was inflicted on the natives; and they trembled with horror when the most holy of the dead were torn from their graves, when the most illustrious of the living were excommunicated by a foreign priest. In the defence of their religion and liberty the Abyssinians rose in arms, with desperate but unsuccessful zeal. Five rebellions were extinguished in the blood of the insurgents: two abunas were slain in battle; whole legions were slaughtered in the field, or suffocated in their caverns; and neither merit, nor rank, nor sex, could save from an ignominious death the enemies of Rome. But the victorious monarch was finally subdued by the constancy of the nation, of his mother, of his son, and of his most faithful friends. Segued listened to the voice of pity, of reason, perhaps of fear: and his edict of liberty of conscience instantly revealed the tyranny and weakness of the Jesuits. On the death of his father, Basilides expelled the Latin patriarch, and restored to the wishes of the nation the faith and discipline of Egypt. The Monophysite churches resounded with a song of triumph, " that the sheep of Æthiopia were now delivered from the hyænas of the West;" and the gates of that solitary realm were for ever shut against the arts, the science, and the fanaticism of Europe.[2]

---

[1] I am aware how tender is the question of circumcision. Yet I will affirm, 1. That the Æthiopians have a physical reason for the circumcision of males, and even of females (Recherches Philosophiques sur les Américains, tom. ii.). 2. That it was practised in Æthiopia long before the introduction of Judaism or Christianity (Herodot. l. ii. c. 104; Marsham, Canon Chron. p. 72, 73). " Infantes circumcidunt ob consuetudinem non ob Judaismum," says Gregory the Abyssinian priest (apud Fabric. Lux Christiana, p. 720). Yet, in the heat of dispute, the Portuguese were sometimes branded with the name of *uncircumcised* (La Croze, p. 80; Ludolph. Hist. and Comment. l. iii. c. 1).

[2] The three Protestant historians, Ludolphus (Hist. Æthiopica, Francofurti, 1681; Commentarius, 1691; Relatio Nova, etc., 1693, in folio), Geddes (Church History of Æthiopia, London, 1696, in 8vo), and La

CHAPTER XLVIII

Plan of the last two [quarto] Volumes—Succession and Characters of the
Greek Emperors of Constantinople, from the Time of Heraclius to the
Latin Conquest

I HAVE now deduced from Trajan to Constantine, from Constantine to Heraclius, the regular series of the Roman emperors;
and faithfully exposed the prosperous and adverse fortunes of
their reigns.   Five centuries of the decline and fall of the empire
have already elapsed; but a period of more than eight hundred
years still separates me from the term of my labours, the taking
of Constantinople by the Turks.   Should I persevere in the
same course, should I observe the same measure, a prolix and
slender thread would be spun through many a'volume, nor would
the patient reader find an adequate reward of instruction or
amusement.   At every step, as we sink deeper in the decline and
fall of the Eastern empire, the annals of each succeeding reign
would impose a more ungrateful and melancholy task.   These
annals must continue to repeat a tedious and uniform tale of
weakness and misery; the natural connection of causes and
events would be broken by frequent and hasty transitions, and
a minute accumulation of circumstances must destroy the light
and effect of those general pictures which compose the use and
ornament of a remote history.   From the time of Heraclius the
Byzantine theatre is contracted and darkened: the line of empire,
which had been defined by the laws of Justinian and the arms of
Belisarius, recedes on all sides from our view; the Roman name,
the proper subject of our inquiries, is reduced to a narrow corner
of Europe, to the lonely suburbs of Constantinople; and the fate
of the Greek empire has been compared to that of the Rhine,
which loses itself in the sands before its waters can mingle with
the ocean.   The scale of dominion is diminished to our view by
the distance of time and place; nor is the loss of external
splendour compensated by the nobler gifts of virtue and genius.

Croze (Hist. du Christianisme d'Ethiopie et d'Arménie, La Haye, 1739,
in 12mo), have drawn their principal materials from the Jesuits, especially
from the General History of Tellez, published in Portuguese at Coimbra,
1660.   We might be surprised at their frankness; but their most flagitious
vice, the spirit of persecution, was in their eyes the most meritorious virtue.
Ludolphus possessed some, though a slight, advantage from the Æthiopic
language, and the personal conversation of Gregory, a free-spirited Abyssinian priest, whom he invited from Rome to the court of Saxe-Gotha.
See the Theologia Æthiopica of Gregory, in Fabricius, Lux Evangelii,
p. 716-734.

In the last moments of her decay Constantinople was doubtless more opulent and populous than Athens at her most flourishing era, when a scanty sum of six thousand talents, or twelve hundred thousand pounds sterling, was possessed by twenty-one thousand male citizens of an adult age. But each of these citizens was a freeman who dared to assert the liberty of his thoughts, words, and actions; whose person and property were guarded by equal law; and who exercised his independent vote in the government of the republic. Their numbers seem to be multiplied by the strong and various discriminations of character; under the shield of freedom, on the wings of emulation and vanity, each Athenian aspired to the level of the national dignity; from this commanding eminence some chosen spirits soared beyond the reach of a vulgar eye; and the chances of superior merit in a great and populous kingdom, as they are proved by experience, would excuse the computation of imaginary millions. The territories of Athens, Sparta, and their allies, do not exceed a moderate province of France or England; but after the trophies of Salamis and Platæa, they expand in our fancy to the gigantic size of Asia, which had been trampled under the feet of the victorious Greeks. But the subjects of the Byzantine empire, who assume and dishonour the names both of Greeks and Romans, present a dead uniformity of abject vices, which are neither softened by the weakness of humanity nor animated by the vigour of memorable crimes. The freemen of antiquity might repeat with generous enthusiasm the sentence of Homer, " that on the first day of his servitude the captive is deprived of one half of his manly virtue." But the poet had only seen the effects of civil or domestic slavery, nor could he foretell that the second moiety of manhood must be annihilated by the spiritual despotism, which shackles not only the actions but even the thoughts of the prostrate votary. By this double yoke the Greeks were oppressed under the successors of Heraclius; the tyrant, a law of eternal justice, was degraded by the vices of his subjects; and on the throne, in the camp, in the schools, we search, perhaps with fruitless diligence, the names and characters that may deserve to be rescued from oblivion. Nor are the defects of the subject compensated by the skill and variety of the painters. Of a space of eight hundred years, the four first centuries are overspread with a cloud interrupted by some faint and broken rays of historic light: in the lives of the emperors, from Maurice to Alexius, Basil the Macedonian has alone been the theme of a separate work; and the absence, or loss, or imperfection of contemporary evidence, must be poorly supplied by the doubtful authority of more recent compilers. The four last centuries are exempt from the reproach of penury: and with the Comnenian family the historic muse of Constantinople again revives, but her apparel is gaudy, her motions are without elegance or grace. A succession of priests, or courtiers, treads in each other's footsteps in the same path of servitude and superstition: their views are narrow, their judgment is feeble or corrupt: and we close the volume of copious barrenness, still ignorant of the causes of events, the characters of the actors, and the manners of the times, which they celebrate or deplore. The observation which has been applied to a man may be extended to a whole people, that the energy of the sword is communicated to the pen; and it will be found by experience that the tone of history will rise or fall with the spirit of the age.

From these considerations I should have abandoned without regret the Greek slaves and their servile historians, had I not reflected that the fate of the Byzantine monarchy is *passively* connected with the most splendid and important revolutions which have changed the state of the world. The space of the lost provinces was immediately replenished with new colonies and rising kingdoms: the active virtues of peace and war deserted from the vanquished to the victorious nations; and it is in their origin and conquests, in their religion and government, that we must explore the causes and effects of the decline and fall of the Eastern empire. Nor will this scope of narrative, the riches and variety of these materials, be incompatible with the unity of design and composition. As, in his daily prayers, the Musulman of Fez or Delhi still turns his face towards the temple of Mecca, the historian's eye shall be always fixed on the city of Constantinople. The excursive line may embrace the wilds of Arabia and Tartary, but the circle will be ultimately reduced to the decreasing limit of the Roman monarchy.

On this principle I shall now establish the plan of the last two volumes of the present work. The first chapter will contain, in a regular series, the emperors who reigned at Constantinople during a period of six hundred years, from the days of Heraclius to the Latin conquest: a rapid abstract, which may be supported by a *general* appeal to the order and text of the original historians. In this introduction I shall confine myself to the revolutions of the throne, the succession of families, the personal characters of the Greek princes, the mode of their life and death, the maxims and influence of their domestic government, and the tendency of their reign to accelerate or suspend the downfall of the Eastern empire. Such a chronological review will serve to illustrate the various argument of the subsequent chapters; and each circumstance of the eventful story of the barbarians will adapt itself in a proper place to the Byzantine annals. The internal state of the empire, and the dangerous heresy of the Paulicians, which shook the East and enlightened the West, will be the subject of two separate chapters; but these inquiries must be postponed till our farther progress shall have opened the view of the world in the ninth and tenth centuries of the Christian era. After this foundation of Byzantine history, the following nations will pass before our eyes, and each will occupy the space to which it may be entitled by greatness or merit, or the degree of connection with the Roman world and the present age. I. The FRANKS; a general appellation which includes all the barbarians of France, Italy, and Germany, who were united by the sword and sceptre of Charlemagne. The persecution of images and their votaries separated Rome and Italy from the Byzantine throne, and prepared the restoration of the Roman empire in the West. II. The ARABS or SARACENS. Three ample chapters will be devoted to this curious and interesting object. In the first, after a picture of the country and its inhabitants, I shall investigate the character of Mohammed; the character, religion, and success of the prophet. In the second I shall lead the Arabs to the conquest of Syria, Egypt, and Africa, the provinces of the Roman empire; nor can I check their victorious career till they have overthrown the monarchies of Persia and Spain. In the third I shall inquire how Constantinople and Europe were saved by the luxury and arts, the division and decay, of the empire of the caliphs. A single chapter will include, III. The BULGARIANS, IV. HUNGARIANS, and V. RUSSIANS, who assaulted by sea or by land the provinces and the capital; but the last of these, so important in their present greatness, will excite some curiosity in their origin and infancy. VI. The NORMANS; or rather the private adventurers of that warlike people, who founded a powerful kingdom in Apulia and Sicily, shook the throne of Constantinople, displayed the trophies of chivalry, and almost realised the wonders of romance. VII. The LATINS; the subjects of the pope, the nations of the West, who enlisted under the banner of the cross for the recovery or relief of the holy sepulchre. The Greek emperors were terrified and preserved by the myriads of pilgrims who marched to Jerusalem with Godfrey of Bouillon and the peers of Christendom. The second and third crusades trod in the footsteps of the first: Asia and Europe were mingled in a sacred war of two hundred years; and the Christian powers were bravely resisted and finally expelled by Saladin and the Mamalukes of Egypt. In these memorable crusades a fleet and army of French and Venetians were diverted from Syria to the Thracian Bosphorus: they assaulted the capital, they subverted the Greek monarchy: and a dynasty of Latin princes was seated near threescore years on the throne of Constantine. VIII. The GREEKS themselves, during this period of captivity and exile, must be considered as a foreign nation; the enemies, and again the sovereigns of Constantinople. Misfortune had rekindled a spark of national virtue; and the Imperial series may be continued with some dignity from their restoration to the Turkish conquest. IX. The MOGULS and TARTARS. By the arms of Zingis and his descendants the globe was shaken from China to Poland and Greece: the sultans were overthrown: the caliphs fell, and the Cæsars trembled on their throne. The victories of Timour suspended above fifty years the final ruin of the Byzantine empire. X. I have already noticed the first appearance of the TURKS; and the names of the fathers, of *Seljuk* and *Othman*, discriminate the two successive dynasties of the nation which emerged in the eleventh century from the Scythian wilderness. The former established a potent and splendid kingdom from the banks of the Oxus to Antioch and Nice; and the first crusade was provoked by the violation of Jerusalem and the danger of Constantinople. From a humble origin the *Ottomans* arose the scourge and terror of Christendom. Constantinople was besieged and taken by Mohammed II., and his triumph annihilates the remnant, the image, the title, of the Roman empire in the East. The schism of the Greeks will be connected with their last calamities and the restoration of learning in the Western world. I shall return from the captivity of the new to the ruins of ancient ROME; and the venerable name, the interesting theme, will shed a ray of glory on the conclusion of my labours.

THE emperor Heraclius had punished a tyrant and ascended his throne; and the memory of his reign is perpetuated by the transient conquest and irreparable loss of the Eastern provinces. After the death of Eudocia, his first wife, he disobeyed the patriarch and violated the laws by his second marriage with his niece Martina; and the superstition of the Greeks beheld the judgment of Heaven in the diseases of the father and the deformity of his offspring. But the opinion of an illegitimate birth is sufficient to distract the choice and loosen the obedience of the people: the ambition of Martina was quickened by maternal love, and perhaps by the envy of a stepmother; and the aged husband was too feeble to withstand the arts of conjugal allurements. Constantine, his eldest son, enjoyed in a mature age the title of Augustus; but the weakness of his constitution required a colleague and a guardian, and he yielded with secret reluctance to the partition of the empire. The senate was summoned to the palace to ratify or attest the association of Heracleonas, the son of Martina: the imposition of the diadem was consecrated by the prayer and blessing of the patriarch; the senators and patricians adored the majesty of the great emperor and the partners of his reign; and as soon as the doors were thrown open they were hailed by the tumultuary but important voice of the soldiers. After an interval of five months the pompous ceremonies which formed the essence of the Byzantine state were celebrated in the cathedral and the hippodrome: the concord of the royal brothers was affectedly displayed by the younger leaning on the arm of the elder; and the name of Martina was mingled in the reluctant or venal acclamations of the people. Heraclius survived this association about two years: his last testimony declared his two sons the equal heirs of the Eastern empire, and commanded them to honour this widow Martina as their mother and their sovereign.

When Martina first appeared on the throne with the name and attributes of royalty, she was checked by a firm, though respectful, opposition; and the dying embers of freedom were kindled by the breath of superstitious prejudice. "We reverence," exclaimed the voice of a citizen, "we reverence the mother of our princes; but to those princes alone our obedience is due; and Constantine, the elder emperor, is of an age to sustain, in his own hands, the weight of the sceptre. Your sex is excluded by nature from the toils of government. How could you combat, how could you answer, the barbarians who, with hostile or friendly intentions, may approach the royal city? May Heaven avert from the Roman republic this national disgrace, which would provoke the patience of the slaves of Persia!" Martina descended from the throne with indignation, and sought a refuge in the female apartment of the palace. The reign of Constantine the Third lasted only one hundred and three days: he expired in the thirtieth year of his age, and, although his life had been a long malady, a belief was entertained that poison had been the means, and his cruel stepmother the author, of his untimely fate. Martina reaped indeed the harvest of his death, and assumed the government in the name of the surviving emperor; but the incestuous widow of Heraclius was universally abhorred; the jealousy of the people was awakened, and the two orphans whom Constantine had left became the objects of the public care. It was in vain that the son of Martina, who was no more than fifteen years of age, was taught to declare himself the guardian of his nephews, one of whom he had presented at the baptismal font: it was in vain that he swore on the wood of the true cross to defend them against all their enemies. On his deathbed the late emperor had despatched a trusty servant to arm the troops and provinces of the East in the defence of his helpless children: the eloquence and liberality of Valentin had been successful, and from his camp of Chalcedon he boldly demanded the punishment of the assassins, and the restoration of the lawful heir. The licence of the soldiers, who devoured the grapes and drank the wine of their Asiatic vineyards, provoked the citizens of Constantinople against the domestic authors of their calamities, and the dome of St. Sophia re-echoed, not with prayers and hymns, but with the clamours and imprecations of an enraged multitude. At their imperious command Heracleonas appeared in the pulpit with the eldest of the royal orphans; Constans alone was saluted as emperor of the Romans, and a crown of gold, which had been taken from the tomb of Heraclius, was placed on his head, with the solemn benediction of the patriarch. But, in the tumult of joy and indignation, the church was pillaged, the sanctuary was polluted by a promiscuous crowd of Jews and barbarians; and the Monothelite Pyrrhus, a creature of the empress, after dropping a protestation on the altar, escaped by a prudent flight from the zeal of the Catholics. A more serious and bloody task was reserved for the senate, who derived a temporary strength from the consent of the soldiers and people. The spirit of Roman freedom revived the ancient and awful examples of the judgment of tyrants, and the Imperial culprits were deposed and condemned as the authors of the death of Constantine. But the severity of the conscript fathers was stained by the indiscriminate punishment of the innocent and the guilty: Martina and Heracleonas were sentenced to the amputation, the former of her tongue, the latter of his nose; and after this cruel execution they consumed the remainder of their days in exile and oblivion. The Greeks who were capable of reflection might find some consolation for their servitude by observing the abuse of power when it was lodged for a moment in the hands of an aristocracy.

We shall imagine ourselves transported five hundred years backwards to the age of the Antonines if we listen to the oration which Constans II. pronounced in the twelfth year of his age before the Byzantine senate. After returning his thanks for the just punishment of the assassins who had intercepted the fairest hopes of his father's reign, " By the divine Providence," said the young emperor, " and by your righteous decree, Martina and her incestuous progeny have been cast headlong from the throne. Your majesty and wisdom have prevented the Roman state from degenerating into lawless tyranny. I therefore exhort and beseech you to stand forth as the counsellors and judges of the common safety." The senators were gratified by the respectful address and liberal donative of their sovereign; but these servile Greeks were unworthy and regardless of freedom; and in his mind the lesson of an hour was quickly erased by the prejudices of the age and the habits of despotism. He retained only a jealous fear lest the senate or people should one day invade the right of primogeniture, and seat his brother Theodosius on an equal throne. By the imposition of holy orders, the grandson of Heraclius was disqualified for the purple; but this ceremony, which seemed to profane the sacraments of the church, was insufficient to appease the suspicions of the tyrant, and the death of the deacon Theodosius could alone expiate the crime of his royal birth. His murder was avenged by the imprecations of the people, and the assassin, in the fulness of power, was driven from his capital into voluntary and perpetual exile. Constans embarked for Greece; and, as if he meant to retort the abhorrence which he deserved, he is said, from the imperial galley, to have spit against the walls of his native city. After passing the winter at Athens, he sailed to Tarentum in Italy, visited Rome, and concluded a long pilgrimage of disgrace and sacrilegious rapine by fixing his residence at Syracuse. But if Constans could fly from his people, he could not fly from himself. The remorse of his conscience created a phantom who pursued him by land and sea, by day and by night; and the visionary Theodosius, presenting to his lips a cup of blood, said, or seemed to say, " Drink, brother, drink "—a sure emblem of the aggravation of his guilt, since he had received from the hands of the deacon the mystic cup of the blood of Christ. Odious to himself and to mankind, Constans perished by domestic, perhaps by episcopal, treason in the capital of Sicily.

A servant who waited in the bath, after pouring warm water on his head, struck him violently with the vase. He fell, stunned by the blow and suffocated by the water; and his attendants, who wondered at the tedious delay, beheld with indifference the corpse of their lifeless emperor. The troops of Sicily invested with the purple an obscure youth, whose inimitable beauty eluded, and it might easily elude, the declining art of the painters and sculptors of the age.

Constans had left in the Byzantine palace three sons, the eldest of whom had been clothed in his infancy with the purple. When the father summoned them to attend his person in Sicily, these precious hostages were detained by the Greeks, and a firm refusal informed him that they were the children of the state. The news of his murder was conveyed with almost supernatural speed from Syracuse to Constantinople; and Constantine, the eldest of his sons, inherited his throne without being the heir of the public hatred. His subjects contributed with zeal and alacrity to chastise the guilt and presumption of a province which had usurped the rights of the senate and people; the young emperor sailed from the Hellespont with a powerful fleet, and the legions of Rome and Carthage were assembled under his standard in the harbour of Syracuse. The defeat of the Sicilian tyrant was easy, his punishment just, and his beauteous head was exposed in the hippodrome; but I cannot applaud the clemency of a prince who, among a crowd of victims, condemned the son of a patrician for deploring with some bitterness the execution of a virtuous father. The youth was castrated: he survived the operation, and the memory of this indecent cruelty is preserved by the elevation of Germanus to the rank of a patriarch and saint. After pouring this bloody libation on his father's tomb, Constantine returned to his capital; and the growth of his young beard during the Sicilian voyage was announced, by the familiar surname of Pogonatus, to the Grecian world. But his reign, like that of his predecessor, was stained with fraternal discord. On his two brothers, Heraclius and Tiberius, he had bestowed the title of Augustus—an empty title, for they continued to languish, without trust or power, in the solitude of the palace. At their secret instigation the troops of the Anatolian *theme* or province approached the city on the Asiatic side, demanded for the royal brothers the partition or exercise of sovereignty, and supported their seditious claim by a theological argument. They were Christians, they cried, and orthodox Catholics, the sincere votaries of the holy and undivided Trinity. Since there are three equal persons in heaven, it is reasonable there should be three equal persons upon earth. The emperor invited these learned divines to a friendly conference, in which they might propose their arguments to the senate: they obeyed the summons, but the prospect of their bodies hanging on the gibbet in the suburb of Galata reconciled their companions to the unity of the reign of Constantine. He pardoned his brothers, and their names were still pronounced in the public acclamations; but on the repetition or suspicion of a similar offence, the obnoxious princes were deprived of their titles and noses, in the presence of the Catholic bishops who were assembled at Constantinople in the sixth general synod. In the close of his life Pogonatus was anxious only to establish the right of primogeniture: the heir of his two sons, Justinian and Heraclius, was offered on the shrine of St. Peter, as a symbol of their spiritual adoption by the pope; but the elder was alone exalted to the rank of Augustus, and the assurance of the empire.

After the decease of his father the inheritance of the Roman world devolved to Justinian II.; and the name of a triumphant lawgiver was dishonoured by the vices of a boy, who imitated his namesake only in the expensive luxury of building. His passions were strong; his understanding was feeble; and he was intoxicated with a foolish pride that his birth had given him the command of millions, of whom the smallest community would not have chosen him for their local magistrate. His favourite ministers were two beings the least susceptible of human sympathy, a eunuch and a monk: to the one he abandoned the palace, to the other the finances; the former corrected the emperor's mother with a scourge, the latter suspended the insolvent tributaries, with their heads downwards, over a slow and smoky fire. Since the days of Commodus and Caracalla the cruelty of the Roman princes had most commonly been the effect of their fear; but Justinian, who possessed some vigour of character, enjoyed the sufferings, and braved the revenge, of his subjects about ten years, till the measure was full of his crimes and of their patience. In a dark dungeon Leontius, a general of reputation, had groaned above three years, with some of the noblest and most deserving of the patricians: he was suddenly drawn forth to assume the government of Greece; and this promotion of an injured man was a mark of the contempt rather than of the confidence of his prince. As he was followed to the port by the kind offices of his friends, Leontius observed, with a sigh, that he was a victim adorned for sacrifice, and that inevitable death would pursue his footsteps. They ventured to reply that glory and empire might be the recompence of a generous resolution, that every order of men abhorred the reign of a monster, and that the hands of two hundred thousand patriots expected only the voice of a leader. The night was chosen for their deliverance; and in the first effort of the conspirators the præfect was slain and the prisons were forced open: the emissaries of Leontius proclaimed in every street, " Christians, to St. Sophia! " and the seasonable text of the patriarch, " This is the day of the Lord! " was the prelude of an inflammatory sermon. From the church the people adjourned to the hippodrome: Justinian, in whose cause not a sword had been drawn, was dragged before these tumultuary judges, and their clamours demanded the instant death of the tyrant. But Leontius, who was already clothed with the purple, cast an eye of pity on the prostrate son of his own benefactor and of so many emperors. The life of Justinian was spared; the amputation of his nose, perhaps of his tongue, was imperfectly performed: the happy flexibility of the Greek language could impose the name of Rhinotmetus; and the mutilated tyrant was banished to Chersonæ in Crim-Tartary, a lonely settlement, where corn, wine, and oil were imported as foreign luxuries.

On the edge of the Scythian wilderness Justinian still cherished the pride of his birth, and the hope of his restoration. After three years' exile, he received the pleasing intelligence that his injury was avenged by a second revolution, and that Leontius in his turn had been dethroned and mutilated by the rebel Apsimar, who assumed the more respectable name of Tiberius. But the claim of lineal succession was still formidable to a plebeian usurper; and his jealousy was stimulated by the complaints and charges of the Chersonites, who beheld the vices of the tyrant in the spirit of the exile. With a band of followers, attached to his person by common hope or common despair, Justinian fled from the inhospitable shore to the horde of the Chozars, who pitched their tents between the Tanais and Borysthenes. The khan entertained with pity and respect the royal suppliant: Phanagoria, once an opulent city, on the Asiatic side of the lake Mæotis, was assigned for his residence; and every Roman prejudice was stifled in his marriage with the sister of the barbarian, who seems, however, from the name of Theodora, to have received the sacrament of baptism. But the faithless Chozar was soon tempted by the gold of Constantinople: and had not the design been revealed by the conjugal love of Theodora, her husband must have been assassinated or betrayed into the power of his enemies. After strangling, with his own hands, the two emissaries of the khan, Justinian sent back his wife to her brother, and embarked on the Euxine in search of new and more faithful allies. His vessel was assaulted by a violent tempest; and one of his pious companions advised him to deserve the mercy of God by a vow of general forgiveness if he should be restored to the throne. " Of forgiveness? " replied the intrepid tyrant: "may I perish this instant—may the Almighty whelm me in the waves, if I consent to spare a single head of my enemies!" He survived this impious menace, sailed into the mouth of the Danube, trusted his person in the royal village of the Bulgarians, and purchased the aid of Terbelis, a pagan conqueror, by the promise of his daughter, and a fair partition of the treasures of the empire. The Bulgarian kingdom extended to the confines of Thrace; and the two princes besieged Constantinople at the head of fifteen thousand horse. Apsimar was dismayed by the sudden and hostile apparition of his rival, whose head had been promised by the Chozar, and of whose evasion he was yet ignorant. After an absence of ten years the crimes of Justinian were faintly remembered, and the birth and misfortunes of their hereditary sovereign excited the pity of the multitude, ever discontented with the ruling powers; and by the active diligence of his adherents he was introduced into the city and palace of Constantine.

In rewarding his allies, and recalling his wife, Justinian displayed some sense of honour and gratitude; and Terbelis retired, after sweeping away a heap of gold coin which he measured with his Scythian whip. But never was vow more religiously performed than the sacred oath of revenge which he had sworn amidst the storms of the Euxine. The two usurpers, for I must reserve the name of tyrant for the conqueror, were dragged into the hippodrome, the one from his prison, the other from his palace. Before their execution Leontius and Apsimar were cast prostrate in chains beneath the throne of the emperor; and Justinian, planting a foot on each of their necks, contemplated above an hour the chariot-race, while the inconstant people shouted, in the words of the Psalmist, " Thou shalt trample on the asp and basilisk, and on the lion and dragon shalt thou set thy foot!" The universal defection which he had once experienced might provoke him to repeat the wish of Caligula,

that the Roman people had but one head. Yet I shall presume
to observe that such a wish is unworthy of an ingenious tyrant,
since his revenge and cruelty would have been extinguished by
a single blow, instead of the slow variety of tortures which
Justinian inflicted on the victims of his anger. His pleasures
were inexhaustible: neither private virtue nor public service
could expiate the guilt of active, or even passive, obedience to
an established government; and, during the six years of his
new reign, he considered the axe, the cord, and the rack as the
only instruments of royalty. But his most implacable hatred
was pointed against the Chersonites, who had insulted his exile
and violated the laws of hospitality. Their remote situation
afforded some means of defence, or at least of escape; and a
grievous tax was imposed on Constantinople to supply the
preparations of a fleet and army. " All are guilty, and all must
perish," was the mandate of Justinian; and the bloody
execution was intrusted to his favourite Stephen, who was
recommended by the epithet of the Savage. Yet even the
savage Stephen imperfectly accomplished the intentions of his
sovereign. The slowness of his attack allowed the greater part
of the inhabitants to withdraw into the country; and the
minister of vengeance contented himself with reducing the youth
of both sexes to a state of servitude, with roasting alive seven
of the principal citizens, with drowning twenty in the sea, and
with reserving forty-two in chains to receive their doom from
the mouth of the emperor. In their return the fleet was driven
on the rocky shores of Anatolia; and Justinian applauded the
obedience of the Euxine, which had involved so many thousands
of his subjects and enemies in a common shipwreck: but the
tyrant was still insatiate of blood; and a second expedition was
commanded to extirpate the remains of the proscribed colony.
In the short interval the Chersonites had returned to their city,
and were prepared to die in arms; the khan of the Chozars
had renounced the cause of his odious brother; the exiles of
every province were assembled in Tauris; and Bardanes, under
the name of Philippicus, was invested with the purple. The
Imperial troops, unwilling and unable to perpetrate the revenge
of Justinian, escaped his displeasure by abjuring his allegiance;
the fleet, under their new sovereign, steered back a more
auspicious course to the harbours of Sinope and Constantinople;
and every tongue was prompt to pronounce, every hand to
execute, the death of the tyrant. Destitute of friends, he was
deserted by his barbarian guards; and the stroke of the assassin

was praised as an act of patriotism and Roman virtue.   His son Tiberius had taken refuge in a church; his aged grandmother guarded the door; and the innocent youth, suspending round his neck the most formidable relics, embraced with one hand the altar, with the other the wood of the true cross.   But the popular fury that dares to trample on superstition, is deaf to the cries of humanity; and the race of Heraclius was extinguished after a reign of one hundred years.

Between the fall of the Heraclian and the rise of the Isaurian dynasty, a short interval of six years is divided into three reigns. Bardanes, or Philippicus, was hailed at Constantinople as a hero who had delivered his country from a tyrant; and he might taste some moments of happiness in the first transports of sincere and universal joy.   Justinian had left behind him an ample treasure, the fruit of cruelty and rapine: but this useful fund was soon and idly dissipated by his successor.   On the festival of his birthday Philippicus entertained the multitude with the games of the hippodrome; from thence he paraded through the streets with a thousand banners and a thousand trumpets; refreshed himself in the baths of Zeuxippus, and, returning to the palace, entertained his nobles with a sumptuous banquet.   At the meridan hour he withdrew to his chamber, intoxicated with flattery and wine, and forgetful that his example had made every subject ambitious, and that every ambitious subject was his secret enemy.   Some bold conspirators introduced themselves in the disorder of the feast; and the slumbering monarch was surprised, bound, blinded, and deposed, before he was sensible of his danger.   Yet the traitors were deprived of their reward; and the free voice of the senate and people promoted Artemius from the office of secretary to that of emperor: he assumed the title of Anastasius the Second, and displayed in a short and troubled reign the virtues both of peace and war.   But after the extinction of the Imperial line the rule of obedience was violated, and every change diffused the seeds of new revolutions.   In a mutiny of the fleet an obscure and reluctant officer of the revenue was forcibly invested with the purple; after some months of a naval war, Anastasius resigned the sceptre; and the conqueror, Theodosius the Third, submitted in his turn to the superior ascendant of Leo, the general and emperor of the Oriental troops.   His two predecessors were permitted to embrace the ecclesiastical profession: the restless impatience of Anastasius tempted him to risk and to lose his life in a treasonable enterprise; but the last

days of Theodosius were honourable and secure. The single
sublime word, "HEALTH," which he inscribed on his tomb,
expresses the confidence of philosophy or religion; and the
fame of his miracles was long preserved among the people of
Ephesus. This convenient shelter of the church might sometimes impose a lesson of clemency; but it may be questioned
whether it is for the public interest to diminish the perils of
unsuccessful ambition.

I have dwelt on the fall of a tyrant; I shall briefly represent
the founder of a new dynasty,[1] who is known to posterity by
the invectives of his enemies, and whose public and private life
is involved in the ecclesiastical story of the Iconoclasts.[2] Yet
in spite of the clamours of superstition, a favourable prejudice
for the character of Leo the Isaurian [3] may be reasonably drawn

---

[1] [With the reign of Leo III. Mr. Finlay's *History of the Byzantine
Empire* commences—a very valuable work.—O. S.]

[2] Genealogy of the Isaurian dynasty:—

LEO III. Imp. *ob.* A.D. 741.
|
Irene,   =   CONSTANTINUS V. COPRONYMUS,   =   Eudocia.
d. of the Khan | Imp. *ob.* 775.
of the Chazars. |

LEO IV.   Nice-   Christo-   Nicetas. Eudoxus. Anthimus.
(Chazarus), phorus.   phorus.
Imp. *ob.* 780,
m. Irene, an
Athenian.
|
Maria = CONSTANTINUS VI. = Theodata.
| Imp. deposed 797, |
| but his mother Irene |
| reigned till 802. |

Euphrosyne,   Leo.
m. Michael II.   —S.

[3] [Though Leo is generally called an Isaurian, he was born at Germanicia,
a city of Armenia Minor, in the mountains near the borders of Cappadocia and Syria. The family of Leo was a foreign one, and Finlay in his
Byzantine Empire observes that he was probably called an Isaurian
because the Isaurians appear to have been the subjects of the empire who
had retained the greatest share of their original nationality.

A strange circumstance must be noted here, that the dates of forty-seven
years in the eighth century from 726-7 to 773-4 are a year wrong. The Anni
Mundi and the indictions, as Bury points out (*Later Roman Empire*,
vol. ii. 425-7), do not correspond. The professor very cogently concluded
from an investigation of the whole circumstances of the case, that Leo III.
had packed two indictions into one year of twelve months, for the purpose
of raising a double capitation tax, and that nearly fifty years later Constantine V. spread one indiction over two years (A.D. 772-4), so restoring
the correspondence between Anni Mundi and Indictions, according to the

from the obscurity of his birth and the duration of his reign.
—I. In an age of manly spirit the prospect of an Imperial
reward would have kindled every energy of the mind, and
produced a crowd of competitors as deserving as they were
desirous to reign.   Even in the corruption and debility of the
modern Greeks the elevation of a plebeian from the last to the
first rank of society supposes some qualifications above the level
of the multitude.   He would probably be ignorant and disdainful
of speculative science; and, in the pursuit of fortune, he might
absolve himself from the obligations of benevolence and justice;
but to his character we may ascribe the useful virtues of
prudence and fortitude, the knowledge of mankind, and the
important art of gaining their confidence and directing their
passions.   It is agreed that Leo was a native of Isauria, and
that Conon was his primitive name.   The writers, whose
awkward satire is praise, describe him as an itinerant pedlar,
who drove an ass with some paltry merchandise to the country
fairs; and foolishly relate that he met on the road some Jewish
fortune-tellers, who promised him the Roman empire, on
condition that he should abolish the worship of idols.   A more
probable account relates the migration of his father from Asia
Minor to Thrace, where he exercised the lucrative trade of a
grazier; and he must have acquired considerable wealth, since
the first introduction of his son was procured by a supply of
five hundred sheep to the Imperial camp.   His first service was
in the guards of Justinian, where he soon attracted the notice,
and by degrees the jealousy, of the tyrant.   His valour and
dexterity were conspicuous in the Colchian war: from Anastasius
he received the command of the Anatolian legions, and by the
suffrage of the soldiers he was raised to the empire with the
general applause of the Roman world.—II. In this dangerous
elevation Leo the Third supported himself against the envy of
his equals, the discontent of a powerful faction, and the assaults
of his foreign and domestic enemies.   The Catholics, who accuse
his religious innovations, are obliged to confess that they were
undertaken with temper and conducted with firmness.   Their
silence respects the wisdom of his administration and the purity

previous method of computation.   This reasoning was confirmed to Prof.
Bury by one fact, the eclipse of the sun noticed by Theophanes under
A.M. 6252, on Friday, August 15, clearly the annular eclipse of A.D. 760
on that day of the month and week.   The received chronology would
imply that the eclipse took place in A.D. 761, August 15, but astronomy
assures us that there was no eclipse on that day, nor was the day Friday.
—O. S.]

of his manners. After a reign of twenty-four years he peaceably expired in the palace of Constantinople; and the purple which he had acquired was transmitted by the right of inheritance to the third generation.[1]

In a long reign of thirty-four years the son and successor of Leo, Constantine the Fifth, surnamed Copronymus, attacked with less temperate zeal the images or idols of the church.[2] Their votaries have exhausted the bitterness of religious gall in their portrait of this spotted panther, this antichrist, this flying dragon of the serpent's seed, who surpassed the vices of Elagabalus and Nero. His reign was a long butchery of whatever was most noble, or holy, or innocent, in his empire. In person, the emperor assisted at the execution of his victims, surveyed their agonies, listened to their groans, and indulged, without satiating, his appetite for blood: a plate of noses was accepted as a grateful offering, and his domestics were often scourged or mutilated by the royal hand. His surname was derived from his pollution of his baptismal font. The infant might be excused; but the manly pleasures of Copronymus degraded him below the level of a·brute; his lust confounded the eternal distinctions of sex and species, and he seemed to extract some unnatural delight from the objects most offensive to human sense. In his religion the Iconoclast was a Heretic, a Jew, a Mohammedan, a Pagan, and an Atheist; and his belief of an invisible power could be discovered only in his magic rites, human victims, and nocturnal sacrifices to Venus and the demons of antiquity. His life was stained with the most opposite vices, and the ulcers which covered his body anticipated before his death the sentiment of hell-tortures. Of these accusations, which I have so patiently copied, a part is refuted by its own absurdity; and in the private anecdotes of the life of princes,

---

[1] [During the latter part of the reign of Leo X., the hostilities of the Saracens, who invested a Pergamenian, named Tiberius, with the purple, and proclaimed him as the son of Justinian, and an earthquake which destroyed the walls of Constantinople, compelled Leo greatly to increase the burden of taxation on his subjects. A twelfth was exacted in addition to every aureus ($\nu\acute{o}\mu\iota\sigma\mu\alpha$) as a wall-tax. Cf. Theophanes; Schlosser, *Geschichte der Bilder-stürmenden Kaiser*, p. 197.—O. S.]

[2] [Gibbon has omitted to mention that on the death of Leo III. Constantine's succession was contested by his brother-in-law, Artavasdus, Count of the Opsikian Theme who had married Leo's daughter Anna. Artavasdus defeated Constantine, was proclaimed emperor, and·associated with him in the empire his eldest son Nicephorus. For nearly two years Constantinople was lost to Constantine (741-3), but in the last-named year Constantinople was taken by the troops of Constantine, and both Artavasdus and his son were put to death. There are coins extant bearing the impression both of Artavasdus and Nicephorus.—O. S.]

the lie is more easy as the detection is more difficult. Without adopting the pernicious maxim, that, where much is alleged, something must be true, I can however discern that Constantine the Fifth was dissolute and cruel. Calumny is more prone to exaggerate than to invent; and her licentious tongue is checked in some measure by the experience of the age and country to which she appeals. Of the bishops and monks, the generals and magistrates, who are said to have suffered under his reign, the numbers are recorded, the names were conspicuous, the execution was public, the mutilation visible and permanent.[1] The Catholics hated the person and government of Copronymus; but even their hatred is a proof of their oppression. They dissembled the provocations which might excuse or justify his rigour, but even these provocations must gradually inflame his resentment and harden his temper in the use or the abuse of despotism. Yet the character of the fifth Constantine was not devoid of merit, nor did his government always deserve the curses or the contempt of the Greeks. From the confession of his enemies I am informed of the restoration of an ancient aqueduct, of the redemption of two thousand five hundred captives, of the uncommon plenty of the times, and of the new colonies with which he repeopled Constantinople and the Thracian cities. They reluctantly praise his activity and courage; he was on horseback in the field at the head of his legions; and, although the fortune of his arms was various, he triumphed by sea and land, on the Euphrates and the Danube, in civil and barbarian war. Heretical praise must be cast into the scale to counterbalance the weight of orthodox invective. The Iconoclasts revered the virtues of the prince: forty years after his death they still prayed before the tomb of the saint. A miraculous vision was propagated by fanaticism or fraud: and the Christian hero appeared on a milk-white steed, brandishing his lance against the pagans of Bulgaria: "An absurd fable," says the Catholic historian, "since Copronymus is chained with the demons in the abyss of hell."

[1] [Constantine V. is accused of burning the library of Constantinople, founded by Julian, but one really cannot credit ninety per cent. of the lies which the monks fabricated against the man who strove to stamp out image-worship among them, and punished the clergy for their superstition. He had many faults, but he was manly and courageous, and he showed himself determined not to be led blindly by priestly advisers. He recovered Germanicia, Melitene, and Theodosiopolis from the Saracens, crushed an expedition sent by the caliph to besiege Cyprus in 746, exhausted the Bulgarian kingdom by a series of campaigns, and showed himself the consistent enemy of all that savoured of superstition.—O. S.]

Leo the Fourth, the son of the fifth and the father of the sixth Constantine, was of a feeble constitution both of mind and body, and the principal care of his reign was the settlement of the succession. The association of the young Constantine was urged by the officious zeal of his subjects; and the emperor, conscious of his decay, complied, after a prudent hesitation, with their unanimous wishes. The royal infant, at the age of five years, was crowned with his mother Irene; and the national consent was ratified by every circumstance of pomp and solemnity that could dazzle the eyes or bind the conscience of the Greeks. An oath of fidelity was administered in the palace, the church, and the hippodrome, to the several orders of the state, who adjured the holy names of the son and mother of God. " Be witness, O Christ! that we will watch over the safety of Constantine the son of Leo, expose our lives in his service, and bear true allegiance to his person and posterity." They pledged their faith on the wood of the true cross, and the act of their engagement was deposited on the altar of St. Sophia. The first to swear, and the first to violate their oath, were the five sons of Copronymus by a second marriage; and the story of these princes is singular and tragic. The right of primogeniture excluded them from the throne; the injustice of their elder brother defrauded them of a legacy of about two millions sterling; some vain titles were not deemed a sufficient compensation for wealth and power; and they repeatedly conspired against their nephew, before and after the death of his father. Their first attempt was pardoned; for the second offence they were condemned to the ecclesiastical state; and for the third treason, Nicephorus, the eldest and most guilty, was deprived of his eyes, and his four brothers, Christopher, Nicetas, Anthimus, and Eudoxus, were punished, as a milder sentence, by the amputation of their tongues. After five years' confinement they escaped to the church of St. Sophia, and displayed a pathetic spectacle to the people. "Countrymen and Christians," cried Nicephorus for himself and his mute brethren, " behold the sons of your emperor, if you can still recognise our features in this miserable state. A life, an imperfect life, is all that the malice of our enemies has spared. It is now threatened, and we now throw ourselves on your compassion." The rising murmur might have produced a revolution had it not been checked by the presence of a minister, who soothed the unhappy princes with flattery and hope, and gently drew them from the sanctuary to the palace. They were speedily embarked for Greece, and

Athens was allotted for the place of their exile. In this calm retreat, and in their helpless condition, Nicephorus and his brothers were tormented by the thirst of power, and tempted by a Sclavonian chief, who offered to break their prison and to lead them in arms, and in the purple, to the gates of Constantinople. But the Athenian people, ever zealous in the cause of Irene, prevented her justice or cruelty; and the five sons of Copronymus were plunged in eternal darkness and oblivion.

For himself, that emperor had chosen a barbarian wife, the daughter of the khan of the Chozars; but in the marriage of his heir he preferred an Athenian virgin, an orphan seventeen years old, whose sole fortune must have consisted in her personal accomplishments. The nuptials of Leo and Irene were celebrated with royal pomp; she soon acquired the love and confidence of a feeble husband, and in his testament he declared the empress guardian of the Roman world, and of their son Constantine the Sixth, who was no more than ten years of age. During his childhood, Irene most ably and assiduously discharged, in her public administration, the duties of a faithful mother; and her zeal in the restoration of images has deserved the name and honours of a saint, which she still occupies in the Greek calendar. But the emperor attained the maturity of youth; the maternal yoke became more grievous; and he listened to the favourites of his own age, who shared his pleasures, and were ambitious of sharing his power. Their reasons convinced him of his right, their praises of his ability, to reign; and he consented to reward the services of Irene by a perpetual banishment to the isle of Sicily. But her vigilance and penetration easily disconcerted their rash projects: a similar, or more severe, punishment was retaliated on themselves and their advisers; and Irene inflicted on the ungrateful prince the chastisement of a boy. After this contest the mother and the son were at the head of two domestic factions; and instead of mild influence and voluntary obedience, she held in chains a captive and an enemy. The empress was overthrown by the abuse of victory; the oath of fidelity, which she exacted to herself alone, was pronounced with reluctant murmurs; and the bold refusal of the Armenian guards encouraged a free and general declaration that Constantine the Sixth was the lawful emperor of the Romans. In this character he ascended his hereditary throne, and dismissed Irene to a life of solitude and repose. But her haughty spirit condescended to the arts of dissimulation: she flattered the bishops and eunuchs, revived the filial tenderness of the prince, regained his confidence, and betrayed his credulity. The character of Constantine was not destitute of sense or spirit; but his education had been studiously neglected; and his ambitious mother exposed to the public censure the vices which she had nourished and the actions which she had secretly advised: his divorce and second marriage offended the prejudices of the clergy, and by his imprudent rigour he forfeited the attachment of the Armenian guards. A powerful conspiracy was formed for the restoration of Irene; and the secret, though widely diffused, was faithfully kept above eight months, till the emperor, suspicious of his danger, escaped from Constantinople with the design of appealing to the provinces and armies. By this hasty flight the empress was left on the brink of the precipice; yet before she implored the mercy of her son, Irene addressed a private epistle to the friends whom she had placed about his person, with a menace, that unless *they* accomplished, *she* would reveal, their treason. Their fear rendered them intrepid; they seized the emperor on the Asiatic shore, and he was transported to the porphyry apartment of the palace, where he had first seen the light. In the mind of Irene ambition had stifled every sentiment of humanity and nature; and it was decreed in her bloody council that Constantine should be rendered incapable of the throne: her emissaries assaulted the sleeping prince, and stabbed their daggers with such violence and precipitation into his eyes as if they meant to execute a mortal sentence. An ambiguous passage of Theophanes persuaded the annalist of the church that death was the immediate consequence of this barbarous execution. The Catholics have been deceived or subdued by the authority of Baronius; and Protestant zeal has re-echoed the words of a cardinal, desirous, as it should seem, to favour the patroness of images. Yet the blind son of Irene survived many years, oppressed by the court and forgotten by the world: the Isaurian dynasty was silently extinguished; and the memory of Constantine was recalled only by the nuptials of his daughter Euphrosyne with the emperor Michael the Second.

The most bigoted orthodoxy has justly execrated the unnatural mother, who may not easily be paralleled in the history of crimes. To her bloody deed superstition has attributed a subsequent darkness of seventeen days, during which many vessels in mid-day were driven from their course, as if the sun, a globe of fire so vast and so remote, could sympathise with the atoms of a revolving planet. On earth, the crime of Irene was left five years unpunished; her reign was crowned with external splendour; and if she could silence the voice of conscience, she neither heard nor regarded the reproaches of mankind. The Roman world bowed to the government of a female; and as she moved through the streets of Constantinople the reins of four milk-white steeds were held by as many patricians, who marched on foot before the golden chariot of their queen. But these patricians were for the most part eunuchs; and their black ingratitude justified, on this occasion, the popular hatred and contempt. Raised, enriched, intrusted with the first dignities of the empire, they basely conspired against their benefactress; the great treasurer Nicephorus was secretly invested with the purple; her successor was introduced into the palace, and crowned at St. Sophia by the venal patriarch. In their first interview she recapitulated with dignity the revolutions of her life, gently accused the perfidy of Nicephorus, insinuated that he owed his life to her unsuspicious clemency, and, for the throne and treasures which she resigned, solicited a decent and honourable retreat. His avarice refused this modest compensation; and, in her exile of the isle of Lesbos, the empress earned a scanty subsistence by the labours of her distaff.

Many tyrants have reigned undoubtedly more criminal than Nicephorus, but none perhaps have more deeply incurred the universal abhorrence of their people. His character was stained with the three odious vices of hypocrisy, ingratitude, and avarice: his want of virtue was not redeemed by any superior talents, nor his want of talents by any pleasing qualifications. Unskilful and unfortunate in war, Nicephorus was vanquished by the Saracens and slain by the Bulgarians; and the advantage of his death overbalanced, in the public opinion, the destruction of a Roman army. His son and heir Stauracius escaped from the field with a mortal wound; yet six months of an expiring life were sufficient to refute his indecent, though popular declaration, that he would in all things avoid the example of his father. On the near prospect of his decease, Michael, the great master of the palace, and the husband of his sister Procopia, was named by every person of the palace and city, except by his envious brother. Tenacious of a sceptre now falling from his hand, he conspired against the life of his successor, and cherished the idea of changing to a democracy the Roman empire. But these rash projects served only to inflame the zeal of the people and to remove the scruples of the candidate: Michael the First accepted the purple, and before he sunk into the grave the son of Nicephorus implored the clemency of his new sovereign. Had Michael in an age of peace ascended an hereditary throne, he might have reigned and died the father of his people: but his mild virtues were adapted to the shade of private life, nor was he capable of controlling the ambition of his equals, or of resisting the arms of the victorious Bulgarians. While his want of ability and success exposed him to the contempt of the soldiers, the masculine spirit of his wife Procopia awakened their indignation. Even the Greeks of the ninth century were provoked by the insolence of a female who, in the front of the standards, presumed to direct their discipline and animate their valour; and their licentious clamours advised the new Semiramis to reverence the majesty of a Roman camp. After an unsuccessful campaign the emperor left, in their winter quarters of Thrace, a disaffected army under the command of his enemies; and their artful eloquence persuaded the soldiers to break the dominion of the eunuchs, to degrade the husband of Procopia, and to assert the right of a military election. They marched towards the capital: yet the clergy, the senate, and the people of Constantinople adhered to the cause of Michael; and the troops and treasures of Asia might have protracted the mischiefs of civil war. But his humanity (by the ambitious it will be termed his weakness) protested that not a drop of Christian blood should be shed in his quarrel, and his messengers presented the conquerors with the keys of the city and the palace They were disarmed by his innocence and submission; his life and his eyes were spared; and the Imperial monk enjoyed the comforts of solitude and religion above thirty-two years after he had been stripped of the purple and separated from his wife.

A rebel, in the time of Nicephorus, the famous and unfortunate Bardanes, had once the curiosity to consult an Asiatic prophet, who, after prognosticating his fall, announced the fortunes of his three principal officers, Leo the Armenian, Michael the Phrygian, and Thomas the Cappadocian, the successive reigns of the two former, the fruitless and fatal enterprise of the third. This prediction was verified, or rather was produced, by the event. Ten years afterwards, when the Thracian camp rejected the husband of Procopia, the crown was presented to the same Leo, the first in military rank and the secret author of the mutiny. As he affected to hesitate, "With this sword," said his companion Michael, "I will open the gates of Constantinople to your Imperial sway, or instantly plunge it into your bosom, if you obstinately resist the just desires of your fellow-soldiers." The compliance of the Armenian was rewarded with the empire, and he reigned seven years and a half under the name of Leo the

Fifth. Educated in a camp, and ignorant both of laws and letters, he introduced into his civil government the rigour and even cruelty of military discipline; but if his severity was sometimes dangerous to the innocent, it was always formidable to the guilty. His religious inconstancy was taxed by the epithet of Chameleon, but the Catholics have acknowledged, by the voice of a saint and confessors, that the life of the Iconoclast was useful to the republic. The zeal of his companion Michael was repaid with riches, honours, and military command; and his subordinate talents were beneficially employed in the public service. Yet the Phrygian was dissatisfied at receiving as a favour a scanty portion of the Imperial prize which he had bestowed on his equal; and his discontent, which sometimes evaporated in hasty discourse, at length assumed a more threatening and hostile aspect against a prince whom he represented as a cruel tyrant. That tyrant, however, repeatedly detected, warned, and dismissed the old companion of his arms, till fear and resentment prevailed over gratitude; and Michael, after a scrutiny into his actions and designs, was convicted of treason, and sentenced to be burnt alive in the furnace of the private baths. The devout humanity of the empress Theophano was fatal to her husband and family. A solemn day, the twenty-fifth of December, had been fixed for the execution: she urged that the anniversary of the Saviour's birth would be profaned by this inhuman spectacle, and Leo consented with reluctance to a decent respite. But on the vigil of the feast his sleepless anxiety prompted him to visit at the dead of night the chamber in which his enemy was confined: he beheld him released from his chain, and stretched on his gaoler's bed in a profound slumber: Leo was alarmed at these signs of security and intelligence; but though he retired with silent steps, his entrance and departure were noticed by a slave who lay concealed in a corner of the prison. Under the pretence of requesting the spiritual aid of a confessor, Michael informed the conspirators that their lives depended on his discretion, and that a few hours were left to assure their own safety, by the deliverance of their friend and country. On the great festivals a chosen band of priests and chanters was admitted into the palace by a private gate to sing matins in the chapel; and Leo, who regulated with the same strictness the discipline of the choir and of the camp, was seldom absent from these early devotions. In the ecclesiastical habit, but with swords under their robes, the conspirators mingled with the procession, lurked in the angles of the chapel, and expected, as a signal of murder, the intonation

of the first psalm by the emperor himself. The imperfect light
and the uniformity of dress, might have favoured his escape,
while their assault was pointed against a harmless priest; but
they soon discovered their mistake, and encompassed on all sides
the royal victim. Without a weapon and without a friend, he
grasped a weighty cross, and stood at bay against the hunters of
his life; but as he asked for mercy, " This is the hour, not of
mercy, but of vengeance," was the inexorable reply. The stroke
of a well-aimed sword separated from his body the right arm and
the cross, and Leo the Armenian was slain at the foot of the altar.

A memorable reverse of fortune was displayed in Michael the
Second, who from a defect in his speech was surnamed the
Stammerer. He was snatched from the fiery furnace to the
sovereignty of an empire; and as in the tumult a smith could not
readily be found, the fetters remained on his legs several hours
after he was seated on the throne of the Cæsars. The royal
blood which had been the price of his elevation was unprofitably
spent; in the purple he retained the ignoble vices of his origin;
and Michael lost his provinces with as supine indifference as if
they had been the inheritance of his fathers. His title was
disputed by Thomas, the last of the military triumvirate, who
transported into Europe fourscore thousand barbarians from the
banks of the Tigris and the shores of the Caspian.[1] He formed
the siege of Constantinople; but the capital was defended with
spiritual and carnal weapons; a Bulgarian king assaulted the
camp of the Orientals, and Thomas had the misfortune or the
weakness to fall alive into the power of the conqueror. The
hands and feet of the rebel were amputated; he was placed on
an ass, and, amidst the insults of the people, was led through the
streets, which he sprinkled with his blood. The depravation of
manners, as savage as they were corrupt, is marked by the
presence of the emperor himself. Deaf to the lamentations of a
fellow-soldier, he incessantly pressed the discovery of more
accomplices, till his curiosity was checked by the question of a
honest or guilty minister: " Would you give credit to an enemy
against the most faithful of your friends? " After the death of
his first wife, the emperor, at the request of the senate, drew
from her monastery Euphrosyne, the daughter of Constantine

[1] [Finlay in his *Byzantine Empire*, speaking of the foreign origin of Thomas
the Cappodocian, or Thomas the Slavonian—for he has both titles: " His
origin, by separating him in an unusual degree from the ruling classes in
the empire—for he was like Michael the Second, of a very low rank in
society—caused him to be regarded as a friend of the people, and all the
subject races in the empire espoused his cause."—O. S.]

the Sixth. Her august birth might justify a stipulation in the marriage-contract that her children should equally share the empire with their elder brother. But the nuptials of Michael and Euphrosyne were barren; and she was content with the title of mother of Theophilus, his son and successor.

The character of Theophilus is a rare example in which religious zeal has allowed and perhaps magnified the virtues of a heretic and a persecutor. His valour was often felt by the enemies, and his justice by the subjects, of the monarchy; but the valour of Theophilus was rash and fruitless, and his justice arbitrary and cruel. He displayed the banner of the cross against the Saracens; but his five expeditions were concluded by a signal overthrow: Amorium, the native city of his ancestors, was levelled with the ground, and from his military toils he derived only the surname of the Unfortunate. The wisdom of a sovereign is comprised in the institution of laws and the choice of magistrates, and, while he seems without action, his civil government revolves round his centre with the silence and order of the planetary system. But the justice of Theophilus was fashioned on the model of the Oriental despots, who, in personal and irregular acts of authority, consult the reason or passion of the moment, without measuring the sentence by the law, or the penalty by the offence.[1] A poor woman threw herself at the emperor's feet to complain of a powerful neighbour, the brother of the empress, who had raised his palace-wall to such an inconvenient height, that her humble dwelling was excluded from light and air! On the proof of the fact, instead of granting, like an ordinary judge, sufficient or ample damages to the plaintiff, the sovereign adjudged to her use and benefit the palace and the ground. Nor was Theophilus content with this extravagant satisfaction: his zeal converted a civil trespass into a criminal act; and the unfortunate patrician was stripped and scourged in the public place of Constantinople. For some venial offences, some defect of equity or vigilance, the principal ministers, a præfect, a quæstor, a captain of the guards, were banished or mutilated, or scalded with boiling pitch, or burnt alive in the hippodrome; and as these dreadful examples might be the effects of error or caprice, they must have alienated from his service the best and wisest of the citizens. But the pride of

[1] [Finlay remarks that Gibbon has exaggerated the cruelty of the punishments inflicted by Theophilus, and Schlosser states that he has found no authority to justify the charge of excessive tyranny. But Bury thinks that Gelzer's opinion is much nearer the mark, who regards him as an insignificant, much-overrated ruler.—O. S.]

the monarch was flattered in the exercise of power, or, as he
thought, of virtue; and the people, safe in their obscurity,
applauded the danger and debasement of their superiors. This
extraordinary rigour was justified in some measure by its salutary consequences; since, after a scrutiny of seventeen days,
not a complaint or abuse could be found in the court or city:
and it might be alleged that the Greeks could be ruled only with
a rod of iron, and that the public interest is the motive and law
of the supreme judge. Yet in the crime, or the suspicion, of
treason, that judge is of all others the most credulous and
partial. Theophilus might inflict a tardy vengeance on the
assassins of Leo and the saviours of his father; but he enjoyed
the fruits of their crime; and his jealous tyranny sacrificed a
brother and a prince to the future safety of his life. A Persian of
the race of the Sassanides died in poverty and exile at Constantinople, leaving an only son, the issue of a plebeian marriage.
At the age of twelve years the royal birth of Theophobus was
revealed, and his merit was not unworthy of his birth. He was
educated in the Byzantine palace, a Christian and a soldier;
advanced with rapid steps in the career of fortune and glory;
received the hand of the emperor's sister; and was promoted to
the command of thirty thousand Persians, who, like his father,
had fled from the Mohammedan conquerors. These troops,
doubly infected with mercenary and fanatic vices, were desirous
of revolting against their benefactor, and erecting the standard
of their native king: but the loyal Theophobus rejected their
offers, disconcerted their schemes, and escaped from their hands
to the camp or palace of his royal brother. A generous confidence
might have secured a faithful and able guardian for his wife and
his infant son, to whom Theophilus, in the flower of his age,
was compelled to leave the inheritance of the empire. But his
jealousy was exasperated by envy and disease: he feared the
dangerous virtues which might either support or oppress their
infancy and weakness; and the dying emperor demanded the
head of the Persian prince. With savage delight he recognised
the familiar features of his brother: "Thou art no longer
Theophobus," he said; and, sinking on his couch, he added,
with a faltering voice, "Soon, too soon, I shall be no more
Theophilus!"

The Russians, who have borrowed from the Greeks the greatest
part of their civil and ecclesiastical policy, preserved, till the
last century, a singular institution in the marriage of the Czar.
They collected, not the virgins of every rank and of every

province, a vain and romantic idea, but the daughters of the
principal nobles, who awaited in the palace the choice of their
sovereign. It is affirmed that a similar method was adopted in
the nuptials of Theophilus. With a golden apple in his hand,
he slowly walked between two lines of contending beauties: his
eye was detained by the charms of Icasia, and, in the awkward-
ness of a first declaration, the prince could only observe, that,
in this world, women had been the cause of much evil; " And
surely, sir," she pertly replied, " they have likewise been the
occasion of much good." This affectation of unseasonable wit
displeased the Imperial lover: he turned aside in disgust;
Icasia concealed her mortification in a convent; and the modest
silence of Theodora was rewarded with the golden apple.
She deserved the love, but did not escape the severity, of her
lord. From the palace garden he beheld a vessel deeply laden,
and steering into the port: on the discovery that the precious
cargo of Syrian luxury was the property of his wife, he condemned the ship to the flames, with a sharp reproach, that her
avarice had degraded the character of an empress into that of a
merchant. Yet his last choice intrusted her with the guardianship of the empire and her son Michael, who was left an orphan
in the fifth year of his age. The restoration of images, and the
final extirpation of the Iconoclasts, has endeared her name to
the devotion of the Greeks; but in the fervour of religious zeal
Theodora entertained a grateful regard for the memory and
salvation of her husband. After thirteen years of a prudent
and frugal administration, she perceived the decline of her
influence; but the second Irene imitated only the virtues of her
predecessor. Instead of conspiring against the life or government of her son, she retired without a struggle, though not without a murmur, to the solitude of private life, deploring the
ingratitude, the vices, and the inevitable ruin of the worthless
youth.

Among the successors of Nero and Elagabalus we have not
hitherto found the imitation of their vices, the character of a
Roman prince who considered pleasure as the object of life, and
virtue as the enemy of pleasure. Whatever might have been the
maternal care of Theodora in the education of Michael the Third,
her unfortunate son was a king before he was a man. If the
ambitious mother laboured to check the progress of reason, she
could not cool the ebullition of passion; and her selfish policy
was justly repaid by the contempt and ingratitude of the headstrong youth. At the age of eighteen he rejected her authority,

without feeling his own incapacity to govern the empire and himself. With Theodora all gravity and wisdom retired from the court; their place was supplied by the alternate dominion of vice and folly; and it was impossible, without forfeiting the public esteem, to acquire or preserve the favour of the emperor. The millions of gold and silver which had been accumulated for the service of the state were lavished on the vilest of men, who flattered his passions and shared his pleasures; and, in a reign of thirteen years, the richest of sovereigns was compelled to strip the palace and the churches of their precious furniture. Like Nero, he delighted in the amusements of the theatre, and sighed to be surpassed in the accomplishments in which he should have blushed to excel. Yet the studies of Nero in music and poetry betrayed some symptoms of a liberal taste; the more ignoble arts of the son of Theophilus were confined to the chariot-race of the hippodrome. The four factions which had agitated the peace, still amused the idleness, of the capital: for himself, the emperor assumed the blue livery: the three rival colours were distributed to his favourites, and in the vile though eager contention he forgot the dignity of his person and the safety of his dominions. He silenced the messenger of an invasion who presumed to divert his attention in the most critical moment of the race; and by his command the importunate beacons were extinguished that too frequently spread the alarm from Tarsus to Constantinople. The most skilful charioteers obtained the first place in his confidence and esteem; their merit was profusely rewarded; the emperor feasted in their houses, and presented their children at the baptismal font; and while he applauded his own popularity, he affected to blame the cold and stately reserve of his predecessors. The unnatural lusts which had degraded even the manhood of Nero were banished from the world; yet the strength of Michael was consumed by the indulgence of love and intemperance. In his midnight revels, when his passions were inflamed by wine, he was provoked to issue the most sanguinary commands; and if any feelings of humanity were left, he was reduced, with the return of sense, to approve the salutary disobedience of his servants. But the most extraordinary feature in the character of Michael is the profane mockery of the religion of his country. The superstition of the Greeks might indeed excite the smile of a philosopher; but his smile would have been rational and temperate, and he must have condemned the ignorant folly of a youth who insulted the objects of public veneration. A buffoon of the court was invested in the robes of the patriarch: his twelve metropolitans, among whom the emperor was ranked, assumed their ecclesiastical garments: they used or abused the sacred vessels of the altar; and in their bacchanalian feasts the holy communion was administered in a nauseous compound of vinegar and mustard. Nor were these impious spectacles concealed from the eyes of the city. On the day of a solemn festival, the emperor, with his bishops or buffoons, rode on asses through the streets, encountered the true patriarch at the head of his clergy, and, by their licentious shouts and obscene gestures, disordered the gravity of the Christian procession. The devotion of Michael appeared only in some offence to reason or piety: he received his theatrical crowns from the statue of the Virgin; and an Imperial tomb was violated for the sake of burning the bones of Constantine the Iconoclast. By this extravagant conduct the son of Theophilus became as contemptible as he was odious: every citizen was impatient for the deliverance of his country; and even the favourites of the moment were apprehensive that a caprice might snatch away what a caprice had bestowed. In the thirtieth year of his age, and in the hour of intoxication and sleep, Michael the Third was murdered in his chamber by the founder of a new dynasty, whom the emperor had raised to an equality of rank and power.

The genealogy of Basil the Macedonian (if it be not the spurious offspring of pride and flattery) exhibits a genuine picture of the revolution of the most illustrious families. The Arsacides, the rivals of Rome, possessed the sceptre of the East near four hundred years: a younger branch of these Parthian kings continued to reign in Armenia,[1] and their royal descendants survived the partition and servitude of that ancient monarchy. Two of these, Artabanus and Chlienes, escaped or retired to the court of Leo the First: his bounty seated them in a safe and hospitable exile in the province of Macedonia; Adrianople was their final settlement. During several generations they maintained the dignity of their birth; and their Roman patriotism rejected the tempting offers of the Persian and Arabian powers,

---

[1] [The family of Basil I. was not Armenian, and the attempt to connect it with the royal line of Armenia must be entirely rejected (says Dr. W. Smith), adding, " there can be little doubt that Basil was a Slav." On the other hand, Prof. Bury says, " The Armenian descent of Basil is set beyond doubt by a notice in the *Vita Euthymii*, combined with the circumstance that a brother of Basil was called Symbatios. The settlement of Armenian families in Thrace by Constantine V. is attested by Theophanes. Hamza of Ispahan states that Basil was a Slav, but there is no evidence to bear this out."—O. S.]

who recalled them to their native country. But their splendour
was insensibly clouded by time and poverty; and the father of
Basil was reduced to a small farm, which he cultivated with his
own hands: yet he scorned to disgrace the blood of the Arsacides
by a plebeian alliance: his wife, a widow of Adrianople, was
pleased to count among her ancestors the great Constantine;
and their royal infant was connected by some dark affinity of
lineage or country with the Macedonian Alexander. No sooner
was he born than the cradle of Basil, his family, and his city,
were swept away by an inundation of the Bulgarians: he was
educated a slave in a foreign land; and in this severe discipline
he acquired the hardiness of body and flexibility of mind which
promoted his future elevation. In the age of youth or manhood
he shared the deliverance of the Roman captives, who generously
broke their fetters, marched through Bulgaria to the shores of
the Euxine, defeated two armies of barbarians, embarked in the
ships which had been stationed for their reception, and returned
to Constantinople, from whence they were distributed to their
respective homes. But the freedom of Basil was naked and
destitute: his farm was ruined by the calamities of war: after
his father's death his manual labour or service could no longer
support a family of orphans; and he resolved to seek a more
conspicuous theatre, in which every virtue and every vice may
lead to the paths of greatness. The first night of his arrival at
Constantinople, without friends or money, the weary pilgrim
slept on the steps of the church of St. Diomede: he was fed by
the casual hospitality of a monk; and was introduced to the
service of a cousin and namesake of the emperor Theophilus,
who, though himself of a diminutive person, was always followed
by a train of tall and handsome domestics. Basil attended his
patron to the government of Peloponnesus; eclipsed, by his
personal merit, the birth and dignity of Theophilus, and formed
a useful connection with a wealthy and charitable matron of
Patras. Her spiritual or carnal love embraced the young
adventurer, whom she adopted as her son. Danielis presented
him with thirty slaves; and the produce of her bounty was
expended in the support of his brothers, and the purchase of
some large estates in Macedonia. His gratitude or ambition
still attached him to the service of Theophilus; and a lucky
accident recommended him to the notice of the court. A
famous wrestler in the train of the Bulgarian ambassadors had
defied, at the royal banquet, the boldest and most robust of the
Greeks. The strength of Basil was praised; he accepted the

challenge; and the barbarian champion was overthrown at the first onset. A beautiful but vicious horse was condemned to be hamstrung: it was subdued by the dexterity and courage of the servant of Theophilus; and his conqueror was promoted to an honourable rank in the Imperial stables. But it was impossible to obtain the confidence of Michael without complying with his vices; and his new favourite, the great chamberlain of the palace, was raised and supported by a disgraceful marriage with a royal concubine, and the dishonour of his sister, who succeeded to her place.[1] The public administration had been abandoned to the Cæsar Bardas, the brother and enemy of Theodora; but the arts of female influence persuaded Michael to hate and to fear his uncle: he was drawn from Constantinople, under the pretence of a Cretan expedition, and stabbed in the tent of audience by the sword of the chamberlain, and in the presence of the emperor. About a month after this execution, Basil was invested with the title of Augustus and the government of the empire. He supported this unequal association till his influence was fortified by popular esteem. His life was endangered by the caprice of the emperor; and his dignity was profaned by a second colleague, who had rowed in the galleys. Yet the murder of his benefactor must be condemned as an act of ingratitude and treason; and the churches which he dedicated to the name of St. Michael were a poor and puerile expiation of his guilt.

The different ages of Basil the First may be compared with those of Augustus. The situation of the Greek did not allow him in his earliest youth to lead an army against his country, or to proscribe the noblest of her sons; but his aspiring genius stooped to the arts of a slave; he dissembled his ambition and even his virtues, and grasped, with the bloody hand of an assassin, the empire which he ruled with the wisdom and tenderness of a parent. A private citizen may feel his interest repugnant to his duty; but it must be from a deficiency of sense or courage that an absolute monarch can separate his happiness from his glory, or his glory from the public welfare. The life or panegyric of Basil has indeed been composed and published under the long reign of his descendants; but even their stability on the throne may be justly ascribed to the superior merit of their ancestor. In his character, his grandson Constantine has attempted to

[1] [Finlay in his *Byzantine Empire* (vol. i. p. 300) controverts this statement, and shows that Thecla, sister of the emperor Michael, became Basil's concubine, not that Basil's sister became Michael's concubine. The royal concubine's name who married the chamberlain was Eudocia Ingerina, mother of Leo VI.—O. S.]

delineate a perfect image of royalty: but that feeble prince, unless he had copied a real model, could not easily have soared so high above the level of his own conduct or conceptions. But the most solid praise of Basil is drawn from the comparison of a ruined and a flourishing monarchy, that which he wrested from the dissolute Michael, and that which he bequeathed to the Macedonian dynasty. The evils which had been sanctified by time and example were corrected by his master-hand; and he revived, if not the national spirit, at least the order and majesty of the Roman empire. His application was indefatigable, his temper cool, his understanding vigorous and decisive; and in his practice he observed that rare and salutary moderation, which pursues each virtue, at an equal distance between the opposite vices. His military service had been confined to the palace; nor was the emperor endowed with the spirit or the talents of a warrior. Yet under his reign the Roman arms were again formidable to the barbarians. As soon as he had formed a new army by discipline and exercise, he appeared in person on the banks of the Euphrates, curbed the pride of the Saracens, and suppressed the dangerous though just revolt of the Manichæans. His indignation against a rebel who had long eluded his pursuit provoked him to wish and to pray that, by the grace of God, he might drive three arrows into the head of Chrysochir. That odious head, which had been obtained by treason rather than by valour, was suspended from a tree, and thrice exposed to the dexterity of the Imperial archer: a base revenge against the dead, more worthy of the times than of the character of Basil. But his principal merit was in the civil administration of the finances and of the laws. To replenish an exhausted treasury it was proposed to resume the lavish and ill-placed gifts of his predecessor: his prudence abated one moiety of the restitution; and a sum of twelve hundred thousand pounds was instantly procured to answer the most pressing demands, and to allow some space for the mature operations of economy. Among the various schemes for the improvement of the revenue, a new mode was suggested of capitation, or tribute, which would have too much depended on the arbitrary discretion of the assessors. A sufficient list of honest and able agents was instantly produced by the minister; but on the more careful scrutiny of Basil himself, only two could be found who might be safely intrusted with such dangerous powers; and they justified his esteem by declining his confidence. But the serious and successful diligence of the emperor established by degrees an equitable balance of property and payment, of receipt and expenditure; a peculiar fund was appropriated to each service; and a public method secured the interest of the prince and the property of the people. After reforming the luxury, he assigned two patrimonial estates to supply the decent plenty, of the Imperial table; the contributions of the subject were reserved for his defence; and the residue was employed in the embellishment of the capital and provinces. A taste for building, however costly, may deserve some praise and much excuse: from thence industry is fed, art is encouraged, and some object is attained of public emolument or pleasure: the use of a road, an aqueduct, or a hospital, is obvious and solid; and the hundred churches that arose by the command of Basil were consecrated to the devotion of the age. In the character of a judge he was assiduous and impartial; desirous to save, but not afraid to strike: the oppressors of the people were severely chastised; but his personal foes, whom it might be unsafe to pardon, were condemned, after the loss of their eyes, to a life of solitude and repentance. The change of language and manners demanded a revision of the obsolete jurisprudence of Justinian: the voluminous body of his Institutes, Pandects, Code, and Novels was digested under forty titles, in the Greek idiom; and the *Basilics*, which were improved and completed by his son and grandson, must be referred to the original genius of the founder of their race. This glorious reign was terminated by an accident in the chase. A furious stag entangled his horns in the belt of Basil, and raised him from his horse: he was rescued by an attendant, who cut the belt and slew the animal; but the fall, or the fever, exhausted the strength of the aged monarch, and he expired in the palace amidst the tears of his family and people. If he struck off the head of the faithful servant for presuming to draw his sword against his sovereign, the pride of despotism, which had lain dormant in his life, revived in the last moments of despair, when he no longer wanted or valued the opinion of mankind.[1]

Of the four sons of the emperor, Constantine died before his father, whose grief and credulity were amused by a flattering impostor and a vain apparition. Stephen, the youngest, was content with the honours of a patriarch and a saint; both Leo and Alexander were alike invested with the purple, but the powers of government were solely exercised by the elder brother. The name of Leo the Sixth has been dignified with the title of

[1] See table on following page.

philosopher; [1] and the union of the prince and the sage, of the
active and speculative virtues, would indeed constitute the
perfection of human nature. But the claims of Leo are far short
of this ideal excellence. Did he reduce his passions and appetites
under the dominion of reason? His life was spent in the pomp
of the palace, in the society of his wives and concubines; and

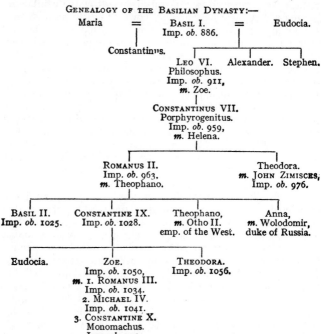

GENEALOGY OF THE BASILIAN DYNASTY:—

Maria = BASIL I. = Eudocia.
Imp. *ob.* 886.

Constantinus.

LEO VI.   Alexander.   Stephen.
Philosophus.
Imp. *ob.* 911,
m. Zoe.

CONSTANTINUS VII.
Porphyrogenitus.
Imp. *ob.* 959,
m. Helena.

ROMANUS II.   Theodora.
Imp. *ob.* 963,   *m.* JOHN ZIMISCES,
m. Theophano.   Imp. *ob.* 976.

BASIL II.   CONSTANTINE IX.   Theophano,   Anna,
Imp. *ob.* 1025.   Imp. *ob.* 1028.   *m.* Otho II.   *m.* Wolodomir,
emp. of the West.   duke of Russia.

Eudocia.   ZOE.   THEODORA.
Imp. *ob.* 1050,   Imp. *ob.* 1056.
m. 1. ROMANUS III.
Imp. *ob.* 1034.
2. MICHAEL IV.
Imp. *ob.* 1041.
3. CONSTANTINE X.
Monomachus.
Imp. *ob.* 1054.

[1] [Leo VI., " the Philosopher " (A.D. 886-912), typifies the idle spirit of
conservatism as correctly as Constantine VI. does the aggressive energy
of progress. He was a man of learning, a lover of luxurious ease, a con-
ceited pedant, and an arbitrary but mild despot. Naturally of a confined
intellect, he owes his title of " the Philosopher," or " the Learned," rather
to the ignorance of the people, who attributed to him an acquaintance with
the secrets of astrological science, than either to his own attainments or to
any remarkable patronage he bestowed on learned men. Leo's works
consist of some poetical oracles and hymns, and a treatise on military
tactics. Leo married four times: (1) Theophano, who died 892; (2) Zoe,
who died 896; (3) Eudocia Baiane, who died 900; (4) Zoe Carbonupsina.
Nicolaus the Mystic, patriarch of Constantinople, refused to celebrate
the fourth marriage, and was banished in February 907, being succeeded
by Euthymius, who complied with the emperor's wishes.—O. S.]

even the clemency which he showed, and the peace which he strove to preserve, must be imputed to the softness and indolence of his character. Did he subdue his prejudices, and those of his subjects? His mind was tinged with the most puerile superstition; the influence of the clergy and the errors of the people were consecrated by his laws; and the oracles of Leo, which reveal, in prophetic style, the fates of the empire, are founded on the arts of astrology and divination. If we still inquire the reason of his sage appellation, it can only be replied, that the son of Basil was less ignorant than the greater part of his contemporaries in church and state; that his education had been directed by the learned Photius; and that several books of profane and ecclesiastical science were composed by the pen, or in the name, of the Imperial *philosopher*. But the reputation of his philosophy and religion was overthrown by a domestic vice, the repetition of his nuptials. The primitive ideas of the merit and holiness of celibacy were preached by the monks and entertained by the Greeks. Marriage was allowed as a necessary means for the propagation of mankind; after the death of either party the survivor might satisfy by a *second* union the weakness or the strength of the flesh; but a *third* marriage was censured as a state of legal fornication; and a *fourth* was a sin or scandal as yet unknown to the Christians of the East. In the beginning of his reign Leo himself had abolished the state of concubines, and condemned, without annulling, third marriages: but his patriotism and love soon compelled him to violate his own laws, and to incur the penance which in a similar case he had imposed on his subjects. In his three first alliances his nuptial bed was unfruitful; the emperor required a female companion, and the empire a legitimate heir. The beautiful Zoe was introduced into the palace as a concubine; and after a trial of her fecundity, and the birth of Constantine, her lover declared his intention of legitimating the mother and the child by the celebration of his fourth nuptials. But the patriarch Nicholas refused his blessing; the Imperial baptism of the young prince was obtained by a promise of separation; and the contumacious husband of Zoe was excluded from the communion of the faithful. Neither the fear of exile, nor the desertion of his brethren, nor the authority of the Latin church, nor the danger of failure or doubt in the succession to the empire, could bend the spirit of the inflexible monk. After the death of Leo he was recalled from exile to the civil and ecclesiastical administration; and the edict of union which was promulgated in the name of Constantine condemned the future scandal of fourth marriages, and left a tacit imputation on his own birth.

In the Greek language *purple* and *porphyry* are the same word: and as the colours of nature are invariable, we may learn that a dark deep red was the Tyrian dye which stained the purple of the ancients. An apartment of the Byzantine palace was lined with porphyry: it was reserved for the use of the pregnant empresses; and the royal birth of their children was expressed by the appellation of *porphyrogenite*, or born in the purple. Several of the Roman princes had been blessed with an heir; but this peculiar surname was first applied to Constantine the Seventh. His life and titular reign were of equal duration: but of fifty-four years six had elapsed before his father's death; and the son of Leo was ever the voluntary or reluctant subject of those who oppressed his weakness or abused his confidence. His uncle Alexander, who had long been invested with the title of Augustus, was the first colleague and governor of the young prince: but in a rapid career of vice and folly the brother of Leo already emulated the reputation of Michael; and when he was extinguished by a timely death, he entertained a project of castrating his nephew and leaving the empire to a worthless favourite. The succeeding years of the minority of Constantine were occupied by his mother Zoe, and a succession or council of seven regents, who pursued their interest, gratified their passions, abandoned the republic, supplanted each other, and finally vanished in the presence of a soldier. From an obscure origin Romanus Lecapenus had raised himself to the command of the naval armies; and in the anarchy of the times had deserved, or at least had obtained, the national esteem. With a victorious and affectionate fleet he sailed from the mouth of the Danube into the harbour of Constantinople, and was hailed as the deliverer of the people and the guardian of the prince. His supreme office was at first defined by the new appellation of father of the emperor; but Romanus soon disdained the subordinate powers of a minister, and assumed, with the titles of Cæsar and Augustus, the full independence of royalty, which he held near five-and-twenty years. His three sons, Christopher, Stephen, and Constantine, were successively adorned with the same honours, and the lawful emperor was degraded from the first to the fifth rank in this college of princes. Yet, in the preservation of his life and crown, he might still applaud his own fortune and the clemency of the usurper. The examples of ancient and modern history would have excused the ambition of

Romanus: the powers and the laws of the empire were in his hand; the spurious birth of Constantine would have justified his exclusion; and the grave or the monastery was open to receive the son of the concubine. But Lecapenus does not appear to have possessed either the virtues or the vices of a tyrant. The spirit and activity of his private life dissolved away in the sunshine of the throne; and in his licentious pleasures he forgot the safety both of the republic and of his family. Of a mild and religious character, he respected the sanctity of oaths, the innocence of the youth, the memory of his parents, and the attachment of the people. The studious temper and retirement of Constantine disarmed the jealousy of power: his books and music, his pen and his pencil, were a constant source of amusement; and if he could improve a scanty allowance by the sale of his pictures, if their price was not enhanced by the name of the artist, he was endowed with a personal talent which few princes could employ in the hour of adversity.

The fall of Romanus was occasioned by his own vices and those of his children. After the decease of Christopher, his eldest son, the two surviving brothers quarrelled with each other, and conspired against their father. At the hour of noon, when all strangers were regularly excluded from the palace, they entered his apartment with an armed force, and conveyed him, in the habit of a monk, to a small island in the Propontis, which was peopled by a religious community. The rumour of this domestic revolution excited a tumult in the city; but Porphyrogenitus alone, the true and lawful emperor, was the object of the public care; and the sons of Lecapenus were taught, by tardy experience, that they had achieved a guilty and perilous enterprise for the benefit of their rival. Their sister Helena, the wife of Constantine, revealed, or supposed, their treacherous design of assassinating her husband at the royal banquet. His loyal adherents were alarmed, and the two usurpers were prevented, seized, degraded from the purple, and embarked for the same island and monastery where their father had been so lately confined. Old Romanus met them on the beach with a sarcastic smile, and, after a just reproach of their folly and ingratitude, presented his Imperial colleagues with an equal share of his water and vegetable diet. In the fortieth year of his reign Constantine the Seventh obtained the possession of the Eastern world, which he ruled, or seemed to rule, near fifteen years. But he was devoid of that energy of character which could emerge into a life of action and glory; and the studies which had amused and dignified his leisure were incompatible with the serious duties of a sovereign. The emperor neglected the practice, to instruct his son Romanus in the theory, of government: while he indulged the habits of intemperance and sloth, he dropped the reins of the administration into the hands of Helena his wife; and, in the shifting scene of her favour and caprice, each minister was regretted in the promotion of a more worthless successor. Yet the birth and misfortunes of Constantine had endeared him to the Greeks; they excused his failings; they respected his learning, his innocence and charity, his love of justice; and the ceremony of his funeral was mourned with the unfeigned tears of his subjects. The body, according to ancient custom, lay in state in the vestibule of the palace; and the civil and military officers, the patricians, the senate, and the clergy approached in due order to adore and kiss the inanimate corpse of their sovereign. Before the procession moved towards the Imperial sepulchre, a herald proclaimed this awful admonition: "Arise, O king of the world, and obey the summons of the King of kings!"

The death of Constantine was imputed to poison; and his son Romanus, who derived that name from his maternal grandfather, ascended the throne of Constantinople. A prince who, at the age of twenty, could be suspected of anticipating his inheritance, must have been already lost in the public esteem; yet Romanus was rather weak than wicked; and the largest share of the guilt was transferred to his wife, Theophano, a woman of base origin, masculine spirit, and flagitious manners. The sense of personal glory and public happiness, the true pleasures of royalty, were unknown to the son of Constantine; and, while the two brothers, Nicephorus and Leo, triumphed over the Saracens, the hours which the emperor owed to his people were consumed in strenuous idleness. In the morning he visited the circus; at noon he feasted the senators; the greater part of the afternoon he spent in the *sphæristerium*, or tennis-court, the only theatre of his victories; from thence he passed over to the Asiatic side of the Bosphorus, hunted and killed four wild boars of the largest size, and returned to the palace, proudly content with the labours of the day. In strength and beauty he was conspicuous above his equals: tall and straight as a young cypress, his complexion was fair and florid, his eyes sparkling, his shoulders broad, his nose long and aquiline. Yet even these perfections were insufficient to fix the love of Theophano; and, after a reign of four years, she mingled for her husband the same deadly draught which she had composed for his father.

By his marriage with this impious woman Romanus the younger left two sons, Basil the Second and Constantine the Ninth, and two daughters, Theophano and Anne. The eldest sister was given to Otho the Second, emperor of the West; the younger became the wife of Wolodomir, great duke and apostle of Russia; and, by the marriage of her granddaughter with Henry the First, king of France, the blood of the Macedonians, and perhaps of the Arsacides, still flows in the veins of the Bourbon line. After the death of her husband the empress aspired to reign in the name of her sons, the elder of whom was five, and the younger only two years of age; but she soon felt the instability of a throne which was supported by a female who could not be esteemed, and two infants who could not be feared. Theophano looked around for a protector, and threw herself into the arms of the bravest soldier; her heart was capacious; but the deformity of the new favourite rendered it more than probable that interest was the motive and excuse of her love. Nicephorus Phocas united, in the popular opinion, the double merit of a hero and a saint. In the former character his qualifications were genuine and splendid: the descendant of a race illustrious by their military exploits, he had displayed in every station and in every province the courage of a soldier and the conduct of a chief; and Nicephorus was crowned with recent laurels from the important conquest of the isle of Crete. His religion was of a more ambiguous cast; and his hair-cloth, his fasts, his pious idiom, and his wish to retire from the business of the world, were a convenient mask for his dark and dangerous ambition. Yet he imposed on a holy patriarch, by whose influence, and by a decree of the senate, he was intrusted, during the minority of the young princes, with the absolute and independent command of the Oriental armies. As soon as he had secured the leaders and the troops he boldly marched to Constantinople, trampled on his enemies, avowed his correspondence with the empress, and, without degrading her sons, assumed, with the title of Augustus, the pre-eminence of rank and the plenitude of power. But his marriage with Theophano was refused by the same patriarch who had placed the crown on his head: by his second nuptials he incurred a year of canonical penance; a bar of spiritual affinity was opposed to their celebration; and some evasion and perjury were required to silence the scruples of the clergy and people. The popularity of the emperor was lost in the purple: in a reign of six years he provoked the hatred of strangers and subjects, and the hypocrisy and avarice of the first Nicephorus were revived in his successor. Hypocrisy I shall never justify or palliate; but I will dare to observe that the odious vice of avarice is of all others most hastily arraigned, and most unmercifully condemned. In a private citizen our judgment seldom expects an accurate scrutiny into his fortune and expense; and in a steward of the public treasure frugality is always a virtue, and the increase of taxes too often an indispensable duty. In the use of his patrimony the generous temper of Nicephorus had been proved; and the revenue was strictly applied to the service of the state: each spring the emperor marched in person against the Saracens; and every Roman might compute the employment of his taxes in triumphs, conquests, and the security of the Eastern barrier.

Among the warriors who promoted his elevation and served under his standard, a noble and valiant Armenian had deserved and obtained the most eminent rewards. The stature of John Zimisces was below the ordinary standard; but this diminutive body was endowed with strength, beauty, and the soul of a hero. By the jealousy of the emperor's brother he was degraded from the office of general of the East to that of director of the posts, and his murmurs were chastised with disgrace and exile. But Zimisces was ranked among the numerous lovers of the empress: on her intercession he was permitted to reside at Chalcedon, in the neighbourhood of the capital: her bounty was repaid in his clandestine and amorous visits to the palace; and Theophano consented with alacrity to the death of an ugly and penurious husband. Some bold and trusty conspirators were concealed in her most private chambers: in the darkness of a winter night, Zimisces, with his principal companions, embarked in a small boat, traversed the Bosphorus, landed at the palace stairs, and silently ascended a ladder of ropes, which was cast down by the female attendants. Neither his own suspicions, nor the warnings of his friends, nor the tardy aid of his brother Leo, nor the fortress which he had erected in the palace, could protect Nicephorus from a domestic foe, at whose voice every door was opened to the assassins. As he slept on a bear-skin on the ground, he was roused by their noisy intrusion, and thirty daggers glittered before his eyes. It is doubtful whether Zimisces imbrued his hands in the blood of his sovereign; but he enjoyed the inhuman spectacle of revenge. The murder was protracted by insult and cruelty; and as soon as the head of Nicephorus was shown from the window, the tumult was hushed, and the Armenian was emperor of the East. On the day of his coronation he was stopped on the threshold of St. Sophia by the intrepid patriarch, who charged his conscience with the deed of treason and blood, and required, as a sign of repentance, that he should separate himself from his more criminal associate. This sally of apostolic zeal was not offensive to the prince, since he could neither love nor trust a woman who had repeatedly violated the most sacred obligations; and Theophano, instead of sharing his Imperial fortune, was dismissed with ignominy from his bed and palace. In their last interview she displayed a frantic and impotent rage, accused the ingratitude of her lover, assaulted, with words and blows, her son Basil, as he stood silent and submissive in the presence of a superior colleague, and avowed her own prostitution in proclaiming the illegitimacy of his birth. The public indignation was appeased by her exile and the punishment of the meaner accomplices: the death of an unpopular prince was forgiven; and the guilt of Zimisces was forgotten in the splendour of his virtues. Perhaps his profusion was less useful to the state than the avarice of Nicephorus; but his gentle and generous behaviour delighted all who approached his person; and it was only in the paths of victory that he trod in the footsteps of his predecessor. The greatest part of his reign was employed in the camp and the field: his personal valour and activity were signalised on the Danube and the Tigris, the ancient boundaries of the Roman world; and by his double triumph over the Russians and the Saracens he deserved the titles of saviour of the empire and conqueror of the East. In his last return from Syria he observed that the most fruitful lands of his new provinces were possessed by the eunuchs. " And is it for them," he exclaimed, with honest indignation, " that we have fought and conquered? Is it for them that we shed our blood and exhaust the treasures of our people? " The complaint was re-echoed to the palace, and the death of Zimisces is strongly marked with the suspicion of poison.

Under this usurpation, or regency, of twelve years, the two lawful emperors, Basil and Constantine, had silently grown to the age of manhood. Their tender years had been incapable of dominion: the respectful modesty of their attendance and salutation was due to the age and merit of their guardians: the childless ambition of those guardians had no temptation to violate their right of succession: their patrimony was ably and faithfully administered; and the premature death of Zimisces was a loss rather than a benefit to the sons of Romanus. Their want of experience detained them twelve years longer the obscure and voluntary pupils of a minister who extended his reign by persuading them to indulge the pleasures of youth, and to disdain the labours of government. In this silken web the weakness of Constantine was for ever entangled; but his elder brother felt the impulse of genius and the desire of action; he frowned, and the minister was no more. Basil was the acknowledged sovereign of Constantinople and the provinces of Europe; but Asia was oppressed by two veteran generals, Phocas and Sclerus, who, alternately friends and enemies, subjects and rebels, maintained their independence, and laboured to emulate the example of successful usurpation. Against these domestic enemies the son of Romanus first drew his sword, and they trembled in the presence of a lawful and high-spirited prince. The first, in the front of battle, was thrown from his horse by the stroke of poison or an arrow; the second, who had been twice loaded with chains, and twice invested with the purple, was desirous of ending in peace the small remainder of his days. As the aged suppliant approached the throne, with dim eyes and faltering steps, leaning on his two attendants, the emperor exclaimed, in the insolence of youth and power, " And is this the man who has so long been the object of our terror? " After he had confirmed his own authority and the peace of the empire, the trophies of Nicephorus and Zimisces would not suffer their royal pupil to sleep in the palace. His long and frequent expeditions against the Saracens were rather glorious than useful to the empire; but the final destruction of the kingdom of Bulgaria appears, since the time of Belisarius, the most important triumph of the Roman arms. Yet, instead of applauding their victorious prince, his subjects detested the rapacious and rigid avarice of Basil; and, in the imperfect narrative of his exploits, we can only discern the courage, patience, and ferociousness of a soldier. A vicious education, which could not subdue his spirit, had clouded his mind; he was ignorant of every science; and the remembrance of his learned and feeble grandsire might encourage his real or affected contempt of laws and lawyers, of artists and arts. Of such a character, in such an age, superstition took a firm and lasting possession: after the first licence of his youth, Basil the Second devoted his life, in the palace and the camp, to the penance of a hermit, wore the monastic habit under his robes and armour, observed a vow of continence, and imposed on his appetites a perpetual abstinence from wine and flesh. In the sixty-eighth year of his age his martial spirit urged him to embark in person for a holy war against the Saracens of Sicily; he was prevented by death, and Basil, surnamed the Slayer of the Bulgarians, was dismissed from the world with the blessings of the clergy and the curses of the people. After his decease, his brother Constantine enjoyed about three years the power or rather the pleasures of royalty; and his only care was the settlement of the succession. He had enjoyed sixty-six years the title of Augustus; and the reign of the two brothers is the longest and most obscure of the Byzantine history.

A lineal succession of five emperors, in a period of one hundred and sixty years, had attached the loyalty of the Greeks to the Macedonian dynasty, which had been thrice respected by the usurpers of their power. After the death of Constantine the Ninth, the last male of the royal race, a new and broken scene presents itself, and the accumulated years of twelve emperors do not equal the space of his single reign. His elder brother had preferred his private chastity to the public interest, and Constantine himself had only three daughters—Eudocia, who took the veil, and Zoe and Theodora, who were preserved till a mature age in a state of ignorance and virginity. When their marriage was discussed in the council of their dying father, the cold or pious Theodora refused to give an heir to the empire, but her sister Zoe presented herself a willing victim at the altar. Romanus Argyrus, a patrician of a graceful person and fair reputation, was chosen for her husband, and, on his declining that honour, was informed that blindness or death was the second alternative. The motive of his reluctance was conjugal affection, but his faithful wife sacrificed her own happiness to his safety and greatness, and her entrance into a monastery removed the only bar to the Imperial nuptials. After the decease of Constantine the sceptre devolved to Romanus the Third; but his labours at home and abroad were equally feeble and fruitless; and the mature age, the forty-eight years of Zoe, were less favourable to the hopes of pregnancy than to the indulgence of pleasure. Her favourite chamberlain was a handsome Paphlagonian of the name of Michael, whose first trade had been that of a money-changer; and Romanus, either from gratitude or equity, connived at their criminal intercourse, or accepted a slight assurance of their innocence. But Zoe soon

justified the Roman maxim, that every adulteress is capable
of poisoning her husband; and the death of Romanus was
instantly followed by the scandalous marriage and elevation of
Michael the Fourth. The expectations of Zoe were, however,
disappointed: instead of a vigorous and grateful lover, she had
placed in her bed a miserable wretch, whose health and reason
were impaired by epileptic fits, and whose conscience was tormented by despair and remorse. The most skilful physicians
of the mind and body were summoned to his aid; and his hopes
were amused by frequent pilgrimages to the baths, and to the
tombs of the most popular saints; the monks applauded his
penance, and, except restitution (but to whom should he have
restored?), Michael sought every method of expiating his guilt.
While he groaned and prayed in sackcloth and ashes, his brother,
the eunuch John, smiled at his remorse, and enjoyed the harvest
of a crime of which himself was the secret and most guilty author.
His administration was only the art of satiating his avarice, and
Zoe became a captive in the palace of her fathers and in the
hands of her slaves. When he perceived the irretrievable
decline of his brother's health, he introduced his nephew,
another Michael, who derived his surname of Calaphates from
his father's occupation in the careening of vessels: at the command of the eunuch, Zoe adopted for her son the son of a
mechanic; and this fictitious heir was invested with the title
and purple of the Cæsars in the presence of the senate and
clergy. So feeble was the character of Zoe, that she was oppressed by the liberty and power which she recovered by the
death of the Paphlagonian; and at the end of four days she
placed the crown on the head of Michael the Fifth, who had
protested with tears and oaths that he should ever reign the
first and most obedient of her subjects. The only act of his
short reign was his base ingratitude to his benefactors, the
eunuch and the empress. The disgrace of the former was
pleasing to the public; but the murmurs, and at length the
clamours, of Constantinople deplored the exile of Zoe, the
daughter of so many emperors; her vices were forgotten, and
Michael was taught that there is a period in which the patience
of the tamest slaves rises into fury and revenge. The citizens
of every degree assembled in a formidable tumult which lasted
three days; they besieged the palace, forced the gates, recalled
their *mothers*, Zoe from her prison, Theodora from her monastery,
and condemned the son of Calaphates to the loss of his eyes or
of his life. For the first time the Greeks beheld with surprise

the two royal sisters seated on the same throne, presiding in the senate, and giving audience to the ambassadors of the nations. But this singular union subsisted no more than two months; the two sovereigns, their tempers, interests, and adherents, were secretly hostile to each other; and as Theodora was still averse to marriage, the indefatigable Zoe, at the age of sixty, consented, for the public good, to sustain the embraces of a third husband, and the censures of the Greek church. His name and number were Constantine the Tenth, and the epithet of *Monomachus*, the single combatant, must have been expressive of his valour and victory in some public or private quarrel. But his health was broken by the tortures of the gout, and his dissolute reign was spent in the alternative of sickness and pleasure. A fair and noble widow had accompanied Constantine in his exile to the isle of Lesbos, and Sclerena gloried in the appellation of his mistress. After his marriage and elevation she was invested with the title and pomp of *Augusta*, and occupied a contiguous apartment in the palace. The lawful consort (such was the delicacy or corruption of Zoe) consented to this strange and scandalous partition; and the emperor appeared in public between his wife and his concubine. He survived them both; but the last measures of Constantine to change the order of succession were prevented by the more vigilant friends of Theodora; and after his decease, she resumed, with the general consent, the possession of her inheritance. In her name, and by the influence of four eunuchs, the Eastern world was peaceably governed about nineteen months; and as they wished to prolong their dominion, they persuaded the aged princess to nominate for her successor Michael the Sixth. The surname of *Stratioticus* declares his military profession; but the crazy and decrepit veteran could only see with the eyes, and execute with the hands, of his ministers. Whilst he ascended the throne, Theodora sunk into the grave—the last of the Macedonian or Basilian dynasty. I have hastily reviewed and gladly dismiss this shameful and destructive period of twenty-eight years, in which the Greeks, degraded below the common level of servitude, were transferred like a herd of cattle by the choice or caprice of two impotent females.

From this night of slavery, a ray of freedom, or at least of spirit, begins to emerge: the Greeks either preserved or revived the use of surnames, which perpetuate the fame of hereditary virtue: and we now discern the rise, succession, and alliances of the last dynasties of Constantinople and Trebizond. The

Comneni, who upheld for a while the fate of the sinking empire, assumed the honour of a Roman origin: but the family had been long since transported from Italy to Asia. Their patrimonial estate was situate in the district of Castamona, in the neighbourhood of the Euxine; and one of their chiefs, who had already entered the paths of ambition, revisited with affection, perhaps with regret, the modest though honourable dwelling of his fathers. The first of their line was the illustrious Manuel, who, in the reign of the second Basil, contributed by war and treaty to appease the troubles of the East: he left in a tender age two sons, Isaac and John, whom, with the consciousness of desert, he bequeathed to the gratitude and favour of his sovereign.[1] The noble youths were carefully trained in the learning of the monastery, the arts of the palace, and the exercises of the camp: and, from the domestic service of the guards, they were rapidly promoted to the command of provinces and armies. Their fraternal union doubled the force and reputation of the Comneni, and their ancient nobility was illustrated by the marriage of the two brothers, with a captive princess of Bulgaria, and the daughter of a patrician who had obtained the name of *Charon* from the number of enemies whom he had sent to the infernal shades. The soldiers had served with reluctant loyalty a series of effeminate masters; the elevation of Michael the Sixth was a personal insult to the more deserving generals; and their discontent was inflamed by the parsimony of the emperor and the insolence of the eunuchs. They secretly assembled in the sanctuary of St. Sophia, and the votes of the military synod would have been unanimous in favour of the old and valiant Catacalon, if the patriotism or modesty of the veteran had not suggested the importance of birth as well as merit in the choice of a sovereign. Isaac Comnenus was approved by general consent, and the associates separated without delay to meet in the plains of Phrygia at the head of their respective squadrons and detachments. The cause of Michael was defended in a single battle by the mercenaries of the imperial guard, who were aliens to the public interest, and animated only by a principle of honour and gratitude. After their defeat the fears of the emperor solicited a treaty, which was almost accepted by the moderation of the Comnenian. But the former was betrayed by his ambassadors, and the latter was prevented by his friends. The solitary Michael submitted to the voice of the people; the patriarch annulled their oath of

---

[1] See table on opposite page.

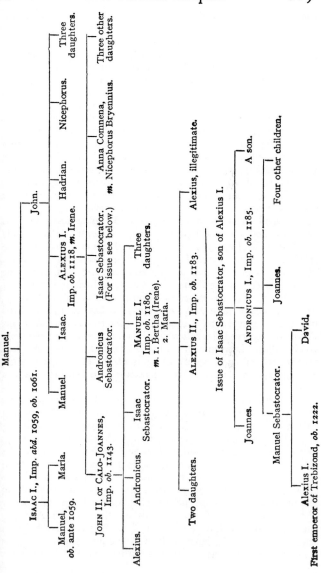

Manuel.

ISAAC I., Imp. *abd.* 1059, *ob.* 1061.

John.

Manuel,
ob. ante 1059.

Maria.

Manuel.

Isaac.

Hadrian.

Nicephorus.

Three
daughters.

ALEXIUS I.,
Imp. *ob.* 1118, *m.* Irene.

Anna Comnena,
m. Nicephorus Bryennius.

Three other
daughters.

JOHN II. or CALO-JOANNES,
Imp. *ob.* 1143.

Andronicus
Sebastocrator.

Isaac Sebastocrator.
(For issue see below.)

Andronicus.

Isaac
Sebastocrator.

MANUEL I.
Imp. *ob.* 1180,
m. 1. Bertha (Irene).
2. Maria.

Three
daughters.

Alexius.

ALEXIUS II., Imp. *ob.* 1183.

Alexius, illegitimate.

Two daughters.

Issue of Isaac Sebastocrator, son of Alexius I.

Joannes.

ANDRONICUS I., Imp. *ob.* 1185.

A son.

Joannes.

Four other children.

Manuel Sebastocrator.

David.

Alexius I.
First emperor of Trebizond, *ob.* 1222.

allegiance; and as he shaved the head of the royal monk, congratulated his beneficial exchange of temporal royalty for the kingdom of heaven; an exchange, however, which the priest, on his own account, would probably have declined. By the hands of the same patriarch, Isaac Comnenus was solemnly crowned; the sword which he inscribed on his coins might be an offensive symbol if it implied his title by conquest; but this sword would have been drawn against the foreign and domestic enemies of the state. The decline of his health and vigour suspended the operation of active virtue; and the prospect of approaching death determined him to interpose some moments between life and eternity. But instead of leaving the empire as the marriage portion of his daughter, his reason and inclination concurred in the preference of his brother John, a soldier, a patriot, and the father of five sons, the future pillars of an hereditary succession. His first modest reluctance might be the natural dictates of discretion and tenderness, but his obstinate and successful perseverance, however it may dazzle with the show of virtue, must be censured as a criminal desertion of his duty, and a rare offence against his family and country. The purple which he had refused was accepted by Constantine Ducas, a friend of the Comnenian house, and whose noble birth was adorned with the experience and reputation of civil policy. In the monastic habit Isaac recovered his health, and survived two years his voluntary abdication. At the command of his abbot, he observed the rule of St. Basil, and executed the most servile offices of the convent: but his latent vanity was gratified by the frequent and respectful visits of the reigning monarch, who revered in his person the character of a benefactor and a saint.

If Constantine the Eleventh were indeed the subject most worthy of empire, we must pity the debasement of the age and nation in which he was chosen. In the labour of puerile declamations he sought, without obtaining, the crown of eloquence, more precious in his opinion than that of Rome; and in the subordinate functions of a judge he forgot the duties of a sovereign and a warrior. Far from imitating the patriotic indifference of the authors of his greatness, Ducas was anxious only to secure, at the expense of the republic, the power and prosperity of his children. His three sons, Michael the Seventh, Andronicus the First, and Constantine the Twelfth, were invested in a tender age with the equal title of Augustus; and the succession was speedily opened by their father's death. His widow,

Eudocia, was intrusted with the administration; but experience had taught the jealousy of the dying monarch to protect his sons from the danger of her second nuptials; and her solemn engagement, attested by the principal senators, was deposited in the hands of the patriarch. Before the end of seven months, the wants of Eudocia or those of the state called aloud for the male virtues of a soldier; and her heart had already chosen Romanus Diogenes, whom she raised from the scaffold to the throne. The discovery of a treasonable attempt had exposed him to the severity of the laws: his beauty and valour absolved him in the eyes of the empress; and Romanus, from a mild exile, was recalled on the second day to the command of the Oriental armies. Her royal choice was yet unknown to the public; and the promise which would have betrayed her falsehood and levity was stolen by a dexterous emissary from the ambition of the patriarch. Xiphilin at first alleged the sanctity of oaths and the sacred nature of a trust; but a whisper that his brother was the future emperor relaxed his scruples, and forced him to confess that the public safety was the supreme law. He resigned the important paper; and when his hopes were confounded by the nomination of Romanus, he could no longer regain his security, retract his declarations, nor oppose the second nuptials of the empress. Yet a murmur was heard in the palace; and the barbarian guards had raised their battle-axes in the cause of the house of Ducas, till the young princes were soothed by the tears of their mother and the solemn assurances of the fidelity of their guardian, who filled the imperial station with dignity and honour. Hereafter I shall relate his valiant but unsuccessful efforts to resist the progress of the Turks. His defeat and captivity inflicted a deadly wound on the Byzantine monarchy of the East; and after he was released from the chains of the sultan, he vainly sought his wife and his subjects. His wife had been thrust into a monastery, and the subjects of Romanus had embraced the rigid maxim of the civil law, that a prisoner in the hands of the enemy is deprived, as by the stroke of death, of all the public and private rights of a citizen. In the general consternation the Cæsar John asserted the indefeasible right of his three nephews: Constantinople listened to his voice: and the Turkish captive was proclaimed in the capital, and received on the frontier, as an enemy of the republic. Romanus was not more fortunate in domestic than in foreign war: the loss of two battles compelled him to yield, on the assurance of fair and honourable treatment; but his enemies were devoid of faith or humanity; and, after the cruel extinction of his sight, his wounds were left to bleed and corrupt, till in a few days he was relieved from a state of misery. Under the triple reign of the house of Ducas, the two younger brothers were reduced to the vain honours of the purple; but the eldest, the pusillanimous Michael, was incapable of sustaining the Roman sceptre; and his surname of *Parapinaces* denotes the reproach which he shared with an avaricious favourite, who enhanced the price and diminished the measure of wheat. In the school of Psellus, and after the example of his mother, the son of Eudocia made some proficiency in philosophy and rhetoric; but his character was degraded rather than ennobled by the virtues of a monk and the learning of a sophist. Strong in the contempt of their sovereign and their own esteem, two generals, at the head of the European and Asiatic legions, assumed the purple at Adrianople and Nice. Their revolt was in the same month; they bore the same name of Nicephorus; but the two candidates were distinguished by the surnames of Bryennius and Botaniates: the former in the maturity of wisdom and courage, the latter conspicuous only by the memory of his past exploits. While Botaniates advanced with cautious and dilatory steps, his active competitor stood in arms before the gates of Constantinople. The name of Bryennius was illustrious; his cause was popular; but his licentious troops could not be restrained from burning and pillaging a suburb; and the people, who would have hailed the rebel, rejected and repulsed the incendiary of his country. This change of the public opinion was favourable to Botaniates, who at length, with an army of Turks, approached the shores of Chalcedon. A formal invitation, in the name of the patriarch, the synod, and the senate, was circulated through the streets of Constantinople; and the general assembly, in the dome of St. Sophia, debated, with order and calmness, on the choice of their sovereign. The guards of Michael would have dispersed this unarmed multitude; but the feeble emperor, applauding his own moderation and clemency, resigned the ensigns of royalty, and was rewarded with the monastic habit, and the title of Archbishop of Ephesus. He left a son, a Constantine, born and educated in the purple; and a daughter of the house of Ducas illustrated the blood and confirmed the succession of the Comnenian dynasty.

John Comnenus, the brother of the emperor Isaac, survived in peace and dignity his generous refusal of the sceptre. By his wife Anne, a woman of masculine spirit and policy, he left eight children: the three daughters multiplied the Comnenian alliances with the noblest of the Greeks: of the five sons, Manuel was stopped by a premature death; Isaac and Alexius restored the Imperial greatness of their house, which was enjoyed without toil or danger by the two younger brethren, Adrian and Nicephorus. Alexius, the third and most illustrious of the brothers, was endowed by nature with the choicest gifts both of mind and body: they were cultivated by a liberal education, and exercised in the school of obedience and adversity. The youth was dismissed from the perils of the Turkish war by the paternal care of the emperor Romanus: but the mother of the Comneni, with her aspiring race, was accused of treason, and banished, by the sons of Ducas, to an island in the Propontis. The two brothers soon emerged into favour and action, fought by each other's side against the rebels and barbarians, and adhered to the emperor Michael, till he was deserted by the world and by himself. In his first interview with Botaniates, " Prince," said Alexius, with a noble frankness, "my duty rendered me your enemy; the decrees of God and of the people have made me your subject. Judge of my future loyalty by my past opposition." The successor of Michael entertained him with esteem and confidence: his valour was employed against three rebels, who disturbed the peace of the empire, or at least of the emperors. Ursel, Bryennius, and Basilacius were formidable by their numerous forces and military fame: they were successively vanquished in the field, and led in chains to the foot of the throne; and whatever treatment they might receive from a timid and cruel court, they applauded the clemency as well as the courage of their conqueror. But the loyalty of the Comneni was soon tainted by fear and suspicion; nor is it easy to settle between a subject and a despot the debt of gratitude which the former is tempted to claim by a revolt, and the latter to discharge by an executioner. The refusal of Alexius to march against a fourth rebel, the husband of his sister, destroyed the merit or memory of his past services: the favourites of Botaniates provoked the ambition which they apprehended and accused; and the retreat of the two brothers might be justified by the defence of their life or liberty. The women of the family were deposited in a sanctuary, respected by tyrants: the men, mounted on horseback, sallied from the city, and erected the standard of civil war. The soldiers who had been gradually assembled in the capital and the neighbourhood were devoted to the cause of a victorious and injured leader: the ties of common interest and domestic alliance secured the attachment of the house of Ducas; and the generous dispute of the Comneni was terminated by the decisive resolution of Isaac, who was the first to invest his younger brother with the name and ensigns of royalty. They returned to Constantinople, to threaten rather than besiege that impregnable fortress; but the fidelity of the guards was corrupted; a gate was surprised, and the fleet was occupied by the active courage of George Palæologus, who fought against his father, without foreseeing that he laboured for his posterity. Alexius ascended the throne; and his aged competitor disappeared in a monastery. An army of various nations was gratified with the pillage of the city; but the public disorders were expiated by the tears and fasts of the Comneni, who submitted to every penance compatible with the possession of the empire.

The life of the emperor Alexius has been delineated by a favourite daughter, who was inspired by a tender regard for his person and a laudable zeal to perpetuate his virtues. Conscious of the just suspicion of her readers, the princess Anna Comnena repeatedly protests that, besides her personal knowledge, she had searched the discourse and writings of the most respectable veterans: that, after an interval of thirty years, forgotten by and forgetful of the world, her mournful solitude was inaccessible to hope and fear; and that truth, the naked perfect truth, was more dear and sacred than the memory of her parent. Yet, instead of the simplicity of style and narrative which wins our belief, an elaborate affectation of rhetoric and science betrays in every page the vanity of a female author. The genuine character of Alexius is lost in a vague constellation of virtues; and the perpetual strain of panegyric and apology awakens our jealousy, to question the veracity of the historian and the merit of the hero. We cannot, however, refuse her judicious and important remark, that the disorders of the times were the misfortune and the glory of Alexius; and that every calamity which can afflict a declining empire was accumulated on his reign by the justice of Heaven and the vices of his predecessors. In the East, the victorious Turks had spread, from Persia to the Hellespont, the reign of the Koran and the Crescent: the West was invaded by the adventurous valour of the Normans; and, in the moments of peace, the Danube poured forth new swarms, who had gained, in the science of war, what they had lost in the ferociousness of manners. The sea was not less hostile than the land; and while the frontiers were assaulted by an open enemy, the palace was distracted with secret treason and conspiracy. On a sudden the banner of the Cross was displayed by the Latins; Europe was precipitated on Asia; and Constantinople had almost been swept away by this impetuous deluge. In the tempest, Alexius steered the Imperial vessel with dexterity and courage. At the head of his armies he was bold in action, skilful in stratagem, patient of fatigue, ready to improve his advantages, and rising from his defeats with inexhaustible vigour. The discipline of the camp was revived, and a new generation of men and soldiers was created by the example and the precepts of their leader. In his intercourse with the Latins, Alexius was patient and artful: his discerning eye pervaded the new system of an unknown world; and I shall hereafter describe the superior policy with which he balanced the interests and passions of the champions of the first crusade. In a long reign of thirty-seven years he subdued and pardoned the envy of his equals: the laws of public and private order were restored: the arts of wealth and science were cultivated: the limits of the empire were enlarged in Europe and Asia; and the Comnenian sceptre was transmitted to his children of the third and fourth generation. Yet the difficulties of the times betrayed some defects in his character; and have exposed his memory to some just or ungenerous reproach. The reader may possibly smile at the lavish praise which his daughter so often bestows on a flying hero: the weakness or prudence of his situation might be mistaken for a want of personal courage; and his political arts are branded by the Latins with the names of deceit and dissimulation. The increase of the male and female branches of his family adorned the throne, and secured the succession; but their princely luxury and pride offended the patricians, exhausted the revenue, and insulted the misery of the people. Anna is a faithful witness that his happiness was destroyed, and his health was broken, by the cares of a public life: the patience of Constantinople was fatigued by the length and severity of his reign; and before Alexius expired, he had lost the love and reverence of his subjects. The clergy could not forgive his application of the sacred riches to the defence of the state; but they applauded his theological learning and ardent zeal for the orthodox faith, which he defended with his tongue, his pen, and his sword. His character was degraded by the superstition of the Greeks; and the same inconsistent principle of human nature enjoined the emperor to found a hospital for the poor and infirm, and to direct the execution of a heretic, who was burnt alive in the square of St. Sophia. Even the sincerity of his moral and religious virtues was suspected by the persons who had passed their lives in his familiar confidence. In his last hours, when he was pressed by his wife Irene to alter the succession, he raised his head, and breathed a pious ejaculation on the vanity of this world. The indignant reply of the empress may be inscribed as an epitaph on his tomb, " You die, as you have lived—A HYPOCRITE ! "

It was the wish of Irene to supplant the eldest of her surviving sons, in favour of her daughter the princess Anna, whose philosophy would not have refused the weight of a diadem. But the order of male succession was asserted by the friends of their country; the lawful heir drew the royal signet from the finger of his insensible or conscious father, and the empire obeyed the master of the palace. Anna Comnena was stimulated by ambition and revenge to conspire against the life of her brother, and, when the design was prevented by the fears or scruples of her husband, she passionately exclaimed that nature had mistaken the two sexes, and had endowed Bryennius with the soul of a woman. The two sons of Alexius, John and Isaac, maintained the fraternal concord, the hereditary virtue of their race, and the younger brother was content with the title of *Sebastocrator*, which approached the dignity without sharing the power of the emperor. In the same person the claims of primogeniture and merit were fortunately united; his swarthy complexion, harsh features, and diminutive stature had suggested the ironical surname of Calo-Johannes, or John the Handsome, which his grateful subjects more seriously applied to the beauties of his mind. After the discovery of her treason, the life and fortune of Anna were justly forfeited to the laws. Her life was spared by the clemency of the emperor; but he visited the pomp and treasures of her palace, and bestowed the rich confiscation on the most deserving of his friends. That respectable friend, Axuch, a slave of Turkish extraction, presumed to decline the gift, and to intercede for the criminal: his generous master applauded and imitated the virtue of his favourite, and the reproach or complaint of an injured brother was the only chastisement of the guilty princess. After this example of clemency, the remainder of his reign was never disturbed by conspiracy or rebellion: feared by his nobles, beloved by his people, John was never reduced to the painful necessity of punishing, or even of pardoning, his personal enemies. During his government of twenty-five years, the penalty of death was abolished in the Roman empire, a law of mercy most delightful to the humane theorist, but of which the practice, in a large and vicious community, is seldom consistent with the public safety. Severe to himself, indulgent to others, chaste, frugal, abstemious, the philosophic Marcus would not have disdained the artless virtues of his successor, derived from his heart, and not borrowed from the schools. He despised and moderated the stately magnificence of the Byzantine court, so oppressive to the people, so contemptible to the eye of reason. Under such a prince innocence had nothing to fear, and merit had everything to hope; and, without assuming the tyrannic office of a censor, he introduced a gradual though visible reformation in the public and private manners of Constantinople. The only defect of this accomplished character was the frailty of noble minds—the love of arms and military glory. Yet the frequent expeditions of John the Handsome may be justified, at least in their principle, by the necessity of repelling the Turks from the Hellespont and the Bosphorus. The sultan of Iconium was confined to his capital, the barbarians were driven to the mountains, and the maritime provinces of Asia enjoyed the transient blessings of their deliverance. From Constantinople to Antioch and Aleppo, he repeatedly marched at the head of a victorious army; and in the sieges and battles of this holy war, his Latin allies were astonished by the superior spirit and prowess of a Greek. As he began to indulge the ambitious hope of restoring the ancient limits of the empire, as he revolved in his mind the Euphrates and Tigris, the dominion of Syria, and the conquest of Jerusalem, the thread of his life and of the public felicity was broken by a singular accident. He hunted the wild boar in the valley of Anazarbus, and had fixed his javelin in the body of the furious animal; but in the struggle a poisoned arrow dropped from his quiver, and a slight wound in his hand, which produced a mortification, was fatal to the best and greatest of the Comnenian princes.

A premature death had swept away the two eldest sons of John the Handsome; of the two survivors, Isaac and Manuel, his judgment or affection preferred the younger; and the choice of their dying prince was ratified by the soldiers, who had applauded the valour of his favourite in the Turkish war. The faithful Axuch hastened to the capital, secured the person of Isaac in honourable confinement, and purchased, with a gift of two hundred pounds of silver, the leading ecclesiastics of St. Sophia, who possessed a decisive voice in the consecration of an emperor. With his veteran and affectionate troops, Manuel soon visited Constantinople; his brother acquiesced in the title of Sebastocrator; his subjects admired the lofty stature and martial graces of their new sovereign, and listened with credulity to the flattering promise that he blended the wisdom of age with the activity and vigour of youth. By the experience of his government they were taught that he emulated the spirit and shared the talents of his father, whose social virtues were buried in the grave. A reign of thirty-seven years is filled by a perpetual though various warfare against the Turks, the Christians, and the hordes of the wilderness beyond the Danube. The arms of Manuel were exercised on Mount Taurus, in the plains of Hungary, on the coast of Italy and Egypt, and on the seas of Sicily and Greece: the influence of his negotiations extended from Jerusalem to Rome and Russia; and the Byzantine monarchy for a while became an object of respect or terror to the powers of Asia and Europe. Educated in the silk and purple of the East, Manuel possessed the iron temper of a soldier, which cannot easily be paralleled, except in the lives of Richard the First of England, and of Charles the Twelfth of Sweden. Such was his strength and exercise in arms, that Raymond, surnamed the Hercules of Antioch, was incapable of wielding the lance and buckler of the Greek emperor. In a famous tournament he entered the lists on a fiery courser, and overturned in his first career two of the stoutest of the Italian knights. The first in the charge, the last in the retreat, his friends and his enemies alike trembled, the former for *his* safety, and the latter for their own. After posting an ambuscade in a wood, he rode forwards in search of some perilous adventure, accompanied only by his brother and the faithful Axuch, who refused to desert their sovereign. Eighteen horsemen, after a short combat, fled before them: but the numbers of the enemy increased; the march of the reinforcement was tardy and fearful, and Manuel, without receiving a wound, cut his way through a squadron of five hundred Turks. In a battle against the Hungarians, impatient of the slowness of his troops, he snatched a standard from the head of the column, and was the first, almost alone, who passed a bridge that separated him from the enemy. In the same country, after transporting his army beyond the Save, he sent back the boats, with an order, under pain of death, to their commander, that he should leave him to conquer or die on that hostile land. In the siege of Corfu, towing after him a captive galley, the emperor stood aloft on the poop, opposing against the volleys of darts and stones a large buckler and a flowing sail; nor could he have escaped inevitable death, had not the Sicilian admiral enjoined his archers to respect the person of a hero. In one day he is said to have slain above forty of the barbarians with his own hand; he returned to the camp, dragging along four Turkish prisoners, whom he had tied to the rings of his saddle: he was ever the foremost to provoke or to accept a single combat; and the *gigantic* champions who encountered his arm were transpierced by the lance, or cut asunder by the sword, of the invincible Manuel. The story of his exploits, which appear as a model or a copy of the romances of chivalry, may induce a reasonable suspicion of the veracity of the Greeks: I will not, to vindicate their credit, endanger my own; yet I may observe that, in the long series of their annals, Manuel is the only prince who has been the subject of similar exaggeration. With the valour of a soldier he did not unite the skill or prudence of a general: his victories were not productive of any permanent or useful conquest; and his Turkish laurels were blasted in his last unfortunate campaign, in which he lost his army in the mountains of Pisidia, and owed his deliverance to the generosity of the sultan. But the most singular feature in the character of Manuel is the contrast and vicissitude of labour and sloth, of hardiness and effeminacy. In war he seemed ignorant of peace, in peace he appeared incapable of war. In the field he slept in the sun or in the snow, tired in the longest marches the strength of his men and horses, and shared with a smile the abstinence or diet of the camp. No sooner did he return to Constantinople, than he resigned himself to the arts and pleasures of a life of luxury: the expense of his dress, his table, and his palace surpassed the measure of his predecessors, and whole summer days were idly wasted in the delicious isles of the Propontis, in the incestuous love of his niece Theodora. The double cost of a warlike and dissolute prince exhausted the revenue and multiplied the taxes; and Manuel, in the distress of his last Turkish camp, endured a bitter reproach from the mouth of a desperate soldier. As he quenched his thirst, he complained that the water of a fountain was mingled with Christian blood. "It is not the first time," exclaimed a voice from the crowd, "that you have drank, O emperor, the blood of your Christian subjects." Manuel Comnenus was twice married, to the virtuous Bertha or Irene of Germany, and to the beauteous Maria, a French or Latin princess of Antioch. The only daughter of his first wife was destined for Bela, an Hungarian prince, who was educated at Constantinople under the name of Alexius; and the consummation of their nuptials might have transferred the Roman sceptre to a race of free and warlike barbarians. But as soon as Maria of Antioch had given a son and heir to the empire, the presumptive rights of Bela were abolished, and he was deprived of his promised bride; but the Hungarian prince resumed his name and the kingdom of his fathers, and displayed such virtues as might excite the regret and envy of the Greeks. The son of Maria was named Alexius; and at the age of ten years he ascended the Byzantine throne, after his father's decease had closed the glories of the Comnenian line.

The fraternal concord of the two sons of the great Alexius had been sometimes clouded by an opposition of interest and passion. By ambition, Isaac the Sebastocrator was excited to flight and rebellion, from whence he was reclaimed by the firmness and clemency of John the Handsome. The errors of Isaac, the father of the emperors of Trebizond, were short and venial; but John, the elder of his sons, renounced for ever his religion. Provoked by a real or imaginary insult of his uncle, he escaped from the Roman to the Turkish camp: his apostacy was rewarded with the sultan's daughter, the title of Chelebi, or noble, and the inheritance of a princely estate; and, in the fifteenth century, Mohammed the Second boasted of his Imperial descent from the Comnenian family. Andronicus, younger brother of John, son of Isaac, and grandson of Alexius Comnenus, is one of the most conspicuous characters of the age; and his genuine adventures might form the subject of a very singular romance. To justify the choice of three ladies of royal birth, it is incumbent on me to observe that their fortunate lover was cast in the best proportions of strength and beauty; and that the want of the softer graces was supplied by a manly countenance, a lofty stature, athletic muscles, and the air and deportment of a soldier. The preservation, in his old age, of health and vigour, was the reward of temperance and exercise. A piece of bread and a draught of water was often his sole and evening repast; and if he tasted of a wild boar or a stag, which he had roasted with his own hands, it was the well-earned fruit of a laborious chase. Dexterous in arms, he was ignorant of fear: his persuasive eloquence could bend to every situation and character of life: his style, though not his practice, was fashioned by the example of St. Paul; and, in every deed of mischief, he had a heart to resolve, a head to contrive, and a hand to execute. In his youth, after the death of the emperor John, he followed the retreat of the Roman army; but, in the march through Asia Minor, design or accident tempted him to wander in the mountains: the hunter was encompassed by the Turkish huntsmen, and he remained some time a reluctant or willing captive in the power of the sultan. His virtues and vices recommended him to the favour of his cousin: he shared the perils and the pleasures of Manuel; and while the emperor lived in public incest with his niece Theodora, the affections of her sister Eudocia were seduced and enjoyed by Andronicus. Above the decencies of her sex and rank, she gloried in the name of his concubine; and both the palace and the camp could witness that she slept, or watched, in the arms of her lover. She accompanied him to his military command of Cilicia, the first scene of his valour and imprudence. He pressed, with active ardour, the siege of Mopsuestia: the day was employed in the boldest attacks; but the night was wasted in song and dance; and a band of Greek comedians formed the choicest part of his retinue. Andronicus was surprised by the sally of a vigilant foe; but, while his troops fled in disorder, his invincible lance transpierced the thickest ranks of the Armenians. On his return to the Imperial camp in Macedonia, he was received by Manuel with public smiles and a private reproof; but the duchies of Naissus, Braniseba, and Castoria were the reward or consolation of the unsuccessful general. Eudocia still attended his motions: at midnight their tent was suddenly attacked by her angry brothers, impatient to expiate her infamy in his blood: his daring spirit refused her advice, and the disguise of a female habit; and, boldly starting from his couch, he drew his sword, and cut his way through the numerous assassins. It was here that he first betrayed his ingratitude and treachery: he engaged in a treasonable correspondence with the king of Hungary and the German emperor; approached the royal tent at a suspicious hour with a drawn sword, and, under the mask of a Latin soldier, avowed an intention of revenge against a mortal foe; and imprudently praised the fleetness of his horse as an instrument of flight and safety. The monarch dissembled his suspicions; but, after the close of the campaign, Andronicus was arrested and strictly confined in a tower of the palace of Constantinople.

In this prison he was left above twelve years; a most painful restraint, from which the thirst of action and pleasure perpetually urged him to escape. Alone and pensive, he perceived some broken bricks in a corner of the chamber, and gradually widened the passage till he had explored a dark and forgotten recess.

Into this hole he conveyed himself and the remains of his provisions, replacing the bricks in their former position, and erasing with care the footsteps of his retreat. At the hour of the customary visit, his guards were amazed by the silence and solitude of the prison, and reported, with shame and fear, his incomprehensible flight. The gates of the palace and city were instantly shut: the strictest orders were despatched into the provinces for the recovery of the fugitive; and his wife, on the suspicion of a pious act, was basely imprisoned in the same tower. At the dead of night she beheld a spectre: she recognised her husband; they shared their provisions, and a son was the fruit of these stolen interviews, which alleviated the tediousness of their confinement. In the custody of a woman the vigilance of the keepers was insensibly relaxed, and the captive had accomplished his real escape, when he was discovered, brought back to Constantinople, and loaded with a double chain. At length he found the moment and the means of his deliverance. A boy, his domestic servant, intoxicated the guards, and obtained in wax the impression of the keys. By the diligence of his friends a similar key, with a bundle of ropes, was introduced into the prison in the bottom of a hogshead. Andronicus employed, with industry and courage, the instruments of his safety, unlocked the doors, descended from the tower, concealed himself all day among the bushes, and scaled in the night the garden-wall of the palace. A boat was stationed for his reception; he visited his own house, embraced his children, cast away his chain, mounted a fleet horse, and directed his rapid course towards the banks of the Danube. At Anchialus, in Thrace, an intrepid friend supplied him with horses and money: he passed the river, traversed with speed the desert of Moldavia and the Carpathian hills, and had almost reached the town of Halicz, in the Polish Russia, when he was intercepted by a party of Walachians, who resolved to convey their important captive to Constantinople. His presence of mind again extricated him from this danger. Under the pretence of sickness he dismounted in the night, and was allowed to step aside from the troop: he planted in the ground his long staff, clothed it with his cap and upper garment, and, stealing into the wood, left a phantom to amuse for some time the eyes of the Walachians. From Halicz he was honourably conducted to Kiow, the residence of the great duke: the subtle Greek soon obtained the esteem and confidence of Ieroslaus; his character could assume the manners of every climate, and the barbarians applauded his strength and courage in the chase of the elks and bears of the forest. In this northern region he deserved the forgiveness of Manuel, who solicited the Russian prince to join his arms in the invasion of Hungary. The influence of Andronicus achieved this important service: his private treaty was signed with a promise of fidelity on one side and of oblivion on the other, and he marched, at the head of the Russian cavalry, from the Borysthenes to the Danube. In his resentment Manuel had ever sympathised with the martial and dissolute character of his cousin, and his free pardon was sealed in the assault of Zemlin, in which he was second, and second only, to the valour of the emperor.

No sooner was the exile restored to freedom and his country than his ambition revived, at first to his own, and at length to the public misfortune. A daughter of Manuel was a feeble bar to the succession of the more deserving males of the Comnenian blood: her future marriage with the prince of Hungary was repugnant to the hopes or prejudices of the princes and nobles. But when an oath of allegiance was required to the presumptive heir, Andronicus alone asserted the honour of the Roman name, declined the unlawful engagement, and boldly protested against the adoption of a stranger. His patriotism was offensive to the emperor; but he spoke the sentiments of the people, and was removed from the royal presence by an honourable banishment, a second command of the Cilician frontier, with the absolute disposal of the revenues of Cyprus. In this station the Armenians again exercised his courage and exposed his negligence; and the same rebel, who baffled all his operations, was unhorsed, and almost slain by the vigour of his lance. But Andronicus soon discovered a more easy and pleasing conquest, the beautiful Philippa, sister of the empress Maria, and daughter of Raymond of Poitou, the Latin prince of Antioch. For her sake he deserted his station, and wasted the summer in balls and tournaments: to his love she sacrificed her innocence, her reputation, and the offer of an advantageous marriage. But the resentment of Manuel for this domestic affront interrupted his pleasures: Andronicus left the indiscreet princess to weep and to repent; and, with a band of desperate adventurers, undertook the pilgrimage of Jerusalem. His birth, his martial renown, and professions of zeal announced him as the champion of the Cross: he soon captivated both the clergy and the king, and the Greek prince was invested with the lordship of Berytus, on the coast of Phœnicia. In his neighbourhood resided a young and handsome queen, of his own nation and family, great-grand-daughter of the emperor Alexis, and widow of Baldwin the Third, king of Jerusalem. She visited and loved her kinsman. Theodora was the third victim of his amorous seduction, and her shame was more public and scandalous than that of her predecessors. The emperor still thirsted for revenge, and his subjects and allies of the Syrian frontier were repeatedly pressed to seize the person and put out the eyes of the fugitive. In Palestine he was no longer safe; but the tender Theodora revealed his danger and accompanied his flight. The queen of Jerusalem was exposed to the East, his obsequious concubine, and two illegitimate children were the living monuments of her weakness. Damascus was his first refuge, and, in the characters of the great Noureddin and his servant Saladin, the superstitious Greek might learn to revere the virtues of the Musulmans. As the friend of Noureddin he visited, most probably, Bagdad and the courts of Persia, and, after a long circuit round the Caspian Sea and the mountains of Georgia, he finally settled among the Turks of Asia Minor, the hereditary enemies of his country. The sultan of Colonia afforded an hospitable retreat to Andronicus, his mistress, and his band of outlaws: the debt of gratitude was paid by frequent inroads in the Roman province of Trebizond, and he seldom returned without an ample harvest of spoil and of Christian captives. In the story of his adventures he was fond of comparing himself to David, who escaped, by a long exile, the snares of the wicked. But the royal prophet (he presumed to add) was content to lurk on the borders of Judæa, to slay an Amalekite, and to threaten, in his miserable state, the life of the avaricious Nabal. The excursions of the Comnenian prince had a wider range, and he had spread over the Eastern world the glory of his name and religion. By a sentence of the Greek church, the licentious rover had been separated from the faithful; but even this excommunication may prove that he never abjured the profession of Christianity.

His vigilance had eluded or repelled the open and secret persecution of the emperor; but he was at length ensnared by the captivity of his female companion. The governor of Trebizond succeeded in his attempt to surprise the person of Theodora: the queen of Jerusalem and her two children were sent to Constantinople, and their loss embittered the tedious solitude of banishment. The fugitive implored and obtained a final pardon, with leave to throw himself at the feet of his sovereign, who was satisfied with the submission of this haughty spirit. Prostrate on the ground, he deplored with tears and groans the guilt of his past rebellion; nor would he presume to arise, unless some faithful subject would drag him to the foot of the throne by an iron chain with which he had secretly encircled his neck. This extraordinary penance excited the wonder and pity of the assembly: his sins were forgiven by the church and state; but the just suspicion of Manuel fixed his residence at a distance from the court, at Oenoe, a town of Pontus, surrounded with rich vineyards, and situate on the coast of the Euxine. The death of Manuel and the disorders of the minority soon opened the fairest field to his ambition. The emperor was a boy of twelve or fourteen years of age, without vigour, or wisdom, or experience: his mother, the empress Mary, abandoned her person and government to a favourite of the Comnenian name; and his sister, another Mary, whose husband, an Italian, was decorated with the title of Cæsar, excited a conspiracy, and at length an insurrection, against her odious stepmother. The provinces were forgotten, the capital was in flames, and a century of peace and order was overthrown in the vice and weakness of a few months. A civil war was kindled in Constantinople; the two factions fought a bloody battle in the square of the palace, and the rebels sustained a regular siege in the cathedral of St. Sophia. The patriarch laboured with honest zeal to heal the wounds of the republic, the most respectable patriots called aloud for a guardian and avenger, and every tongue repeated the praise of the talents and even the virtues of Andronicus. In his retirement he affected to revolve the solemn duties of his oath: " If the safety or honour of the Imperial family be threatened, I will reveal and oppose the mischief to the utmost of my power." His correspondence with the patriarch and patricians was seasoned with apt quotations from the Psalms of David and the Epistles of St. Paul; and he patiently waited till he was called to her deliverance by the voice of his country. In his march from Oenoe to Constantinople, his slender train insensibly swelled to a crowd and an army; his professions of religion and loyalty were mistaken for the language of his heart; and the simplicity of a foreign dress, which showed to advantage his majestic stature, displayed a lively image of his poverty and exile. All opposition sunk before him; he reached the straits of the Thracian Bosphorus; the Byzantine navy sailed from the harbour to receive and transport the saviour of the empire: the torrent was loud and irresistible, and the insects who had basked in the sunshine of royal favour disappeared at the blast of the storm. It was the

first care of Andronicus to occupy the palace, to salute the
emperor, to confine his mother, to punish her minister, and to
restore the public order and tranquillity. He then visited the
sepulchre of Manuel: the spectators were ordered to stand
aloof, but, as he bowed in the attitude of prayer, they heard, or
thought they heard, a murmur of triumph and revenge: " I no
longer fear thee, my old enemy, who hast driven me a vagabond
to every climate of the earth. Thou art safely deposited under
a seven-fold dome, from whence thou canst never arise till the
signal of the last trumpet. It is now my turn, and speedily
will I trample on thy ashes and thy posterity." From his
subsequent tyranny we may impute such feelings to the man
and the moment; but it is not extremely probable that he gave
an articulate sound to his secret thoughts. In the first months
of his administration his designs were veiled by a fair semblance
of hypocrisy, which could delude only the eyes of the multitude:
the coronation of Alexius was performed with due solemnity,
and his perfidious guardian, holding in his hands the body and
blood of Christ, most fervently declared that he lived, and was
ready to die, for the service of his beloved pupil. But his
numerous adherents were instructed to maintain that the
sinking empire must perish in the hands of a child; that the
Romans could only be saved by a veteran prince, bold in arms,
skilful in policy, and taught to reign by the long experience of
fortune and mankind; and that it was the duty of every citizen
to force the reluctant modesty of Andronicus to undertake the
burden of the public care. The young emperor was himself
constrained to join his voice to the general acclamation, and
to solicit the association of a colleague, who instantly degraded
him from the supreme rank, secluded his person, and verified
the rash declaration of the patriarch, that Alexius might be
considered as dead so soon as he was committed to the custody
of his guardian. But his death was preceded by the imprisonment and execution of his mother. After blackening her reputation, and inflaming against her the passions of the multitude,
the tyrant accused and tried the empress for a treasonable
correspondence with the king of Hungary. His own son, a
youth of honour and humanity, avowed his abhorrence of this
flagitious act, and three of the judges had the merit of preferring
their conscience to their safety; but the obsequious tribunal,
without requiring any proof or hearing any defence, condemned
the widow of Manuel, and her unfortunate son subscribed the
sentence of her death. Maria was strangled, her corpse was

buried in the sea, and her memory was wounded by the insult most offensive to female vanity, a false and ugly representation of her beauteous form. The fate of her son was not long deferred: he was strangled with a bowstring, and the tyrant, insensible to pity or remorse, after surveying the body of the innocent youth, struck it rudely with his foot. "Thy father," he cried, "was a *knave*, thy mother a *whore*, and thyself a *fool !*"

The Roman sceptre, the reward of his crimes, was held by Andronicus about three years and a half as the guardian or sovereign of the empire. His government exhibited a singular contrast of vice and virtue. When he listened to his passions, he was the scourge; when he consulted his reason, the father of his people. In the exercise of private justice he was equitable and rigorous; a shameful and pernicious venality was abolished, and the offices were filled with the most deserving candidates by a prince who had sense to choose and severity to punish. He prohibited the inhuman practice of pillaging the goods and persons of shipwrecked mariners; the provinces, so long the objects of oppression or neglect, revived in prosperity and plenty; and millions applauded the distant blessings of his reign, while he was cursed by the witnesses of his daily cruelties. The ancient proverb, that bloodthirsty is the man who returns from banishment to power, had been applied, with too much truth, to Marius and Tiberius, and was now verified for the third time in the life of Andronicus. His memory was stored with a black list of the enemies and rivals who had traduced his merit, opposed his greatness, or insulted his misfortunes; and the only comfort of his exile was the sacred hope and promise of revenge. The necessary extinction of the young emperor and his mother imposed the fatal obligation of extirpating the friends who hated, and might punish, the assassin; and the repetition of murder rendered him less willing and less able to forgive. A horrid narrative of the victims whom he sacrificed by poison or the sword, by the sea or the flames, would be less expressive of his cruelty than the appellation of the Halcyon-days, which was applied to a rare and bloodless week of repose: the tyrant strove to transfer on the laws and the judges some portion of his guilt, but the mask was fallen, and his subjects could no longer mistake the true author of their calamities. The noblest of the Greeks, more especially those who, by descent or alliance, might dispute the Comnenian inheritance, escaped from the monster's den: Nice or Prusa, Sicily or Cyprus, were their places of refuge; and as their flight

was already criminal, they aggravated their offence by an open
revolt and the Imperial title. Yet Andronicus resisted the
daggers and swords of his most formidable enemies: Nice and
Prusa were reduced and chastised; the Sicilians were content
with the sack of Thessalonica; and the distance of Cyprus was
not more propitious to the rebel than to the tyrant. His throne
was subverted by a rival without a merit, and a people without
arms. Isaac Angelus, a descendant in the female line from the
great Alexius, was marked as a victim by the prudence or superstition of the emperor. In a moment of despair Angelus
defended his life and liberty, slew the executioner, and fled to
the church of St. Sophia. The sanctuary was insensibly filled
with a curious and mournful crowd, who, in his fate, prognosticated their own. But their lamentations were soon turned to
curses, and their curses to threats: they dared to ask, " Why
do we fear? why do we obey? We are many, and he is one;
our patience is the only bond of our slavery." With the dawn
of day the city burst into a general sedition, the prisons were
thrown open, the coldest and most servile were roused to the
defence of their country, and Isaac, the second of the name, was
raised from the sanctuary to the throne. Unconscious of his
danger, the tyrant was absent—withdrawn from the toils of
state, in the delicious islands of the Propontis. He had contracted an indecent marriage with Alice, or Agnes, daughter of
Lewis the Seventh, of France, and relict of the unfortunate
Alexius; and his society, more suitable to his temper than to his
age, was composed of a young wife and a favourite concubine.
On the first alarm he rushed to Constantinople, impatient for
the blood of the guilty; but he was astonished by the silence of
the palace, the tumult of the city, and the general desertion of
mankind. Andronicus proclaimed a free pardon to his subjects;
they neither desired nor would grant forgiveness: he offered to
resign the crown to his son Manuel; but the virtues of the son
could not expiate his father's crimes. The sea was still open
for his retreat; but the news of the revolution had flown along
the coast; when fear had ceased, obedience was no more; the
Imperial galley was pursued and taken by an armed brigantine,
and the tyrant was dragged to the presence of Isaac Angelus,
loaded with fetters, and a long chain round his neck. His
eloquence and the tears of his female companions pleaded in
vain for his life; but, instead of the decencies of a legal execution,
the new monarch abandoned the criminal to the numerous
sufferers whom he had deprived of a father, a husband, or a

friend. His teeth and hair, an eye and a hand, were torn from him, as a poor compensation for their loss; and a short respite was allowed, that he might feel the bitterness of death. Astride on a camel, without any danger of a rescue, he was carried through the city, and the basest of the populace rejoiced to trample on the fallen majesty of their prince. After a thousand blows and outrages, Andronicus was hung by the feet between two pillars that supported the statues of a wolf and a sow; and every hand that could reach the public enemy inflicted on his body some mark of ingenious or brutal cruelty, till two friendly or furious Italians, plunging their swords into his body, released him from all human punishment. In this long and painful agony, " Lord have mercy upon me!" and " Why will you bruise a broken reed?" were the only words that escaped from his mouth. Our hatred for the tyrant is lost in pity for the man; nor can we blame his pusillanimous resignation, since a Greek Christian was no longer master of his life.

I have been tempted to expatiate on the extraordinary character and adventures of Andronicus; but I shall here terminate the series of the Greek emperors since the time of Heraclius. The branches that sprang from the Comnenian trunk had insensibly withered, and the male line was continued only in the posterity of Andronicus himself, who, in the public confusion, usurped the sovereignty of Trebizond, so obscure in history, and so famous in romance. A private citizen of Philadelphia, Constantine Angelus, had emerged to wealth and honours by his marriage with the daughter of the emperor Alexius. His son Andronicus is conspicuous only by his cowardice. His grandson Isaac punished and succeeded the tyrant; but he was dethroned by his own vices and the ambition of his brother; and their discord introduced the Latins to the conquest of Constantinople, the first great period in the fall of the Eastern empire.

If we compute the number and duration of the reigns, it will be found that a period of six hundred years is filled by sixty emperors, including in the Augustan list some female sovereigns, and deducting some usurpers who were never acknowledged in the capital, and some princes who did not live to possess their inheritance. The average proportion will allow ten years for each emperor—far below the chronological rule of Sir Isaac Newton, who, from the experience of more recent and regular monarchies, has defined about eighteen or twenty years as the term of an ordinary reign. The Byzantine empire was most tranquil and prosperous when it could acquiesce in hereditary succession: five dynasties, the Heraclian, Isaurian, Amorian, Basilian, and Comnenian families, enjoyed and transmitted the royal patrimony during their respective series of five, four, three, six, and four generations; several princes number the years of their reign with those of their infancy; and Constantine the Seventh and his two grandsons occupy the space of an entire century. But in the intervals of the Byzantine dynasties the succession is rapid and broken, and the name of a successful candidate is speedily erased by a more fortunate competitor. Many were the paths that led to the summit of royalty: the fabric of rebellion was overthrown by the stroke of conspiracy, or undermined by the silent arts of intrigue: the favourites of the soldiers or people, of the senate or clergy, of the women and eunuchs, were alternately clothed with the purple: the means of their elevation were base, and their end was often contemptible or tragic. A being of the nature of man, endowed with the same faculties, but with a longer measure of existence, would cast down a smile of pity and contempt on the crimes and follies of human ambition, so eager, in a narrow span, to grasp at a precarious and short-lived enjoyment. It is thus that the experience of history exalts and enlarges the horizon of our intellectual view. In a composition of some days, in a perusal of some hours, six hundred years have rolled away, and the duration of a life or reign is contracted to a fleeting moment: the grave is ever beside the throne; the success of a criminal is almost instantly followed by the loss of his prize; and our immortal reason survives and disdains the sixty phantoms of kings who have passed before our eyes, and faintly dwell on our remembrance. The observation, that in every age and climate ambition has prevailed with the same commanding energy, may abate the surprise of a philosopher; but while he condemns the vanity, he may search the motive of this universal desire to obtain and hold the sceptre of dominion. To the greater part of the Byzantine series we cannot reasonably ascribe the love of fame and of mankind. The virtue alone of John Comnenus was beneficent and pure: the most illustrious of the princes who precede or follow that respectable name have trod with some dexterity and vigour the crooked and bloody paths of a selfish policy: in scrutinising the imperfect characters of Leo the Isaurian, Basil the First, and Alexius Comnenus, of Theophilus, the second Basil, and Manuel Comnenus, our esteem and censure are almost equally balanced; and the remainder of the Imperial crowd could only desire and expect to be forgotten by posterity. Was personal happiness the aim and object of their ambition? I shall not descant on the vulgar topics of the misery of kings; but I may surely observe that their condition, of all others, is the most pregnant with fear, and the least susceptible of hope. For these opposite passions a larger scope was allowed in the revolutions of antiquity than in the smooth and solid temper of the modern world, which cannot easily repeat either the triumph of Alexander or the fall of Darius. But the peculiar infelicity of the Byzantine princes exposed them to domestic perils, without affording any lively promise of foreign conquest. From the pinnacle of greatness Andronicus was precipitated by a death more cruel and shameful than that of the vilest malefactor; but the most glorious of his predecessors had much more to dread from their subjects than to hope from their enemies. The army was licentious without spirit, the nation turbulent without freedom: the barbarians of the East and West pressed on the monarchy, and the loss of the provinces was terminated by the final servitude of the capital.

The entire series of Roman emperors, from the first of the Cæsars to the last of the Constantines, extends above fifteen hundred years: and the term of dominion, unbroken by foreign conquest, surpasses the measure of the ancient monarchies—the Assyrians or Medes, the successors of Cyrus, or those of Alexander.

CHAPTER XLIX

Introduction, Worship, and Persecution of Images—Revolt of Italy and Rome—Temporal Dominion of the Popes—Conquest of Italy by the Franks—Establishment of Images—Character and Coronation of Charlemagne—Restoration and Decay of the Roman Empire in the West—Independence of Italy—Constitution of the Germanic Body

In the connection of the church and state I have considered the former as subservient only, and relative, to the latter; a salutary maxim, if in fact as well as in narrative it had ever been held sacred. The oriental philosophy of the Gnostics, the dark abyss of predestination and grace, and the strange transformation of the Eucharist from the sign to the substance of Christ's body,[1]

[1] The learned Selden has given the history of transubstantiation in a comprehensive and pithy sentence: "This opinion is only rhetoric turned into logic." (His Works, vol. iii. p. 2073, in his Table-Talk.)

I have purposely abandoned to the curiosity of speculative divines. But I have reviewed with diligence and pleasure the objects of ecclesiastical history by which the decline and fall of the Roman empire were materially affected, the propagation of Christianity, the constitution of the Catholic church, the ruin of Paganism, and the sects that arose from the mysterious controversies concerning the Trinity and incarnation. At the head of this class we may justly rank the worship of images, so fiercely disputed in the eighth and ninth centuries; since a question of popular superstition produced the revolt of Italy, the temporal power of the popes, and the restoration of the Roman empire in the West.

The primitive Christians were possessed with an unconquerable repugnance to the use and abuse of images; and this aversion may be ascribed to their descent from the Jews, and their enmity to the Greeks. The Mosaic law had severely proscribed all representations of the Deity; and that precept was firmly established in the principles and practice of the chosen people. The wit of the Christian apologists was pointed against the foolish idolaters who bowed before the workmanship of their own hands; the images of brass and marble, which, had *they* been endowed with sense and motion, should have started rather from the pedestal to adore the creative powers of the artist.[1] Perhaps some recent and imperfect converts of the Gnostic tribe might crown the statues of Christ and St. Paul with the profane honours which they paid to those of Aristotle and Pythagoras;[2] but the public religion of the Catholics was uniformly simple and spiritual; and the first notice of the use of pictures is in the censure of the council of Illiberis, three hundred years after the Christian æra. Under the successors of Constantine, in the peace and luxury of the triumphant church, the more prudent bishops condescended to indulge a visible superstition for the benefit of the multitude; and after the ruin of Paganism they were no longer restrained by the apprehension of an odious parallel. The first introduction of a symbolic worship was in the veneration of the cross and of relics. The

---

[1] Nec intelligunt homines ineptissimi, quôd si sentire simulacra et moveri possent, [ultro] adoratura hominem fuissent à quo sunt expolita. (Divin. Institut. l. ii. c. 2.) Lactantius is the last, as well as the most eloquent, of the Latin apologists. Their raillery of idols attacks not only the object, but the form and matter.

[2] See Irenæus, Epiphanius, and Augustin (Basnage, Hist. des Eglises Réformées, tom. ii. p. 1313). This Gnostic practice has a singular affinity with the private worship of Alexander Severus (Lampridius, c. 29; Lardner, Heathen Testimonies, vol. iii. p. 34).

saints and martyrs, whose intercession was implored, were seated on the right hand of God; but the gracious and often super-natural favours which, in the popular belief, were showered round their tomb, conveyed an unquestionable sanction of the devout pilgrims who visited, and touched, and kissed these lifeless remains, the memorials of their merits and sufferings.[1] But a memorial more interesting than the skull or the sandals of a departed worthy is the faithful copy of his person and features, delineated by the arts of painting or sculpture. In every age such copies, so congenial to human feelings, have been cherished by the zeal of private friendship or public esteem: the images of the Roman emperors were adored with civil and almost religious honours; a reverence less ostentatious, but more sincere, was applied to the statues of sages and patriots; and these profane virtues, these splendid sins, disappeared in the presence of the holy men who had died for their celestial and everlasting country. At first the experiment was made with caution and scruple; and the venerable pictures were discreetly allowed to instruct the ignorant, to awaken the cold, and to gratify the prejudices of the heathen proselytes. By a slow though inevitable progression the honours of the original were transferred to the copy: the devout Christian prayed before the image of a saint; and the Pagan rites of genuflexion, luminaries, and incense again stole into the Catholic church. The scruples of reason or piety were silenced by the strong evidence of visions and miracles; and the pictures which speak, and move, and bleed, must be endowed with a divine energy, and may be considered as the proper objects of religious adora-tion. The most audacious pencil might tremble in the rash attempt of defining by forms and colours the infinite Spirit, the eternal Father, who pervades and sustains the universe.[2] But the superstitious mind was more easily reconciled to paint and to worship the angels, and, above all, the Son of God, under the human shape which on earth they have condescended to assume. The second person of the Trinity had been clothed with a real and mortal body; but that body had ascended into heaven:

---

[1] See this History, vol. ii. p. 229, 382; iii. p. 139, *seq.*

[2] Οὐ γὰρ τὸ Θεῖον ἁπλοῦν ὑπάρχον καὶ ἄληπτον μορφαῖς τισι καὶ σχήμασιν ἀπεικάζομεν, οὔτε κηρῷ καὶ ξύλοις τὴν ὑπερούσιον καὶ προάναρχον οὐσίαν τιμᾶν ἥμεις διεγνώκαμεν. (Concilium Nicenum, ii. in Collect. Labb. tom. viii. p. 1025, edit. Venet.) Il seroit peut-être à-propos de ne point souffrir d'images de la Trinité ou de la Divinité; les défenseurs les plus zélés des images ayant condamné celles-ci, et le concile de Trente ne parlant que des images de Jésus-Christ et des Saints (Dupin, Biblioth. Ecclés. tom. vi. p. 154).

and had not some similitude been presented to the eyes of
his disciples, the spiritual worship of Christ might have been
obliterated by the visible relics and representations of the saints.
A similar indulgence was requisite and propitious for the Virgin
Mary: the place of her burial was unknown; and the assumption of her soul and body into heaven was adopted by the
credulity of the Greeks and Latins. The use, and even the
worship, of images was firmly established before the end of the
sixth century: they were fondly cherished by the warm imagination of the Greeks and Asiatics: the Pantheon and Vatican
were adorned with the emblems of a new superstition; but this
semblance of idolatry was more coldly entertained by the rude
barbarians and the Arian clergy of the West. The bolder forms
of sculpture, in brass or marble, which peopled the temples of
antiquity, were offensive to the fancy or conscience of the
Christian Greeks; and a smooth surface of colours has ever been
esteemed a more descent and harmless mode of imitation.[1]

The merit and effect of a copy depends on its resemblance
with the original; but the primitive Christians were ignorant of
the genuine features of the Son of God, his mother, and his
apostles: the statue of Christ at Paneas, in Palestine,[2] was
more probably that of some temporal saviour; the Gnostics
and their profane monuments were reprobated, and the fancy
of the Christian artists could only be guided by the clandestine
imitation of some heathen model. In this distress a bold and
dexterous invention assured at once the likeness of the image
and the innocence of the worship. A new superstructure of
fable was raised on the popular basis of a Syrian legend on the
correspondence of Christ and Abgarus, so famous in the days
of Eusebius, so reluctantly deserted by our modern advocates.

[1] This general history of images is drawn from the twenty-second book
of the Hist. des Eglises Réformées of Basnage, tom. ii. p. 1310-1337. He
was a Protestant, but of a manly spirit; and on this head the Protestants
are so notoriously in the right, that they can venture to be impartial.
See the perplexity of poor Friar Pagi, Critica, tom. i. p. 42.

[2] After removing some rubbish of miracle and inconsistency, it may be
allowed that, as late as the year 300, Paneas in Palestine was decorated
with a bronze statue, representing a grave personage wrapped in a cloak,
with a grateful or suppliant female kneeling before him, and that an in-
scription—$\tau\hat{\wp}$ $\Sigma\hat{\omega}\tau\eta\rho\iota$, $\tau\hat{\wp}$ $\epsilon\hat{\upsilon}\epsilon\rho\gamma\acute{\epsilon}\tau\eta$—was perhaps inscribed on the pedestal.
By the Christians this group was foolishly explained of their founder and
the *poor* woman whom he had cured of the bloody flux (Euseb. vii. 18;
Philostorg. vii. 3, etc.). M. de Beausobre more reasonably conjectures
the philosopher Apollonius, or the emperor Vespasian; in the latter supposition the female is a city, a province, or perhaps the queen Berenice
(Bibliothèque Germanique, tom. xiii. p. 1-92).

The bishop of Cæsarea [1] records the epistle,[2] but he most strangely forgets the picture of Christ [3]—the perfect impression of his face on a linen, with which he gratified the faith of the royal stranger who had invoked his healing power, and offered the strong city of Edessa to protect him against the malice of the Jews. The ignorance of the primitive church is explained by the long imprisonment of the image in a niche of the wall, from whence, after an oblivion of five hundred years, it was released by some prudent bishop, and seasonably presented to the devotion of the times. Its first and most glorious exploit was the deliverance of the city from the arms of Chosroes Nushirvan; and it was soon revered as a pledge of the divine promise that Edessa should never be taken by a foreign enemy. It is true, indeed, that the text of Procopius ascribes the double deliverance of Edessa to the wealth and valour of her citizens, who purchased the absence and repelled the assaults of the Persian monarch. He was ignorant, the profane historian, of the testimony which he is compelled to deliver in the ecclesiastical page of Evagrius, that the Palladium was exposed on the rampart, and that the water which had been sprinkled on the holy face, instead of quenching, added new fuel to the flames of the besieged. After this important service the image of Edessa was preserved with respect and gratitude; and if the Armenians rejected the legend, the more credulous Greeks adored the similitude, which was not the work of any mortal pencil, but the immediate creation of the divine original. The

[1] Euseb. Hist. Ecclés. l. i. c. 13. The learned Assemannus has brought up the collateral aid of three Syrians, St. Ephrem, Josua Stylites, and James bishop of Sarug; but I do not find any notice of the Syriac original or the archives of Edessa (Biblioth. Orient. tom. i. p. 318, 420, 554); their vague belief is probably derived from the Greeks.

[2] The evidence for these epistles is stated and rejected by the candid Lardner (Heathen Testimonies, vol. i. p. 297-309). Among the herd of bigots who are forcibly driven from this convenient but untenable post, I am ashamed—with the Grabes, Caves, Tillemonts, etc., to discover Mr. Addison, an English gentleman (his Works, vol. i. p. 528, Baskerville's edition); but his superficial tract on the Christian religion owes its credit to his name, his style, and the interested applause of our clergy.

[3] From the silence of James of Sarug (Asseman. Biblioth. Orient. p. 289, 318), and the testimony of Evagrius (Hist. Ecclés. l. iv. c. 27), I conclude that this fable was invented between the years 521 and 594, most probably after the siege of Edessa in 540 (Asseman. tom. i. p. 416; Procopius, de Bell. Persic. l. ii. [c. 12, tom. i. p. 208 *sq.*, ed. Bonn]). It is the sword and buckler of Gregory II. (in Epist. i. ad Leon. Isaur. Concil. tom. viii. p. 656, 657), of John Damascenus (Opera, tom. i. p. 281, edit. Lequien [De Fide Orthod. l. iv. c. 16]), and of the second Nicene Council (Actio v. p. 1030). The most perfect edition may be found in Cedrenus (Compend. p. 175-178 [ed. Par.; tom. i. p. 308-314, ed. Bonn]).

style and sentiments of a Byzantine hymn will declare how far their worship was removed from the grossest idolatry. " How can we with mortal eyes contemplate this image, whose celestial splendour the host of heaven presumes not to behold? HE who dwells in heaven condescends this day to visit us by his venerable image; HE who is seated on the cherubim visits us this day by a picture, which the Father has delineated with his immaculate hand, which he has formed in an ineffable manner, and which we sanctify by adoring it with fear and love." Before the end of the sixth century these images, *made without hands* (in Greek it is a single word [1]), were propagated in the camps and cities of the Eastern empire; [2] they were the objects of worship, and the instruments of miracles; and in the hour of danger or tumult their venerable presence could revive the hope, rekindle the courage, or repress the fury of the Roman legions. Of these pictures the far greater part, the transcripts of a human pencil, could only pretend to a secondary likeness and improper title; but there were some of higher descent, who derived their resemblance from an immediate contact with the original, endowed for that purpose with a miraculous and prolific virtue. The most ambitious aspired from a filial to a fraternal relation with the image of Edessa; and such is the *veronica* of Rome, or Spain, or Jerusalem, which Christ in his agony and bloody sweat applied to his face, and delivered to a holy matron. The fruitful precedent was speedily transferred to the Virgin Mary, and the saints and martyrs. In the church of Diospolis, in Palestine, the features of the Mother of God [3] were deeply inscribed in a marble column: the East and West have been decorated by the pencil of St. Luke; and the Evangelist, who was perhaps a physician, has been forced to exercise the occupation of a painter,

[1] Ἀχειροποίητος. See Ducange, in Gloss. Græ. et Lat. The subject is treated with equal learning and bigotry by the Jesuit Gretser (Syntagma de Imaginibus non Manû factis, ad calcem Codini de Officiis, p. 289-330), the ass, or rather the fox, of Ingoldstadt (see the Scaligerana); with equal reason and wit by the Protestant Beausobre, in the ironical controversy which he has spread through many volumes of the Bibliothèque Germanique (tom. xviii. p. 1-50; xx. p. 27-68; xxv. p. 1-36; xxvii. p. 85-118; xxviii. p. 1-33; xxxi. p. 111-148; xxxii. p. 75-107; xxxiv. p. 67-96).

[2] Theophylact. Simocatta (l. ii. c. 3, p. 34 [ed. Par.; p. 70, ed. Bonn]; l. iii. c. 1, p. 63 [p. 114, ed Bonn]) celebrates the θεανδρικὸν εἰκασμα, which he styles ἀχειροποίητον; yet it was no more than a copy, since he adds, ἀρχέτυπον γὰρ ἐκεῖνο (of Edessa) θρησκεύουσι 'Ρωμαιοί τι ἀῤῥητον. See Pagi, tom. ii. A.D. 586, No. 11.

[3] See, in the genuine or supposed works of John Damascenus, two passages on the Virgin and St. Luke, which have not been noticed by Gretser, nor consequently by Beausobre (Opera Joh. Damascen. tom. i. p. 618, 631 (Adv. Constantinum Cabal. c. 6; Epist. ad Theophilum Imp. c. 4]).

so profane and odious in the eyes of the primitive Christians. The Olympian Jove, created by the muse of Homer and the chisel of Phidias, might inspire a philosophic mind with momentary devotion; but these Catholic images were faintly and flatly delineated by monkish artists in the last degeneracy of taste and genius.[1]

The worship of images had stolen into the church by insensible degrees, and each petty step was pleasing to the superstitious mind, as productive of comfort and innocent of sin. But in the beginning of the eighth century, in the full magnitude of the abuse, the more timorous Greeks were awakened by an apprehension that, under the mask of Christianity, they had restored the religion of their fathers: they heard, with grief and impatience, the name of idolaters—the incessant charge of the Jews and Mohammedans,[2] who derived from the Law and the Koran an immortal hatred to graven images and all relative worship. The servitude of the Jews might curb their zeal and depreciate their authority; but the triumphant Musulmans, who reigned at Damascus, and threatened Constantinople, cast into the scale of reproach the accumulated weight of truth and victory. The cities of Syria, Palestine, and Egypt had been fortified with the images of Christ, his mother, and his saints; and each city presumed on the hope or promise of miraculous defence. In a rapid conquest of ten years the Arabs subdued those cities and these images; and, in their opinion, the Lord of Hosts pronounced a decisive judgment between the adoration and contempt of these mute and inanimate idols.[3] For a while Edessa had braved the Persian assaults; but the chosen city, the spouse of Christ, was involved in the common ruin; and his divine resemblance became the slave and trophy of the infidels. After a servitude of three hundred years, the Palladium was yielded to the devotion of Constantinople, for a ransom of twelve thousand pounds of silver, the redemption of two hundred

---

[1] " Your scandalous figures stand quite out from the canvas: they are as bad as a group of statues! " It was thus that the ignorance and bigotry of a Greek priest applauded the pictures of Titian, which he had ordered, and refused to accept.

[2] By Cedrenus, Zonaras, Glycas, and Manasses, the origin of the Iconoclasts is imputed to the caliph Yezid and two Jews, who promised the empire to Leo; and the reproaches of these hostile sectaries are turned into an absurd conspiracy for restoring the purity of the Christian worship (see Spanheim, Hist. Imag. c. 2).

[3] [Yezid, ninth caliph of the race of the Ommiadæ, caused all the images in Syria to be destroyed about the year 720; hence the orthodox reproached the sectarians with following the example of the Saracens and the Jews.— O. S.]

Musulmans, and a perpetual truce for the territory of Edessa.[1]
In this season of distress and dismay the eloquence of the monks
was exercised in the defence of images; and they attempted to
prove that the sin and schism of the greatest part of the Orientals
had forfeited the favour and annihilated the virtue of these
precious symbols. But they were now opposed by the murmurs
of many simple or rational Christians, who appealed to the
evidence of texts, of facts, and of the primitive times, and
secretly desired the reformation of the church. As the worship
of images had never been established by any general or positive
law, its progress in the Eastern empire had been retarded, or
accelerated, by the differences of men and manners, the local
degrees of refinement, and the personal characters of the bishops.
The splendid devotion was fondly cherished by the levity of the
capital and the inventive genius of the Byzantine clergy; while
the rude and remote districts of Asia were strangers to this
innovation of sacred luxury. Many large congregations of
Gnostics and Arians maintained, after their conversion, the
simple worship which had preceded their separation; and the
Armenians, the most warlike subjects of Rome, were not
reconciled, in the twelfth century, to the sight of images.[2]
These various denominations of men afforded a fund of prejudice
and aversion, of small account in the villages of Anatolia or
Thrace, but which, in the fortune of a soldier, a prelate, or a
eunuch, might be often connected with the powers of the church
and state.

Of such adventurers the most fortunate was the emperor Leo
the Third,[3] who, from the mountains of Isauria, ascended the

[1] See Elmacin (Hist. Saracen. p. 267), Abulpharagius (Dynast. p. 201),
and Abulfeda (Annal. Moslem. p. 264), and the criticisms of Pagi (tom. iii.
A.D. 944). The prudent Franciscan refuses to determine whether the image
of Edessa now reposes at Rome or Genoa; but its repose is inglorious, and
this ancient object of worship is no longer famous or fashionable.

[2] Ἀρμενίοις καὶ Ἀλαμανοῖς ἐπ' ἴσης ἡ τῶν ἁγίων εἰκόνων προσκύνησις ἀπηγό-
ρευται (Nicetas, l. ii. p. 258 [ed. Par.; p. 527, ed. Bonn]). The Armenian
churches are still content with the Cross (Missions du Levant, tom. iii. p.
148); but surely the superstitious Greek is unjust to the superstition of the
Germans of the twelfth century.

[3] Our original but not impartial monuments of the Iconoclasts must be
drawn from the Acts of the Councils, tom. viii. and ix. Collect. Labbé,
edit. Venet., and the historical writings of Theophanes, Nicephorus,
Manasses, Cedrenus, Zonaras, etc. Of the modern Catholics, Baronius,
Pagi, Natalis Alexander (Hist. Eccles. Seculum viii. and ix.), and Maimbourg (Hist. des Iconoclastes), have treated the subject with learning,
passion, and credulity. The Protestant labours of Frederick Spanheim
(Historia Imaginum restituta) and James Basnage (Hist des Eglises Réformées, tom. ii. l. xxiii. p. 1339-1385) are cast into the Iconoclast scale.
With this mutual aid and opposite tendency it is easy for *us* to poise the
balance with philosophic indifference.

throne of the East. He was ignorant of sacred and profane letters; but his education, his reason, perhaps his intercourse with the Jews and Arabs, had inspired the martial peasant with a hatred of images; and it was held to be the duty of a prince to impose on his subjects the dictates of his own conscience. But in the outset of an unsettled reign, during ten years of toil and danger, Leo submitted to the meanness of hypocrisy, bowed before the idols which he despised, and satisfied the Roman pontiff with the annual professions of his orthodoxy and zeal. In the reformation of religion his first steps were moderate and cautious: he assembled a great council of senators and bishops, and enacted, with their consent, that all the images should be removed from the sanctuary and altar to a proper height in the churches, where they might be visible to the eyes, and inaccessible to the superstition, of the people. But it was impossible on either side to check the rapid though adverse impulse of veneration and abhorrence: in their lofty position the sacred images still edified their votaries and reproached the tyrant. He was himself provoked by resistance and invective; and his own party accused him of an imperfect discharge of his duty, and urged for his imitation the example of the Jewish king, who had broken without scruple the brazen serpent of the temple. By a second edict he proscribed the existence as well as the use of religious pictures; the churches of Constantinople and the provinces were cleansed from idolatry; the images of Christ, the Virgin, and the saints were demolished, or a smooth surface of plaster was spread over the walls of the edifice. The sect of the Iconoclasts was supported by the zeal and despotism of six emperors, and the East and West were involved in a noisy conflict of one hundred and twenty years. It was the design of Leo the Isaurian to pronounce the condemnation of images as an article of faith, and by the authority of a general council: but the convocation of such an assembly was reserved for his son Constantine;[1] and though it is stigmatised by triumphant bigotry as a meeting of fools and atheists, their own partial and mutilated acts betray many symptoms of reason and piety. The debates and decrees of many provincial synods introduced

---

[1] Some flowers of rhetoric are Σύνοδον παράνομον καὶ ἄθεον, and the bishops τοῖς ματαιόφροσιν. By Damascenus it is styled ἄκυρος καὶ ἄδεκτος (Opera, tom. i. p. 623 [Adv. Constant. Cabal. c. 16]). Spanheim's Apology for the Synod of Constantinople (p. 171, etc.) is worked up with truth and ingenuity from such materials as he could find in the Nicene Acts (p. 1046, etc.). The witty John of Damascus converts ἐπισκόπους into ἐπισκότους; makes them κοιλιοδούλους, slaves of their belly, etc. Opera, tom. i. p. 306.

the summons of the general council which met in the suburbs of Constantinople, and was composed of the respectable number of three hundred and thirty-eight bishops of Europe and Anatolia; for the patriarchs of Antioch and Alexandria were the slaves of the caliph, and the Roman pontiff had withdrawn the churches of Italy and the West from the communion of the Greeks. This Byzantine synod assumed the rank and powers of the seventh general council; yet even this title was a recognition of the six preceding assemblies, which had laboriously built the structure of the Catholic faith. After a serious deliberation of six months, the three hundred and thirty-eight bishops pronounced and subscribed a unanimous decree, that all visible symbols of Christ, except in the Eucharist, were either blasphemous or heretical; that image-worship was a corruption of Christianity and a renewal of Paganism; that all such monuments of idolatry should be broken or erased; and that those who should refuse to deliver the objects of their private superstition were guilty of disobedience to the authority of the church and of the emperor. In their loud and loyal acclamations they celebrated the merits of their temporal redeemer; and to his zeal and justice they intrusted the execution of their spiritual censures. At Constantinople, as in the former councils, the will of the prince was the rule of episcopal faith; but on this occasion I am inclined to suspect that a large majority of the prelates sacrificed their secret conscience to the temptations of hope and fear. In the long night of superstition the Christians had wandered far away from the simplicity of the Gospel: nor was it easy for them to discern the clue, and tread back the mazes of the labyrinth. The worship of images was inseparably blended, at least to a pious fancy, with the Cross, the Virgin, the saints and their relics; the holy ground was involved in a cloud of miracles and visions; and the nerves of the mind, curiosity and scepticism, were benumbed by the habits of obedience and belief. Constantine himself is accused of indulging a royal licence to doubt, or deny, or deride the mysteries of the Catholics,[1] but they were deeply inscribed in the public and private creed of his bishops; and the boldest Iconoclast might assault with a secret horror the monuments of popular devotion, which were consecrated to the honour of his celestial patrons.

[1] He is accused of proscribing the title of saint; styling the Virgin, Mother of *Christ*; comparing her after her delivery to an empty purse; of Arianism, Nestorianism, etc. In his defence, Spanheim (c. iv. p. 207) is somewhat embarrassed between the interest of a Protestant and the duty of an orthodox divine.

In the reformation of the sixteenth century freedom and knowledge had expanded all the faculties of man: the thirst of innovation superseded the reverence of antiquity; and the vigour of Europe could disdain those phantoms which terrified the sickly and servile weakness of the Greeks.

The scandal of an abstract heresy can be only proclaimed to the people by the blast of the ecclesiastical trumpet; but the most ignorant can perceive, the most torpid must feel, the profanation and downfall of their visible deities. The first hostilities of Leo were directed against a lofty Christ on the vestibule, and above the gate, of the palace. A ladder had been planted for the assault, but it was furiously shaken by a crowd of zealots and women: they beheld, with pious transport, the ministers of sacrilege tumbling from on high and dashed against the pavement; and the honours of the ancient martyrs were prostituted to these criminals, who justly suffered for murder and rebellion.[1] The execution of the Imperial edicts was resisted by frequent tumults in Constantinople and the provinces: the person of Leo was endangered, his officers were massacred, and the popular enthusiasm was quelled by the strongest efforts of the civil and military power. Of the Archipelago, or Holy Sea, the numerous islands were filled with images and monks: their votaries abjured, without scruple, the enemy of Christ, his mother, and the saints; they armed a fleet of boats and galleys, displayed their consecrated banners, and boldly steered for the harbour of Constantinople, to place on the throne a new favourite of God and the people. They depended on the succour of a miracle: but their miracles were inefficient against the *Greek fire ;* and, after the defeat and conflagration of their fleet, the naked islands were abandoned to the clemency or justice of the conqueror. The son of Leo, in the first year of his reign, had undertaken an expedition against the Saracens: during his absence the capital, the palace, and the purple were occupied by his kinsman Artavasdes, the ambitious champion of the orthodox faith. The worship of images was triumphantly restored: the patriarch renounced his dissimulation, or dissembled his sentiments; and the righteous claim of the usurper was acknowledged, both in the new and in ancient Rome. Constantine flew for refuge to his paternal

---

[1] The holy confessor Theophanes approves the principle of their rebellion, θείῳ κινούμενοι ζήλῳ (p. 339). Gregory II. (in Epist. i. ad Imp. Leon. Concil. tom. viii. p. 661, 664) applauds the zeal of the Byzantine women who killed the Imperial officers.

mountains; but he descended at the head of the bold and affectionate Isaurians; and his final victory confounded the arms and predictions of the fanatics. His long reign was distracted with clamour, sedition, conspiracy, and mutual hatred and sanguinary revenge: the persecution of images was the motive or pretence of his adversaries; and, if they missed a temporal diadem, they were rewarded by the Greeks with the crown of martyrdom. In every act of open and clandestine treason the emperor felt the unforgiving enmity of the monks, the faithful slaves of the superstition to which they owed their riches and influence. They prayed, they preached, they absolved, they inflamed, they conspired; the solitude of Palestine poured forth a torrent of invective; and the pen of St. John Damascenus,[1] the last of the Greek fathers, devoted the tyrant's head, both in this world and the next.[2] I am not at leisure to examine how far the monks provoked, nor how much they have exaggerated, their real and pretended sufferings, nor how many lost their lives or limbs, their eyes or their beards, by the cruelty of the emperor. From the chastisement of individuals he proceeded to the abolition of the order; and, as it was wealthy and useless, his resentment might be stimulated by avarice, and justified by patriotism. The formidable name and mission of the *Dragon*,[3] his visitor-general, excited the terror and abhorrence of the *black* nation: the religious communities were dissolved, the buildings were converted into magazines or barracks; the lands, movables, and cattle were confiscated; and our modern precedents will support the charge, that much wanton

---

[1] John, or Mansur, was a noble Christian of Damascus, who held a considerable office in the service of the caliph. His zeal in the cause of images exposed him to the resentment and treachery of the Greek emperor; and, on the suspicion of a treasonable correspondence, he was deprived of his right hand, which was miraculously restored by the Virgin. After this deliverance he resigned his office, distributed his wealth, and buried himself in the monastery of St. Sabas, between Jerusalem and the Dead Sea. The legend is famous; but his learned editor, Father Lequien, has unluckily proved that St. John Damascenus was already a monk before the Iconoclast dispute (Opera, tom. i. Vit. St. Joan. Damascen. p. 10-13, et Notas ad loc.).

[2] After sending Leo to the devil, he introduces his heir—τὸ μιαρὸν αὐτοῦ γέννημα, καὶ τῆς κακίας αὐτοῦ κληρονόμος ἐν διπλῷ γενόμενος (Opera Damascen. tom. i. p. 625 [Adv. Constant. Cabal. c. 20]). If the authenticity of this piece be suspicious, we are sure that in other works, no longer extant, Damascenus bestowed on Constantine the titles of νέον Μωαμέθ, Χριστομάχον, μισάγιον (tom. i. p. 306).

[3] In the narrative of this persecution from Theophanes and Cedrenus, Spanheim (p. 235-238) is happy to compare the *Draco* of Leo with the dragoons (*Dracones*) of Louis XIV., and highly solaces himself with this controversial pun.

or malicious havoc was exercised against the relics, and even the books, of the monasteries. With the habit and profession of monks, the public and private worship of images was rigorously proscribed; and it should seem that a solemn abjuration of idolatry was exacted from the subjects, or at least from the clergy, of the Eastern empire.[1]

The patient East abjured with reluctance her sacred images; they were fondly cherished, and vigorously defended, by the independent zeal of the Italians. In ecclesiastical rank and jurisdiction the patriarch of Constantinople and the pope of Rome were nearly equal. But the Greek prelate was a domestic slave under the eye of his master, at whose nod he alternately passed from the convent to the throne, and from the throne to the convent. A distant and dangerous station, amidst the barbarians of the West, excited the spirit and freedom of the Latin bishops. Their popular election endeared them to the Romans: the public and private indigence was relieved by their ample revenue; and the weakness or neglect of the emperors compelled them to consult, both in peace and war, the temporal safety of the city. In the school of adversity the priest insensibly imbibed the virtues and the ambition of a prince; the same character was assumed, the same policy was adopted, by the Italian, the Greek, or the Syrian, who ascended the chair of St. Peter; and, after the loss of her legions and provinces, the genius and fortune of the popes again restored the supremacy of Rome. It is agreed that in the eighth century their dominion was founded on rebellion, and that the rebellion was produced, and justified, by the heresy of the Iconoclasts; but the conduct of the second and third Gregory, in this memorable contest, is variously interpreted in the wishes of their friends and enemies. The Byzantine writers unanimously declare that, after a fruitless admonition, they pronounced the separation of the East and West, and deprived the sacrilegious tyrant of the revenue and sovereignty of Italy. Their excommunication is still more clearly expressed by the Greeks, who beheld the accomplishment of the papal triumphs; and as they are more strongly attached to their religion than to their country, they praise, instead of blaming, the zeal and orthodoxy of these apostolical

---

[1] Πρόγραμμα γὰρ ἐξεπέμψε κατὰ πᾶσαν ἐξαρχίαν τὴν ὑπὸ τῆς χειρὸς αὐτοῦ, πάντας ὑπογράψαι καὶ ὀμνύναι· τοῦ ἀθετῆσαι τὴν προσκύνησιν τῶν σεπτῶν εἰκόνων (Damascen. Op. tom. i. p. 625 [Adv. Constant. Cabal. c. 21]). This oath and subscription I do not remember to have seen in any modern compilation.

men.[1] The modern champions of Rome are eager to accept the praise and the precedent: this great and glorious example of the deposition of royal heretics is celebrated by the cardinals Baronius and Bellarmine; [2] and if they are asked why the same thunders were not hurled against the Neros and Julians of antiquity? they reply, that the weakness of the primitive church was the sole cause of her patient loyalty.[3] On this occasion the effects of love and hatred are the same; and the zealous Protestants, who seek to kindle the indignation and to alarm the fears of princes and magistrates, expatiate on the insolence and treason of the two Gregories against their lawful sovereign.[4] They are defended only by the moderate Catholics, for the most part of the Gallican church,[5] who respect the saint without approving the sin. These common advocates of the crown and the mitre circumscribe the truth of facts by the rule of equity, Scripture, and tradition, and appeal to the evidence of the Latins,[6] and the lives[7] and epistles of the popes themselves.

[1] Καὶ τὴν Ῥώμην σὺν πάσῃ [τῇ] Ἰταλίᾳ τῆς βασιλείας αὐτοῦ ἀπέστησε, says Theophanes (Chronograph. p. 343 [tom. i. p. 630, ed. Bonn]). For this Gregory is styled by Cedrenus ἀνὴρ ἀποστολικός (p. 450). Zonaras specifies the thunder, ἀναθέματι συνοδικῷ (tom. ii. l. xv. [c. 4] p. 104, 105). It may be observed that the Greeks are apt to confound the times and actions of two Gregories.

[2] See Baronius, Annal. Eccles. A.D. 730, No. 4, 5: dignum exemplum! Bellarmin. de Romano Pontifice, l. v. c. 8: mulctavit eum parte imperii. Sigonius, de Regno Italiæ, l. iii. Opera, tom. ii. p. 169. Yet such is the change of Italy, that Sigonius is corrected by the editor of Milan, Philippus Argelatus, a Bolognese, and subject of the pope.

[3] Quod si Christiani olim non deposuerunt Neronem aut Julianum, id fuit quia deerant vires temporales Christianis (honest Bellarmine, de Rom. Pont. l. v. c. 7). Cardinal Perron adds a distinction more honourable to the first Christians, but not more satisfactory to modern princes—the treason of heretics and apostates, who break their oath, belie their coin, and renounce their allegiance to Christ and his vicar (Perroniana, p. 89).

[4] Take, as a specimen, the cautious Basnage (Hist. de l'Eglise, p. 1350, 1351) and the vehement Spanheim (Hist. Imaginum), who, with a hundred more, tread in the footsteps of the centuriators of Magdeburg.

[5] See Launoy (Opera, tom. v. pars ii. Epist. vii. 7, p. 456-474), Natalis Alexander (Hist. Nov. Testamenti, secul. viii. dissert. i. p. 92-96), Pagi (Critica, tom. iii. p. 215, 216), and Giannone (Istoria Civile di Napoli, tom. i. p. 317-320), a disciple of the Gallican school. In the field of controversy I always pity the moderate party, who stand on the open middle ground exposed to the fire of both sides.

[6] They appeal to Paul Warnefrid, or Diaconus (de Gestis Langobard. l. vi. c. 49, p. 506, 507, in Script. Ital. Muratori, tom. i. pars i.), and the nominal Anastasius (de Vit. Pont. in Muratori, tom. iii. pars. i.; Gregorius II., p. 154; Gregorius III., p. 158; Zacharias, p. 161; Stephanus III., p. 165; Paulus, p. 172; Stephanus IV., p. 174; Hadrianus, p. 179; Leo III., p. 195). Yet I may remark that the true Anastasius (Hist. Eccles. p. 134, edit. Reg.) and the Historia Miscella (l. xxi. p. 151, in tom. i. Script. Ital.), both of the ninth century, translate and approve the Greek text of Theophanes.

[7] With some minute difference, the most learned critics, Lucas Holstenius,

Two original epistles, from Gregory the Second to the emperor Leo, are still extant;[1] and if they cannot be praised as the most perfect models of eloquence and logic, they exhibit the portrait, or at least the mask, of the founder of the papal monarchy. " During ten pure and fortunate years," says Gregory to the emperor, " we have tasted the annual comfort of your royal letters, subscribed in purple ink with your own hand, the sacred pledges of your attachment to the orthodox creed of our fathers. How deplorable is the change! how tremendous the scandal! You now accuse the Catholics of idolatry; and, by the accusation, you betray your own impiety and ignorance. To this ignorance we áre compelled to adapt the grossness of our style and arguments: the first elements of holy letters are sufficient for your confusion; and were you to enter a grammar-school, and avow yourself the enemy of our worship, the simple and pious children would be provoked to cast their horn-books at your head." After this decent saluta-tion the pope attempts the usual distinction between the idols of antiquity and the Christian images. The former were the fanciful representations of phantoms or demons, at a time when the true God had not manifested his person in any visible like-ness. The latter are the genuine forms of Christ, his mother, and his saints, who had approved, by a crowd of miracles, the innocence and merit of this relative worship. He must indeed have trusted to the ignorance of Leo, since he could assert the perpetual use of images from the apostolic age, and their venerable presence in the six synods of the Catholic church. A more specious argument is drawn from present possession and recent practice: the harmony of the Christian world supersedes the demand of a general council; and Gregory frankly confesses that such assemblies can only be useful under the reign of an orthodox prince. To the impudent and inhuman Leo, more guilty than a heretic, he recommends peace, silence, and implicit

Schelestrate, Ciampini, Bianchini, Muratori (Prolegomena ad tom. iii. pars. i.), are agreed that the Liber Pontificalis was composed and continued by the apostolical librarians and notaries of the eighth and ninth centuries, and that the last and smallest part is the work of Anastasius, whose name it bears. The style is barbarous, the narrative partial, the details are trifling; yet it must be read as a curious and authentic record of the times. The epistles of the popes are dispersed in the volumes of Councils.
[1] The two epistles of Gregory II. have been preserved in the Acts of the Nicene Council (tom. viii. p. 651-674). They are without a date, which is variously fixed—by Baronius in the year 726, by Muratori (Annali d'Italia, tom. vi. p. 120) in 729, and by Pagi in 730. Such is the force of prejudice, that some *papists* have praised the good sense and moderation of these letters.

obedience to his spiritual guides of Constantinople and Rome. The limits of civil and ecclesiastical powers are defined by the pontiff. To the former he appropriates the body; to the latter the soul: the sword of justice is in the hands of the magistrate: the more formidable weapon of excommunication is intrusted to the clergy; and in the exercise of their divine commission a zealous son will not spare his offending father: the successor of St. Peter may lawfully chastise the kings of the earth. "You assault us, O tyrant! with a carnal and military hand: unarmed and naked we can only implore the Christ, the prince of the heavenly host, that he will send unto you a devil for the destruction of your body and the salvation of your soul. You declare, with foolish arrogance, I will despatch my orders to Rome: I will break in pieces the image of St. Peter; and Gregory, like his predecessor Martin, shall be transported in chains and in exile to the foot of the imperial throne. Would to God that I might be permitted to tread in the footsteps of the holy Martin! but may the fate of Constans serve as a warning to the persecutors of the church! After his just condemnation by the bishops of Sicily, the tyrant was cut off in the fulness of his sins, by a domestic servant: the saint is still adored by the nations of Scythia, among whom he ended his banishment and his life. But it is our duty to live for the edification and support of the faithful people; nor are we reduced to risk our safety on the event of a combat. Incapable as you are of defending your Roman subjects, the maritime situation of the city may perhaps expose it to your depredation; but we can remove to the distance of four-and-twenty *stadia*,[1] to the first fortress of the Lombards, and then——you may pursue the winds. Are you ignorant that the popes are the bond of union, the mediators of peace between the East and West? The eyes of the nations are fixed on our humility; and they revere, as a God upon earth, the apostle St. Peter, whose image you threaten to destroy.[2] The remote and interior kingdoms of the West present their homage to Christ and his vicegerent; and we now

---

[1] Εἴκοσι τέσσαρα στάδια ὑποχωρήσει ὁ Ἀρχιερεὺς Ῥώμης εἰς τὴν χώραν Καμπανίας, καὶ ὕπαγε δίωξον τοὺς ἀνέμους (Epist. i. p. 664). This proximity of the Lombards is hard of digestion. Camillo Pellegrini (Dissert. iv. de Ducatû Beneventi, in the Script. Ital. tom. v. p. 172, 173) forcibly reckons the twenty-fourth stadia, not from Rome, but from the limits of the Roman duchy, to the first fortress, perhaps Sora, of the Lombards. I rather believe that Gregory, with the pedantry of the age, employs *stadia* for miles, without much inquiry into the genuine measure.

[2] Ὃν αἱ πᾶσαι βασιλεῖαι τῆς δύσεως ὡς Θεὸν ἐπίγειον ἔχουσι.

prepare to visit one of their most powerful monarchs who desires to receive from our hands the sacrament of baptism.[1] The barbarians have submitted to the yoke of the Gospel, while you alone are deaf to the voice of the shepherd. These pious barbarians are kindled into rage: they thirst to avenge the persecution of the East. Abandon your rash and fatal enterprise; reflect, tremble, and repent. If you persist, we are innocent of the blood that will be spilt in the contest; may it fall on your own head! "

The first assault of Leo against the images of Constantinople had been witnessed by a crowd of strangers from Italy and the West, who related with grief and indignation the sacrilege of the emperor. But on the reception of his proscriptive edict they trembled for their domestic deities; the images of Christ and the Virgin, of the angels, martyrs, and saints, were abolished in all the churches of Italy; and a strong alternative was proposed to the Roman pontiff, the royal favour as the price of his compliance, degradation and exile as the penalty of his disobedience. Neither zeal nor policy allowed him to hesitate; and the haughty strain in which Gregory addressed the emperor displays his confidence in the truth of his doctrine or the powers of resistance. Without depending on prayers or miracles, he boldly armed against the public enemy, and his pastoral letters admonished the Italians of their danger and their duty.[2] At this signal, Ravenna, Venice, and the cities of the Exarchate and Pentapolis adhered to the cause of religion; their military force by sea and land consisted, for the most part, of the natives; and the spirit of patriotism and zeal was transfused into the mercenary strangers. The Italians swore to live and die in the defence of the pope and the holy images; the Roman people was devoted to their father, and even the Lombards were ambitious

---

[1] Ἀπὸ τῆς ἐσωτέρου δύσεως τοῦ λεγομένου Σεπτετοῦ (p. 665). The Pope appears to have imposed on the ignorance of the Greeks: he lived and died in the Lateran, and in his time all the kingdoms of the West had embraced Christianity. May not this unknown *Septetus* have some reference to the chief of the Saxon *Heptarchy*, to Ina king of Wessex, who, in the pontificate of Gregory the Second, visited Rome for the purpose, not of baptism, but of pilgrimage (Pagi, A.D. 689, No. 2; A.D. 726, No. 15)?

[2] I shall transcribe the important and decisive passage of the Liber Pontificalis. Respiciens ergo pius vir profanam principis jussionem, jam contra Imperatorem quasi contra *hostem* se armavit, renuens hæresim ejus, scribens ubique se cavere Christianos, eo quod orta fuisset impietas talis. *Igitur* permoti omnes Pentapolenses, atque Venetiarum exercitus contra Imperatoris jussionem restiterunt: dicentes se nunquam in ejusdem pontificis condescendere necem, sed pro ejus magis defensione viriliter decertare (p. 156).

to share the merit and advantage of this holy war. The most treasonable act, but the most obvious revenge, was the destruction of the statues of Leo himself: the most effectual and pleasing measure of rebellion was the withholding the tribute of Italy, and depriving him of a power which he had recently abused by the imposition of a new capitation.[1] A form of administration was preserved by the election of magistrates and governors; and so high was the public indignation, that the Italians were prepared to create an orthodox emperor, and to conduct him with a fleet and army to the palace of Constantinople. In that palace the Roman bishops, the second and third Gregory, were condemned as the authors of the revolt, and every attempt was made, either by fraud or force, to seize their persons and to strike at their lives. The city was repeatedly visited or assaulted by captains of the guards, and dukes and exarchs of high dignity or secret trust; they landed with foreign troops, they obtained some domestic aid, and the superstition of Naples may blush that her fathers were attached to the cause of heresy. But these clandestine or open attacks were repelled by the courage and vigilance of the Romans; the Greeks were overthrown and massacred, their leaders suffered an ignominious death, and the popes, however inclined to mercy, refused to intercede for these guilty victims. At Ravenna,[2] the several quarters of the city had long exercised a bloody and hereditary feud; in religious controversy they found a new aliment of faction: but the votaries of images were superior in numbers or spirit, and the exarch, who attempted to stem the torrent, lost his life in a popular sedition. To punish this flagitious deed, and restore his dominion in Italy, the emperor sent a fleet and army into the Hadriatic gulf. After suffering from the winds and waves much loss and delay, the Greeks made their descent in the neighbourhood of Ravenna: they threatened to depopulate the guilty capital, and to imitate, perhaps to surpass,

---

[1] A *census*, or capitation, says Anastasius (p. 156): a most cruel tax, unknown to the Saracens themselves, exclaims the zealous Maimbourg (Hist. des Iconoclastes, l. i.), and Theophanes (p. 344 [tom. i. p. 631, ed. Bonn]), who talks of Pharaoh's numbering the male children of Israel. This mode of taxation was familiar to the Saracens; and, most unluckily for the historian, it was imposed a few years afterwards in France by his patron Louis XIV.

[2] See the Liber Pontificalis of Agnellus (in the Scriptores Rerum Italicarum of Muratori, tom. ii. pars. i), whose deeper shade of barbarism marks the difference between Rome and Ravenna. Yet we are indebted to him for some curious and domestic facts—the quarters and factions of Ravenna (p. 154), the revenge of Justinian II. (p. 160, 161), the defeat of the Greeks (p. 170, 171), etc.

the example of Justinian the Second, who had chastised a former rebellion by the choice and execution of fifty of the principal inhabitants. The women and clergy, in sackcloth and ashes, lay prostrate in prayer; the men were in arms for the defence of their country; the common danger had united the factions, and the event of a battle was preferred to the slow miseries of a siege. In a hard-fought day, as the two armies alternately yielded and advanced, a phantom was seen, a voice was heard, and Ravenna was victorious by the assurance of victory. The strangers retreated to their ships, but the populous sea-coast poured forth a multitude of boats; the waters of the Po were so deeply infected with blood, that during six years the public prejudice abstained from the fish of the river; and the institution of an annual feast perpetuated the worship of images and the abhorrence of the Greek tyrant. Amidst the triumph of the Catholic arms, the Roman pontiff convened a synod of ninety-three bishops against the heresy of the Iconoclasts. With their consent, he pronounced a general excommunication against all who by word or deed should attack the tradition of the fathers and the images of the saints: in this sentence the emperor was tacitly involved,[1] but the vote of a last and hopeless remonstrance may seem to imply that the anathema was yet suspended over his guilty head. No sooner had they confirmed their own safety, the worship of images, and the freedom of Rome and Italy, than the popes appear to have relaxed of their severity, and to have spared the relics of the Byzantine dominion. Their moderate counsels delayed and prevented the election of a new emperor, and they exhorted the Italians not to separate from the body of the Roman monarchy. The exarch was permitted to reside within the walls of Ravenna, a captive rather than a master; and till the Imperial coronation of Charlemagne, the government of Rome and Italy was exercised in the name of the successors of Constantine.[2]

[1] Yet Leo was undoubtedly comprised in the si quis . . . imaginum sacrarum . . . destructor . . . extiterit, sit extorris a corpore D.N. Jesu Christi vel totius ecclesiæ unitate. The canonists may decide whether the guilt or the name constitutes the excommunication; and the decision is of the last importance of their safety, since, according to the oracle (Gratian, Caus. xxiii. q. 5, c. 47, apud Spanheim, Hist. Imag. p. 112), homicidas non esse qui excommunicatos trucidant.

[2] Compescuit tale consilium Pontifex, sperans conversionem principis (Anastas. p. 156). Sed ne desisterent ab amore et fide R.J. admonebat (p. 157). The popes style Leo and Constantine Copronymus, Imperatores et Domini, with the strange epithet of *Piissimi*. A famous mosaic of the Lateran (A.D. 798) represents Christ, who delivers the keys to St. Peter and the banner to Constantine V. (Muratori, Annali d'Italia, tom. vi. p. 337).

The liberty of Rome, which had been oppressed by the arms and arts of Augustus, was rescued, after seven hundred and fifty years of servitude, from the persecution of Leo the Isaurian. By the Cæsars the triumphs of the consuls had been annihilated: in the decline and fall of the empire, the god Terminus, the sacred boundary, had insensibly receded from the ocean, the Rhine, the Danube, and the Euphrates; and Rome was reduced to her ancient territory from Viterbo to Terracina, and from Narni to the mouth of the Tiber.[1] When the kings were banished, the republic reposed on the firm basis which had been founded by their wisdom and virtue. Their perpetual jurisdiction was divided between two annual magistrates: the senate continued to exercise the powers of administration and counsel; and the legislative authority was distributed in the assemblies of the people by a well-proportioned scale of property and service. Ignorant of the arts of luxury, the primitive Romans had improved the science of government and war: the will of the community was absolute: the rights of individuals were sacred: one hundred and thirty thousand citizens were armed for defence or conquest; and a band of robbers and outlaws was moulded into a nation, deserving of freedom and ambitious of glory.[2] When the sovereignty of the Greek emperors was extinguished, the ruins of Rome presented the sad image of depopulation and decay: her slavery was a habit, her liberty an accident; the effect of superstition, and the object of her own amazement and terror. The last vestige of the substance, or even the forms, of the constitution, was obliterated from the practice and memory of the Romans; and they were devoid of knowledge, or virtue, again to build the fabric of a commonwealth. Their scanty remnant, the offspring of slaves and strangers, was despicable in the eyes of the victorious barbarians. As often as the Franks or Lombards expressed their most bitter contempt of a foe, they called him a Roman; " and in this name," says the bishop Liutprand, " we include whatever is base, whatever is cowardly, whatever is perfidious, the extremes of avarice and luxury, and every vice that can prostitute the

---

[1] I have traced the Roman duchy according to the maps, and the maps according to the excellent dissertation of Father Beretti (de Chorographia Italiæ Medii Ævi, sect. xx. p. 216-232). Yet I must nicely observe that Viterbo is of Lombard foundation (p. 211), and that Terracina was usurped by the Greeks.

[2] On the extent, population, etc., of the Roman kingdom, the reader may peruse with pleasure the *Discours Préliminaire* to the République Romaine of M. de Beaufort (tom. i.), who will not be accused of too much credulity for the early ages of Rome.

dignity of human nature." [1] By the necessity of their situation, the inhabitants of Rome were cast into the rough model of a republican government: they were compelled to elect some judges in peace and some leaders in war: the nobles assembled to deliberate, and their resolves could not be executed without the union and consent of the multitude. The style of the Roman senate and people was revived,[2] but the spirit was fled; and their new independence was disgraced by the tumultuous conflict of licentiousness and oppression. The want of laws could only be supplied by the influence of religion, and their foreign and domestic counsels were moderated by the authority of the bishop. His alms, his sermons, his correspondence with the kings and prelates of the West, his recent services, their gratitude and oath, accustomed the Romans to consider him as the first magistrate or prince of the city. The Christian humility of the popes was not offended by the name of *Dominus*, or Lord; and their face and inscription are still apparent on the most ancient coins.[3] Their temporal dominion is now confirmed by the reverence of a thousand years; and their noblest title

---

[1] Quos (*Romanos*) nos, Longobardi scilicet, Saxones, Franci, Lotharingi, Bajoarii, Suevi, Burgundiones, tanto dedignamur ut inimicos nostros commoti, nil aliud contumeliarum nisi Romane, dicamus: hoc solo, id est Romanorum nomine, quicquid ignobilitatis, quicquid timiditatis, quicquid avaritiæ, quicquid luxuriæ, quicquid mendacii, immo quicquid vitiorum est comprehendentes (Liutprand, in Legat. Script. Ital. tom. ii. pars. i. p. 481). For the sins of Cato or Tully, Minos might have imposed as a fit penance the daily perusal of this barbarous passage.

[2] Pipino regi Francorum [et Patricio Romanorum] omnis senatus atque universa populi generalitas a Deo servatæ Romanæ urbis. Codex Carolin. epist. 36 in Script. Ital. tom. iii. pars ii. p. 160. The names of senatus and senator were never totally extinct (Dissert. Chorograph. p. 216, 217); but in the middle ages they signified little more than nobiles, optimates, etc. (Ducange, Gloss. Latin.).

[3] See Muratori, Antiquit. Italiæ Medii Ævi, tom. ii. Dissertat. xxvii. p. 548. On one of these coins we read Hadrianus Papa (A.D. 772); on the reverse. Vict. DDNN. with the word *CONOB*, which the Père Joubert (Science des Médailles, tom. ii. p. 42) explains by *CON*stantinopoli *O*fficina *B* (*secunda*).

[The letters CONOB, which frequently appear on the Byzantine coins, and which have given rise to much dispute, have been satisfactorily explained by Pinder and Friedländer, *Die Münzen Justinians, mit sechs Kupfertafeln*, Berlin, 1843. That the letters CON should be separated from OB, and that they signify Constantinople, seems clear from the epigraphs AQUOB, TESOB, and TROB, which indicate respectively Aquileia, Thessalonica, and Trèves. The above-mentioned writers suppose that OB are the Greek numerals, and that they consequently indicate the number 72. In the time of Augustus 40 gold coins (aure or solidi) were equal to a pound; but as these coins were gradually struck lighter and lighter, it was at length enacted by Valentinian I., in A.D. 367, that henceforth 72 solidi should be coined out of a pound of gold; and accordingly we find CONOB for the first time on the coins of this emperor.—O. S.]

is the free choice of a people whom they had redeemed from slavery.

In the quarrels of ancient Greece, the holy people of Elis enjoyed a perpetual peace, under the protection of Jupiter, and in the exercise of the Olympic games.[1] Happy would it have been for the Romans if a similar privilege had guarded the patrimony of St. Peter from the calamities of war; if the Christians who visited the holy threshold would have sheathed their swords in the presence of the apostle and his successor. But this mystic circle could have been traced only by the wand of a legislator and a sage: this pacific system was incompatible with the zeal and ambition of the popes: the Romans were not addicted, like the inhabitants of Elis, to the innocent and placid labours of agriculture; and the barbarians of Italy, though softened by the climate, were far below the Grecian states in the institutions of public and private life. A memorable example of repentance and piety was exhibited by Liutprand, king of the Lombards. In arms, at the gate of the Vatican, the conqueror listened to the voice of Gregory the Second,[2] withdrew his troops, resigned his conquests, respectfully visited the church of St. Peter, and, after performing his devotions, offered his sword and dagger, his cuirass and mantle, his silver cross, and his crown of gold, on the tomb of the apostle. But this religious fervour was the illusion, perhaps the artifice, of the moment; the sense of interest is strong and lasting; the love of arms and rapine was congenial to the Lombards; and both the prince and people were irresistibly tempted by the disorders of Italy, the nakedness of Rome, and the unwarlike profession of her new chief. On the first edicts of the emperor, they declared themselves the champions of the holy images: Liutprand invaded the province of Romagna, which had already assumed that distinctive appellation; the Catholics of the Exarchate yielded without reluctance to his civil and military power; and a foreign enemy was introduced for the first time into the impregnable fortress of Ravenna. That city and fortress were speedily recovered by the active diligence and maritime forces of the Venetians; and those faithful subjects obeyed the exhortation of Gregory himself, in separating the personal guilt of Leo from

[1] See West's Dissertation on the Olympic Games (Pindar, vol. ii. p. 32-36, edition in 12mo) and the judicious reflections of Polybius (tom. i. l. iv. [c. 73] p. 466, edit. Gronov.).
[2] The speech of Gregory to the Lombard is finely composed by Sigonius (de Regno Italiæ, l. iii. Opera, tom. ii. p. 173), who imitates the licence and the spirit of Sallust or Livy.

the general cause of the Roman empire.[1] The Greeks were less mindful of the service than the Lombards of the injury: the two nations, hostile in their faith, were reconciled in a dangerous and unnatural alliance: the king and the exarch marched to the conquest of Spoleto and Rome; the storm evaporated without effect, but the policy of Liutprand alarmed Italy with a vexatious alternative of hostility and truce. His successor Astolphus declared himself the equal enemy of the emperor and the pope: Ravenna was subdued by force or treachery,[2] and this final conquest extinguished the series of the exarchs, who had reigned with a subordinate power since the time of Justinian and the ruin of the Gothic kingdom. Rome was summoned to acknowledge the victorious Lombard as her lawful sovereign; the annual tribute of a piece of gold was fixed as the ransom of each citizen, and the sword of destruction was unsheathed to exact the penalty of her disobedience. The Romans hesitated; they entreated; they complained; and the threatening barbarians were checked by arms and negotiations, till the popes had engaged the friendship of an ally and avenger beyond the Alps.[3]

In his distress the first Gregory had implored the aid of the hero of the age, of Charles Martel, who governed the French monarchy with the humble title of mayor or duke; and who, by his signal victory over the Saracens, had saved his country, and perhaps Europe, from the Mohammedan yoke. The ambassadors of the pope were received by Charles with decent reverence; but the greatness of his occupations, and the shortness of his life, prevented his interference in the affairs of Italy, except by a friendly and ineffectual mediation. His son Pepin, the heir of his power and virtues, assumed the office of champion of the Roman church; and the zeal of the French prince appears to have been prompted by the love of glory and religion. But

---

[1] The Venetian historians, John Sagorninus (Chron. Venet. p. 13) and the doge Andrew Dandolo (Scriptores Rer. Ital. tom. xii. p. 135), have preserved this epistle of Gregory. The loss and recovery of Ravenna are mentioned by Paulus Diaconus (de Gest. Langobard. l. vi. c. 49, 54, in Script. Ital. tom. i. pars. i. p. 506, 508); but our chronologists, Pagi, Muratori, etc., cannot ascertain the date or circumstances.

[2] The option will depend on the various readings of the MSS. of Anastasius—*deceperat*, or *decerpserat* (Script. Ital. tom. iii. pars. i. p. 167).

[3] The Codex Carolinus is a collection of the epistles of the popes to Charles Martel (whom they style *Subregulus*), Pepin, and Charlemagne, as far as the year 791, when it was formed by the last of these princes. His original and authentic MS (Bibliothecæ Cubicularis) is now in the Imperial library of Vienna, and has been published by Lambecius and Muratori (Script. Rerum Ital. tom. iii. pars ii. p. 75, etc.).

the danger was on the banks of the Tiber, the succour on those of the Seine; and our sympathy is cold to the relation of distant misery. Amidst the tears of the city, Stephen the Third embraced the generous resolution of visiting in person the courts of Lombardy and France, to deprecate the injustice of his enemy, or to excite the pity and indignation of his friend. After soothing the public despair by litanies and orations, he undertook this laborious journey with the ambassadors of the French monarch and the Greek emperor. The king of the Lombards was inexorable; but his threats could not silence the complaints, nor retard the speed, of the Roman pontiff, who traversed the Pennine Alps, reposed in the abbey of St. Maurice, and hastened to grasp the right hand of his protector; a hand which was never lifted in vain, either in war or friendship. Stephen was entertained as the visible successor of the apostle; at the next assembly, the field of March or of May, his injuries were exposed to a devout and warlike nation, and he repassed the Alps, not as a suppliant, but as a conqueror, at the head of a French army, which was led by the king in person. The Lombards, after a weak resistance, obtained an ignominious peace, and swore to restore the possessions, and to respect the sanctity, of the Roman church. But no sooner was Astolphus delivered from the presence of the French arms, than he forgot his promise and resented his disgrace. Rome was again encompassed by his arms; and Stephen, apprehensive of fatiguing the zeal of his Transalpine allies, enforced his complaint and request by an eloquent letter in the name and person of St. Peter himself.[1] The apostle assures his adoptive sons, the king, the clergy, and the nobles of France, that, dead in the flesh, he is still alive in the spirit; that they now hear, and must obey, the voice of the founder and guardian of the Roman church; 'that the Virgin, the angels, the saints, and the martyrs, and all the host of heaven, unanimously urge the request, and will confess the obligation; that riches, victory, and paradise will crown their pious enterprise, and that eternal damnation will be the penalty of their neglect, if they suffer his tomb, his temple, and his people to fall into the hands of the perfidious Lombards. The second expedition of Pepin was not less rapid and fortunate than

---

[1] See this most extraordinary letter in the Codex Carolinus, epist. iii. p. 92. The enemies of the popes have charged them with fraud and blasphemy; yet they surely meant to persuade rather than deceive. This introduction of the dead, or of immortals, was familiar to the ancient orators, though it is executed on this occasion in the rude fashion of the age.

the first: St. Peter was satisfied, Rome was again saved, and Astolphus was taught the lessons of justice and sincerity by the scourge of a foreign master. After this double chastisement, the Lombards languished about twenty years in a state of languor and decay. But their minds were not yet humbled to their condition; and instead of affecting the pacific virtues of the feeble, they peevishly harassed the Romans with a repetition of claims, evasions, and inroads, which they undertook without reflection and terminated without glory. On either side, their expiring monarchy was pressed by the zeal and prudence of Pope Adrian the First, the genius, the fortune, and greatness of Charlemagne the son of Pepin; these heroes of the church and state were united in public and domestic friendship, and, while they trampled on the prostrate, they varnished their proceedings with the fairest colours of equity and moderation.[1] The passes of the Alps and the walls of Pavia were the only defence of the Lombards; the former were surprised, the latter were invested, by the son of Pepin; and after a blockade of two years, Desiderius, the last of their native princes, surrendered his sceptre and his capital. Under the dominion of a foreign king, but in the possession of their national laws, the Lombards became the brethren, rather than the subjects, of the Franks; who derived their blood, and manners, and language from the same Germanic origin.[2]

The mutual obligations of the popes and the Carlovingian family form the important link of ancient and modern, of civil and ecclesiastical, history. In the conquest of Italy, the champions of the Roman church obtained a favourable occasion, a specious title, the wishes of the people, the prayers and intrigues of the clergy. But the most essential gifts of the popes to the Carlovingian race were the dignities of king of France[3] and of patrician of Rome. I. Under the sacerdotal

---

[1] Except in the divorce of the daughter of Desiderius, whom Charlemagne repudiated sine aliquo crimine. Pope Stephen IV. had most furiously opposed the alliance of a noble Frank—cum perfidâ, horridâ, nec dicendâ, fœtentissimâ natione Longobardorum—to whom he imputes the first stain of leprosy (Cod. Carolin. epist. 45, p. 178, 179). Another reason against the marriage was the existence of a first wife (Muratori, Annali d'Italia, tom. vi. p. 232, 233, 236, 237). But Charlemagne indulged himself in the freedom of polygamy or concubinage.

[2] See the Annali d'Italia of Muratori, tom. vi., and the three first Dissertations of his Antiquitates Italiæ Medii Ævi, tom. i.

[3] Besides the common historians, three French critics, Launoy (Opera, tom. v. pars ii. l. vii. epist. 9, p. 477-487), Pagi (Critica, A.D. 751, No. 1-6, A.D. 752, No. 1-10), and Natalis Alexander (Hist. Novi Testamenti, dissertat. ii. p. 96-107), have treated this subject of the deposition of Childeric

monarchy of St. Peter the nations began to resume the practice of seeking, on the banks of the Tiber, their kings, their laws, and the oracles of their fate. The Franks were perplexed between the name and substance of their government. All the powers of royalty were exercised by Pepin, mayor of the palace; and nothing, except the regal title, was wanting to his ambition. His enemies were crushed by his valour; his friends were multiplied by his liberality; his father had been the saviour of Christendom; and the claims of personal merit were repeated and ennobled in a descent of four generations. The name and image of royalty was still preserved in the last descendant of Clovis, the feeble Childeric; but his obsolete right could only be used as an instrument of sedition: the nation was desirous of restoring the simplicity of the constitution; and Pepin, a subject and a prince, was ambitious to ascertain his own rank and the fortune of his family. The mayor and the nobles were bound, by an oath of fidelity, to the royal phantom: the blood of Clovis was pure and sacred in their eyes; and their common ambassadors addressed the Roman pontiff to dispel their scruples or to absolve their promise. The interest of Pope Zachary, the successor of the two Gregories, prompted him to decide, and to decide in their favour: he pronounced that the nation might lawfully unite, in the same person, the title and authority of king; and that the unfortunate Childeric, a victim of the public safety, should be degraded, shaved, and confined in a monastery for the remainder of his days. An answer so agreeable to their wishes was accepted by the Franks, as the opinion of a casuist, the sentence of a judge, or the oracle of a prophet: the Merovingian race disappeared from the earth; and Pepin was exalted on a buckler by the suffrage of a free people, accustomed to obey his laws and to march under his standard. His coronation was twice performed, with the sanction of the popes, by their most faithful servant St. Boniface, the apostle of Germany, and by the grateful hands of Stephen the Third, who, in the monastery of St. Denys, placed the diadem on the head of his benefactor. The royal unction of the kings of Israel was dexterously applied: [1] the successor of St. Peter assumed the

with learning and attention, but with a strong bias to save the independence of the crown. Yet they are hard pressed by the texts which they produce of Eginhard, Theophanes, and the old annals, Laureshamenses, Fuldenses, Loisielani.

[1] Not absolutely for the first time. On a less conspicuous theatre it had been used, in the sixth and seventh centuries, by the provincial bishops of Britain and Spain. The royal unction of Constantinople was borrowed

character of a divine ambassador: a German chieftain was transformed into the Lord's anointed; and this Jewish rite has been diffused and maintained by the superstition and vanity of modern Europe. The Franks were absolved from their ancient oath; but a dire anathema was thundered against them and their posterity, if they should dare to renew the same freedom of choice, or to elect a king, except in the holy and meritorious race of the Carlovingian princes. Without apprehending the future danger, these princes gloried in their present security: the secretary of Charlemagne affirms that the French sceptre was transferred by the authority of the popes;[1] and, in their boldest enterprises, they insist, with confidence, on this signal and successful act of temporal jurisdiction.

II. In the change of manners and language the patricians of Rome[2] were far removed from the senate of Romulus, or the palace of Constantine—from the free nobles of the republic, or the fictitious parents of the emperor. After the recovery of Italy and Africa by the arms of Justinian, the importance and danger of those remote provinces required the presence of a supreme magistrate; he was indifferently styled the exarch or the patrician; and these governors of Ravenna, who fill their place in the chronology of princes, extended their jurisdiction over the Roman city. Since the revolt of Italy and the loss of the Exarchate, the distress of the Romans had exacted some sacrifice of their independence. Yet, even in this act, they exercised the right of disposing of themselves; and the decrees of the senate and people successively invested Charles Martel and his posterity with the honours of patrician of Rome. The leaders of a powerful nation would have disdained a servile title and subordinate office; but the reign of the Greek emperors was suspended; and, in the vacancy of the empire, they derived a more glorious commission from the pope and the republic.

from the Latins in the last age of the empire. Constantine Manasses mentions that of Charlemagne as a foreign, Jewish, incomprehensible ceremony. See Selden's Titles of Honour, in his Works, vol. iii. part i. p. 234-249.

[1] See Eginhard, in Vitâ Caroli Magni, c. i. p. 9, etc., c. iii. p. 24 [ed. Schminck]. Childeric was deposed—*jussû*, the Carlovingians were established—*auctoritate*, Pontificis Romani. Launoy, etc., pretend that these strong words are susceptible of a very soft interpretation. Be it so; yet Eginhard understood the world, the court, and the Latin language.

[2] For the title and powers of patrician of Rome, see Ducange (Gloss. Latin. tom. v. p. 149-151), Pagi (Critica, A.D. 740, No. 6-11), Muratori (Annali d'Italia, tom. vi. p. 308-329), and St. Marc (Abrégé Chronologique de l'Italie, tom. i. p. 379-382). Of these the Franciscan Pagi is the most disposed to make the patrician a lieutenant of the church, rather than of the empire.

The Roman ambassadors presented these patricians with the keys of the shrine of St. Peter, as a pledge and symbol of sovereignty; with a holy banner which it was their right and duty to unfurl in the defence of the church and city.[1] In the time of Charles Martel and of Pepin, the interposition of the Lombard kingdom covered the freedom, while it threatened the safety, of Rome; and the *patriciate* represented only the title, the service, the alliance, of these distant protectors. The power and policy of Charlemagne annihilated an enemy and imposed a master. In his first visit to the capital he was received with all the honours which had formerly been paid to the exarch, the representative of the emperor; and these honours obtained some new decorations from the joy and gratitude of Pope Adrian the First.[2] No sooner was he informed of the sudden approach of the monarch, than he despatched the magistrates and nobles of Rome to meet him, with the banner, about thirty miles from the city. At the distance of one mile the Flaminian Way was lined with the *schools*, or national communities, of Greeks, Lombards, Saxons, etc.: the Roman youth was under arms; and the children of a more tender age, with palms and olive branches in their hands, chanted the praises of their great deliverer. At the aspect of the holy crosses, and ensigns of the saints, he dismounted from his horse, led the procession of his nobles to the Vatican, and, as he ascended the stairs, devoutly kissed each step of the threshold of the apostles. In the portico, Adrian expected him at the head of his clergy: they embraced, as friends and equals; but in their march to the altar, the king or patrician assumed the right hand of the pope. Nor was the Frank content with these vain and empty demonstrations of respect. In the twenty-six years that elapsed between the conquest of Lombardy and his Imperial coronation, Rome, which had been delivered by the sword, was subject, as his own, to the sceptre of Charlemagne. The people swore allegiance to his person and family: in his name money was coined and

---

[1] The papal advocates can soften the symbolic meaning of the banner and the keys; but the style of ad *regnum* dimisimus, or direximus (Codex Carolin. epist. i. tom. iii. pars ii. p. 76), seems to allow of no palliation or escape. In the MS. of the Vienna library, they read, instead of *regnum, rogum*, prayer or request (see Ducange); and the royalty of Charles Martel is subverted by this important correction (Catalani, in his Critical Prefaces, Annali d'Italia, tom. xvii. p. 95-99).

[2] In the authentic narrative of this reception, the Liber Pontificalis observes—obviam illi ejus sanctitas dirigens venerabiles [venerandas] cruces, id est signa; sicut mos est ad exarchum, aut patricium suscipiendum, eum cum ingenti honore suscipi fecit (tom. iii. pars. i. p. 185).

justice was administered; and the election of the popes was examined and confirmed by his authority. Except an original and self-inherent claim of sovereignty, there was not any prerogative remaining which the title of emperor could add to the patrician of Rome.[1]

The gratitude of the Carlovingians was adequate to these obligations, and their names are consecrated as the saviours and benefactors of the Roman church. Her ancient patrimony of farms and houses was transformed by their bounty into the temporal dominion of cities and provinces; and the donation of the Exarchate was the first-fruits of the conquests of Pepin.[2] Astolphus with a sigh relinquished his prey; the keys and the hostages of the principal cities were delivered to the French ambassador; and, in his master's name, he presented them before the tomb of St. Peter. The ample measure of the Exarchate[3] might comprise all the provinces of Italy which had obeyed the emperor and his vicegerent; but its strict and proper limits were included in the territories of Ravenna, Bologna, and Ferrara: its inseparable dependency was the Pentapolis, which stretched along the Hadriatic from Rimini to Ancona, and advanced into the midland country as far as the ridges of the Apennine. In this transaction the ambition and avarice of the popes has been severely condemned. Perhaps the humility of a Christian priest should have rejected an earthly kingdom, which it was not easy for him to govern without renouncing the virtues of his profession. Perhaps a faithful subject, or even a generous enemy, would have been less impatient to divide the spoils of the barbarian; and if the emperor had intrusted Stephen to solicit in his name the restitution of the Exarchate, I will not absolve the pope from the reproach of treachery and falsehood. But in the rigid interpretation of

---

[1] Paulus Diaconus, who wrote before the *empire* of Charlemagne, describes Rome as his subject city—vestræ civitates (ad Pompeium Festum), suis addidit sceptris (de Metensis Ecclesiæ Episcopis). Some Carlovingian medals, struck at Rome, have engaged Le Blanc to write an elaborate, though partial, dissertation on their authority at Rome, both as patricians and emperors (Amsterdam, 1692, in 4to).

[2] Mosheim (Institution Hist. Eccles. p. 263) weighs this donation with fair and deliberate prudence. The original act has never been produced; but the Liber Pontificalis represents (p. 171), and the Codex Carolinus supposes, this ample gift. Both are contemporary records; and the latter is the more authentic, since it has been preserved, not in the Papal, but the Imperial, library.

[3] Between the exorbitant claims, and narrow concessions, of interest and prejudice, from which even Muratori (Antiquitat. tom. i. p. 63-68) is not exempt I have been guided, in the limits of the Exarchate and Pentapolis, by the Dissertatio Chorographica Italiæ Medii Ævi, tom. x. p. 160-180.

the laws, every one may accept, without injury, whatever his benefactor can bestow without injustice. The Greek emperor had abdicated or forfeited his right to the Exarchate; and the sword of Astolphus was broken by the stronger sword of the Carlovingian. It was not in the cause of the Iconoclast that Pepin had exposed his person and army in a double expedition beyond the Alps: he possessed, and might lawfully alienate, his conquests: and to the importunities of the Greeks he piously replied that no human consideration should tempt him to resume the gift which he had conferred on the Roman pontiff for the remission of his sins and the salvation of his soul. The splendid donation was granted in supreme and absolute dominion, and the world beheld for the first time a Christian bishop invested with the prerogatives of a temporal prince—the choice of magistrates, the exercise of justice, the imposition of taxes, and the wealth of the palace of Ravenna. In the dissolution of the Lombard kingdom the inhabitants of the duchy of Spoleto [1] sought a refuge from the storm, shaved their heads after the Roman fashion, declared themselves the servants and subjects of St. Peter, and completed, by this voluntary surrender, the present circle of the ecclesiastical state. That mysterious circle was enlarged to an indefinite extent by the verbal or written donation of Charlemagne,[2] who, in the first transports of his victory, despoiled himself and the Greek emperor of the cities and islands which had formerly been annexed to the Exarchate. But in the cooler moments of absence and reflection he viewed with an eye of jealousy and envy the recent greatness of his ecclesiastical ally. The execution of his own and his father's promises was respectfully eluded: the king of the Franks and Lombards asserted the inalienable rights of the empire; and, in his life and death, Ravenna,[3] as well as Rome,

---

[1] Spoletini deprecati sunt, ut eos in servitio B. Petri reciperet et more Romanorum tonsurari faceret (Anastasius, p. 185). Yet it may be a question whether they gave their own persons or their country.

[2] The policy and donations of Charlemagne are carefully examined by St. Marc (Abrégé, tom. i. p. 390-408), who has well studied the Codex Carolinus. I believe, with him, that they were only verbal. The most ancient act of donation that pretends to be extant is that of the emperor Lewis the Pious (Sigonius, de Regno Italiæ, l. iv. Opera, tom. ii. p. 267-270). Its authenticity, or at least its integrity, are much questioned (Pagi, A.D. 817, No. 7, etc.; Muratori, Annali, tom. vi. p. 432, etc.; Dissertat. Chorographica, p. 33, 34); but I see no reasonable objection to these princes so freely disposing of what was not their own.

[3] Charlemagne solicited and obtained from the proprietor, Adrian I., the mosaics of the palace of Ravenna, for the decoration of Aix-la-Chapelle (Cod. Carolin. epist. 67, p. 223).

was numbered in the list of his metropolitan cities. The sovereignty of the Exarchate melted away in the hands of the popes; they found in the archbishops of Ravenna a dangerous and domestic rival:[1] the nobles and people disdained the yoke of a priest; and in the disorders of the times they could only retain the memory of an ancient claim, which, in a more prosperous age, they have revived and realised.

Fraud is the resource of weakness and cunning; and the strong, though ignorant, barbarian was often entangled in the net of sacerdotal policy. The Vatican and Lateran were an arsenal and manufacture which, according to the occasion, have produced or concealed a various collection of false or genuine, of corrupt or suspicious acts, as they tended to promote the interest of the Roman church. Before the end of the eighth century some apostolical scribe, perhaps the notorious Isidore, composed the decretals and the donation of Constantine, the two magic pillars of the spiritual and temporal monarchy of the popes. This memorable donation was introduced to the world by an epistle of Adrian the First, who exhorts Charlemagne to imitate the liberality and revive the name of the great Constantine.[2] According to the legend, the first of the Christian emperors was healed of the leprosy, and purified in the waters of baptism, by St. Silvester, the Roman bishop; and never was physician more gloriously recompensed. His royal proselyte withdrew from the seat and patrimony of St. Peter; declared his resolution of founding a new capital in the East; and resigned to the popes the free and perpetual sovereignty of Rome, Italy, and the provinces of the West.[3] This fiction was productive of the most beneficial effects. The Greek princes were convicted of the

---

[1] The popes often complain of the usurpations of Leo of Ravenna (Codex Carolin. epist. 51, 52, 53, p. 200-205). Si corpus St. Andreæ germani St. Petri hîc humasset, nequaquam nos Romani pontifices sic subjugassent (Agnellus, Liber Pontificalis, in Scriptores Rerum Ital. tom. ii. pars i. p. 107).

[2] Piissimo Constantino magno, per ejus largitatem S. R. Ecclesia elevata et exaltata est, et potestatem in his Hesperiæ partibus largiri dignatus est. . . . Quia ecce novus Constantinus his temporibus, etc. (Codex Carolin. epist. 49, in tom. iii. part. ii. p. 195). Pagi (Critica, A.D. 324, No. 16) ascribes them to an imposter of the eighth century, who borrowed the name of St. Isidore: his humble title of *Peccator* was ignorantly, but aptly, turned into *Mercator ;* his merchandise was indeed profitable, and a few sheets of paper were sold for much wealth and power.

[3] Fabricius (Biblioth. Græc. tom. vi. p. 4-7) has enumerated the several editions of this Act, in Greek and Latin. The copy which Laurentius Valla recites and refutes appears to be taken either from the spurious Acts of St. Silvester or from Gratian's Decree, to which, according to him and others, it has been surreptitiously tacked.

guilt of usurpation; and the revolt of Gregory was the claim of his lawful inheritance. The popes were delivered from their debt of gratitude; and the nominal gifts of the Carlovingians were no more than the just and irrevocable restitution of a scanty portion of the ecclesiastical state. The sovereignty of Rome no longer depended on the choice of a fickle people; and the successors of St. Peter and Constantine were invested with the purple and prerogatives of the Cæsars. So deep was the ignorance and credulity of the times that the most absurd of fables was received with equal reverence in Greece and in France, and is still enrolled among the decrees of the canon law.[1] The emperors and the Romans were incapable of discerning a forgery that subverted their rights and freedom; and the only opposition proceeded from a Sabine monastery, which in the beginning of the twelfth century disputed the truth and validity of the donation of Constantine.[2] In the revival of letters and liberty this fictitious deed was transpierced by the pen of Laurentius Valla, the pen of an eloquent critic and a Roman patriot.[3] His contemporaries of the fifteenth century were astonished at his sacrilegious boldness; yet such is the silent and irresistible progress of reason, that before the end of the next age the fable was rejected by the contempt of historians [4] and

[1] In the year 1059 it was believed (was it believed?) by Pope Leo IX., Cardinal Peter Damianus, etc. Muratori places (Annali d'Italia, tom. ix. p. 23, 24) the fictitious donations of Lewis the Pious, the Othos, etc., de Donatione Constantini. See a Dissertation of Natalis Alexander, seculum iv. diss. 25, p. 335-350.

[2] See a large account of the controversy (A.D. 1105), which arose from a private lawsuit, in the Chronicon Farsense (Script. Rerum Italicarum, tom. ii. pars. ii. p. 637, etc.), a copious extract from the archives of that Benedictine abbey. They were formerly accessible to curious foreigners (Le Blanc and Mabillon), and would have enriched the first volume of the Historia Monastica Italiæ of Quirini. But they are now imprisoned (Muratori, Scriptores R. I. tom. ii. pars ii. p. 269) by the timid policy of the court of Rome; and the future cardinal yielded to the voice of authority and the whispers of ambition (Quirini, Comment. pars ii. p. 123-136).

[3] I have read in the collection of Schardius (de Potestate Imperiali Ecclesiasticâ, p. 734-780) this animated discourse, which was composed by the author A.D. 1440, six years after the flight of Pope Eugenius IV. It is a most vehement party pamphlet; Valla justifies and animates the revolt of the Romans, and would even approve the use of a dagger against their sacerdotal tyrant. Such a critic might expect the persecution of the clergy; yet he made his peace, and is buried in the Lateran (Bayle, Dictionnaire Critique, VALLA; Vossius, de Historicis Latinis, p. 580).

[4] See Guicciardini, a servant of the popes, in that long and valuable digression, which has resumed its place in the last edition, correctly published from the author's MS., and printed in four volumes in quarto, under the name of Friburgo, 1775 (Istoria d'Italia, tom. i. p. 385-395).

poets,[1] and the tacit or modest censure of the advocates of the Roman church.[2] The popes themselves have indulged a smile at the credulity of the vulgar;[3] but a false and obsolete title still sanctifies their reign; and by the same fortune which has attended the decretals and the Sibylline oracles, the edifice has subsisted after the foundations have been undermined.

While the popes established in Italy their freedom and dominion, the images, the first cause of their revolt, were restored in the Eastern empire.[4] Under the reign of Constantine the Fifth, the union of civil and ecclesiastical power had overthrown the tree, without extirpating the root, of superstition. The idols, for such they were now held, were secretly cherished by the order and the sex most prone to devotion; and the fond alliance of the monks and females obtained a final victory over the reason and authority of man. Leo the Fourth maintained with less rigour the religion of his father and grandfather; but his wife, the fair and ambitious Irene, had imbibed the zeal of the Athenians, the heirs of the idolatry, rather than the philosophy, of their ancestors. During the life of her husband these sentiments were inflamed by danger and dissimulation, and she could only labour to protect and promote some favourite monks whom she drew from their caverns and seated on the metropolitan thrones of the East. But as soon as she reigned in her

[1] The Paladin Astolpho found it in the moon, among the things that were lost upon earth (Orlando Furioso, xxxiv. 80).

> Di vari fiori ad un gran monte passa,
> Ch' ebbe già buono odore, or puzza forte:
> Questo era il dono (se però dir lece)
> Che Costantino al buon Silvestro fece.

Yet this incomparable poem has been approved by a bull of Leo X.

[2] See Baronius, A.D. 324, No. 117-123; A.D. 1191, No. 51, etc. The cardinal wishes to suppose that Rome was offered by Constantine, and *refused* by Silvester. The act of donation he considers, strangely enough, as a forgery of the Greeks.

[3] Baronius n'en dit guères contre; encore en a-t-il trop dit, et l'on vouloit sans moi (*Cardinal du Perron*), qui l'empêchai, censurer cette partie de son histoire. J'en devisai un jour avec le Pape, et il ne me répondit autre chose "che volete? i Canonici la tengono," il le disoit *en riant* (Perroniana, p. 77).

[4] The remaining history of images, from Irene to Theodora, is collected for the Catholics by Baronius and Pagi (A.D. 780-840), Natalis Alexander (Hist. N. T. seculum viii.; Panoplia adversus Hæreticos, p. 118-178), and Dupin (Biblioth. Ecclés. tom. vi. p. 136-154); for the Protestants, by Spanheim (Hist. Imag. p. 305-639), Basnage (Hist. de l'Eglise, tom. i. p. 556-572; tom. ii. p. 1362-1385), and Mosheim (Institut. Hist. Eccles. secul. viii. et ix.). The Protestants, except Mosheim, are soured with controversy; but the Catholics, except Dupin, are inflamed by the fury and superstition of the monks; and even Le Beau (Hist. du Bas Empire), a gentleman and a scholar, is infected by the odious contagion.

own name and that of her son, Irene more seriously undertook
the ruin of the Iconoclasts; and the first step of her future persecution was a general edict for liberty of conscience. In the
restoration of the monks a thousand images were exposed to the
public veneration; a thousand legends were invented of their
sufferings and miracles. By the opportunities of death or removal the episcopal seats were judiciously filled; the most eager
competitors for earthly or celestial favour anticipated and
flattered the judgment of their sovereign; and the promotion
of her secretary Tarasius gave Irene the patriarch of Constantinople, and the command of the Oriental church. But the
decrees of a general council could only be repealed by a similar
assembly: [1] the Iconoclasts whom she convened were bold in
possession, and averse to debate; and the feeble voice of the
bishops was re-echoed by the more formidable clamour of the
soldiers and people of Constantinople. The delay and intrigues
of a year, the separation of the disaffected troops, and the choice
of Nice for a second orthodox synod, removed these obstacles;
and the episcopal conscience was again, after the Greek fashion,
in the hands of the prince. No more than eighteen days were
allowed for the consummation of this important work: the
Iconoclasts appeared, not as judges, but as criminals or penitents:
the scene was decorated by the legates of Pope Adrian and the
Eastern patriarchs; [2] the decrees were framed by the president
Tarasius, and ratified by the acclamations and subscriptions
of three hundred and fifty bishops. They unanimously pronounced that the worship of images is agreeable to Scripture
and reason, to the fathers and councils of the church: but they
hesitate whether that worship be relative or direct; whether
the Godhead and the figure of Christ be entitled to the same
mode of adoration. Of this second Nicene council the acts are
still extant; a curious monument of superstition and ignorance,
of falsehood and folly. I shall only notice the judgment of
the bishops, on the comparative merit of image-worship and
morality. A monk had concluded a truce with the demon of

[1] See the Acts, in Greek and Latin, of the second Council of Nice, with a
number of relative pieces, in the eighth volume of the Councils, p. 645-1600.
A faithful version, with some critical notes, would provoke, in different
readers, a sigh or a smile.
[2] The pope's legates were casual messengers, two priests without any
special commission, and who were disavowed on their return. Some
vagabond monks were persuaded by the Catholics to represent the Oriental
patriarchs. This curious anecdote is revealed by Theodore Studites
(Epist. i. 38, in Sirmond. Opp. tom. v. p. 1319), one of the warmest
Iconoclasts of the age.

fornication, on condition of interrupting his daily prayers to a picture that hung in his cell. His scruples prompted him to consult the abbot. " Rather than abstain from adoring Christ and his Mother in their holy images, it would be better for you," replied the casuist, " to enter every brothel, and visit every prostitute, in the city." [1] For the honour of orthodoxy, at least the orthodoxy of the Roman church, it is somewhat unfortunate that the two princes who convened the two councils of Nice are both stained with the blood of their sons. The second of these assemblies was approved and rigorously executed by the despotism of Irene, and she refused her adversaries the toleration which at first she had granted to her friends. During the five succeeding reigns, a period of thirty-eight years, the contest was maintained with unabated rage and various success between the worshippers and the breakers of the images; but I am not inclined to pursue with minute diligence the repetition of the same events. Nicephorus allowed a general liberty of speech and practice; and the only virtue of his reign is accused by the monks as the cause of his temporal and eternal perdition. Superstition and weakness formed the character of Michael the First, but the saints and images were incapable of supporting their votary on the throne. In the purple, Leo the Fifth asserted the name and religion of an Armenian; and the idols, with their seditious adherents, were condemned to a second exile. Their applause would have sanctified the murder of an impious tyrant, but his assassin and successor, the second Michael, was tainted from his birth with the Phrygian heresies: he attempted to mediate between the contending parties; and the intractable spirit of the Catholics insensibly cast him into the opposite scale. His moderation was guarded by timidity; but his son Theophilus, alike ignorant of fear and pity, was the last and most cruel of the Iconoclasts. The enthusiasm of the times ran strongly against them; and the emperors, who stemmed the torrent, were exasperated and punished by the public hatred. After the death of Theophilus the final victory of the images was achieved by a second female, his widow Theodora, whom he left the guardian of the empire. Her measures were bold and decisive. The fiction of a tardy repentance absolved the fame

---

[1] Συμφέρει δέ σοι μὴ καταλιπεῖν ἐν τῇ πόλει ταύτῃ πορνεῖον εἰς ὃ μὴ εἰσέλθῃς, ἢ ἵνα ἀρνήσῃ τὸ προσκύνειν τὸν κύριον ἡμῶν καὶ θεὸν Ἰησοῦν Χριστὸν μετὰ τῆς ἰδίας αὐτοῦ μήτρος ἐν εἰκονι. These visits could not be innocent, since the Δαίμων πορνείας (the demon of fornication) ἐπολέμει δὲ αὐτὸν . . . . ἐν μιᾷ οὖν ὡς ἐπέκειτο αὐτῷ σφόδρα, etc. Actio iv. p. 901 : Actio v. p. 1031.

and the soul of her deceased husband; the sentence of the Iconoclast patriarch was commuted from the loss of his eyes to a whipping of two hundred lashes: the bishops trembled, the monks shouted, and the festival of orthodoxy preserves the annual memory of the triumph of the images. A single question yet remained, whether they are endowed with any proper and inherent sanctity; it was agitated by the Greeks of the eleventh century;[1] and as this opinion has the strongest recommendation of absurdity, I am surprised that it was not more explicitly decided in the affirmative. In the West Pope Adrian the First accepted and announced the decrees of the Nicene assembly, which is now revered by the Catholics as the seventh in rank of the general councils. Rome and Italy were docile to the voice of their father; but the greatest part of the Latin Christians were far behind in the race of superstition. The churches of France, Germany, England, and Spain steered a middle course between the adoration and the destruction of images, which they admitted into their temples, not as objects of worship, but as lively and useful memorials of faith and history. An angry book of controversy was composed and published in the name of Charlemagne:[2] under his authority a synod of three hundred bishops was assembled at Frankfort:[3] they blamed the fury of the Iconoclasts, but they pronounced a more severe censure against the superstition of the Greeks, and the decrees of their pretended council, which was long despised by the barbarians of the West.[4] Among them the worship of images

[1] See an account of this controversy in the Alexias of Anna Comnena (l. v. p. 129 [ed. Par.; c. 2, p. 229, ed. Bonn]) and Mosheim (Institut. Hist. Eccles. p. 371, 372).

[The edict of Theophilus against the worship of images was promulgated A.D. 832. The principal sufferers were the brothers Theodore and Theophanes who were tortured, and Lazarus the painter who was scourged and then imprisoned.—O. S.]

[2] The Libri Carolini (Spanheim, p. 443-529), composed in the palace or winter quarters of Charlemagne, at Worms, A.D. 790, and sent by Engebert to Pope Adrian I., who answered them by a grandis et verbosa epistola (Concil. tom. viii. p. 1553). The Carolines propose 120 objections against the Nicene synod, and such words as these are the flowers of their rhetoric —Dementiam . . . priscæ Gentilitatis obsoletum errorem . . . argumenta insanissima et absurdissima . . . derisione dignas næniis, etc. etc.

[3] The assemblies of Charlemagne were political as well as ecclesiastical; and the three hundred members (Nat. Alexander, sect. viii. p. 53) who sat and voted at Frankfort must include not only the bishops, but the abbots, and even the principal laymen.

[4] Qui supra sanctissima patres nostri (episcopi et sacerdotes) omnimodis servitium et adorationem imaginum renuentes contempserunt, atque consentientes condemnaverunt (Concil. tom. ix. p. 101; Canon ii. Franckfurd). A polemic must be hard-hearted indeed who does not pity the efforts of Baronius, Pagi, Alexander, Maimbourg, etc., to elude this unlucky sentence.

advanced with a silent and insensible progress; but a large atonement is made for their hesitation and delay by the gross idolatry of the ages which precede the reformation, and of the countries, both in Europe and America, which are still immersed in the gloom of superstition.

It was after the Nicene synod, and under the reign of the pious Irene, that the popes consummated the separation of Rome and Italy, by the translation of the empire to the less orthodox Charlemagne. They were compelled to choose between the rival nations: religion was not the sole motive of their choice; and while they dissembled the failings of their friends, they beheld, with reluctance and suspicion, the Catholic virtues of their foes. The difference of language and manners had perpetuated the enmity of the two capitals; and they were alienated from each other by the hostile opposition of seventy years. In that schism the Romans had tasted of freedom, and the popes of sovereignty: their submission would have exposed them to the revenge of a jealous tyrant; and the revolution of Italy had betrayed the impotence, as well as the tyranny, of the Byzantine court. The Greek emperors had restored the images, but they had not restored the Calabrian estates [1] and the Illyrian diocese,[2] which the Iconoclasts had torn away from the successors of St. Peter; and Pope Adrian threatens them with a sentence of excommunication unless they speedily abjure this practical heresy.[3] The Greeks were now orthodox; but their religion might be tainted by the breath of the reigning monarch: the

---

[1] Theophanes (p. 343 [tom. i. p. 631, ed. Bonn]) specifies those of Sicily and Calabria, which yielded an annual rent of three talents and a half of gold (perhaps £7000 sterling). Liutprand more pompously enumerates the patrimonies of the Roman church in Greece, Judæa, Persia, Mesopotamia, Babylonia, Egypt, and Libya, which were detained by the injustice of the Greek emperor (Legat. ad Nicephorum, in Script. Rerum Italicarum, tom. ii. pars i. p. 481).

[2] The great diocese of the Eastern Illyricum, with Apulia, Calabria, and Sicily (Thomassin, Discipline de l'Eglise, tom. i. p. 145). By the confession of the Greeks, the patriarch of Constantinople had detached from Rome the metropolitans of Thessalonica, Athens, Corinth, Nicopolis, and Patræ (Luc. Holsten. Geograph. Sacra, p. 22); and his spiritual conquests extended to Naples and Amalfi (Giannone, Istoria Civile di Napoli, tom. i. p. 517-524; Pagi, A.D. 730, No. 11).

[3] In hoc ostenditur, quia ex uno capitulo ab errore reversis, in aliis duobus, in *eodem* (was it the same?) permaneant errore . . . de diocesi S. R. E. seu de patrimoniis iterum increpantes commonemus, ut si ea restituere noluerit hereticum eum pro hujusmodi errore perseverantiâ decernemus (Epist. Hadrian. Papæ ad Carolum Magnum, in Concil. tom. viii. p. 1598); to which he adds a reason most directly opposite to his conduct, that he preferred the salvation of souls and rule of faith to the goods of this transitory world.

Franks were now contumacious; but a discerning eye might discern their approaching conversion, from the use, to the adoration, of images. The name of Charlemagne was stained by the polemic acrimony of his scribes; but the conqueror himself conformed, with the temper of a statesman, to the various practice of France and Italy. In his four pilgrimages or visits to the Vatican he embraced the popes in the communion of friendship and piety; knelt before the tomb, and consequently before the image, of the apostle; and joined, without scruple, in all the prayers and processions of the Roman liturgy. Would prudence or gratitude allow the pontiffs to renounce their benefactor? Had they a right to alienate his gift of the Exarchate? Had they power to abolish his government of Rome? The title of patrician was below the merit and greatness of Charlemagne; and it was only by reviving the Western empire that they could pay their obligations or secure their establishment. By this decisive measure they would finally eradicate the claims of the Greeks: from the debasement of a provincial town, the majesty of Rome would be restored; the Latin Christians would be united, under a supreme head, in their ancient metropolis; and the conquerors of the West would receive their crown from the successors of St. Peter. The Roman church would acquire a zealous and respectable advocate; and, under the shadow of the Carlovingian power, the bishop might exercise, with honour and safety, the government of the city.[1]

Before the ruin of Paganism in Rome the competition for a wealthy bishopric had often been productive of tumult and bloodshed. The people was less numerous, but the times were more savage, the prize more important, and the chair of St. Peter was fiercely disputed by the leading ecclesiastics who aspired to the rank of sovereign. The reign of Adrian the First [2]

---

[1] Fontanini considers the emperors as no more than the advocates of the church (advocatus et defensor S. R. E. See Ducange, Gloss. Lat. tom. i. p. 97). His antagonist Muratori reduces the popes to be no more than the exarchs of the emperor. In the more equitable view of Mosheim (Institut. Hist. Eccles. p. 264, 265), they held Rome under the empire as the most honourable species of fief or benefice—premuntur nocte caliginosâ!

[2] His merits and hopes are summed up in an epitaph of thirty-eight verses, of which Charlemagne declares himself the author (Concil. tom. viii. p. 520).

> Post patrem lacrymans Carolus hæc carmina scripsi.
> Tu mihi dulcis amor, te modo plango pater . .
> Nomina jungo simul titulis, clarissime, nostra
> Adrianus, Carolus, rex ego, tuque pater.

The poetry might be supplied by Alcuin; but the tears, the most glorious tribute, can only belong to Charlemagne.

surpasses the measure of past or succeeding ages;[1] the walls of Rome, the sacred patrimony, the ruin of the Lombards, and the friendship of Charlemagne, were the trophies of his fame: he secretly edified the throne of his successors, and displayed in a narrow space the virtues of a great prince. His memory was revered; but in the next election, a priest of the Lateran, Leo the Third, was preferred to the nephew and the favourite of Adrian, whom he had promoted to the first dignities of the church. Their acquiescence or repentance disguised, above four years, the blackest intention of revenge, till the day of a procession, when a furious band of conspirators dispersed the unarmed multitude, and assaulted with blows and wounds the sacred person of the pope. But their enterprise on his life or liberty was disappointed, perhaps by their own confusion and remorse. Leo was left for dead on the ground: on his revival from the swoon, the effect of his loss of blood, he recovered his speech and sight; and this natural event was improved to the miraculous restoration of his eyes and tongue, of which he had been deprived, twice deprived, by the knife of the assassins.[2] From his prison he escaped to the Vatican: the duke of Spoleto hastened to his rescue, Charlemagne sympathised in his injury, and in his camp of Paderborn in Westphalia accepted, or solicited, a visit from the Roman pontiff. Leo repassed the Alps with a commission of counts and bishops, the guards of his safety and the judges of his innocence; and it was not without reluctance that the conqueror of the Saxons delayed till the ensuing year the personal discharge of this pious office. In his fourth and last pilgrimage he was received at Rome with the due honours of king and patrician: Leo was permitted to purge himself by oath of the crimes imputed to his charge: his enemies were silenced, and the sacrilegious attempt against his life was punished by the mild and insufficient penalty of exile. On the festival of Christmas, the last year of the eighth century, Charlemagne appeared in the church of St. Peter; and, to gratify the vanity

---

[1] Every new pope is admonished—" Sancte Pater, non videbis annos Petri," twenty-five years. On the whole series the average is about eight years—a short hope for an ambitious cardinal.

[2] The assurance of Anastasius (tom. iii. pars i. p. 197, 198) is supported by the credulity of some French annalists; but Eginhard, and other writers of the same age, are more natural and sincere. " Unus ei oculus paululum est læsus," says John the deacon of Naples (Vit. Episcop. Napol. in Scriptores Muratori, tom. i. pars ii. p. 312). Theodolphus, a contemporary bishop of Orleans, observes with prudence (l. iii. carm. 3):—

Reddita sunt? mirum est: mirum est auferre nequisse.
Est tamen in dubio, hinc mirer an inde magis.

of Rome, he had exchanged the simple dress of his country for the habit of a patrician.[1] After the celebration of the holy mysteries, Leo suddenly placed a precious crown on his head,[2] and the dome resounded with the acclamations of the people, " Long life and victory to Charles, the most pious Augustus, crowned by God the great and pacific emperor of the Romans!" The head and body of Charlemagne were consecrated by the royal unction: after the example of the Cæsars, he was saluted or adored by the pontiff: his coronation oath represents a promise to maintain the faith and privileges of the church; and the first-fruits were paid in his rich offerings to the shrine of the apostle. In his familiar conversation the emperor protested his ignorance of the intentions of Leo, which he would have disappointed by his absence on that memorable day. But the preparations of the ceremony must have disclosed the secret; and the journey of Charlemagne reveals his knowledge and expectation: he had acknowledged that the Imperial title was the object of his ambition, and a Roman synod had pronounced that it was the only adequate reward of his merit and services.[3]

The appellation of *great* has been often bestowed, and sometimes deserved, but CHARLEMAGNE is the only prince in whose favour the title has been indissolubly blended with the name. That name, with the addition of *saint*, is inserted in the Roman calendar; and the saint, by a rare felicity, is crowned with the praises of the historians and philosophers of an enlightened age.[4]

---

[1] Twice, at the request of Adrian and Leo, he appeared at Rome—longâ tunicâ et chlamyde amictus, et calceamentis quoque Romano more formatis. Eginhard (c. xxiii. p. 109-113) describes, like Suetonius, the simplicity of his dress, so popular in the nation, that, when Charles the Bald returned to France in a foreign habit, the patriotic dogs barked at the apostate (Gaillard, Vie de Charlemagne, tom. iv. p. 109).

[2] See Anastasius (p. 199) and Eginhard (c. xxviii. p. 124-128). The unction is mentioned by Theophanes (p. 399 [tom. i. p. 733, ed. Bonn]), the oath by Sigonius (from the Ordo Romanus), and the pope's adoration, more antiquorum principum, by the Annales Bertiniani (Script. Murator. tom. ii. pars ii. p. 505).

[3] This great event of the translation or restoration of the empire is related and discussed by Natalis Alexander (secul. ix. dissert. i. p. 390-397), Pagi (tom. iii. p. 418), Muratori (Annali d'Italia, tom. vi. p. 339-352), Sigonius (de Regno Italiæ, l. iv. Opp. tom. ii. p. 247-251), Spanheim (de fictâ Translatione Imperii), Giannone (tom. i. p. 395-405), St. Marc (Abrégé Chronologique, tom. i. p. 438-450), Galliard (Hist. de Charlemagne, tom. ii. p. 386-446). Almost all these moderns have some religious or national bias.

[4] By Mably (Observations sur l'Histoire de France), Voltaire (Histoire Générale), Robertson (History of Charles V.), and Montesquieu (Esprit des Loix, l. xxxi. c. 18). In the year 1782 M. Gaillard published his Histoire de Charlemagne (in 4 vols. in 12mo), which I have freely and profitably used. The author is a man of sense and humanity, and his work is laboured

His *real* merit is doubtless enhanced by the barbarism of the nation and the times from which he emerged: but the *apparent* magnitude of an object is likewise enlarged by an unequal comparison; and the ruins of Palmyra derive a casual splendour from the nakedness of the surrounding desert. Without injustice to his fame, I may discern some blemishes in the sanctity and greatness of the restorer of the Western empire. Of his moral virtues, chastity is not the most conspicuous: [1] but the public happiness could not be materially injured by his nine wives or concubines, the various indulgence of meaner or more transient amours, the multitude of his bastards whom he bestowed on the church, and the long celibacy and licentious manners of his daughters,[2] whom the father was suspected of loving with too fond a passion. I shall be scarcely permitted to accuse the ambition of a conqueror; but in a day of equal retribution, the sons of his brother Carloman, the Merovingian princes of Aquitain, and the four thousand five hundred Saxons who were beheaded on the same spot, would have something to allege against the justice and humanity of Charlemagne. His treatment of the vanquished Saxons [3] was an abuse of the right of conquest; his laws were not less sanguinary than his arms, and, in the discussion of his motives, whatever is subtracted from bigotry must be imputed to temper. The sedentary reader is amazed by his incessant activity of mind and body; and his subjects and enemies were not less astonished at his sudden presence at the moment when they believed him at the most distant extremity of the empire; neither peace nor war, nor summer nor winter, were a season of repose; and our fancy cannot easily reconcile the annals of his reign with the geography

with industry and elegance. But I have likewise examined the original monuments of the reigns of Pepin and Charlemagne, in the fifth volume of the Historians of France.

[1] The vision of Weltin, composed by a monk eleven years after the death of Charlemagne, shows him in purgatory, with a vulture, who is perpetually gnawing the guilty member, while the rest of his body, the emblem of his virtues, is sound and perfect (see Galliard, tom. ii. p. 317-360).

[2] The marriage of Eginhard with Imma, daughter of Charlemagne, is, in my opinion, sufficiently refuted by the *probrum* and *suspicio* that sullied these fair damsels, without excepting his own wife (c. xix. p. 98-100, cum Notis Schmincke). The husband must have been too strong for the historian.

[3] Besides the massacres and transmigrations, the pain of death was pronounced against the following crimes:—1. The refusal of baptism. 2. The false pretence of baptism. 3. A relapse to idolatry. 4. The murder of a priest or bishop. 5. Human sacrifices. 6. Eating meat in Lent. But every crime might be expiated by baptism or penance (Galliard, tom. ii. p. 241-247); and the Christian Saxons became the friends and equals of the Franks (Struv. Corpus Hist. Germanicæ, p. 133).

of his expeditions.[1] But this activity was a national, rather than a personal virtue: the vagrant life of a Frank was spent in the chase, in pilgrimage, in military adventures; and the journeys of Charlemagne were distinguished only by a more numerous train and a more important purpose. His military renown must be tried by the scrutiny of his troops, his enemies, and his actions. Alexander conquered with the arms of Philip, but the *two* heroes who preceded Charlemagne bequeathed him their name, their examples, and the companions of their victories. At the head of his veteran and superior armies he oppressed the savage or degenerate nations, who were incapable of confederating for their common safety; nor did he ever encounter an equal antagonist in numbers, in discipline, or in arms. The science of war has been lost and revived with the arts of peace; but his campaigns are not illustrated by any siege or battle of singular difficulty and success; and he might behold with envy the Saracen trophies of his grandfather. After his Spanish expedition his rear-guard was defeated in the Pyrenæan mountains; and the soldiers, whose situation was irretrievable, and whose valour was useless, might accuse, with their last breath, the want of skill or caution of their general.[2] I touch with reverence the laws of Charlemagne, so highly applauded by a respectable judge. They compose not a system, but a series, of occasional and minute edicts, for the correction of abuses, the reformation of manners, the economy of his farms, the care of his poultry, and even the sale of his eggs. He wished to improve the laws and the character of the Franks; and his attempts, however feeble and imperfect, are deserving of praise: the inveterate evils of the times were suspended or mollified by his government;[3] but in his institutions I can seldom discover the general views and the immortal spirit of a legislator, who survives

---

[1] [M. Guizot, in his Cours d'Histoire Moderne, has compiled the following statement of Charlemagne's military campaigns, viz.:—

1 against the Aquitanians.			1 against the Bavarians.
18	,,	Saxons.	4	,,	Slaves beyond the Elbe.
5	,,	Lombards.	5	,,	Saracens in Italy.
7	,,	Arabs in Spain.	3	,,	Danes.
1	,,	Thuringians.	2	,,	Greeks.
4	,,	Avars.	—		
2	,,	Bretons.	53 campaigns.—O. S.]		

[2] In this action the famous Rutland, Rolando, Orlando, was slain—cum compluribus aliis. See the truth in Eginhard (c. 9, p. 51-56), and the fable in an ingenious Supplement of M. Gaillard (tom. iii. p. 474). The Spaniards are too proud of a victory which history ascribes to the Gascons, and romance to the Saracens.

[3] Yet Schmidt, from the best authorities, represents the interior disorders and oppression of his reign (Hist. des Allemands, tom. ii. p. 45-49).

himself for the benefit of posterity.   The union and stability of his empire depended on 'the life of a single man: he imitated the dangerous practice of dividing his kingdoms among his sons; and, after his numerous diets, the whole constitution was left to fluctuate between the disorders of anarchy and despotism. His esteem for the piety and knowledge of the clergy tempted him to intrust that aspiring order with temporal dominion and civil jurisdiction; and his son Lewis, when he was stripped and degraded by the bishops, might accuse, in some measure, the imprudence of his father.   His laws enforced the imposition of tithes, because the demons had proclaimed in the air that the default of payment had been the cause of the last scarcity.[1] The literary merits of Charlemagne are attested by the foundation of schools, the introduction of arts, the works which were published in his name, and his familiar connection with the subjects and strangers whom he invited to his court to educate both the prince and people.   His own studies were tardy, laborious, and imperfect; if he spoke Latin, and understood Greek, he derived the rudiments of knowledge from conversation, rather than from books; and, in his mature age, the emperor strove to acquire the practice of writing, which every peasant now learns in his infancy.[2]   The grammar and logic, the music and astronomy, of the times were only cultivated as the handmaids of superstition; but the curiosity of the human mind must ultimately tend to its improvement, and the encouragement of learning reflects the purest and most pleasing lustre on the character of Charlemagne.[3]   The dignity of his person,[4] the length of his reign, the prosperity of his arms, the

[1] Omnis homo ex suâ proprietate legitimam decimam ad ecclesiam conferat.   Experimento enim didicimus, in anno, quo illa valida fames irrepsit, ebullire vacuas annonas à dæmonibus devoratas, et voces exprobrationis auditas.   Such is the decree and assertion of the great Council of Frankfort (Canon xxv. tom. ix. p. 105)   Both Selden (Hist. of Tithes; Works, vol. iii. part ii. p. 1146) and Montesquieu (Esprit des Loix, l. xxxi. c. 12) represent Charlemagne as the first *legal* author of tithes.   Such obligations have country gentlemen to his memory!

[2] Eginhard (c. 25, p. 119) clearly affirms, tentabat et scribere . . . sed parum prospere successit labor præposterus et sero inchoatus.   The moderns have perverted and corrected this obvious meaning, and the title of M. Gaillard's Dissertation (tom. iii. p. 247-260) betrays his partiality.

[3] See Gaillard, tom. iii. p. 138-176, and Schmidt, tom. ii. p. 121-129.

[4] M. Gaillard (tom. iii. p. 372) fixes the true stature of Charlemagne (see a Dissertation of Marquard Freher ad calcem Eginhard, p. 220, etc.) at five feet nine inches of French, about six feet one inch and a fourth English, measure.   The romance-writers have increased it to eight feet, and the giant was endowed with matchless strength and appetite: at a single stroke of his good sword *Joyeuse*, he cut asunder a horseman and his horse; at a single repast he devoured a goose, two fowls, a quarter of mutton, etc.

vigour of his government, and the reverence of distant nations, distinguish him from the royal crowd; and Europe dates a new era from his restoration of the Western empire.

That empire was not unworthy of its title,[1] and some of the fairest kingdoms of Europe were the patrimony or conquest of a prince who reigned at the same time in France, Spain, Italy, Germany, and Hungary.[2]   I. The Roman province of Gaul had been transformed into the name and monarchy of FRANCE: but, in the decay of the Merovingian line, its limits were contracted by the independence of the *Britons* and the revolt of *Aquitain*. Charlemagne pursued and confined the Britons on the shores of the ocean; and that ferocious tribe, whose origin and language are so different from the French, was chastised by the imposition of tribute, hostages, and peace. After a long and evasive contest, the rebellion of the dukes of Aquitain was punished by the forfeiture of their province, their liberty, and their lives. Harsh and rigorous would have been such treatment of ambitious governors, who had too faithfully copied the mayors of the palace. But a recent discovery[3] has proved that these unhappy princes were the last and lawful heirs of the blood and sceptre of Clovis, a younger branch, from the brother of Dagobert, of the Merovingian house. Their ancient kingdom was reduced to the duchy of Gascogne, to the counties of Fesenzac and Armagnac, at the foot of the Pyrenees: their race was propagated till the beginning of the sixteenth century, and, after surviving their Carlovingian tyrants, they were reserved to feel the injustice or the favours of a third dynasty. By the re-union of Aquitain, France was enlarged to its present boundaries, with the additions of the Netherlands and Spain, as far as the Rhine.   II. The Saracens had been expelled from

[1] See the concise, but correct and original, work of D'Anville (Etats formés en Europe après la Chute de l'Empire Romain en Occident, Paris, 1771, in 4to), whose map includes the empire of Charlemagne; the different parts are illustrated—by Valesius (Notitia Galliarum) for France, Beretti (Dissertatio Chorographica) for Italy, De Marca (Marca Hispanica) for Spain. For the middle geography of Germany I confess myself poor and destitute.

[2] After a brief relation of his wars and conquests (Vit. Carol. c. 5-14), Eginhard recapitulates, in a few words (c. 15), the countries subject to his empire. Struvius (Corpus Hist. German. p. 118-149) has inserted in his Notes the texts of the old Chronicles.

[3] Of a charter granted to the monastery of Alaon (A.D. 845) by Charles the Bald, which deduces this royal pedigree. I doubt whether some subsequent links of the ninth and tenth centuries are equally firm; yet the whole is approved and defended by M. Gaillard (tom. ii. p. 60-81, 203-206), who affirms that the family of Montesquiou (not of the President de Montesquieu) is descended, in the female line, from Clotaire and Clovis—an innocent pretension!

France by the grandfather and father of Charlemagne; but they still possessed the greatest part of SPAIN, from the rock of Gibraltar to the Pyrenees. Amidst their civil divisions, an Arabian emir of Saragossa implored his protection in the diet of Paderborn. Charlemagne undertook the expedition, restored the emir, and, without distinction of faith, impartially crushed the resistance of the Christians, and rewarded the obedience and service of the Mohammedans. In his absence he instituted the *Spanish march*,[1] which extended from the Pyrenees to the river Ebro: Barcelona was the residence of the French governor; he possessed the counties of *Rousillon* and *Catalonia*, and the infant kingdoms of *Navarre* and *Arragon* were subject to his jurisdiction. III. As king of the Lombards and patrician of Rome he reigned over the greatest part of ITALY,[2] a tract of a thousand miles from the Alps to the borders of Calabria. The duchy of *Beneventum*, a Lombard fief, had spread, at the expense of the Greeks, over the modern kingdom of Naples. But Arrechis, the reigning duke, refused to be included in the slavery of his country, assumed the independent title of prince, and opposed his sword to the Carlovingian monarchy. His defence was firm, his submission was not inglorious, and the emperor was content with an easy tribute, the demolition of his fortresses, and the acknowledgment, on his coins, of a supreme lord. The artful flattery of his son Grimoald added the appellation of father, but he asserted his dignity with prudence, and Beneventum insensibly escaped from the French yoke.[3] IV. Charlemagne was the first who united GERMANY under the same sceptre. The name of *Oriental France* is preserved in the circle of *Franconia*; and the people of *Hesse* and *Thuringia* were recently incorporated with the victors by the conformity of religion and government. The *Alemanni*, so formidable to the Romans, were the faithful vassals and confederates of the Franks, and their country was inscribed within the modern limits of *Alsace*, *Swabia*, and *Switzerland*. The *Bavarians*, with a similar indulgence of their laws and manners, were less patient of a master: the repeated treasons of Tasillo justified the abolition

[1] The governors or counts of the Spanish march revolted from Charles the Simple about the year 900; and a poor pittance, the Rousillon, has been recovered in 1642 by the kings of France (Longuerue, Description de la France, tom. i. p. 220-222). Yet the Rousillon contains 188,900 subjects, and annually pays 2,600,000 livres (Necker, Administration des Finances, tom. i. p. 278, 279); more people, perhaps, and doubtless more money, than the march of Charlemagne.

[2] Schmidt, Hist. des Allemands, tom. ii. p. 200, etc.

[3] See Giannone, tom. i. p. 374, 375, and the Annals of Muratori.

of their hereditary dukes, and their power was shared among the counts who judged and guarded that important frontier. But the north of Germany, from the Rhine and beyond the Elbe, was still hostile and Pagan; nor was it till after a war of thirty-three years that the Saxons bowed under the yoke of Christ and of Charlemagne. The idols and their votaries were extirpated; the foundation of eight bishoprics, of Munster, Osnaburgh, Paderborn, and Minden, of Bremen, Verden, Hildesheim, and Halberstadt, define, on either side of the Weser, the bounds of ancient Saxony; these episcopal seats were the first schools and cities of that savage land, and the religion and humanity of the children atoned, in some degree, for the massacre of the parents. Beyond the Elbe, the *Slavi*, or Sclavonians, of similar manners and various denominations, overspread the modern dominions of Prussia, Poland, and Bohemia, and some transient marks of obedience have tempted the French historian to extend the empire to the Baltic and the Vistula. The conquest or conversion of those countries is of a more recent age, but the first union of *Bohemia* with the Germanic body may be justly ascribed to the arms of Charlemagne. V. He retaliated on the Avars, or Huns of Pannonia, the same calamities which they had inflicted on the nations. Their rings, the wooden fortifications which encircled their districts and villages, were broken down by the triple effort of a French army that was poured into their country by land and water, through the Carpathian mountains and along the plain of the Danube. After a bloody conflict of eight years, the loss of some French generals was avenged by the slaughter of the most noble Huns: the relics of the nation submitted: the royal residence of the chagan was left desolate and unknown; and the treasures, the rapine of two hundred and fifty years, enriched the victorious troops, or decorated the churches, of Italy and Gaul.[1] After the reduction of Pannonia, the empire of Charlemagne was bounded only by the conflux of the Danube with the Theiss and the Save: the provinces of Istria, Liburnia, and Dalmatia were an easy though unprofitable accession; and it was an effect of his moderation that he left the maritime cities under the real or nominal sovereignty of the Greeks. But these distant possessions added more to the reputation than to the power of the

---

[1] Quot prælia in eo gesta! quantum sanguinis effusum sit! Testatur vacua omni habitatione Pannonia, et locus in quo regia Cagani fuit ita desertus, ut ne vestigium quidem humanæ habitationis appareat. Tota in hoc bello Hunnorum nobilitas periit, tota gloria decidit, omnis pecunia et congesti ex longo tempore thesauri direpti sunt. Eginhard, c. 13.

Latin emperor; nor did he risk any ecclesiastical foundations to reclaim the barbarians from their vagrant life and idolatrous worship. Some canals of communication between the rivers, the Saône and the Meuse, the Rhine and the Danube, were faintly attempted.[1] Their execution would have vivified the empire; and more cost and labour were often wasted in the structure of a cathedral.

If we retrace the outlines of this geographical picture, it will be seen that the empire of the Franks extended, between east and west, from the Ebro to the Elbe or Vistula; between the north and south, from the duchy of Beneventum to the river Eyder, the perpetual boundary of Germany and Denmark. The personal and political importance of Charlemagne was magnified by the distress and division of the rest of Europe. The islands of Great Britain and Ireland were disputed by a crowd of princes of Saxon or Scottish origin; and, after the loss of Spain, the Christian and Gothic kingdom of Alphonso the Chaste was confined to the narrow range of the Asturian mountains. These petty sovereigns revered the power or virtue of the Carlovingian monarch, implored the honour and support of his alliance, and styled him their common parent, the sole and supreme emperor of the West.[2] He maintained a more equal intercourse with the caliph Harun al Rashid,[3] whose dominion stretched from Africa to India, and accepted from his ambassadors a tent, a water-clock, an elephant, and the keys of the Holy Sepulchre. It is not easy to conceive the private friendship of a Frank and an Arab, who were strangers to each other's person, and language, and religion: but their public correspondence was founded on vanity, and their remote situation left no room for a competition of interest. Two-thirds of the Western empire of Rome were subject to Charlemagne, and the deficiency was amply supplied by his command of the inaccessible or invincible nations of

[1] The junction of the Rhine and Danube was undertaken only for the service of the Pannonian war (Gaillard, Vie de Charlemagne, tom. ii. p. 312-315). The canal, which would have been only two leagues in length, and of which some traces are still extant in Swabia, was interrupted by excessive rains, military avocations, and superstitious fears (Schæpflin, Hist. de l'Académie des Inscriptions, tom. xviii. p. 256; Molimina fluviorum, etc., jungendorum, p. 59-62).

[2] See Eginhard, c. 16; and Galliard, tom. ii. p. 361-385, who mentions with a loose reference, the intercourse of Charlemagne and Egbert, the emperor's gift of his own sword, and the modest answer of his Saxon disciple. The anecdote, if genuine, would have adorned our English histories.

[3] The correspondence is mentioned only in the French annals, and the Orientals are ignorant of the caliph's friendship for the *Christian dog*—a polite appellation, which Harun bestows on the emperor of the Greeks.

Germany. But in the choice of his enemies we may be reasonably surprised that he so often preferred the poverty of the north to the riches of the south. The three-and-thirty campaigns laboriously consumed in the woods and morasses of Germany would have sufficed to assert the amplitude of his title by the expulsion of the Greeks from Italy and the Saracens from Spain. The weakness of the Greeks would have insured an easy victory: and the holy crusade against the Saracens would have been prompted by glory and revenge, and loudly justified by religion and policy. Perhaps, in his expeditions beyond the Rhine and the Elbe, he aspired to save his monarchy from the fate of the Roman empire, to disarm the enemies of civilised society, and to eradicate the seed of future emigrations. But it has been wisely observed, that, in a light of precaution, all conquest must be ineffectual, unless it could be universal, since the increasing circle must be involved in a larger sphere of hostility.[1] The subjugation of Germany withdrew the veil which had so long concealed the continent or islands of Scandinavia from the knowledge of Europe, and awakened the torpid courage of their barbarous natives. The fiercest of the Saxon idolaters escaped from the Christian tyrant to their brethren of the North; the Ocean and Mediterranean were covered with their piratical fleets; and Charlemagne beheld with a sigh the destructive progress of the Normans, who, in less than seventy years, precipitated the fall of his race and monarchy.

Had the pope and the Romans revived the primitive constitution, the titles of emperor and Augustus were conferred on Charlemagne for the term of his life; and his successors, on each vacancy, must have ascended the throne by a formal or tacit election. But the association of his son Lewis the Pious asserts the independent right of monarchy and conquest, and the emperor seems on this occasion to have foreseen and prevented the latent claims of the clergy. The royal youth was commanded to take the crown from the altar, and with his own hands to place it on his head, as a gift which he held from God, his father, and the nation.[2] The same ceremony was repeated,

[1] Gaillard, tom. ii. p. 361-365, 471-476, 492. I have borrowed his judicious remarks on Charlemagne's plan of conquest, and the judicious distinction of his enemies of the first and the second *enceinte* (tom. ii. p. 184, 509, etc.).

[2] Thegan, the biographer of Lewis, relates this coronation; and Baronius has honestly transcribed it (A.D. 813, No. 13, etc.; see Gaillard, tom. ii. p. 506, 507, 508), howsoever adverse to the claims of the popes. For the series of the Carlovingians, see the historians of France, Italy, and Germany; Pfeffel, Schmidt, Velly, Muratori, and even Voltaire, whose pictures are sometimes just, and always pleasing.

though with less energy, in the subsequent associations of Lothaire and Lewis the Second: the Carlovingian sceptre was transmitted from father to son in a lineal descent of four generations; and the ambition of the popes was reduced to the empty honour of crowning and anointing these hereditary princes, who were already invested with their power and dominions. The pious Lewis survived his brothers, and embraced the whole empire of Charlemagne; but the nations and the nobles, his bishops and his children, quickly discerned that this mighty mass was no longer inspired by the same soul; and the foundations were undermined to the centre, while the external surface was yet fair and entire. After a war, or battle, which consumed one hundred thousand Franks, the empire was divided by treaty between his three sons, who had violated every filial and fraternal duty. The kingdoms of Germany and France were for ever separated; the provinces of Gaul, between the Rhone and the Alps, the Meuse and the Rhine, were assigned, with Italy, to the Imperial dignity of Lothaire. In the partition of his share, Lorraine and Arles, two recent and transitory kingdoms, were bestowed on the younger children: and Lewis the Second, his eldest son, was content with the realm of Italy, the proper and sufficient patrimony of a Roman emperor. On his death, without any male issue, the vacant throne was disputed by his uncles and cousins and the popes most dexterously seized the occasion of judging the claims and merits of the candidates, and of bestowing on the most obsequious, or most liberal, the Imperial office of advocate of the Roman church. The dregs of the Carlovingian race no longer exhibited any symptoms of virtue or power, and the ridiculous epithets of the *bald*, the *stammerer*, the *fat*, and the *simple*, distinguished the tame and uniform features of a crowd of kings alike deserving of oblivion. By the failure of the collateral branches the whole inheritance devolved to Charles the Fat, the last emperor of his family: his insanity authorised the desertion of Germany, Italy, and France: he was deposed in a diet, and solicited his daily bread from the rebels by whose contempt his life and liberty had been spared. According to the measure of their force, the governors, the bishops, and the lords usurped the fragments of the falling empire; and some preference was shown to the female or illegitimate blood of Charlemagne. Of the greater part, the title and possession were alike doubtful, and the merit was adequate to the contracted scale of their dominions.. Those who could appear with an army at the gates of Rome were crowned emperors in the Vatican; but their modesty was more frequently satisfied with the appellation of kings of Italy: and the whole term of seventy-four years may be deemed a vacancy, from the abdication of Charles the Fat to the establishment of Otho the First.

Otho [1] was of the noble race of the dukes of Saxony; and if he truly descended from Witikind, the adversary and proselyte of Charlemagne, the posterity of a vanquished people was exalted to reign over their conquerors. His father, Henry the Fowler, was elected, by the suffrage of the nation, to save and institute the kingdom of Germany. Its limits [2] were enlarged on every side by his son, the first and greatest of the Othos. A portion of Gaul, to the west of the Rhine, along the banks of the Meuse and the Moselle, was assigned to the Germans, by whose blood and language it has been tinged since the time of Cæsar and Tacitus. Between the Rhine, the Rhone, and the Alps, the successors of Otho acquired a vain supremacy over the broken kingdoms of Burgundy and Arles. In the North, Christianity was propagated by the sword of Otho, the conqueror and apostle of the Slavic nations of the Elbe and Oder: the marches of Brandenburg and Sleswick were fortified with German colonies; and the king of Denmark, the dukes of Poland and Bohemia, confessed themselves his tributary vassals. At the head of a victorious army he passed the Alps, subdued the kingdom of Italy, delivered the pope, and for ever fixed the Imperial crown in the name and nation of Germany. From that memorable era two maxims of public jurisprudence were introduced by force and ratified by time. I. *That* the prince, who was elected in the German diet, acquired from that instant the subject kingdoms of Italy and Rome. II. But that he might not legally assume the titles of emperor and Augustus, till he had received the crown from the hands of the Roman pontiff.[3]

[1] He was the son of Otho, the son of Ludolph, in whose favour the duchy of Saxony had been instituted, A.D. 858. Ruotgerus, the biographer of a St. Bruno (Biblioth. Bunavianæ Catalog. tom. iii. vol. ii. p. 679), gives a splendid character of his family. Atavorum atavi usque ad hominum memoriam omnes nobilissimi; nullus in eorum stirpe ignotus, nullus degener facile reperitur (apud Struvium, Corp. Hist. German. p. 216). Yet Gundling (in Henrico Aucupe) is not satisfied of his descent from Witikind.

[2] See the treatise of Conringius (de Finibus Imperii Germanici, Francofurt. 1680, in 4to); he rejects the extravagant and improper scale of the Roman and Carlovingian empires, and discusses with moderation the rights of Germany, her vassals, and her neighbours.

[3] The power of custom forces me to number Conrad I. and Henry I., the Fowler, in the list of emperors, a title which was never assumed by those

The imperial dignity of Charlemagne was announced to the East by the alteration of his style; and instead of saluting his fathers, the Greek emperors, he presumed to adopt the more equal and familiar appellation of brother.[1] Perhaps in his connection with Irene he aspired to the name of husband: his embassy to Constantinople spoke the language of peace and friendship, and might conceal a treaty of marriage with that ambitious princess, who had renounced the most sacred duties of a mother. The nature, the duration, the probable consequences of such a union between two distant and dissonant empires, it is impossible to conjecture; but the unanimous silence of the Latins may teach us to suspect that the report was invented by the enemies of Irene, to charge her with the guilt of betraying the church and state to the strangers of the West.[2] The French ambassadors were the spectators, and had nearly been the victims, of the conspiracy of Nicephorus, and the national hatred. Constantinople was exasperated by the treason and sacrilege of ancient Rome: a proverb, " That the Franks were good friends and bad neighbours," was in every one's mouth; but it was dangerous to provoke a neighbour who might be tempted to reiterate, in the church of St. Sophia, the ceremony of his Imperial coronation. After a tedious journey of circuit and delay, the ambassadors of Nicephorus found him in his camp, on the banks of the river Sala; and Charlemagne affected to confound their vanity by displaying, in a Franconian village, the pomp, or at least the pride, of the Byzantine palace.[3] The Greeks were successively led through four halls of audience: in the first they were ready to fall prostrate before a splendid personage in a chair of state, till he informed them that he was only a servant, the constable, or master of the horse, of the emperor. The same mistake and the same answer were repeated

kings of Germany. The Italians, Muratori for instance, are more scrupulous and correct, and only reckon the princes who have been crowned at Rome.

[1] Invidiam tamen suscepti nominis (C. P. imperatoribus super hoc indignantibus) magnâ tulit patientiâ, vicitque eorum contumaciam . . . mittendo ad eos crebras legationes, et in epistolis fratres eos appellando. Eginhard, c. 28, p. 128. Perhaps it was on their account that, like Augustus, he affected some reluctance to receive the empire.

[2] Theophanes speaks of the coronation and unction of Charles, Κάρουλος (Chronograph. p. 399 [tom. i. p. 733, ed. Bonn]), and of his treaty of marriage with Irene (p. 402 [p. 737, ed. Bonn]), which is unknown to the Latins. Gaillard relates his transactions with the Greek empire (tom. ii. p. 446-468).

[3] Gaillard very properly observes that this pageant was a farce suitable to children only; but that it was indeed represented in the presence, and for the benefit, of children of a larger growth.

in the apartments of the count palatine, the steward, and the chamberlain; and their impatience was gradually heightened, till the doors of the presence-chamber were thrown open, and they beheld the genuine monarch on his throne, enriched with the foreign luxury which he despised, and encircled with the love and reverence of his victorious chiefs. A treaty of peace and alliance was concluded between the two empires, and the limits of the East and West were defined by the right of present possession. But the Greeks [1] soon forgot this humiliating equality, or remembered it only to hate the barbarians by whom it was extorted. During the short union of virtue and power, they respectfully saluted the *august* Charlemagne with the acclamations of *basileus*, and emperor of the Romans. As soon as these qualities were separated in the person of his pious son, the Byzantine letters were inscribed, " To the king, or, as he styles " himself, the emperor, of the Franks and Lombards." When both power and virtue were extinct, they despoiled Lewis the Second of his hereditary title, and, with the barbarous appellation of rex or *rega*, degraded him among the crowd of Latin princes. His reply [2] is expressive of his weakness: he proves, with some learning, that both in sacred and profane history the name of king is synonymous with the Greek word *basileus* : if, at Constantinople, it were assumed in a more exclusive and imperial sense, he claims from his ancestors, and from the pope, a just participation of the honours of the Roman purple. The same controversy was revived in the reign of the Othos; and their ambassador describes in lively colours the insolence of the Byzantine court.[3] The Greeks affected to despise the poverty and ignorance of the Franks and Saxons; and in their last decline refused to prostitute to the kings of Germany the title of Roman emperors.

---

[1] Compare in the original texts collected by Pagi (tom. iii. A.D. 812, No. 7, A.D. 824, No. 10, etc.) the contrast of Charlemagne and his son: to the former the ambassadors of Michael (who were indeed disavowed) more suo, id est linguâ Græcâ laudes dixerunt, imperatorem eum et Βασιλέα appellantes; to the latter, *Vocato* imperatori *Francorum*, etc.

[2] See the epistle, in Paralipomena, of the anonymous writer of Salerno (Script. Ital. tom. ii. pars ii. p. 243-254, c. 93¹107), whom Baronius (A.D. 871, No. 51-71) mistook for Erchempert, when he transcribed it in his Annals.

[3] Ipse enim vos, non *imperatorem*, id est Βασιλέα suâ linguâ, sed ob indignationem Ῥῆγα, id est *regem* nostrâ vocabat (Liutprand, in Legat. in Script. Ital. tom. ii. pars i. p. 479). The pope had exhorted Nicephorus, emperor of the *Greeks*, to make peace with Otho, the august emperor of the *Romans*—quæ inscriptio secundum Græcos peccatoria [peccatrix] et temeraria . . . imperatorem inquiunt, *universalem Romanorum, Augustum, magnum, solum*, Nicephorum (ib. p. 486).

These emperors, in the election of the popes, continued to exercise the powers which had been assumed by the Gothic and Grecian princes; and the importance of this prerogative increased with the temporal estate and spiritual jurisdiction of the Roman church. In the Christian aristocracy the principal members of the clergy still formed a senate to assist the administration, and to supply the vacancy, of the bishop. Rome was divided into twenty-eight parishes, and each parish was governed by a cardinal-priest, or presbyter—a title which, however common and modest in its origin, has aspired to emulate the purple of kings. Their number was enlarged by the association of the seven deacons of the most considerable hospitals, the seven palatine judges of the Lateran, and some dignitaries of the church. This ecclesiastical senate was directed by the seven cardinal-bishops of the Roman province, who were less occupied in the suburb dioceses of Ostia, Porto, Velitræ, Tusculum, Præneste, Tibur, and the Sabines, than by their weekly service in the Lateran, and their superior share in the honours and authority of the apostolic see. On the death of the pope these bishops recommended a successor to the suffrage of the college of cardinals,[1] and their choice was ratified or rejected by the applause or clamour of the Roman people. But the election was imperfect; nor could the pontiff be legally consecrated till the emperor, the advocate of the church, had graciously signified his approbation and consent. The royal commissioner examined on the spot the form and freedom of the proceedings; nor was it till after a previous scrutiny into the qualifications of the candidates that he accepted an oath of fidelity, and confirmed the donations which had successively enriched the patrimony of St. Peter. In the frequent schisms the rival claims were submitted to the sentence of the emperor; and in a synod of bishops he presumed to judge, to condemn, and to punish the crimes of a guilty pontiff. Otho the First imposed a treaty on the senate and people, who engaged to prefer the candidate most acceptable to his majesty:[2] his successors anticipated or prevented

---

[1] The origin and progress of the title of cardinal may be found in Thomassin (Discipline de l'Eglise, tom. i. p. 1261-1298), Muratori (Antiquitat. Italiæ Medii Ævi, tom. vi. Dissert. lxi. p. 159-182), and Mosheim (Institut. Hist. Eccles. p. 345-347), who accurately remarks the forms and changes of the election. The cardinal-bishops, so highly exalted by Peter Damianus, are sunk to a level with the rest of the sacred college.

[2] Firmiter jurantes, nunquam se papam electuros aut ordinaturos, præter consensum et electionem Othonis et filii sui (Liutprand, l. vi. c. 6, p. 472). This important concession may either supply or confirm the decree of the clergy and people of Rome, so fiercely rejected by Baronius, Pagi,

their choice: they bestowed the Roman benefice, like the bishoprics of Cologne or Bamberg, on their chancellors or preceptors; and whatever might be the merit of a Frank or Saxon, his name sufficiently attests the interposition of foreign power. These acts of prerogative were most speciously excused by the vices of a popular election. The competitor who had been excluded by the cardinals appealed to the passions or avarice of the multitude; the Vatican and the Lateran were stained with blood; and the most powerful senators, the marquises of Tuscany and the counts of Tusculum, held the apostolic see in a long and disgraceful servitude. The Roman pontiffs of the ninth and tenth centuries were insulted, imprisoned, and murdered by their tyrants; and such was their indigence, after the loss and usurpation of the ecclesiastical patrimonies, that they could neither support the state of a prince, nor exercise the charity of a priest.[1] The influence of two sister prostitutes, Marozia and Theodora, was founded on their wealth and beauty, their political and amorous intrigues: the most strenuous of their lovers were rewarded with the Roman mitre, and their reign [2] may have suggested to the darker ages [3] the fable [4] of a

and Muratori (A.D. 964), and so well defended and explained by St. Marc (Abrégé, tom. ii. p. 808-816, tom. iv. p. 1167-1185). Consult that historical critic, and the Annals of Muratori, for the election and confirmation of each pope.

[1] The oppression and vices of the Roman church in the tenth century are strongly painted in the history and legation of Liutprand (see p. 440, 450, 471-476, 479, etc.); and it is whimsical enough to observe Muratori tempering the invectives of Baronius against the popes. But these popes had been chosen, not by the cardinals, but by lay-patrons.

[2] The time of Pope Joan (*papissa Joanna*) is placed somewhat earlier than Theodora or Marozia; and the two years of her imaginary reign are forcibly inserted between Leo IV. and Benedict III. But the contemporary Anastasius indissolubly links the death of Leo and the elevation of Benedict (illico, mox, p. 247); and the accurate chronology of Pagi, Muratori, and Leibnitz fixes both events to the year 857.

[3] The advocates for Pope Joan produce one hundred and fifty witnesses, or rather echoes, of the fourteenth, fifteenth, and sixteenth centuries. They bear testimony against themselves and the legend, by multiplying the proof that so curious a story *must* have been repeated by writers of every description to whom it was known. On those of the ninth and tenth centuries the recent event would have flashed with a double force. Would Photius have spared such a reproach? Could Liutprand have missed such scandal? It is scarcely worth while to discuss the various readings of Martinus Polonus, Sigebert of Gemblours, or even Marianus Scotus; but a most palpable forgery is the passage of Pope Joan which has been foisted into some MSS. and editions of the Roman Anastasius.

[4] As *false*, it deserves that name; but I would not pronounce it incredible. Suppose a famous French chevalier of our own times to have been born in Italy, and educated in the church, instead of the army: *her* merit or fortune *might* have raised her to St. Peter's chair; her amours would have been natural; her delivery in the streets unlucky, but not improbable.

female pope.[1] The bastard son, the grandson, and the great-grandson of Marozia, a rare genealogy, were seated in the chair of St. Peter; and it was at the age of nineteen years that the second of these became the head of the Latin church. His youth and manhood were of a suitable complexion; and the nations of pilgrims could bear testimony to the charges that were urged against him in a Roman synod, and in the presence of Otho the Great. As John XII. had renounced the dress and decencies of his profession, the *soldier* may not perhaps be dishonoured by the wine which he drank, the blood that he spilt, the flames that he kindled, or the licentious pursuits of gaming and hunting. His open simony might be the consequence of distress; and his blasphemous invocation of Jupiter and Venus, if it be true, could not possibly be serious. But we read, with some surprise, that the worthy grandson of Marozia lived in public adultery with the matrons of Rome; that the Lateran palace was turned into a school for prostitution; and that his rapes of virgins and widows had deterred the female pilgrims from visiting the tomb of St. Peter, lest, in the devout act, they should be violated by his successor.[2] The Protestants have dwelt with malicious pleasure on these characters of antichrist; but to a philosophic eye the vices of the clergy are far less dangerous than their virtues. After a long series of scandal the apostolic see was reformed and exalted by the austerity and zeal of Gregory VII. That ambitious monk devoted his life to the execution of two projects. I. To fix in the college of cardinals the freedom and independence of election, and for ever to abolish the right or usurpation of the emperors and the Roman people. II. To bestow and resume the Western empire as a fief or benefice[3] of the church, and to extend his temporal

---

[1] Till the Reformation the tale was repeated and believed without offence: and Joan's female statue long occupied her place among the popes in the cathedral of Sienna (Pagi, Critica, tom. iii. p. 624-626). She has been annihilated by two learned Protestants, Blondel and Bayle (Dictionnaire Critique, PAPESSE, POLONUS, BLONDEL): but their brethren were scandalised by this equitable and generous criticism. Spanheim and Lenfant attempt to save this poor engine of controversy; and even Mosheim condescends to cherish some doubt and suspicion (p. 289).

[2] Lateranense palatium . . . prostibulum meretricum . . . Testis omnium gentium, præterquam Romanorum, absentia mulierum, quæ sanctorum apostolorum limina orandi gratiâ timent visere, cum nonnullas ante dies paucos, hunc audierint conjugatas, viduas, virgines vi oppressisse (Liutprand, Hist. l. vi. c. 6, p. 471. See the whole affair of John XII. p. 471-476).

[3] A new example of the mischief of equivocation is the *beneficium* (Ducange, tom. i. p. 617, etc.), which the pope conferred on the emperor Frederic I., since the Latin word may signify either a legal fief, of a simple

dominion over the kings and kingdoms of the earth. After a contest of fifty years the first of these designs was accomplished by the firm support of the ecclesiastical order, whose liberty was connected with that of their chief. But the second attempt, though it was crowned with some partial and apparent success, has been vigorously resisted by the secular power, and finally extinguished by the improvement of human reason.

In the revival of the empire of Rome neither the bishop nor the people could bestow on Charlemagne or Otho the provinces which were lost, as they had been won by the chance of arms. But the Romans were free to choose a master for themselves; and the powers which had been delegated to the patrician were irrevocably granted to the French and Saxon emperors of the West. The broken records of the times [1] preserve some remembrance of their palace, their mint, their tribunal, their edicts, and the sword of justice, which, as late as the thirteenth century, was derived from Cæsar to the præfect of the city.[2] Between the arts of the popes and the violence of the people this supremacy was crushed and annihilated. Content with the titles of emperor and Augustus, the successors of Charlemagne neglected to assert this local jurisdiction. In the hour of prosperity their ambition was diverted by more alluring objects; and in the decay and division of the empire they were oppressed by the defence of their hereditary provinces. Amidst the ruins of Italy the famous Marozia invited one of the usurpers to assume the character of her third husband; and Hugh king of Burgundy was introduced by her faction into the mole of Hadrian or castle of St. Angelo, which commands the principal bridge and entrance of Rome. Her son by the first marriage, Alberic, was compelled to attend at the nuptial banquet; but his reluctant and ungraceful service was chastised with a blow by his new father. The blow was productive of a revolution. "Romans," exclaimed the youth, "once you were the masters of the world, and these Burgundians the most abject of your slaves. They now reign, these voracious and brutal savages,

---

favour, an obligation (we want the word *bienfait*). See Schmidt, Hist. des Allemands, tom. iii. p. 393-408. Pfeffel, Abrégé Chronologique, tom. i. p. 229, 296, 317, 324, 420, 430, 500. 505, 509, etc.)

[1] For the history of the emperors in Rome and Italy, see Sigonius, de Regno Italiæ, Opp. tom. ii., with the Notes of Saxius, and the Annals of Muratori, who might refer more distinctly to the authors of his great collection.

[2] See the Dissertation of Le Blanc at the end of his treatise des Monnoyes de France, in which he produces some Roman coins of the French emperors.

and my injury is the commencement of your servitude." [1]
The alarum-bell rang to arms in every quarter of the city: the
Burgundians retreated with haste and shame; Marozia was
imprisoned by her victorious son; and his brother, Pope John XI.,
was reduced to the exercise of his spiritual functions. With
the title of prince, Alberic possessed above twenty years the
government of Rome; and he is said to have gratified the
popular prejudice by restoring the office, or at least the title, of
consuls and tribunes. His son and heir Octavian assumed,
with the pontificate, the name of John XII.: like his predecessor,
he was provoked by the Lombard princes to seek a deliverer for
the church and republic; and the services of Otho were rewarded
with the Imperial dignity. But the Saxon was imperious, the
Romans were impatient, the festival of the coronation was disturbed by the secret conflict of prerogative and freedom, and
Otho commanded his swordbearer not to stir from his person
lest he should be assaulted and murdered at the foot of the
altar.[2] Before he repassed the Alps, the emperor chastised the
revolt of the people and the ingratitude of John XII. The pope
was degraded in a synod; the præfect was mounted on an ass,
whipped through the city, and cast into a dungeon; thirteen
of the most guilty were hanged, others were mutilated or
banished; and this severe process was justified by the ancient
laws of Theodosius and Justinian. The voice of fame has
accused the second Otho of a perfidious and bloody act, the
massacre of the senators, whom he had invited to his table
under the fair semblance of hospitality and friendship.[3] In the
minority of his son Otho the Third, Rome made a bold attempt
to shake off the Saxon yoke, and the consul Crescentius was the
Brutus of the republic. From the condition of a subject and an
exile he twice rose to the command of the city, oppressed,
expelled, and created the popes, and formed a conspiracy for
restoring the authority of the Greek emperors. In the fortress
of St. Angelo he maintained an obstinate siege, till the un-

---

[1] Romanorum aliquando servi, scilicet Burgundiones, Romanis im-
perent? . . . Romanæ urbis dignitas ad tantam est stultitiam ducta,
ut meretricum etiam imperio pareat? (Liutprand, l. iii. c. 12, p. 450).
Sigonius (l. vi. p. 400) positively affirms the renovation of the consulship;
but in the old writers Albericus is more frequently styled princeps Romanorum.

[2] Ditmar, p. 354, apud Schmidt, tom. iii. p. 439.

[3] This bloody feast is described in Leonine verse in the Pantheon of
Godfrey of Viterbo (Script. Ital. tom. vii. p. 436, 437), who flourished
towards the end of the twelfth century (Fabricius, Biblioth. Latin. med. et
infimi Ævi, tom. iii. p. 69, edit. Mansi); but his evidence, which imposed
on Sigonius, is reasonably suspected by Muratori (Annali, tom. viii. p. 177).

fortunate consul was betrayed by a promise of safety: his body was suspended on a gibbet, and his head was exposed on the battlements of the castle. By a reverse of fortune, Otho, after separating his troops, was besieged three days, without food, in his palace, and a disgraceful escape saved him from the justice or fury of the Romans. The senator Ptolemy was the leader of the people, and the widow of Crescentius enjoyed the pleasure or the fame of revenging her husband by a poison which she administered to her Imperial lover. It was the design of Otho the Third to abandon the ruder countries of the North, to erect his throne in Italy, and to revive the institutions of the Roman monarchy. But his successors only once in their lives appeared on the banks of the Tiber to receive their crown in the Vatican.[1] Their absence was contemptible, their presence odious and formidable. They descended from the Alps at the head of their barbarians, who were strangers and enemies to the country; and their transient visit was a scene of tumult and bloodshed.[2] A faint remembrance of their ancestors still tormented the Romans; and they beheld with pious indignation the succession of Saxons, Franks, Swabians, and Bohemians, who usurped the purple and prerogatives of the Cæsars.

There is nothing perhaps more adverse to nature and reason than to hold in obedience remote countries and foreign nations in opposition to their inclination and interest. A torrent of barbarians may pass over the earth, but an extensive empire must be supported by a refined system of policy and oppression: in the centre an absolute power, prompt in action and rich in resources: a swift and easy communication with the extreme parts: fortifications to check the first effort of rebellion: a regular administration to protect and punish; and a well-disciplined army to inspire fear, without provoking discontent and despair. Far different was the situation of the German Cæsars, who were ambitious to enslave the kingdom of Italy. Their patrimonial estates were stretched along the Rhine, or scattered in the provinces; but this ample domain was alienated by the imprudence or distress of successive princes; and their

---

[1] The coronation of the emperor, and some original ceremonies of the tenth century, are preserved in the Panegyric on Berengarius (Script. Ital. tom. ii. pars i. p. 405-414), illustrated by the Notes of Hadrian Valesius and Leibnitz. Sigonius has related the whole process of the Roman expedition, in good Latin, but with some errors of time and fact (l. vii. p. 441-446).

[2] In a quarrel at the coronation of Conrad II. Muratori takes leave to observe—doveano ben essere allora indisciplinati, barbari, e *bestiali* i Tedeschi. Annal. tom. viii. p. 368.

revenue, from minute and vexatious prerogative, was scarcely sufficient for the maintenance of their household. Their troops were formed by the legal or voluntary service of their feudal vassals, who passed the Alps with reluctance, assumed the licence of rapine and disorder, and capriciously deserted before the end of the campaign. Whole armies were swept away by the pestilential influence of the climate: the survivors brought back the bones of their princes and nobles; [1] and the effects of their own intemperance were often imputed to the treachery and malice of the Italians, who rejoiced at least in the calamities of the barbarians. This irregular tyranny might contend on equal terms with the petty tyrants of Italy; nor can the people, or the reader, be much interested in the event of the quarrel. But in the eleventh and twelfth centuries the Lombards rekindled the flame of industry and freedom, and the generous example was at length imitated by the republics of Tuscany. In the Italian cities a municipal government had never been totally abolished; and their first privileges were granted by the favour and policy of the emperors, who were desirous of erecting a plebeian barrier against the independence of the nobles. But their rapid progress, the daily extension of their power and pretensions, were founded on the numbers and spirit of these rising communities. [2] Each city filled the measure of her diocese or district: the jurisdiction of the counts and bishops, of the marquises and counts, was banished from the land; and the proudest nobles were persuaded or compelled to desert their solitary castles, and to embrace the more honourable character of freemen and magistrates. The legislative authority was inherent in the general assembly; but the executive powers were intrusted to three consuls, annually chosen from the three orders of *captains, valvassors*, [3] and commons, into which the republic was divided. Under the protection of equal law the labours of agriculture and commerce were gradually revived; but the martial spirit of the Lombards was nourished by the presence

[1] After boiling away the flesh. The caldrons for that purpose were a necessary piece of travelling furniture; and a German, who was using it for his brother, promised it to a friend, after it should have been employed for himself (Schmidt, tom. iii. p. 423, 424). The same author observes that the whole Saxon line was extinguished in Italy (tom. ii. p. 440).

[2] Otho, bishop of Frisingen, has left an important passage on the Italian cities (l. ii. c. 13, in Script. Ital. tom. vi. p. 707-710): and the rise, progress, and government of these republics are perfectly illustrated by Muratori (Antiquitat. Ital. Medii Ævi, tom. iv. dissert. xlv.-lii. p. 1-675; Annal tom. viii. ix. x.).

[3] For these titles, see Selden (Titles of Honour, vol. iii. part i. p. 488), Ducange (Gloss. Latin. tom. ii. p. 140, tom. vi. p. 776), and St. Marc (Abrégé Chronologique, tom. ii. p. 719).

of danger; and as often as the bell was rung, or the standard [1]
erected, the gates of the city poured forth a numerous and
intrepid band, whose zeal in their own cause was soon·guided by
the use and discipline of arms. At the foot of these popular
ramparts the pride of the Cæsars was overthrown; and the
invincible genius of liberty prevailed over the two Frederics,
the greatest princes of the middle age: the first, superior perhaps
in military prowess; the second, who undoubtedly excelled in
the softer accomplishments of peace and learning.

Ambitious of restoring the splendour of the purple, Frederic
the First invaded the republics of Lombardy with the arts of a
statesman, the valour of a soldier, and the cruelty of a tyrant.
The recent discovery of the Pandects had renewed a science
most favourable to despotism; and his venal advocates proclaimed the emperor the absolute master of the lives and
properties of his subjects. His royal prerogatives, in a less
odious sense, were acknowledged in the diet of Roncaglia, and
the revenue of Italy was fixed at thirty thousand pounds of
silver,[2] which were multiplied to an indefinite demand by the
rapine of the fiscal officers. The obstinate cities were reduced
by the terror or the force of his arms; his captives were delivered
to the executioner, or shot from his military engines; and after
the siege and surrender of Milan the buildings of that stately
capital were razed to the ground, three hundred hostages were
sent into Germany, and the inhabitants were dispersed in four
villages, under the yoke of the inflexible conqueror.[3] But Milan
soon rose from her ashes; and the league of Lombardy was
cemented by distress: their cause was espoused by Venice, Pope
Alexander the Third, and the Greek emperor: the fabric of oppression was overturned in a day; and in the treaty of Constance, Frederic subscribed, with some reservations, the freedom
of four-and-twenty cities. His grandson contended with their
vigour and maturity; but Frederic the Second [4] was endowed
with some personal and peculiar advantages. His birth and

---

[1] The Lombards invented and used the *carocium*, a standard planted on
a car or waggon, drawn by a team of oxen (Ducange, tom. ii. p. 194, 195;
Muratori, Antiquitat. tom. ii. diss. xxvi. p. 489-493).

[2] Gunther Ligurinus, l. viii. 584, et seq. apud Schmidt, tom. iii. p. 399.

[3] Solus imperator faciem suam firmavit ut petram (Burcard. de Excidio
Mediolani, Script. Ital. tom. vi. p. 917). This volume of Muratori contains
the originals of the history of Frederic the First, which must be compared
with due regard to the circumstances and prejudices of each German or
Lombard writer.

[4] For the history of Frederic II. and the House of Swabia at Naples, see
Giannone, Istoria Civile, tom. ii. 1. xiv-xix.

education recommended him to the Italians; and in the implacable discord of the two factions the Ghibelins were attached to the emperor, while the Guelfs displayed the bannner of liberty and the church. The court of Rome had slumbered when his father Henry the Sixth was permitted to unite with the empire the kingdoms of Naples and Sicily; and from these hereditary realms the son derived an ample and ready supply of troops and treasure. Yet Frederic the Second was finally oppressed by the arms of the Lombards and the thunders of the Vatican: his kingdom was given to a stranger, and the last of his family was beheaded at Naples on a public scaffold. During sixty years no emperor appeared in Italy, and the name was remembered only by the ignominious sale of the last relics of sovereignty.

The barbarian conquerors of the West were pleased to decorate their chief with the title of emperor; but it was not their design to invest him with the despotism of Constantine and Justinian. The persons of the Germans were free, their conquests were their own, and their national character was animated by a spirit which scorned the servile jurisprudence of the new or the ancient Rome. It would have been a vain and dangerous attempt to impose a monarch on the armed freemen, who were impatient of a magistrate; on the bold, who refused to obey; on the powerful, who aspired to command. The empire of Charlemagne and Otho was distributed among the dukes of the nations or provinces, the counts of the smaller districts, and the margraves of the marches or frontiers, who all united the civil and military authority as it had been delegated to the lieutenants of the first Cæsars. The Roman governors, who for the most part were soldiers of fortune, seduced their mercenary legions, assumed the Imperial purple, and either failed or succeeded in their revolt, without wounding the power and unity of government. If the dukes, margraves, and counts of Germany were less audacious in their claims, the consequences of their success were more lasting and pernicious to the state. Instead of aiming at the supreme rank, they silently laboured to establish and appropriate their provincial independence. Their ambition was seconded by the weight of their estates and vassals, their mutual example and support, the common interest of the subordinate nobility, the change of princes and families, the minorities of Otho the Third and Henry the Fourth, the ambition of the popes, and the vain pursuit of the fugitive crowns of Italy and Rome. All the attributes of regal and territorial jurisdiction were gradually usurped by the commanders of the provinces; the right of peace and war, of life and death, of coinage and taxation, of foreign alliance and domestic economy. Whatever had been seized by violence was ratified by favour or distress, was granted as the price of a doubtful vote or a voluntary service; whatever had been granted to one could not without injury be denied to his successor or equal; and every act of local or temporary possession was insensibly moulded into the constitution of the Germanic kingdom. In every province the visible presence of the duke or count was interposed between the throne and the nobles; the subjects of the law became the vassals of a private chief; and the standard which *he* received from his sovereign was often raised against him in the field. The temporal power of the clergy was cherished and exalted by the superstition or policy of the Carlovingian and Saxon dynasties, who blindly depended on their moderation and fidelity; and the bishoprics of Germany were made equal in extent and privilege, superior in wealth and population, to the most ample states of the military order. As long as the emperors retained the prerogative of bestowing on every vacancy these ecclesiastic and secular benefices, their cause was maintained by the gratitude or ambition of their friends and favourites. But in the quarrel of the investitures they were deprived of their influence over the episcopal chapters; the freedom of election was restored, and the sovereign was reduced, by a solemn mockery, to his *first prayers*, the recommendation, once in his reign, to a single prebend in each church. The secular governors, instead of being recalled at the will of a superior, could be degraded only by the sentence of their peers. In the first age of the monarchy the appointment of the son to the duchy or county of his father was solicited as a favour; it was gradually obtained as a custom, and extorted as a right: the lineal succession was often extended to the collateral or female branches; the states of the empire (their popular, and at length their legal, appellation) were divided and alienated by testament and sale; and all idea of a public trust was lost in that of a private and perpetual inheritance. The emperor could not even be enriched by the casualties of forfeiture and extinction: within the term of a year he was obliged to dispose of the vacant fief; and in the choice of the candidate it was his duty to consult either the general or the provincial diet.

After the death of Frederic the Second, Germany was left a monster with a hundred heads. A crowd of princes and prelates disputed the ruins of the empire: the lords of innumerable castles were less prone to obey than to imitate their superiors; and, according to the measure of their strength, their incessant hostilities received the names of conquest or robbery. Such anarchy was the inevitable consequence of the laws and manners of Europe; and the kingdoms of France and Italy were shivered into fragments by the violence of the same tempest. But the Italian cities and the French vassals were divided and destroyed, while the union of the Germans has produced, under the name of an empire, a great system of a federative republic. In the frequent and at last the perpetual institution of diets, a national spirit was kept alive, and the powers of a common legislature are still exercised by the three branches or colleges of the electors, the princes, and the free and Imperial cities of Germany. I. Seven of the most powerful feudatories were permitted to assume, with a distinguished name and rank, the exclusive privilege of choosing the Roman emperor; and these electors were the king of Bohemia, the duke of Saxony, the margrave of Brandenburg, the count palatine of the Rhine, and the three archbishops of Mentz, of Trèves, and of Cologne.[1] II. The college of princes and prelates purged themselves of a promiscuous multitude: they reduced to four representative votes the long series of independent counts, and excluded the nobles or equestrian order, sixty thousand of whom, as in the Polish diets, had appeared on horseback in the field of election. III. The pride of birth and dominion, of the sword and the mitre, wisely adopted the commons as the third branch of the legislature, and, in the progress of society, they were introduced about the same era into the national assemblies of France, England, and Germany. The Hanseatic League commanded the trade and navigation of the north: the confederates of the Rhine secured the peace and intercourse of the inland country; the influence of the cities has been adequate to their wealth and policy, and their negative still invalidates the acts of the two superior colleges of electors and princes.[2]

---

[1] [With regard to the method of electing the Roman emperor, as well as all the events leading up to the formation of what Bury aptly calls the Electoral College, see Bryce, *Holy Roman Empire* (pp. 229, 230). The Electoral College " is mentioned A.D. 1152, and in somewhat clearer terms in 1198, as a distinct body, but without anything to show who composed it. First in A.D. 1263 does a letter from Pope Urban IV. say that by immemorial custom the right of choosing the Roman king belonged to seven persons, the seven who had just divided their votes on Richard of Cornwall and Alphonso of Castile."—O. S.]

[2] In the immense labyrinth of the *jus publicum* of Germany, I must either quote one writer or a thousand; and I had rather trust to one faithful guide than transcribe, on credit, a multitude of names and passages. That guide is M. Pfeffel, the author of the best legal and constitutional

It is in the fourteenth century that we may view in the strongest light the state and contrast of the Roman empire of Germany, which no longer held, except on the borders of the Rhine and Danube, a single province of Trajan or Constantine. Their unworthy successors were the counts of Hapsburg, of Nassau, of Luxemburg, and of Schwartzenburg: the emperor Henry the Seventh procured for his son the crown of Bohemia, and his grandson Charles the Fourth was born among a people strange and barbarous in the estimation of the Germans themselves.[1] After the excommunication of Lewis of Bavaria, he received the gift or promise of the vacant empire from the Roman pontiffs, who, in the exile and captivity of Avignon, affected the dominion of the earth. The death of his competitors united the electoral college, and Charles was unanimously saluted king of the Romans, and future emperor; a title which in the same age was prostituted to the Cæsars of Germany and Greece. The German emperor was no more than the elective and impotent magistrate of an aristocracy of princes, who had not left him a village that he might call his own. His best prerogative was the right of presiding and proposing in the national senate, which was convened at his summons; and his native kingdom of Bohemia, less opulent than the adjacent city of Nuremberg, was the firmest seat of his power and the richest source of his revenue. The army with which he passed the Alps consisted of three hundred horse. In the cathedral of St. Ambrose, Charles was crowned with the *iron* crown, which tradition ascribed to the Lombard monarchy; but he was admitted only with a peaceful train; the gates of the city were shut upon him; and the king of Italy was held a captive by the arms of the Visconti, whom he confirmed in the sovereignty of Milan. In the Vatican he was again crowned with the *golden* crown of the empire; but, in

history that I know of any country (Nouvel Abrégé Chronologique de l'Histoire et du Droit Public d'Allemagne; Paris, 1776, 2 vols. in 4to). His learning and judgment have discerned the most interesting facts; his simple brevity comprises them in a narrow space; his chronological order distributes them under the proper dates; and an elaborate index collects them under their respective heads. To this work, in a less perfect state, Dr. Robertson was gratefully indebted for that masterly sketch which traces even the modern changes of the Germanic body. The Corpus Historiæ Germanicæ of Struvius has been likewise consulted, the more usefully, as that huge compilation is fortified in every page with the original texts.

[1] Yet, *personally*, Charles IV. must not be considered as a barbarian. After his education at Paris, he recovered the use of the Bohemian, his native, idiom; and the emperor conversed and wrote with equal facility in French, Latin, Italian, and German (Struvius, p. 615, 616). Petrarch always represents him as a polite and learned prince.

obedience to a secret treaty, the Roman emperor immediately withdrew, without reposing a single night within the walls of Rome. The eloquent Petrarch,[1] whose fancy revived the visionary glories of the Capitol, deplores and upbraids the ignominious flight of the Bohemian; and even his contemporaries could observe that the sole exercise of his authority was in the lucrative sale of privileges and titles. The gold of Italy secured the election of his son; but such was the shameful poverty of the Roman emperor, that his person was arrested by a butcher in the streets of Worms, and was detained in the public inn as a pledge or hostage for the payment of his expenses.

From this humiliating scene let us turn to the apparent majesty of the same Charles in the diets of the empire. The golden bull, which fixes the Germanic constitution, is promulgated in the style of a sovereign and legislator. A hundred princes bowed before his throne, and exalted their own dignity by the voluntary honours which they yielded to their chief or minister. At the royal banquet the hereditary great officers, the seven electors, who in rank and title were equal to kings, performed their solemn and domestic service of the palace. The seals of the triple kingdom were borne in state by the archbishops of Mentz, Cologne, and Trèves, the perpetual arch-chancellors of Germany, Italy, and Arles. The great marshal, on horseback, exercised his function with a silver measure of oats, which he emptied on the ground, and immediately dismounted to regulate the order of the guests. The great steward, the count palatine of the Rhine, placed the dishes on the table. The great chamberlain, the margrave of Brandenburg, presented, after the repast, the golden ewer and basin, to wash. The king of Bohemia, as great cupbearer, was represented by the emperor's brother, the duke of Luxemburg and Brabant; and the procession was closed by the great huntsmen, who introduced a boar and a stag, with a loud chorus of horns and hounds.[2] Nor was the supremacy of the emperor confined to Germany alone: the hereditary monarchs of Europe confessed the pre-eminence of his rank and dignity: he was the first of the Christian princes, the temporal head of the great republic of the West:[3] to his

---

[1] Besides the German and Italian historians, the expedition of Charles IV. is painted in lively and original colours in the curious Mémoires sur la Vie de Petrarque, tom. iii. p. 376-430, by the Abbé de Sade, whose prolixity has never been blamed by any reader of taste and curiosity.

[2] See the whole ceremony, in Struvius, p. 629.

[3] The republic of Europe, with the pope and emperor at its head, was never represented with more dignity than in the council of Constance. See Lenfant's History of that assembly.

person the title of majesty was long appropriated; and he disputed with the pope the sublime prerogative of creating kings and assembling councils. The oracle of the civil law, the learned Bartolus, was a pensioner of Charles the Fourth; and his school resounded with the doctrine that the Roman emperor was the rightful sovereign of the earth, from the rising to the setting sun. The contrary opinion was condemned, not as an error, but as a heresy, since even the Gospel had pronounced, " And there went forth a decree from Cæsar Augustus, that *all the world* should be taxed." [1]

If we annihilate the interval of time and space between Augustus and Charles, strong and striking will be the contrast between the two Cæsars: the Bohemian, who concealed his weakness under the mask of ostentation, and the Roman, who disguised his strength under the semblance of modesty. At the head of his victorious legions, in his reign over the sea and land, from the Nile and Euphrates to the Atlantic Ocean, Augustus professed himself the servant of the state and the equal of his fellow-citizens. The conqueror of Rome and her provinces assumed the popular and legal form of a censor, a consul, and a tribune. His will was the law of mankind, but in the declaration of his laws he borrowed the voice of the senate and people; and, from their decrees, their master accepted and renewed his temporary commission to administer the republic. In his dress, his domestics,[2] his titles, in all the offices of social life, Augustus maintained the character of a private Roman; and his most artful flatterers respected the secret of his absolute and perpetual monarchy.

[1] Gravina, Origines Juris Civilis, p. 108.
[2] Six thousand urns have been discovered of the slaves and freedmen of Augustus and Livia. So minute was the division of office, that one slave was appointed to weigh the wool which was spun by the empress's maids, another for the care of her lapdog, etc. (Camere Sepolchrale, etc., by Bianchini. Extract of his work, in the Bibliothèque Italique, tom. iv. p. 175. His Eloge, by Fontenelle, tom. vi. p. 356.) But these servants were of the same rank, and possibly not more numerous than those of Pollio or Lentulus. They only prove the general riches of the city.

CHAPTER L

Description of Arabia and its Inhabitants—Birth, Character, and Doctrine of Mohammed—He preaches at Mecca—Flies to Medina—Propagates his Religion by the Sword—Voluntary or reluctant Submission of the Arabs—His Death and Successors—The Claims and Fortunes of Ali and his Descendants

AFTER pursuing above six hundred years the fleeting Cæsars of Constantinople and Germany, I now descend, in the reign of Heraclius, on the eastern borders of the Greek monarchy. While the state was exhausted by the Persian war, and the church was distracted by the Nestorian and Monophysite sects, Mohammed, with the sword in one hand and the Koran in the other, erected his throne on the ruins of Christianity and of Rome. The genius of the Arabian prophet, the manners of his nation, and the spirit of his religion, involve the causes of the decline and fall of the Eastern empire; and our eyes are curiously intent on one of the most memorable revolutions which have impressed a new and lasting character on the nations of the globe.[1]

In the vacant space between Persia, Syria, Egypt, and Æthiopia, the Arabian peninsula [2] may be conceived as a triangle of spacious but irregular dimensions. From the northern point

[1] As in this and the following chapter I shall display much Arabic learning, I must profess my total ignorance of the Oriental tongues, and my gratitude to the learned interpreters, who have transfused their science into the Latin, French, and English languages. Their collections, versions, and histories, I shall occasionally notice.

[2] The geographers of Arabia may be divided into three classes:—1. The *Greeks* and *Latins*, whose progressive knowledge may be traced in Agatharchides (de Mari Rubro, in Hudson, Geograph. Minor. tom. i.), Diodorus Siculus (tom. i. l. ii. [c. 48-54] p. 159-167; l. iii. [c. 14 *sqq.*] p. 211-216, edit. Wesseling), Strabo (l. xvi. p. 1112-1114 [p. 767-769, ed. Casaub.], from Eratosthenes, p. 1122-1132 [776-785, ed. Casaub.], from Artemidorus), Dionysius (Periegesis, v. 927-969), Pliny (Hist. Natur. v. 12; vi. 32), and Ptolemy (Descript. et Tabulæ Urbium, in Hudson, tom. iii.). 2. The *Arabic writers*, who have treated the subject with the zeal of patriotism or devotion: the extracts of Pocock (Specimen Hist. Arabum, p. 125-128) from the Geography of the Sherif al Edrissi, render us still more dissatisfied with the version or abridgment (p. 24-27, 44-56, 108, etc., 119, etc.) which the Maronites have published under the absurd title of Geographia Nubiensis (Paris, 1619); but the Latin and French translators, Greaves (in Hudson, tom. iii.) and Galland (Voyage de la Palestine par La Roque, p. 265-346), have opened to us the Arabia of Abulfeda, the most copious and correct account of the peninsula, which may be enriched, however, from the Bibliothèque Orientale of D'Herbelot, p. 120, et alibi passim. 3. The *European travellers*, among whom Shaw (p. 438-455) and Niebuhr (Description, 1773; Voyages, tom. i. 1776) deserve an honourable distinction: Busching (Géographie par Berenger, tom. viii. p. 416-510) has compiled with judgment; and D'Anville's Maps (Orbis Veteribus Notus, and 1re

of Beles,[1] on the Euphrates, a line of fifteen hundred miles is terminated by the Straits of Babelmandeb and the land of frankincense. About half this length may be allowed for the middle breadth, from east to west, from Bassora to Suez, from the Persian Gulf to the Red Sea.[2] The sides of the triangle are gradually enlarged, and the southern basis presents a front of a thousand miles to the Indian Ocean. The entire surface of the peninsula exceeds in a fourfold proportion that of Germany or France; but the far greater part has been justly stigmatised with the epithets of the *stony* and the *sandy*. Even the wilds of Tartary are decked, by the hand of nature, with lofty trees and luxuriant herbage; and the lonesome traveller derives a sort of comfort and society from the presence of vegetable life. But in the dreary waste of Arabia a boundless level of sand is intersected by sharp and naked mountains; and the face of the desert, without shade or shelter, is scorched by the direct and intense rays of a tropical sun. Instead of refreshing breezes, the winds, particularly from the south-west, diffuse a noxious and even deadly vapour; the hillocks of sand which they alternately raise and scatter are compared to the billows of the ocean, and whole caravans, whole armies, have been lost and buried in the whirl-wind. The common benefits of water are an object of desire and contest; and such is the scarcity of wood, that some art is requisite to preserve and propagate the element of fire. Arabia is destitute of navigable rivers, which fertilise the soil, and convey its produce to the adjacent regions: the torrents that fall from the hills are imbibed by the thirsty earth: the rare and hardy plants, the tamarind or the acacia, that strike their roots into the clefts of the rocks, are nourished by the dews of the

Partie de l'Asie) should lie before the reader, with his Géographie Ancienne, tom. ii. p. 208-231.

[Among additional authorities slightly later in time may be mentioned J. L. Burckhardt, *Travels in Arabia*; J. R. Wellsted, *Travels in Arabia*; the Rev. Charles Foster, *Historical Geography of Arabia*; A. P. Caussin de Perceval, *Essai sur l'Histoire des Arabes avant l'Islamisme, pendant l'époque de Mahomet, et jusqu'à la réduction de toutes les tribus sous la loi Musulmane.*—O. S.]

[1] Abulfed. Descript. Arabiæ, p. 1; D'Anville, l'Euphrate et le Tigre, p. 19, 20. It was in this place, the paradise or garden of a satrap, that Xenophon and the Greeks first passed the Euphrates (Anabasis, l. i. c. 10 [c. 4, § 10] p. 29, edit. Wells).

[2] Reland has proved, with much superfluous learning, 1. That our Red Sea (the Arabian Gulf) is no more than a part of the *Mare Rubrum*, the Ἐρυθρὰ θαλάσση of the ancients, which was extended to the indefinite space of the Indian Ocean. 2. That the synonymous words ἐρυθρος, αἰθίοψ, allude to the colour of the blacks or negroes (Dissert. Miscell. tom. i. p. 59-117).

night: a scanty supply of rain is collected in cisterns and aqueducts: the wells and springs are the secret treasure of the desert; and the pilgrim of Mecca,[1] after many a dry and sultry march, is disgusted by the taste of the waters which have rolled over a bed of sulphur or salt. Such is the general and genuine picture of the climate of Arabia. The experience of evil enhances the value of any local or partial enjoyments. A shady grove, a green pasture, a stream of fresh water, are sufficient to attract a colony of sedentary Arabs to the fortunate spots which can afford food and refreshment to themselves and their cattle, and which encourage their industry in the cultivation of the palm-tree and the vine. The high lands that border on the Indian Ocean are distinguished by their superior plenty of wood and water: the air is more temperate, the fruits are more delicious, the animals and the human race more numerous: the fertility of the soil invites and rewards the toil of the husbandman; and the peculiar gifts of frankincense[2] and coffee have attracted in different ages the merchants of the world. If it be compared with the rest of the peninsula, this sequestered region may truly deserve the appellation of the *happy;* and the splendid colouring of fancy and fiction has been suggested by contrast and countenanced by distance. It was for this earthly paradise that nature had reserved her choicest favours and her most curious workmanship: the incompatible blessings of luxury and innocence were ascribed to the natives: the soil was impregnated with gold[3] and gems, and both the land and sea were taught to exhale the odours of aromatic sweets. This division of the *sandy,* the *stony,* and the *happy,* so familiar to the Greeks and Latins, is unknown to the Arabians themselves; and it is singular enough, that a country whose language and inhabitants have ever been the same should scarcely retain a vestige of its

---

[1] In the thirty days, or stations, between Cairo and Mecca, there are fifteen destitute of good water. See the route of the Hadjees, in Shaw's Travels, p. 477.

[2] The aromatics, especially the *thus* or frankincense, of Arabia, occupy the twelfth book of Pliny. Our great poet (Paradise Lost, l. iv.) introduces, in a simile, the spicy odours that are blown by the north-east wind from the Sabæan coast:—

—— Many a league,
Pleas'd with the grateful scent, old Ocean smiles.
(Plin. Hist. Natur. xii. 42.)

[3] Agatharchides affirms that lumps of pure gold were found from the size of an olive to that of a nut; that iron was twice, and silver ten times, the value of gold (de Mari Rubro, p. 60 [Hudson, Geogr. M., tom. i.]). These real or imaginary treasures are vanished; and no gold-mines are at present known in Arabia (Niebuhr, Description, p. 124).

ancient geography. The maritime districts of *Bahrein* and *Oman* are opposite to the realm of Persia. The kingdom of *Yemen* displays the limits, or at least the situation, of Arabia Felix: the name of *Neged* is extended over the inland space; and the birth of Mohammed has illustrated the province of *Hejaz* along the coast of the Red Sea.[1]

The measure of population is regulated by the means of subsistence; and the inhabitants of this vast peninsula might be out-numbered by the subjects of a fertile and industrious province. Along the shores of the Persian Gulf, of the ocean, and even of the Red Sea, the *Ichthyophagi*,[2] or fish-eaters, continued to wander in quest of their precarious food. In this primitive and abject state, which ill deserves the name of society, the human brute, without arts or laws, almost without sense or language, is poorly distinguished from the rest of the animal creation. Generations and ages might roll away in silent oblivion, and the helpless savage was restrained from multiplying his race by the wants and pursuits which confined his existence to the narrow margin of the sea-coast. But in an early period of antiquity the great body of the Arabs had emerged from this scene of misery; and as the naked wilderness could not maintain a people of hunters, they rose at once to the more secure and plentiful condition of the pastoral life. The same life is uniformly pursued by the roving tribes of the desert; and in the portrait of the modern *Bedoweens* we may trace the features of their ancestors,[3] who, in the age of Moses or Mohammed, dwelt

[1] Consult, peruse, and study the Specimen Historiæ Arabum of Pocock (Oxon. 1650, in 4to). The thirty pages of text and version are extracted from the Dynasties of Gregory Abulpharagius, which Pocock afterwards translated (Oxon. 1663, in 4to): the three hundred and fifty-eight notes form a classic and original work on the Arabian antiquities.

[Hejaz means the " barrier " or " frontier," as lying between the southern and northern merchants, or, in other words, between Arabia Felix and Arabia Petræa. It is a mountainous district, and includes Medina as well as Mecca. It occupies the space between Neged (Najd) and the Red Sea. Cf. Ewing, *Arab and Druze at Home*, 1907.—O. S.]

[2] Arrian remarks the Ichthyophagi of the coast of Hejaz (Periplus Maris Erythræi, p. 12) and beyond Aden (p. 15 [Hudson, Geogr. M., t. i.]). It seems probable that the shores of the Red Sea (in the largest sense) were occupied by these savages in the time perhaps of Cyrus; but I can hardly believe that any cannibals were left among the savages in the reign of Justinian (Procop. de Bell. Persic. l. i. c. 19 [t. i. p. 100, ed. Bonn]).

[3] See the Specimen Historiæ Arabum of Pocock, p. 2, 5, 86, etc. The journey of M. d'Arvieux, in 1664, to the camp of the emir of Mount Carmel (Voyage de la Palestine, Amsterdam, 1718) exhibits a pleasing and original picture of the life of the Bedoweens, which may be illustrated from Niebuhr (Description de l'Arabie, p. 327-344), and Volney (tom. i. p. 343-385), the last and most judicious of our Syrian travellers.

[There is no such word as Bedouins (Bedoweens) in the language of the

under similar tents, and conducted their horses, and camels, and sheep to the same springs and the same pastures. Our toil is lessened, and our wealth is increased, by our dominion over the useful animals; and the Arabian shepherd had acquired the absolute possession of a faithful friend and a laborious slave.[1] Arabia, in the opinion of the naturalist, is the genuine and original country of the *horse*; the climate most propitious, not indeed to the size, but to the spirit and swiftness, of that generous animal. The merit of the Barb, the Spanish, and the English breed is derived from a mixture of Arabian blood:[2] the Bedoweens preserve, with superstitious care, the honours and the memory of the purest race: the males are sold at a high price, but the females are seldom alienated; and the birth of a noble foal was esteemed among the tribes as a subject of joy and mutual congratulation. These horses are educated in the tents, among the children of the Arabs, with a tender familiarity, which trains them in the habits of gentleness and attachment. They are accustomed only to walk and to gallop: their sensations are not blunted by the incessant abuse of the spur and the whip: their powers are reserved for the moments of flight and pursuit: but no sooner do they feel the touch of the hand or the stirrup, than they dart away with the swiftness of the wind; and if their friend be dismounted in the rapid career, they instantly stop till he has recovered his seat. In the sands of Afric and Arabia the *camel* is a sacred and precious gift. That strong and patient beast of burden can perform, without eating or drinking, a journey of several days; and a reservoir of fresh water is preserved in a large bag, a fifth stomach of the animal, whose body is imprinted with the marks of servitude: the larger breed is capable of transporting a weight of a thousand pounds; and the dromedary, of a lighter and more active frame, outstrips the fleetest courser in the race. Alive or dead, almost every part

desert. The singular term is Bedawi meaning an Arab, the plural Bedawa, Arabs, but never Bedaween. See *Arab and Druze at Home*, by the Rev. W. Ewing, M.A. (1907), in which the whole question is treated by a ripe scholar, and Ewing and Thomson's *Dictionary of the Bible* (1910).—O. S.]

[1] Read (it is no unpleasing task) the incomparable articles of the *Horse* and the *Camel*, in the Natural History of M. de Buffon.

[2] For the Arabian horses, see D'Arvieux (p. 159-173) and Niebuhr (p. 142-144). At the end of the thirteenth century the horses of Neged were esteemed sure-footed, those of Yemen strong and serviceable, those of Hejaz most noble. The horses of Europe, the tenth and last class, were generally despised as having too much body and too little spirit (D'Herbelot, Biblioth. Orient. p. 339): their strength was requisite to bear the weight of the knight and his armour.

of the camel is serviceable to man: her milk is plentiful and
nutritious: the young and tender flesh has the taste of veal: [1]
a valuable salt is extracted from the urine: the dung supplies
the deficiency of fuel; and the long hair, which falls each year
and is renewed, is coarsely manufactured into the garments, the
furniture, and the tents of the Bedoweens. In the rainy seasons
they consume the rare and insufficient herbage of the desert:
during the heats of summer and the scarcity of winter they
remove their encampments to the sea-coast, the hills of Yemen,
or the neighbourhood of the Euphrates, and have often extorted
the dangerous licence of visiting the banks of the Nile and the
villages of Syria and Palestine. The life of a wandering Arab
is a life of danger and distress; and though sometimes, by rapine
or exchange, he may appropriate the fruits of industry, a private
citizen in Europe is in the possession of more solid and pleasing
luxury than the proudest emir who marches in the field at the
head of ten thousand horse.

Yet an essential difference may be found between the hordes of
Scythia and the Arabian tribes; since many of the latter were
collected into towns, and employed in the labours of trade and
agriculture. A part of their time and industry was still devoted
to the management of their cattle: they mingled, in peace and
war, with their brethren of the desert; and the Bedoweens
derived from their useful intercourse some supply of their wants,
and some rudiments of art and knowledge. Among the forty-
two cities of Arabia,[2] enumerated by Abulfeda, the most ancient
and populous were situate in the *happy* Yemen: the towers of
Saana,[3] and the marvellous reservoir of Merab,[4] were constructed
by the kings of the Homerites; but their profane lustre was

---

[1] Qui carnibus camelorum vesci solent odii tenaces sunt, was the opinion
of an Arabian physician (Pocock, Specimen, p. 88). Mohammed himself,
who was fond of milk, prefers the cow, and does not even mention the
camel; but the diet of Mecca and Medina was already more luxurious
(Gagnier, Vie de Mahomet, tom. iii. p. 404).

[2] Yet Marcian of Heraclea (in Periplo, p. 16, in tom. i. Hudson, Minor
Geograph.) reckons one hundred and sixty-four towns in Arabia Felix.
The size of the towns might be small, the faith of the writer might be large.

[3] It is compared by Abulfeda (in Hudson, tom. iii. p. 54) to Damascus,
and is still the residence of the Imam of Yemen (Voyages de Niebuhr, tom. i.
p. 331-342). Saana is twenty-four parasangs from Dafar (Abulfeda, p. 51)
and sixty-eight from Aden (p. 53).

[4] Pocock, Specimen, p. 57; Geograph. Nubiensis, p. 52. Mariaba, or
Merab, six miles in circumference, was destroyed by the legions of Augustus
(Plin. Hist. Nat. vi. 32), and had not revived in the fourteenth century
(Abulfed. Descript. Arab. p. 58).

eclipsed by the prophetic glories of MEDINA [1] and MECCA,[2] near the Red Sea, and at the distance from each other of two hundred and seventy miles. The last of these holy places was known to the Greeks under the name of Macoraba; and the termination of the word is expressive of its greatness, which has not indeed, in the most flourishing period, exceeded the size and populousness of Marseilles. Some latent motive, perhaps of superstition, must have impelled the founders in the choice of a most unpromising situation. They erected their habitations of mud or stone in a plain about two miles long and one mile broad, at the foot of three barren mountains: the soil is a rock; the water even of the holy well of Zemzem is bitter or brackish; the pastures are remote from the city; and grapes are transported above seventy miles from the gardens of Tayef. The fame and spirit of the Koreishites, who reigned in Mecca, were conspicuous among the Arabian tribes; but their ungrateful soil refused the labours of agriculture, and their position was favourable to the enterprises of trade. By the seaport of Gedda, at the distance only of forty miles, they maintained an easy correspondence with Abyssinia; and that Christian kingdom afforded the first refuge to the disciples of Mohammed. The treasures of Africa were conveyed over the peninsula to Gerrha or Katif, in the province of Bahrein, a city built, as it is said, of rock-salt, by the Chaldæan exiles; [3] and from thence, with the native pearls of the Persian Gulf, they were floated on rafts to the mouth of the Euphrates. Mecca is placed almost at an equal distance, a month's journey, between Yemen on the right and Syria on the left hand. The former was the winter, the latter the summer,

[1] The name of *city*, Medina, was appropriated, κατ᾽ ἐξόχην, to Yatreb (the Iatrippa of the Greeks), the seat of the prophet. The distances from Medina are reckoned by Abulfeda in stations, or days' journey of a caravan (p. 15): to Bahrein, fifteen; to Bassora, eighteen; to Cufah, twenty; to Damascus or Palestine, twenty; to Cairo, twenty-five; to Mecca, ten; from Mecca to Saana (p. 52) or Aden, thirty; to Cairo, thirty-one days, or 412 hours (Shaw's Travels, p. 477); which, according to the estimate of D'Anville (Mesures Itinéraires, p. 99), allows about twenty-five English miles for a day's journey. From the land of frankincense (Hadramaut, in Yemen, between Aden and Cape Fartasch) to Gaza, in Syria, Pliny (Hist. Nat. xii. 32) computes sixty-five mansions of camels. These measures may assist fancy and elucidate facts.

[2] Our notions of Mecca must be drawn from the Arabians (D'Herbelot, Bibliothèque Orientale, p. 368-371; Pocock, Specimen, p. 125-128; Abulfeda, p. 11-40). As no unbeliever is permitted to enter the city, our travellers are silent; and the short hints of Thevenot (Voyages du Levant, part i. 490) are taken from the suspicious mouth of an African renagado. Some Persians counted 6000 houses (Chardin, tom. iv. p. 167).

[3] Strabo, l. xvi. p. 1110 [p. 766, ed. Casaub.]. See one of these salt houses near Bassora, in D'Herbelot, Biblioth. Orient. p. 6.

station of her caravans; and their seasonable arrival relieved the ships of India from the tedious and troublesome navigation of the Red Sea. In the markets of Saana and Merab, in the harbours of Oman and Aden, the camels of the Koreishites were laden with a precious cargo of aromatics; a supply of corn and manufactures was purchased in the fairs of Bostra and Damascus; the lucrative exchange diffused plenty and riches in the streets of Mecca; and the noblest of her sons united the love of arms with the profession of merchandise.[1]

The perpetual independence of the Arabs has been the theme of praise among strangers and natives; and the arts of controversy transform this singular event into a prophecy and a miracle in favour of the posterity of Ismael.[2] Some exceptions, that can neither be dissembled nor eluded, render this mode of reasoning as indiscreet as it is superfluous; the kingdom of Yemen has been successively subdued by the Abyssinians, the Persians, the sultans of Egypt,[3] and the Turks:[4] the holy cities of Mecca and Medina have repeatedly bowed under a Scythian tyrant; and the Roman province of Arabia[5] embraced the

[1] Mirum dictû ex innumeris populis pars æqua in *commerciis* aut in latrociniis degit (Plin. Hist. Nat. vi. 32). See Sale's Koran, Sûra. cvi. p. 503; Pocock, Specimen, p. 2; D'Herbelot, Biblioth. Orient. p. 361; Prideaux's Life of Mahomet, p. 5; Gagnier, Vie de Mahomet, tom. i. p. 72, 120, 126, etc.

[2] A nameless doctor (Universal Hist. vol. xx. octavo edition) has formerly *demonstrated* the truth of Christianity by the independence of the Arabs. A critic, besides the exceptions of fact, might dispute the meaning of the text (Gen. xvi. 12), the extent of the application, and the foundation of the pedigree.

[3] It was subdued, A.D. 1173, by a brother of the great Saladin, who founded a dynasty of Curds or Ayoubites (Guignes, Hist. des Huns, tom. i. p. 425; D'Herbelot, p. 477).

[4] By the lieutenant of Soliman I. (A.D. 1538) and Selim II. (1568). See Cantemir's Hist. of the Othman Empire, p. 201, 221. The pasha, who resided at Saana, commanded twenty-one beys; but no revenue was ever remitted to the Porte (Marsigli, Stato Militare dell' Imperio Ottomanno, p. 124), and the Turks were expelled about the year 1630 (Niebuhr, p. 167, 168).

[5] Of the Roman province, under the name of Arabia and the third Palestine, the principal cities were Bostra and Petra, which dated their era from the year 105, when they were subdued by Palma, a lieutenant of Trajan (Dion Cassius, l. lxviii. [c. 14]). Petra was the capital of the Nabathæans, whose name is derived from the eldest of the sons of Ismael (Gen. xxv. 12, etc., with the Commentaries of Jerom, Le Clerc, and Calmet). Justinian relinquished a palm country of ten days' journey to the south of Ælah (Procop. de Bell. Persic. l. i. c. 19 [t. i. p. 101, ed. Bonn]), and the Romans maintained a centurion and a custom-house (Arrian in Periplo Maris Erythræi, p. 11, in Hudson, tom. i.) at a place (λεύκη κώμη, Pagus Albus, Hawarà) in the territory of Medina (D'Anville, Mémoire sur l'Egypte, p. 243). These real possessions, and some naval inroads of Trajan (Peripl. p. 14, 15), are magnified by history and medals into the Roman conquest of Arabia.

peculiar wilderness in which Ismael and his sons must have pitched their tents in the face of their brethren. Yet these exceptions are temporary or local; the body of the nation has escaped the yoke of the most powerful monarchies: the arms of Sesostris and Cyrus, of Pompey and Trajan, could never achieve the conquest of Arabia; the present sovereign of the Turks [1] may exercise a shadow of jurisdiction, but his pride is reduced to solicit the friendship of a people whom it is dangerous to provoke and fruitless to attack. The obvious causes of their freedom are inscribed on the character and country of the Arabs. Many ages before Mohammed,[2] their intrepid valour had been severely felt by their neighbours in offensive and defensive war. The patient and active virtues of a soldier are insensibly nursed in the habits and discipline of a pastoral life. The care of the sheep and camels is abandoned to the women of the tribe; but the martial youth, under the banner of the emir, is ever on horseback, and in the field, to practise the exercise of the bow, the javelin, and the scymetar. The long memory of their independence is the firmest pledge of its perpetuity, and succeeding generations are animated to prove their descent and to maintain their inheritance. Their domestic feuds are suspended on the approach of a common enemy; and in their last hostilities against the Turks, the caravan of Mecca was attacked and pillaged by fourscore thousand of the confederates. When they advance to battle, the hope of victory is in the front; in the rear, the assurance of a retreat. Their horses and camels, who in eight or ten days can perform a march of four or five hundred miles, disappear before the conqueror; the secret waters of the desert elude his search; and his victorious troops are consumed with thirst, hunger, and fatigue in the pursuit of an invisible foe, who scorns his efforts, and safely reposes in the heart of the burning solitude. The arms and deserts of the Bedoweens are not only the safeguards of their own freedom, but the barriers also of the happy Arabia, whose inhabitants, remote from war, are enervated by the luxury of the soil and climate. The legions of Augustus melted away in disease and lassitude;[3] and it is only by a naval power that the reduction

---

[1] Niebuhr (Description de l'Arabie, p. 302, 303, 329-331) affords the most recent and authentic intelligence of the Turkish empire in Arabia.

[2] Diodorus Siculus (tom. ii. l. xix. [c. 94] p. 390-393, edit. Wesseling) has clearly exposed the freedom of the Nabathæan Arabs, who resisted the arms of Antigonus and his son.

[3] Strabo, l. xvi. p. 1127-1129 [p. 781 sq. ed. Casaub.]; Plin. Hist. Natur. vi. 32. Ælius Gallus landed near Medina, and marched near a thousand

of Yemen has been successfully attempted. When Mohammed erected his holy standard,[1] that kingdom was a province of the Persian empire; yet seven princes of the Homerites still reigned in the mountains; and the vicegerent of Chosroes was tempted to forget his distant country and his unfortunate master. The historians of the age of Justinian represent the state of the independent Arabs, who were divided by interest or affection in the long quarrel of the East: the tribe of *Gassan* was allowed to encamp on the Syrian territory: the princes of *Hira* were permitted to form a city about forty miles to the southward of the ruins of Babylon. Their service in the field was speedy and vigorous; but their friendship was venal, their faith inconstant, their enmity capricious: it was an easier task to excite than to disarm these roving barbarians; and, in the familiar intercourse of war, they learned to see and to despise the splendid weakness both of Rome and of Perisa. From Mecca to the Euphrates, the Arabian tribes [2] were confounded by the Greeks and Latins under the general appellation of SARACENS,[3] a name which every Christian mouth has been taught to pronounce with terror and abhorrence.

The slaves of domestic tyranny may vainly exult in their national independence: but the Arab is personally free; and he enjoys, in some degree, the benefits of society, without forfeiting the prerogatives of nature. In every tribe, superstition, or gratitude, or fortune has exalted a particular family above

miles into the part of Yemen between Mareb and the ocean. The non ante devictis Sabææ regibus (Od. i. 29) and the intacti Arabum thesauri (Od. iii. 24) of Horace, attest the virgin purity of Arabia.

[1] See the imperfect history of Yemen in Pocock, Specimen, p. 55-66; of Hira, p. 66-74; of Gassan, p. 75-78; as far as it could be known or preserved in the time of ignorance.

[2] The Σαρακηνικὰ φῦλα, μυριάδες ταῦτα, καὶ τὸ πλεῖστον αὐτῶν ἐρημονόμοι καὶ ἀδέσποτοι, are described by Menander (Excerpt. Legation. p. 149 [ed. Par.; p. 375, ed. Bonn]), Procopius (de Bell. Persic. l. i. c. 17, 19; l. ii. c. 10), and in the most lively colours by Ammianus Marcellinus (l. xiv. c. 4), who had spoken of them as early as the reign of Marcus.

[3] The name which, used by Ptolemy and Pliny in a more confined, by Ammianus and Procopius in a larger, sense, has been derived, ridiculously, from *Sarah*, the wife of Abraham, obscurely from the village of *Saraka* (μετὰ τοὺς Ναβαταίους, Stephan. de Urbibus [s. v. Σάρακα]), more plausibly from the Arabic words, which signify a *thievish* character, or *Oriental* situation (Hottinger, Hist. Oriental. l. i. c. i. p. 7, 8; Pocock, Specimen, p. 33-35; Asseman. Biblioth. Orient. tom. iv. p. 567). Yet the last and most popular of these etymologies is refuted by Ptolemy (Arabia, p. 2, 18, in Hudson, tom. iii.), who expressly remarks the western and southern position of the Saracens, then an obscure tribe on the borders of Egypt. The appellation cannot therefore allude to any *national* character; and, since it was imposed by strangers, it must be found, not in the Arabic, but in a foreign language.

the heads of their equals. The dignities of sheick and emir invariably descend in this chosen race; but the order of succession is loose and precarious; and the most worthy or aged of the noble kinsmen are preferred to the simple though important office of composing disputes by their advice, and guiding valour by their example. Even a female of sense and spirit has been permitted to command the countrymen of Zenobia.[1] The momentary junction of several tribes produces an army: their more lasting union constitutes a nation: and the supreme chief, the emir of emirs, whose banner is displayed at their head, may deserve, in the eyes of strangers, the honours of the kingly name. If the Arabian princes abuse their power, they are quickly punished by the desertion of their subjects, who had been accustomed to a mild and parental jurisdiction. Their spirit is free, their steps are unconfined, the desert is open, and the tribes and families are held together by a mutual and voluntary compact. The softer natives of Yemen supported the pomp and majesty of a monarch; but if he could not leave his palace without endangering his life,[2] the active powers of government must have been devolved on his nobles and magistrates. The cities of Mecca and Medina present, in the heart of Asia, the form, or rather the substance, of a commonwealth. The grandfather of Mohammed, and his lineal ancestors, appear in foreign and domestic transactions as the princes of their country; but they reigned, like Pericles at Athens, or the Medici at Florence, by the opinion of their wisdom and integrity; their influence was divided with their patrimony; and the sceptre was transferred from the uncles of the prophet to a younger branch of the tribe of Koreish. On solemn occasions they convened the assembly of the people; and, since mankind must be either compelled or persuaded to obey, the use and reputation of oratory among the ancient Arabs is the clearest evidence of public freedom.[3] But their simple freedom was of a very different cast from the nice

---

[1] Saraceni . . . mulieres aiunt in eos regnare (Expositio totius Mundi, p. 3, in Hudson, tom. iii.). The reign of Mavia is famous in ecclesiastical story. Pocock, Specimen, p. 69, 83.

[2] Ἐκ τῶν βασιλείων μὴ ἐξελθεῖν is the report of Agatharchides (de Mari Rubro, p. 63, 64, in Hudson, tom. i.), Diodorus Siculus (tom. i. l. iii. c. 47, p. 215), and Strabo (l. xvi. p. 1124 [p. 778, ed. Casaub.]). But I much suspect that this is one of the popular tales, or extraordinary accidents, which the credulity of travellers so often transforms into a fact, a custom, and a law.

[3] Non gloriabantur antiquitus Arabes, nisi gladio, hospite, et *eloquentiâ* (Sephadius apud Pocock, Specimen, p. 161, 162). This gift of speech they shared only with the Persians; and the sententious Arabs would probably have disdained the simple and sublime logic of Demosthenes.

and artificial machinery of the Greek and Roman republics, in which each member possessed an undivided share of the civil and political rights of the community. In the more simple state of the Arabs, the nation is free, because each of her sons disdains a base submission to the will of a master. His breast is fortified with the austere virtues of courage, patience, and sobriety; the love of independence prompts him to exercise the habits of self-command; and the fear of dishonour guards him from the meaner apprehension of pain, of danger, and of death. The gravity and firmness of the mind is conspicuous in his outward demeanour: his speech is slow, weighty, and concise; he is seldom provoked to laughter; his only gesture is that of stroking his beard, the venerable symbol of manhood; and the sense of his own importance teaches him to accost his equals without levity, and his superiors without awe.[1] The liberty of the Saracens survived their conquests: the first caliphs indulged the bold and familiar language of their subjects: they ascended the pulpit to persuade and edify the congregation; nor was it before the seat of empire was removed to the Tigris that the Abbassides adopted the proud and pompous ceremonial of the Persian and Byzantine courts.

In the study of nations and men we may observe the causes that render them hostile or friendly to each other, that tend to narrow or enlarge, to mollify or exasperate, the social character. The separation of the Arabs from the rest of mankind has accustomed them to confound the ideas of stranger and enemy; and the poverty of the land has introduced a maxim of jurisprudence which they believe and practise to the present hour. They pretend that, in the division of the earth, the rich and fertile climates were assigned to the other branches of the human family; and that the posterity of the outlaw Ismael might recover, by fraud or force, the portion of inheritance of which he had been unjustly deprived. According to the remark of Pliny, the Arabian tribes are equally addicted to theft and merchandise: the caravans that traverse the desert are ransomed or pillaged; and their neighbours, since the remote times of Job and Sesostris,[2] have been the victims of their rapacious spirit. If a Bedoween

---

[1] I must remind the reader that D'Arvieux, D'Herbelot, and Niebuhr represent in the most lively colours the manners and government of the Arabs, which are illustrated by many incidental passages in the Life of Mahomet.

[2] Observe the first chapter of Job, and the long wall of 1500 stadia which Sesostris built from Pelusium to Heliopolis (Diodor. Sicul. tom. i. l. i. [c. 57] p. 67). Under the name of *Hycsos*, the shepherd kings, they had formerly subdued Egypt (Marsham, Canon. Chron. p. 98-163, etc.).

discovers from afar a solitary traveller, he rides furiously against him, crying, with a loud voice, " Undress thyself, thy aunt (*my wife*) is without a garment." A ready submission entitles him to mercy; resistance will provoke the aggressor, and his own blood must expiate the blood which he presumes to shed in legitimate defence. A single robber, or a few associates, are branded with their genuine name; but the exploits of a numerous band assume the character of lawful and honourable war. The temper of a people thus armed against mankind was doubly inflamed by the domestic licence of rapine, murder, and revenge. In the constitution of Europe, the right of peace and war is now confined to a small, and the actual exercise to a much smaller, list of respectable potentates; but each Arab, with impunity and renown, might point his javelin against the life of his countrymen. The union of the nation consisted only in a vague resemblance of language and manners; and in each community the jurisdiction of the magistrate was mute and impotent. Of the time of ignorance which preceded Mohammed, seventeen hundred battles [1] are recorded by tradition: hostility was embittered with the rancour of civil faction: and the recital, in prose or verse, of an obsolete feud, was sufficient to rekindle the same passions among the descendants of the hostile tribes. In private life every man, at least every family, was the judge and avenger of its own cause. The nice sensibility of honour, which weighs the insult rather than the injury, sheds its deadly venom on the quarrels of the Arabs: the honour of their women, and of their *beards*, is most easily wounded; an indecent action, a contemptuous word, can be expiated only by the blood of the offender; and such is their patient inveteracy, that they expect whole months and years the opportunity of revenge. A fine or compensation for murder is familiar to the barbarians of every age: but in Arabia the kinsmen of the dead are at liberty to accept the atonement, or to exercise with their own hands the law of retaliation. The refined malice of the Arabs refuses even the head of the murderer, substitutes an innocent to the guilty person, and transfers the penalty to the best and most considerable of the race by whom they have been injured. If he falls by their hands, they are exposed in their turn to the danger of reprisals; the interest and principal of the bloody debt are

[1] Or, according to another account, 1200 (D'Herbelot, Bibliothèque Orientale, p. 75): the two historians who wrote of the *Ayam al Arab*, the battles of the Arabs, lived in the ninth and tenth century. The famous war of Dahes and Gabrah was occasioned by two horses, lasted forty years, and ended in a proverb (Pocock, Specimen, p. 48).

accumulated: the individuals of either family lead a life of malice and suspicion, and fifty years may sometimes elapse before the account of vengeance be finally settled.[1] This sanguinary spirit, ignorant of pity or forgiveness, has been moderated, however, by the maxims of honour, which require in every private encounter some decent equality of age and strength, of numbers and weapons. An annual festival of two, perhaps of four, months, was observed by the Arabs before the time of Mohammed, during which their swords were religiously sheathed both in foreign and domestic hostility; and this partial truce is more strongly expressive of the habits of anarchy and warfare.[2]

But the spirit of rapine and revenge was attempered by the milder influence of trade and literature. The solitary peninsula is encompassed by the most civilised nations of the ancient world; the merchant is the friend of mankind; and the annual caravans imported the first seeds of knowledge and politeness into the cities and even the camps of the desert. Whatever may be the pedigree of the Arabs, their language is derived from the same original stock with the Herbew, the Syriac, and the Chaldæan tongues; the independence of the tribes was marked by their peculiar dialects;[3] but each, after their own, allowed a just preference to the pure and perspicuous idiom of Mecca. In Arabia, as well as in Greece, the perfection of language outstripped the refinement of manners; and her speech could diversify the fourscore names of honey, the two hundred of a serpent, the five hundred of a lion, the thousand of a sword, at a time when this copious dictionary was intrusted to the memory of an illiterate people. The monuments of the Homerites were inscribed with an obsolete and mysterious character; but the Cufic letters, the groundwork of the present alphabet, were invented on the banks of the Euphrates; and

[1] The modern theory and practice of the Arabs in the revenge of murder are described by Niebuhr (Description, p. 26-31). The harsher features of antiquity may be traced in the Koran, c. 2, p. 20, c. 17, p. 230, with Sale's Observations.

[2] Procopius (de Bell. Persic. l. i. c. 16) places the *two* holy months about the summer solstice. The Arabians consecrate *four* months of the year— the first, seventh, eleventh, and twelfth; and pretend that, in a long series of ages, the truce was infringed only four or six times (Sale's Preliminary Discourse, p. 147-150, and Notes on the ninth chapter of the Koran, p. 154, etc.; Casiri, Biblioth. Hispano-Arabica, tom. ii. p. 20, 21).

[3] Arrian, in the second century, remarks (in Periplo Maris Erythræi, p. 12 [Hudson, Geog. M., t. i.]) the partial or total difference of the dialects of the Arabs. Their language and letters are copiously treated by Pocock (Specimen, p. 150-154), Casiri (Biblioth. Hispano-Arabica, tom. i. p. 1, 83, 292; tom. ii. p. 25, etc.), and Niebuhr (Description de l'Arabie, p. 72-86), I pass slightly; I am not fond of repeating words like a parrot.

the recent invention was taught at Mecca by a stranger who settled in that city after the birth of Mohammed. The arts of grammar, of metre, and of rhetoric were unknown to the free-born eloquence of the Arabians; but their penetration was sharp, their fancy luxuriant, their wit strong and sententious,[1] and their more elaborate compositions were addressed with energy and effect to the minds of their hearers. The genius and merit of a rising poet was celebrated by the applause of his own and the kindred tribes. A solemn banquet was prepared, and a chorus of women, striking their tymbals, and displaying the pomp of their nuptials, sung in the presence of their sons and husbands the felicity of their native tribe—that a champion had now appeared to vindicate their rights—that a herald had raised his voice to immortalise their renown. The distant or hostile tribes resorted to an annual fair, which was abolished by the fanaticism of the first Moslems—a national assembly that must have contributed to refine and harmonise the barbarians. Thirty days were employed in the exchange, not only of corn and wine, but of eloquence and poetry. The prize was disputed by the generous emulation of the bards; the victorious performance was deposited in the archives of princes and emirs; and we may read in our own language the seven original poems which were inscribed in letters of gold, and suspended in the temple of Mecca.[2] The Arabian poets were the historians and moralists of the age; and if they sympathised with the prejudices, they inspired and crowned the virtues, of their countrymen. The indissoluble union of generosity and valour was the darling theme of their song; and when they pointed their keenest satire against a despicable race, they affirmed, in the bitterness of reproach, that the men knew not how to give, nor the women to deny.[3] The same hospitality, which was practised by Abraham, and celebrated by Homer, is still renewed in the camps of the Arabs.

---

[1] A familiar tale in Voltaire's Zadig (le Chien et le Cheval) is related to prove the natural sagacity of the Arabs (D'Herbelot, Biblioth. Orient. p. 120, 121; Gagnier, Vie de Mahomet, tom. i. p. 37-46); but D'Arvieux, or rather La Roque (Voyage de Palestine, p. 92), denies the boasted superiority of the Bedoweens. The one hundred and sixty-nine sentences of Ali (translated by Ockley, London, 1718) afford a just and favourable specimen of Arabian wit.

[2] Pocock (Specimen, p. 158-161) and Casiri (Biblioth. Hispano-Arabica, tom. i. p. 48, 84, etc., 119, tom. ii. p. 17, etc.) speak of the Arabian poets before Mohammed: the seven poems of the Caaba have been published in English by Sir William Jones; but his honourable mission to India has deprived us of his own notes, far more interesting than the obscure and obsolete text.

[3] Sale's Preliminary Discourse, p. 29, 30.

The ferocious Bedoweens, the terror of the desert, embrace, without inquiry or hesitation, the stranger who dares to confide in their honour and to enter their tent. His treatment is kind and respectful: he shares the wealth or the poverty of his host; and, after a needful repose, he is dismissed on his way with thanks, with blessings, and perhaps with gifts. The heart and hand are more largely expanded by the wants of a brother or a friend; but the heroic acts that could deserve the public applause must have surpassed the narrow measure of discretion and experience. A dispute had arisen, who among the citizens of Mecca was entitled to the prize of generosity; and a successive application was made to the three who were deemed most worthy of the trial. Abdallah, the son of Abbas, had undertaken a distant journey, and his foot was in the stirrup, when he heard the voice of a suppliant, " O son of the uncle of the apostle of God, I am a traveller, and in distress! " He instantly dismounted to present the pilgrim with his camel, her rich caparison, and a purse of four thousand pieces of gold, excepting only the sword, either for its intrinsic value, or as the gift of an honoured kinsman. The servant of Kais informed the second suppliant that his master was asleep: but he immediately added, " Here is a purse of seven thousand pieces of gold (it is all we have in the house), and here is an order that will entitle you to a camel and a slave; " the master, as soon as he awoke, praised and enfranchised his faithful steward, with a gentle reproof, that by respecting his slumbers he had stinted his bounty. The third of these heroes, the blind Arabah, at the hour of prayer, was supporting his steps on the shoulders of two slaves. " Alas! " he replied, " my coffers are empty! but these you may sell; if you refuse, I renounce them." At these words, pushing away the youths, he groped along the wall with his staff. The character of Hatem is the perfect model of Arabian virtue: [1] he was brave and liberal, an eloquent poet, and a successful robber: forty camels were roasted at his hospitable feasts; and at the prayer of a suppliant enemy he restored both the captives and the spoil. The freedom of his countrymen disdained the laws of justice; they proudly indulged the spontaneous impulse of pity and benevolence.

---

[1] D'Herbelot, Biblioth. Orient. p. 458; Gagnier, Vie de Mahomet, tom. iii. p. 118; Caab and Hesnus (Pocock, Specimen, p. 43, 46, 48) were likewise conspicuous for their liberality; and the latter is elegantly praised by an Arabian poet: " Videbis eum cum accesseris exultantem, ac si dares illi quod ab illo petis."

The religion of the Arabs,[1] as well as of the Indians, consisted in the worship of the sun, the moon, and the fixed stars; a primitive and specious mode of superstition. The bright luminaries of the sky display the visible image of a Deity: their number and distance convey to a philosophic, or even a vulgar, eye the idea of boundless space: the character of eternity is marked on these solid globes, that seem incapable of corruption or decay: the regularity of their motions may be ascribed to a principle of reason or instinct; and their real or imaginary influence encourages the vain belief that the earth and its inhabitants are the object of their peculiar care. The science of astronomy was cultivated at Babylon; but the school of the Arabs was a clear firmament and a naked plain. In their nocturnal marches they steered by the guidance of the stars; their names, and order, and daily station were familiar to the curiosity and devotion of the Bedoween; and he was taught by experience to divide in twenty-eight parts the zodiac of the moon, and to bless the constellations who refreshed with salutary rains the thirst of the desert. The reign of the heavenly orbs could not be extended beyond the visible sphere; and some metaphysical powers were necessary to sustain the transmigration of souls and the resurrection of bodies: a camel was left to perish on the grave, that he might serve his master in another life; and the invocation of departed spirits implies that they were still endowed with consciousness and power. I am ignorant, and I am careless, of the blind mythology of the barbarians—of the local deities, of the stars, the air, and the earth, of their sex or titles, their attributes or subordination. Each tribe, each family, each independent warrior, created and changed the rites and the object of his fantastic worship; but the nation, in every age, has bowed to the religion as well as to the language of Mecca. The genuine antiquity of the CAABA ascends beyond the Christian era: in describing the coast of the Red Sea the Greek historian Diodorus [2] has remarked, between the Thamudites and the Sabæans, a famous temple, whose superior sanctity was

---

[1] Whatever can now be known of the idolatry of the ancient Arabians may be found in Pocock (Specimen, p. 89-136, 163, 164). His profound erudition is more clearly and concisely interpreted by Sale (Preliminary Discourse, p. 14-24); and Assemanni (Biblioth. Orient. tom. iv. p. 580-590) has added some valuable remarks.

[2] Ἱερὸν ἁγιώτατον ἵδρυται τιμώμενον ὑπὸ πάντων Ἀράβων περιττότερον (Diodor. Sicul. tom. i. l. iii. [c. 43] p. 211). The character and position are so correctly apposite, that I am surprised how this curious passage should have been read without notice or application. Yet this famous temple had been overlooked by Agatharchides (de Mari Rubro, p. 58, in

revered by *all* the Arabians; the linen or silken veil, which is annually renewed by the Turkish emperor, was first offered by a pious king of the Homerites, who reigned seven hundred years before the time of Mohammed.[1]   A tent or a cavern might suffice for the worship of the savages, but an edifice of stone and clay has been erected in its place; and the art and power of the monarchs of the East have been confined to the simplicity of the original model.[2]   A spacious portico encloses the quadrangle of the Caaba—a square chapel twenty-four cubits long, twenty-three broad, and twenty-seven high: a door and a window admit the light; the double roof is supported by three pillars of wood; a spout (now of gold) discharges the rain-water, and the well Zemzem is protected by a dome from accidental pollution.   The tribe of Koreish, by fraud or force, had acquired the custody of the Caaba: the sacerdotal office devolved through four lineal descents to the grandfather of Mohammed; and the family of the Hashemites, from whence he sprung, was the most respectable and sacred in the eyes of their country.[3]   The precincts of Mecca enjoyed the rights of sanctuary; and in the last month of each year the city and the temple were crowded with a long train of pilgrims, who presented their vows and offerings in the house of God.   The same rites which are now accomplished by the faithful Musulman were invented and practised by the superstition of the idolaters.   At an awful distance they cast away their garments: seven times with hasty steps they encircled the

Hudson, tom. i.), whom Diodorus copies in the rest of the description. Was the Sicilian more knowing than the Egyptian? Or was the Caaba built between the years of Rome 650 and 746, the dates of their respective histories? (Dodwell, in Dissert. ad tom. i. Hudson, p. 72; Fabricius, Biblioth. Græc. tom. ii. p. 770).

[Mr. Forster (*Historical Geography of Arabia*) has raised an objection fatal to this hypothesis of Gibbon. The temple, situated in the country of the Banizomeneis, was not between the Thamudites and Sabæans, but higher up than the coast inhabited by the former. Mr. Forster would place it as far north as Moilah. I am not quite satisfied that this will agree with the whole description of Diodorus.—O. S.]

[1] Pocock, Specimen, p. 60, 61. From the death of Mohammed we ascend to 68, from his birth to 129, years before the Christian era. The veil or curtain, which is now of silk and gold, was no more than a piece of Egyptian linen (Abulfeda, in Vit. Mohammed. c. 6, p. 14 [ed. Gagnier, Oxon. 1723]).

[2] The original plan of the Caaba (which is servilely copied in Sale, the Universal History, etc.) was a Turkish draught, which Reland (de Religione Mohammedicâ, p. 113-123) has corrected and explained from the best authorities. For the description and legend of the Caaba, consult Pocock (Specimen, p. 115-122), the Bibliothèque Orientale of D'Herbelot (*Caaba, Hagiar, Zemzem,* etc.), and Sale (Preliminary Discourse, p. 114-122).

[3] Cosa [Kussai], the fifth ancestor of Mohammed, must have usurped the Caaba A.D. 440; but the story is differently told by Jannabi (Gagnier, Vie de Mahomet, tom. i. p. 65-69) and by Abulfeda (in Vit. Moham. c. 6, p. 13).

Caaba, and kissed the black stone: seven times they visited and adored the adjacent mountains: seven times they threw stones into the valley of Mina: and the pilgrimage was achieved, as at the present hour, by a sacrifice of sheep and camels, and the burial of their hair and nails in the consecrated ground. Each tribe either found or introduced in the Caaba their domestic worship: the temple was adorned, or defiled, with three hundred and sixty idols of men, eagles, lions, and antelopes; and most conspicuous was the statue of Hebal, of red agate, holding in his hand seven arrows without heads or feathers, the instruments and symbols of profane divination. But this statue was a monument of Syrian arts: the devotion of the ruder ages was content with a pillar or a tablet; and the rocks of the desert were hewn into gods or altars in imitation of the black stone [1] of Mecca, which is deeply tainted with the reproach of an idolatrous origin. From Japan to Peru the use of sacrifice has universally prevailed; and the votary has expressed his gratitude or fear by destroying or consuming, in honour of the gods, the dearest and most precious of their gifts. The life of a man [2] is the most precious oblation to deprecate a public calamity: the altars of Phœnicia and Egypt, of Rome and Carthage, have been polluted with human gore: the cruel practice was long preserved among the Arabs; in the third century a boy was annually sacrificed by the tribe of the Dumatians; [3] and a royal captive was piously slaughtered by the prince of the Saracens, the ally and soldier of the emperor Justinian. [4]   A parent who drags his son to the altar

---

[1] In the second century, Maximus of Tyre attributes to the Arabs the worship of a stone—'Ἀράβιοι σέβουσι μὲν, ὅντινα δὲ οὐκ οἶδα, τὸ δὲ ἄγαλμα [ὃ] εἶδον λίθος ἦν τετράγωνος (Dissert. viii. tom. i. p. 142, edit. Reiske); and the reproach is furiously re-echoed by the Christians (Clemens Alex. in Protreptico, p. 40 [ed. Oxon. 1715]; Arnobius contra Gentes, l. vi. p. 246 [t. i. p. 196, ed. Lugd. B. 1651]). Yet these stones were no other than the βαίτυλα of Syria and Greece, so renowned in sacred and profane antiquity (Euseb. Præp. Evangel. l. i. p. 37; Marsham, Canon. Chron. p. 54-56).

[2] The two horrid subjects of 'Ἀνδροθυσία and Παιδοθυσία are accurately discussed by the learned Sir John Marsham (Canon. Chron. p. 76-78, 301-304). Sanchoniatho derives the Phœnician sacrifices from the example of Chronus; but we are ignorant whether Chronus lived before or after Abraham, or indeed whether he lived at all.

[3] Κατ' ἔτος ἔκαστον παῖδα ἔθυον, is the reproach of Porphyry; but he likewise imputes to the Romans the same barbarous custom, which, A.U.C. 657, had been finally abolished. Dumætha, Daumat al Gendal, is noticed by Ptolemy (Tabul. p. 37, Arabia, p. 9-29) and Abulfeda (p. 57); and may be found in D'Anville's maps, in the mid-desert between Chaibar and Tadmor.

[4] Procopius (de Bell. Persico, l. ii. c. 28), Evagrius (l. vi. c. 21), and Pocock (Specimen, p. 72, 86) attest the human sacrifices of the Arabs in the sixth century. The danger and escape of Abdallah is a tradition rather than a fact (Gagnier, Vie. de Mahomet. tom. i. p. 82-84).

exhibits the most painful and sublime effort of fanaticism: the deed or the intention was sanctified by the example of saints and heroes; and the father of Mohammed himself was devoted by a rash vow, and hardly ransomed for the equivalent of a hundred camels. In the time of ignorance the Arabs, like the Jews and Egyptians, abstained from the taste of swine's flesh;[1] they circumcised[2] their children at the age of puberty: the same customs, without the censure or the precept of the Koran, have been silently transmitted to their posterity and proselytes. It has been sagaciously conjectured that the artful legislator indulged the stubborn prejudices of his countrymen. It is more simple to believe that he adhered to the habits and opinions of his youth, without foreseeing that a practice congenial to the climate of Mecca might become useless or inconvenient on the banks of the Danube or the Volga.

Arabia was free: the adjacent kingdoms were shaken by the storms of conquest and tyranny, and the persecuted sects fled to the happy land where they might profess what they thought, and practise what they professed. The religions of the Sabians and Magians, of the Jews and Christians, were disseminated from the Persian Gulf to the Red Sea. In a remote period of antiquity Sabianism was diffused over Asia by the science of the Chaldæans[3] and the arms of the Assyrians. From the observations of two thousand years the priests and astronomers of Babylon[4] deduced the eternal laws of nature and providence. They adored the seven gods, or angels, who directed the course of the seven

---

[1] Suillis carnibus abstinent, says Solinus (Polyhistor. c. 33), who copies Pliny (l. viii. c. 78) in the strange supposition that hogs cannot live in Arabia. The Egyptians were actuated by a natural and superstitious horror for that unclean beast (Marsham, Canon. p. 205). The old Arabians likewise practised, *post coitum*, the rite of ablution (Herodot. l. i. c. 189), which is sanctified by the Mohammedan law (Reland, p. 75, etc.; Chardin, or rather the *Mollah* of Shah Abbas, tom. iv. p. 71, etc.).

[2] The Mohammedan doctors are not fond of the subject; yet they hold circumcision necessary to salvation, and even pretend that Mohammed was miraculously born without a foreskin (Pocock, Specimen, p. 319, 320; Sale's Preliminary Discourse, p. 106, 107).

[3] Diodorus Siculus (tom. i. l. ii. [c. 29 sqq.] p. 142-145) has cast on their religion the curious but superficial glance of a Greek. Their astronomy would be far more valuable; they had looked through the telescope of reason, since they could doubt whether the sun were in the number of the planets or of the fixed stars.

[4] Simplicius (who quotes Porphyry), de Cœlo, l. ii. com. xlvi. p. 123, lin. 18, apud Marsham, Canon. Chron. p. 474, who doubts the fact, because it is adverse to his systems. The earliest date of the Chaldæan observations is the year 2234 before Christ. After the conquest of Babylon by Alexander, they were communicated, at the request of Aristotle, to the astronomer Hipparchus. What a moment in the annals of science!

planets, and shed their irresistible influence on the earth. The
attributes of the seven planets, with the twelve signs of the
zodiac, and the twenty-four constellations of the northern and
southern hemisphere, were represented by images and talismans;
the seven days of the week were dedicated to their respective
deities; the Sabians prayed thrice each day; and the temple of
the moon at Haran was the term of their pilgrimage.[1] But the
flexible genius of their faith was always ready either to teach or
to learn: in the tradition of the creation, the deluge, and the
patriarchs, they held a singular agreement with their Jewish
captives; they appealed to the secret books of Adam, Seth, and
Enoch; and a slight infusion of the Gospel has transformed the
last remnant of the Polytheists into the Christians of St. John,
in the territory of Bassora.[2] The altars of Babylon were overturned by the Magians; but the injuries of the Sabians were
revenged by the sword of Alexander; Persia groaned above
five hundred years under a foreign yoke; and the purest disciples
of Zoroaster escaped from the contagion of idolatry, and breathed
with their adversaries the freedom of the desert.[3] Seven
hundred years before the death of Mohammed the Jews were
settled in Arabia; and a far greater multitude was expelled from
the Holy Land in the wars of Titus and Hadrian. The industrious exiles aspired to liberty and power: they erected
synagogues in the cities, and castles in the wilderness; and their
Gentile converts were confounded with the children of Israel,
whom they resembled in the outward mark of circumcision.
The Christian missionaries were still more active and successful:
the Catholics asserted their universal reign; the sects whom
they oppressed successively retired beyond the limits of the

[1] Pocock (Specimen, p. 138-146), Hottinger (Hist. Orient. p. 162-203),
Hyde (de Religione Vet. Persarum, p. 124, 128, etc.), D'Herbelot (Sabi,
p. 725, 726), and Sale (Preliminary Discourse, p. 14, 15), rather excite than
gratify our curiosity; and the last of these writers confounds Sabianism
with the primitive religion of the Arabs.

[2] D'Anville (l'Euphrate et le Tigre, p. 130-147) will fix the position of
these ambiguous Christians; Assemannus (Biblioth. Oriental. tom. iv.
p. 607-614) may explain their tenets. But it is a slippery task to ascertain
the creed of an ignorant people, afraid and ashamed to disclose their secret
traditions.
[The Codex Nasiræus, their sacred book, has been published by Norberg,
whose researches contain almost all that is known of this singular people.
But their origin is almost as obscure as ever: if ancient, their creed has
been so corrupted with mysticism and Mohammedanism, that its native
lineaments are very indistinct.—O. S.]

[3] The Magi were fixed in the province of Bahrein (Gagnier, Vie de
Mahomet, tom. iii. p. 114), and mingled with the old Arabians (Pocock,
Specimen, p. 146-150).

Roman empire; the Marcionites and Manichæans dispersed their *fantastic* opinions and apocryphal gospels; the churches of Yemen, and the princes of Hira and Gassan, were instructed in a purer creed by the Jacobite and Nestorian bishops.[1]   The liberty of choice was presented to the tribes: each Arab was free to elect or to compose his private religion; and the rude superstition of his house was mingled with the sublime theology of saints and philosophers.   A fundamental article of faith was inculcated by the consent of the learned strangers; the existence of one supreme God, who is exalted above the powe:s of heaven and earth, but who has often revealed himself to mankind by the ministry of his angels and prophets, and whose grace or justice has interrupted, by seasonable miracles, the order of nature.   The most rational of the Arabs acknowledged his power, though they neglected his worship;[2] and it was habit rather than conviction that still attached them to the relics of idolatry.   The Jews and Christians were the people of the *Book ;* the Bible was already translated into the Arabic language,[3] and the volume of the Old Testament was accepted by the concord of these implacable enemies.   In the story of the Hebrew patriarchs the Arabs were pleased to discover the fathers of their nation.   They applauded the birth and promises of Ismael; revered the faith and virtue of Abraham; traced his pedigree and their own to the creation of the first man, and imbibed with equal credulity the prodigies of the holy text, and the dreams and traditions of the Jewish rabbis.

The base and plebeian origin of Mohammed is an unskilful calumny of the Christians,[4] who exalt instead of degrading the

[1] The state of the Jews and Christians in Arabia is described by Pocock from Sharestani, etc. (Specimen, p. 60, 134, etc.), Hottinger (Hist. Orient. p. 212-238), D'Herbelot (Biblioth. Orient. p. 474-476), Basnage (Hist. des Juifs, tom. vii. p. 185; tom. viii. p. 280), and Sale (Preliminary Discourse, p. 22, etc., 33, etc.).

[2] In their offerings it was a maxim to defraud God for the profit of the idol—not a more potent, but a more irritable, patron (Pocock, Specimen, p. 108, 109).

[3] Our versions now extant, whether Jewish or Christian, appear more recent than the Koran; but the existence of a prior translation may be fairly inferred—1. From the perpetual practice of the synagogue, of expounding the Hebrew lesson by a paraphrase in the vulgar tongue of the country. 2. From the analogy of the Armenian, Persian, Æthiopic versions expressly quoted by the fathers of the fifth century, who assert that the Scriptures were translated into *all* the barbaric languages (Walton, Prolegomena ad Biblia Polyglot. p. 34, 93-97; Simon, Hist. Critique du V. et du N. Testament, tom. i. p. 180, 181, 282-286, 293, 305, 306, tom. iv. p. 206).

[4] In eo conveniunt omnes, ut plebeio vilique genere ortum, etc. (Hottinger, Hist. Orient. p. 136).   Yet Theophanes, the most ancient of the

merit of their adversary. His descent from Ismael was a
national privilege or fable; but if the first steps of the pedigree [1]
are dark and doubtful, he could produce many generations of
pure and genuine nobility: he sprung from the tribe of Koreish
and the family of Hashem, the most illustrious of the Arabs, the
princes of Mecca, and the hereditary guardians of the Caaba.[2]
The grandfather of Mohammed was Abdol Motalleb, the son of
Hashem, a wealthy and generous citizen, who relieved the
distress of famine with the supplies of commerce. Mecca,
which had been fed by the liberality of the father, was saved
by the courage of the son. The kingdom of Yemen was subject
to the Christian princes of Abyssinia: their vassal Abrahah was
provoked by an insult to avenge the honour of the cross; and
the holy city was invested by a train of elephants and an army
of Africans. A treaty was proposed; and, in the first audience,
the grandfather of Mohammed demanded the restitution of his
cattle. " And why," said Abrahah, " do you not rather implore
my clemency in favour of your temple, which I have threatened
to destroy?" "Because," replied the intrepid chief, "the
cattle is my own; the Caaba belongs to the gods, and *they* will
defend their house from injury and sacrilege." The want of
provisions, or the valour of the Koreish, compelled the Abyssinians to a disgraceful retreat: their discomfiture has been

Greeks, and the father of many a lie, confesses that Mohammed was of the
race of Ismael, ἐκ μιᾶς γενικωτάτης φυλῆς (Chronograph. p. 277 [ed. Par.;
tom. i. p. 512, ed. Bonn]).

[1] Abulfeda (in Vit. Mohammed. c. 1, 2) and Gagnier (Vie de Mahomet,
p. 25-97) describe the popular and approved genealogy of the prophet.
At Mecca, I would not dispute its authenticity: at Lausanne, I will
venture to observe—1. *That*, from Ismael to Mohammed, a period of 2500
years, they reckon thirty, instead of seventy-five, generations. 2. *That*
the modern Bedoweens are ignorant of their history, and careless of their
pedigree (Voyage de D'Arvieux, p. 100, 103).

[According to the usually received tradition, Koreish was originally
an epithet conferred upon Fihr (born about A.D. 200), who was the ancestor,
at the distance of eight generations, of the famous Kussai mentioned in
the next note. Sprenger, however, maintains that the tribe of Koreish
was first formed by Kussai, and that the members of the new tribe called
themselves the children of Fihr as a symbol of unity. He regards Fihr
as a mythical personage.—O. S.]

[2] [Kussai (born about A.D. 400), great-grandfather of Abdol Motalleb,
and consequently fifth in the ascending line from Mohammed, obtained
supreme power at Mecca. His office and privileges were—to supply the
numerous pilgrims with food and fresh water, the latter a rare article at
Mecca; to conduct the business of the temple; and to preside in the senate
or council. His revenues were a tenth of all merchandise brought to Mecca.
After the death of Kussai these offices became divided among his descendants; and, though the branch from which Mohammed sprang belonged to
the reigning line, yet his family, especially after the death of his grandfather, had but little to do with the actual government of Mecca.—O. S.]

adorned with a miraculous flight of birds, who showered down stones on the heads of the infidels; and the deliverance was long commemorated by the era of the elephant.[1] The glory of Abdol Motalleb was crowned with domestic happiness; his life was prolonged to the age of one hundred and ten years; and he became the father of six daughters and thirteen sons. His best beloved Abdallah was the most beautiful and modest of the Arabian youth; and in the first night, when he consummated his marriage with Amina, of the noble race of the Zahrites, two hundred virgins are said to have expired of jealousy and despair. Mohammed,[2] the only son of Abdallah and Amina,[3] was born at Mecca, four years after the death of Justinian, and two months after the defeat of the Abyssinians,[4] whose victory would have

---

[1] The seed of this history, or fable, is contained in the cvth chapter of the Koran; and Gagnier (in Præfat. ad Vit. Moham. p. 18, etc.) has translated the historical narrative of Abulfeda, which may be illustrated from D'Herbelot (Biblioth. Orientale, p. 12) and Pocock (Specimen, p. 64). Prideaux (Life of Mahomet, p. 48) calls it a lie of the coinage of Mohammed; but Sale (Koran, p. 501-503), who is half a Musulman, attacks the inconsistent faith of the Doctor for believing the miracles of the Delphic Apollo. Maracci (Alcoran, tom. i. part ii. p. 14; tom. ii. p. 823) ascribes the miracle to the devil, and extorts from the Mohammedans the confession that God would not have defended against the Christians the idols of the Caaba.

[The apparent miracle which caused the retreat from the Hejaz was nothing else than the smallpox which broke out in the army of Abrahah. This seems to have been the first appearance of the smallpox in Arabia. Sprenger, *Life of Mohammed.*—O. S.]

[2] [Mohammed means " the praised," the name given to him by his grandfather on account of the favourable omen attending his birth. When Amina had given birth to the prophet, she sent for his grandfather, and related to him that she had seen in a dream a light proceeding from her body which illuminated the palaces of Bostra. We learn from Sir W. Muir and Burckhardt that among the Arabs a name is given to the infant immediately on its birth. The name is derived from some trifling accident or from some object which had struck the fancy of the mother or any of the women present at the child's birth.—O. S.]

[3] [Amina, the mother of Mohammed, was of Jewish birth. Sprenger, on the other hand, says she was a Koreishite, and the daughter of Wahab, an elder of the Zohrah family.—O. S.]

[4] The safest eras of Abulfeda (in Vit. c. i. p. 2), of Alexander, or the Greeks, 882, of Bocht Naser, or Nabonassar, 1316, equally lead us to the year 569. The old Arabian calendar is too dark and uncertain to support the Benedictines (Art de vérifier les Dates, p. 15), who, from the day of the month and week, deduce a new mode of calculation, and remove the birth of Mohammed to the year of Christ 570, the 10th of November. Yet this date would agree with the year 882 of the Greeks, which is assigned by Elmacin (Hist. Saracen. p. 5) and Abulpharagius (Dynast. p. 101; and Errata, Pocock's version). While we refine our chronology, it is possible that the illiterate prophet was ignorant of his own age.

[The latest authority (Mr. P. de Lacy Johnstone, M.A.) states that Mohammed was born in 571, on a Monday in the first half of Raby' I. He also comes to the conclusion that he died at the age of sixty-three years. All good Mussulmans celebrate the birth of Mohammed on the 12th of Raby' I., and for this day almost all traditions agree. But that day was a Thursday

introduced into the Caaba the religion of the Christians. In his early infancy [1] he was deprived of his father, his mother, and his grandfather; his uncles were strong and numerous; and, in the division of the inheritance, the orphan's share was reduced to five camels and an Æthiopian maid-servant.[2] At home and abroad, in peace and war, Abu Taleb, the most respectable of his uncles, was the guide and guardian of his youth; in his twenty-fifth year he entered into the service of Cadijah, a rich and noble widow of Mecca, who soon rewarded his fidelity with the gift of her hand and fortune. The marriage contract, in the simple style of antiquity, recites the mutual love of Mohammed and Cadijah; describes him as the most accomplished of the tribe of Koreish; and stipulates a dowry of twelve ounces of gold and twenty camels, which was supplied by the liberality of his uncle.[3] By this alliance the son of Abdallah was restored to the station of his ancestors; and the judicious matron was content with his domestic virtues, till, in the fortieth year of his age,[4]

in 571. But there are reasons for believing that the Meccan year was originally a lunar one, and continued so until the beginning of the fifth century, when in imitation of the Jews it was turned by the intercalation of a month at the close of every third year into a luni-solar one. Hence it follows that all calculations made up to the end of Mohammed's life must be made in luni-solar years and not in lunar years, involving a yearly difference of ten days. See *Calcutta Review*, No. 41, p. 49; De Lacy Johnstone's " Mohammed " in World's Epoch-makers Series.—O. S.]

[1] [The father of Mohammed died two months before his birth: and to the ill state of health which the shock of this premature bereavement entailed on the widow, Sprenger, Muir, and Johnstone all attribute the sickly and nervous temperament of the prophet. His mother died in his seventh year, his grandfather two years later.—O. S.]

[2] [His poverty was due, however, not to the injustice of his uncles, but, as De Lacy Johnstone points out, to his own inactivity and unfitness for the ordinary duties of life. He had the same patrimony with which his father began his life, viz., a house, five camels, a flock of sheep, and a female slave, yet he was reduced to the necessity of pasturing sheep, an occupation considered by the Arabs as peculiarly humiliating.—Cf. Weil's *Mahomet*. The same author adds that Mohammed afterwards entered into the linen trade in partnership with a man named Saïb.—O. S.]

[3] I copy the honourable testimony of Abu Taleb to his family and nephew. Laus Deo, qui nos a stirpe Abrahami et semine Ismaelis constituit, et nobis regionem sacram dedit, et nos judices hominibus statuit. Porro Mohammed filius Abdollahi nepotis mei (*nepos meus*) quo cum [non] ex æquo librabitur e Koraishidis quispiam cui non præponderaturus est bonitate, et excellentiâ, et intellectû, et gloriâ, et acumine, etsi opum inops fuerit (et certe opes umbra transiens sunt et depositum quod reddi debet), desiderio Chadijæ filiæ Chowailedi tenetur, et illa vicissim ipsius, quicquid autem dotis vice petieritis, ego in me suscipiam (Pocock, Specimen, e septimâ parte libri Ebn Hamduni [p. 171]).

[4] The private life of Mohammed, from his birth to his mission, is preserved by Abulfeda (in Vit. c. 3-7), and the Arabian writers of genuine or apocryphal note, who are alleged by Hottinger (Hist. Orient. p. 204-211), Maracci (tom. i. p. 10-14), and Gagnier (Vie de Mahomet, tom. i. p. 97-134).

he assumed the title of a prophet, and proclaimed the religion of the Koran.

According to the tradition of his companions, Mohammed [1] was distinguished by the beauty of his person, an outward gift which is seldom despised, except by those to whom it has been refused. Before he spoke, the orator engaged on his side the affections of a public or private audience. They applauded his commanding presence, his majestic aspect, his piercing eye, his gracious smile, his flowing beard, his countenance that painted every sensation of the soul, and his gestures that enforced each expression of the tongue.[2] In the familiar offices of life he scrupulously adhered to the grave and ceremonious politeness of his country: his respectful attention to the rich and powerful was dignified by his condescension and affability to the poorest citizens of Mecca: the frankness of his manner concealed the artifice of his views; and the habits of courtesy were imputed to personal friendship or universal benevolence. His memory was capacious and retentive; his wit easy and social; his imagination sublime; his judgment clear, rapid, and decisive. He possessed the courage both of thought and action; and, although his designs might gradually expand with his success, the first idea which he entertained of his divine mission bears the stamp of an original and superior genius. The son of Abdallah was educated in the bosom of the noblest race, in the use of the purest dialect of Arabia; and the fluency of his speech

---

[1] Abulfeda, in Vit. c. 65, 66; Gagnier, Vie de Mahomet, tom. iii. p. 272-289; the best traditions of the person and conversation of the prophet are derived from Ayesha, Ali, and Abu Horaira (Gagnier, tom. ii. p. 267; Ockley's Hist. of the Saracens, vol. ii. p. 149), surnamed the Father of a Cat, who died in the year 59 of the Hegira.

[2] [The following is the description of Mohammed's person given by Dr. Sprenger:—" He was of middle size, had broad shoulders, a wide chest, and large bones, and he was fleshy but not stout. The immoderate size of his head was partly disguised by the long locks of hair, which in slight curls came down nearly to the lobes of his ears. His oval face, though tawny, was rather fair for an Arab, but neither pale nor high coloured. The forehead was broad, and his fine and long, but narrow, eyebrows were separated by a vein, which you could see throbbing if he was angry. Under long eyelashes sparkled bloodshot black eyes through wide-slit eyelids. His nose was large, prominent, and slightly hooked, and the tip of it seemed to be turned up, but was not so in reality. The mouth was wide, and he had a good set of teeth, and the fore-teeth were asunder. His beard rose from the cheek-bones and came down to the collar-bone; he clipped his mustachios, but did not shave them. He stooped, and was slightly humpbacked. His gait was careless, and he walked fast but heavily, as if he were ascending a hill; and if he looked back, he turned his whole body. The mildness of his countenance gained him the confidence of every one; but he could not look straight into a man's face; he turned his eyes usually outwards.—O. S.]

was corrected and enhanced by the practice of discreet and seasonable silence. With these powers of eloquence, Mohammed was an illiterate barbarian: his youth had never been instructed in the arts of reading and writing;[1] the common ignorance exempted him from shame or reproach, but he was reduced to a narrow circle of existence, and deprived of those faithful mirrors which reflect to our mind the minds of sages and heroes. Yet the book of nature and of man was open to his view; and some fancy has been indulged in the political and philosophical observations which are ascribed to the Arabian *traveller*.[2] He compares the nations and the religions of the earth; discovers the weakness of the Persian and Roman monarchies; beholds with pity and indignation the degeneracy of the times; and resolves to unite under one God and one king the invincible spirit and primitive virtues of the Arabs. Our more accurate inquiry will suggest, that, instead of visiting the courts, the camps, the temples of the East, the two journeys of Mohammed into Syria were confined to the fairs of Bostra and Damascus; that he was only thirteen years of age when he accompanied the caravan of his uncle; and that his duty compelled him to return as soon as he had disposed of the merchandise of Cadijah. In these hasty

[1] Those who believe that Mohammed could read or write are incapable of reading what is written, with another pen, in the Suras, or chapters of the Koran, vii. xxix. xcvi. These texts, and the tradition of the Sonna, are admitted, without doubt, by Abulfeda (in Vit. c. 7), Gagnier (Not. ad Abulfed. p. 15), Pocock (Specimen, p. 151), Reland (de Religione Mohammedicâ, p. 236), and Sale (Preliminary Discourse, p. 42). Mr. White, almost alone, denies the ignorance, to accuse the imposture, of the prophet. His arguments are far from satisfactory. Two short trading journeys to the fairs of Syria were surely not sufficient to infuse a science so rare among the citizens of Mecca: it was not in the cool, deliberate act of a treaty that Mohammed would have dropped the mask; nor can any conclusion be drawn from the words of disease and delirium. The *lettered* youth, before he aspired to the prophetic character, must have often exercised, in private life, the arts of reading and writing; and his first converts, of his own family, would have been the first to detect and upbraid his scandalous hypocrisy (White's Sermons, p. 203, 204, Notes, p. xxxvi.-xxxviii.).

[Modern Orientalists are now inclined to answer the question, " Could Mohammed read and write? " in the affirmative! The point hinges upon the critical interpretation of certain important passages in the Koran. Moslem authors are at variance. Almost all the modern writers, and many of the old, deny the ability of their prophet to read and write: but good authors, especially of the Shiite sect, admit that he could read, though they describe him as an unskilful penman.—O. S.]

[2] The Count de Boulainvilliers (Vie de Mahomet, p. 202-228) leads his Arabian pupil, like the Telemachus of Fenélon, or the Cyrus of Ramsay. His journey to the court of Persia is probably a fiction, nor can I trace the origin of his exclamation, " Les Grecs sont pourtant des hommes." The two Syrian journeys are expressed by almost all the Arabian writers, both Mohammedans and Christians (Gagnier, ad Abulfed. p. 10).

and superficial excursions the eye of genius might discern some objects invisible to his grosser companions; some seeds of knowledge might be cast upon a fruitful soil; but his ignorance of the Syriac language must have checked his curiosity; and I cannot perceive in the life or writings of Mohammed that his prospect was far extended beyond the limits of the Arabian world. From every region of that solitary world the pilgrims of Mecca were annually assembled by the calls of devotion and commerce: in the free concourse of multitudes, a simple citizen, in his native tongue, might study the political state and character of the tribes, the theory and practice of the Jews and Christians. Some useful strangers might be tempted, or forced, to implore the rights of hospitality; and the enemies of Mohammed have named the Jew, the Persian, and the Syrian monk, whom they accuse of lending their secret aid to the composition of the Koran.[1] Conversation enriches the understanding, but solitude is the school of genius; and the uniformity of a work denotes the hand of a single artist. From his earliest youth Mohammed was addicted to religious contemplation; each year, during the month of Ramadan, he withdrew from the world and from the arms of Cadijah: in the cave of Hera, three miles from Mecca,[2] he consulted the spirit of fraud or enthusiasm, whose abode is not in the heavens, but in the mind of the prophet. The faith which, under the name of *Islam*, he preached to his family and nation, is compounded of an eternal truth and a necessary fiction, THAT THERE IS ONLY ONE GOD, AND THAT MOHAMMED IS THE APOSTLE OF GOD.[3]

It is the boast of the Jewish apologists, that, while the learned nations of antiquity were deluded by the fables of polytheism, their simple ancestors of Palestine preserved the knowledge and

---

[1] I am not at leisure to pursue the fables or conjectures which name the strangers accused or suspected by the infidels of Mecca (Koran, c. 16, p. 223, c. 35, p. 297, with Sale's Remarks; Prideaux's Life of Mahomet, p. 22-27; Gagnier, Not. ad Abulfed. p. 11, 74; Maracci, tom. ii. p. 400). Even Prideaux has observed that the transaction must have been secret, and that the scene lay in the heart of Arabia.

[2] Abulfeda in Vit. c. 7, p. 15; Gagnier, tom. i. p. 133, 135. The situation of Mount Hera is remarked by Abulfeda (Geograph. Arab. p. 4). Yet Mohammed had never read of the cave of Egeria, ubi nocturnæ Numa constituebat amicæ, of the Idæan mount, where Minos conversed with Jove, etc.

[3] [*Islám* is the verbal noun or infinitive, and Moslim, which has been corrupted into Mussulman, is the participle or causative form of *salm*, which means peace. The signification of Islám is to make peace, either by compact or by doing homage to the stronger, acknowledging his superiority. In the Koran it means to do homage to God, to acknowledge him as our absolute Lord to the exclusion of idols.—O. S.]

worship of the true God. The moral attributes of Jehovah may not easily be reconciled with the standard of *human* virtue: his metaphysical qualities are darkly expressed; but each page of the Pentateuch and the Prophets is an evidence of his power: the unity of his name is inscribed on the first table of the law; and his sanctuary was never defiled by any visible image of the invisible essence. After the ruin of the temple, the faith of the Hebrew exiles was purified, fixed, and enlightened by the spiritual devotion of the synagogue; and the authority of Mohammed will not justify his perpetual reproach that the Jews of Mecca or Medina adored Ezra as the son of God.[1] But the children of Israel had ceased to be a people; and the religions of the world were guilty, at least in the eyes of the prophet, of giving sons, or daughters, or companions to the supreme God. In the rude idolatry of the Arabs the crime is manifest and audacious: the Sabians are poorly excused by the pre-eminence of the first planet, or intelligence, in their celestial hierarchy; and in the Magian system the conflict of the two principles betrays the imperfection of the conqueror. The Christians of the seventh century had insensibly relapsed into a semblance of paganism; their public and private vows were addressed to the relics and images that disgraced the temples of the East: the throne of the Almighty was darkened by a cloud of martyrs, and saints, and angels, the objects of popular veneration; and the Collyridian heretics, who flourished in the fruitful soil of Arabia, invested the Virgin Mary with the name and honours of a goddess.[2] The mysteries of the Trinity and Incarnation *appear* to contradict the principle of the divine unity. In their obvious sense, they introduce three equal deities, and transform the man Jesus into the substance of the Son of God:[3] an orthodox

[1] Koran, c. 9, p. 153. Al Beidawi, and the other commentators quoted by Sale, adhere to the charge; but I do not understand that it is coloured by the most obscure or absurd tradition of the Talmudists.

[2] Hottinger, Hist. Orient. p. 225-228. The Collyridian heresy was carried from Thrace to Arabia by some women, and the name was borrowed from the κολλυρις, or cake, which they offered to the goddess. This example, that of Beryllus bishop of Bostra (Euseb. Hist. Eccles. l. vi. c. 33), and several others, may excuse the reproach, Arabia hæreseon ferax.

[3] The three gods in the Koran (c. 4, p. 81, c. 5, p. 92) are obviously directed against our Catholic mystery: but the Arabic commentators understand them of the Father, the Son, and the Virgin Mary, an heretical Trinity, maintained, as it is said, by some barbarians at the Council of Nice (Eutych. Annal. tom. i. p. 440). But the existence of the *Marianites* is denied by the candid Beausobre (Hist. de Manichéisme, tom. i. p. 532); and he derives the mistake from the word *Rouah*, the Holy Ghost, which in some Oriental tongues is of the feminine gender, and is figuratively styled the mother of Christ in the gospel of the Nazarenes.

commentary will satisfy only a believing mind: intemperate curiosity and zeal had torn the veil of the sanctuary: and each of the Oriental sects was eager to confess that all, except themselves, deserved the reproach of idolatry and polytheism. The creed of Mohammed is free from suspicion or ambiguity; and the Koran is a glorious testimony to the unity of God. The prophet of Mecca rejected the worship of idols and men, of stars and planets, on the rational principle that whatever rises must set, that whatever is born must die, that whatever is corruptible must decay and perish.[1] In the Author of the universe his rational enthusiasm confessed and adored an infinite and eternal being, without form or place, without issue or similitude, present to our most secret thoughts, existing by the necessity of his own nature, and deriving from himself all moral and intellectual perfection. These sublime truths, thus announced in the language of the prophet,[2] are firmly held by his disciples, and defined with metaphysical precision by the interpreters of the Koran. A philosophic theist might subscribe the popular creed of the Mohammedans:[3] a creed too sublime perhaps for our present faculties. What object remains for the fancy, or even the understanding, when we have abstracted from the unknown substance all ideas of time and space, of motion and matter, of sensation and reflection? The first principle of reason and revelation was confirmed by the voice of Mohammed: his proselytes, from India to Morocco, are distinguished by the name of *Unitarians;* and the danger of idolatry has been prevented by the interdiction of images. The doctrine of eternal decrees and absolute predestination is strictly embraced by the Mohammedans; and they struggle with the common difficulties, *how* to reconcile the prescience of God with the freedom and responsibility of man; *how* to explain the permission of evil under the reign of infinite power and infinite goodness.[4]

[1] This train of thought is philosophically exemplified in the character of Abraham, who opposed in Chaldæa the first introduction of idolatry (Koran, c. 6, p. 106; D'Herbelot, Biblioth. Orient. p. 13).

[2] See the Koran, particularly the second (p. 30), the fifty-seventh (p. 437), the fifty-eighth (p. 441) chapters, which proclaim the omnipotence of the Creator.

[3] The most orthodox creeds are translated by Pocock (Specimen, p. 274, 284-292), Ockley (Hist. of the Saracens, vol. ii. p. lxxxii.-xcv.), Reland (de Religion. Moham. l. i. p. 7-13), and Chardin (Voyages en Perse, tom. iv. p. 4-28). The great truth, that God is without similitude, is foolishly criticised by Maracci (Alcoran, tom. i. part iii. p. 87-94), because he made man after his own image.

[4] [Gibbon's estimate of the prophet's system is much too favourable on the score of its originality. Mohammed simply gathered up into one system what he found floating in the minds of men around him. The

The God of nature has written his existence on all his works, and his law in the heart of man. To restore the knowledge of the one, and the practice of the other, has been the real or pretended aim of the prophets of every age: the liberality of Mohammed allowed to his predecessors the same credit which he claimed for himself; and the chain of inspiration was prolonged from the fall of Adam to the promulgation of the Koran.[1] During that period some rays of prophetic light had been imparted to one hundred and twenty-four thousand of the elect, discriminated by their respective measure of virtue and grace; three hundred and thirteen apostles were sent with a special commission to recall their country from idolatry and vice; one hundred and four volumes have been dictated by the Holy Spirit; and six legislators of transcendent brightness have announced to mankind the six successive revelations of various rites, but of one immutable religion. The authority and station of Adam, Noah, Abraham, Moses, Christ, and Mohammed, rise in just gradation above each other; but whosoever hates or rejects any one of the prophets is numbered with the infidels. The writings of the patriarchs were extant only in the apocryphal copies of the Greeks and Syrians: [2] the conduct of Adam had not entitled him to the gratitude or respect of his children; the seven precepts of Noah were observed by an inferior and imperfect class of the proselytes of the synagogue; [3] and the memory of Abraham was obscurely revered by the Sabians in his native land of Chaldæa: of the myriads of prophets, Moses and Christ alone lived and reigned; and the remnant of the inspired writings was comprised in the books of the Old and the New Testament. The miraculous story of Moses is consecrated and embellished

Koreishites charged Mohammed with taking his whole doctrine from a book called the " Asatyr of the Ancients," which is several times quoted in the Koran, and appears to have contained the doctrine of the resurrection. Qoss had preached the unity of God, and other preachers, before Mohammed.—O. S.]

[1] Reland, de Relig. Moham. l. i. p. 17-47; Sale's Preliminary Discourse, p. 73-76; Voyage de Chardin, tom. iv. p. 28-37 and 37-47, for the Persian addition, " Ali is the Vicar of God! " Yet the precise number of prophets is not an article of faith.

[2] For the apocryphal books of Adam, see Fabricius, Codex Pseudepigraphus V. T. p. 27-29; of Seth, p. 154-157; of Enoch, p. 160-219. But the book of Enoch is consecrated, in some measure, by the quotation of the apostle St. Jude; and a long legendary fragment is alleged by Syncellus and Scaliger.

[3] The seven precepts of Noah are explained by Marsham (Canon. Chronicus, p. 154-180) who adopts, on this occasion, the learning and credulity of Selden.

in the Koran;[1] and the captive Jews enjoy the secret revenge of imposing their own belief on the nations whose recent creeds they deride. For the author of Christianity, the Mohammedans are taught by the prophet to entertain a high and mysterious reverence.[2] " Verily, Christ Jesus, the son of Mary, is the apostle of God, and his word, which he conveyed unto Mary, and a Spirit proceeding from him: honourable in this world, and in the world to come; and one of those who approach near to the presence of God." [3] The wonders of the genuine and apocryphal gospels [4] are profusely heaped on his head; and the Latin church has not disdained to borrow from the Koran the immaculate conception [5] of his virgin mother. Yet Jesus was a mere mortal; and, at the day of judgment, his testimony will serve to condemn both the Jews, who reject him as a prophet, and the Christians, who adore him as the Son of God. The malice of his enemies aspersed his reputation, and conspired against his life; but their intention only was guilty; a phantom or a criminal was substituted on the cross; and the innocent saint was translated to the seventh heaven.[6] During six hundred years the Gospel was the way of truth and salvation; but the Christians insensibly forgot both the laws and the example of their founder; and Mohammed was instructed by the Gnostics to accuse the church, as well as the synagogue, of corrupting the integrity of the sacred

[1] The articles of *Adam, Noah, Abraham, Moses*, etc., in the Bibliothèque of D'Herbelot, are gaily bedecked with the fanciful legends of the Mohammedans, who have built on the groundwork of Scripture and the Talmud.
[2] Koran, c. 7, p. 128, etc., c. 10, p. 173, etc.; D'Herbelot, p. 647, etc.
[3] Koran, c. 3, p. 40, c. 4, p. 80; D'Herbelot, p. 399, etc.
[4] See the gospel of St. Thomas, or of the Infancy, in the Codex Apocryphus N. T. of Fabricius, who collects the various testimonies concerning it (p. 128-158). It was published in Greek by Cotelier, and in Arabic by Sike, who thinks our present copy more recent than Mohammed. Yet his quotations agree with the original about the speech of Christ in his cradle, his living birds of clay, etc. (*Sike*, c. i. p. 168, 169, c. 36, p. 198, 199, c. 46, p. 206; *Cotelier*, c. 2, p. 160, 161).
[5] It is darkly hinted in the Koran (c. 3, p. 39), and more clearly explained by the tradition of the Sonnites (Sale's Note, and Maracci, tom. ii. p. 112). In the twelfth century, the immaculate conception was condemned by St. Bernard as a presumptuous novelty (Fra Paolo, Istoria del Concilio di Trento, l. ii.).
[6] See the Koran, c. 3, v. 53, and c. 4, v. 156, of Maracci's edition. Deus est præstantissimus dolose agentium (an odd praise) . . . nec crucifixerunt eum, sed objecta est eis similitudo: an expression that may suit with the system of the Docetes; but the commentators believe (Maracci, tom. ii. p. 113-115, 173; Sale, p. 42, 43, 79) that another man, a friend or an enemy, was crucified in the likeness of Jesus; a fable which they had read in the gospel of St. Barnabas, and which had been started as early as the time of Irenæus, by some Ebionite heretics (Beausobre, Hist. du Manichéisme, tom. ii. p. 25; Mosheim de Reb. Christ. p. 353).

text.[1] The piety of Moses and of Christ rejoiced in the assurance of a future Prophet, more illustrious than themselves: the evangelic promise of the *Paraclete*, or Holy Ghost, was prefigured in the name, and accomplished in the person, of Mohammed,[2] the greatest and the last of the apostles of God.

The communication of ideas requires a similitude of thought and language: the discourse of a philosopher would vibrate without effect on the ear of a peasant; yet how minute is the distance of *their* understandings, if it be compared with the contact of an infinite and a finite mind, with the word of God expressed by the tongue or the pen of a mortal? The inspiration of the Hebrew prophets, of the apostles and evangelists of Christ, might not be incompatible with the exercise of their reason and memory; and the diversity of their genius is strongly marked in the style and composition of the books of the Old and New Testament. But Mohammed was content with a character more humble, yet more sublime, of a simple editor; the substance of the Koran,[3] according to himself or his disciples, is uncreated and eternal; subsisting in the essence of the Deity, and inscribed with a pen of light on the table of his everlasting decrees. A paper copy, in a volume of silk and gems, was brought down to the lowest heaven by the angel Gabriel, who, under the Jewish economy, had indeed been despatched on the most important errands; and this trusty messenger successively revealed the chapters and verses to the Arabian prophet. Instead of a perpetual and perfect measure of the divine will, the fragments of the Koran were produced at the discretion of Mohammed; each revelation is suited to the emergencies of his policy or passion; and all contradiction is removed by the saving maxim that any text of Scripture is abrogated or modified by any subsequent passage. The word of God and of the apostle was diligently recorded by his disciples on palm-leaves and the shoulder-bones

---

[1] This charge is obscurely urged in the Koran (c. 3, p. 45); but neither Mohammed nor his followers are sufficiently versed in languages and criticism to give any weight or colour to their suspicions. Yet the Arians and Nestorians could relate some stories, and the illiterate prophet might listen to the bold assertions of the Manichæans. See Beausobre, tom. i. p. 291-305.

[2] Among the prophecies of the Old and New Testament, which are perverted by the fraud or ignorance of the Musulmans, they apply to the prophet the promise of the *Paraclete*, or Comforter, which had been already usurped by the Montanists and Manichæans (Beausobre, Hist. Critique du Manichéisme, tom. i. p. 263, etc.); and the easy change of letters, περικλυτὸς for παράκλητος, affords the etymology of the name of Mohammed (Maracci, tom. i. part i. p. 15-28).

[3] For the Koran, see D'Herbelot, p. 85-88; Maracci, tom. i. in Vit. Mohammed. p. 32-45; Sale, Preliminary Discourse, p. 56-70.

of mutton; and the pages, without order or connection, were cast into a domestic chest in the custody of one of his wives. Two years after the death of Mohammed, the sacred volume was collected and published by his friend and successor Abubeker: the work was revised by the caliph Othman, in the thirtieth year of the Hegira; and the various editions of the Koran assert the same miraculous privilege of a uniform and incorruptible text.[1]   In the spirit of enthusiasm or vanity, the prophet rests the truth of his mission on the merit of his book; audaciously challenges both men and angels to imitate the beauties of a single page; and presumes to assert that God alone could dictate this incomparable performance.[2]   This argument is most powerfully addressed to a devout Arabian, whose mind is attuned to faith and rapture; whose ear is delighted by the music of sounds; and whose ignorance is incapable of comparing the productions of human genius.[3]   The harmony and copiousness of style will not reach, in a version, the European infidel: he will peruse with impatience the endless incoherent rhapsody of fable, and precept, and declamation, which seldom excites a sentiment or an idea, which sometimes crawls in the dust, and is sometimes lost in the clouds.   The divine attributes exalt the fancy of the Arabian missionary; but his loftiest strains must yield to the sublime simplicity of the book of Job, composed in a remote age, in the same country, and in the same language.[4]   If

[1] [Abubeker, at the suggestion of Omar, gave orders for the collection and publication of the Koran; but the editorial work was actually performed by Zeid Ibn Thâbit, who had been one of Mohammed's secretaries. He is related to have gathered the text " from date-leaves and tablets of white stone, and from the breasts of men." The recension of Othman has been handed down to the present day unaltered.   So carefully has it been preserved that there are no variations of importance among the innumerable copies scattered throughout the world.   Contending and embittered factions, originating in the murder of Othman himself, within a quarter of a century after the death of Mohammed, have ever since rent the Moslem world.   Yet but one Koran has been current among them, and the consentaneous use of it by all proves that we have now before us the self-same text prepared by the commands of that unfortunate caliph who was a Moslem martyr.—O. S.]

[2] Koran, c. 17, v. 89.   In Sale, p. 235, 236.   In Maracci, p. 410.

[3] Yet a sect of Arabians was persuaded that it might be equalled or surpassed by a human pen (Pocock, Specimen, p. 221, etc.); and Maracci (the polemic is too hard for the translator) derides the rhyming affectation of the most applauded passage (tom. i. part. ii. p. 69-75).

[4] Colloquia (whether real or fabulous) in mediâ Arabiâ atque ab Arabibus habita (Lowth, de Poesi Hebræorum Prælect. xxxii. xxxiii. xxxiv. with his German editor Michaelis, Epimetron iv.).   Yet Michaelis (p. 671-673) has detected many Egyptian images, the elephantiasis, papyrus, Nile, crocodile, etc.   The language is ambiguously styled *Arabico-Hebræa*.   The resemblance of the sister dialects was much more visible in their childhood than in their mature age (Michaelis, p. 682; Schultens, in Præfat. Job).

the composition of the Koran exceeds the faculties of a man, to what superior intelligence should we ascribe the Iliad of Homer, or the Philippics of Demosthenes? In all religions the life of the founder supplies the silence of his written revelation: the sayings of Mohammed were so many lessons of truth; his actions so many examples of virtue; and the public and private memorials were preserved by his wives and companions. At the end of two hundred years the *Sonna*, or oral law, was fixed and consecrated by the labours of Al Bochari, who discriminated seven thousand two hundred and seventy-five genuine traditions from a mass of three hundred thousand reports of a more doubtful or spurious character. Each day the pious author prayed in the temple of Mecca, and performed his ablutions with the water of Zemzem: the pages were successively deposited on the pulpit and the sepulchre of the apostle; and the work has been approved by the four orthodox sects of the Sonnites.[1]

The mission of the ancient prophets, of Moses and of Jesus, had been confirmed by many splendid prodigies; and Mohammed was repeatedly urged, by the inhabitants of Mecca and Medina, to produce a similar evidence of his divine legation; to call down from heaven the angel or the volume of his revelation, to create a garden in the desert, or to kindle a conflagration in the unbelieving city. As often as he is pressed by the demands of the Koreish, he involves himself in the obscure boast of vision and prophecy, appeals to the internal proofs of his doctrine, and shields himself behind the providence of God, who refuses those signs and wonders that would depreciate the merit of faith and aggravate the guilt of infidelity. But the modest or angry tone of his apologies betrays his weakness and vexation; and these passages of scandal established beyond suspicion the integrity of the Koran.[2] The votaries of Mohammed are more assured than himself of his miraculous gifts; and their confidence and credulity increase as they are farther removed from the time and place of his spiritual exploits. They believe or affirm that trees went forth to meet him; that he was saluted by stones; that water gushed from his fingers; that he fed the hungry, cured the sick, and raised the dead; that a beam groaned to him;

---

[1] Al Bochari died A.H. 224. See D'Herbelot, p. 208, 416, 827; Gagnier, Not. ad Abulfed. c. 19, p. 33.

[2] See, more remarkably, Koran, c. 2, 6, 12, 13, 17. Prideaux (Life of Mahomet, p. 18, 19) has confounded the impostor. Maracci, with a more learned apparatus, has shown that the passages which deny his miracles are clear and positive (Alcoran, tom. i. part. ii. p. 7-12), and those which seem to assert them are ambiguous and insufficient (p. 12-22).

that a camel complained to him; that a shoulder of mutton
informed him of its being poisoned; and that both animate and
inanimate nature were equally subject to the apostle of God.[1]
His dream of a nocturnal journey is seriously described as
a real and corporeal transaction. A mysterious animal, the
Borak, conveyed him from the temple of Mecca to that of Jerusalem: with his companion Gabriel he successively ascended the
seven heavens, and received and repaid the salutations of the
patriarchs, the prophets, and the angels, in their respective
mansions. Beyond the seventh heaven Mohammed alone was
permitted to proceed; he passed the veil of unity, approached
within two bow-shots of the throne, and felt a cold that pierced
him to the heart, when his shoulder was touched by the hand of
God. After this familiar though important conversation, he
again descended to Jerusalem, remounted the Borak, returned
to Mecca, and performed in the tenth part of a night the journey
of many thousand years.[2] According to another legend, the
apostle confounded in a national assembly the malicious
challenge of the Koreish. His resistless word split asunder the
orb of the moon: the obedient planet stooped from her station
in the sky, accomplished the seven revolutions round the Caaba,
saluted Mohammed in the Arabian tongue, and, suddenly con-
tracting her dimensions, entered at the collar, and issued forth
through the sleeve, of his shirt.[3] The vulgar are amused with

[1] See the Specimen Hist. Arabum, the text of Abulpharagius, p. 17; the
notes of Pocock, p. 187-190; D'Herbelot, Bibliothèque Orientale, p. 76,
77; Voyages de Chardin, tom. iv. p. 200-203; Maracci (Alcoran, tom. i.
p. 22-64) has most laboriously collected and confuted the miracles and
prophecies of Mohammed, which, according to some writers, amount to
three thousand.

[2] The nocturnal journey is circumstantially related by Abulfeda (in Vit.
Mohammed. c. 19, p. 33), who wishes to think it a vision; by Prideaux
(p. 31-40), who aggravates the absurdities; and by Gagnier (tom. i. p. 252-
343), who declares, from the zealous Al Jannabi, that to deny this journey
is to disbelieve the Koran. Yet the Koran, without naming either heaven,
or Jerusalem, or Mecca, has only dropped a mysterious hint: Laus illi qui
transtulit servum suum ab oratorio Haram ad oratorium remotissimum
(Koran, c. 17, v. 1; in Maracci, tom. ii. p. 407; for Sale's version is more
licentious). A slender basis for the aërial structure of tradition.

[3] In the prophetic style, which uses the present or past for the future,
Mohammed had said, Appropinquavit hora et scissa est luna (Koran, c. 54,
v. 1; in Maracci, tom. ii. p. 688). This figure of rhetoric has been converted into a fact, which is said to be attested by the most respectable eye-
witnesses (Maracci, tom. ii. p. 690). The festival is still celebrated by the
Persians (Chardin, tom. iv. p. 201); and the legend is tediously spun out
by Gagnier (Vie de Mahomet, tom. i. p. 183-234), on the faith, as it should
seem, of the credulous Al Jannabi. Yet a Mohammedan doctor has arraigned the credit of the principal witness (apud Pocock, Specimen, p. 187);
the best interpreters are content with the simple sense of the Koran (Al

these marvellous tales; but the gravest of the Musulman doctors imitate the modesty of their master, and indulge a latitude of faith or interpretation.[1] They might speciously allege, that in preaching the religion it was needless to violate the harmony of nature; that a creed unclouded with mystery may be excused from miracles; and that the sword of Mohammed was not less potent than the rod of Moses.

The polytheist is oppressed and distracted by the variety of superstition: a thousand rites of Egyptian origin were interwoven with the essence of the Mosaic law; and the spirit of the Gospel had evaporated in the pageantry of the church. The prophet of Mecca was tempted by prejudice, or policy, or patriotism, to sanctify the rites of the Arabians, and the custom of visiting the holy stone of the Caaba. But the precepts of Mohammed himself inculcate a more simple and rational piety: prayer, fasting, and alms are the religious duties of a Musulman; and he is encouraged to hope that prayer will carry him half way to God, fasting will bring him to the door of his palace, and alms will gain him admittance.[2] I. According to the tradition of the nocturnal journey, the apostle, in his personal conference with the Deity, was commanded to impose on his disciples the daily obligation of fifty prayers. By the advice of Moses, he applied for an alleviation of this intolerable burden; the number was gradually reduced to five; without any dispensation of business or pleasure, or time or place: the devotion of the faithful is repeated at daybreak, at noon, in the afternoon, in the evening, and at the first watch of the night; and in the present decay of religious fervour, our travellers are edified by the profound humility and attention of the Turks and Persians. Cleanliness is the key of prayer: the frequent lustration of the hands, the face, and the body, which was practised of old by the Arabs, is solemnly enjoined by the Koran; and a permission is formally granted to supply with sand the scarcity of water. The words

Beidawi, apud Hottinger, Hist. Orient. l. ii. p. 302), and the silence of Abulfeda is worthy of a prince and a philosopher.

[1] Abulpharagius, in Specimen Hist. Arab. p. 17; and his scepticism is justified in the notes of Pocock, p. 190-194, from the purest authorities.

[2] The most authentic account of these precepts, pilgrimage, prayer, fasting, alms, and ablutions, is extracted from the Persian and Arabian theologians by Maracci (Prodrom. part iv. p. 9-24), Reland (in his excellent treatise de Religione Mohammedicâ, Utrecht, 1717, p. 67-123), and Chardin (Voyages en Perse, tom. iv. p. 47-195). Maracci is a partial accuser; but the jeweller, Chardin, had the eyes of a philosopher; and Reland, a judicious student, had travelled over the East in his closet at Utrecht. The fourteenth letter of Tournefort (Voyage du Levant, tom. ii. p. 325-360, in octavo) describes what he had seen of the religion of the Turks.

and attitudes of supplication, as it is performed either sitting, or standing, or prostrate on the ground, are prescribed by custom or authority; but the prayer is poured forth in short and fervent ejaculations; the measure of zeal is not exhausted by a tedious liturgy; and each Musulman for his own person is invested with the character of a priest. Among the theists, who reject the use of images, it has been found necessary to restrain the wanderings of the fancy, by directing the eye and the thought towards a *kebla* or visible point of the horizon. The prophet was at first inclined to gratify the Jews by the choice of Jerusalem; but he soon returned to a more natural partiality; and five times every day the eyes of the nations at Astracan, at Fez, at Delhi, are devoutly turned to the holy temple of Mecca.[1] Yet every spot for the service of God is equally pure: the Mohammedans indifferently pray in their chamber or in the street. As a distinction from the Jews and Christians, the Friday in each week is set apart for the useful institution of public worship: the people is assembled in the mosch; and the imam, some respectable elder, ascends the pulpit, to begin the prayer and pronounce the sermon. But the Mohammedan religion is destitute of priesthood or sacrifice; and the independent spirit of fanaticism looks down with contempt on the ministers and the slaves of superstition. II. The voluntary[2] penance of the ascetics, the torment and glory of their lives, was odious to a prophet who censured in his companions a rash vow of abstaining from flesh, and women, and sleep; and firmly declared that he would suffer no monks in his religion.[3] Yet he instituted, in each year, a fast of thirty days; and strenuously recommended the observance as a discipline which purifies the soul and subdues the body, as a salutary exercise of obedience to the will of God and his apostle. During

---

[1] [Mohammed at first granted the Jews many privileges in observing their ancient customs and their Sabbath, and he himself kept the fast of ten days with which the Jewish year begins. But when he found himself deceived in his expectations of converting them their privileges were withdrawn. Mecca was substituted for Jerusalem as the Kebla, or quarter to which the face is directed during prayer, and in place of the Jewish fast that of Ramadhan was instituted.—O. S.]

[2] Mohammed (Sale's Koran, c. 9, p. 153) reproaches the Christians with taking their priests and monks for their lords, besides God. Yet Maracci (Prodromus, part iii. p. 69, 70) excuses the worship, especially of the pope, and quotes, from the Koran itself, the case of Eblis, or Satan, who was cast from heaven for refusing to adore Adam.

[3] Koran, c. 5, p. 94, and Sale's note, which refers to the authority of Jallaloddin and Al Beidawi. D'Herbelot declares that Mohammed condemned *la vie religieuse*, and that the first swarms of fakirs, dervises, etc., did not appear till after the year 300 of the Hegira (Biblioth. Orient. p. 292, 718).

the month of Ramadan, from the rising to the setting of the sun, the Musulman abstains from eating, and drinking, and women, and baths, and perfumes; from all nourishment that can restore his strength, from all pleasure that can gratify his senses. In the revolution of the lunar year, the Ramadan coincides, by turns, with the winter cold and the summer heat; and the patient martyr, without assuaging his thirst with a drop of water, must expect the close of a tedious and sultry day. The interdiction of wine, peculiar to some orders of priests or hermits, is converted by Mohammed alone into a positive and general law; [1] and a considerable portion of the globe has abjured, at his command, the use of that salutary, though dangerous, liquor. These painful restraints are, doubtless, infringed by the libertine, and eluded by the hypocrite; but the legislator, by whom they are enacted, cannot surely be accused of alluring his proselytes by the indulgence of their sensual appetites. III. The charity of the Mohammedans descends to the animal creation; and the Koran repeatedly inculcates, not as a merit, but as a strict and indispensable duty, the relief of the indigent and unfortunate. Mohammed, perhaps, is the only lawgiver who has defined the precise measure of charity: the standard may vary with the degree and nature of property, as it consists either in money, in corn or cattle, in fruits or merchandise: but the Musulman does not accomplish the law, unless he bestows a *tenth* of his revenue; and if his conscience accuses him of fraud or extortion, the tenth, under the idea of restitution, is enlarged to a *fifth*. [2] Benevolence is the foundation of justice, since we are forbid to injure those whom we are bound to assist. A prophet may reveal the secrets of heaven and of futurity; but in his moral precepts he can only repeat the lessons of our own hearts.

The two articles of belief, and the four practical duties, of Islam, [3] are guarded by rewards and punishments; and the faith

---

[1] See the double prohibition (Koran, c. 2, p. 25, c. 5, p. 94); the one in the style of a legislator, the other in that of a fanatic. The public and private motives of Mohammed are investigated by Prideaux (Life of Mahomet, p. 62, 64) and Sale (Preliminary Discourse, p. 124).

[2] The jealousy of Maracci (Prodromus, part iv. p. 33) prompts him to enumerate the more liberal alms of the Catholics of Rome. Fifteen great hospitals are open to many thousand patients and pilgrims; fifteen hundred maidens are annually portioned; fifty-six charity-schools are founded for both sexes; one hundred and twenty confraternities relieve the wants of their brethren, etc. The benevolence of London is still more extensive; but I am afraid that much more is to be ascribed to the humanity than to the religion of the people.

[3] [The four practical duties of Islam are prayer, fasting, alms, and pilgrimage.—O. S.]

of the Musulman is devoutly fixed on the event of the judgment and the last day. The prophet has not presumed to determine the moment of that awful catastrophe, though he darkly announces the signs, both in heaven and earth, which will precede the universal dissolution, when life shall be destroyed, and the order of creation shall be confounded in the primitive chaos. At the blast of the trumpet new worlds will start into being; angels, genii, and men will arise from the dead, and the human soul will again be united to the body. The doctrine of the resurrection was first entertained by the Egyptians;[1] and their mummies were embalmed, their pyramids were constructed, to preserve the ancient mansion of the soul during a period of three thousand years. But the attempt is partial and unavailing; and it is with a more philosophic spirit that Mohammed relies on the omnipotence of the Creator, whose word can re-animate the breathless clay, and collect the innumerable atoms that no longer retain their form or substance.[2] The intermediate state of the soul it is hard to decide; and those who most firmly believe her immaterial nature, are at a loss to understand how she can think or act without the agency of the organs of sense.

The re-union of the soul and body will be followed by the final judgment of mankind; and in his copy of the Magian picture, the prophet has too faithfully represented the forms of proceeding, and even the slow and successive operations, of an earthly tribunal. By his intolerant adversaries he is upbraided for extending, even to themselves, the hope of salvation; for asserting the blackest heresy, that every man who believes in God, and accomplishes good works, may expect in the last day a favourable sentence. Such rational indifference is ill adapted to the character of a fanatic; nor is it probable that a messenger from heaven should depreciate the value and necessity of his own revelation. In the idiom of the Koran,[3] the belief of God is inseparable from that of Mohammed: the good works are those which he has enjoined; and the two qualifications imply the

[1] See Herodotus (l. ii. c. 123) and our learned countryman Sir John Marsham (Canon. Chronicus, p. 46). The Ἅδης of the same writer (p. 254-274) is an elaborate sketch of the infernal regions, as they were painted by the fancy of the Egyptians and Greeks, of the poets and philosophers of antiquity.

[2] The Koran (c. 2, p. 259, etc.; of Sale, p. 32; of Maracci, p. 97) relates an ingenious miracle, which satisfied the curiosity and confirmed the faith of Abraham.

[3] The candid Reland has demonstrated that Mohammed damns all unbelievers (de Religione Moham. p. 128-142); that devils will not be finally saved (p. 196-199); that paradise will not *solely* consist of corporeal delights (p. 199-205); and that women's souls are immortal (p. 205-209).

profession of Islam, to which all nations and all sects are equally invited. Their spiritual blindness, though excused by ignorance and crowned with virtue, will be scourged with everlasting torments; and the tears which Mohammed shed over the tomb of his mother, for whom he was forbidden to pray, display a striking contrast of humanity and enthusiasm.[1] The doom of the infidels is common: the measure of their guilt and punishment is determined by the degree of evidence which they have rejected, by the magnitude of the errors which they have entertained: the eternal mansions of the Christians, the Jews, the Sabians, the Magians, and the idolaters are sunk below each other in the abyss; and the lowest hell is reserved for the faithless hypocrites who have assumed the mask of religion. After the greater part of mankind has been condemned for their opinions, the true believers only will be judged by their actions. The good and evil of each Musulman will be accurately weighed in a real or allegorical balance; and a singular mode of compensation will be allowed for the payment of injuries: the aggressor will refund an equivalent of his own good actions, for the benefit of the person whom he has wronged; and if he should be destitute of any moral property, the weight of his sins will be loaded with an adequate share of the demerits of the sufferer. According as the shares of guilt or virtue shall preponderate, the sentence will be pronounced, and all, without distinction, will pass over the sharp and perilous bridge of the abyss; but the innocent, treading in the footsteps of Mohammed, will gloriously enter the gates of paradise, while the guilty will fall into the first and mildest of the seven hells. The term of expiation will vary from nine hundred to seven thousand years; but the prophet has judiciously promised that *all* his disciples, whatever may be their sins, shall be saved, by their own faith and his intercession, from eternal damnation. It is not surprising that superstition should act most powerfully on the fears of her votaries, since the human fancy can paint with more energy the misery than the bliss of a future life. With the two simple elements of darkness and fire we create a sensation of pain, which may be aggravated to an infinite degree by the idea of endless duration. But the same idea operates with an opposite effect on the continuity of pleasure; and too much of our present enjoyments is obtained

---

[1] Al Beidawi, apud Sale, Koran, c. 9, p. 164. The refusal to pray for an unbelieving kindred is justified, according to Mohammed, by the duty of a prophet, and the example of Abraham, who reprobated his own father as an enemy of God. Yet Abraham (he adds, c. 9, v. 116; Maracci, tom. ii. p. 317) fuit sane pius, mitis.

from the relief, or the comparison, of evil. It is natural enough that an Arabian prophet should dwell with rapture on the groves, the fountains, and the rivers of paradise; but instead of inspiring the blessed inhabitants with a liberal taste for harmony and science, conversation and friendship, he idly celebrates the pearls and diamonds, the robes of silk, palaces of marble, dishes of gold, rich wines, artificial dainties, numerous attendants, and the whole train of sensual and costly luxury, which becomes insipid to the owner, even in the short period of this mortal life. Seventy-two *Houris*, or black-eyed girls, of resplendent beauty, blooming youth, virgin purity, and exquisite sensibility, will be created for the use of the meanest believer; a moment of pleasure will be prolonged to a thousand years, and his faculties will be increased a hundred fold, to render him worthy of his felicity. Notwithstanding a vulgar prejudice, the gates of heaven will be open to both sexes; but Mohammed has not specified the male companions of the female elect, lest he should either alarm the jealousy of their former husbands, or disturb their felicity by the suspicion of an everlasting marriage. This image of a carnal paradise has provoked the indignation, perhaps the envy, of the monks: they declaim against the impure religion of Mohammed; and his modest apologists are driven to the poor excuse of figures and allegories. But the sounder and more consistent party adhere, without shame, to the literal interpretation of the Koran: useless would be the resurrection of the body, unless it were restored to the possession and exercise of its worthiest faculties; and the union of sensual and intellectual enjoyment is requisite to complete the happiness of the double animal, the perfect man. Yet the joys of the Mohammedan paradise will not be confined to the indulgence of luxury and appetite; and the prophet has expressly declared that all meaner happiness will be forgotten and despised by the saints and martyrs, who shall be admitted to the beatitude of the divine vision.[1]

The first and most arduous conquests of Mohammed [2] were

[1] For the day of judgment, hell, paradise, etc., consult the Koran (c. 2, v. 25, c. 56, 78, etc.), with Maracci's virulent but learned refutation (in his notes, and in the Prodromus, part iv. p. 78, 120, 122, etc.); D'Herbelot (Bibliothèque Orientale, p. 368, 375); Reland, (p. 47-61); and Sale (p. 76-103). The original ideas of the Magi are darkly and doubtfully explored by their apologist Dr. Hyde (Hist. Religionis Persarum, c. 33, p. 402-412, Oxon. 1760). In the article of Mohammed, Bayle has shown how indifferently wit and philosophy supply the absence of genuine information.

[2] Before I enter on the history of the prophet, it is incumbent on me to produce my evidence. The Latin, French, and English versions of the Koran are preceded by historical discourses, and the three translators, Maracci (tom. i. p. 10-32), Savary (tom. i. p. 1-248), and Sale (Preliminary

those of his wife, his servant, his pupil, and his friend; [1] since he presented himself as a prophet to those who were most conversant with his infirmities as a man. Yet Cadijah believed the words, and cherished the glory, of her husband; the obsequious and affectionate Zeid was tempted by the prospect of freedom; the illustrious Ali, the son of Abu Taleb,[2] embraced the sentiments of his cousin with the spirit of a youthful hero; and the wealth, the moderation, the veracity of Abubeker, confirmed the religion of the prophet whom he was destined to succeed. By his persuasion ten of the most respectable citizens of Mecca were introduced to the private lessons of Islam; they yielded to the voice of reason and enthusiasm; they repeated the fundamental creed, " There is but one God, and Mohammed is the apostle of God; " and their faith, even in this life, was rewarded with riches and honours, with the command of armies and the government of kingdoms. Three years were silently employed in the conversion of fourteen proselytes, the first-fruits of his mission; but in the fourth year he assumed the prophetic office,

Discourse, p. 33-56), had accurately studied the language and character of their author. Two professed Lives of Mahomet have been composed by Dr. Prideaux (Life of Mahomet, seventh edition, London, 1718, in octavo) and the Count de Boulainvilliers (Vie de Mahomed, Londres, 1730, in octavo); but the adverse wish of finding an impostor or a hero has too often corrupted the learning of the Doctor and the ingenuity of the Count. The article in D'Herbelot (Biblioth. Orient. p. 598-603) is chiefly drawn from Novairi and Mirkond; but the best and most authentic of our guides is M. Gagnier, a Frenchman by birth, and professor at Oxford of the Oriental tongues. In two elaborate works (Ismael Abulfeda de Vita et Rebus gestis Mohammedis, etc., Latine vertit, Præfatione et Notis illustravit Johannes Gagnier, Oxon. 1723, in folio; La Vie de Mahomet traduite et compilée de l'Alcoran, des Traditions Authentiques de la Sonna et des meilleurs Auteurs Arabes, Amsterdam, 1748, 3 vols. in 12mo) he has interpreted, illustrated, and supplied the Arabic text of Abulfeda and Al Jannabi; the first an enlightened prince, who reigned at Hamah, in Syria, A.D. 1310-1332 (see Gagnier, Præfat. ad Abulfed.); the second a credulous doctor, who visited Mecca A.D. 1556. (D'Herbelot, p. 397; Gagnier, tom. iii. p. 209, 210.) These are my general vouchers, and the inquisitive reader may follow the order of time and the division of chapters. Yet I must observe that both Abulfeda and Al Jannabi are modern historians, and that they cannot appeal to any writers of the first century of the Hegira.

[1] After the Greeks, Prideaux (p. 8) discloses the secret doubts of the wife of Mohammed. As if he had been a privy counsellor of the prophet, Boulainvilliers (p. 272, etc.) unfolds the sublime and patriotic views of Cadijah and the first disciples.

[2] [Abubeker, or more probably Abu Bakr, literally " the father of the virgin "—so called because his daughter Ayesha was the only maiden whom Mohammed married—was a wealthy merchant of the Taym family, much respected for his benevolence and straightforward dealing. He was one of the first to accept the mission of the prophet, and is said to have believed in the unity of God before Mohammed himself. He did more for the success of Islam even than the prophet himself.—O. S.]

and, resolving to impart to his family the light of divine truth, he prepared a banquet, a lamb, as it is said, and a bowl of milk, for the entertainment of forty guests of the race of Hashem. "Friends and kinsmen," said Mohammed to the assembly, "I offer you, and I alone can offer, the most precious of gifts, the treasures of this world and of the world to come. God has commanded me to call you to his service. Who among you will support my burden? Who among you will be my companion and my vizir?"[1] No answer was returned, till the silence of astonishment, and doubt, and contempt was at length broken by the impatient courage of Ali, a youth in the fourteenth year of his age. "O prophet, I am the man: whosoever rises against thee, I will dash out his teeth, tear out his eyes, break his legs, rip up his belly. O prophet, I will be thy vizir over them." Mohammed accepted his offer with transport, and Abu Taleb was ironically exhorted to respect the superior dignity of his son. In a more serious tone, the father of Ali advised his nephew to relinquish his impracticable design. "Spare your remonstrances," replied the intrepid fanatic to his uncle and benefactor; "if they should place the sun on my right hand, and the moon on my left, they should not divert me from my course." He persevered ten years in the exercise of his mission; and the religion which has overspread the East and the West advanced with a slow and painful progress within the walls of Mecca. Yet Mohammed enjoyed the satisfaction of beholding the increase of his infant congregation of Unitarians, who revered him as a prophet, and to whom he seasonably dispensed the spiritual nourishment of the Koran. The number of proselytes may be esteemed by the absence of eighty-three men and eighteen women, who retired to Æthiopia in the seventh year of his mission; and his party was fortified by the timely conversion of his uncle Hamza, and of the fierce and inflexible Omar, who signalised in the cause of Islam the same zeal which he had exerted for its destruction. Nor was the charity of Mohammed confined to the tribe of Koreish, or the precincts of Mecca: on solemn festivals, in the days of pilgrimage, he frequented the Caaba, accosted the strangers of every tribe, and urged, both in private converse and public discourse, the belief and worship of a sole Deity. Conscious of his reason and of his weakness, he asserted the liberty of conscience, and disclaimed the use of

[1] *Vezirus, portitor, bajulus, onus ferens:* and this plebeian name was transferred by an apt metaphor to the pillars of the state (Gagnier, Not. ad Abulfed. p. 19). I endeavour to preserve the Arabian idiom, as far as I can feel it myself in a Latin or French translation.

religious violence:[1] but he called the Arabs to repentance, and conjured them to remember the ancient idolaters of Ad and Thamud, whom the divine justice had swept away from the face of the earth.[2]

The people of Mecca were hardened in their unbelief by superstition and envy. The elders of the city, the uncles of the prophet, affected to despise the presumption of an orphan, the reformer of his country: the pious orations of Mohammed in the Caaba were answered by the clamours of Abu Taleb. "Citizens and pilgrims, listen not to the tempter, hearken not to his impious novelties. Stand fast in the worship of Al Lâta and Al Uzzah." Yet the son of Abdallah was ever dear to the aged chief: and he protected the fame and person of his nephew against the assaults of the Koreishites, who had long been jealous of the pre-eminence of the family of Hashem. Their malice was coloured with the pretence of religion: in the age of Job the crime of impiety was punished by the Arabian magistrate;[3] and Mohammed was guilty of deserting and denying the national deities. But so loose was the policy of Mecca, that the leaders of the Koreish, instead of accusing a criminal, were compelled to employ the measures of persuasion or violence. They repeatedly addressed Abu Taleb in the style of reproach and menace. "Thy nephew reviles our religion; he accuses our wise forefathers of ignorance and folly; silence him quickly, lest he kindle tumult and discord in the city. If he persevere, we shall draw our swords against him and his adherents, and thou wilt be responsible for the blood of thy fellow-citizens." The weight and moderation of Abu Taleb eluded the violence of religious faction; the most helpless or timid of the disciples retired to Æthiopia, and the prophet withdrew himself to various

[1] The passages of the Koran in behalf of toleration are strong and numerous: c. 2, v. 257, c. 16, 129, c. 17, 54, c. 45, 15, c. 50, 39, c. 88, 21, etc., with the notes of Maracci and Sale. This character alone may generally decide the doubts of the learned, whether a chapter was revealed at Mecca or Medina.

[2] See the Koran (passim, and especially c. 7, p. 123, 124, etc.), and the tradition of the Arabs (Pocock, Specimen, p. 35-37). The caverns of the tribe of Thamud, fit for men of the ordinary stature, were shown in the midway between Medina and Damascus (Abulfed. Arabiæ Descript. p. 43, 44), and may be probably ascribed to the Troglodytes of the primitive world (Michaelis, ad Lowth de Poesi Hebræor. p. 131-134; Recherches sur les Egyptiens, tom. ii. p. 48, etc.).

[3] In the time of Job the crime of impiety was punished by the Arabian magistrate (c. 31, v. 26, 27, 28). I blush for a respectable prelate (de Poesi Hebræorum, p. 650, 651, edit. Michaelis; and letter of a late professor in the university of Oxford, p. 15-53), who justifies and applauds this patriarchal inquisition.

places of strength in the town and country. As he was still
supported by his family, the rest of the tribe of Koreish engaged
themselves to renounce all intercourse with the children of
Hashem—neither to buy nor sell, neither to marry nor to give
in marriage, but to pursue them with implacable enmity, till
they should deliver the person of Mohammed to the justice of the
gods. The decree was suspended in the Caaba before the eyes
of the nation: the messengers of the Koreish pursued the Musulman exiles in the heart of Africa; they besieged the prophet
and his most faithful followers, intercepted their water, and
inflamed their mutual animosity by the retaliation of injuries
and insults. A doubtful truce restored the appearances of concord, till the death of Abu Taleb abandoned Mohammed to the
power of his enemies, at the moment when he was deprived of
his domestic comforts by the loss of his faithful and generous
Cadijah. Abu Sophian, the chief of the branch of Ommiyah,
succeeded to the principality of the republic of Mecca. A
zealous votary of the idols, a mortal foe of the line of Hashem, he
convened an assembly of the Koreishites and their allies to decide
the fate of the apostle. His imprisonment might provoke the
despair of his enthusiasm; and the exile of an eloquent and
popular fanatic would diffuse the mischief through the provinces
of Arabia. His death was resolved; and they agreed that a
sword from each tribe should be buried in his heart, to divide
the guilt of his blood, and baffle the vengeance of the Hashemites.
An angel or a spy revealed their conspiracy, and flight was the
only resource of Mohammed.[1] At the dead of night, accompanied by his friend Abubeker, he silently escaped from his
house: the assassins watched at the door; but they were
deceived by the figure of Ali, who reposed on the bed, and was
covered with the green vestment, of the apostle. The Koreish
respected the piety of the heroic youth; but some verses of
Ali, which are still extant, exhibit an interesting picture of his
anxiety, his tenderness, and his religious confidence. Three days
Mohammed and his companion were concealed in the cave of
Thor, at the distance of a league from Mecca; and in the close
of each evening they received from the son and daughter of
Abubeker a secret supply of intelligence and food. The diligence
of the Koreish explored every haunt in the neighbourhood of the
city: they arrived at the entrance of the cavern; but the providential deceit of a spider's web and a pigeon's nest is supposed

---

[1] D'Herbelot, Biblioth. Orient. p. 445. He quotes a particular history of
the flight of Mohammed.

to convince them that the place was solitary and inviolate.
" We are only two," said the trembling Abubeker. " There is
a third," replied the prophet; " it is God himself." No sooner
was the pursuit abated than the two fugitives issued from the
rock and mounted their camels: on the road to Medina they were
overtaken by the emissaries of the Koreish; they redeemed
themselves with prayers and promises from their hands. In
this eventful moment the lance of an Arab might have changed
the history of the world. The flight of the prophet from Mecca
to Medina has fixed the memorable era of the *Hegira*,[1] which, at
the end of twelve centuries, still discriminates the lunar years
of the Mohammedan nations.[2]

The religion of the Koran might have perished in its cradle
had not Medina embraced with faith and reverence the holy
outcasts of Mecca. Medina, or the *city*, known under the name
of Yathreb before it was sanctified by the throne of the prophet,
was divided between the tribes of the Charegites and the Awsites,
whose hereditary feud was rekindled by the slightest provocations: two colonies of Jews, who boasted a sacerdotal race, were
their humble allies, and, without converting the Arabs, they
introduced the taste of science and religion, which distinguished
Medina as the city of the Book. Some of her noblest citizens, in
a pilgrimage to the Caaba, were converted by the preaching of
Mohammed; on their return they diffused the belief of God and
his prophet, and the new alliance was ratified by their deputies
in two secret and nocturnal interviews on a hill in the suburbs
of Mecca. In the first, ten Charegites and two Awsites, united
in faith and love, protested, in the name of their wives, their
children and their absent brethren, that they would for ever
profess the creed and observe the precepts of the Koran. The
second was a political association, the first vital spark of the
empire of the Saracens.[3] Seventy-three men and two women
of Medina held a solemn conference with Mohammed, his
kinsmen, and his disciples, and pledged themselves to each other

---

[1] The *Hegira* was instituted by Omar, the second caliph, in imitation of
the era of the martyrs of the Christians (D'Herbelot, p. 444); and properly
commenced sixty-eight days before the flight of Mohámmed, with the first
of Moharren, or first day of that Arabian year, which coincides with Friday,
July 16th, A.D. 622 (Abulfeda, Vit. Moham. c. 22, 23, p. 45-50; and
Greaves's edition of Ullug Beg's Epochæ Arabum, etc., c. 1, p. 8, 10, etc.).

[2] Mohammed's life, from his mission to the Hegira, may be found in
Abulfeda (p. 14-45) and Gagnier (tom. i. p. 134-251, 342-383). The legend
from p. 187-234 is vouched by Al Jannabi, and disdained by Abulfeda.

[3] The triple inauguration of Mohammed is described by Abulfeda (p. 30,
33, 40, 86), and Gagnier (tom. i. p. 342, etc., 349, etc., tom. ii. p. 223, etc.).

by a mutual oath of fidelity. They promised, in the name of the city, that if he should be banished they would receive him as a confederate, obey him as a leader, and defend him to the last extremity, like their wives and children. "But if you are recalled by your country," they asked with a flattering anxiety, " will you not abandon your new allies?" " All things," replied Mohammed, with a smile, " are now common between us; your blood is as my blood, your ruin as my ruin. We are bound to each other by the ties of honour and interest. I am your friend, and the enemy of your foes." " But if we are killed in your service, what," exclaimed the deputies of Medina, " will be our reward?" " PARADISE," replied the prophet. " Stretch forth thy hand." He stretched it forth, and they reiterated the oath of allegiance and fidelity. Their treaty was ratified by the people, who unanimously embraced the profession of Islam; they rejoiced in the exile of the apostle, but they trembled for his safety, and impatiently expected his arrival. After a perilous and rapid journey along the sea-coast, he halted at Koba, two miles from the city, and made his public entry into Medina, sixteen days after his flight from Mecca. Five hundred of the citizens advanced to meet him; he was hailed with acclamations of loyalty and devotion; Mohammed was mounted on a she-camel, an umbrella shaded his head, and a turban was unfurled before him to supply the deficiency of a standard. His bravest disciples, who had been scattered by the storm, assembled round his person; and the equal, though various, merit of the Moslems was distinguished by the names of *Mohagerians* and *Ansars*, the fugitives of Mecca, and the auxiliaries of Medina. To eradicate the seeds of jealousy, Mohammed judiciously coupled his principal followers with the rights and obligations of brethren; and when Ali found himself without a peer, the prophet tenderly declared that *he* would be the companion and brother of the noble youth. The expedient was crowned with success; the holy fraternity was respected in peace and war, and the two parties vied with each other in a generous emulation of courage and fidelity. Once only the concord was slightly ruffled by an accidental quarrel: a patriot of Medina arraigned the insolence of the strangers, but the hint of their expulsion was heard with abhorrence; and his own son most eagerly offered to lay at the apostle's feet the head of his father.

From his establishment at Medina, Mohammed assumed the exercise of the regal and sacerdotal office; and it was impious to appeal from a judge whose decrees were inspired by the divine wisdom. A small portion of ground, the patrimony of two orphans, was acquired by gift or purchase; [1] on that chosen spot he built a house and a mosch, more venerable in their rude simplicity than the palaces and temples of the Assyrian caliphs. His seal of gold, or silver, was inscribed with the apostolic title; when he prayed and preached in the weekly assembly, he leaned against the trunk of a palm tree; and it was long before he indulged himself in the use of a chair or pulpit of rough timber. [2] After a reign of six years fifteen hundred Moslems, in arms and in the field, renewed their óath of allegiance; and their chief repeated the assurance of protection till the death of the last member, or the final dissolution of the party. It was in the same camp that the deputy of Mecca was astonished by the attention of the faithful to the words and looks of the prophet, by the eagerness with which they collected his spittle, a hair that dropped on the ground, the refuse water of his lustrations, as if they participated in some degree of the prophetic virtue. " I have seen," said he, " the Chosroes of Persia and the Cæsar of Rome, but never did I behold a king among his subjects like Mohammed among his companions." The devout fervour of enthusiasm acts with more energy and truth than the cold and formal servility of courts.

In the state of nature every man has a right to defend, by force of arms, his person and his possessions; to repel, or even to prevent, the violence of his enemies, and to extend his hostilities to a reasonable measure of satisfaction and retaliation. In the free society of the Arabs, the duties of subject and citizen imposed a feeble restraint; and Mohammed, in the exercise of a peaceful and benevolent mission, had been despoiled and banished by the injustice of his countrymen. The choice of an independent people had exalted the fugitive of Mecca to the rank of a sovereign; and he was invested with the just prerogative

---

[1] Prideaux (Life of Mahomet, p. 44) reviles the wickedness of the impostor, who despoiled two poor orphans, the sons of a carpenter; a reproach which he drew from the Disputatio contra Saracenos, composed in Arabic before the year 1130; but the honest Gagnier (ad Abulfed. p. 53) has shown that they were deceived by the word *Al Nagjar*, which signifies, in this place, not an obscure trade, but a noble tribe of Arabs. The desolate state of the ground is described by Abulfeda; and his worthy interpreter has proved, from Al Bochari, the offer of a price; from Al Jannabi, the fair purchase; and from Ahmed Ben Joseph, the payment of the money by the generous Abubeker. On these grounds the prophet must be honourably acquitted.

[2] Al Jannabi (apud Gagnier, tom. ii. p. 246, 324) describes the seal and pulpit as two venerable relics of the apostle of God; and the portrait of his court is taken from Abulfeda (c. 44, p. 85).

of forming alliances, and of waging offensive or defensive war.
The imperfection of human rights was supplied and armed by
the plenitude of divine power: the prophet of Medina assumed,
in his new revelations, a fiercer and more sanguinary tone, which
proves that his former moderation was the effect of weakness: [1]
the means of persuasion had been tried, the season of forbear-
ance was elapsed, and he was now commanded to propagate his
religion by the sword, to destroy the monuments of idolatry,
and, without regarding the sanctity of days or months, to pursue
the unbelieving nations of the earth. The same bloody precepts,
so repeatedly inculcated in the Koran, are ascribed by the author
to the Pentateuch and the Gospel. But the mild tenor of the
evangelic style may explain an ambiguous text, that Jesus did
not bring peace on the earth, but a sword: his patient and
humble virtues should not be confounded with the intolerant
zeal of princes and bishops, who have disgraced the name of his
disciples. In the prosecution of religious war, Mohammed might
appeal with more propriety to the example of Moses, of the
Judges, and the kings of Israel. The military laws of the
Hebrews are still more rigid than those of the Arabian legislator.[2]
The Lord of hosts marched in person before the Jews: if a city
resisted their summons, the males, without distinction, were put
to the sword: the seven nations of Canaan were devoted to
destruction; and neither repentance nor conversion could shield
them from the inevitable doom, that no creature within their
precincts should be left alive. The fair option of friendship, or
submission, or battle, was proposed to the enemies of Mohammed.
If they professed the creed of Islam, they were admitted to all
the temporal and spiritual benefits of his primitive disciples, and
marched under the same banner to extend the religion which
they had embraced. The clemency of the prophet was decided
by his interest: yet he seldom trampled on a prostrate enemy;
and he seems to promise that on the payment of a tribute the
least guilty of his unbelieving subjects might be indulged in
their worship, or at least in their imperfect faith. In the first
months of his reign he practised the lessons of holy warfare, and
displayed his white banner before the gates of Medina: the

[1] The eighth and ninth chapters of the Koran are the loudest and most
vehement; and Maracci (Prodromus, part iv. p. 59-64) has inveighed with
more justice than discretion against the double dealing of the impostor.
[2] The tenth and twentieth chapters of Deuteronomy, with the practical
comments of Joshua, David, etc., are read with more awe than satisfaction
by the pious Christians of the present age. But the bishops, as well as the
rabbis of former times, have beat the drum-ecclesiastic with pleasure and
success. (Sale's Preliminary Discourse, p. 142, 143).

martial apostle fought in person at nine battles or sieges; [1] and fifty enterprises of war were achieved in ten years by himself or his lieutenants. The Arab continued to unite the professions of a merchant and a robber; and his petty excursions for the defence or the attack of a caravan insensibly prepared his troops for the conquest of Arabia. The distribution of the spoil was regulated by a divine law: [2] the whole was faithfully collected in one common mass: a fifth of the gold and silver, the prisoners and cattle, the movables and immovables, was reserved by the prophet for pious and charitable uses; the remainder was shared in adequate portions by the soldiers who had obtained the victory or guarded the camp: the rewards of the slain devolved to their widows and orphans; and the increase of cavalry was encouraged by the allotment of a double share to the horse and to the man. From all sides the roving Arabs were allured to the standard of religion and plunder: the apostle sanctified the licence of embracing the female captives as their wives or concubines; and the enjoyment of wealth and beauty was a feeble type of the joys of paradise prepared for the valiant martyrs of the faith. "The sword," says Mohammed, "is the key of heaven and of hell: a drop of blood shed in the cause of God, a night spent in arms, is of more avail than two months of fasting or prayer: whosoever falls in battle, his sins are forgiven: at the day of judgment his wounds shall be resplendent as vermilion, and odoriferous as musk; and the loss of his limbs shall be supplied by the wings of angels and cherubim." The intrepid souls of the Arabs were fired with enthusiasm: the picture of the invisible world was strongly painted on their imagination; and the death which they had always despised became an object of hope and desire. The Koran inculcates, in the most absolute sense, the tenets of fate and predestination, which would extinguish both industry and virtue, if the actions of man were governed by his speculative belief. Yet their influence in every age has exalted the courage of the Saracens and Turks. The first companions of Mohammed advanced to battle with a fearless confidence: there is no danger

---

[1] Abulfeda, in Vit. Moham. p. 156. The private arsenal of the apostle consisted of nine swords, three lances, seven pikes or half-pikes, a quiver and three bows, seven cuirasses, three shields, and two helmets (Gagnier, tom. iii. p. 328-334), with a large white standard, a black banner (p. 335), twenty horses (p. 322), etc. Two of his martial sayings are recorded by tradition (Gagnier, tom. ii. p. 88, 337).

[2] The whole subject de jure belli Mohammedanorum is exhausted in a separate dissertation by the learned Reland (Dissertationes Miscellaneæ, tom. iii. Dissertat. x. p. 3-53).

where there is no chance: they were ordained to perish in their beds; or they were safe and invulnerable amidst the darts of the enemy.[1]

Perhaps the Koreish would have been content with the flight of Mohammed, had they not been provoked and alarmed by the vengeance of an enemy who could intercept their Syrian trade as it passed and repassed through the territory of Medina. Abu Sophian himself, with only thirty or forty followers, conducted a wealthy caravan of a thousand camels; the fortune or dexterity of his march escaped the vigilance of Mohammed; but the chief of the Koreish was informed that the holy robbers were placed in ambush to await his return. He despatched a messenger to his brethren of Mecca, and they were roused, by the fear of losing their merchandise and their provisions, unless they hastened to his relief with the military force of the city. The sacred band of Mohammed was formed of three hundred and thirteen Moslems, of whom seventy-seven were fugitives, and the rest auxiliaries: they mounted by turns a train of seventy camels (the camels of Yathreb were formidable in war); but such was the poverty of his first disciples, that only two could appear on horseback in the field.[2] In the fertile and famous vale of Beder,[3] three stations from Medina, he was informed by his scouts of the caravan that approached on one side; of the Koreish, one hundred horse, eight hundred and fifty foot, who advanced on the other. After a short debate he sacrificed the prospect of wealth to the pursuit of glory and revenge; and a slight intrenchment was formed to cover his troops, and a stream of fresh water that glided through the valley. " O God," he exclaimed as the numbers of the Koreish descended from the hills, " O God, if these are destroyed, by whom wilt thou be worshipped on the earth?—Courage, my

---

[1] The doctrine of absolute predestination, on which few religions can reproach each other, is sternly exposed in the Koran (c. 3, p. 52, 53, c. 4, p. 70, etc., with the notes of Sale, and c. 17, p. 413, with those of Maracci). Reland (de Relig. Moham. p. 61-64) and Sale (Prelim. Discourse, p. 103) represent the opinions of the doctors, and our modern travellers the confidence, the fading confidence, of the Turks.

[2] Al Jannabi (apud Gagnier, tom. ii. p. 9) allows him seventy or eighty horse; and on two other occasions, prior to the battle of Ohud, he enlists a body of thirty (p. 10) and of 500 (p. 66) troopers. Yet the Musulmans, in the field of Ohud, had no more than two horses, according to the better sense of Abulfeda (in Vit. Mohamm. c. 31, p. 65). In the *Stony* province the camels are numerous; but the horse appears to have been less common than in the *Happy* or the *Desert* Arabia.

[3] Bedder Houneene, twenty miles from Medina, and forty from Mecca, is on the high road of the caravan of Egypt; and the pilgrims annually commemorate the prophet's victory by illuminations, rockets, etc. Shaw's Travels, p. 477.

children; close your ranks; discharge your arrows, and the day is your own." At these words he placed himself, with Abubeker, on a throne or pulpit,[1] and instantly demanded the succour of Gabriel and three thousand angels. His eye was fixed on the field of battle: the Musulmans fainted and were pressed: in that decisive moment the prophet started from his throne, mounted his horse, and cast a handful of sand into the air; " Let their faces be covered with confusion." Both armies heard the thunder of his voice: their fancy beheld the angelic warriors:[2] the Koreish trembled and fled: seventy of the bravest were slain; and seventy captives adorned the first victory of the faithful.[3] The dead bodies of the Koreish were despoiled and insulted: two of the most obnoxious prisoners were punished with death; and the ransom of the others, four thousand drachms of silver, compensated in some degree the escape of the caravan. But it was in vain that the camels of Abu Sophian explored a new

[1] The place to which Mohammed retired during the action is styled by Gagnier (in Abulfeda, c. 27. p. 58; Vie de Mahomet, tom. ii. p. 30, 33) *Umbraculum, une loge de bois avec une porte.* The same Arabic word is rendered by Reiske (Annales Moslemici Abulfedæ, p. 23) by *Solium, Suggestus editior ;* and the difference is of the utmost moment for the honour both of the interpreter and of the hero. I am sorry to observe the pride and acrimony with which Reiske chastises his fellow-labourer. Sæpe sic vertit, ut integræ paginæ nequeant nisi unâ liturâ corrigi: Arabice non satis callebat, et carebat judicio critico. J. J. Reiske, Prodidagmata ad Hagji Chalisæ Tabulas, p. 228, ad calcem Abulfedæ Syriæ Tabulæ; Lipsiæ, 1766, in 4to.

[Mohammed was by no means the courageous individual Gibbon makes him out to be. Weil, in his *Life of Mohammed,* says, " His behaviour in his different campaigns, as well as in the first years of his appearance as a prophet, and also towards the close of his life, when he was become very powerful, compels us, despite his endurance and perseverance, to characterise him as very timorous. It was not until after the conversion of Omar and Hamza that he ventured openly to appear in the mosque along with the professors of his faith as a Moslem. He not only took no part in the fight at the battle of Bedr, but kept at some distance from the field, and had some dromedaries ready before his tent in order to flee in case of a reverse."—O. S.]

[2] The loose expressions of the Koran (c. 3, p. 124, 125, c. 8, p. 9) allow the commentators to fluctuate between the numbers of 1000, 3000, or 9000 angels; and the smallest of these might suffice for the slaughter of seventy of the Koreish (Maracci, Alcoran, tom. ii. p. 131). Yet the same scholiasts confess that this angelic band was not visible to any mortal eye (Maracci, p. 297). They refine on the words (c. 8, 16), " not thou, but God," etc. (D'Herbelot, Biblioth. Orientale, p. 600, 601.)

[3] [Among the captives was Abbas, the rich uncle of Mohammed, who was obliged to pay ransom, though he alleged that inwardly he was a believer and had been forced to take part in the expedition against the prophet. He returned to Mecca, where he served Mohammed as a spy. On the occasion of the second battle, at Mount Ohud, six miles north of Medina, Abd Allah, with 200 men, deserted Mohammed at a critical moment, so that the disproportion of the forces was vastly greater than at Bedr.—O. S.]

road through the desert and along the Euphrates: they were overtaken by the diligence of the Musulmans; and wealthy must have been the prize, if twenty thousand drachms could be set apart for the fifth of the apostle. The resentment of the public and private loss stimulated Abu Sophian to collect a body of three thousand men, seven hundred of whom were armed with cuirasses, and two hundred were mounted on horseback; three thousand camels attended his march; and his wife Henda, with fifteen matrons of Mecca, incessantly sounded their timbrels to animate the troops, and to magnify the greatness of Hobal, the most popular deity of the Caaba. The standard of God and Mohammed was upheld by nine hundred and fifty believers: the disproportion of numbers was not more alarming than in the field of Beder, and their presumption of victory prevailed against the divine and human sense of the apostle. The second battle was fought on Mount Ohud, six miles to the north of Medina:[1] the Koreish advanced in the form of a crescent; and the right wing of cavalry was led by Caled, the fiercest and most successful of the Arabian warriors. The troops of Mohammed were skilfully posted on the declivity of the hill; and their rear was guarded by a detachment of fifty archers. The weight of their charge impelled and broke the centre of the idolaters: but in the pursuit they lost the advantage of their ground: the archers deserted their station: the Musulmans were tempted by the spoil, disobeyed their general, and disordered their ranks. The intrepid Caled, wheeling his cavalry on their flank and rear, exclaimed, with a loud voice, that Mohammed was slain. He was indeed wounded in the face with a javelin: two of his teeth were shattered with a stone; yet, in the midst of tumult and dismay, he reproached the infidels with the murder of a prophet; and blessed the friendly hand that stanched his blood, and conveyed him to a place of safety.[2] Seventy martyrs died for the sins of the people; they fell, said the apostle, in pairs, each brother embracing his lifeless companion;[3] their bodies were mangled by the inhuman females of Mecca; and the wife of

---

[1] Geograph. Nubiensis, p. 47.

[2] [At this engagement the person of the prophet was protected by a helmet and a double coat of mail. He was recognised among the wounded by Caab, the son of Malek, by whom, Abubekr, Omar, and ten or twelve others he was carried to a cave upon an eminence. Thither he was pursued by Ubejj Ibn Challaf, who had been long keeping a horse in extraordinary condition for the purpose of surprising and killing Mohammed. But the latter killed him by one blow.—O. S.]

[3] In the third chapter of the Koran (p. 50-53, with Sale's notes) the prophet alleges some poor excuses for the defeat of Ohud.

Abu Sophian tasted the entrails of Hamza, the uncle of Mohammed. They might applaud their superstition and satiate their fury; but the Musulmans soon rallied in the field, and the Koreish wanted strength or courage to undertake the siege of Medina. It was attacked the ensuing year by an army of ten thousand enemies; and this third expedition is variously named, from the *nations* which marched under the banner of Abu Sophian, from the *ditch* which was drawn before the city, and a camp of three thousand Musulmans. The prudence of Mohammed declined a general engagement: the valour of Ali was signalised in single combat; and the war was protracted twenty days, till the final separation of the confederates. A tempest of wind, rain, and hail overturned their tents: their private quarrels were fomented by an insidious adversary; and the Koreish, deserted by their allies, no longer hoped to subvert the throne, or to check the conquests, of their invincible exile.[1]

The choice of Jerusalem for the first kebla of prayer discovers the early propensity of Mohammed in favour of the Jews; and happy would it have been for their temporal interest had they recognised in the Arabian prophet the hope of Israel and the promised Messiah. Their obstinacy converted his friendship into implacable hatred, with which he pursued that unfortunate people to the last moment of his life; and in the double character of an apostle and a conqueror, his persecution was extended to both worlds.[2] The Kainoka dwelt at Medina under the protection of the city: he seized the occasion of an accidental tumult, and summoned them to embrace his religion or contend with him in battle. "Alas," replied the trembling Jews, "we are ignorant of the use of arms, but we persevere in the faith and worship of our fathers; why wilt thou reduce us to the necessity of a just defence?" The unequal conflict was terminated in fifteen days; and it was with extreme reluctance that Mohammed yielded to the importunity of his allies, and consented to spare the lives of the captives. But their riches were confiscated, their arms became more effectual in the hands of the Musulmans; and a wretched colony of seven hundred exiles was driven with their wives and children to implore a refuge on

[1] For the detail of the three Koreish wars, of Beder, of Ohud, and of the ditch, peruse Abulfeda (p. 56-61, 64-69, 73-77), Gagnier (tom. ii. p. 23-45, 70-96, 120-139), with the proper articles of D'Herbelot, and the abridgments of Elmacin (Hist. Saracen. p. 6, 7) and Abulpharagius (Dynast. p. 102).

[2] The wars of Mohammed against the Jewish tribes of Kainoka, the Nadhirites, Koraidha, and Chaibar, are related by Abulfeda (p. 61, 71, 77, 87, etc.) and Gagnier (tom. ii. p. 61-65, 107-112, 139-148, 268-294).

the confines of Syria. The Nadhirites were more guilty, since they conspired in a friendly interview to assassinate the prophet. He besieged their castle, three miles from Medina; but their resolute defence obtained an honourable capitulation; and the garrison, sounding their trumpets and beating their drums, was permitted to depart with the honours of war. The Jews had excited and joined the war of the Koreish: no sooner had the *nations* retired from the *ditch*, than Mohammed, without laying aside his armour, marched on the same day to extirpate the hostile race of the children of Koraidha. After a resistance of twenty-five days they surrendered at discretion. They trusted to the intercession of their old allies of Medina: they could not be ignorant that fanaticism obliterates the feelings of humanity. A venerable elder, to whose judgment they appealed, pronounced the sentence of their death: seven hundred Jews were dragged in chains to the market-place of the city; they descended alive into the grave prepared for their execution and burial; and the apostle beheld with an inflexible eye the slaughter of his helpless enemies. Their sheep and camels were inherited by the Musulmans: three hundred cuirasses, five hundred pikes, a thousand lances, composed the most useful portion of the spoil. Six days' journey to the north-east of Medina, the ancient and wealthy town of Chaibar was the seat of the Jewish power in Arabia: the territory, a fertile spot in the desert, was covered with plantations and cattle, and protected by eight castles, some of which were esteemed of impregnable strength. The forces of Mohammed consisted of two hundred horse and fourteen hundred foot: in the succession of eight regular and painful sieges they were exposed to danger, and fatigue, and hunger; and the most undaunted chiefs despaired of the event. The apostle revived their faith and courage by the example of Ali, on whom he bestowed the surname of the Lion of God: perhaps we may believe that a Hebrew champion of gigantic stature was cloven to the chest by his irresistible scimitar; but we cannot praise the modesty of romance, which represents him as tearing from its hinges the gate of a fortress and wielding the ponderous buckler in his left hand.[1] After the reduction of the castles the town of Chaibar submitted to the yoke. The chief of the tribe was tortured, in the presence of Mohammed, to force a confession of his hidden treasure: the industry of the shepherds and husband-

---

[1] Abu Rafe, the servant of Mohammed, is said to affirm that he himself and seven other men afterwards tried, without success, to move the same gate from the ground (Abulfeda, p. 90). Abu Rafe was an eye-witness, but who will be witness for Abu Rafe?

men was rewarded with a precarious toleration: they were permitted, so long as it should please the conqueror, to improve their patrimony, in equal shares, for *his* emolument and their own. Under the reign of Omar, the Jews of Chaibar were transplanted to Syria; and the caliph alleged the injunction of his dying master, that one and the true religion should be professed in his native land of Arabia.[1]

Five times each day the eyes of Mohammed were turned towards Mecca,[2] and he was urged by the most sacred and powerful motives to revisit, as a conqueror, the city and the temple from whence he had been driven as an exile. The Caaba was present to his waking and sleeping fancy: an idle dream was translated into vision and prophecy; he unfurled the holy banner; and a rash promise of success too hastily dropped from the lips of the apostle. His march from Medina to Mecca displayed the peaceful and solemn pomp of a pilgrimage: seventy camels, chosen and bedecked for sacrifice, preceded the van; the sacred territory was respected; and the captives were dismissed without ransom to proclaim his clemency and devotion. But no sooner did Mohammed descend into the plain, within a day's journey of the city, than he exclaimed, " They have clothed themselves with the skins of tigers: " the numbers and resolution of the Koreish opposed his progress; and the roving Arabs of the desert might desert or betray a leader whom they had followed for the hopes of spoil. The intrepid fanatic sunk into a cool and cautious politician: he waved in the treaty his title of apostle of God; concluded with the Koreish and their allies a truce of ten years; engaged to restore the fugitives of Mecca who should embrace his religion; and stipulated only, for the ensuing year, the humble privilege of entering the city as a friend, and of remaining three days to accomplish the rites of the pilgrimage. A cloud of shame and sorrow hung on the retreat of the Musulmans, and their disappointment might justly accuse the failure of a prophet who had so often appealed to the evidence of success. The faith and hope of the pilgrims were

---

[1] The banishment of the Jews is attested by Elmacin (Hist. Saracen. p. 9) and the great Al Zabari (Gagnier, tom. ii. p. 285). Yet Niebuhr (Description de l'Arabie, p. 324) believes that the Jewish religion and Karaite sect are still professed by the tribe of Chaibar; and that, in the plunder of the caravans, the disciples of Moses are the confederates of those of Mohammed.

[2] The successive steps of the reduction of Mecca are related by Abulfeda (p. 84-87, 97-100, 102-111) and Gagnier (tom. ii. p. 209-245, 309-322; tom. iii. p. 1-58), Elmacin (Hist. Saracen. p. 8, 9, 10), Abulpharagius (Dynast. p. 103).

rekindled by the prospect of Mecca: their swords were sheathed: seven times in the footsteps of the apostle they encompassed the Caaba: the Koreish had retired to the hills, and Mohammed, after the customary sacrifice, evacuated the city on the fourth day. The people was edified by his devotion; the hostile chiefs were awed, or divided, or seduced; and both Caled and Amrou, the future conquerors of Syria and Egypt, most seasonably deserted the sinking cause of idolatry. The power of Mohammed was increased by the submission of the Arabian tribes; ten thousand soldiers were assembled for the conquest of Mecca; and the idolators, the weaker party, were easily convicted of violating the truce. Enthusiasm and discipline impelled the march, and preserved the secret, till the blaze of ten thousand fires proclaimed to the astonished Koreish the design, the approach, and the irresistible force of the enemy. The haughty Abu Sophian presented the keys of the city; admired the variety of arms and ensigns that passed before him in review; observed that the son of Abdallah had acquired a mighty kingdom; and confessed, under the scimitar of Omar, that he was the apostle of the true God. The return of Marius and Sylla was stained with the blood of the Romans: the revenge of Mohammed was stimulated by religious zeal, and his injured followers were eager to execute or to prevent the order of a massacre. Instead of indulging their passions and his own,[1] the victorious exile forgave the guilt, and united the factions, of Mecca. His troops, in three divisions, marched into the city: eight-and-twenty of the inhabitants were slain by the sword of Caled; eleven men and six women were proscribed by the sentence of Mohammed;[2]

[1] After the conquest of Mecca, the Mohammed of Voltaire imagines and perpetrates the most horrid crimes. The poet confesses that he is not supported by the truth of history, and can only allege, que celui qui fait la guerre à sa patrie au nom de Dieu est capable de tout (Œuvres de Voltaire, tom. xv. p. 282). The maxim is neither charitable nor philosophic; and some reverence is surely due to the fame of heroes and the religion of nations. I am informed that a Turkish ambassador at Paris was much scandalised at the representation of this tragedy.

[2] [Of these eleven men and six women who were proscribed, only four really met with the death sentence. The eight and twenty inhabitants of Mecca slain by Chaled brought on the latter the censure of the prophet. The same thing happened on another occasion. The prophet had sent him on an expedition to the province of Tehama, and on passing through the territory of the Beni Djasima, Chaled caused a considerable number of them to be put to death, although they were already Mussulmans. Unfortunately, when required to confess their faith, they had, from ancient custom, used the word Saba'na (converts or renegades) instead of the usual Moslem expression Aslamna. On hearing of the act, Mohammed raised his hands to heaven and exclaimed, " O God, I am pure before thee, and

but he blamed the cruelty of his lieutenant; and several of the most obnoxious victims were indebted for their lives to his clemency or contempt. The chiefs of the Koreish were prostrate at his feet. "What mercy can you expect from the man whom you have wronged?" "We confide in the generosity of our kinsman." "And you shall not confide in vain: begone! you are safe, you are free." The people of Mecca deserved their pardon by the profession of Islam; and after an exile of seven years, the fugitive missionary was enthroned as the prince and prophet of his native country.[1] But the three hundred and sixty idols of the Caaba were ignominiously broken: the house of God was purified and adorned: as an example to future times, the apostle again fulfilled the duties of a pilgrim; and a perpetual law was enacted that no unbeliever should dare to set his foot on the territory of the holy city.[2]

The conquest of Mecca determined the faith and obedience of the Arabian tribes;[3] who, according to the vicissitudes of fortune, had obeyed, or disregarded, the eloquence or the arms of the prophet. Indifference for rites and opinions still marks the character of the Bedoweens; and they might accept, as loosely as they hold, the doctrine of the Koran. Yet an obstinate remnant still adhered to the religion and liberty of their ancestors, and the war of Honain derived a proper appellation from the *idols*, whom Mohammed had vowed to destroy, and whom the confederates of Tayef had sworn to defend.[4] Four thousand Pagans advanced with secrecy and speed to surprise the conqueror: they pitied and despised the supine negligence

have taken no part in Chaled's deed." Mohammed compensated the Beni Djasima for the slaughter of their kinsmen, but the services of Chaled obliged him to overlook his offence.—O. S.]

[1] The Mohammedan doctors still dispute whether Mecca was reduced by force or consent (Abulfeda, p. 107, et Gagnier ad locum); and this verbal controversy is of as much moment as our own about William the *Conqueror*.

[2] In excluding the Christians from the peninsula of Arabia, the province of Hejaz, or the navigation of the Red Sea, Chardin (Voyages en Perse, tom. iv. p. 166) and Reland (Dissertat. Miscell. tom. iii. p. 51) are more rigid than the Musulmans themselves. The Christians are received without scruple into the ports of Mocha, and even of Gedda; and it is only the city and precincts of Mecca that are inaccessible to the profane (Niebuhr, Description de l'Arabie, p. 308, 309; Voyage en Arabie, tom. i. p. 205, 248, etc.).

[3] Abulfeda, p. 112-115; Gagnier, tom. iii. p. 67-88; D'Herbelot MOHAMMED.

[4] The siege of Tayef, division of the spoil, etc., are related by Abulfeda (p. 117-123) and Gagnier (tom. iii. p. 88-111). It is Al Jannabi who mentions the engines and engineers of the tribe of Daws. The fertile spot of Tayef was supposed to be a piece of the land of Syria detached and dropped in the general deluge.

of the Koreish, but they depended on the wishes, and perhaps the aid, of a people who had so lately renounced their gods, and bowed beneath the yoke of their enemy. The banners of Medina and Mecca were displayed by the prophet; a crowd of Bedoweens increased the strength or numbers of the army, and twelve thousand Musulmans entertained a rash and sinful presumption of their invincible strength. They descended without precaution into the valley of Honain: the heights had been occupied by the archers and slingers of the confederates; their numbers were oppressed, their discipline was confounded, their courage was appalled, and the Koreish smiled at their impending destruction. The prophet, on his white mule, was encompassed by the enemies: he attempted to rush against their spears in search of a glorious death: ten of his faithful companions interposed their weapons and their breasts; three of these fell dead at his feet: " O my brethren," he repeatedly cried with sorrow and indignation, " I am the son of Abdallah, I am the apostle of truth! O man, stand fast in the faith! O God, send down thy succour!" His uncle Abbas, who, like the heroes of Homer, excelled in the loudness of his voice, made the valley resound with the recital of the gifts and promises of God: the flying Moslems returned from all sides to the holy standard; and Mohammed observed with pleasure that the furnace was again rekindled: his conduct and example restored the battle, and he animated his victorious troops to inflict a merciless revenge on the authors of their shame. From the field of Honain he marched without delay to the siege of Tayef, sixty miles to the south-east of Mecca, a fortress of strength, whose fertile lands produce the fruits of Syria in the midst of the Arabian desert. A friendly tribe, instructed (I know not how) in the art of sieges, supplied him with a train of battering-rams and military engines, with a body of five hundred artificers. But it was in vain that he offered freedom to the slaves of Tayef; that he violated his own laws by the extirpation of the fruit-trees; that the ground was opened by the miners; that the breach was assaulted by the troops. After a siege of twenty days the prophet sounded a retreat; but he retreated with a song of devout triumph, and affected to pray for the repentance and safety of the unbelieving city. The spoil of this fortunate expedition amounted to six thousand captives, twenty-four thousand camels, forty thousand sheep, and four thousand ounces of silver: a tribe who had fought at Honain redeemed their prisoners by the sacrifice of their idols: but Mohammed compensated the loss by resigning to the soldiers his fifth of the plunder, and wished, for their sake, that he possessed as many head of cattle as there were trees in the province of Tehama. Instead of chastising the disaffection of the Koreish, he endeavoured to cut out their tongues (his own expression), and to secure their attachment, by a superior measure of liberality: Abu Sophian alone was presented with three hundred camels and twenty ounces of silver; and Mecca was sincerely converted to the profitable religion of the Koran.

The *fugitives* and *auxiliaries* complained that they who had borne the burden were neglected in the season of victory. "Alas!" replied their artful leader, "suffer me to conciliate these recent enemies, these doubtful proselytes, by the gift of some perishable goods. To your guard I intrust my life and fortunes. You are the companions of my exile, of my kingdom, of my paradise." He was followed by the deputies of Tayef, who dreaded the repetition of a siege. "Grant us, O apostle of God! a truce of three years with the toleration of our ancient worship." "Not a month, not an hour." "Excuse us at least from the obligation of prayer." "Without prayer religion is of no avail." They submitted in silence: their temples were demolished, and the same sentence of destruction was executed on all the idols of Arabia. His lieutenants, on the shores of the Red Sea, the Ocean, and the Gulf of Persia, were saluted by the acclamations of a faithful people; and the ambassadors who knelt before the throne of Medina were as numerous (says the Arabian proverb) as the dates that fall from the maturity of a palm-tree. The nation submitted to the God and the sceptre of Mohammed: the opprobrious name of tribute was abolished: the spontaneous or reluctant oblations of alms and tithes were applied to the service of religion; and one hundred and fourteen thousand Moslems accompanied the last pilgrimage of the apostle.[1]

When Heraclius returned in triumph from the Persian war, he entertained, at Emesa, one of the ambassadors of Mohammed, who invited the princes and nations of the earth to the profession of Islam. On this foundation the zeal of the Arabians has supposed the secret conversion of the Christian emperor: the vanity of the Greeks has feigned a personal visit of the prince of Medina, who accepted from the royal bounty a rich domain, and

---

[1] The last conquests and pilgrimage of Mohammed are contained in Abulfeda (p. 121-133), Gagnier (tom. iii. p. 119-219), Elmacin (p. 10, 11 [4to ed., Lugd. Bat. 1625]), Abulpharagius (p. 103). The ninth of the Hegira was styled the Year of Embassies (Gagnier, Not. ad Abulfed. p. 121).

a secure retreat, in the province of Syria.[1] But the friendship of
Heraclius and Mohammed was of short continuance: the new
religion had inflamed rather than assuaged the rapacious spirit
of the Saracens; and the murder of an envoy afforded a decent
pretence for invading, with three thousand soldiers, the territory
of Palestine, that extends to the eastward of the Jordan. The
holy banner was intrusted to Zeid; and such was the discipline
or enthusiasm of the rising sect, that the noblest chiefs served
without reluctance under the slave of the prophet. On the
event of his decease, Jaafar and Abdallah were successively
substituted to the command; and if the three should perish in
the war, the troops were authorised to elect their general. The
three leaders were slain in the battle of Muta,[2] the first military
action which tried the valour of the Moslems against a foreign
enemy. Zeid fell, like a soldier, in the foremost ranks: the
death of Jaafar was heroic and memorable: he lost his right
hand: he shifted the standard to his left: the left was severed
from his body; he embraced the standard with his bleeding
stumps, till he was transfixed to the ground with fifty honourable
wounds. "Advance," cried Abdallah, who stepped into the
vacant place, "advance with confidence: either victory or
paradise is our own." The lance of a Roman decided the
alternative; but the falling standard was rescued by Caled, the
proselyte of Mecca: nine swords were broken in his hand; and
his valour withstood and repulsed the superior numbers of the
Christians. In the nocturnal council of the camp he was chosen
to command: his skilful evolutions of the ensuing day secured
either the victory or the retreat of the Saracens; and Caled is
renowned among his brethren and his enemies by the glorious
appellation of the *Sword of God*. In the pulpit, Mohammed
described, with prophetic rapture, the crowns of the blessed
martyrs; but in private he betrayed the feelings of human
nature: he was surprised as he wept over the daughter of Zeid:
"What do I see?" said the astonished votary. "You see,"
replied the apostle, "a friend who is deploring the loss of his
most faithful friend." After the conquest of Mecca the sovereign of Arabia affected to prevent the hostile preparations of

---

[1] Compare the bigoted Al Jannabi (apud Gagnier, tom. ii. p. 232-255)
with the no less bigoted Greeks, Theophanes (p. 276-278 [tom. i. p. 511-
514, ed. Bonn]), Zonaras (tom. ii. l. xiv. [c. 16] p. 86), and Cedrenus (p. 421
[tom. i. p. 737, ed. Bonn]).

[2] For the battle of Muta, and its consequences, see Abulfeda (p. 100-102)
and Gagnier (tom. ii. p. 327-343). Χάλεδος (says Theophanes) ὃν λέγουσι
μάχαιραν τοῦ Θεοῦ [t. i. p. 515, ed. Bonn].

Heraclius; and solemnly proclaimed war against the Romans, without attempting to disguise the hardships and dangers of the enterprise.[1] The Moslems were discouraged: they alleged the want of money, or horses, or provisions; the season of harvest, and the intolerable heat of the summer: " Hell is much hotter," said the indignant prophet. He disdained to compel their service: but on his return he admonished the most guilty, by an excommunication of fifty days. Their desertion enhanced the merit of Abubeker, Othman, and the faithful companions who devoted their lives and fortunes; and Mohammed displayed his banner at the head of ten thousand horse and twenty thousand foot. Painful indeed was the distress of the march: lassitude and thirst were aggravated by the scorching and pestilential winds of the desert: ten men rode by turns on the same camel; and they were reduced to the shameful necessity of drinking the water from the belly of that useful animal. In the mid-way, ten days' journey from Medina and Damascus, they reposed near the grove and fountain of Tabuc. Beyond that place Mohammed declined the prosecution of the war: he declared himself satisfied with the peaceful intentions, he was more probably daunted by the martial array, of the emperor of the East. But the active and intrepid Caled spread around the terror of his name; and the prophet received the submission of the tribes and cities, from the Euphrates to Ailah, at the head of the Red Sea. To his Christian subjects Mohammed readily granted the security of their persons, the freedom of their trade, the property of their

[1] The expedition of Tabuc is recorded by our ordinary historians, Abulfeda (Vit. Moham. p. 123-127) and Gagnier (Vie de Mahomet, tom. iii. p. 147-163); but we have the advantage of appealing to the original evidence of the Koran (c. 9, p. 154, 165), with Sale's learned and rational notes.

[The expedition to Tabuc was undertaken in the month Radjab of the ninth year of the Hegira (A.D. 631). Mohammed's friends gave a great part of their substance towards defraying its expenses. Abu Bekr gave the whole of his property, consisting of 4000 drachms, and when Mohammed asked, " What then hast thou left for thy family? " the answer was " God, and his prophet." The traditions vary exceedingly respecting the number of the army assembled on this occasion. About 30,000 is the lowest estimate given; but this is probably exaggerated, and a large number deserted at the outset of the march. When Mohammed at Tabuc consulted his companions as to the further prosecution of the enterprise, Omar said, " If you are commanded by God to go further, do it." The prophet answered, " If I had the command of God I should not ask your advice." Omar replied, " O prophet of God! the Greeks are a numerous people, and there is not a single Mussulman among them. Moreover, we have already nearly approached them, and your neighbourhood has struck them with terror. This year, therefore, let us return, till you find it convenient to undertake another campaign against them; or till God offers some other opportunity."—O. S.]

goods, and the toleration of their worship.[1]   The weakness of
their Arabian brethren had restrained them from opposing his
ambition; the disciples of Jesus were endeared to the enemy of
the Jews; and it was the interest of a conqueror to propose a fair
capitulation to the most powerful religion of the earth.

Till the age of sixty-three years the strength of Mohammed
was equal to the temporal and spiritual fatigues of his mission.
His epileptic fits, an absurd calumny of the Greeks, would be an
object of pity rather than abhorrence; [2] but he seriously believed
that he was poisoned at Chaibar by the revenge of a Jewish
female.[3]   During four years the health of the prophet declined;
his infirmities increased; but his mortal disease was a fever of
fourteen days, which deprived him by intervals of the use of
reason.   As soon as he was conscious of his danger, he edified
his brethren by the humility of his virtue or penitence.   " If
there be any man," said the apostle from the pulpit, " whom I
have unjustly scourged, I submit my own back to the lash of
retaliation.   Have I aspersed the reputation of a Musulman?
let him proclaim *my* faults in the face of the congregation.   Has
any one been despoiled of his goods? the little that I possess
shall compensate the principal and the interest of the debt."
" Yes," replied a voice from the crowd, " I am entitled to three
drachms of silver."   Mohammed heard the complaint, satisfied

---

[1] The *Diploma securitatis Aïlensibus* is attested by Ahmed Ben Joseph,
and the author *Libri Splendorum* (Gagnier, Not. ad Abulfedam, p. 125);
but Abulfeda himself, as well as Elmacin (Hist. Saracen. p. 11), though he
owns Mohammed's regard for the Christians (p. 13), only mention peace
and tribute.   In the year 1630 Sionita published at Paris the text and
version of Mohammed's patent in favour of the Christians; which was
admitted and reprobated by the opposite taste of Salmasius and Grotius
(Bayle, MAHOMET, Rem. AA).   Hottinger doubts of its authenticity (Hist.
Orient. p. 237);   Renaudot urges the consent of the Mohammedans (Hist.
Patriarch. Alex. p. 169); but Mosheim (Hist. Eccles. p. 244) shows the
futility of their opinion, and inclines to believe it spurious.   Yet Abulpharagius quotes the impostor's treaty with the Nestorian patriarch (Asseman. Biblioth. Orient. tom. ii. p. 418); but Abulpharagius was primate of
the Jacobites.

[2] The epilepsy, or falling sickness of Mohammed, is asserted by Theophanes, Zonaras, and the rest of the Greeks; and is greedily swallowed by
the gross bigotry of Hottinger (Hist. Orient. p. 10, 11), Prideaux (Life of
Mahomet, p. 12), and Maracci (tom. ii. Alcoran. p. 762, 763).   The titles
(*the wrapped-up, the covered*) of two chapters of the Koran (73, 74) can
hardly be strained to such an interpretation: the silence, the ignorance of
the Mohammedan commentators, is more conclusive than the most peremptory denial; and the charitable side is espoused by Ockley (Hist. of the
Saracens, tom. i. p. 301), Gagnier (ad Abulfedam, p. 9; Vie de Mahomet,
tom. i. p. 118), and Sale (Koran, p. 469-474).

[3] This poison (more ignominious since it was offered as a test of his
prophetic knowledge) is frankly confessed by his zealous votaries, Abulfeda (p. 92) and Al Jannabi (apud Gagnier, tom. ii. p. 286-288).

the demand, and thanked his creditor for accusing him in this world rather than at the day of judgment. He beheld with temperate firmness the approach of death; enfranchised his slaves (seventeen men, as they are named, and eleven women); minutely directed the order of his funeral; and moderated the lamentations of his weeping friends, on whom he bestowed the benediction of peace. Till the third day before his death he regularly performed the function of public prayer: the choice of Abubeker to supply his place appeared to mark that ancient and faithful friend as his successor in the sacerdotal and regal office; but he prudently declined the risk and envy of a more explicit nomination. At a moment when his faculties were visibly impaired, he called for pen and ink to write, or, more properly, to dictate, a divine book, the sum and accomplishment of all his revelations: a dispute arose in the chamber whether he should be allowed to supersede the authority of the Koran; and the prophet was forced to reprove the indecent vehemence of his disciples. If the slightest credit may be afforded to the traditions of his wives and companions, he maintained, in the bosom of his family, and to the last moments of his life, the dignity of an apostle, and the faith of an enthusiast; described the visits of Gabriel, who bid an everlasting farewell to the earth; and expressed his lively confidence, not only of the mercy, but of the favour, of the Supreme Being. In a familiar discourse he had mentioned his special prerogative, that the angel of death was not allowed to take his soul till he had respectfully asked the permission of the prophet. The request was granted; and Mohammed immediately fell into the agony of his dissolution: his head was reclined on the lap of Ayesha, the best beloved of all his wives; he fainted with the violence of pain; recovering his spirits, he raised his eyes towards the roof of the house, and, with a steady look, though a faltering voice, uttered the last broken, though articulate, words: " O God! . . . pardon my sins. . . . Yes . . . I come . . . among my fellow citizens on high; " and thus peaceably expired on a carpet spread upon the floor. An expedition for the conquest of Syria was stopped by this mournful event: the army halted at the gates of Medina; the chiefs were assembled round their dying master. The city, more especially the house, of the prophet, was a scene of clamorous sorrow or silent despair: fanaticism alone could suggest a ray of hope and consolation. " How can he be dead, our witness, our intercessor, our mediator, with God? By God he is not dead: like Moses and Jesus, he is wrapt in a holy trance, and speedily will he return to his faithful people." The evidence of sense was disregarded; and Omar, unsheathing his scimitar, threatened to strike off the heads of the infidels who should dare to affirm that the prophet was no more. The tumult was appeased by the weight and moderation of Abubeker. " Is it Mohammed," said he to Omar and the multitude, " or the God of Mohammed, whom you worship? The God of Mohammed liveth for ever; but the apostle was a mortal like ourselves, and, according to his own prediction, he has experienced the common fate of mortality." He was piously interred by the hands of his nearest kinsman, on the same spot on which he expired: [1] Medina has been sanctified by the death and burial of Mohammed; and the innumerable pilgrims of Mecca often turn aside from the way, to bow, in voluntary devotion, [2] before the simple tomb of the prophet. [3]

At the conclusion of the life of Mohammed it may perhaps be expected that I should balance his faults and virtues, that I should decide whether the title of enthusiast or impostor more properly belongs to that extraordinary man. Had I been intimately conversant with the son of Abdallah, the task would still be difficult, and the success uncertain: at the distance of twelve centuries I darkly contemplate his shade through a cloud of religious incense; and could I truly delineate the portrait of an hour, the fleeting resemblance would not equally apply to the

[1] The Greeks and Latins have invented and propagated the vulgar and ridiculous story that Mohammed's iron tomb is suspended in the air at *Mecca* (σῆμα μετεωριζόμενον. Laonicus Chalcocondyles de Rebus Turcicis, l. iii. p. 66 [ed. Par.; p. 126, ed. Bonn.]), by the action of equal and potent loadstones (Dictionnaire de Bayle, MAHOMET, Rem. EE. FF.). Without any philosophical inquiries, it may suffice, that, 1. The prophet was not buried at Mecca; and, 2. That his tomb at Medina, which has been visited by millions, is placed on the ground (Reland, de Relig. Moham. l. ii. c. 19, p. 209-211; Gagnier, Vie de Mahomet, tom. iii. p. 263-268).

[Most of the biographers of Mohammed state that he died on Monday the 12th Rabia-l-Awwl, in the year 11 of the Hegira, which answers to the 7th June, 632. This, however, fell on a Sunday. But as a contemporary poem mentions the day of his death as Monday, it is probable that a mistake has been made in the day of the month, and that he died on the 8th.—O. S.]

[2] Al Jannabi enumerates (Vie de Mahomet, tom. iii. p. 372-391) the multifarious duties of a pilgrim who visits the tombs of the prophet and his companions; and the learned casuist decides that this act of devotion is nearest in obligation and merit to a divine precept. The doctors are divided which, of Mecca or Medina, be the most excellent (p. 391-394).

[3] The last sickness, death, and burial of Mohammed are described by Abulfeda and Gagnier (Vit. Moham. p. 133-142; Vie de Mahomet, tom. iii. p. 220-271). The most private and interesting circumstances were originally received from Ayesha, Ali, the sons of Abbas, etc.; and as they dwelt at Medina, and survived the prophet many years, they might repeat the pious tale to a second or third generation of pilgrims.

solitary of Mount Hera, to the preacher of Mecca, and to the conqueror of Arabia. The author of a mighty revolution appears to have been endowed with a pious and contemplative disposition: so soon as marriage had raised him above the pressure of want, he avoided the paths of ambition and avarice; and till the age of forty he lived with innocence, and would have died without a name. The unity of God is an idea most congenial to nature and reason; and a slight conversation with the Jews and Christians would teach him to despise and detest the idolatry of Mecca. It was the duty of a man and a citizen to impart the doctrine of salvation, to rescue his country from the dominion of sin and error. The energy of a mind incessantly bent on the same object would convert a general obligation into a particular call; the warm suggestions of the understanding or the fancy would be felt as the inspirations of Heaven; the labour of thought would expire in rapture and vision; and the inward sensation, the invisible monitor, would be described with the form and attributes of an angel of God.[1] From enthusiasm to imposture the step is perilous and slippery; the demon of Socrates [2] affords a memorable instance how a wise man may deceive himself, how a good man may deceive others, how the conscience may slumber in a mixed and middle state between self-illusion and voluntary fraud. Charity may believe that the original motives of Mohammed were those of pure and genuine benevolence; but a human missionary is incapable of cherishing the obstinate unbelievers who reject his claims, despise his arguments, and persecute his life; he might forgive his personal adversaries, he may lawfully hate the enemies of God; the stern

---

[1] The Christians, rashly enough, have assigned to Mohammed a tame pigeon, that seemed to descend from heaven and whisper in his ear. As this pretended miracle is urged by Grotius (de Veritate Religionis Christianæ), his Arabic translator, the learned Pocock, inquired of him the names of his authors; and Grotius confessed that it is unknown to the Mohammedans themselves. Lest it should provoke their indignation and laughter, the pious *lie* is suppressed in the Arabic version; but it has maintained an edifying place in the numerous editions of the Latin text (Pocock, Specimen Hist. Arabum, p. 186, 187; Reland, de Religion. Moham. l. ii. c. 39, p. 259-262).

[2] Ἐμοὶ δὲ τοῦτό ἐστιν ἐκ παιδὸς ἀρξάμενον, φωνή τις γιγνομένη· ἢ ὅταν γένηται ἀεὶ ἀποτρέπει με τούτου ὃ ἂν μέλλω πράττειν, προτρέπει δὲ οὔποτε (Plato, in Apolog. Socrat. c. 19, p. 121, 122, edit. Fischer). The familiar examples which Socrates urges in his Dialogue with Theages (Platon. Opera, tom. i. p. 128, 129, edit. Hen. Stephan.) are beyond the reach of human foresight; and the divine inspiration (the Δαιμόνιον) of the philosopher is clearly taught in the Memorabilia of Xenophon. The ideas of the most rational Platonists are expressed by Cicero (de Divinat. i. 54), and in the fourteenth and fifteenth Dissertations of Maximus of Tyre (p. 153-172, edit. Davis).

passions of pride and revenge were kindled in the bosom of Mohammed, and he sighed, like the prophet of Nineveh, for the destruction of the rebels whom he had condemned. The injustice of Mecca and the choice of Medina transformed the citizen into a prince, the humble preacher into the leader of armies; but his sword was consecrated by the example of the saints; and the same God who afflicts a sinful world with pestilence and earthquakes might inspire for their conversion or chastisement the valour of his servants. In the exercise of political government he was compelled to abate of the stern rigour of fanaticism, to comply in some measure with the prejudices and passions of his followers, and to employ even the vices of mankind as the instruments of their salvation. The use of fraud and perfidy, of cruelty and injustice, were often subservient to the propagation of the faith; and Mohammed commanded or approved the assassination of the Jews and idolaters who had escaped from the field of battle. By the repetition of such acts the character of Mohammed must have been gradually stained; and the influence of such pernicious habits would be poorly compensated by the practice of the personal and social virtues which are necessary to maintain the reputation of a prophet among his sectaries and friends. Of his last years ambition was the ruling passion; and a politician will suspect that he secretly smiled (the victorious impostor!) at the enthusiasm of his youth, and the credulity of his proselytes.[1] A philosopher will observe that *their* credulity and *his* success would tend more strongly to fortify the assurance of his divine mission, that his interest and religion were inseparably connected, and that his conscience would be soothed by the persuasion that he alone was absolved by the Deity from the obligation of positive and moral laws. If he retained any vestige of his native innocence, the sins of Mohammed may be allowed as an evidence of his sincerity. In the support of truth, the arts of fraud and fiction may be deemed less criminal; and he would have started at the foulness of the means, had he not been satisfied of the importance and justice of the end. Even in a conqueror or a priest I can surprise a word or action of unaffected humanity; and the decree of Mohammed, that, in the sale of captives, the mothers should never be separated from their children, may suspend, or moderate, the censure of the historian.[2]

[1] In some passage of his voluminous writings, Voltaire compares the prophet, in his old age, to a fakir " qui détache la chaîne de son cou pour en donner sur les oreilles à ses confrères."

[2] Gagnier relates, with the same impartial pen, this humane law of the

The good sense of Mohammed [1] despised the pomp of royalty; the apostle of God submitted to the menial offices of the family; he kindled the fire, swept the floor, milked the ewes, and mended with his own hands his shoes and his woollen garment. Disdaining the penance and merit of a hermit, he observed, without effort or vanity, the abstemious diet of an Arab and a soldier. On solemn occasions he feasted his companions with rustic and hospitable plenty; but in his domestic life many weeks would elapse without a fire being kindled on the hearth of the prophet. The interdiction of wine was confirmed by his example; his hunger was appeased with a sparing allowance of barley-bread: he delighted in the taste of milk and honey; but his ordinary food consisted of dates and water. Perfumes and women were the two sensual enjoyments which his nature required, and his religion did not forbid; and Mohammed affirmed that the fervour of his devotion was increased by these innocent pleasures. The heat of the climate inflames the blood of the Arabs, and their libidinous complexion has been noticed by the writers of antiquity.[2] Their incontinence was regulated by the civil and religious laws of the Koran: their incestuous alliances were blamed: the boundless licence of polygamy was reduced to four legitimate wives or concubines; their rights both of bed and of dowry were equitably determined; the freedom of divorce was discouraged; adultery was condemned as a capital offence; and fornication, in either sex, was punished with a hundred stripes.[3] Such were the calm and rational precepts of the legislator; but in his private conduct Mohammed indulged the appetites of a man, and abused the claims of a prophet. A special revelation dispensed him from the laws which he had imposed on his nation; the female sex, without reserve, was abandoned to his desires; and this singular prerogative excited the envy rather than the

prophet, and the murders of Caab and Sophian, which he prompted and approved (Vie de Mahomet, tom. ii. p. 69, 97, 208).

[1] For the domestic life of Mohammed, consult Gagnier, and the corresponding chapters of Abulfeda; for his diet (tom. iii. p. 285-288); his children (p. 189, 289); his wives (p. 290-303); his marriage with Zeineb (tom. ii. p. 152-160); his amour with Mary (p. 303-309); the false accusation of Ayesha (p. 186-199). The most original evidence of the three last transactions is contained in the twenty-fourth, thirty-third, and sixty-sixth chapters of the Koran, with Sale's Commentary. Prideaux (Life of Mahomet, p. 80-90) and Maracci (Prodrom. Alcoran, part iv. p. 49-59) have maliciously exaggerated the frailties of Mohammed.

[2] Incredibile est quo ardore apud eos in Venerem uterque solvitur sexus (Ammian. Marcellin. l. xiv. c. 4).

[3] Sale (Preliminary Discourse, p. 133-137) has recapitulated the laws of marriage, divorce, etc.; and the curious reader of Selden's Uxor Hebraica will recognise many Jewish ordinances.

scandal, the veneration rather than the envy, of the devout Musulmans. If we remember the seven hundred wives and three hundred concubines of the wise Solomon, we shall applaud the modesty of the Arabian, who espoused no more than seventeen or fifteen wives; eleven are enumerated who occupied at Medina their separate apartments round the house of the apostle, and enjoyed in their turns the favour of his conjugal society. What is singular enough, they were all widows, excepting only Ayesha, the daughter of Abubeker. *She* was doubtless a virgin, since Mohammed consummated his nuptials (such is the premature ripeness of the climate) when she was only nine years of age. The youth, the beauty, the spirit of Ayesha gave her a superior ascendant: she was beloved and trusted by the prophet; and, after his death, the daughter of Abubeker was long revered as the mother of the faithful. Her behaviour had been ambiguous and indiscreet: in a nocturnal march she was accidentally left behind, and in the morning Ayesha returned to the camp with a man. The temper of Mohammed was inclined to jealousy; but a divine revelation assured him of her innocence: he chastised her accusers, and published a law of domestic peace, that no woman should be condemned unless four male witnesses had seen her in the act of adultery.[1] In his adventures with Zeineb, the wife of Zeid, and with Mary, an Egyptian captive, the amorous prophet forgot the interest of his reputation. At the house of Zeid, his freedman and adopted son, he beheld, in a loose undress, the beauty of Zeineb, and burst forth into an ejaculation of devotion and desire. The servile, or grateful, freedman understood the hint, and yielded without hesitation to the love of his benefactor. But as the filial relation had excited some doubt and scandal, the angel Gabriel descended from heaven to ratify the deed, to annul the adoption, and gently to reprove the apostle for distrusting the indulgence of his God. One of his wives, Hafna, the daughter of Omar, surprised him on her own bed in the embraces of his Egyptian captive: she promised secrecy and forgiveness: he swore that he would renounce the possession of Mary. Both parties forgot their engagements; and Gabriel again descended with a chapter of the Koran to absolve him from his oath, and to exhort him freely to enjoy his captives and concubines without listening to the clamours of his wives. In a solitary retreat of thirty days he

[1] In a memorable case, the Caliph Omar decided that all presumptive evidence was of no avail; and that all the four witnesses must have actually seen stylum in pyxide (Abulfedæ Annales Moslemici, p. 71, vers. Reiske [Lips. 1754]).

laboured alone with Mary to fulfil the commands of the angel. When his love and revenge were satiated, he summoned to his presence his eleven wives, reproached their disobedience and indiscretion, and threatened them with a sentence of divorce, both in this world and in the next—a dreadful sentence, since those who had ascended the bed of the prophet were for ever excluded from the hope of a second marriage. Perhaps the incontinence of Mohammed may be palliated by the tradition of his natural or preternatural gifts: [1] he united the manly virtue of thirty of the children of Adam; and the apostle might rival the thirteenth labour [2] of the Grecian Hercules.[3] A more serious and decent excuse may be drawn from his fidelity to Cadijah. During the twenty-four years of their marriage her youthful husband abstained from the right of polygamy, and the pride or tenderness of the venerable matron was never insulted by the society of a rival. After her death he placed her in the rank of the four perfect women, with the sister of Moses, the mother of Jesus, and Fatima, the best beloved of his daughters. " Was she not old? " said Ayesha, with the insolence of a blooming beauty; " has not God given you a better in her place? " " No, by God," said Mohammed, with an effusion of honest gratitude, " there never can be a better! She believed in me when men despised me; she relieved my wants when I was poor and persecuted by the world." [4]

In the largest indulgence of polygamy, the founder of a religion and empire might aspire to multiply the chances of a numerous posterity and a lineal succession. The hopes of Mohammed were fatally disappointed. The virgin Ayesha, and his ten widows of mature age and approved fertility, were barren in his

---

[1] Sibi robur ad generationem, quantum triginta viri habent, inesse jactaret: ita ut unicâ horâ posset undecim fœminis *satisfacere*, ut ex Arabum libris refert Stus. Petrus Paschasius, c. 2 (Maracci, Prodromus Alcoran, p. iv. p. 55. See likewise Observations de Belon, l. iii. c. 10, fol. 179, recto). Al Jannabi (Gagnier, tom. iii. p. 287) records his own testimony, that he surpassed all men in conjugal vigour; and Abulfeda mentions the exclamation of Ali, who washed his body after his death, " O propheta, certa penis tuus cœlum versus erectus est," in Vit. Mohammed, p. 140.

[2] I borrow the style of a father of the church, ἐναθλεύων Ἡρακλῆς τρισκαιδέκατον ἆθλον (Greig. Nazianzen, Orat. iii. p. 108 [ed. Par. 1609]).

[3] The common and most glorious legend includes, in a single night, the fifty victories of Hercules over the virgin daughters of Thestius (Diodor. Sicul. tom. i. l. iv. [c. 29] p. 274; Pausanias, l. ix. [c. 27, § 6] p. 763; Statius Silv. l. i. eleg. iii. v. 42). But Athenæus allows seven nights (Deipnosophist, l. xiii. [c. 4] p. 556), and Apollodorus fifty, for this arduous achievement of Hercules, who was then no more than eighteen years of age (Biblioth. l. ii. c. 4 [§ 10] p. 111, cum notis Heyne, part i. p. 332).

[4] Abulfeda in Vit. Moham. p. 12, 13, 16, 17, cum notis Gagnier.

potent embraces. The four sons of Cadijah died in their infancy. Mary, his Egyptian concubine, was endeared to him by the birth of Ibrahim. At the end of fifteen months the prophet wept over his grave; but he sustained with firmness the raillery of his enemies, and checked the adulation or credulity of the Moslems by the assurance that an eclipse of the sun was *not* occasioned by the death of the infant. Cadijah had likewise given him four daughters, who were married to the most faithful of his disciples: the three eldest died before their father; but Fatima, who possessed his confidence and love, became the wife of her cousin Ali, and the mother of an illustrious progeny. The merit and misfortunes of Ali and his descendants will lead me to anticipate, in this place, the series of the Saracen caliphs, a title which describes the commanders of the faithful as the vicars and successors of the apostle of God.[1]

The birth, the alliance, the character of Ali, which exalted him above the rest of his countrymen, might justify his claim to the vacant throne of Arabia. The son of Abu Taleb was, in his own right, the chief of the family of Hashem, and the hereditary prince or guardian of the city and temple of Mecca. The light of prophecy was extinct; but the husband of Fatima might expect the inheritance and blessing of her father: the Arabs had sometimes been patient of a female reign; and the two grandsons of the prophet had often been fondled in his lap, and shown in his pulpit, as the hope of his age, and the chief of the youth of paradise. The first of the true believers might aspire to march before them in this world and in the next; and if some were of a graver and more rigid cast, the zeal and virtue of Ali were never outstripped by any recent proselyte. He united the qualifications of a poet, a soldier, and a saint: his wisdom still breathes in a collection of moral and religious sayings;[2] and every antagonist, in the combats of the tongue or of the sword, was

---

[1] This outline of the Arabian history is drawn from the Bibliothèque Orientale of D'Herbelot (under the names of *Aboubecre*, *Omar*, *Othman*, *Ali*, etc.), from the Annals of Abulfeda, Abulpharagius, and Elmacin (under the proper years of the *Hegira*), and especially from Ockley's History of the Saracens (vol. i. p. 1-10, 115-122, 229, 249, 363-372, 378-391, and almost the whole of the second volume). Yet we should weigh with caution the traditions of the hostile sects; a stream which becomes still more muddy as it flows farther from the source. Sir John Chardin has too faithfully copied the fables and errors of the modern Persians (Voyages, tom. ii. p. 235-250, etc.).

[2] Ockley (at the end of his second volume) has given an English version of 169 sentences, which he ascribes, with some hesitation, to Ali, the son of Abu Taleb. His preface is coloured by the enthusiasm of a translator; yet these sentences delineate a characteristic, though dark, picture of human life.

subdued by his eloquence and valour. From the first hour of his mission to the last rites of his funeral, the apostle was never forsaken by a generous friend, whom he delighted to name his brother, his vicegerent, and the faithful Aaron of a second Moses. The son of Abu Taleb was afterwards reproached for neglecting to secure his interest by a solemn declaration of his right, which would have silenced all competition, and sealed his succession by the decrees of Heaven. But the unsuspecting hero confided in himself: the jealousy of empire, and perhaps the fear of opposition, might suspend the resolutions of Mohammed; and the bed of sickness was besieged by the artful Ayesha, the daughter of Abubeker, and the enemy of Ali.

The silence and death of the prophet restored the liberty of the people; and his companions convened an assembly to deliberate on the choice of his successor. The hereditary claim and lofty spirit of Ali were offensive to an aristocracy of elders, desirous of bestowing and resuming the sceptre by a free and frequent election: the Koreish could never be reconciled to the proud pre-eminence of the line of Hashem: the ancient discord of the tribes was rekindled; the *fugitives* of Mecca and the *auxiliaries* of Medina asserted their respective merits; and the rash proposal of choosing two independent caliphs would have crushed in their infancy the religion and empire of the Saracens. The tumult was appeased by the disinterested resolution of Omar, who, suddenly renouncing his own pretensions, stretched forth his hand and declared himself the first subject of the mild and venerable Abubeker. The urgency of the moment, and the acquiescence of the people, might excuse this illegal and precipitate measure; but Omar himself confessed from the pulpit, that, if any Musulman should hereafter presume to anticipate the suffrage of his brethren, both the elector and the elected would be worthy of death.[1] After the simple inauguration of Abubeker, he was obeyed in Medina, Mecca, and the provinces of Arabia: the Hashemites alone declined the oath of fidelity; and their chief, in his own house, maintained above six months a sullen and independent reserve, without listening to the threats of Omar, who attempted to consume with fire the habitation of the daughter of the apostle. The death of Fatima, and the decline of his party, subdued the indignant spirit of Ali: he condescended

---

[1] Ockley (Hist. of the Saracens, vol. i. p. 5, 6) from an Arabian MS. represents Ayesha as adverse to the substitution of her father in the place of the apostle. This fact, so improbable in itself, is unnoticed by Abulfeda, Al Jannabi, and Al Bochari, the last of whom quotes the tradition of Ayesha herself (Vit. Mohammed. p. 136; Vie de Mahomet, tom. iii. p. 236.)

to salute the commander of the faithful, accepted his excuse of
the necessity of preventing their common enemies, and wisely
rejected his courteous offer of abdicating the government of the
Arabians. After a reign of two years the aged caliph was
summoned by the angel of death. In his testament, with the
tacit approbation of the companions, he bequeathed the sceptre
to the firm and intrepid virtue of Omar. " I have no occasion,"
said the modest candidate, " for the place." " But the place
has occasion for you," replied Abubeker; who expired with a
fervent prayer that the God of Mohammed would ratify his
choice, and direct the Musulmans in the way of concord and
obedience. The prayer was not ineffectual, since Ali himself, in
a life of privacy and prayer, professed to revere the superior
worth and dignity of his rival, who comforted him for the loss of
empire by the most flattering marks of confidence and esteem.
In the twelfth year of his reign Omar received a mortal wound
from the hand of an assassin: he rejected with equal impartiality
the names of his son and of Ali, refused to load his conscience
with the sins of his successor, and devolved on six of the most
respectable companions the arduous task of electing a commander of the faithful. On this occasion Ali was again blamed
by his friends [1] for submitting his right to the judgment of men,
for recognising their jurisdiction by accepting a place among the
six electors. He might have obtained their suffrage had he
deigned to promise a strict and servile conformity, not only to
the Koran and tradition, but likewise to the determinations of
two *seniors*.[2] With these limitations, Othman, the secretary of
Mohammed, accepted the government; nor was it till after the
third caliph, twenty-four years after the death of the prophet,
that Ali was invested by the popular choice with the regal and
sacerdotal office. The manners of the Arabians retained their
primitive simplicity, and the son of Abu Taleb despised the pomp
and vanity of this world. At the hour of prayer he repaired to
the mosch of Medina, clothed in a thin cotton gown, a coarse
turban on his head, his slippers in one hand, and his bow in
the other, instead of a walking-staff. The companions of the

---

[1] Particularly by his friend and cousin Abdallah, the son of Abbas, who
died A.D. 687, with the title of grand doctor of the Moslems. In Abulfeda
[Ann. Moslem.] he recapitulates the important occasions in which Ali had
neglected his salutary advice (p. 76, vers. Reiske); and concludes (p. 85),
O princeps fidelium, absque controversia tu quidem vere [vir] fortis es, at
inops boni consilii, et rerum gerendarum parum callens.

[2] I suspect that the two seniors (Abulpharagius, p. 115; Ockley, tom. i.
p. 371) may signify not two actual counsellors, but his two predecessors,
Abubeker and Omar.]

prophet and the chiefs of the tribe saluted their new sovereign, and gave him their right hands as a sign of fealty and allegiance.

The mischiefs that flow from the contests of ambition are usually confined to the times and countries in which they have been agitated. But the religious discord of the friends and enemies of Ali has been renewed in every age of the Hegira, and is still maintained in the immortal hatred of the Persians and Turks.[1] The former, who are branded with the appellation of *Shiites* or sectaries, have enriched the Mohammedan creed with a new article of faith; and if Mohammed be the apostle, his companion Ali is the vicar, of God. In their private converse, in their public worship, they bitterly execrate the three usurpers who intercepted his indefeasible right to the dignity of Imam and Caliph; and the name of Omar expresses in their tongue the perfect accomplishment of wickedness and impiety.[2] The *Sonnites*, who are supported by the general consent and orthodox tradition of the Musulmans, entertain a more impartial, or at least a more decent, opinion. They respect the memory of Abubeker, Omar, Othman, and Ali, the holy and legitimate successors of the prophet. But they assign the last and most humble place to the husband of Fatima, in the persuasion that the order of succession was determined by the degrees of sanctity.[3] An historian who balances the four caliphs with a hand unshaken by superstition will calmly pronounce that their manners were alike pure and exemplary; that their zeal was fervent, and probably sincere; and that, in the midst of riches and power, their lives were devoted to the practice of moral and religious duties. But the public virtues of Abubeker and Omar, the prudence of the first, the severity of the second, maintained the peace and prosperity of their reigns. The feeble temper and declining age of Othman

---

[1] The schism of the Persians is explained by all our travellers of the last century, especially in the second and fourth volumes of their master Chardin. Niebuhr, though of inferior merit, has the advantage of writing so late as the year 1764 (Voyages en Arabie, etc., tom. ii. p. 208-233), since the ineffectual attempt of Nadir Shah to change the religion of the nation (see his Persian History translated into French by Sir William Jones, tom. ii. p. 5, 6, 47, 48, 144-155).

[2] Omar is the name of the devil; his murderer is a saint. When the Persians shoot with the bow, they frequently cry, " May this arrow go to the heart of Omar! " (Voyages de Chardin, tom. ii. p. 239, 240, 259, etc.).

[3] This gradation of merit is distinctly marked in a creed illustrated by Reland (de Relig. Mohamm. l. i. p. 37); and a Sonnite argument inserted by Ockley (Hist. of the Saracens, tom. ii. p. 230). The practice of cursing the memory of Ali was abolished, after forty years, by the Ommiades themselves (D'Herbelot, p. 690); and there are few among the Turks who presume to revile him as an infidel (Voyages de Chardin, tom. iv. p. 46).

were incapable of sustaining the weight of conquest and empire. He chose, and he was deceived; he trusted, and he was betrayed: the most deserving of the faithful became useless or hostile to his government, and his lavish bounty was productive only of ingratitude and discontent. The spirit of discord went forth in the provinces: their deputies assembled at Medina; and the Charegites, the desperate fanatics who disclaimed the yoke of subordination and reason, were confounded among the free-born Arabs, who demanded the redress of their wrongs and the punishment of their oppressors. From Cufa, from Bassora, from Egypt, from the tribes of the desert, they rose in arms, encamped about a league from Medina, and despatched a haughty mandate to their sovereign, requiring him to execute justice or to descend from the throne. His repentance began to disarm and disperse the insurgents; but their fury was rekindled by the arts of his enemies; and the forgery of a perfidious secretary was contrived to blast his reputation and precipitate his fall. The caliph had lost the only guard of his predecessors, the esteem and confidence of the Moslems: during a siege of six weeks his water and provisions were intercepted, and the feeble gates of the palace were protected only by the scruples of the more timorous rebels. Forsaken by those who had abused his simplicity, the helpless and venerable caliph expected the approach of death: the brother of Ayesha marched at the head of the assassins; and Othman, with the Koran in his lap, was pierced with a multitude of wounds. A tumultuous anarchy of five days was appeased by the inauguration of Ali: his refusal would have provoked a general massacre. In this painful situation he supported the becoming pride of the chief of the Hashemites; declared that he had rather serve than reign; rebuked the presumption of the strangers; and required the formal if not the voluntary assent of the chiefs of the nation. He has never been accused of prompting the assassin of Omar; though Persia indiscreetly celebrates the festival of that holy martyr. The quarrel between Othman and his subjects was assuaged by the early mediation of Ali; and Hassan, the eldest of his sons, was insulted and wounded in the defence of the caliph. Yet it is doubtful whether the father of Hassan was strenuous and sincere in his opposition to the rebels; and it is certain that he enjoyed the benefit of their crime. The temptation was indeed of such magnitude as might stagger and corrupt the most obdurate virtue. The ambitious candidate no longer aspired to the barren sceptre of Arabia; the Saracens had been victorious in the East and West; and the wealthy kingdoms of Persia,

Syria, and Egypt were the patrimony of the commander of the faithful.

A life of prayer and contemplation had not chilled the martial activity of Ali; but in a mature age, after a long experience of mankind, he still betrayed in his conduct the rashness and indiscretion of youth. In the first days of his reign he neglected to secure, either by gifts or fetters, the doubtful allegiance of Telha and Zobeir, two of the most powerful of the Arabian chiefs. They escaped from Medina to Mecca, and from thence to Bassora; erected the standard of revolt; and usurped the government of Irak, or Assyria, which they had vainly solicited as the reward of their services. The mask of patriotism is allowed to cover the most glaring inconsistencies; and the enemies, perhaps the assassins, of Othman now demanded vengeance for his blood. They were accompanied in their flight by Ayesha, the widow of the prophet, who cherished to the last hour of her life an implacable hatred against the husband and the posterity of Fatima. The most reasonable Moslems were scandalised that the mother of the faithful should expose in a camp her person and character; but the superstitious crowd was confident that her presence would sanctify the justice and assure the success of their cause. At the head of twenty thousand of his loyal Arabs, and nine thousand valiant auxiliaries of Cufa, the caliph encountered and defeated the superior numbers of the rebels under the walls of Bassora. Their leaders, Telha and Zobeir, were slain in the first battle that stained with civil blood the arms of the Moslems. After passing through the ranks to animate the troops, Ayesha had chosen her post amidst the dangers of the field. In the heat of the action, seventy men who held the bridle of her camel were successively killed or wounded; and the cage, or litter, in which she sat was stuck with javelins and darts like the quills of a porcupine. The venerable captive sustained with firmness the reproaches of the conqueror, and was speedily dismissed to her proper station, at the tomb of Mohammed, with the respect and tenderness that was still due to the widow of the apostle. After this victory, which was styled the Day of the Camel, Ali marched against a more formidable adversary; against Moawiyah, the son of Abu Sophian, who had assumed the title of caliph, and whose claim was supported by the forces of Syria and the interest of the house of Ommiyah. From the passage of Thapsacus, the plain of Siffin [1] extends along the Western bank of the Euphrates. On

[1] The plain of Siffin is determined by D'Anville (l'Euphrate et le Tigre, p. 29) to be the Campus Barbaricus of Procopius.

this spacious and level theatre the two competitors waged a desultory war of one hundred and ten days. In the course of ninety actions or skirmishes, the loss of Ali was estimated at twenty-five, that of Moawiyah at forty-five, thousand soldiers; and the list of the slain was dignified with the names of five-and-twenty veterans who had fought at Beder under the standard of Mohammed. In this sanguinary contest the lawful caliph displayed a superior character of valour and humanity. His troops were strictly enjoined to await the first onset of the enemy, to spare their flying brethren, and to respect the bodies of the dead, and the chastity of the female captives. He generously proposed to save the blood of the Moslems by a single combat; but his trembling rival declined the challenge as a sentence of inevitable death. The ranks of the Syrians were broken by the charge of a hero who was mounted on a piebald horse, and wielded with irresistible force his ponderous and two-edged sword. As often as he smote a rebel, he shouted the Allah Acbar, " God is victorious! " and in the tumult of a nocturnal battle he was heard to repeat four hundred times that tremendous exclamation. The prince of Damascus already meditated his flight; but the certain victory was snatched from the grasp of Ali by the disobedience and enthusiasm of his troops. Their conscience was awed by the solemn appeal to the books of the Koran which Moawiyah exposed on the foremost lances; and Ali was compelled to yield to a disgraceful truce and an insidious compromise. He retreated with sorrow and indignation to Cufa; his party was discouraged; the distant provinces of Persia, of Yemen, and of Egypt were subdued or seduced by his crafty rival; and the stroke of fanaticism, which was aimed against the three chiefs of the nation, was fatal only to the cousin of Mohammed. In the temple of Mecca three Charegites or enthusiasts discoursed of the disorders of the church and state: they soon agreed that the deaths of Ali, of Moawiyah, and of his friend Amrou, the viceroy of Egypt, would restore the peace and unity of religion. Each of the assassins chose his victim, poisoned his dagger, devoted his life, and secretly repaired to the scene of action. Their resolution was equally desperate: but the first mistook the person of Amrou, and stabbed the deputy who occupied his seat; the prince of Damascus was dangerously hurt by the second; the lawful caliph, in the mosch of Cufa, received a mortal wound from the hand of the third. He expired in the sixty-third year of his age, and mercifully recommended to his children that they would despatch the murderer by a single stroke. The sepulchre of

Ali[1] was concealed from the tyrants of the house of Ommiyah;[2] but in the fourth age of the Hegira, a tomb, a temple, a city, arose near the ruins of Cufa.[3] Many thousands of the Shiites repose in holy ground at the feet of the vicar of God; and the desert is vivified by the numerous and annual visits of the Persians, who esteem their devotion not less meritorious than the pilgrimage of Mecca.

The persecutors of Mohammed usurped the inheritance of his children; and the champions of idolatry became the supreme heads of his religion and empire. The opposition of Abu Sophian had been fierce and obstinate; his conversion was tardy and reluctant; his new faith was fortified by necessity and interest; he served, he fought, perhaps he believed; and the sins of the time of ignorance were expiated by the recent merits of the family of Ommiyah. Moawiyah, the son of Abu Sophian, and of the cruel Henda, was dignified in his early youth with the office or title of secretary of the prophet: the judgment of Omar intrusted him with the government of Syria; and he administered that important province above forty years, either in a subordinate or supreme rank. Without renouncing the fame of valour and liberality, he affected the reputation of humanity and moderation: a grateful people was attached to their benefactor; and the victorious Moslems were enriched with the spoils of Cyprus and Rhodes. The sacred duty of pursuing the assassins of Othman was the engine and pretence of his ambition. The bloody shirt of the martyr was exposed in the mosch of Damascus: the emir deplored the fate of his injured kinsman; and sixty thousand Syrians were engaged in his service by an oath of fidelity and revenge. Amrou, the conqueror of Egypt, himself an army, was the first who saluted the new monarch, and divulged the dangerous secret that the Arabian caliphs might be created

---

[1] Abulfeda, a moderate Sonnite, relates the different opinions concerning the burial of Ali, but adopts the sepulchre of Cufa, hodie famâ numeroque religiose frequentantium celebratum. This number is reckoned by Niebuhr to amount annually to 2000 of the dead and 5000 of the living (tom. ii. p. 208, 209).

[2] All the tyrants of Persia, from Adhad el Dowlat (A.D. 977, D'Herbelot, p. 58, 59, 95) to Nadir Shah (A.D. 1743, Hist. de Nadir Shah, tom. ii. p. 155), have enriched the tomb of Ali with the spoils of the people. The dome is copper, with a bright and massy gilding, which glitters to the sun at the distance of many a mile.

[3] The city of Meshed Ali, five or six miles from the ruins of Cufa, and one hundred and twenty to the south of Bagdad, is of the size and form of the modern Jerusalem. Meshed Hosein, larger and more populous, is at the distance of thirty miles.

elsewhere than in the city of the prophet.[1] The policy of
Moawiyah eluded the valour of his rival; and, after the death of
Ali, he negotiated the abdication of his son Hassan, whose mind
was either above or below the government of the world, and who
retired without a sigh from the palace of Cufa to a humble cell
near the tomb of his grandfather. The aspiring wishes of the
caliph were finally crowned by the important change of an
elective to an hereditary kingdom. Some murmurs of freedom
or fanaticism attested the reluctance of the Arabs, and four
citizens of Medina refused the oath of fidelity; but the designs of
Moawiyah were conducted with vigour and address; and his son
Yezid, a feeble and dissolute youth, was proclaimed as the commander of the faithful and the successor of the apostle of God.

A familiar story is related of the benevolence of one of the
sons of Ali. In serving at table a slave had inadvertently
dropped a dish of scalding broth on his master: the heedless
wretch fell prostrate, to deprecate his punishment, and repeated
a verse of the Koran: " Paradise is for those who command
their anger: "—" I am not angry: "—" and for those who
pardon offences: "—" I pardon your offence: "—" and for
those who return good for evil: "—" I give you your liberty,
and four hundred pieces of silver." With an equal measure of
piety, Hosein, the younger brother of Hassan, inherited a
remnant of his father's spirit, and served with honour against
the Christians in the siege of Constantinople. The primogeniture of the line of Hashem, and the holy character of grandson of
the apostle, had centered in his person, and he was at liberty to
prosecute his claim against Yezid, the tyrant of Damascus,
whose vices he despised, and whose title he had never deigned
to acknowledge. A list was secretly transmitted from Cufa to
Medina, of one hundred and forty thousand Moslems, who professed their attachment to his cause, and who were eager to
draw their swords so soon as he should appear on the banks of
the Euphrates. Against the advice of his wisest friends, he
resolved to trust his person and family in the hands of a
perfidious people. He traversed the desert of Arabia with a
timorous retinue of women and children; but as he approached
the confines of Irak he was alarmed by the solitary or hostile
face of the country, and suspected either the defection or ruin
of his party. His fears were just: Obeidollah, the governor of

---

[1] I borrow, on this occasion, the strong sense and expression of Tacitus
(Hist. i. 4): Evulgato imperii arcano, posse imperatorem [principem] alibi
quam Romæ fieri.

Cafu, had extinguished the first sparks of an insurrection; and Hosein, in the plain of Kerbela, was encompassed by a body of five thousand horse, who intercepted his communication with the city and the river. He might still have escaped to a fortress in the desert that had defied the power of Cæsar and Chosroes, and confided in the fidelity of the tribe of Tai, which would have armed ten thousand warriors in his defence. In a conference with the chief of the enemy he proposed the option of three honourable conditions: that he should be allowed to return to Medina, or be stationed in a frontier garrison against the Turks, or safely conducted to the presence of Yezid. But the commands of the caliph, or his lieutenant, were stern and absolute; and Hosein was informed that he must either submit as a captive and a criminal to the commander of the faithful, or expect the consequences of his rebellion. "Do you think," replied he, "to terrify me with death?" And, during the short respite of a night, he prepared with calm and solemn resignation to encounter his fate. He checked the lamentations of his sister Fatima, who deplored the impending ruin of his house. "Our trust," said Hosein, "is in God alone. All things, both in heaven and earth, must perish and return to their Creator. My brother, my father, my mother, were better than me, and every Musulman has an example in the prophet." He pressed his friends to consult their safety by a timely flight: they unanimously refused to desert or survive their beloved master: and their courage was fortified by a fervent prayer and the assurance of paradise. On the morning of the fatal day, he mounted on horseback, with his sword in one hand and the Koran in the other: his generous band of martyrs consisted only of thirty-two horse and forty foot; but their flanks and rear were secured by the tent-ropes, and by a deep trench which they had filled with lighted faggots, according to the practice of the Arabs. The enemy advanced with reluctance, and one of their chiefs deserted, with thirty followers, to claim the partnership of inevitable death. In every close onset, or single combat, the despair of the Fatimites was invincible; but the surrounding multitudes galled them from a distance with a cloud of arrows, and the horses and men were successively slain: a truce was allowed on both sides for the hour of prayer; and the battle at length expired by the death of the last of the companions of Hosein. Alone, weary, and wounded, he seated himself at the door of his tent. As he tasted a drop of water, he was pierced in the mouth with a dart; and his son and nephew, two beautiful

youths, were killed in his arms. He lifted his hands to heaven
—they were full of blood—and he uttered a funeral prayer for
the living and the dead. In a transport of despair his sister
issued from the tent, and adjured the general of the Cufians
that he would not suffer Hosein to be murdered before his eyes:
a tear trickled down his venerable beard; and the boldest of his
soldiers fell back on every side as the dying hero threw himself
among them. The remorseless Shamer, a name detested by
the faithful, reproached their cowardice; and the grandson of
Mohammed was slain with three-and-thirty strokes of lances
and swords. After they had trampled on his body, they carried
his head to the castle of Cufa, and the inhuman Obeidollah
struck him on the mouth with a cane: " Alas," exclaimed an
aged Musulman, " on these lips have I seen the lips of the apostle
of God ! " In a distant age and climate the tragic scene of the
death of Hosein will awaken the sympathy of the coldest
reader.[1] On the annual festival of his martyrdom, in the devout
pilgrimage to his sepulchre, his Persian votaries abandon their
souls to the religious frenzy of sorrow and indignation.[2]

When the sisters and children of Ali were brought in chains to
the throne of Damascus, the caliph was advised to extirpate
the enmity of a popular and hostile race, whom he had injured
beyond the hope of reconciliation. But Yezid preferred the
counsels of mercy; and the mourning family was honourably
dismissed to mingle their tears with their kindred at Medina.
The glory of martyrdom superseded the right of primogeniture;
and the twelve IMAMS,[3] or pontiffs, of the Persian creed, are Ali,
Hassan, Hosein, and the lineal descendants of Hosein to the
ninth generation. Without arms, or treasures, or subjects,
they successively enjoyed the veneration of the people, and
provoked the jealousy of the reigning caliphs: their tombs, at
Mecca or Medina, on the banks of the Euphrates, or in the
province of Chorasan, are still visited by the devotion of their
sect. Their names were often the pretence of sedition and civil

[1] I have abridged the interesting narrative of Ockley (tom. ii. p. 170-
231). It is long and minute; but the pathetic, almost always, consists in
the detail of little circumstances.

[2] Niebuhr the Dane (Voyages en Arabie, etc., tom. ii. p. 208, etc.) is,
perhaps, the only European traveller who has dared to visit Meshed Ali
and Meshed Hosein. The two sepulchres are in the hands of the Turks,
who tolerate and tax the devotion of the Persian heretics. The festival of
the death of Hosein is amply described by Sir John Chardin, a traveller
whom I have often praised.

[3] The general article of *Imam*, in D'Herbelot's Bibliothèque, will indicate
the succession, and the lives of the *twelve* are given under their respective
names.

war: but these royal saints despised the pomp of the world; submitted to the will of God and the injustice of man; and devoted their innocent lives to the study and practice of religion. The twelfth and last of the Imams, conspicuous by the title of *Mahadi*, or the Guide, surpassed the solitude and sanctity of his predecessors. He concealed himself in a cavern near Bagdad: the time and place of his death are unknown; and his votaries pretend that he still lives, and will appear before the day of judgment to overthrow the tyranny of Dejal, or the Antichrist.[1] In the lapse of two or three centuries, the posterity of Abbas, the uncle of Mohammed, had multiplied to the number of thirty-three thousand:[2] the race of Ali might be equally prolific: the meanest individual was above the first and greatest of princes; and the most eminent were supposed to excel the perfection of angels. But their adverse fortune, and the wide extent of the Musulman empire, allowed an ample scope for every bold and artful impostor who claimed affinity with the holy seed: the sceptre of the Almohades, in Spain and Afric; of the Fatimites, in Egypt and Syria;[3] of the Sultans of Yemen; and of the Sophis of Persia;[4] has been consecrated by this vague and ambiguous title. Under their reigns it might be dangerous to dispute the legitimacy of their birth; and one of the Fatimite caliphs silenced an indiscreet question by drawing his scimitar: "This," said Moez, "is my pedigree; and these," casting a handful of gold to his soldiers—"and these are my kindred and my children." In the various conditions of princes, or

[1] The name of *Antichrist* may seem ridiculous, but the Mohammedans have liberally borrowed the fables of every religion (Sale's Preliminary Discourse, p. 80, 82). In the royal stable of Ispahan two horses were always kept saddled, one for the Mahadi himself, the other for his lieutenant, Jesus the son of Mary.

[2] In the year of the Hegira 200 (A.D. 815). See D'Herbelot, p. 546.

[3] D'Herbelot, p. 342. The enemies of the Fatimites disgraced them by a Jewish origin. Yet they accurately deduced their genealogy from Jaafar, the sixth Imam; and the impartial Abulfeda allows (Annal. Moslem. p. 230) that they were owned by many, qui absque controversiâ genuini sunt Alidarum, homines propaginum suæ gentis exacte callentes. He quotes some lines from the celebrated *Scherif* or *Radhi*, Egone humilitatem induam in terris hostium? (I suspect him to be an Edrissite of Sicily) cum in Ægypto sit Chalifa de gente Alii, quocum ego communem habeo patrem et vindicem.

[4] The kings of Persia of the last dynasty are descended from Sheik Sefi, a saint of the fourteenth century, and, through him, from Moussa Cassem, the son of Hosein, the son of Ali (Olearius, p. 957; Chardin, tom. iii. p. 288). But I cannot trace the intermediate degrees in any genuine or fabulous pedigree. If they were truly Fatimites, they might draw their origin from the princes of Mazanderan, who reigned in the ninth century (D'Herbelot, p. 96).

doctors, or nobles, or merchants, or beggars, a swarm of the genuine or fictitious descendants of Mohammed and Ali is honoured with the appellation of sheiks, or sherifs, or emirs. In the Ottoman empire they are distinguished by a green turban; receive a stipend from the treasury; are judged only by their chief; and, however debased by fortune or character, still assert the proud pre-eminence of their birth. A family of three hundred persons, the pure and orthodox branch of the caliph Hassan, is preserved without taint or suspicion in the holy cities of Mecca and Medina, and still retains, after the revolutions of twelve centuries, the custody of the temple and the sovereignty of their native land. The fame and merit of Mohammed would ennoble a plebeian race, and the ancient blood of the Koreish transcends the recent majesty of the kings of the earth.[1]

The talents of Mohammed are entitled to our applause; but his success has, perhaps, too strongly attracted our admiration. Are we surprised that a multitude of proselytes should embrace the doctrine and the passions of an eloquent fanatic? In the heresies of the church the same seduction has been tried and repeated from the time of the apostles to that of the reformers. Does it seem incredible that a private citizen should grasp the sword and the sceptre, subdue his native country, and erect a monarchy by his victorious arms? In the moving picture of the dynasties of the East, a hundred fortunate usurpers have arisen from a baser origin, surmounted more formidable obstacles, and filled a larger scope of empire and conquest. Mohammed was alike instructed to preach and to fight; and the union of these opposite qualities, while it enhanced his merit, contributed to his success: the operation of force and persuasion, of enthusiasm and fear, continually acted on each other, till every barrier yielded to their irresistible power. His voice invited the Arabs to freedom and victory, to arms and rapine, to the indulgence of their darling passions in this world and the other: the restraints which he imposed were requisite to establish the credit of the prophet, and to exercise the obedience of the people; and the only objection to his success was his rational creed of the unity and perfections of God. It is not the propagation, but the permanency of his religion, that deserves our

[1] The present state of the family of Mohammed and Ali is most accurately described by Demetrius Cantemir (Hist. of the Othman Empire, p. 94) and Niebuhr (Description de l'Arabie, p. 9-16, 317, etc.). It is much to be lamented that the Danish traveller was unable to purchase the chronicles of Arabia.

wonder: the same pure and perfect impression which he engraved at Mecca and Medina is preserved, after the revolutions of twelve centuries, by the Indian, the African, and the Turkish proselytes of the Koran. If the Christian apostles, St. Peter or St. Paul, could return to the Vatican, they might possibly inquire the name of the Deity who is worshipped with such mysterious rites in that magnificent temple: at Oxford or Geneva they would experience less surprise; but it might still be incumbent on them to peruse the catechism of the church, and to study the orthodox commentators on their own writings and the words of their Master. But the Turkish dome of St. Sophia, with an increase of splendour and size, represents the humble tabernacle erected at Medina by the hands of Mohammed. The Mohammedans have uniformly withstood the temptation of reducing the object of their faith and devotion to a level with the senses and imagination of man. " I believe in one God, and Mohammed the apostle of God," is the simple and invariable profession of Islam. The intellectual image of the Deity has never been degraded by any visible idol; the honours of the prophet have never transgressed the measure of human virtue; and his living precepts have restrained the gratitude of his disciples within the bounds of reason and religion. The votaries of Ali have, indeed, consecrated the memory of their hero, his wife, and his children; and some of the Persian doctors pretend that the divine essence was incarnate in the person of the Imams; but their superstition is universally condemned by the Sonnites; and their impiety has afforded a seasonable warning against the worship of saints and martyrs. The metaphysical questions on the attributes of God, and the liberty of man, have been agitated in the schools of the Mohammedans as well as in those of the Christians; but among the former they have never engaged the passions of the people, or disturbed the tranquillity of the state. The cause of this important difference may be found in the separation or union of the regal and sacerdotal characters. It was the interest of the caliphs, the successors of the prophet and commanders of the faithful, to repress and discourage all religious innovations: the order, the discipline, the temporal and spiritual ambition of the clergy, are unknown to the Moslems; and the sages of the law are the guides of their conscience and the oracles of their faith. From the Atlantic to the Ganges the Koran is acknowledged as the fundamental code, not only of theology but of civil and criminal jurisprudence; and the laws which regulate the actions and the property of mankind are guarded by the infallible and immutable sanction of the will of God. This religious servitude is attended with some practical disadvantage; the illiterate legislator had been often misled by his own prejudices and those of his country; and the institutions of the Arabian desert may be ill adapted to the wealth and numbers of Ispahan and Constantinople. On these occasions the Cadhi respectfully places on his head the holy volume, and substitutes a dexterous interpretation more apposite to the principles of equity and the manners and policy of the times.

His beneficial or pernicious influence on the public happiness is the last consideration in the character of Mohammed. The most bitter or most bigoted of his Christian or Jewish foes will surely allow that he assumed a false commission to inculcate a salutary doctrine, less perfect only than their own. He piously supposed, as the basis of his religion, the truth and sanctity of *their* prior revelations, the virtues and miracles of their founders. The idols of Arabia were broken before the throne of God; the blood of human victims was expiated by prayer, and fasting, and alms, the laudable or innocent arts of devotion; and his rewards and punishments of a future life were painted by the images most congenial to an ignorant and carnal generation. Mohammed was, perhaps, incapable of dictating a moral and political system for the use of his countrymen: but he breathed among the faithful a spirit of charity and friendship; recommended the practice of the social virtues; and checked, by his laws and precepts, the thirst of revenge, and the oppression of widows and orphans. The hostile tribes were united in faith and obedience, and the valour which had been idly spent in domestic quarrels was vigorously directed against a foreign enemy. Had the impulse been less powerful, Arabia, free at home, and formidable abroad, might have flourished under a succession of her native monarchs. Her sovereignty was lost by the extent and rapidity of conquest. The colonies of the nation were scattered over the East and West, and their blood was mingled with the blood of their converts and captives. After the reign of three caliphs, the throne was transported from Medina to the valley of Damascus and the banks of the Tigris; the holy cities were violated by impious war; Arabia was ruled by the rod of a subject, perhaps of a stranger; and the Bedoweens of the desert, awakening from their dream of dominion, resumed their old and solitary independence.[1]

[1] The writers of the Modern Universal History (vols. i. and ii.) have compiled in 850 folio pages the life of Mohammed and the annals of the

CHAPTER LI

The Conquest of Persia, Syria, Egypt, Africa, and Spain, by the Arabs or
Saracens—Empire of the Caliphs, or Successors of Mohammed—
State of the Christians, etc., under their Government

THE revolution of Arabia had not changed the character of the
Arabs: the death of Mohammed was the signal of independence;
and the hasty structure of his power and religion tottered to its
foundations. A small and faithful band of his primitive disciples had listened to his eloquence, and shared his distress; had
fled with the apostle from the persecution of Mecca, or had
received the fugitive in the walls of Medina. The increasing
myriads who acknowledged Mohammed as their king and prophet
had been compelled by his arms, or allured by his prosperity.
The polytheists were confounded by the simple idea of a solitary
and invisible God; the pride of the Christians and Jews disdained
the yoke of a mortal and contemporary legislator. Their habits
of faith and obedience were not sufficiently confirmed; and
many of the new converts regretted the venerable antiquity of
the law of Moses; or the rites and mysteries of the Catholic
church; or the idols, the sacrifices, the joyous festivals of their
Pagan ancestors. The jarring interests and hereditary feuds
of the Arabian tribes had not yet coalesced in a system of union
and subordination; and the barbarians were impatient of the
mildest and most salutary laws that curbed their passions or
violated their customs. They submitted with reluctance to the
religious precepts of the Koran, the abstinence from wine, the
fast of the Ramadan, and the daily repetition of five prayers;
and the alms and tithes which were collected for the treasury
of Medina could be distinguished only by a name from the payment of a perpetual and ignominious tribute. The example of
Mohammed had excited a spirit of fanaticism or imposture, and
several of his rivals presumed to imitate the conduct, and defy
the authority, of the living prophet. At the head of the *fugitives*
and *auxiliaries*, the first caliph was reduced to the cities of

caliphs. They enjoyed the advantage of reading, and sometimes correct-
ing, the Arabic text; yet, notwithstanding their high-sounding boasts, I
cannot find, after the conclusion of my work, that they have afforded me
much (if any) additional information. The dull mass is not quickened by
a spark of philosophy or taste; and the compilers indulge the criticism
of acrimonious bigotry against Boulainvilliers, Sale, Gagnier, and all who
have treated Mohammed with favour, or even justice.

Mecca, Medina, and Tayef; and perhaps the Koreish would have restored the idols of the Caaba, if their levity had not been checked by a seasonable reproof. " Ye men of Mecca, will ye be the last to embrace, and the first to abandon, the religion of Islam?" After exhorting the Moslems to confide in the aid of God and his apostle, Abubeker resolved, by a vigorous attack, to prevent the junction of the rebels. The women and children were safely lodged in the cavities of the mountains: the warriors, marching under eleven banners, diffused the terror of their arms; and the appearance of a military force revived and confirmed the loyalty of the faithful. The inconstant tribes accepted, with humble repentance, the duties of prayer, and fasting, and alms; and, after some examples of success and severity, the most daring apostates fell prostrate before the sword of the Lord and of Caled. In the fertile province of Yemanah,[1] between the Red Sea and the Gulf of Persia, in a city not inferior to Medina itself, a powerful chief, his name was Moseilama, had assumed the character of a prophet, and the tribe of Hanifa listened to his voice. A female prophetess was attracted by his reputation: the decencies of words and actions were spurned by these favourites of heaven;[2] and they employed several days in mystic and amorous converse. An obscure sentence of his Koran, or book, is yet extant;[3] and, in the pride of his mission, Moseilama condescended to offer a partition of the earth. The proposal was answered by Mohammed with contempt; but the rapid progress of the impostor awakened the fears of his successor: forty thousand Moslems were assembled under the standard of Caled;

---

[1] See the description of the city and country of Al Yamanah, in Abulfeda, Descript. Arabiæ, p. 60, 61. In the thirteenth century there were some ruins and a few palms; but in the present century the same ground is occupied by the visions and arms of a modern prophet, whose tenets are imperfectly known (Niebuhr, Description de l'Arabie, p. 296-302).

[2] Their first salutation may be transcribed, but cannot be translated. It was thus that Moseilama said or sung:—

Surge tandem itaque strenue permolenda; nam stratus tibi thorus est.
Aut in propatulo tentorio si velis, aut in abditiore cubiculo si malis;
Aut supinam te humi exporrectam fustigabo, si velis, aut si malis manibus pedibusque nixam.
Aut si velis ejus (*Priapi*) gemino triente, aut si malis totus veniam.
Imo, totus venito, O Apostole Dei, clamabat fœmina. Id ipsum, dicebat Moseilama, mihi quoque suggessit Deus.

The prophetess Segjah, after the fall of her lover, returned to idolatry; but, under the reign of Moawiyah, she became a Musulman, and died at Bassora (Abulfeda, Annal. vers. Reiske, p. 63).

[3] See this text, which demonstrates a God from the work of generation, in Abulpharagius (Specimen Hist. Arabum, p. 13; and Dynast. p. 103) and Abulfeda (Annal. p. 63).

and the existence of their faith was resigned to the event of a decisive battle. In the first action they were repulsed with the loss of twelve hundred men; but the skill and perseverance of their general prevailed: their defeat was avenged by the slaughter of ten thousand infidels; and Moseilama himself was pierced by an Æthiopian slave with the same javelin which had mortally wounded the uncle of Mohammed.[1] The various rebels of Arabia, without a chief or a cause, were speedily suppressed by the power and discipline of the rising monarchy; and the whole nation again professed, and more steadfastly held, the religion of the Koran. The ambition of the caliphs provided an immediate exercise for the restless spirit of the Saracens: their valour was united in the prosecution of a holy war; and their enthusiasm was equally confirmed by opposition and victory.

From the rapid conquests of the Saracens a presumption will naturally arise, that the first caliphs commanded in person the armies of the faithful, and sought the crown of martyrdom in the foremost ranks of the battle. The courage of Abubeker,[2] Omar,[3] and Othman[4] had indeed been tried in the persecution and wars of the prophet: and the personal assurance of paradise must have taught them to despise the pleasures and dangers of the present world. But they ascended the throne in a venerable or mature age; and esteemed the domestic cares of religion and justice the most important duties of a sovereign. Except the presence of Omar at the siege of Jerusalem, their longest expeditions were the frequent pilgrimage from Medina to Mecca; and they calmly received the tidings of victory as they prayed or preached before the sepulchre of the prophet. The austere and frugal measure of their lives was the effect of virtue or habit, and the pride of their simplicity insulted the vain magnificence of the kings of the earth. When Abubeker assumed the office of caliph, he enjoined his daughter Ayesha to take a strict account of his private patrimony, that it might be evident whether he were enriched or impoverished by the service of the state. He thought himself entitled to a stipend of three pieces of gold, with

---

[1] [The great loss sustained by the Moslems in this campaign was the occasion of Abu Bekr's ordering the Koran to be collected, being fearful that much of it might perish by the death of those in whose memory it was deposited.—O. S.]

[2] His reign in Eutychius, tom. ii. p. 251. Elmacin, p. 18. Abulpharagius, p. 108. Abulfeda, p. 60. D'Herbelot, p. 58.

[3] His reign in Eutychius, p. 264. Elmacin, p. 24. Abulpharagius, p. 110. Abulfeda, p. 66. D'Herbelot, p. 686.

[4] His reign in Eutychius, p. 323. Elmacin, p. 36. Abulpharagius. p. 115. Abulfeda, p. 75. D'Herbelot, p. 695.

the sufficient maintenance of a single camel and a black slave; but on the Friday of each week he distributed the residue of his own and the public money, first to the most worthy, and then to the most indigent, of the Moslems. The remains of his wealth, a coarse garment and five pieces of gold, were delivered to his successor, who lamented with a modest sigh his own inability to equal such an admirable model. Yet the abstinence and humility of Omar were not inferior to the virtues of Abubeker; his food consisted of barley-bread or dates; his drink was water; he preached in a gown that was torn or tattered in twelve places; and a Persian satrap, who paid his homage to the conqueror, found him asleep among the beggars on the steps of the mosch of Medina. Economy is the source of liberality, and the increase of the revenue enabled Omar to established a just and perpetual reward for the past and present services of the faithful. Careless of his own emolument, he assigned to Abbas, the uncle of the prophet, the first and most ample allowance of twenty-five thousand drachms or pieces of silver. Five thousand were allotted to each of the aged warriors, the relics of the field of Beder; and the last and meanest of the companions of Mohammed was distinguished by the annual reward of three thousand pieces. One thousand was the stipend of the veterans who had fought in the first battles against the Greeks and Persians; and the decreasing pay, as low as fifty pieces of silver, was adapted to the respective merit and seniority of the soldiers of Omar. Under his reign, and that of his predecessor, the conquerors of the East were the trusty servants of God and the people; the mass of the public treasure was consecrated to the expenses of peace and war; a prudent mixture of justice and bounty maintained the discipline of the Saracens, and they united, by a rare felicity, the despatch and execution of despotism with the equal and frugal maxims of a republican government. The heroic courage of Ali,[1] the consummate prudence of Moawiyah,[2] excited the emulation of their subjects; and the talents which had been exercised in the school of civil discord were more usefully applied to propagate the faith and dominion of the prophet. In the sloth and vanity of the palace of Damascus the succeeding princes of the house of Ommiyah were alike destitute of the qualifications of statesmen and of

[1] His reign in Eutychius, p. 343. Elmacin, p. 51. Abulpharagius, p. 117. Abulfeda, p. 83. D'Herbelot, p. 89.
[2] His reign in Eutychius, p. 344. Elmacin, p. 54. Abulpharagius, p. 123. Abulfeda, p. 101. D'Herbelot, p. 586.

saints.[1] Yet the spoils of unknown nations were continually laid at the foot of their throne, and the uniform ascent of the Arabian greatness must be ascribed to the spirit of the nation rather than the abilities of their chiefs. A large deduction must be allowed for the weakness of their enemies. The birth of Mohammed was fortunately placed in the most degenerate and disorderly period of the Persians, the Romans, and the barbarians of Europe: the empires of Trajan, or even of Constantine or Charlemagne, would have repelled the assault of the naked Saracens, and the torrent of fanaticism might have been obscurely lost in the sands of Arabia.

In the victorious days of the Roman republic it had been the aim of the senate to confine their councils and legions to a single war, and completely to suppress a first enemy before they provoked the hostilities of a second. These timid maxims of policy were disdained by the magnanimity or enthusiasm of the Arabian caliphs. With the same vigour and success they invaded the successors of Augustus and those of Artaxerxes; and the rival monarchies at the same instant became the prey of an enemy whom they had been so long accustomed to despise. In the ten years of the administration of Omar, the Saracens reduced to his obedience thirty-six thousand cities or castles, destroyed four thousand churches or temples of the unbelievers, and edified fourteen hundred moschs for the exercise of the religion of Mohammed. One hundred years after his flight from Mecca the arms and the reign of his successors extended from India to the Atlantic Ocean, over the various and distant provinces which may be comprised under the names of, I. Persia; II. Syria; III. Egypt; IV. Africa; and V. Spain. Under this general division I shall proceed to unfold these memorable transactions, despatching with brevity the remote and less interesting conquests of the East, and reserving a fuller narrative for those domestic countries which had been included within the pale of the Roman empire. Yet I must excuse my own defects by a just complaint of the blindness and insufficiency of my guides. The Greeks, so loquacious in controversy, have not been anxious to celebrate the triumphs of their enemies.[2] After

[1] Their reigns in Eutychius, tom. ii. p. 360-395. Elmacin, p. 59-108. Abulpharagius, Dynast. ix. p. 124-139. Abulfeda, p. 111-141. D'Herbelot, Bibliothèque Orientale, p. 691, and the particular articles of the Ommiades.

[2] For the seventh and eighth century, we have scarcely any original evidence of the Byzantine historians, except the chronicles of Theophanes (Theophanis Confessoris Chronographia, Gr. et Lat. cum notis Jacobi Goar. Paris, 1655, in folio), and the Abridgment of Nicephorus (Nicephori

a century of ignorance the first annals of the Musulmans were collected in a great measure from the voice of tradition.[1] Among the numerous productions of Arabic and Persian literature,[2] our interpreters have selected the imperfect sketches of a more recent age.[3] The art and genius of history have ever been unknown to the Asiatics;[4] they are ignorant of the laws of criticism; and our monkish chronicles of the same period may be compared to their most popular works, which are never vivified by the spirit of philosophy and freedom.   The *Oriental*

Patriarchæ C. P. Breviarium Historicum, Gr. et Lat. Paris, 1648, in folio), who both lived in the beginning of the ninth century (see Hanckius de Scriptor. Byzant. p. 200-246). Their contemporary, Photius, does not seem to be more opulent. After praising the style of Nicephorus, he adds, Καὶ ὅλως πολλούς ἐστι τῶν πρὸ αὐτοῦ ἀποκρυπτόμενος τῇδε τῆς ἱστορίας τῇ συγγραφῇ, and only complains of his extreme brevity (Phot. Biblioth. Cod. lxvi. p. 100 [p. 33, ed Bekk.]).   Some additions may be gleaned from the more recent histories of Cedrenus and Zonaras of the twelfth century.

[1] Tabari, or Al Tabari, a native of Taborestan, a famous Imam of Bagdad, and the Livy of the Arabians, finished his general history in the year of the Hegira 302 (A.D. 914). At the request of his friends he reduced a work of 30,000 sheets to a more reasonable size. But his Arabic original is known only by the Persian and Turkish versions. The Saracenic history of Ebn Amid, or Elmacin, is said to be an abridgment of the great Tabari (Ockley's Hist. of the Saracens, vol. ii. preface, p. xxxix.; and, list of authors, D'Herbelot, p. 866, 870, 1014).

[2] Besides the lists of authors framed by Prideaux (Life of Mahomet, p. 179-189), Ockley (at the end of his second volume), and Petit de la Croix (Hist. de Gengiscan, p. 525-550), we find in the Bibliothèque Orientale *Tarikh*, a catalogue of two or three hundred histories or chronicles of the East, of which not more than three or four are older than Tabari. A lively sketch of Oriental literature is given by Reiske (in his Prodidagmata ad Hagji Chalifæ librum memorialem ad calcem Abulfedæ Tabulæ Syriæ, Lipsiæ, 1766); but his project and the French version of Petit de la Croix (Hist. de Timur Bec, tom. i. preface, p. xlv.) have fallen to the ground.

[3] The particular historians and geographers will be occasionally introduced. The four following titles represent the Annals which have guided me in this general narrative:—1. *Annales Eutychii, Patriarchæ Alexandrini, ab Edwardo Pocockio, Oxon.* 1656, 2 vols. in 4to. A pompous edition of an indifferent author, translated by Pocock to gratify the presbyterian prejudices of his friend Selden. 2. *Historia Saracenica Georgii Elmacini, operâ et studio Thomæ Erpenii*, in 4to, *Lugd. Batavorum*, 1625. He is said to have hastily translated a corrupt MS., and his version is often deficient in style and sense. 3. *Historia compendiosa Dynastiarum a Gregorio Abulpharagio, interprete Edwardo Pocockio*, in 4to, *Oxon.* 1663. More useful for the literary than the civil history of the East. 4. *Abulfedæ Annales Moslemici ad Ann. Hegiræ ccccvi. a Jo. Jac. Reiske*, in 4to, *Lipsiæ*, 1754. The best of our chronicles, both for the original and version, yet how far below the name of Abulfeda! We know that he wrote at Hamah in the fourteenth century. The three former were Christians of the tenth, twelfth, and thirteenth centuries; the two first, natives of Egypt—a Melchite patriarch, and a Jacobite scribe.

[4] M. de Guignes (Hist. des Huns, tom. i. pref. p. xix. xx.) has characterised, with truth and knowledge, the two sorts of Arabian historians—the dry annalist, and the tumid and flowery orator.

library of a Frenchman [1] would instruct the most learned mufti of the East; and perhaps the Arabs might not find in a single historian so clear and comprehensive a narrative of their own exploits as that which will be deduced in the ensuing sheets.

I. In the first year of the first caliph, his lieutenant Chaled, the Sword of God, and the scourge of the infidels, advanced to the banks of the Euphrates, and reduced the cities of Anbar and Hira. Westward of the ruins of Babylon, a tribe of sedentary Arabs had fixed themselves on the verge of the desert; and Hira was the seat of a race of kings who had embraced the Christian religion, and reigned above six hundred years under the shadow of the throne of Persia. [2] The last of the Mondars was defeated and slain by Chaled; his son was sent a captive to Medina; his nobles bowed before the successor of the prophet; the people was tempted by the example and success of their countrymen; and the caliph accepted as the first-fruits of foreign conquest an annual tribute of seventy thousand pieces of gold. The conquerors, and even their historians, were astonished by the dawn of their future greatness: " In the same year," says Elmacin, " Chaled fought many signal battles: an immense multitude of the infidels was slaughtered, and spoils infinite and innumerable were acquired by the victorious Moslems." [3] But the invincible Chaled was soon transferred to the Syrian war: the invasion of the Persian frontier was conducted by less active or less prudent commanders: the Saracens were repulsed with loss in the passage of the Euphrates; and, though they chastised the insolent pursuit of the Magians, their remaining forces still hovered in the desert of Babylon.

[1] Bibliothèque Orientale, par M. D'Herbelot, in folio, Páris, 1697. For the character of the respectable author consult his friend Thevenot (Voyages du Levant, part i. chap. 1). His work is an agreeable miscellany, which must gratify every taste; but I never can digest the alphabetical order; and I find him more satisfactory in the Persian than the Arabic history. The recent supplement from the papers of MM. Visdelou and Galland (in folio, La Haye, 1779) is of a different cast, a medley of tales, proverbs, and Chinese antiquities.

[2] Pocock will explain the chronology (Specimen Hist. Arabum, p. 66-74), and D'Anville the geography (l'Euphrate et le Tigre, p. 125), of the dynasty of the Almondars. The English scholar understood more Arabic than the mufti of Aleppo (Ockley, vol. ii. p. 34); the French geographer is equally at home in every age and every climate of the world.
[Hira was situated only a few miles north-west of the more modern Cufa. It was founded by the Arabs about A.D. 190, and therefore could not have existed six centuries as represented in the text.—O. S.]

[3] Fecit et Chaled plurima in hoc anno prælia, in quibus vicerunt Muslimi, et *infidelium* immensâ multitudine occisâ spolia infinita et innumera sunt nacti (Hist. Saracenica, p. 20). The Christian annalist slides into the national and compendious term of *infidels*, and I often adopt (I hope without scandal) this characteristic mode of expression.

The indignation and fears of the Persians suspended for a
moment their intestine divisions. By the unanimous sentence of
the priests and nobles, their queen Arzema was deposed; the
sixth of the transient usurpers who had arisen and vanished in
three or four years since the death of Chosroes and the retreat of
Heraclius. Her tiara was placed on the head of Yezdegerd, the
grandson of Chosroes; and the same era, which coincides with an
astronomical period,[1] has recorded the fall of the Sassanian
dynasty and the religion of Zoroaster.[2] The youth and inex-
perience of the prince—he was only fifteen years of age—declined
a perilous encounter; the royal standard was delivered into the
hands of his general Rustam; and a remnant of thirty thousand
regular troops was swelled in truth, or in opinion, to one hundred
and twenty thousand subjects, or allies, of the Great King. The
Moslems, whose numbers were reinforced from twelve to thirty
thousand, had pitched their camp in the plains of Cadesia:[3] and
their line, though it consisted of fewer *men*, could produce more
soldiers, than the unwieldy host of the infidels. I shall here
observe what I must often repeat, that the charge of the Arabs
was not, like that of the Greeks and Romans, the effort of a firm
and compact infantry: their military force was chiefly formed of

---

[1] A cycle of 120 years, at the end of which an intercalary month of 30
days supplied the use of our Bissextile, and restored the integrity of the
solar year. In a great revolution of 1440 years this intercalation was successively removed from the first to the twelfth month; but Hyde and
Freret are involved in a profound controversy, whether the twelve, or only
eight of these changes were accomplished before the era of Yezdegerd,
which is unanimously fixed to the 16th of June, A.D. 632. How laboriously
does the curious spirit of Europe explore the darkest and most distant
antiquities (Hyde, de Religione Persarum, c. 14-18, p. 181-211; Freret in
the Mém. de l'Académie des Inscriptions, tom. xvi. p. 233-267)!

[2] Nine days after the death of Mahomet (7th June, A.D. 632) we find the
era of Yezdegerd (16th June, A.D. 632), and his accession cannot be postponed beyond the end of the first year. His predecessors could not therefore resist the arms of the caliph Omar; and these unquestionable dates
overthrow the thoughtless chronology of Abulpharagius. See Ockley's
Hist. of the Saracens, vol. i. p. 130.

[3] Cadesia, says the Nubian geographer (p. 121), is, in margine solitudinis,
61 leagues from Bagdad, and two stations from Cufa. Otter (Voyage, tom.
i. p. 163) reckons 15 leagues, and observes that the place is supplied with
dates and water.

[The battle of Cadesia was one of the decisive battles of the world.
Layard, in his *Nineveh and Babylon*, says, " The ruins of Cadesia may be
seen on both sides of the Tigris. Sailing down the Tigris the traveller
perceives huge masses of brickwork jutting out from the falling banks, or
overhanging the precipice of earth that hems in the stream. Here and
there are more perfect ruins of buildings, walls of solid masonry of the
Sassanian period, and cupolas fretted with the elegant tracery of early
Arabic architecture. These are the remains of the palaces and castles of
the last Persian kings and of the first caliphs."—O. S.]

cavalry and archers; and the engagement, which was often interrupted and often renewed by single combats and flying skirmishes, might be protracted without any decisive event to the continuance of several days. The periods of the battle of Cadesia were distinguished by their peculiar appellations. The first, from the well-timed appearance of six thousand of the Syrian brethren, was denominated the day of *succour*. The day of *concussion* might express the disorder of one, or perhaps of both, of the contending armies. The third, a nocturnal tumult, received the whimsical name of the night of *barking*, from the discordant clamours, which were compared to the inarticulate sounds of the fiercest animals. The morning of the succeeding day determined the fate of Persia; and a seasonable whirlwind drove a cloud of dust against the faces of the unbelievers. The clangour of arms was re-echoed to the tent of Rustam, who, far unlike the ancient hero of his name, was gently reclining in a cool and tranquil shade, amidst the baggage of his camp, and the train of mules that were laden with gold and silver. On the sound of danger he started from his couch; but his flight was overtaken by a valiant Arab, who caught him by the foot, struck off his head, hoisted it on a lance, and, instantly returning to the field of battle, carried slaughter and dismay among the thickest ranks of the Persians. The Saracens confess a loss of seven thousand five hundred men; and the battle of Cadesia is justly described by the epithets of obstinate and atrocious.[1] The standard of the monarchy was overthrown and captured in the field—a leathern apron of a blacksmith who in ancient times had arisen the deliverer of Persia; but this badge of heroic poverty was disguised and almost concealed by a profusion of precious gems.[2] After this victory the wealthy province of Irak, or Assyria, submitted to the caliph, and his conquests were firmly established by the speedy foundation of Bassora,[3] a place which ever commands the trade and navigation of the Persians. At the distance of fourscore miles from the Gulf the Euphrates and Tigris unite in a broad and direct current, which is aptly styled

---

[1] Atrox, contumax, plus semel renovatum, are the well-chosen expressions of the translator of Abulfeda (Reiske, p. 69).

[2] D'Herbelot, Bibliothèque Orientale, p. 297, 348.

[3] The reader may satisfy himself on the subject of Bassora by consulting the following writers:—Geograph. Nubiens. p. 121; D'Herbelot, Bibliothèque Orientale, p. 192; D'Anville, L'Euphrate et le Tigre, p. 130, 133, 145; Raynal, Hist. Philosophique des deux Indes, tom. ii. p. 92-100; Voyages di Pietro della Valle, tom. iv. p. 370-391; De Tavernier, tom. i. p. 240-247; De Thevenot, tom. ii. p. 545-584; D'Otter, tom. ii. p. 45-78; De Niebuhr, tom. ii. p. 172-199.

the river of the Arabs. In the midway, between the junction and the mouth of these famous streams, the new settlement was planted on the western bank: the first colony was composed of eight hundred Moslems; but the influence of the situation soon reared a flourishing and populous capital. The air, though excessively hot, is pure and healthy; the meadows are filled with palm-trees and cattle; and one of the adjacent valleys has been celebrated among the four paradises or gardens of Asia. Under the first caliphs the jurisdiction of this Arabian colony extended over the southern provinces of Persia; the city has been sanctified by the tombs of the companions and martyrs; and the vessels of Europe still frequent the port of Bassora, as a convenient station and passage of the Indian trade.

After the defeat of Cadesia, a country intersected by rivers and canals might have opposed an insuperable barrier to the victorious cavalry; and the walls of Ctesiphon or Madayn, which had resisted the battering-rams of the Romans, would not have yielded to the darts of the Saracens. But the flying Persians were overcome by the belief that the last day of their religion and empire was at hand; the strongest posts were abandoned by treachery or cowardice; and the king, with a part of his family and treasures, escaped to Holwan, at the foot of the Median hills. In the third month after the battle, Said, the lieutenant of Omar, passed the Tigris without opposition; the capital was taken by assault; and the disorderly resistance of the people gave a keener edge to the sabres of the Moslems, who shouted with religious transport, " This is the white palace of Chosroes; this is the promise of the apostle of God!" The naked robbers of the desert were suddenly enriched beyond the measure of their hope or knowledge. Each chamber revealed a new treasure secreted with art, or ostentatiously displayed; the gold and silver, the various wardrobes and precious furniture, surpassed (says Abulfeda) the estimate of fancy or numbers; and another historian defines the untold and almost infinite mass by the fabulous computation of three thousands of thousands of thousands of pieces of gold.[1] Some minute though curious facts represent the contrast of riches and ignorance. From the remote islands of the Indian Ocean a large provision of camphire [2]

[1] Mente vix potest numerove comprehendi quanta spolia . . . nostris cesserint. Abulfeda, p. 69. Yet I still suspect that the extravagant numbers of Elmacin may be the error, not of the text, but of the version. The best translators from the Greek, for instance, I find to be very poor arithmeticians.

[2] The camphire-tree grows in China and Japan, but many hundredweight

had been imported, which is employed with a mixture of wax to illuminate the palaces of the East. Strangers to the name and properties of that odoriferous gum, the Saracens, mistaking it for salt, mingled the camphire in their bread, and were astonished at the bitterness of the taste. One of the apartments of the palace was decorated with a carpet of silk, sixty cubits in length, and as many in breadth: a paradise or garden was depictured on the ground; the flowers, fruits, and shrubs were imitated by the figures of the gold embroidery, and the colours of the precious stones; and the ample square was encircled by a variegated and verdant border. The Arabian general persuaded his soldiers to relinquish their claim, in the reasonable hope that the eyes of the caliph would be delighted with the splendid workmanship of nature and industry. Regardless of the merit of art and the pomp of royalty, the rigid Omar divided the prize among his brethren of Medina: the picture was destroyed; but such was the intrinsic value of the materials, that the share of Ali alone was sold for twenty thousand drams. A mule that carried away the tiara and cuirass, the belt and bracelets of Chosroes, was overtaken by the pursuers; the gorgeous trophy was presented to the commander of the faithful; and the gravest of the companions condescended to smile when they beheld the white beard, hairy arms, and uncouth figure of the veteran who was invested with the spoils of the Great King.[1] The sack of Ctesiphon was followed by its desertion and gradual decay. The Saracens disliked the air and situation of the place, and Omar was advised by his general to remove the seat of government to the Western side of the Euphrates. In every age the foundation and ruin of the Assyrian cities has been easy and rapid: the country is destitute of stone and timber; and the most solid structures [2] are composed of bricks baked in the sun, and joined by a cement of the native bitumen. The name of *Cufa* [3] describes an habitation of reeds and earth; but the importance of the new capital was

---

of those meaner sorts are exchanged for a single pound of the more precious gum of Borneo and Sumatra (Raynal, Hist. Philosoph. tom. i. p. 362-365; Dictionnaire d'Hist. Naturelle par Bomare; Miller's Gardener's Dictionary). These may be the islands of the first climate from whence the Arabians imported their camphire (Geograph. Nub. p. 34, 35; D'Herbelot, p. 232).

[1] See Gagnier, Vie de Mahomet, tom. i. p. 376, 377. I may credit the fact without believing the prophecy.

[2] The most considerable ruins of Assyria are the tower of Belus, at Babylon, and the hall of Chosroes, at Ctesiphon: they have been visited by that vain and curious traveller Pietro della Valle (tom. i. p. 713-718, 731-735).

[3] Consult the article of *Coufah* in the Bibliothèque of D'Herbelot (p. 277, 278), and the second volume of Ockley's History, particularly p. 40 and 153.

supported by the numbers, wealth, and spirit of a colony of veterans; and their licentiousness was indulged by the wisest caliphs, who were apprehensive of provoking the revolt of a hundred thousand swords: " Ye men of Cufa," said Ali, who solicited their aid, " you have been always conspicuous by your valour. You conquered the Persian king and scattered his forces, till you had taken possession of his inheritance." This mighty conquest was achieved by the battles of Jalula and Nehavend. After the loss of the former, Yezdegerd fled from Holwan, and concealed his shame and despair in the mountains of Farsistan, from whence Cyrus had descended with his equal and valiant companions. The courage of the nation survived that of the monarch: among the hills to the south of Ecbatana or Hamadan one hundred and fifty thousand Persians made a third and final stand for their religion and country; and the decisive battle of Nehavend was styled by the Arabs the victory of victories. If it be true that the flying general of the Persians was stopped and overtaken in a crowd of mules and camels laden with honey, the incident, however slight or singular, will denote the luxurious impediments of an Oriental army.[1]

The geography of Persia is darkly delineated by the Greeks and Latins; but the most illustrious of her cities appear to be more ancient than the invasion of the Arabs. By the reduction of Hamadan and Ispahan, of Caswin, Tauris, and Rei, they gradually approached the shores of the Caspian Sea: and the orators of Mecca might applaud the success and spirit of the faithful, who had already lost sight of the northern bear, and had almost transcended the bounds of the habitable world.[2] Again turning towards the West and the Roman empire, they repassed the Tigris over the bridge of Mosul, and, in the captive provinces of Armenia and Mesopotamia, embraced their victorious brethren of the Syrian army. From the palace of Madayn their Eastern progress was not less rapid or extensive. They advanced along the Tigris and the Gulf, penetrated through the passes of the

---

[1] See the article of *Nehavena*, in D'Herbelot, p. 667, 668; and Voyages en Turquie et en Perse, par Otter, tom. i. p. 191.

[2] It is in such a style of ignorance and wonder that the Athenian orator describes the Arctic conquests of Alexander, who never advanced beyond the shores of the Caspian. Ἀλέξανδρος ἔξω τῆς ἄρκτου καὶ τῆς οἰκουμένης, ὀλίγου δεῖν, πάσης μεθειστήκει. Æschines contra Ctesiphontem, tom. iii. p. 554, edit. Græc. Orator. Reiske. This memorable cause was pleaded at Athens, Olymp. cxii. 3 (before Christ 330), in the autumn (Taylor, præfat. p. 370, etc.), about a year after the battle of Arbela; and Alexander, in the pursuit of Darius, was marching towards Hyrcania and Bactriana.

mountains into the valley of Estachar or Persepolis, and profaned the last sanctuary of the Magian empire. The grandson of Chosroes was nearly surprised among the falling columns and mutilated figures—a sad emblem of the past and present fortune of Persia:[1] he fled with accelerated haste over the desert of Kirman, implored the aid of the warlike Segestans, and sought a humble refuge on the verge of the Turkish and Chinese power. But a victorious army is insensible of fatigue: the Arabs divided their forces in the pursuit of a timorous enemy; and the caliph Othman promised the government of Chorasan to the first general who should enter that large and populous country, the kingdom of the ancient Bactrians. The condition was accepted; the prize was deserved; the standard of Mohammed was planted on the walls of Herat, Merou, and Balch; and the successful leader neither halted nor reposed till his foaming cavalry had tasted the waters of the Oxus. In the public anarchy the independent governors of the cities and castles obtained their separate capitulations; the terms were granted or imposed by the esteem, the prudence, or the compassion of the victors; and a simple profession of faith established the distinction between a brother and a slave. After a noble defence, Harmozan, the prince or satrap of Ahwaz and Susa, was compelled to surrender his person and his state to the discretion of the caliph; and their interview exhibits a portrait of the Arabian manners. In the presence, and by the command, of Omar the gay barbarian was despoiled of his silken robes embroidered with gold, and of his tiara bedecked with rubies and emeralds: " Are you now sensible," said the conqueror to his naked captive, " are you now sensible of the judgment of God, and of the different rewards of infidelity and obedience? " " Alas! " replied Harmozan, " I feel them too deeply. In the days of our common ignorance we fought with the weapons of the flesh, and my nation was superior. God was then neuter: since he has espoused your quarrel, you have subverted our kingdom and religion." Oppressed by this painful dialogue, the Persian complained of intolerable thirst, but discovered some apprehension lest he should be killed whilst he was drinking a cup of water. " Be of good courage," said the caliph; " your life is safe till you have drunk this water: " the crafty satrap accepted the assurance, and instantly dashed the vase against the ground. Omar would have avenged the deceit, but

---

[1] We are indebted for this curious particular to the Dynasties of Abulpharagius, p. 116; but it is needless to prove the identity of Estachar and Persepolis (D'Herbelot, p. 327); and still more needless to copy the drawings and descriptions of Sir John Chardin, or Corneille le Bruyn.

his companions represented the sanctity of an oath; and the speedy conversion of Harmozan entitled him not only to a free pardon, but even to a stipend of two thousand pieces of gold. The administration of Persia was regulated by an actual survey of the people, the cattle, and the fruits of the earth; [1] and this monument, which attests the vigilance of the caliphs, might have instructed the philosophers of every age. [2]

The flight of Yezdegerd had carried him beyond the Oxus, and as far as the Jaxartes, two rivers [3] of ancient and modern renown, which descend from the mountains of India towards the Caspian Sea. He was hospitably entertained by Tarkhan, prince of Fargana, [4] a fertile province on the Jaxartes: the king of Samarcand, with the Turkish tribes of Sogdiana and Scythia, were moved by the lamentations and promises of the fallen monarch; and he solicited, by a suppliant embassy, the more solid and powerful friendship of the emperor of China. [5] The virtuous Taitsong, [6] the first of the dynasty of the Tang, may be justly compared with the Antonines of Rome: his people enjoyed the blessings of prosperity and peace; and his dominion was acknowledged by forty-four hordes of the barbarians of Tartary. His last garrisons of Cashgar and Khoten maintained a frequent intercourse with their neighbours of the Jaxartes and Oxus; a recent colony of Persians had introduced into China the astronomy of the Magi; and Taitsong might be alarmed by the rapid progress and dangerous vicinity of the Arabs. The influence, and perhaps the supplies, of China revived the hopes of

---

[1] After the conquest of Persia, Theophanes adds, αὐτῷ δὲ τῷ χρόνῳ ἐκέλευσεν Οὔμαρος ἀναγραφῆναι πᾶσαν τὴν ὑπ' αὐτὸν οἰκουμένην· ἐγένετο δὲ ἡ ἀναγραφὴ καὶ ἀνθρώπων καὶ κτηνῶν καὶ θυτῶν (Chronograph. p. 283 [tom. i. p. 522, ed. Bonn]).

[2] Amidst our meagre relations, I must regret that D'Herbelot has not found and used a Persian translation of Tabari, enriched, as he says, with many extracts from the native historians of the Ghebers or Magi (Bibliothèque Orientale, p. 1014).

[3] The most authentic accounts of the two rivers, the Sihon (Jaxartes) and the Gihon (Oxus), may be found in Sherif al Edrisi (Geograph. Nubiens. p. 138); Abulfeda (Descript. Chorasan. in Hudson, tom. iii. p. 23); Abulghazi Khan, who reigned on their banks (Hist. Généalogique des Tatars, p. 32, 57, 766); and the Turkish Geographer, a MS. in the king of France's library (Examen Critique des Historiens d'Alexandre, p. 194-360).

[4] The territory of Fargana is described by Abulfeda, p. 76, 77.

[5] Eo redegit angustiarum eundem regem exsulem, ut Turcici regis, et Sogdiani, et Sinensis, auxilia missis literis imploraret (Abulfed. Annal. p. 74). The connection of the Persian and Chinese history is illustrated by Freret (Mém. de l'Académie, tom. xvi. p. 245-255), and De Guignes (Hist. des Huns, tom. i. p. 54-59; and for the geography of the borders, tom. ii. p. 1-43).

[6] Hist. Sinica, p. 41-46, in the third part of the Relations Curieuses of Thevenot.

Yezdegerd and the zeal of the worshippers of fire; and he returned with an army of Turks to conquer the inheritance of his fathers. The fortunate Moslems, without unsheathing their swords, were the spectators of his ruin and death. The grandson of Chosroes was betrayed by his servant, insulted by the seditious inhabitants of Merou, and oppressed, defeated, and pursued by his barbarian allies. He reached the banks of a river, and offered his rings and bracelets for an instant passage in a miller's boat. Ignorant or insensible of royal distress, the rustic replied that four drams of silver were the daily profit of his mill, and that he would not suspend his work unless the loss were repaid. In this moment of hesitation and delay the last of the Sassanian kings was overtaken and slaughtered by the Turkish cavalry, in the nineteenth year of his unhappy reign.[1] His son Firuz, a humble client of the Chinese emperor, accepted the station of captain of his guards; and the Magian worship was long preserved by a colony of loyal exiles in the province of Bucharia. His grandson inherited the regal name; but after a faint and fruitless enterprise he returned to China, and ended his days in the palace of Sigan. The male line of the Sassanides was extinct; but the female captives, the daughters of Persia, were given to the conquerors in servitude or marriage; and the race of the caliphs and imams was ennobled by the blood of their royal mothers.[2]

After the fall of the Persian kingdom, the river Oxus divided the territories of the Saracens and of the Turks. This narrow boundary was soon overleaped by the spirit of the Arabs; the governors of Chorasan extended their successive inroads; and one of their triumphs was adorned with the buskin of a Turkish queen, which she dropped in her precipitate flight beyond the hills of Bochara.[3] But the final conquest of Transoxiana,[4] as

[1] I have endeavoured to harmonise the various narratives of Elmacin (Hist. Saracen. p. 37), Abulpharagius (Dynast. p. 116), Abulfeda (Annal. p. 74, 79), and D'Herbelot (p. 485). The end of Yezdegerd was not only unfortunate, but obscure.

[2] The two daughters of Yezdegerd married Hassan, the son of Ali, and Mohammed, the son of Abubeker; and the first of these was the father of a numerous progeny. The daughter of Phirouz became the wife of the caliph Walid, and their son Yezid derived his genuine or fabulous descent from the Chosroes of Persia, the Cæsars of Rome, and the Chagans of the Turks or Avars (D'Herbelot, Biblioth. Orientale, p. 96, 487).

[3] It was valued at 2000 pieces of gold, and was the prize of Obeidollah, the son of Ziyad, a name afterwards infamous by the murder of Hosein (Ockley's History of the Saracens, vol. ii. p. 142, 143). His brother Salem was accompanied by his wife, the first Arabian woman (A.D. 680) who passed the Oxus: she borrowed, or rather stole, the crown and jewels of the princess of the Sogdians (p. 231, 232).

[4] A part of Abulfeda's geography is translated by Greaves, inserted in

well as of Spain, was reserved for the glorious reign of the inactive Walid; and the name of Catibah, the camel-driver, declares
the origin and merit of his successful lieutenant. While one of
his colleagues displayed the first Mohammedan banner on the
banks of the Indus, the spacious regions between the Oxus, the
Jaxartes, and the Caspian Sea were reduced by the arms of
Catibah to the obedience of the prophet and of the caliph.[1] A
tribute of two millions of pieces of gold was imposed on the
infidels; their idols were burnt or broken; the Musulman chief
pronounced a sermon in the new mosch of Carizme; after several
battles the Turkish hordes were driven back to the desert; and
the emperors of China solicited the friendship of the victorious
Arabs. To their industry the prosperity of the province, the
Sogdiana of the ancients, may in a great measure be ascribed;
but the advantages of the soil and climate had been understood
and cultivated since the reign of the Macedonian kings. Before
the invasion of the Saracens, Carizme, Bochara, and Samarcand
were rich and populous under the yoke of the shepherds of the
north. These cities were surrounded with a double wall; and
the exterior fortification, of a larger circumference, enclosed the
fields and gardens of the adjacent district. The mutual wants of
India and Europe were supplied by the diligence of the Sogdian
merchants; and the inestimable art of transforming linen into
paper has been diffused from the manufacture of Samarcand
over the Western world.[2]

II. No sooner had Abubeker restored the unity of faith and
government than he despatched a circular letter to the Arabian
tribes. "In the name of the most merciful God, to the rest of
the true believers. Health and happiness, and the mercy and
blessing of God, be upon you. I praise the most high God, and I
pray for his prophet Mohammed. This is to acquaint you that I

Hudson's collection of the minor geographers (tom. iii.), and entitled,
Descriptio Chorasmiæ et *Mawaralnahræ*, id est, regionum extra fluvium,
Oxum, p. 80. The name of *Transoxiana*, softer in sound, equivalent in
sense, is aptly used by Petit de la Croix (Hist. de Gengiscan, etc.) and
some modern Orientalists, but they are mistaken in ascribing it to the
writers of antiquity.

[1] The conquests of Catibah are faintly marked by Elmacin (Hist. Saracen.
p. 84), D'Herbelot (Biblioth. Orient. *Catbah, Samarcand Valid.*), and De
Guignes (Hist. des Huns, tom. i. p. 58, 59).

[2] A curious description of Samarcand is inserted in the Bibliotheca
Arabico-Hispana, tom. i. p. 208, etc. The librarian Casiri (tom. ii. 9)
relates from credible testimony that paper was first imported from China
to Samarcand, A.H. 30, and *invented*, or rather introduced, at Mecca,
A.H. 88. The Escurial library contains paper MSS. as old as the fourth or
fifth century of the Hegira.

intend to send the true believers into Syria [1] to take it out of the hands of the infidels. And I would have you know that the fighting for religion is an act of obedience to God." His messengers returned with the tidings of pious and martial ardour which they had kindled in every province; and the camp of Medina was successively filled with the intrepid bands of the Saracens, who panted for action, complained of the heat of the season and the scarcity of provisions, and accused with impatient murmurs the delays of the caliph. As soon as their numbers were complete, Abubeker ascended the hill, reviewed the men, the horses, and the arms, and poured forth a fervent prayer for the success of their undertaking. In person and on foot he accompanied the first day's march; and when the blushing leaders attempted to dismount, the caliph removed their scruples by a declaration that those who rode and those who walked in the service of religion were equally meritorious. His instructions [2] to the chiefs of the Syrian army were inspired by the warlike fanaticism which advances to seize and affects to despise the objects of earthly ambition. "Remember," said the successor of the prophet, "that you are always in the presence of God, on the verge of death, in the assurance of judgment, and the hope of paradise. Avoid injustice and oppression; consult with your brethren, and study to preserve the love and confidence of your troops. When you fight the battles of the Lord, acquit yourselves like men, without turning your backs; but let not your victory be stained with the blood of women or children. Destroy no palm-trees, nor burn any fields of corn. Cut down no fruit-trees, nor do any mischief to cattle, only such as you kill to eat. When you make any covenant or article, stand to it, and be as good as your word. As you go on, you will find some religious persons who live retired

---

[1] A separate history of the conquest of Syria has been composed by Al Wakidi, cadi of Bagdad, who was born A.D. 748, and died A.D. 822: he likewise wrote the conquest of Egypt, of Diarbekir, etc. Above the meagre and recent chronicles of the Arabians, Al Wakidi has the double merit of antiquity and copiousness. His tales and traditions afford an artless picture of the men and the times. Yet his narrative is too often defective, trifling, and improbable. Till something better shall be found, his learned and spirited interpreter (Ockley, in his History of the Saracens, vol. i. p. 21-342) will not deserve the petulant animadversion of Reiske (Prodidagmata ad Hagji Chalifæ Tabulas, p. 236). I am sorry to think that the labours of Ockley were consummated in a jail (see his two prefaces to the first vol. A.D. 1708, to the second, 1718, with the list of authors at the end).

[2] The instructions, etc., of the Syrian war are described by Al Wakidi and Ockley, tom. i. p. 22-27, etc. In the sequel it is necessary to contract, and needless to quote, their circumstantial narrative. My obligations to others shall be noticed.

in monasteries, and propose to themselves to serve God that way: let them alone, and neither kill them nor destroy their monasteries:[1] and you will find another sort of people, that belong to the synagogue of Satan, who have shaven crowns;[2] be sure you cleave their skulls, and give them no quarter till they either turn Mohammedans or pay tribute." All profane or frivolous conversation, all dangerous recollection of ancient quarrels, was severely prohibited among the Arabs: in the tumult of a camp the exercises of religion were assiduously practised; and the intervals of action were employed in prayer, meditation, and the study of the Koran. The abuse, or even the use, of wine was chastised by fourscore strokes on the soles of the feet, and in the fervour of their primitive zeal many secret sinners revealed their fault and solicited their punishment. After some hesitation, the command of the Syrian army was delegated to Abu Obeidah, one of the fugitives of Mecca, and companions of Mohammed; whose zeal and devotion were assuaged, without being abated, by the singular mildness and benevolence of his temper. But in all the emergencies of war the soldiers demanded the superior genius of Chaled; and whoever might be the choice of the prince, the *Sword of God* was both in fact and fame the foremost leader of the Saracens. He obeyed without reluctance; he was consulted without jealousy; and such was the spirit of the man, or rather of the times, that Chaled professed his readiness to serve under the banner of the faith, though it were in the hands of a child or an enemy. Glory and riches and dominion were indeed promised to the victorious Musulman; but he was carefully instructed, that, if the goods of this life were his only incitement, *they* likewise would be his only reward.

One of the fifteen provinces of Syria, the cultivated lands to the eastward of the Jordan, had been decorated by Roman vanity with the name of *Arabia*;[3] and the first arms of the

---

[1] Notwithstanding this precept, M. Pauw (Recherches sur les Egyptiens, tom. ii. p. 192, edit. Laûsanne) represents the Bedoweens as the implacable enemies of the Christian monks. For my own part, I am more inclined to suspect the avarice of the Arabian robbers and the prejudices of the German philosopher.

[2] Even in the seventh century the monks were generally laymen: they wore their hair long and dishevelled, and shaved their heads when they were ordained priests. The circular tonsure was sacred and mysterious: it was the crown of thorns; but it was likewise a royal diadem, and every priest was a king, etc. (Thomassin, Discipline de l'Eglise, tom. i. p. 721-758, especially p. 737, 738.)

[3] Huic Arabia est conserta, ex alio latere Nabathæis contigua; opima varietate commerciorum, castrisque oppleta validis et castellis, quæ ad repellendos gentium vicinarum excursus, solicitudo pervigil veterum per

Saracens were justified by the semblance of a national right.
The country was enriched by the various benefits of trade; by
the vigilance of the emperors it was covered with a line of forts;
and the populous cities of Gerasa, Philadelphia, and Bosra [1]
were secure, at least from a surprise, by the solid structure of
their walls. The last of these cities was the eighteenth station
from Medina: the road was familiar to the caravans of Hejaz
and Irak, who annually visited this plenteous market of the province and the desert: the perpetual jealousy of the Arabs had
trained the inhabitants to arms; and twelve thousand horse
could sally from the gates of Bosra, an appellation which signifies,
in the Syriac language, a strong tower of defence. Encouraged
by their first success against the open towns and flying parties of
the borders, a detachment of four thousand Moslems presumed
to summon and attack the fortress of Bosra. They were
oppressed by the numbers of the Syrians; they were saved by
the presence of Chaled, with fifteen hundred horse: he blamed the
enterprise, restored the battle, and rescued his friend, the venerable Serjabil, who had vainly invoked the unity of God and the
promises of the apostle. After a short repose the Moslems performed their ablutions with sand instead of water; [2] and the
morning prayer was recited by Chaled before they mounted on
horseback. Confident in their strength, the people of Bosra
threw open their gates, drew their forces into the plain, and
swore to die in the defence of their religion. But a religion of
peace was incapable of withstanding the fanatic cry of " Fight,
fight! Paradise, paradise! " that re-echoed in the ranks of the
Saracens; and the uproar of the town, the ringing of bells,[3] and
the exclamations of the priests and monks, increased the dismay

opportunos saltus erexit et cautos. Ammian. Marcellin. xiv. 8; Reland,
Palestin. tom. i. p. 85, 86.

[1] With Gerasa and Philadelphia, Ammianus praises the fortifications of
Bosra, [murorum] firmitate cautissimas. They deserved the same praise
in the time of Abulfeda (Tabul. Syriæ, p. 99), who describes this city, the
metropolis of Hawran (Auranitis), four days' journey from Damascus.
The Hebrew etymology I learn from Reland, Palestin. tom. ii. p. 666.

[2] The apostle of a desert and an army was obliged to allow this ready
succedaneum for water (Koran, c. iii. p. 66; c. v. p. 83); but the Arabian
and Persian casuists have embarrassed his free permission with many
niceties and distinctions (Reland, de Relig. Mohammed. l. i. p. 82, 83;
Chardin, Voyages en Perse, tom. iv.).

[3] *The bells rung !* Ockley, vol. i. p. 38. Yet I much doubt whether this
expression can be justified by the text of Al Wakidi, or the practice of the
times. Ad Græcos, says the learned Ducange (Glossar. med. et infim.
Græcitat. tom. i. p. 774) campanarum usus serius transit et etiamnum
rarissimus est. The oldest example which he can find in the Byzantine
writers is of the year 1040; but the Venetians pretend that they introduced
bells at Constantinople in the ninth century.

and disorder of the Christians. With the loss of two hundred and thirty men, the Arabs remained masters of the field; and the ramparts of Bosra, in expectation of human or divine aid, were crowded with holy crosses and consecrated banners. The governor Romanus had recommended an early submission: despised by the people, and degraded from his office, he still retained the desire and opportunity of revenge. In a nocturnal interview he informed the enemy of a subterraneous passage from his house under the wall of the city; the son of the caliph, with a hundred volunteers, were committed to the faith of this new ally, and their successful intrepidity gave an easy entrance to their companions. After Chaled had imposed the terms of servitude and tribute, the apostate or convert avowed in the assembly of the people his meritorious treason: " I renounce your society," said Romanus, " both in this world and the world to come. And I deny him that was crucified, and whosoever worships him. And I choose God for my Lord, Islam for my faith, Mecca for my temple, the Moslems for my brethren, and Mohammed for my prophet; who was sent to lead us into the right way, and to exalt the true religion in spite of those who join partners with God."

The conquest of Bosra, four days' journey from Dasmacus,[1] encouraged the Arabs to besiege the ancient capital of Syria.[2] At some distance from the walls they encamped among the groves and fountains of that delicious territory,[3] and the usual option, of the Mohammedan faith, of tribute, or of war, was proposed to the resolute citizens, who had been lately strengthened by a reinforcement of five thousand Greeks. In the decline, as

---

[1] Damascus is amply described by the Sherif al Edrisi (Geograph. Nub. p. 116, 117), and his translator, Sionita (Appendix, c. 4); Abulfeda (Tabula Syriæ, p. 100); Schultens (Index Geograph. ad Vit. Saladin.); D'Herbelot (Biblioth. Orient. p. 291); Thevenot (Voyage du Levant, part i. p. 688 698); Maundrell (Journey from Aleppo to Jerusalem, p. 122-130); and Pocock (Description of the East, vol. ii. p. 117-127).

[2] Nobilissima civitas, says Justin. According to the Oriental traditions, it was older than Abraham or Semiramis. Joseph. Antiq. Jud. l. i. c. 6 [§ 4], 7 [§ 2], p. 24, 29, edit. Havercamp. Justin. xxxvi. 2.

[3] Ἔδει γὰρ, οἶμαι, τὴν Διὸς πόλιν ἀληθῶς, καὶ τὸν τῆς Ἑώας ἀπάσης ὀφθαλμόν, τὴν ἱερὰν καὶ μεγίστην Δάμασκον λέγω, τοῖς τε ἄλλοις σύμπασιν, οἷον ἱερῶν κάλλει, καὶ νεῶν μεγέθει, καὶ ὡρῶν εὐκαιρίᾳ, καὶ πηγῶν ἀγλαΐᾳ, καὶ ποταμῶν πλήθει, καὶ γῆς εὐφορίᾳ νικῶσαν, etc. Julian. Epist. xxiv. p. 392. These splendid epithets are occasioned by the figs of Damascus, of which the author sends a hundred to his friend Serapion, and this rhetorical theme is inserted by Petavius, Spanheim, etc. (p. 390-396), among the genuine epistles of Julian. How could they overlook that the writer is an inhabitant of Damascus (he thrice affirms that this peculiar fig grows only (παρ' ἡμῖν), a city which Julian never entered or approached?

in the infancy of the military art, a hostile defiance was frequently offered and accepted by the generals themselves: [1] many a lance was shivered in the plain of Damascus, and the personal prowess of Caled was signalised in the first sally of the besieged. After an obstinate combat he had overthrown and made prisoner one of the Christian leaders, a stout and worthy antagonist. He instantly mounted a fresh horse, the gift of the governor of Palmyra, and pushed forwards to the front of the battle. " Repose yourself for a moment," said his friend Derar, " and permit me to supply your place: you are fatigued with fighting with this dog." " O Derar," replied the indefatigable Saracen, " we shall rest in the world to come. He that labours to-day shall rest to-morrow." With the same unabated ardour Chaled answered, encountered, and vanquished a second champion; and the heads of his two captives, who refused to abandon their religion, were indignantly hurled into the midst of the city. The event of some general and partial actions reduced the Damascenes to a closer defence: but a messenger, whom they dropped from the walls, returned with the promise of speedy and powerful succour, and their tumultuous joy conveyed the intelligence to the camp of the Arabs. After some debate, it was resolved by the generals to raise, or rather to suspend, the siege of Damascus till they had given battle to the forces of the emperor. In the retreat Chaled would have chosen the more perilous station of the rear-guard; he modestly yielded to the wishes of Abu Obeidah. But in the hour of danger he flew to the rescue of his companion, who was rudely pressed by a sally of six thousand horse and ten thousand foot, and few among the Christians could relate at Damascus the circumstances of their defeat. The importance of the contest required the junction of the Saracens, who were dispersed on the frontiers of Syria and Palestine; and I shall transcribe one of the circular mandates which was addressed to Amrou, the future conqueror of Egypt: " In the name of the most merciful God: from Chaled to Amrou, health and happiness. Know that thy brethren the Moslems design to march to Aiznadin, where there is an army of seventy thousand Greeks, who purpose to come against us, *that they may extinguish the light of God with their mouths ; but God preserveth his light in spite of the infidels*.[2] As soon therefore as this letter of mine shall be

---

[1] Voltaire, who casts a keen and lively glance over the surface of history, has been struck with the resemblance of the first Moslems and the heroes of the Iliad—the siege of Troy and that of Damascus (Hist. Générale, tom. i. p. 348).

[2] These words are a text of the Koran, c. ix. 32, lxi. 8. Like our fanatics

delivered to thy hands, come with those that are with thee to Aiznadin, where thou shalt find us if it please the most high God." The summons was cheerfully obeyed, and the forty-five thousand Moslems, who met on the same day, on the same spot, ascribed to the blessing of Providence the effects of their activity and zeal.

About four years after the triumphs of the Persian war the repose of Heraclius and the empire was again disturbed by a new enemy, the power of whose religion was more strongly felt than it was clearly understood by the Christians of the East. In his palace of Constantinople or Antioch he was awakened by the invasion of Syria, the loss of Bosra, and the danger of Damascus. An army of seventy thousand veterans, or new levies, was assembled at Hems or Emesa, under the command of his general Werdan:[1] and these troops, consisting chiefly of cavalry, might be indifferently styled either Syrians, or Greeks, or Romans: *Syrians*, from the place of their birth or warfare; *Greeks*, from the religion and language of their sovereign; and *Romans*, from the proud appellation which was still profaned by the successors of Constantine. On the plain of Aiznadin,[2] as Werdan rode on a white mule decorated with gold chains, and surrounded with ensigns and standards, he was surprised by the near approach of a fierce and naked warrior, who had undertaken to view the state of the enemy. The adventurous valour of Derar was inspired, and has perhaps been adorned, by the enthusiasm of his age and country. The hatred of the Christians, the love of spoil, and the contempt of danger, were the ruling passions of the audacious Saracen; and the prospect of instant death could never shake his religious confidence, or ruffle the calmness of his resolution, or even suspend the frank and martial pleasantry of his humour. In the most hopeless enterprises he was bold, and prudent, and

of the last century, the Moslems, on every familiar or important occasion, spoke the language of *their* Scriptures—a style more natural in their mouths than the Hebrew idiom, transplanted into the climate and dialect of Britain.

[1] The name of Werdan is unknown to Theophanes; and, though it might belong to an Armenian chief, has very little of a Greek aspect or sound. If the Byzantine historians have mangled the Oriental names, the Arabs, in this instance, likewise have taken ample revenge on their enemies. In transposing the Greek character from right to left, might they not produce, from the familiar appellation of *Andrew*, something like the anagram *Werdan* ?

[2] [The exact site of Aiznadin is uncertain, but the place where this great battle occurred probably lay between Ramla and Beit Djibrin, the ancient Beto-Gabra, in the south of Palestine. With regard to the name Werdan which Gibbon seeks to prove may be an anagram of the word " Andrew," it is hard to understand what was in Gibbon's mind at this time. The name Werdan is of Armenian origin and is akin to Bardanes.—O. S.]

fortunate: after innumerable hazards, after being thrice a prisoner in the hands of the infidels, he still survived to relate the achievements, and to enjoy the rewards, of the Syrian conquest. On this occasion his single lance maintained a flying fight against thirty Romans, who were detached by Werdan; and, after killing or unhorsing seventeen of their number, Derar returned in safety to his applauding brethren. When his rashness was mildly censured by the general, he excused himself with the simplicity of a soldier. "Nay," said Derar, "I did not begin first: but they came out to take me, and I was afraid that God should see me turn my back: and indeed I fought in good earnest, and without doubt God assisted me against them; and had I not been apprehensive of disobeying your orders, I should not have come away as I did; and I perceive already that they will fall into our hands." In the presence of both armies a venerable Greek advanced from the ranks with a liberal offer of peace; and the departure of the Saracens would have been purchased by a gift to each soldier of a turban, a robe, and a piece of gold; ten robes and a hundred pieces to their leader; one hundred robes and a thousand pieces to the caliph. A smile of indignation expressed the refusal of Caled. "Ye Christian dogs, you know your option; the Koran, the tribute, or the sword. We are a people whose delight is in war rather than in peace: and we despise your pitiful alms, since we shall be speedily masters of your wealth, your families, and your persons." Notwithstanding this apparent disdain, he was deeply conscious of the public danger: those who had been in Persia, and had seen the armies of Chosroes, confessed that they never beheld a more formidable array. From the superiority of the enemy the artful Saracen derived a fresh incentive of courage: "You see before you," said he, "the united force of the Romans; you cannot hope to escape, but you may conquer Syria in a single day. The event depends on your discipline and patience. Reserve yourselves till the evening. It was in the evening that the Prophet was accustomed to vanquish." During two successive engagements, his temperate firmness sustained the darts of the enemy and the murmurs of his troops. At length, when the spirits and quivers of the adverse line were almost exhausted, Chaled gave the signal of onset and victory. The remains of the Imperial army fled to Antioch, or Cæsarea, or Damascus; and the death of four hundred and seventy Moslems was compensated by the opinion that they had sent to hell above fifty thousand of the infidels. The spoil was inestimable; many banners and crosses of gold and silver, precious stones, silver and gold chains, and innumerable suits of the richest armour and apparel. The general distribution was postponed till Damascus should be taken; but the seasonable supply of arms became the instrument of new victories. The glorious intelligence was transmitted to the throne of the caliph; and the Arabian tribes, the coldest or most hostile to the prophet's mission, were eager and importunate to share the harvest of Syria.

The sad tidings were carried to Damascus by the speed of grief and terror; and the inhabitants beheld from their walls the return of the heroes of Aiznadin. Amrou led the van at the head of nine thousand horse: the bands of the Saracens succeeded each other in formidable review; and the rear was closed by Chaled in person, with the standard of the black eagle. To the activity of Derar he intrusted the commission of patrolling round the city with two thousand horse, of scouring the plain, and of intercepting all succour or intelligence. The rest of the Arabian chiefs were fixed in their respective stations before the seven gates of Damascus; and the siege was renewed with fresh vigour and confidence. The art, the labour, the military engines of the Greeks and Romans are seldom to be found in the simple, though successful, operations of the Saracens: it was sufficient for them to invest a city with arms rather than with trenches; to repel the sallies of the besieged; to attempt a stratagem or an assault; or to expect the progress of famine and discontent. Damascus would have acquiesced in the trial of Aiznadin, as a final and peremptory sentence between the emperor and the caliph: her courage was rekindled by the example and authority of Thomas, a noble Greek, illustrious in a private condition by the alliance of Heraclius.[1] The tumult and illumination of the night proclaimed the design of the morning sally; and the Christian hero, who affected to despise the enthusiasm of the Arabs, employed the resource of a similar superstition. At the principal gate, in the sight of both armies, a lofty crucifix was erected; the bishop, with his clergy, accompanied the march, and laid the volume of the New Testament before the image of Jesus; and the contending parties were scandalised or edified by a prayer that the Son of God would defend his servants and vindicate his truth. The

[1] Vanity prompted the Arabs to believe that Thomas was the son-in-law of the emperor. We know the children of Heraclius by his two wives; and his *august* daughter would not have married in exile at Damascus (see Ducange, Fam. Byzantin. p. 118, 119). Had he been less religious, I might only suspect the legitimacy of the damsel.

battle raged with incessant fury; and the dexterity of Thomas,[1] an incomparable archer, was fatal to the boldest Saracens, till their death was revenged by a female heroine. The wife of Aban, who had followed him to the holy war, embraced her expiring husband. "Happy," said she, "happy art thou, my dear: thou art gone to thy Lord, who first joined us together, and then parted us asunder. I will revenge thy death, and endeavour to the utmost of my power to come to the place where thou art, because I love thee. Henceforth shall no man ever touch me more, for I have dedicated myself to the service of God." Without a groan, without a tear, she washed the corpse of her husband, and buried him with the usual rites. Then grasping the manly weapons, which in her native land she was accustomed to wield, the intrepid widow of Aban sought the place where his murderer fought in the thickest of the battle. Her first arrow pierced the hand of his standard-bearer; her second wounded Thomas in the eye; and the fainting Christians no longer beheld their ensign or their leader. Yet the generous champion of Damascus refused to withdraw to his palace: his wound was dressed on the rampart; the fight was continued till the evening; and the Syrians rested on their arms. In the silence of the night, the signal was given by a stroke on the great bell; the gates were thrown open, and each gate discharged an impetuous column on the sleeping camp of the Saracens. Chaled was the first in arms: at the head of four hundred horse he flew to the post of danger, and the tears trickled down his iron cheeks as he uttered a fervent ejaculation: "O God, who never sleepest, look upon thy servants, and do not deliver them into the hands of their enemies." The valour and victory of Thomas were arrested by the presence of the *Sword of God*; with the knowledge of the peril, the Moslems recovered their ranks, and charged the assailants in the flank and rear. After the loss of thousands, the Christian general retreated with a sigh of despair, and the pursuit of the Saracens was checked by the military engines of the rampart.

After a siege of seventy days,[2] the patience, and perhaps the

---

[1] Al Wakidi (Ockley, p. 101) says, "with poisoned arrows;" but this savage invention is so repugnant to the practice of the Greeks and Romans, that I must suspect on this occasion the malevolent credulity of the Saracens.

[2] Abulfeda allows only seventy days for the siege of Damascus (Annal. Moslem. p. 67, vers. Reiske); but Elmacin, who mentions this opinion, prolongs the term to six months, and notices the use of *balistæ* by the Saracens (Hist. Saracen. p. 25, 32). Even this longer period is insufficient to fill the interval between the battle of Aiznadin (July, A.D. 633) and the

provisions, of the Damascenes were exhausted; and the bravest of their chiefs submitted to the hard dictates of necessity. In the occurrences of peace and war, they had been taught to dread the fierceness of Chaled and to revere the mild virtues of Abu Obeidah. At the hour of midnight one hundred chosen deputies of the clergy and people were introduced to the tent of that venerable commander. He received and dismissed them with courtesy. They returned with a written agreement, on the faith of a companion of Mohammed, that all hostilities should cease; that the voluntary emigrants might depart in safety, with as much as they could carry away of their effects; and that the tributary subjects of the caliph should enjoy their lands and houses, with the use and possession of seven churches. On these terms, the most respectable hostages, and the gate nearest to his camp, were delivered into his hands: his soldiers imitated the moderation of their chief; and he enjoyed the submissive gratitude of a people whom he had rescued from destruction. But the success of the treaty had relaxed their vigilance, and in the same moment the opposite quarter of the city was betrayed and taken by assault. A party of a hundred Arabs had opened the eastern gate to a more inexorable foe. "No quarter," cried the rapacious and sanguinary Chaled, "no quarter to the enemies of the Lord:" his trumpets sounded, and a torrent of Christian blood was poured down the streets of Damascus. When he reached the church of St. Mary, he was astonished and provoked by the peaceful aspect of his companions; their swords were in the scabbard, and they were surrounded by a multitude of priests and monks. Abu Obeidah saluted the general: "God," said he, "has delivered the city into my hands by way of surrender, and has saved the believers the trouble of fighting." "And am I not," replied the indignant Chaled, "am I not the lieutenant of the commander of the faithful? Have I not taken the city by storm? The unbelievers shall perish by the sword. Fall on." The hungry and cruel Arabs would have obeyed the welcome command; and Damascus was lost, if the benevolence of Abu Obeidah had not been supported by a decent and dignified firmness. Throwing himself between the trembling citizens and the most eager of the barbarians, he adjured them, by the holy name of God, to respect his promise, to suspend their fury, and to wait

accession of Omar (24th July, A.D. 634), to whose reign the conquest of Damascus is unanimously ascribed (Al Wakidi, apud Ockley, vol. i. p. 115; Abulpharagius, Dynast. p. 112, vers. Pocock). Perhaps, as in the Trojan war, the operations were interrupted by excursions and detachments till the last seventy days of the siege.

the determination of their chiefs. The chiefs retired into the church of St. Mary; and after a vehement debate, Chaled submitted in some measure to the reason and authority of his colleague; who urged the sanctity of a covenant, the advantage as well as the honour which the Moslems would derive from the punctual performance of their word, and the obstinate resistance which they must encounter from the distrust and despair of the rest of the Syrian cities. It was agreed that the sword should be sheathed, that the part of Damascus which had surrendered to Abu Obeidah should be immediately entitled to the benefit of his capitulation, and that the final decision should be referred to the justice and wisdom of the caliph.[1] A large majority of the people accepted the terms of toleration and tribute; and Damascus is still peopled by twenty thousand Christians. But the valiant Thomas, and the free-born patriots who had fought under his banner, embraced the alternative of poverty and exile. In the adjacent meadow a numerous encampment was formed of priests and laymen, of soldiers and citizens, of women and children: they collected, with haste and terror, their most precious movables; and abandoned, with loud lamentations or silent anguish, their native homes and the pleasant banks of the Pharpar. The inflexible soul of Chaled was not touched by the spectacle of their distress: he disputed with the Damascenes the property of a magazine of corn; endeavoured to exclude the garrison from the benefit of the treaty; consented, with reluctance, that each of the fugitives should arm himself with a sword, or a lance, or a bow; and sternly declared, that, after a respite of three days, they might be pursued and treated as the enemies of the Moslems.

The passion of a Syrian youth completed the ruin of the exiles of Damascus. A nobleman of the city, of the name of Jonas,[2] was betrothed to a wealthy maiden; but her parents delayed the

---

[1] It appears from Abulfeda (p. 125) and Elmacin (p. 32) that this distinction of the two parts of Damascus was long remembered, though not always respected, by the Mohammedan sovereigns. See likewise Eutychius (Annal. tom. ii. p. 379, 390, 383).

[2] On the fate of these lovers, whom he names Phocyas and Eudocia, Mr. Hughes has built the Siege of Damascus, one of our most popular tragedies, and which possesses the rare merit of blending nature and history, the manners of the times and the feelings of the heart. The foolish delicacy of the players compelled him to soften the guilt of the hero and the despair of the heroine. Instead of a base renegado, Phocyas serves the Arabs as an honourable ally; instead of prompting their pursuit, he flies to the succour of his countrymen, and, after killing Caled and Derar, is himself mortally wounded, and expires in the presence of Eudocia, who professes her resolution to take the veil at Constantinople. A frigid catastrophe!

consummation of his nuptials, and their daughter was persuaded to escape with the man whom she had chosen. They corrupted the nightly watchmen of the gate Keisan; the lover, who led the way, was encompassed by a squadron of Arabs; but his exclamation in the Greek tongue, " the bird is taken," admonished his mistress to hasten her return. In the presence of Chaled, and of death, the unfortunate Jonas professed his belief in one God and his apostle Mohammed; and continued, till the season of his martyrdom, to discharge the duties of a brave and sincere Musulman. When the city was taken, he flew to the monastery where Eudocia had taken refuge; but the lover was forgotten; the apostate was scorned; she preferred her religion to her country; and the justice of Chaled, though deaf to mercy, refused to detain by force a male or female inhabitant of Damascus. Four days was the general confined to the city by the obligation of the treaty and the urgent cares of his new conquest. His appetite for blood and rapine would have been extinguished by the hopeless computation of time and distance; but he listened to the importunities of Jonas, who assured him that the weary fugitives might yet be overtaken. At the head of four thousand horse, in the disguise of Christian Arabs, Chaled undertook the pursuit. They halted only for the moments of prayer; and their guide had a perfect knowledge of the country. For a long way the footsteps of the Damascenes were plain and conspicuous: they vanished on a sudden; but the Saracens were comforted by the assurance that the caravan had turned aside into the mountains, and must speedily fall into their hands. In traversing the ridges of the Libanus they endured intolerable hardships, and the sinking spirits of the veteran fanatics were supported and cheered by the unconquerable ardour of a lover. From a peasant of the country they were informed that the emperor had sent orders to the colony of exiles to pursue without delay the road of the sea-coast and of Constantinople, apprehensive, perhaps, that the soldiers and people of Antioch might be discouraged by the sight and the story of their sufferings. The Saracens were conducted through the territories of Gabala [1] and Laodicea, at a cautious distance from the walls of the cities; the rain was incessant, the

---

[1] The towns of Gabala and Laodicea, which the Arabs passed, still exist in a state of decay (Maundrell, p. 11, 12; Pocock, vol. ii. p. 13). Had not the Christians been overtaken, they must have crossed the Orontes on some bridge in the sixteen miles between Antioch and the sea, and might have rejoined the high road of Constantinople at Alexandria. The Itineraries will represent the directions and distances (p. 146, 148, 581, 582, edit. Wesseling).

night was dark, a single mountain separated them from the Roman army; and Chaled, ever anxious for the safety of his brethren, whispered an ominous dream in the ear of his companion. With the dawn of day the prospect again cleared, and they saw before them, in a pleasant valley, the tents of Damascus. After a short interval of repose and prayer Chaled divided his cavalry into four squadrons, committing the first to his faithful Derar, and reserving the last for himself. They successively rushed on the promiscuous multitude, insufficiently provided with arms, and already vanquished by sorrow and fatigue. Except a captive, who was pardoned and dismissed, the Arabs enjoyed the satisfaction of believing that not a Christian of either sex escaped the edge of their scimitars. The gold and silver of Damascus was scattered over the camp, and a royal wardrobe of three hundred load of silk might clothe an army of naked barbarians. In the tumult of the battle Jonas sought and found the object of his pursuit: but her resentment was inflamed by the last act of his perfidy; and as Eudocia struggled in his hateful embraces, she struck a dagger to her heart. Another female, the widow of Thomas, and the real or supposed daughter of Heraclius, was spared and released without a ransom: but the generosity of Chaled was the effect of his contempt; and the haughty Saracen insulted, by a message of defiance, the throne of the Cæsars. Chaled had penetrated above a hundred and fifty miles into the heart of the Roman province: he returned to Damascus with the same secrecy and speed. On the accession of Omar, the *Sword of God* was removed from the command; but the caliph, who blamed the rashness, was compelled to applaud the vigour and conduct of the enterprise.

Another expedition of the conquerors of Damascus will equally display their avidity and their contempt for the riches of the present world. They were informed that the produce and manufactures of the country were annually collected in the fair of Abyla,[1] about thirty miles from the city; that the cell of a devout hermit was visited at the same time by a multitude of pilgrims; and that the festival of trade and superstition would be ennobled by the nuptials of the daughter of the governor of Tripoli. Abdallah, the son of Jaafar, a glorious and holy martyr, undertook, with a banner of five hundred horse, the

---

[1] *Dair Abil Kodos.* After retrenching the last word, the epithet *holy*, I discover the Abila of Lysanias between Damascus and Heliopolis: the name (*Abil* signifies a vineyard) concurs with the situation to justify my conjecture (Reland, Palestin. tom. i. p. 317, tom. ii. p. 525, 527).

pious and profitable commission of despoiling the infidels.   As he
approached the fair of Abyla, he was astonished by the report
of the mighty concourse of Jews and Christians, Greeks and
Armenians, of natives of Syria and of strangers of Egypt, to the
number of ten thousand, besides a guard of five thousand horse
that attended the person of the bride.   The Saracens paused:
" For my own part," said Abdallah, " I *dare not* go back: our
foes are many, our danger is great, but our reward is splendid and
secure, either in this life or in the life to come.   Let every man,
according to his inclination, advance or retire."   Not a Musulman deserted his standard.   " Lead the way," said Abdallah to
his Christian guide, " and you shall see what the companions of
the prophet can perform."   They charged in five squardons;
but after the first advantage of the surprise they were encompassed and almost overwhelmed by the multitude of their enemies;
and their valiant band is fancifully compared to a white spot in
the skin of a black camel.[1]   About the hour of sunset, when their
weapons dropped from their hands, when they panted on the
verge of eternity, they discovered an approaching cloud of dust,
they heard the welcome sound of the *tecbir*,[2] and they soon perceived the standard of Chaled, who flew to their relief with the
utmost speed of his cavalry.   The Christians were broken by his
attack, and slaughtered in their flight, as far as the river of
Tripoli.   They left behind them the various riches of the fair;
the merchandises that were exposed for sale, the money that was
brought for purchase, the gay decorations of the nuptials, and the
governor's daughter, with forty of her female attendants.   The
fruits, provisions, and furniture, the money, plate, and jewels,
were diligently laden on the backs of horses, asses, and mules;
and the holy robbers returned in triumph to Damascus.   The
hermit, after a short and angry controversy with Chaled, declined
the crown of martyrdom, and was left alive in the solitary scene
of blood and devastation.

[1] I am bolder than Mr. Ockley (vol. i. p. 164), who dares not insert this
figurative expression in the text, though he observes in a marginal note
that the Arabians often borrow their similes from that useful and familiar
animal.   The reindeer may be equally famous in the songs of the Laplanders.

> [2] We heard the *tecbir* ; so the Arabs call
> Their shout of onset, when with loud appeal
> They challenge heaven, as if demanding conquest.

This word, so formidable in their holy wars, is a verb active (says Ockley
in his index) of the second conjugation, from *Kabbara*, which signifies saying *Alla Acbar*, God is most mighty

Syria,[1] one of the countries that have been improved by the most early cultivation, is not unworthy of the preference.[2] The heat of the climate is tempered by the vicinity of the sea and mountains, by the plenty of wood and water; and the produce of a fertile soil affords the subsistence, and encourages the propagation, of men and animals. From the age of David to that of Heraclius, the country was overspread with ancient and flourishing cities: the inhabitants were numerous and wealthy; and, after the slow ravage of despotism and superstition, after the recent calamities of the Persian war, Syria could still attract and reward the rapacious tribes of the desert. A plain, of ten days' journey, from Damascus to Aleppo and Antioch, is watered, on the western side, by the winding course of the Orontes. The hills of Libanus and Anti-Libanus are planted from north to south, between the Orontes and the Mediterranean; and the epithet of *hollow* (Cœlesyria) was applied to a long and fruitful valley, which is confined in the same direction by the two ridges of snowy mountains.[3] Among the cities which are enumerated by Greek and Oriental names in the geography and conquest of Syria, we may distinguish Emesa or Hems, Heliopolis or Baalbec, the former as the metropolis of the plain, the latter as the capital of the valley. Under the last of the Cæsars they were strong and populous; the turrets glittered from afar: an ample space was covered with public and private buildings; and the citizens were illustrious by their spirit, or at least by their pride; by

[1] In the Geography of Abulfeda, the description of Syria, his native country, is the most interesting and authentic portion. It was published in Arabic and Latin, Lipsiæ, 1766, in quarto, with the learned notes of Kochler and Reiske, and some extracts of geography and natural history from Ibn Ol Wardii. Among the modern travels, Pocock's Description of the East (of Syria and Mesopotamia, vol. ii. p. 88-209) is a work of superior learning and dignity; but the author too often confounds what he had seen and what he had read.

[2] The praises of Dionysius are just and lively. Καὶ τὴν μὲν (Syria) πολλοί τε καὶ ὄλβιοι ἄνδρες ἔχουσιν (in Periegesi, v. 902, in tom. iv. Geograph. Minor. Hudson). In another place he styles the country πολύπτολιν αἶαν (v. 898). He proceeds to say,

Πᾶσα δέ τοι λιπαρή τε καὶ εὔβοτος ἔπλετο χώρη,
Μῆλά τε φερβέμεναι καὶ δένδρεσι καρπὸν ἀέξειν.   v. 921, 922.

This poetical geographer lived in the age of Augustus, and his description of the world is illustrated by the Greek commentary of Eustathius, who paid the same compliment to Homer and Dionysius (Fabric. Biblioth. Græc. l. iv. c. 2, tom. iii. p. 21, etc.).
[With regard to Dionysius, Gibbon is wrong. Though his date is still uncertain, he probably wrote during the reign of Hadrian and in all probability at Alexandria.—O. S.]

[3] The topography of the Libanus and Anti-Libanus is excellently described by the learning and sense of Reland (Palestin. tom. i. p. 311-326).

their riches, or at least by their luxury. In the days of paganism, both Emesa and Heliopolis were addicted to the worship of Baal, or the sun; but the decline of their superstition and splendour has been marked by a singular variety of fortune. Not a vestige remains of the temple of Emesa, which was equalled in poetic style to the summits of Mount Libanus,[1] while the ruins of Baalbec, invisible to the writers of antiquity, excite the curiosity and wonder of the European traveller.[2] The measure of the temple is two hundred feet in length and one hundred in breadth: the front is adorned with a double portico of eight columns; fourteen may be counted on either side; and each column, forty-five feet in height, is composed of three massy blocks of stone or marble. The proportions and orna-ments of the Corinthian order express the architecture of the Greeks: but as Baalbec has never been the seat of a monarch, we are at a loss to conceive how the expense of these magnificent structures could be supplied by private or municipal liberality.[3] From the conquest of Damascus the Saracens proceeded to Heliopolis and Emesa: but I shall decline the repetition of the sallies and combats which have been already shown on a larger scale. In the prosecution of the war their policy was not less effectual than their sword. By short and separate truces they dissolved the union of the enemy; accustomed the Syrians to compare their friendship with their enmity; familiarised the idea of their language, religion, and manners; and exhausted,

---

[1] —— Emesæ fastigia celsa renident.
Nam diffusa solo latus explicat, ac subit auras
Turribus in cœlum nitentibus: incola claris
Cor studiis acuit . . .
Denique flammicomo devoti pectora soli
Vitam agitant:—Libanus frondosa cacumina turget,
Et tamen his celsi certant fastigia templi.

These verses of the Latin version of Rufus Avienus [vv. 1085, *seq.*] are wanting in the Greek original of Dionysius; and since they are likewise unnoticed by Eustathius, I must, with Fabricius (Biblioth. Latin. tom. iii. p. 153, edit. Ernesti), and against Salmasius (ad Vopiscum, p. 366, 367, in Hist. August.), ascribe them to the fancy, rather than the MSS., of Avienus.

[2] I am much better satisfied with Maundrell's slight octavo (Journey, p. 134-139) than with the pompous folio of Dr. Pocock (Description of the East, vol. ii. p. 106-113); but every preceding account is eclipsed by the magnificent description and drawings of MM. Dawkins and Wood, who have transported into England the ruins of Palmyra and Baalbec.

[3] The Orientals explain the prodigy by a never-failing expedient. The edifices of Baalbec were constructed by the fairies or the genii (Hist. de Timour Bec, tom. iii. l. v. c. 23, p. 311, 312; Voyage d'Otter, tom. i. p. 83). With less absurdity, but with equal ignorance, Abulfeda and Ibn Chaukel ascribe them to the Sabæans or Aadites. Non sunt in omni Syria ædificia magnificentiora his (Tabula Syriæ, p. 103).

636 a.d. The Roman Empire 325

by clandestine purchase, the magazines and arsenals of the cities which they returned to besiege. They aggravated the ransom of the more wealthy or the more obstinate; and Chalcis alone was taxed at five thousand ounces of gold, five thousand ounces of silver, two thousand robes of silk, and as many figs and olives as would load five thousand asses. But the terms of truce or capitulation were faithfully observed; and the lieutenant of the caliph, who had promised not to enter the walls of the captive Baalbec, remained tranquil and immovable in his tent till the jarring factions solicited the interposition of a foreign master. The conquest of the plain and valley of Syria was achieved in less than two years. Yet the commander of the faithful reproved the slowness of their progress; and the Saracens, bewailing their fault with tears of rage and repentance, called aloud on their chiefs to lead them forth to fight the battles of the Lord. In a recent action, under the walls of Emesa, an Arabian youth, the cousin of Chaled, was heard aloud to exclaim, "Methinks I see the black-eyed girls looking upon me; one of whom, should she appear in this world, all mankind would die for love of her. And I see in the hand of one of them a handkerchief of green silk and a cap of precious stones, and she beckons me, and calls out, Come hither quickly, for I love thee." With these words, charging the Christians, he made havoc wherever he went, till, observed at length by the governor of Hems, he was struck through with a javelin.

It was incumbent on the Saracens to exert the full powers of their valour and enthusiasm against the forces of the emperor, who was taught, by repeated losses, that the rovers of the desert had undertaken, and would speedily achieve, a regular and permanent conquest. From the provinces of Europe and Asia, fourscore thousand soldiers were transported by sea and land to Antioch and Cæsarea: the light troops of the army consisted of sixty thousand Christian Arabs of the tribe of Gassan. Under the banner of Jabalah, the last of their princes, they marched in the van; and it was a maxim of the Greeks, that, for the purpose of cutting diamond, a diamond was the most effectual. Heraclius withheld his person from the dangers of the field; but his presumption, or perhaps his despondency, suggested a peremptory order, that the fate of the province and the war should be decided by a single battle. The Syrians were attached to the standard of Rome and of the cross; but the noble, the citizen, the peasant, were exasperated by the injustice and cruelty of a licentious host, who oppressed them as subjects and despised them as strangers and aliens.[1] A report of these mighty preparations was conveyed to the Saracens in their camp of Emesa; and the chiefs, though resolved to fight, assembled a council: the faith of Abu Obeidah would have expected on the same spot the glory of martyrdom; the wisdom of Chaled advised an honourable retreat to the skirts of Palestine and Arabia, where they might await the succours of their friends and the attack of the unbelievers. A speedy messenger soon returned from the throne of Medina, with the blessings of Omar and Ali, the prayers of the widows of the prophet, and a reinforcement of eight thousand Moslems. In their way they overturned a detachment of Greeks; and when they joined at Yermuk the camp of their brethren, they found the pleasing intelligence that Chaled had already defeated and scattered the Christian Arabs of the tribe of Gassan. In the neighbourhood of Bosra, the springs of Mount Hermon descend in a torrent to the plain of Decapolis, or ten cities; and the Hieromax, a name which has been corrupted to Yermuk, is lost, after a short course, in the lake of Tiberias.[2] The banks of this obscure stream were illustrated by a long and bloody encounter. On this momentous occasion the public voice and the modesty of Abu Obeidah restored the command to the most deserving of the Moslems. Chaled assumed his station in the front, his colleague was posted in the rear, that the disorder of the fugitives might be checked by his venerable aspect, and the sight of the yellow banner which Mohammed had displayed before the walls of Chaibar. The last line was occupied by the sister of Derar, with the Arabian women who had enlisted in this holy war, who were accustomed to wield the bow and the lance, and who in a moment of captivity had defended, against the uncircumcised ravishers, their chastity and religion.[3] The exhortation of the generals was

[1] I have read somewhere in Tacitus, or Grotius, Subjectos habent tanquam suos, viles tanquam alienos. Some Greek officers ravished the wife, and murdered the child, of their Syrian landlord; and Manuel smiled at his undutiful complaint.

[2] See Reland, Palestin. tom. i. p. 272, 283, tom. ii. p. 773, 775. This learned professor was equal to the task of describing the Holy Land, since he was alike conversant with Greek and Latin, with Hebrew and Arabian literature. The Yermuk, or Hieromax, is noticed by Cellarius (Geograph. Antiq. tom. ii. p. 392) and D'Anville (Géographie Ancienne, tom. ii. p. 185). The Arabs, and even Abulfeda himself, do not seem to recognise the scene of their victory.

[3] These women were of the tribe of the Hamyarites, who derived their origin from the ancient Amalekites. Their females were accustomed to ride on horseback, and to fight like the Amazons of old (Ockley, vol. i. p. 67).

brief and forcible: "Paradise is before you, the devil and hell-fire in your rear." Yet such was the weight of the Roman cavalry that the right wing of the Arabs was broken and separated from the main body. Thrice did they retreat in disorder, and thrice were they driven back to the charge by the reproaches and blows of the women. In the intervals of action, Abu Obeidah visited the tents of his brethren, prolonged their repose by repeating at once the prayers of two different hours; bound up their wounds with his own hands, and administered the comfortable reflection, that the infidels partook of their sufferings without partaking of their reward. Four thousand and thirty of the Moslems were buried in the field of battle; and the skill of the Armenian archers enabled seven hundred to boast that they had lost an eye in that meritorious service. The veterans of the Syrian war acknowledged that it was the hardest and most doubtful of the days which they had seen. But it was likewise the most decisive: many thousands of the Greeks and Syrians fell by the swords of the Arabs; many were slaughtered, after the defeat, in the woods and mountains; many, by mistaking the ford, were drowned in the waters of the Yermuk; and however the loss may be magnified,[1] the Christian writers confess and bewail the bloody punishment of their sins.[2] Manuel, the Roman general, was either killed at Damascus, or took refuge in the monastery of Mount Sinai. An exile in the Byzantine court, Jabalah lamented the manners of Arabia, and his unlucky preference of the Christian cause.[3] He had once inclined to the profession of Islam; but in the pilgrimage of Mecca, Jabalah was provoked to strike one of his brethren, and fled with amaze-

[1] We killed of them, says Abu Obeidah to the caliph, one hundred and fifty thousand, and made prisoners forty thousand (Ockley, vol. i. p. 241). As I cannot doubt his veracity, nor believe his computation, I must suspect that the Arabic historians indulged themselves in the practice of composing speeches and letters for their heroes.

[2] After deploring the sins of the Christians, Theophanes adds (Chronograph. p 276 [tom. i. p. 510, ed. Bonn]), ἀνέστη ὁ ἐρημικὸς [ἐρημικώτατος] 'Αμαλὴκ τύπτων ἡμᾶς τὸν λαὸν τοῦ Χριστοῦ, καὶ γίνεται πρώτῃ φορᾷ πτῶσις τοῦ 'Ρωμαϊκοῦ στρατοῦ ἡ κατὰ τὸ Γαβιθὰν [Γαβιθᾶ] λέγω (does he mean Aiznadin?) καὶ 'Ιερμουχὰν, καὶ τὴν ἄθεσμον αἱματοχυσίαν. His account is brief and obscure, but he accuses the numbers of the enemy, the adverse wind, and the cloud of dust: μὴ δυνηθέντες (the Romans) ἀντιπροσωπῆσαι [ἀντωπῆσαι] ἐχθροῖς διὰ τὸν κονιορτὸν ἡττῶνται· καὶ ἑαυτοὺς βάλλοντες εἰς τὰς στενόδους τοῦ 'Ιερμοχθοῦ ποταμοῦ ἐκεῖ ἀπώλοντο ἄρδην (Chronograph. p. 280 [t. i. p. 518, ed. Bonn]).

[3] See Abulfeda (Annal. Moslem. p. 70, 71), who transcribes the poetical complaint of Jabalah himself, and some panegyrical strains of an Arabian poet, to whom the chief of Gassan sent from Constantinople a gift of five hundred pieces of gold by the hands of the ambassador of Omar.

ment from the stern and equal justice of the caliph. The victorious Saracens enjoyed at Damascus a month of pleasure and repose: the spoil was divided by the discretion of Abu Obeidah: an equal share was allotted to a soldier and to his horse, and a double portion was reserved for the noble coursers of the Arabian breed.

After the battle of Yermuk the Roman army no longer appeared in the field; and the Saracens might securely choose among the fortified towns of Syria the first object of their attack. They consulted the caliph whether they should march to Cæsarea or Jerusalem; and the advice of Ali determined the immediate siege of the latter. To a profane eye Jerusalem was the first or second capital of Palestine; but after Mecca and Medina, it was revered and visited by the devout Moslems as the temple· of the Holy Land, which had been sanctified by the revelation of Moses, of Jesus, and of Mohammed himself. The son of Abu Sophian was sent with five thousand Arabs to try the first experiment of surprise or treaty; but on the eleventh day the town was invested by the whole force of Abu Obeidah. He addressed the customary summons to the chief commanders and people of *Ælia*.[1] " Health and happiness to every one that follows the right way! We require of you to testify that there is but one God, and that Mohammed is his apostle. If you refuse this, consent to pay tribute, and be under us forthwith. Otherwise I shall bring men against you who love death better than you do the drinking of wine or eating hog's flesh. Nor will I ever stir from you, if it please God, till I have destroyed those that fight for you, and made slaves of your children." But the city was defended on every side by deep valleys and steep ascents; since the invasion of Syria the walls and towers had been anxiously restored; the bravest of the fugitives of Yermuk had stopped in the nearest place of refuge; and in the defence of the sepulchre of Christ the natives and strangers might feel some sparks of the enthusiasm which so fiercely glowed in the bosoms of the Saracens. The siege of Jerusalem lasted four months; not a day was lost without some action of sally or assault; the military engines incessantly played from the

---

[1] In the name of the city, the profane prevailed over the sacred: *Jerusalem* was known to the devout Christians (Euseb. de Martyr. Palest. c. xi.); but the legal and popular appellation of *Ælia* (the colony of Ælius Hadrianus) has passed from the Romans to the Arabs. (Reland, Palestin. tom. i. p. 207, tom. ii. p. 835; D'Herbelot, Bibliothèque Orientale, *Cods*, p. 269; *Ilia*, p. 420.) The epithet of *Al Cods*, the Holy, is used as the proper name of Jerusalem.

ramparts; and the inclemency of the winter was still more painful and destructive to the Arabs. The Christians yielded at
length to the perseverance of the besiegers. The patriarch
Sophronius appeared on the walls, and by the voice of an interpreter demanded a conference. After a vain attempt to
dissuade the lieutenant of the caliph from his impious enterprise,
he proposed, in the name of the people, a fair capitulation,
with this extraordinary clause, that the articles of security should
be ratified by the authority and presence of Omar himself. The
question was debated in the council of Medina; the sanctity of
the place, and the advice of Ali, persuaded the caliph to gratify
the wishes of his soldiers and enemies; and the simplicity of his
journey is more illustrious than the royal pageants of vanity
and oppression. The conqueror of Persia and Syria was mounted
on a red camel, which carried, besides his person, a bag of corn,
a bag of dates, a wooden dish, and a leathern bottle of water.
Wherever he halted, the company, without distinction, was invited to partake of his homely fare, and the repast was consecrated by the prayer and exhortation of the commander of the
faithful.[1] But in this expedition or pilgrimage his power was
exercised in the administration of justice: he reformed the
licentious polygamy of the Arabs, relieved the tributaries from
extortion and cruelty, and chastised the luxury of the Saracens
by despoiling them of their rich silks, and dragging them on their
faces in the dirt. When he came within sight of Jerusalem, the
caliph cried with a loud voice, " God is victorious: O Lord, give
us an easy conquest!" and, pitching his tent of coarse hair,
calmly seated himself on the ground. After signing the capitulation, he entered the city without fear or precaution, and
courteously discoursed with the patriarch concerning its religious
antiquities.[2] Sophronius bowed before his new master, and
secretly muttered, in the words of Daniel, " The abomination of
desolation is in the holy place." [3] At the hour of prayer they
stood together in the church of the Resurrection; but the caliph

---

[1] The singular journey and equipage of Omar are described (besides
Ockley, vol. i. p. 250) by Murtadi (Merveilles de l'Egypte, p. 200-202).

[2] The Arabs boast of an old prophecy preserved at Jerusalem, and describing the name, the religion, and the person of Omar, the future conqueror. By such arts the Jews are said to have soothed the pride of their
foreign masters, Cyrus and Alexander (Joseph. Ant. Jud. l. xi. c. 1 [§ 1,
2], 8 [§ 5], p. 547, 579-582).

[3] Τὸ βδέλυγμα τῆς ἐρημώσεως τὸ ῥηθὲν διὰ Δανιὴλ τοῦ προφήτου ἑστὼς ἐν
τόπῳ ἁγίῳ. Theophan. Chronograph. p. 281 [tom. i. p. 520, ed. Bonn].
This prediction, which had already served for Antiochus and the Romans,
was again refitted for the present occasion, by the economy of Sophronius,
one of the deepest theologians of the Monothelite controversy.

refused to perform his devotions, and contented himself with praying on the steps of the church of Constantine. To the patriarch he disclosed his prudent and honourable motive. " Had I yielded," said Omar, " to your request, the Moslems of a future age would have infringed the treaty under colour of imitating my example." By his command the ground of the temple of Solomon was prepared for the foundation of a mosch;[1] and, during a residence of ten days, he regulated the present and future state of his Syrian conquests. Medina might be jealous lest the caliph should be detained by the sanctity of Jerusalem or the beauty of Damascus; her apprehensions were dispelled by his prompt and voluntary return to the tomb of the apostle.[2]

To achieve what yet remained of the Syrian war, the caliph had formed two separate armies; a chosen detachment, under Amrou and Yezid, was left in the camp of Palestine; while the larger division, under the standard of Abu Obeidah and Chaled, marched away to the north against Antioch and Aleppo. The latter of these, the Berœa of the Greeks, was not yet illustrious as the capital of a province or a kingdom; and the inhabitants, by anticipating their submission and pleading their poverty, obtained a moderate composition for their lives and religion. But the castle of Aleppo,[3] distinct from the city, stood erect on a lofty artificial mound: the sides were sharpened to a precipice, and faced with freestone; and the breadth of the ditch might be filled with water from the neighbouring springs. After the loss of three thousand men, the garrison was still equal to the defence; and Youkinna, their valiant and hereditary chief, had murdered his brother, a holy monk, for daring to pronounce the name of peace. In a siege of four or five months, the hardest

---

[1] According to the accurate survey of D'Anville (Dissertation sur l'ancienne Jerusalem, p. 42-54), the mosch of Omar, enlarged and embellished by succeeding caliphs, covered the ground of the ancient temple (παλαιον του μεγαλου ναου δαπεδον, says Phocas), a length of 215, a breadth of 172, toises. The Nubian geographer declares that this magnificent structure was second only in size and beauty to the great mosch of Cordova (p. 113), whose present state Mr. Swinburne has so elegantly represented (Travels into Spain, p. 296-302).

[2] Of the many Arabic tarikhs or chronicles of Jerusalem (D'Herbelot, p. 867), Ockley found one among the Pocock MSS. of Oxford (vol. i. p. 257), which he has used to supply the defective narrative of Al Wakidi.

[3] The Persian historian of Timur (tom. iii. l. v. c. 21, p. 300) describes the castle of Aleppo as founded on a rock one hundred cubits in height; a proof, says the French translator, that he had never visited the place. It is now in the midst of the city, of no strength, with a single gate, the circuit is about 500 or 600 paces, and the ditch half full of stagnant water (Voyages de Tavernier, tom. i. p. 149; Pocock, vol. ii. part i. p. 150). The fortresses of the East are contemptible to a European eye.

of the Syrian war, great numbers of the Saracens were killed and wounded: their removal to the distance of a mile could not seduce the vigilance of Youkinna; nor could the Christians be terrified by the execution of three hundred captives, whom they beheaded before the castle wall. The silence, and at length the complaints, of Abu Obeidah informed the caliph that their hope and patience were consumed at the foot of this impregnable fortress. "I am variously affected," replied Omar, "by the difference of your success; but I charge you by no means to raise the siege of the castle. Your retreat would diminish the reputation of our arms, and encourage the infidels to fall upon you on all sides. Remain before Aleppo till God shall determine the event, and forage with your horse round the adjacent country." The exhortation of the commander of the faithful was fortified by a supply of volunteers from all the tribes of Arabia, who arrived in the camp on horses or camels. Among these was Dames, of a servile birth, but of gigantic size and intrepid resolution. The forty-seventh day of his service he proposed, with only thirty men, to make an attempt on the castle. The experience and testimony of Chaled recommended his offer; and Abu Obeidah admonished his brethren not to despise the baser origin of Dames, since he himself, could he relinquish the public care, would cheerfully serve under the banner of the slave. His design was covered by the appearance of a retreat; and the camp of the Saracens was pitched about a league from Aleppo. The thirty adventurers lay in ambush at the foot of the hill; and Dames at length succeeded in his inquiries, though he was provoked by the ignorance of his Greek captives. "God curse these dogs," said the illiterate Arab, "what a strange barbarous language they speak!" At the darkest hour of the night he scaled the most accessible height, which he had diligently surveyed, a place where the stones were less entire, or the slope less perpendicular, or the guard less vigilant. Seven of the stoutest Saracens mounted on each other's shoulders, and the weight of the column was sustained on the broad and sinewy back of the gigantic slave. The foremost in this painful ascent could grasp and climb the lowest part of the battlements; they silently stabbed and cast down the sentinels; and the thirty brethren, repeating a pious ejaculation, "O apostle of God, help and deliver us!" were successively drawn up by the long folds of their turbans. With bold and cautious footsteps Dames explored the palace of the governor, who celebrated, in riotous merriment, the festival of his deliverance. From thence, returning to his companions, he assaulted on the inside the entrance of the castle. They overpowered the guard, unbolted the gate, let down the drawbridge, and defended the narrow pass, till the arrival of Chaled, with the dawn of day, relieved their danger and assured their conquest. Youkinna, a formidable foe, became an active and useful proselyte; and the general of the Saracens expressed his regard for the most humble merit, by detaining the army at Aleppo till Dames was cured of his honourable wounds. The capital of Syria was still covered by the castle of Aazaz and the iron bridge of the Orontes. After the loss of those important posts, and the defeat of the last of the Roman armies, the luxury of Antioch [1] trembled and obeyed. Her safety was ransomed with three hundred thousand pieces of gold; but the throne of the successors of Alexander, the seat of the Roman government in the East, which had been decorated by Cæsar with the titles of free, and holy, and inviolate, was degraded under the yoke of the caliphs to the secondary rank of a provincial town. [2]

In the life of Heraclius the glories of the Persian war are clouded on either hand by the disgrace and weakness of his more early and his later days. When the successors of Mohammed unsheathed the sword of war and religion, he was astonished at the boundless prospect of toil and danger; his nature was indolent, nor could the infirm and frigid age of the emperor be kindled to a second effort. The sense of shame, and the importunities of the Syrians, prevented his hasty departure from the scene of action; but the hero was no more; and the loss of Damascus and Jerusalem, the bloody fields of Aiznadin and Yermuk, may be imputed in some degree to the absence or misconduct of the sovereign. Instead of defending the sepulchre of Christ, he involved the church and state in a metaphysical

---

[1] The date of the conquest of Antioch by the Arabs is of some importance. By comparing the years of the world in the Chronography of Theophanes with the years of the Hegira in the history of Elmacin, we shall determine that it was taken between January 23rd and September 1st of the year of Christ 638 (Pagi, Critica, in Baron. Annal. tom. ii. p. 812, 813). Al Wakidi (Ockley, vol. i. p. 314) assigns that event to Tuesday, August 21st, an inconsistent date; since Easter fell that year on April 5th, the 21st of August must have been a Friday (see the Tables of the Art de Vérifier les Dates).

[2] His bounteous edict, which tempted the grateful city to assume the victory of Pharsalia for a perpetual era, is given ἐν Ἀντιοχείᾳ τῇ μητροπόλει, ἱερᾷ καὶ ἀσύλῳ καὶ αὐτονόμῳ, καὶ ἀρχούσῃ καὶ προκαθεμένῃ τῆς ἀνατολῆς. John Malala, in Chron. p. 91, edit. Venet. [p. 216, ed. Bonn.]. We may distinguish his authentic information of domestic facts from his gross ignorance of general history.

controversy for the unity of his will; and while Heraclius crowned the offspring of his second nuptials, he was tamely stripped of the most valuable part of their inheritance. In the cathedral of Antioch, in the presence of the bishops, at the foot of the crucifix, he bewailed the sins of the prince and people; but his confession instructed the world that it was vain, and perhaps impious, to resist the judgment of God. The Saracens were invincible in fact, since they were invincible in opinion; and the desertion of Youkinna, his false repentance and repeated perfidy, might justify the suspicion of the emperor that he was encompassed by traitors and apostates who conspired to betray his person and their country to the enemies of Christ. In the hour of adversity his superstition was agitated by the omens and dreams of a falling crown; and after bidding an eternal farewell to Syria, he secretly embarked with a few attendants, and absolved the faith of his subjects.[1] Constantine, his eldest son, had been stationed with forty thousand men at Cæsarea, the civil metropolis of the three provinces of Palestine. But his private interest recalled him to the Byzantine court; and, after the flight of his father, he felt himself an unequal champion to the united force of the caliph. His vanguard was boldly attacked by three hundred Arabs and a thousand black slaves, who, in the depth of winter, had climbed the snowy mountains of Libanus, and who were speedily followed by the victorious squadrons of Chaled himself. From the north and south the troops of Antioch and Jerusalem advanced along the sea-shore till their banners were joined under the walls of the Phœnician cities: Tripoli and Tyre were betrayed; and a fleet of fifty transports, which entered without distrust the captive harbours, brought a seasonable supply of arms and provisions to the camp of the Saracens. Their labours were terminated by the unexpected surrender of Cæsarea: the Roman prince had embarked in the night;[2] and the defenceless citizens solicited their pardon

---

[1] See Ockley (vol. i. p. 308, 312), who laughs at the credulity of his author. When Heraclius bade farewell to Syria, Vale Syria et ultimum vale, he prophesied that the Romans should never re-enter the province till the birth of an inauspicious child, the future scourge of the empire. Abulfeda, p. 68. I am perfectly ignorant of the mystic sense, or nonsense, of this prediction.

[2] In the loose and obscure chronology of the times, I am guided by an authentic record (in the book of ceremonies of Constantine Porphyrogenitus), which certifies that June 4, A.D. 638, the emperor crowned his younger son Heraclius, in the presence of his eldest, Constantine, and in the palace of Constantinople; that January 1, A.D. 639, the royal procession visited the great church, and, on the 4th of the same month, the hippodrome.

with an offering of two hundred thousand pieces of gold. The remainder of the province, Ramlah, Ptolemais or Acre, Sichem or Neapolis, Gaza, Ascalon, Berytus, Sidon, Gabala, Laodicea, Apamea, Hierapolis, no longer presumed to dispute the will of the conqueror; and Syria bowed under the sceptre of the caliphs seven hundred years after Pompey had despoiled the last of the Macedonian kings.[1]

The sieges and battles of six campaigns had consumed many thousands of the Moslems. They died with the reputation and the cheerfulness of martyrs; and the simplicity of their faith may be expressed in the words of an Arabian youth, when he embraced, for the last time, his sister and mother: " It is not," said he, " the delicacies of Syria, or the fading delights of this world, that have prompted me to devote my life in the cause of religion. But I seek the favour of God and his apostle; and I have heard, from one of the companions of the prophet, that the spirits of the martyrs will be lodged in the crops of green birds, who shall taste the fruits, and drink of the rivers, of paradise. Farewell: we shall meet again among the groves and fountains which God has provided for his elect." The faithful captives might exercise a passive and more arduous resolution; and a cousin of Mohammed is celebrated for refusing, after an abstinence of three days, the wine and pork, the only nourishment that was allowed by the malice of the infidels. The frailty of some weaker brethren exasperated the implacable spirit of fanaticism; and the father of Amer deplored, in pathetic strains, the apostasy and damnation of a son, who had renounced the promises of God and the intercession of the prophet, to occupy, with the priests and deacons, the lowest mansions of hell. The more fortunate Arabs who survived the war and persevered in the faith were restrained by their abstemious leader from the abuse of prosperity. After a refreshment of three days Abu Obeidah withdrew his troops from the pernicious contagion of the luxury of Antioch, and assured the caliph that their religion and virtue could only be preserved by the hard discipline of poverty and labour. But the virtue of Omar, however rigorous to himself, was kind and liberal to his brethren. After a just tribute of praise and thanksgiving, he dropped a tear of compassion; and sitting down on the ground wrote an answer

---

[1] Sixty-five years before Christ, *Syria Pontusque* Cn. Pompeii virtutis monumenta sunt (Vell. Patercul. ii. 38), rather of his fortune and power; he adjudged Syria to be a Roman province, and the last of the Seleucides were incapable of drawing a sword in the defence of their patrimony (see the original texts collected by Usher, Annal. p. 420).

in which he mildly censured the severity of his lieutenant: " God," said the successor of the prophet, " has not forbidden the use of the good things of this world to faithful men, and such as have performed good works. Therefore you ought to have given them leave to rest themselves, and partake freely of those good things which the country affordeth. If any of the Saracens have no family in Arabia, they may marry in Syria; and whosoever of them wants any female slaves, he may purchase as many as he hath occasion for." The conquerors prepared to use, or to abuse, this gracious permission; but the year of their triumph was marked by a mortality of men and cattle, and twenty-five thousand Saracens were snatched away from the possession of Syria. The death of Abu Obeidah might be lamented by the Christians; but his brethren recollected that he was one of the ten elect whom the prophet had named as the heirs of paradise.[1] Chaled survived his brethren about three years; and the tomb of the Sword of God is shown in the neighbourhood of Emesa. His valour, which founded in Arabia and Syria the empire of the caliphs, was fortified by the opinion of a special providence; and as long as he wore a cap which had been blessed by Mohammed, he deemed himself invulnerable amidst the darts of the infidels.[2]

The place of the first conquerors was supplied by a new generation of their children and countrymen: Syria became the seat and support of the house of Ommiyah; and the revenue, the soldiers, the ships of that powerful kingdom were consecrated to enlarge on every side the empire of the caliphs. But the Saracens despise a superfluity of fame; and their historians scarcely condescend to mention the subordinate conquests which are lost in the splendour and rapidity of their victorious career. To the *north* of Syria they passed Mount Taurus, and reduced to their obedience the province of Cilicia, with its capital Tarsus, the ancient monument of the Assyrian kings. Beyond a second ridge of the same mountains, they spread the flame of war, rather than the light of religion, as far as the shores of the Euxine and

---

[1] Abulfeda, Annal. Moslem. p. 73. Mohammed could artfully vary the praises of his disciples. Of Omar he was accustomed to say, that, if a prophet could arise after himself, it would be Omar, and that in a general calamity Omar would be accepted by the divine justice (Ockley, vol. i. p. 221.)

[2] [Khaled (or Caled), for both spellings occur according to the Rouzont Uzzuffa, after having been deprived of his ample share of the plunder of Syria by the jealousy of Omar, died possessed only of his horse, his arms, and a single slave. Yet Omar was obliged to acknowledge to his lamenting parent that never mother had produced a son like Khaled.—O. S.]

the neighbourhood of Constantinople. To the *east* they advanced to the banks and sources of the Euphrates and Tigris: [1] the long-disputed barrier of Rome and Persia was for ever confounded; the walls of Edessa and Amida, of Dara and Nisibis, which had resisted the arms and engines of Sapor or Nushirvan, were levelled in the dust; and the holy city of Abgarus might vainly produce the epistle or the image of Christ to an unbelieving conqueror. To the *west* the Syrian kingdom is bounded by the sea: and the ruin of Aradus, a small island or peninsula on the coast, was postponed during ten years. But the hills of Libanus abounded in timber; the trade of Phœnicia was populous in mariners: and a fleet of seventeen hundred barks was equipped and manned by the natives of the desert. The Imperial navy of the Romans fled before them from the Pamphylian rocks to the Hellespont; but the spirit of the emperor, a grandson of Heraclius, had been subdued before the combat by a dream and a pun.[2] The Saracens rode masters of the sea; and the islands of Cyprus, Rhodes, and the Cyclades were successively exposed to their rapacious visits. Three hundred years before the Christian era, the memorable though fruitless siege of Rhodes,[3] by Demetrius, had furnished that maritime republic with the materials and the subject of a trophy. A gigantic statue of Apollo, or the sun, seventy cubits in height, was erected at the entrance of the harbour, a monument of the freedom and the arts of Greece. After standing fifty-six years, the colossus of Rhodes was overthrown by an earthquake; but the massy trunk, and huge fragments, lay scattered eight centuries on the ground, and are often described as one of the

---

[1] Al Wakidi had likewise written a history of the conquest of Diarbekir or Mesopotamia (Ockley, at the end of the second vol.), which our interpreters do not appear to have seen. The Chronicle of Dionysius of Telmar, the Jacobite patriarch, records the taking of Edessa A.D. 637, and of Dara A.D. 641 (Asseman. Biblioth. Orient. tom. ii. p. 103); and the attentive may glean some doubtful information from the Chronography of Theophanes (p. 285-287 [t. i. p. 526, *sqq.* ed. Bonn]). Most of the towns of Mesopotamia yielded by surrender (Abulpharag. p. 112).

[2] He dreamt that he was at Thessalonica, a harmless and unmeaning vision; but his soothsayer, or his cowardice, understood the sure omen of a defeat concealed in that inauspicious word θὲς ἀλλῷ νίκην, Give to another the victory (Theoph. p. 287 [vol. i. p. 529, ed. Bonn.]; Zonaras, tom. ii. l. xiv. [c. 19] p. 88).

[3] Every passage and every fact that relates to the isle, the city, and the colossus of Rhodes, are compiled in the laborious treatise of Meursius, who has bestowed the same diligence on the two larger islands of Crete and Cyprus. See, in the third vol. of his works, the *Rhodus* of Meursius (l. i. c. 15, p. 715-719). The Byzantine writers, Theophanes and Constantine, have ignorantly prolonged the term to 1360 years, and ridiculously divide the weight among 30,000 camels.

wonders of the ancient world. They were collected by the diligence of the Saracens, and sold to a Jewish merchant of Edessa, who is said to have laden nine hundred camels with the weight of the brass metal: an enormous weight, though we should include the hundred colossal figures,[1] and the three thousand statues, which adorned the prosperity of the city of the sun.

III. The conquest of Egypt may be explained by the character of the victorious Saracen, one of the first of his nation, in an age when the meanest of the brethren was exalted above his nature by the spirit of enthusiasm. The birth of Amrou was at once base and illustrious; his mother, a notorious prostitute, was unable to decide among five of the Koreish; but the proof of resemblance adjudged the child to Aasi, the oldest of her lovers.[2] The youth of Amrou was impelled by the passions and prejudices of his kindred: his poetic genius was exercised in satirical verses against the person and doctrine of Mohammed; his dexterity was employed by the reigning faction to pursue the religious exiles who had taken refuge in the court of the Æthiopian king.[3] Yet he returned from this embassy a secret proselyte; his reason or his interest determined him to renounce the worship of idols; he escaped from Mecca with his friend Chaled; and the prophet of Medina enjoyed at the same moment the satisfaction of embracing the two firmest champions of his cause. The impatience of Amrou to lead the armies of the faithful was checked by the reproof of Omar, who advised him not to seek power and dominion, since he who is a subject to-day may be a prince to-morrow. Yet his merit was not overlooked by the two first successors of Mohammed; they were indebted to his arms for the conquest of Palestine; and in all the battles and sieges of Syria he united with the temper of a chief the valour of an adventurous soldier. In a visit to Medina the caliph expressed a wish to survey the sword which had cut down so many Christian warriors: the son of Aasi unsheathed a short and ordinary scimitar; and as he perceived the surprise of Omar, " Alas," said the modest Saracen, " the sword itself, without the arm of

---

[1] Centum colossi alium nobilitaturi locum, says Pliny, with his usual spirit. Hist. Natur. xxxiv. 18.

[2] We learn this anecdote from a spirited old woman, who reviled to their faces the caliph and his friend. She was encouraged by the silence of Amrou and the liberality of Moawiyah (Abulfeda, Annal. Moslem. p. 111).

[3] Gagnier, Vie de Mahomet, tom. ii. p. 46, etc., who quotes the Abyssinian history, or romance, of Abdel Balcides. Yet the fact of the embassy and ambassador may be allowed.

its master, is neither sharper nor more weighty than the sword
of Pharezdak the poet." [1]   After the conquest of Egypt he was
recalled by the jealousy of the caliph Othman; but in the subsequent troubles, the ambition of a soldier, a statesman, and an
orator, emerged from a private station.   His powerful support,
both in council and in the field, established the throne of the
Ommiades; the administration and revenue of Egypt were
restored by the gratitude of Moawiyah to a faithful friend who
had raised himself above the rank of a subject; and Amrou
ended his days in the palace and city which he had founded on
the banks of the Nile.   His dying speech to his children is celebrated by the Arabians as a model of eloquence and wisdom:
he deplored the errors of his youth; but if the penitent was still
infected by the vanity of a poet, he might exaggerate the venom
and mischief of his impious compositions.[2]

From his camp in Palestine Amrou had surprised or anticipated
the caliph's leave for the invasion of Egypt.[3]   The magnanimous
Omar trusted in his God and his sword, which had shaken the
thrones of Chosroes and Cæsar: but when he compared the
slender force of the Moslems with the greatness of the enterprise,
he condemned his own rashness, and listened to his timid companions.   The pride and the greatness of Pharaoh were familiar
to the readers of the Koran; and a tenfold repetition of prodigies
had been scarcely sufficient to effect, not the victory, but the
flight, of six hundred thousand of the children of Israel: the
cities of Egypt were many and populous; their architecture was
strong and solid; the Nile, with its numerous branches, was alone
an insuperable barrier; and the granary of the Imperial city
would be obstinately defended by the Roman powers.   In this
perplexity the commander of the faithful resigned himself to the
decision of chance, or, in his opinion, of Providence.   At the
head of only four thousand Arabs, the intrepid Amrou had

[1] This saying is preserved by Pocock (Not. ad Carmen Tograi, p. 184),
and justly applauded by Mr. Harris (Philosophical Arrangements, p. 350).

[2] For the life and character of Amrou, see Ockley (Hist. of the Saracens,
vol. i. p. 28, 63, 94, 328, 342, 344, and to the end of the volume; vol. ii.
p. 51, 55, 57, 74, 110-112, 162) and Otter (Mém. de l'Académie des Inscriptions, tom. xxi. p. 131, 132).   The readers of Tacitus may aptly compare
Vespasian and Mucianus with Moawiyah and Amrou.   Yet the resemblance is still more in the situation, than in the characters, of the men.

[3] Al Wakidi had likewise composed a separate history of the conquest of
Egypt, which Mr. Ockley could never procure; and his own inquiries
(vol. i. p. 344-362) have added very little to the original text of Eutychius
(Annal. tom. ii. p. 296-323, vers. Pocock), the Melchite patriarch of Alex
andria, who lived three hundred years after the revolution.

[The invasion of Egypt took place either in the eighteenth or nineteenth
year of the Hegira, that being A.D. 639 or 640.—O. S.]

marched away from his station of Gaza when he was overtaken
by the messenger of Omar. " If you are still in Syria," said the
ambiguous mandate, " retreat without delay; but if, at the
receipt of this epistle, you have already reached the frontiers of
Egypt, advance with confidence, and depend on the succour of
God and of your brethren." The experience, perhaps the secret
intelligence, of Amrou had taught him to suspect the mutability
of courts; and he continued his march till his tents were un-
questionably pitched on Egyptian ground. He there assembled
his officers, broke the seal, perused the epistle, gravely inquired
the name and situation of the place, and declared his ready
obedience to the commands of the caliph. After a siege of thirty
days he took possession of Farmah or Pelusium; and that key
of Egypt, as it has been justly named, unlocked the entrance of
the country as far as the ruins of Heliopolis and the neighbourhood of the modern Cairo.

On the western side of the Nile, at a small distance to the east
of the Pyramids, at a small distance to the south of the Delta,
Memphis, one hundred and fifty furlongs in circumference, displayed the magnificence of ancient kings. Under the reign of
the Ptolemies and Cæsars, the seat of government was removed
to the sea-coast; the ancient capital was eclipsed by the arts
and opulence of Alexandria; the palaces, and at length the
temples, were reduced to a desolate and ruinous condition: yet,
in the age of Augustus, and even in that of Constantine, Memphis
was still numbered among the greatest and most populous of
the provincial cities.[1] The banks of the Nile, in this place of
the breadth of three thousand feet, were united by two bridges
of sixty and of thirty boats, connected in the middle stream by
the small island of Rouda, which was covered with gardens and
habitations.[2] The eastern extremity of the bridge was terminated
by the town of Babylon and the camp of a Roman legion, which
protected the passage of the river and the second capital of
Egypt. This important fortress, which might fairly be described

---

[1] Strabo, an accurate and attentive spectator, observes of Heliopolis
νυνὶ μὲν οὖν ἐστὶ πανέρημος ἡ πόλις (Geograph. l. xvii. p. 1158 [p. 805, ed.
Casaub.]); but of Memphis he declares πόλις δ' ἐστὶ μεγαλή τε καὶ εὔανδρος,
δευτέρα μετ' 'Αλεξάνδρειαν (p. 1161 [p. 807, ed. Casaub.]): he notices, however, the mixture of inhabitants, and the ruin of the palaces. In the proper
Egypt, Ammianus enumerates Memphis among the four cities, maximis
urbibus quibus provincia nitet (xxii. 16); and the name of Memphis
appears with distinction in the Roman Itinerary and episcopal lists.

[2] These rare and curious facts, the breadth (2946 feet) and the bridge of
the Nile, are only to be found in the Danish traveller and the Nubian
geographer (p. 98).

as a part of Memphis or *Misrah*, was invested by the arms of the lieutenant of Omar: a reinforcement of four thousand Saracens soon arrived in his camp; and the military engines, which battered the walls, may be imputed to the art and labour of his Syrian allies. Yet the siege was protracted to seven months; and the rash invaders were encompassed and threatened by the inundation of the Nile.[1] Their last assault was bold and successful: they passed the ditch, which had been fortified with iron spikes, applied their scaling-ladders, entered the fortress with the shout of " God is victorious! " and drove the remnant of the Greeks to their boats and the isle of Rouda. The spot was afterwards recommended to the conqueror by the easy communication with the gulf and the peninsula of Arabia; the remains of Memphis were deserted; the tents of the Arabs were converted into permanent habitations; and the first mosch was blessed by the presence of fourscore companions of Mohammed.[2] A new city arose in their camp on the eastward bank of the Nile; and the contiguous quarters of Babylon and Fostat are confounded in their present decay by the appellation of Old Misrah, or Cairo, of which they form an extensive suburb. But the name of Cairo, the town of victory, more strictly belongs to the modern capital, which was founded in the tenth century by the Fatimite caliphs.[3] It has gradually receded from the river; but the continuity of buildings may be traced by an attentive eye from the monuments of Sesostris to those of Saladin.[4]

Yet the Arabs, after a glorious and profitable enterprise, must

[1] From the month of April the Nile begins imperceptibly to rise; the swell becomes strong and visible in the moon after the summer solstice (Plin. Hist. Nat. v. 10), and is usually proclaimed at Cairo on St. Peter's day (June 29). A register of thirty successive years marks the greatest height of the waters between July 25 and August 18 (Maillet, Description de l'Egypte, lettre xi. p. 67, etc.; Pocock's Description of the East, vol. i. p. 200; Shaw's Travels, p. 383).

[2] Murtadi, Merveilles de l'Egypte, p. 243-259. He expatiates on the subject with the zeal and minuteness of a citizen and a bigot, and his local traditions have a strong air of truth and accuracy.

[3] D'Herbelot, Bibliothèque Orientale, p. 233.

[4] The position of New and of Old Cairo is well known, and has been often described. Two writers who were intimately acquainted with ancient and modern Egypt have fixed, after a learned inquiry, the city of Memphis at *Gizeh*, directly opposite the Old Cairo (Sicard, Nouveaux Mémoires des Missions du Levant, tom. vi. p. 5, 6; Shaw's Observations and Travels, p. 296-304). Yet we may not disregard the authority or the arguments of Pocock (vol. i. p. 25-41), Niebuhr (Voyage, tom. i. p. 77-106), and, above all, of D'Anville (Description de l'Egypte, p. 111, 112, 130-149), who have removed Memphis towards the village of Mohannah, some miles farther to the south. In their heat the disputants have forgot that the ample space of a metropolis covers and annihilates the far greater part of the controversy.

have retreated to the desert, had they not found a powerful
alliance in the heart of the country. The rapid conquest of
Alexander was assisted by the superstition and revolt of the
natives; they abhorred their Persian oppressors, the disciples
of the Magi, who had burnt the temples of Egypt, and feasted
with sacrilegious appetite on the flesh of the god Apis.[1] After a
period of ten centuries the same revolution was renewed by a
similar cause; and in the support of an incomprehensible creed
the zeal of the Coptic Christians was equally ardent. I have
already explained the origin and progress of the Monophysite
controversy, and the persecution of the emperors, which converted
a sect into a nation, and alienated Egypt from their religion and
government. The Saracens were received as the deliverers of
the Jacobite church; and a secret and effectual treaty was
opened during the siege of Memphis between a victorious army
and a people of slaves. A rich and noble Egyptian, of the name
of Mokawkas, had dissembled his faith to obtain the administration of his province: in the disorders of the Persian war he
aspired to independence: the embassy of Mohammed ranked him
among princes; but he declined, with rich gifts and ambiguous
compliments, the proposal of a new religion.[2] The abuse of his
trust exposed him to the resentment of Heraclius: his submission was delayed by arrogance and fear; and his conscience
was prompted by interest to throw himself on the favour of the
nation and the support of the Saracens. In his first conference
with Amrou he heard without indignation the usual option, of
the Koran, the tribute, or the sword. " The Greeks," replied
Mokawkas, " are determined to abide the determination of the
sword; but with the Greeks I desire no communion, either in this
world or in the next, and I abjure for ever the Byzantine tyrant,
his synod of Chalcedon, and his Melchite slaves. For myself and
my brethren, we are resolved to live and die in the profession
of the gospel and unity of Christ. It is impossible for us to
embrace the revelations of your prophet; but we are desirous of
peace, and cheerfully submit to pay tribute and obedience to his

---

[1] See Herodotus, l. iii. c. 27, 28, 29; Ælian. Hist. Var. l. iv. c. 8; Suidas
in Ὦχος,, tom. ii. p. 774; Diodor. Sicul. tom. ii. l. xvii. [c. 49] p. 197, ed.
Wesseling. Τῶν Περσῶν ἠσεβηκότων εἰς τὰ ἱερά, says the last of these
historians.

[2] Mokawkas sent the prophet two Coptic damsels, with two maids and
one eunuch, an alabaster vase, an ingot of pure gold, oil, honey, and the
finest white linen of Egypt, with a horse, a mule, and an ass, distinguished
by their respective qualifications. The embassy of Mohammed was despatched from Medina in the seventh year of the Hegira (A.D. 628). See
Gagnier (Vie de Mahomet, tom. ii. p. 255, 256, 303), from Al Jannabi.

temporal successors." The tribute was ascertained at two
pieces of gold for the head of every Christian; but old men,
monks, women, and children of both sexes under sixteen years
of age, were exempted from this personal assessment: the
Copts above and below Memphis swore allegiance to the caliph,
and promised an hospitable entertainment of three days to every
Musulman who should travel through their country. By this
charter of security the ecclesiastical and civil tyranny of the
Melchites was destroyed: [1] the anathemas of St. Cyril were
thundered from every pulpit; and the sacred edifices, with the
patrimony of the church, were restored to the national communion of the Jacobites, who enjoyed without moderation the
moment of triumph and revenge. At the pressing summons
of Amrou, their patriarch Benjamin emerged from his desert;
and, after the first interview, the courteous Arab affected to
declare that he had never conversed with a Christian priest of
more innocent manners and a more venerable aspect.[2] In the
march from Memphis to Alexandria the lieutenant of Omar intrusted his safety to the zeal and gratitude of the Egyptians:
the roads and bridges were diligently repaired; and in every
step of his progress he could depend on a constant supply of
provisions and intelligence. The Greeks of Egypt, whose
numbers could scarcely equal a tenth of the natives, were overwhelmed by the universal defection: they had ever been hated,
they were no longer feared: the magistrate fled from his tribunal,
the bishop from his altar; and the distant garrisons were surprised or starved by the surrounding multitudes. Had not the
Nile afforded a safe and ready conveyance to the sea, not an
individual could have escaped who by birth, or language, or
office, or religion, was connected with their odious name.

By the retreat of the Greeks from the provinces of Upper
Egypt a considerable force was collected in the island of Delta;
the natural and artificial channels of the Nile afforded a succession of strong and defensible posts; and the road to Alexandria

[1] The præfecture of Egypt, and the conduct of the war, had been trusted
by Heraclius to the patriarch Cyrus (Theophan. p. 280, 281 [t. i. p. 516,
519, ed. Bonn.]). " In Spain," said James II., " do you not consult your
priests? " " We do," replied the Catholic ambassador, " and our affairs
succeed accordingly." I know not how to relate the plans of Cyrus, of
paying tribute without impairing the revenue, and of converting Omar by
his marriage with the emperor's daughter (Nicephor. Breviar. p. 17, 18
[ed. Par. 1648]).
[2] See the Life of Benjamin, in Renaudot (Hist. Patriarch. Alexandrin.
p. 156-172), who has enriched the conquest of Egypt with some facts from
the Arabic text of Severus the Jacobite historian.

was laboriously cleared by the victory of the Saracens in two-and-twenty days of general or partial combat. In their annals of conquest the siege of Alexandria [1] is perhaps the most arduous and important enterprise. The first trading city in the world was abundantly replenished with the means of subsistence and defence. Her numerous inhabitants fought for the dearest of human rights, religion and property; and the enmity of the natives seemed to exclude them from the common benefit of peace and toleration. The sea was continually open; and if Heraclius had been awake to the public distress, fresh armies of Romans and barbarians might have been poured into the harbour to save the second capital of the empire. A circumference of ten miles would have scattered the forces of the Greeks, and favoured the stratagems of an active enemy; but the two sides of an oblong square were covered by the sea and the lake Maræotis, and each of the narrow ends exposed a front of no more than ten furlongs. The efforts of the Arabs were not inadequate to the difficulty of the attempt and the value of the prize. From the throne of Medina the eyes of Omar were fixed on the camp and city: his voice excited to arms the Arabian tribes and the veterans of Syria; and the merit of a holy war was recommended by the peculiar fame and fertility of Egypt. Anxious for the ruin or expulsion of their tyrants, the faithful natives devoted their labours to the service of Amrou; some sparks of martial spirit were perhaps rekindled by the example of their allies; and the sanguine hopes of Mokawkas had fixed his sepulchre in the church of St. John of Alexandria. Eutychius, the patriarch, observes that the Saracens fought with the courage of lions; they repulsed the frequent and almost daily sallies of the besieged, and soon assaulted in their turn the walls and towers of the city. In every attack the sword, the banner of Amrou, glittered in the van of the Moslems. On a memorable day he was betrayed by his imprudent valour: his followers who had entered the citadel were driven back; and the general, with a friend and a slave, remained a prisoner in the hands of the Christians. When Amrou was conducted before the præfect, he remembered his dignity, and forgot his situation: a lofty

[1] The local description of Alexandria is perfectly ascertained by the master-hand of the first of geographers (D'Anville, Mémoire sur l'Egypte, p. 52-63); but we may borrow the eyes of the modern travellers, more especially of Thevenot (Voyage au Levant, part i. p. 381-395), Pocock (vol. i. p. 2-13), and Niebuhr (Voyage en Arabie, tom. i. p. 34-43). Of the two modern rivals, Savary and Volney, the one may amuse, the other will instruct.

demeanour and resolute language revealed the lieutenant of the caliph, and the battle-axe of a soldier was already raised to strike off the head of the audacious captive. His life was saved by the readiness of his slave, who instantly gave his master a blow on the face, and commanded him with an angry tone to be silent in the presence of his superiors. The credulous Greek was deceived: he listened to the offer of a treaty, and his prisoners were dismissed in the hope of a more respectable embassy, till the joyful acclamations of the camp announced the return of their general, and insulted the folly of the infidels. At length, after a siege of fourteen months,[1] and the loss of three-and-twenty thousand men, the Saracens prevailed: the Greeks embarked their dispirited and diminished numbers, and the standard of Mohammed was planted on the walls of the capital of Egypt. " I have taken," said Amrou to the caliph, " the great city of the West. It is impossible for me to enumerate the variety of its riches and beauty; and I shall content myself with observing that it contains four thousand palaces, four thousand baths, four hundred theatres or places of amusement, twelve thousand shops for the sale of vegetable food, and forty thousand tributary Jews. The town has been subdued by force of arms, without treaty or capitulation, and the Moslems are impatient to seize the fruits of their victory." [2] The commander of the faithful rejected with firmness the idea of pillage, and directed his lieutenant to reserve the wealth and revenue of Alexandria for the public service and the propagation of the faith: the inhabitants were numbered; a tribute was imposed; the zeal and resentment of the Jacobites were curbed, and the Melchites who submitted to the Arabian yoke were indulged in the obscure but tranquil exercise of their worship. The intelligence of this disgraceful and calamitous event afflicted the declining health of the emperor; and Heraclius died of a dropsy

---

[1] Both Eutychius (Annal. tom. ii. p. 319) and Elmacin (Hist. Saracen. p. 28) concur in fixing the taking of Alexandria to Friday of the new moon of Moharram of the twentieth year of the Hegira (December 22, A.D. 640). In reckoning backwards fourteen months, seven months before Babylon, etc., Amrou might have invaded Egypt about the end of the year 638: but we are assured that he entered the country the 12th of Bayni, 6th of June (Murtadi, Merveilles de l'Egypte, p. 164; Severus, apud Renaudot, p. 162). The Saracen, and afterwards Lewis IX. of France, halted at Pelusium, or Damietta, during the season of the inundation of the Nile.

[The capture of Alexandria took place, according to Brook's chronology, October 17, 641.—O. S.]

[2] Eutych. Annal. tom. ii. p. 316, 319.

about seven weeks after the loss of Alexandria.[1] Under the minority of his grandson the clamours of the people deprived of their daily sustenance compelled the Byzantine court to undertake the recovery of the capital of Egypt. In the space of four years the harbour and fortifications of Alexandria were twice occupied by a fleet and army of Romans. They were twice expelled by the valour of Amrou, who was recalled by the domestic peril from the distant wars of Tripoli and Nubia. But the facility of the attempt, the repetition of the insult, and the obstinacy of the resistance, provoked him to swear that, if a third time he drove the infidels into the sea, he would render Alexandria as accessible on all sides as the house of a prostitute. Faithful to his promise, he dismantled several parts of the walls and towers; but the people was spared in the chastisement of the city, and the mosch of *Mercy* was erected on the spot where the victorious general had stopped the fury of his troops.

I should deceive the expectation of the reader if I passed in silence the fate of the Alexandrian library, as it is described by the learned Abulpharagius. The spirit of Amrou was more curious and liberal than that of his brethren, and in his leisure hours the Arabian chief was pleased with the conversation of John, the last disciple of Ammonius, and who derived the surname of *Philoponus* from his laborious studies of grammar and philosophy.[2] Emboldened by this familiar intercourse, Philoponus presumed to solicit a gift, inestimable in *his* opinion, contemptible in that of the barbarians—the royal library, which alone, among the spoils of Alexandria, had not been appropriated by the visit and the seal of the conqueror. Amrou was inclined to gratify the wish of the grammarian, but his rigid integrity refused to alienate the minutest object without the consent of the caliph: and the well-known answer of Omar was inspired by the ignorance of a fanatic. " If these writings of the Greeks agree with the book of God, they are useless and

---

[1] Notwithstanding some inconsistencies of Theophanes and Cedrenus, the accuracy of Pagi (Critica, tom. ii. p. 824) has extracted from Nicephorus and the Chronicon Orientale the true date of the death of Heraclius, February 11th, A.D. 641, fifty days after the loss of Alexandria. A fourth of that time was sufficient to convey the intelligence.

[2] Many treatises of this lover of labour (φιλόπονος) are still extant; but for readers of the present age, the printed and unpublished are nearly in the same predicament. Moses and Aristotle are the chief objects of his verbose commentaries, one of which is dated as early as May 10th, A.D. 617 (Fabric. Biblioth. Græc. tom. ix. p. 458-468). A modern (John Le Clerc), who sometimes assumed the same name, was equal to old Philoponus in diligence, and far superior in good sense and real knowledge.

need not be preserved: if they disagree, they are pernicious and ought to be destroyed." The sentence was executed with blind obedience: the volumes of paper or parchment were distributed to the four thousand baths of the city; and such was their incredible multitude, that six months were barely sufficient for the consumption of this precious fuel. Since the Dynasties of Abulpharagius [1] have been given to the world in a Latin version, the tale has been repeatedly transcribed; and every scholar, with pious indignation, has deplored the irreparable shipwreck of the learning, the arts, and the genius of antiquity. For my own part, I am strongly tempted to deny both the fact and the consequences. The fact is indeed marvellous. " Read and wonder! " says the historian himself: and the solitary report of a stranger who wrote at the end of six hundred years on the confines of Media is overbalanced by the silence of two annalists of a more early date, both Christians, both natives of Egypt, and the most ancient of whom, the patriarch Eutychius, has amply described the conquest of Alexandria.[2] The rigid sentence of Omar is repugnant to the sound and orthodox precept of the Mohammedan casuists: they expressly declare that the religious books of the Jews and Christians, which are acquired by the right of war, should never be committed to the flames; and that the works of profane science, historians or poets, physicians or philosophers, may be lawfully applied to the use of the faithful.[3] A more destructive zeal may perhaps

---

[1] Abulpharag. Dynast. p. 114, vers. Pocock. Audi quid factum sit et mirare. It would be endless to enumerate the moderns who have wondered and believed, but I may distinguish with honour the rational scepticism of Renaudot (Hist. Alex. Patriarch. p. 170): historia . . . habet aliquid ἄπιστον ut Arabibus familiare est.

[2] This curious anecdote will be vainly sought in the annals of Eutychius, and the Saracenic history of Elmacin. The silence of Abulfeda, Murtadi, and a crowd of Moslems, is less conclusive, from their ignorance of Christian literature.

[3] See Reland, de Jure Militari Mohammedanorum, in his third volume of Dissertations, p. 37. The reason for not burning the religious books of the Jews or Christians is derived from the respect that is due to the *name* of God.

[There seems now to be grave doubt thrown upon the story of the burning of the Alexandrian library. Prof. Bury here states a circumstance that must weigh strongly with all who wish to reach the truth in regard to this matter. The origin of the story is perhaps to be sought in the actual destruction of religious books in Persia. Ibn Khaldun, as quoted by Hajji Khalifa, states that Omar authorised some Persian books to be thrown into the water, basing his decision on the same dilemma which, according to Abulpharagius, he enunciated to Amrou. It is quite credible that books of the fire worshippers were destroyed by Omar's orders; and this incident might have originated legends of the destruction of books elsewhere.—O. S.]

be attributed to the first successors of Mohammed; yet in this instance the conflagration would have speedily expired in the deficiency of materials. I shall not recapitulate the disasters of the Alexandrian library, the involuntary flame that was kindled by Cæsar in his own defence,[1] or the mischievous bigotry of the Christians, who studied to destroy the monuments of idolatry.[2] But if we gradually descend from the age of the Antonines to that of Theodosius, we shall learn from a chain of contemporary witnesses that the royal palace and the temple of Serapis no longer contained the four, or the seven, hundred thousand volumes which had been assembled by the curiosity and magnificence of the Ptolemies.[3] Perhaps the church and seat of the patriarchs might be enriched with a repository of books; but if the ponderous mass of Arian and Monophysite controversy were indeed consumed in the public baths,[4] a philosopher may allow, with a smile, that it was ultimately devoted to the benefit of mankind. I sincerely regret the more valuable libraries which have been involved in the ruin of the Roman empire; but when I seriously compute the lapse of ages, the waste of ignorance, and the calamities of war, our treasures, rather than our losses, are the object of my surprise. Many curious and interesting facts are buried in oblivion: the three great historians of Rome have been transmitted to our hands in a mutilated state; and we are deprived of many pleasing compositions of the lyric, iambic, and dramatic poetry of the Greeks. Yet we should gratefully remember that the mischances of time and accident have spared the classic works to which the suffrage of antiquity [5] had adjudged the first place of genius and glory: the teachers of ancient knowledge, who are

[1] Consult the collections of Frensheim (Supplement. Livian. c. 12, 43) and Usher (Annal. p. 469). Livy himself had styled the Alexandrian library, elegantiæ regum curæque egregium opus—a liberal encomium, for which he is pertly criticised by the narrow stoicism of Seneca (De Tranquillitate Animi, c. 9), whose wisdom on this occasion deviates into nonsense.

[2] See this History, vol. iii. p. 132.

[3] Aulus Gellius (Noctes Atticæ, vi. 17), Ammianus Marcellinus (xxii. 16), and Orosius (l. vi. c. 15 [p. 421]). They all speak in the *past* tense, and the words of Ammianus are remarkably strong: fuerunt Bibliothecæ innumerabiles [inæstimabiles]; et loquitur monumentorum veterum concinens fides, etc.

[4] Renaudot answers for versions of the Bible, Hexapla, Catenæ Patrum, Commentaries, etc. (p. 170). Our Alexandrian MS., if it came from Egypt, and not from Constantinople or Mount Athos (Wetstein, Prolegom. ad N. T. p. 8, etc.), might *possibly* be among them.

[5] I have often perused with pleasure a chapter of Quintilian (Institut. Orator. x. 1) in which that judicious critic enumerates and appreciates the series of Greek and Latin classics.

still extant, had perused and compared the writings of their predecessors; [1] nor can it fairly be presumed that any important truth, any useful discovery in art or nature, has been snatched away from the curiosity of modern ages.

In the administration of Egypt,[2] Amrou balanced the demands of justice and policy; the interest of the people of the law, who were defended by God; and of the people of the alliance, who were protected by man. In the recent tumult of conquest and deliverance, the tongue of the Copts and the sword of the Arabs were most adverse to the tranquillity of the province. To the former, Amrou declared that faction and falsehood would be doubly chastised—by the punishment of the accusers, whom he should detest as his personal enemies, and by the promotion of their innocent brethren, whom their envy had laboured to injure and supplant. He excited the latter by the motives of religion and honour to sustain the dignity of their character, to endear themselves by a modest and temperate conduct to God and the caliph, to spare and protect a people who had trusted to their faith, and to content themselves with the legitimate and splendid rewards of their victory. In the management of the revenue he disapproved the simple but oppressive mode of a capitation, and preferred with reason a proportion of taxes deducted on every branch from the clear profits of agriculture and commerce. A third part of the tribute was appropriated to the annual repairs of the dykes and canals, so essential to the public welfare. Under his administration the fertility of Egypt supplied the dearth of Arabia; and a string of camels, laden with corn and provisions, covered almost without an interval the long road from Memphis to Medina.[3] But the genius of Amrou soon renewed the maritime communication which had been attempted or achieved by the Pharaohs, the Ptolemies, or the Cæsars; and a canal, at least eighty miles in length, was opened from the Nile to the Red Sea. This inland navigation, which would have joined the Mediterranean and the Indian Ocean, was soon discontinued as useless and dangerous: the throne was removed from Medina to

---

[1] Such as Galen, Pliny, Aristotle, etc. On this subject Wotton (Reflections on Ancient and Modern Learning, p. 85-95) argues with solid sense against the lively exotic fancies of Sir William Temple. The contempt of the Greeks for *barbaric* science would scarcely admit the Indian or Æthiopic books into the library of Alexandria; nor is it proved that philosophy has sustained any real loss from their exclusion.

[2] This curious and authentic intelligence of Murtadi (p. 284-289) has not been discovered either by Mr. Ockley or by the self-sufficient compilers of the Modern Universal History.

[3] Eutychius, Annal. tom. ii. p. 320. Elmacin, Hist. Saracen. p. 35.

Damascus, and the Grecian fleets might have explored a passage to the holy cities of Arabia.[1]

Of his new conquest the caliph Omar had an imperfect knowledge from the voice of fame and the legends of the Koran. He requested that his lieutenant would place before his eyes the realm of Pharaoh and the Amalekites; and the answer of Amrou exhibits a lively and not unfaithful picture of that singular country.[2] " O commander of the faithful, Egypt is a compound of black earth and green plants, between a pulverised mountain and a red sand. The distance from Syene to the sea is a month's journey for a horseman. Along the valley descends a river, on which the blessing of the Most High reposes both in the evening and morning, and which rises and falls with the revolutions of the sun and moon. When the annual dispensation of Providence unlocks the springs and fountains that nourish the earth, the Nile rolls his swelling and sounding waters through the realm of Egypt: the fields are overspread by the salutary flood; and the villages communicate with each other in their painted barks. The retreat of the inundation deposits a fertilising mud for the

---

[1] On these *obscure* canals the reader may try to satisfy himself from D'Anville (Mém. sur l'Egypte, p. 108-110, 124, 132), and a learned thesis, maintained and printed at Strasburg in the year 1770 (Jungendorum marium fluviorumque molimina, p. 39-47, 68-70). Even the supine Turks have agitated the old project of joining the two seas (Mémoires du Baron de Tott, tom. iv.).
[It is unquestionable that there was anciently a canal following a line something similar to that of the Suez Canal of to-day. Both classical authority and Arabian tradition unite in testifying to the existence of a canal between the Nile and the Red Sea. It was begun by Nechos, the son of Psammetichus, but left unfinished till completed by Darius, the son of Hystaspes. This line began a little above Bubastis on the Pelusiac branch of the Nile (Herodot. ii. 158). Having become choked with sand, it was restored by Ptolemy Philadelphus, who, however, placed its head farther north, in the neighbourhood of Phacusa. Another line, derived from the Nile above the Delta, seems to have been subsequently added. The canal was evidently navigable in the time of Augustus, but it seems to have become useless in the time of Pliny the elder. It was, however, repaired by Trajan, and we know from Lucian that it was navigable in the second century in his time. The line, as restored by Amrou, began at Babylon (or Fostat), ran northward to Bilbeis, then eastward through the valley of Tomlat, to the ruins of Heroopolis, whence it took a southerly direction and entered the Red Sea at Kolzum, near the spot where Suez has subsequently risen. It must, therefore, have followed the same line as in the time of Trajan; and as Amrou succeeded in a year or two in rendering it again navigable, we may conclude that the ancient works remained in a tolerable degree of preservation.—O. S.]
[2] A small volume, des Merveilles, etc., de l'Egypte, composed in the thirteenth century by Murtadi of Cairo, and translated from an Arabic MS. of Cardinal Mazarin, was published by Pierre Vatier, Paris, 1666. The antiquities of Egypt are wild and legendary; but the writer deserves credit and esteem for his account of the conquest and geography of his native country (see the Correspondence of Amrou and Omar, p. 279-289).

reception of the various seeds: the crowds of husbandmen who blacken the land may be compared to a swarm of industrious ants; and their native indolence is quickened by the lash of the taskmaster and the promise of the flowers and fruits of a plentiful increase. Their hope is seldom deceived; but the riches which they extract from the wheat, the barley, and the rice, the legumes, the fruit-trees, and the cattle, are unequally shared between those who labour and those who possess. According to the vicissitudes of the seasons, the face of the country is adorned with a *silver* wave, a verdant *emerald*, and the deep yellow of a *golden* harvest." [1] Yet this beneficial order is sometimes interrupted; and the long delay and sudden swell of the river in the first year of the conquest might afford some colour to an edifying fable. It is said that the annual sacrifice of a virgin [2] had been interdicted by the piety of Omar; and that the Nile lay sullen and inactive in his shallow bed, till the mandate of the caliph was cast into the obedient stream, which rose in a single night to the height of sixteen cubits. The admiration of the Arabs for their new conquest encouraged the licence of their romantic spirit. We may read, in the gravest authors, that Egypt was crowded with twenty thousand cities or villages: [3] *that*, exclusive of the Greeks and Arabs, the Copts alone were found, on the assessment, six millions of tributary subjects,[4] or twenty millions of either sex and of every age: *that* three hundred millions of gold

---

[1] In a twenty years' residence at Cairo, the consul Maillet had contemplated that varying scene—the Nile (Lettre ii., particularly p. 70, 75); the fertility of the land (Lettre ix.). From a college at Cambridge the poetic eye of Gray had *seen* the same objects with a keener glance:—

> What wonder in the sultry climes that spread,
> Where Nile, redundant o'er his summer bed,
> From his broad bosom life and verdure flings,
> And broods o'er Egypt with his wat'ry wings,
> If with advent'rous oar, and ready sail,
> The dusky people drive before the gale,
> Or on frail floats to neighbouring cities ride,
> That rise and glitter o'er the ambient tide.

(Mason's Works and Memoirs of Gray, p. 199, 200.)

[2] Murtadi, p. 164-167. The reader will not easily credit a human sacrifice under the Christian emperors, or a miracle of the successors of Mohammed.

[3] Maillet, Description de l'Egypte, p. 22. He mentions this number as the *common* opinion; and adds that the generality of these villages contain two or three thousand persons, and that many of them are more populous than our large cities.

[4] Eutych. Annal. tom. ii. p. 308, 311. The twenty millions are computed from the following *data :* one-twelfth of mankind above sixty, one-third below sixteen, the proportion of men to women as seventeen to sixteen (Recherches sur la Population de la France, p. 71, 72). The president Goguet (Origine des Arts, etc. tom. iii. p. 26, etc.) bestows

or silver were annually paid to the treasury of the caliph.[1]   Our reason must be startled by these extravagant assertions; and they will become more palpable if we assume the compass and measure the extent of habitable ground: a valley from the tropic to Memphis seldom broader than twelve miles, and the triangle of the Delta, a flat surface of two thousand one hundred square leagues, compose a twelfth part of the magnitude of France.[2]   A more accurate research will justify a more reasonable estimate.   The three hundred millions, created by the error of a scribe, are reduced to the decent revenue of four millions three hundred thousand pieces of gold, of which nine hundred thousand were consumed by the pay of the soldiers.[3]   Two authentic lists, of the present and of the twelfth century, are circumscribed within the respectable number of two thousand seven hundred villages and towns.[4]   After a long residence at Cairo, a French consul has ventured to assign about four millions of Mohammedans, Christians, and Jews, for the ample, though not incredible, scope of the population of Egypt.[5]

twenty-seven millions on ancient Egypt, because the seventeen hundred companions of Sesostris were born on the same day.
[The number of six million Copts may be credible, says Clinton, if we understand it of the total Coptic population and not (with Eutychius) of the male adults alone.   In the reign of Nero, A.D. 66, Egypt, exclusive of Alexandria, contained 7,500,000 inhabitants.—O. S.]

[1] Elmacin, Hist. Saracen. p. 218; and this gross lump is swallowed without scruple by D'Herbelot (Biblioth. Orient. p. 1031), Arbuthnot (Tables of Ancient Coins, p. 262), and De Guignes (Hist. des Huns, tom. iii. p. 135). They might allege the not less extravagant liberality of Appian in favour of the Ptolemies (in præfat.) of seventy-four myriads, 740,000 talents, an annual income of 185, or near 300, millions of pounds sterling, according as we reckon by the Egyptian or the Alexandrian talent (Bernard de Ponderibus Antiq. p. 186).

[2] See the measurement of D'Anville (Mém. sur l'Egypte, p. 23, etc.). After some peevish cavils, M. Pauw (Recherches sur les Egyptiens, tom. i. p. 118-121) can only enlarge his reckoning to 2250 square leagues.

[3] Renaudot, Hist. Patriarch. Alexand. p. 334, who calls the common reading or version of Elmacin *error librarii*.   His own emendation, of 4,300,000 pieces, in the ninth century, maintains a probable medium between the 3,000,000 which the Arabs acquired by the conquest of Egypt (idem, p. 168), and the 2,400,000 which the sultan of Constantinople levied in the last century (Pietro della Valle, tom. i. p. 352; Thevenot, part i. p. 824).   Pauw (Recherches, .tom. ii. p. 365-373) gradually raises the revenue of the Pharaohs, the Ptolemies, and the Cæsars, from six to fifteen millions of German crowns.

[4] The list of Schultens (Index Geograph. ad calcem Vit. Saladin. p. 5) contains 2396 places; that of D'Anville (Mém. sur l'Egypte, p. 29), from the divan of Cairo, enumerates 2696.

[5] See Maillet (Description de l'Égypte, p. 28), who seems to argue with candour and judgment.   I am much better satisfied with the observations than with the reading of the French consul.   He was ignorant of Greek and Latin literature, and his fancy is too much delighted with the fictions of the Arabs.   Their best knowledge is collected by Abulfeda (Descript.

IV. The conquest of Africa, from the Nile to the Atlantic Ocean,[1] was first attempted by the arms of the caliph Othman. The pious design was approved by the companions of Mohammed and the chiefs of the tribes; and twenty thousand Arabs marched from Medina, with the gifts and the blessing of the commander of the faithful. They were joined in the camp of Memphis by twenty thousand of their countrymen; and the conduct of the war was intrusted to Abdallah,[2] the son of Said and the foster-brother of the caliph, who had lately supplanted the conqueror and lieutenant of Egypt. Yet the favour of the prince, and the merit of his favourite, could not obliterate the guilt of his apostasy. The early conversion of Abdallah, and his skilful pen, had recommended him to the important office of transcribing the sheets of the Koran: he betrayed his trust, corrupted the text, derided the errors which he had made, and fled to Mecca to escape the justice, and expose the ignorance, of the apostle. After the conquest of Mecca he fell prostrate at the feet of Mohammed: his tears, and the entreaties of Othman, extorted a reluctant pardon; but the prophet declared that he had so long hesitated, to allow time for some zealous disciple to avenge his injury in the blood of the apostate. With apparent fidelity and effective merit he served the religion which it was no longer his interest to desert: his birth and talents gave him an honourable rank among the Koreish; and, in a nation of cavalry, Abdallah was renowned as the boldest and most dexterous horse-

Ægypt. Arab. et Lat. à Joh. David Michaelis, Göttingæ, in 4to, 1776); and in two recent voyages into Egypt, we are amused by Savary, and instructed by Volney. I wish the latter could travel over the globe.

[1] My conquest of Africa is drawn from two French interpreters of Arabic literature, Cardonne (Hist. de l'Afrique et de l'Espagne sous la Domination des Arabes, tom. i. p. 8-55) and Otter (Hist. de l'Académie des Inscriptions, tom. xxi. p. 111-125 and 136). They derive their principal information from Novairi, who composed, A.D. 1331, an Encyclopædia in more than twenty volumes. The five general parts successively treat of, 1. Physics; 2. Man; 3. Animals; 4. Plants; and 5. History; and the African affairs are discussed in the sixth chapter of the fifth section of this last part (Reiske, Prodidagmata ad Hagji Chalifæ Tabulas, p. 232-234). Among the older historians who are quoted by Novairi we may distinguish the original narrative of a soldier who led the van of the Moslems.

[The following chronology of the Moslem conquests in Egypt and Africa may be found useful:—

> Amrou begins his campaign in Egypt, December, 639.
> Battle of Heliopolis, July or August, 640.
> Alexandria and Babylon besieged, September, 640.
> Babylon captured, April 641.
> Alexandria capitulates, October 17, 641.
> Reduction of Tripoli and Sabrata, 642-3.—O. S.]

[2] See the history of Abdallah, in Abulfeda (Vit. Mohammed. p. 109) and Gagnier (Vie de Mahomet, tom. iii. p. 45-48).

man of Arabia. At the head of forty thousand Moslems he advanced from Egypt into the unknown countries of the West. The sands of Barca might be impervious to a Roman legion; but the Arabs were attended by their faithful camels; and the natives of the desert beheld without terror the familiar aspect of the soil and climate. After a painful march they pitched their tents before the walls of Tripoli,[1] a maritime city in which the *name*, the wealth, and the inhabitants of the province had gradually centred, and which now maintains the third rank among the states of Barbary. A reinforcement of Greeks was surprised and cut in pieces on the sea-shore; but the fortifications of Tripoli resisted the first assaults; and the Saracens were tempted by the approach of the præfect Gregory[2] to relinquish the labours of the siege for the perils and the hopes of a decisive action. If his standard was followed by one hundred and twenty thousand men, the regular bands of the empire must have been lost in the naked and disorderly crowd of Africans and Moors, who formed the strength, or rather the numbers, of his host. He rejected with indignation the option of the Koran or the tribute; and during several days the two armies were fiercely engaged from the dawn of light to the hour of noon, when their fatigue and the excessive heat compelled them to seek shelter and refreshment in their respective camps. The daughter of Gregory, a maid of incomparable beauty and spirit, is said to have fought by his side: from her earliest youth she was trained to mount on horseback, to draw the bow, and to wield the scimitar; and the richness of her arms and apparel were conspicuous in the foremost ranks of the battle. Her hand, with a hundred thousand pieces of gold, was offered for the head of the Arabian general, and the youths of Africa were excited by the prospect of the glorious prize. At the pressing solicitation of his

---

[1] The province and city of Tripoli are described by Leo Africanus (in Navigatione et Viaggi di Ramusio, tom. i. Venetia, 1550, fol. 76 *verso*) and Marmol (Description de l'Afrique, tom. ii. p. 562). The first of these writers was a Moor, a scholar, and a traveller, who composed or translated his African geography in a state of captivity at Rome, where he had assumed the name and religion of Pope Leo X. In a similar captivity among the Moors, the Spaniard Marmol, a soldier of Charles V., compiled his Description of Africa, translated by D'Ablancourt into French (Paris, 1667, 3 vols. in 4to). Marmol had read and seen, but he is destitute of the curious and extensive observation which abounds in the original work of Leo the African.

[2] Theophanes, who mentions the defeat, rather than the death, of Gregory. He brands the præfect with the name of Τύραννος: he had probably assumed the purple (Chronograph. p. 285 [tom. i. p. 525, ed. Bonn.]).

brethren, Abdallah withdrew his person from the field; but the Saracens were discouraged by the retreat of their leader, and the repetition of these equal or unsuccessful conflicts.

A noble Arabian, who afterwards became the adversary of Ali, and the father of a caliph, had signalised his valour in Egypt, and Zobeir [1] was the first who planted the scaling-ladder against the walls of Babylon. In the African war he was detached from the standard of Abdallah. On the news of the battle, Zobeir, with twelve companions, cut his way through the camp of the Greeks, and pressed forwards, without tasting either food or repose, to partake of the dangers of his brethren. He cast his eyes round the field: " Where," said he, " is our general? " " In his tent." " Is the tent a station for the general of the Moslems? " Abdallah represented with a blush the importance of his own life, and the temptation that was held forth by the Roman præfect. " Retort," said Zobeir, " on the infidels their ungenerous attempt. Proclaim through the ranks that the head of Gregory shall be repaid with his captive daughter, and the equal sum of one hundred thousand pieces of gold." To the courage and discretion of Zobeir the lieutenant of the caliph intrusted the execution of his own stratagem, which inclined the long-disputed balance in favour of the Saracens. Supplying by activity and artifice the deficiency of numbers, a part of their forces lay concealed in their tents, while the remainder prolonged an irregular skirmish with the enemy till the sun was high in the heavens. On both sides they retired with fainting steps: their horses were unbridled, their armour was laid aside, and the hostile nations prepared, or seemed to prepare, for the refreshment of the evening, and the encounter of the ensuing day. On a sudden the charge was sounded; the Arabian camp poured forth a swarm of fresh and intrepid warriors; and the long line of the Greeks and Africans was surprised, assaulted, overturned, by new squadrons of the faithful, who, to the eye of fanaticism, might appear as a band of angels descending from the sky. The præfect himself was slain by the hand of Zobeir: his daughter, who sought revenge and death, was surrounded and made prisoner; and the fugitives involved in their disaster the town of Sufetula, to which they escaped from the sabres and lances of the Arabs. Sufetula was built one hundred and fifty miles to the south of Carthage: a

[1] See in Ockley (Hist. of the Saracens, vol. ii. p. 45) the death of Zobier, which was honoured with the tears of Ali, against whom he had rebelled. *His* valour at the siege of Babylon, if indeed it be the same person, is mentioned by Eutychius (Annal. tom. ii. p. 308).

gentle declivity is watered by a running stream, and shaded by a grove of juniper-trees; and, in the ruins of a triumphal arch, a portico, and three temples of the Corinthian order, curiosity may yet admire the magnificence of the Romans.[1] After the fall of this opulent city, the provincials and barbarians implored on all sides the mercy of the conqueror. His vanity or his zeal might be flattered by offers of tribute or professions of faith: but his losses, his fatigues, and the progress of an epidemical disease prevented a solid establishment; and the Saracens, after a campaign of fifteen months, retreated to the confines of Egypt, with the captives and the wealth of their African expedition. The caliph's fifth was granted to a favourite, on the nominal payment of five hundred thousand pieces of gold;[2] but the state was doubly injured by this fallacious transaction, if each foot-soldier had shared one thousand, and each horseman three thousand pieces, in the real division of the plunder. The author of the death of Gregory was expected to have claimed the most precious reward of the victory: from his silence it might be presumed that he had fallen in the battle, till the tears and exclamations of the præfect's daughter at the sight of Zobeir revealed the valour and modesty of that gallant soldier. The unfortunate virgin was offered, and almost rejected, as a slave, by her father's murderer, who coolly declared that his sword was consecrated to the service of religion; and that he laboured for a recompense far above the charms of mortal beauty or the riches of this transitory life. A reward congenial to his temper was the honourable commission of announcing to the caliph Othman the success of his arms. The companions, the chiefs, and the people were assembled in the mosch of Medina, to hear the interesting narrative of Zobeir; and, as the orator forgot nothing except the merit of his own counsels and actions, the name of Abdallah was joined by the Arabians with the heroic names of Chaled and Amrou.[3]

The Western conquests of the Saracens were suspended near twenty years, till their dissensions were composed by the establishment of the house of Ommiyah; and the caliph Moawiyah

---

[1] Shaw's Travels, p. 118, 119.

[2] Mimica emptio, says Abulfeda, erat hæc, et mira donatio; quandoquidem Othman, ejus nomine nummos ex ærario prius ablatos ærario præstabat (Annal. Moslem. p. 78). Elmacin (in his cloudy version, p. 39) seems to report the same job. When the Arabs besieged the palace of Othman, it stood high in their catalogue of grievances.

[3] Ἐπεστράτευσαν Σαρακηνοὶ τὴν Ἀφρικήν, καὶ συμβάλοντες τῷ τυράννῳ Γρηγορίῳ τοῦτον τρέπουσι, καὶ τοὺς σὺν αὐτῷ κτείνουσι, καὶ στοιχήσαντες φόρους μετὰ τῶν Ἄφρων ὑπέστρεψαν. Theophan. Chronograph. p. 285, edit. Paris [vol. i. p. 525, ed. Bonn.]. His chronology is loose and inaccurate.

was invited by the cries of the Africans themselves.   The successors of Heraclius had been informed of the tribute which they had been compelled to stipulate with the Arabs; but instead of being moved to pity and relieve their distress, they imposed, as an equivalent or a fine, a second tribute of a similar amount. The ears of the Byzantine ministers were shut against the complaints of their poverty and ruin; their despair was reduced to prefer the dominion of a single master; and the extortions of the patriarch of Carthage, who was invested with civil and military power, provoked the sectaries, and even the Catholics, of the Roman province, to abjure the religion as well as the authority of their tyrants.   The first lieutenant of Moawiyah acquired a just renown, subdued an important city, defeated an army of thirty thousand Greeks, swept away fourscore thousand captives, and enriched with their spoils the bold adventurers of Syria and Egypt.[1]   But the title of conqueror of Africa is more justly due to his successor Akbah.   He marched from Damascus at the head of ten thousand of the bravest Arabs; and the genuine force of the Moslems was enlarged by the doubtful aid and conversion of many thousand barbarians.   It would be difficult, nor is it necessary, to trace the accurate line of the progress of Akbah.   The interior regions have been peopled by the Orientals with fictitious armies and imaginary citadels.   In the warlike province of Zab, or Numidia, fourscore thousand of the natives might assemble in arms; but the number of three hundred and sixty towns is incompatible with the ignorance or decay of husbandry;[2] and a circumference of three leagues will not be justified by the ruins of Erbe or Lambesa, the ancient metropolis of that inland country.   As we approach the sea-coast, the well-known cities of Bugia[3] and Tangier[4] define the more certain limits of the Saracen victories.   A remnant of trade still adheres to the commodious harbour of Bugia, which in a more prosperous age is said to have contained about twenty thousand houses; and the plenty of iron which is dug from the adjacent mountains might have supplied a braver people with the instruments of

[1] Theophanes (in Chronograph. p. 293 [vol. i. p. 539]) inserts the vague rumours that might reach Constantinople of the Western conquests of the Arabs; and I learn from Paul Warnefrid, deacon of Aquileia (de Gestis Langobard. l. v. c. 13), that at this time they sent a fleet from Alexandria into the Sicilian and African seas.

[2] See Novairi (apud Otter, p. 118), Leo Africanus (fol. 81, *verso*), who reckons only cinque città e infinite casale, Marmol (Description de l'Afrique, tom. iii. p. 33), and Shaw (Travels, p. 57, 65-68).

[3] Leo African. fol. 58, *verso*; 59, *recto*; Marmol, tom. ii. p. 415; Shaw, p. 43.

[4] Leo African. fol. 52; Marmol, tom. ii. p. 228.

defence. The remote position and venerable antiquity of Tingi, or Tangier, have been decorated by the Greek and Arabian fables; but the figurative expressions of the latter, that the walls were constructed of brass, and that the roofs were covered with gold and silver, may be interpreted as the emblems of strength and opulence. The province of Mauritania Tingitana,[1] which assumed the name of the capital, had been imperfectly discovered and settled by the Romans; the five colonies were confined to a narrow pale, and the more southern parts were seldom explored except by the agents of luxury, who searched the forests for ivory and the citron-wood,[2] and the shores of the ocean for the purple shell-fish. The fearless Akbah plunged into the heart of the country, traversed the wilderness in which his successors erected the splendid capitals of Fez and Morocco,[3] and at length penetrated to the verge of the Atlantic and the great desert. The river Sus descends from the western sides of Mount Atlas, fertilises, like the Nile, the adjacent soil, and falls into the sea at a moderate distance from the Canary, or Fortunate, islands. Its banks were inhabited by the last of the Moors, a race of savages, without laws or discipline or religion: they were astonished by the strange and irresistible terrors of the Oriental arms; and as they possessed neither gold nor silver, the richest spoil was the beauty of the female captives, some of whom were afterwards sold for a thousand pieces of gold. The career, though not the

[1] Regio ignobilis, et vix quicquam illustre sortita, parvis oppidis habitatur, parva flumina emittit, solo quam viris melior, et segnitie gentis obscura. Pomponius Mela, i. 5; iii. 10. Mela deserves the more credit, since his own Phœnician ancestors had migrated from Tingitana to Spain (see, in ii. 6, a passage of that geographer so cruelly tortured by Salmasius, Isaac Vossius, and the most virulent of critics, James Gronovius). He lived at the time of the final reduction of that country by the emperor Claudius; yet, almost thirty years afterwards, Pliny (Hist. Nat. v. i.) complains of his authors, too lazy to inquire, too proud to confess their ignorance of that wild and remote province.

[2] The foolish fashion of this citron-wood prevailed at Rome among the men, as much as the taste for pearls among the women. A round board or table, four or five feet in diameter, sold for the price of an estate (latifundii taxatione), eight, ten, or twelve thousand pounds sterling (Plin. Hist. Natur. xiii. 29). I conceive that I must not confound the tree *citrus* with that of the fruit *citrum*. But I am not botanist enough to define the former (it is like the wild cypress) by the vulgar or Linnæan name; nor will I decide whether the *citrum* be the orange or the lemon. Salmasius appears to exhaust the subject, but he too often involves himself in the web of his disorderly erudition (Plinian. Exercitat. tom. ii. p. 666, etc.).

[3] Leo African. fol. 16, *verso*. Marmol. tom. ii. p. 28. This province, the first scene of the exploits and greatness of the *cherifs*, is often mentioned in the curious history of that dynasty at the end of the third volume of Marmol, Description de l'Afrique. The third volume of the Recherches Historiques sur les Maures (lately published at Paris) illustrates the history and geography of the kingdoms of Fez and Morocco.

zeal, of Akbah was checked by the prospect of a boundless ocean. He spurred his horse into the waves, and, raising his eyes to heaven, exclaimed with the tone of a fanatic, " Great God! if my course were not stopped by this sea, I would still go on, to the unknown kingdoms of the West, preaching the unity of thy holy name, and putting to the sword the rebellious nations who worship any other gods than thee." [1] Yet this Mohammedan Alexander, who sighed for new worlds, was unable to preserve his recent conquests. By the universal defection of the Greeks and Africans he was recalled from the shores of the Atlantic, and the surrounding multitudes left him only the resource of an honourable death. The last scene was dignified by an example of national virtue. An ambitious chief, who had disputed the command and failed in the attempt, was led about as a prisoner in the camp of the Arabian general. The insurgents had trusted to his discontent and revenge; he disdained their offers and revealed their designs. In the hour of danger the grateful Akbah unlocked his fetters and advised him to retire; he chose to die under the banner of his rival. Embracing as friends and martyrs, they unsheathed their scimitars, broke their scabbards, and maintained an obstinate combat till they fell by each other's side on the last of their slaughtered countrymen. The third general or governor of Africa, Zuheir, avenged and encountered the fate of his predecessor. He vanquished the natives in many battles; he was overthrown by a powerful army which Constantinople had sent to the relief of Carthage.

It had been the frequent practice of the Moorish tribes to join the invaders, to share the plunder, to profess the faith, and to revolt to their savage state of independence and idolatry on the first retreat or misfortune of the Moslems. The prudence of Akbah had proposed to found an Arabian colony in the heart of Africa; a citadel that might curb the levity of the barbarians, a place of refuge to secure, against the accidents of war, the wealth and the families of the Saracens. With this view, and under the modest title of the station of a caravan, he planted this colony in the fiftieth year of the Hegira. In its present decay, Cairoan [2] still holds the second rank in the kingdom of

---

[1] Otter (p. 119) has given the strong tone of fanaticism to this exclamation, which Cardonne (p. 37) has softened to a pious wish of *preaching* the Koran. Yet they had both the same text of Novairi before their eyes.

[2] The foundation of Cairoan is mentioned by Ockley (Hist. of the Saracens, vol. ii. p. 129, 130); and the situation, mosch, etc., of the city are described by Leo Africanus (fol. 75), Marmol (tom. ii. p. 532), and Sha (p. 115).

Tunis, from which it is distant about fifty miles to the south: [1] its inland situation, twelve miles westward of the sea, has protected the city from the Greek and Sicilian fleets. When the wild beasts and serpents were extirpated, when the forest, or rather wilderness, was cleared, the vestiges of a Roman town were discovered in a sandy plain: the vegetable food of Cairoan is brought from afar; and the scarcity of springs constrains the inhabitants to collect in cisterns and reservoirs a precarious supply of rain-water. These obstacles were subdued by the industry of Akbah; he traced a circumference of three thousand and six hundred paces, which he encompassed with a brick wall; in the space of five years the governor's palace was surrounded with a sufficient number of private habitations; a spacious mosch was supported by five hundred columns of granite, porphyry, and Numidian marble; and Cairoan became the seat of learning as well as of empire. But these were the glories of a later age; the new colony was shaken by the successive defeats of Akbah and Zuheir, and the western expeditions were again interrupted by the civil discord of the Arabian monarchy. The son of the valiant Zobeir maintained a war of twelve years, a siege of seven months, against the house of Ommiyah. Abdallah was said to unite the fierceness of the lion with the subtlety of the fox; but if he inherited the courage, he was devoid of the generosity, of his father.[2]

The return of domestic peace allowed the caliph Abdalmalek to resume the conquest of Africa; the standard was delivered to Hassan, governor of Egypt, and the revenue of that kingdom, with an army of forty thousand men, was consecrated to the important service. In the vicissitudes of war, the interior provinces had been alternately won and lost by the Saracens. But the sea-coast still remained in the hands of the Greeks; the predecessors of Hassan had respected the name and fortifications of Carthage; and the number of its defenders was recruited by

[1] A portentous, though frequent, mistake has been the confounding, from a slight similitude of name, the *Cyrene* of the Greeks and the *Cairoan* of the Arabs, two cities which are separated by an interval of a thousand miles along the sea-coast. The great Thuanus has not escaped this fault, the less excusable as it is connected with a formal and elaborate description of Africa (Historiar. l. vii. c. 2, in tom. i. p. 240, edit. Buckley).

[2] Besides the Arabic chronicles of Abulfeda, Elmacin, and Abulpharagius, under the seventy-third year of the Hegira, we may consult D'Herbelot (Biblioth. Orient. p. 7) and Ockley (Hist. of the Saracens, vol. ii. p. 339-349). The latter has given the last and pathetic dialogue between Abdallah and his mother, but he has forgot a physical effect of *her* grief for his death, the return, at the age of ninety, and fatal consequences, of her *menses*.

the fugitives of Cabes and Tripoli. The arms of Hassan were bolder and more fortunate: he reduced and pillaged the metropolis of Africa; and the mention of scaling-ladders may justify the suspicion that he anticipated by a sudden assault the more tedious operations of a regular siege. But the joy of the conquerors was soon disturbed by the appearance of the Christian succours. The præfect and patrician John, a general of experience and renown, embarked at Constantinople the forces of the Eastern empire;[1] they were joined by the ships and soldiers of Sicily, and a powerful reinforcement of Goths[2] was obtained from the fears and religion of the Spanish monarch. The weight of the confederate navy broke the chain that guarded the entrance of the harbour; the Arabs retired to Cairoan, or Tripoli; the Christians landed; the citizens hailed the ensign of the cross, and the winter was idly wasted in the dream of victory or deliverance. But Africa was irrecoverably lost; the zeal and resentment of the commander of the faithful[3] prepared in the ensuing spring a more numerous armament by sea and land; and the patrician in his turn was compelled to evacuate the post and fortifications of Carthage. A second battle was fought in the neighbourhood of Utica: the Greeks and Goths were again defeated; and their timely embarkation saved them from the sword of Hassan, who had invested the slight and insufficient rampart of their camp. Whatever yet remained of Carthage was delivered to the flames, and the colony of Dido[4] and Cæsar

---

[1] Λεόντιος ——— ἅπαντα τὰ 'Ρωμαϊκὰ ἐξώπλισε πλοῖμα, στρατηγόν τε ἐπ' αὐτοῖς 'Ιωάννην τὸν Πατρίκιον ἔμπειρον τῶν πολεμίων προχειρισάμενος πρὸς Καρχηδόνα κατὰ τῶν Σαρακηνῶν ἐξέπεμψεν. Nicephori Constantinopolitani Breviar. p. 26. The patriarch of Constantinople, with Theophanes (Chronograph. p. 309 [vol. i. p. 566, sq., ed. Bonn]), have slightly mentioned this last attempt for the relief of Africa. Pagi (Critica, tom. iii. p. 129, 141) has nicely ascertained the chronology by a strict comparison of the Arabic and Byzantine historians, who often disagree both in time and fact. See likewise a note of Otter (p. 121).

[2] Dove s'erano ridotti i nobili Romani e i *Gotti*; and afterwards, i Romani suggirono e i *Gotti* lasciarono Carthagine (Leo African. fol. 72, recto.). I know not from what Arabic writer the African derived his Goths; but the fact, though new, is so interesting and so probable, that I will accept it on the slightest authority.

[3] This commander is styled by Nicephorus Βασιλεὺς Σαρακήνων, a vague though not improper definition of the caliph. Theophanes introduces the strange appellation of Πρωτοσύμβολος, which his interpreter Goar explains by *Vizir Azem*. They may approach the truth, in assigning the active part to the minister rather than the prince; but they forget that the Ommiades had only a *kateb*, or secretary, and that the office of Vizir was not revived or instituted till the 132nd year of the Hegira (D'Herbelot, p. 912).

[4] According to Solinus (c. 27 [§ 11], p. 36, edit. Salmas.), the Carthage of Dido stood either 677 or 737 years—a various reading, which proceeds

lay desolate above two hundred years, till a part, perhaps a twentieth, of the old circumference was repeopled by the first of the Fatimite caliphs. In the beginning of the sixteenth century the second capital of the West was represented by a mosch, a college without students, twenty-five or thirty shops, and the huts of five hundred peasants, who, in their abject poverty, displayed the arrogance of the Punic senators. Even that paltry village was swept away by the Spaniards whom Charles the Fifth had stationed in the fortress of the Goletta. The ruins of Carthage have perished; and the place might be unknown if some broken arches of an aqueduct did not guide the footsteps of the inquisitive traveller.[1]

The Greeks were expelled, but the Arabians were not yet masters of the country. In the interior provinces the Moors or *Berbers*,[2] so feeble under the first Cæsars, so formidable to the Byzantine princes, maintained a disorderly resistance to the religion and power of the successors of Mohammed. Under the standard of their queen Cahina the independent tribes acquired some degree of union and discipline; and as the Moors respected in their females the character of a prophetess, they attacked the invaders with an enthusiasm similar to their own. The veteran bands of Hassan were inadequate to the defence of Africa: the conquests of an age were lost in a single day; and the Arabian chief, overwhelmed by the torrent, retired to the confines of Egypt, and expected, five years, the promised succours of the caliph. After the retreat of the Saracens, the victorious

from the difference of MSS. or editions (Salmas. Plin. Exercit. tom. i. p. 228). The former of these accounts, which gives 823 years before Christ, is more consistent with the well-weighed testimony of Velleius Paterculus; but the latter is preferred by our chronologist (Marsham, Canon. Chron. p. 398) as more agreeable to the Hebrew and Tyrian annals.

[1] Leo African. fol. 71, *verso* ; 72, *recto*. Marmol. tom. ii. p. 445-447. Shaw, p. 80.

[2] The history of the word *Barbar* may be classed under four periods. 1. In the time of Homer, when the Greeks and Asiatics might probably use a common idiom, the imitative sound of Bar-bar was applied to the ruder tribes, whose pronunciation was most harsh, whose grammar was most defective. Κάρες Βαρβαρόφωνοι (Iliad, ii. 867, with the Oxford Scholiast Clarke's Annotation, and Henry Stephens's Greek Thesaurus, tom. i. p. 720). 2. From the time, at least, of Herodotus, it was extended to *all* the nations who were strangers to the language and manners of the Greeks. 3. In the age of Plautus, the Romans submitted to the insult (Pompeius Festus, l. ii. p. 48, edit. Dacier), and freely gave themselves the name of barbarians. They insensibly claimed an exemption for Italy and her subject provinces; and at length removed the disgraceful appellation to the savage or hostile nations beyond the pale of the empire. 4. In every sense it was due to the Moors: the familiar word was borrowed from the Latin provincials by the Arabian conquerors, and has justly settled as a local denomination (Barbary) along the northern coast of Africa.

prophetess assembled the Moorish chiefs, and recommended a measure of strange and savage policy. " Our cities," said she, " and the gold and silver which they contain, perpetually attract the arms of the Arabs. These vile metals are not the objects of *our* ambition; we content ourselves with the simple productions of the earth. Let us destroy these cities; let us bury in their ruins those pernicious treasures; and when the avarice of our foes shall be destitute of temptation, perhaps they will cease to disturb the tranquillity of a warlike people." The proposal was accepted with unanimous applause. From Tangier to Tripoli the buildings, or at least the fortifications, were demolished, the fruit-trees were cut down, the means of subsistence were extirpated, a fertile and populous garden was changed into a desert, and the historians of a more recent period could discern the frequent traces of the prosperity and devastation of their ancestors. Such is the tale of the modern Arabians. Yet I strongly suspect that their ignorance of antiquity, the love of the marvellous, and the fashion of extolling the philosophy of barbarians, has induced them to describe, as one voluntary act, the calamities of three hundred years since the first fury of the Donatists and Vandals. In the progress of the revolt Cahina had most probably contributed her share of destruction; and the alarm of universal ruin might terrify and alienate the cities that had reluctantly yielded to her unworthy yoke. They no longer hoped, perhaps they no longer wished, the return of their Byzantine sovereigns: their present servitude was not alleviated by the benefits of order and justice; and the most zealous Catholic must prefer the imperfect truths of the Koran to the blind and rude idolatry of the Moors. The general of the Saracens was again received as the saviour of the province: the friends of civil society conspired against the savages of the land; and the royal prophetess was slain in the first battle, which overturned the baseless fabric of her superstition and empire. The same spirit revived under the successor of Hassan: it was finally quelled by the activity of Musa and his two sons; but the number of the rebels may be presumed from that of three hundred thousand captives; sixty thousand of whom, the caliph's fifth, were sold for the profit of the public treasury. Thirty thousand of the barbarian youth were enlisted in the troops; and the pious labours of Musa, to inculcate the knowledge and practice of the Koran, accustomed the Africans to obey the apostle of God and the commander of the faithful. In their climate and government, their diet and habitation, the wandering Moors resembled the Bedoweens of the desert. With the religion they were proud to adopt the language, name, and origin of Arabs: the blood of the strangers and natives was insensibly mingled; and from the Euphrates to the Atlantic the same nation might seem to be diffused over the sandy plains of Asia and Africa. Yet I will not deny that fifty thousand tents of pure Arabians might be transported over the Nile, and scattered through the Libyan desert; and I am not ignorant that five of the Moorish tribes still retain their *barbarous* idiom, with the appellation and character of *white* Africans.[1]

V. In the progress of conquest from the north and south, the Goths and the Saracens encountered each other on the confines of Europe and Africa. In the opinion of the latter, the difference of religion is a reasonable ground of enmity and warfare.[2]

As early as the time of Othman,[3] their piratical squadrons had ravaged the coast of Andalusia,[4] nor had they forgotten the relief of Carthage by the Gothic succours. In that age, as well as in the present, the kings of Spain were possessed of the fortress of Ceuta; one of the Columns of Hercules, which is divided by a narrow strait from the opposite pillar or point of Europe. A small portion of Mauritania was still wanting to the African conquest; but Musa, in the pride of victory, was repulsed from the walls of Ceuta, by the vigilance and courage of Count Julian, the general of the Goths. From his disappointment and perplexity Musa was relieved by an unexpected message of the Christian chief, who offered his place, his person, and his sword to the successors of Mohammed, and solicited the disgraceful honour of introducing their arms into the heart of Spain.[5] If

[1] The first book of Leo Africanus, and the observations of Dr. Shaw (p. 220, 223, 227, 247, etc.), will throw some light on the roving tribes of Barbary, of Arabian or Moorish descent. But Shaw had seen these savages with distant terror; and Leo, a captive in the Vatican, appears to have lost more of his Arabic than he could acquire of Greek or Roman learning. Many of his gross mistakes might be detected in the first period of the Mohammedan history.

[2] In a conference with a prince of the Greeks, Amrou observed that their religion was different; upon which score it was lawful for brothers to quarrel. Ockley's History of the Saracens, vol. i. p. 328.

[3] Abulfeda, Annal. Moslem. p. 78, vers. Reiske.

[4] The name of Andalusia is applied by the Arabs not only to the modern province, but to the whole peninsula of Spain (Geograph. Nub. p. 151; D'Herbelot, Biblioth. Orient. p. 114, 115). The etymology has been most improbably deduced from Vandalusia, country of the Vandals (D'Anville, Etats de l'Europe, p. 146, 147, etc.). But the Handalusia of Casiri, which signifies, in Arabic, the region of the evening, of the West, in a word, the Hesperia of the Greeks, is perfectly apposite (Biblioth. Arabico-Hispana, tom. ii. p. 327, etc.).

[5] The fall and resurrection of the Gothic monarchy are related by Mariana

we inquire into the cause of his treachery, the Spaniards will repeat the popular story of his daughter Cava;[1] of a virgin who was seduced, or ravished, by her sovereign; of a father who sacrificed his religion and country to the thirst of revenge. The passions of princes have often been licentious and destructive; but this well-known tale, romantic in itself, is indifferently supported by external evidence; and the history of Spain will suggest some motives of interest and policy more congenial to the breast of a veteran statesman.[2] After the decease or deposition of Witiza, his two sons were supplanted by the ambition of Roderic, a noble Goth, whose father, the duke or governor of a province, had fallen a victim to the preceding tyranny. The monarchy was still elective; but the sons of Witiza, educated on the steps of the throne, were impatient of a private station. Their resentment was the more dangerous, as it was varnished with the dissimulation of courts; their followers were excited by the remembrance of favours and the promise of a revolution; and their uncle Oppas, archbishop of Toledo and Seville, was the first person in the church, and the second in the state. It is probable that Julian was involved in the disgrace of the unsuccessful faction; that he had little to hope and much to fear from the new reign; and that the imprudent king could not forget or forgive the injuries which Roderic and his family had sustained. The merit and influence of the count rendered him a useful or formidable subject; his estates were ample, his followers bold and numerous; and it was too fatally shown that, by his

---

(tom. i. p. 238-260; l. vi. c. 19-26; l. vii. c. 1, 2). That historian has infused into his noble work (Historiæ de Rebus Hispaniæ, libri xxx.; Hagæ Comitum, 1733, in four volumes in folio, with the Continuation of Miniana) the style and spirit of a Roman classic; and, after the twelfth century, his knowledge and judgment may be safely trusted. But the Jesuit is not exempt from the prejudices of his order; he adopts and adorns, like his rival Buchanan, the most absurd of the national legends; he is too careless of criticism and chronology, and supplies, from a lively fancy, the chasms of historical evidence. These chasms are large and frequent; Roderic, archbishop of Toledo, the father of the Spanish history, lived five hundred years after the conquest of the Arabs; and the more early accounts are comprised in some meagre lines of the blind chronicles of Isidore of Badajoz (Pacensis) and of Alphonso III. king of Leon, which I have seen only in the annals of Pagi.

[1] Le viol (says Voltaire) est aussi difficile à faire qu'à prouver. Des Evêques se seroient-ils ligués pour une fille? (Hist. Générale, c. xxvi.) His argument is not logically conclusive.

[2] In the story of Cava, Mariana (l. vi. c. 21, p. 241, 242) seems to vie with the Lucretia of Livy. Like the ancients, he seldom quotes; and the oldest testimony of Baronius (Annal. Eccles. A.D. 713, No. 19), that of Lucas Tudensis, a Gallician deacon of the thirteenth century, only says, Cava quam pro concubinâ utebatur.

Andalusian and Mauritanian commands, he held in his hand the keys of the Spanish monarchy. Too feeble, however, to meet his sovereign in arms, he sought the aid of a foreign power; and his rash invitation of the Moors and Arabs produced the calamities of eight hundred years. In his epistles, or in a personal interview, he revealed the wealth and nakedness of his country; the weakness of an unpopular prince; the degeneracy of an effeminate people. The Goths were no longer the victorious barbarians, who had humbled the pride of Rome, despoiled the queen of nations, and penetrated from the Danube to the Atlantic Ocean. Secluded from the world by the Pyrenæan mountains, the successors of Alaric had slumbered in a long peace: the walls of the cities were mouldered into dust: the youth had abandoned the exercise of arms; and the presumption of their ancient renown would expose them in a field of battle to the first assault of the invaders. The ambitious Saracen was fired by the ease and importance of the attempt; but the execution was delayed till he had consulted the commander of the faithful; and his messenger returned with the permission of Walid to annex the unknown kingdoms of the West to the religion and throne of the caliphs. In his residence of Tangier, Musa, with secrecy and caution, continued his correspondence and hastened his preparations. But the remorse of the conspirators was soothed by the fallacious assurance that he should content himself with the glory and spoil, without aspiring to establish the Moslems beyond the sea that separates Africa from Europe.[1]

Before Musa would trust an army of the faithful to the traitors and infidels of a foreign land, he made a less dangerous trial of their strength and veracity. One hundred Arabs, and four hundred Africans, passed over, in four vessels, from Tangier or Ceuta: the place of their descent on the opposite shore of the strait is marked by the name of Tarif their chief; and the

---

[1] The Orientals, Elmacin, Abulpharagius, Abulfeda, pass over the conquest of Spain in silence, or with a single word. The text of Novairi, and the other Arabian writers, is represented, though with some foreign alloy, by M. de Cardonne (Hist. de l'Afrique et de l'Espagne sous la Domination des Arabes, Paris, 1765, 3 vols. in 12mo, tom. i. p. 55-114), and more concisely by M. de Guignes (Hist. des Huns, tom. i. p. 347-350). The librarian of the Escurial has not satisfied my hopes: yet he appears to have searched with diligence his broken materials; and the history of the conquest is illustrated by some valuable fragments of the *genuine* Razis (who wrote at Corduba, A.H. 300), of Ben Hazil, etc. See Biblioth. Arabico-Hispana, tom. ii. p. 32, 105, 106, 182, 252, 319-332. On this occasion the industry of Pagi has been aided by the Arabic learning of his friend the Abbé de Longuerue, and to their joint labours I am deeply indebted.

date of this memorable event [1] is fixed to the month of Ramadan, of the ninety-first year of the Hegira, to the month of July, seven hundred and forty-eight years from the Spanish era of Cæsar,[2] seven hundred and ten after the birth of Christ. From their first station, they marched eighteen miles through a hilly country to the castle and town of Julian;[3] on which (it is still called Algezire) they bestowed the name of the Green Island, from a verdant cape that advances into the sea. Their hospitable entertainment, the Christians who joined their standard, their inroad into a fertile and unguarded province, the richness of their spoil, and the safety of their return, announced to their brethren the most favourable omens of victory. In the ensuing spring five thousand veterans and volunteers were embarked under the command of Tarik, a dauntless and skilful soldier, who surpassed the expectation of his chief; and the necessary transports were provided by the industry of their too faithful ally. The Saracens landed [4] at the pillar or point of Europe; the corrupt and familiar appellation of Gibraltar (*Gebel al Tarik*) describes the mountain of Tarik; and the entrenchments of his camp were the first outline of those fortifications which, in the hands of our countrymen, have resisted the art and power of the house of Bourbon. The adjacent governors informed the court of Toledo of the descent and progress of the Arabs; and the defeat of his lieutenant Edeco, who had been commanded to seize and bind the presumptuous strangers, admonished Roderic

---

[1] A mistake of Roderic of Toledo, in comparing the lunar years of the Hegira with the Julian years of the Era, has determined Baronius, Mariana, and the crowd of Spanish historians to place the first invasion in the year 713, and the battle of Xeres in November, 714. This anachronism of three years has been detected by the more correct industry of modern chronologists, above all, of Pagi (Critica, tom. iii. p. 169, 171-174), who have restored the genuine date of the revolution. At the present time an Arabian scholar, like Cardonne, who adopts the ancient error (tom. i. p. 75), is inexcusably ignorant or careless.

[2] The Era of Cæsar, which in Spain was in legal and popular use till the fourteenth century, begins thirty-eight years before the birth of Christ. I would refer the origin to the general peace by sea and land, which confirmed the power and *partition* of the Triumvirs (Dion Cassius, l. xlviii. p. 547, 553 [c. 28 and 36]. Appian de Bell. Civil. l. v. [c. 72] p. 1034, edit. fol.). Spain was a province of Cæsar Octavian; and Tarragona, which raised the first temple to Augustus (Tacit. Annal. i. 78), might borrow from the Orientals this mode of flattery.

[3] The road, the country, the old castle of Count Julian, and the superstitious belief of the Spaniards of hidden treasures, etc., are described by Père Labat (Voyages en Espagne et en Italie, tom. i. p. 207-217) with his usual pleasantry.

[4] The Nubian Geographer (p. 154) explains the topography of the war; but it is highly incredible that the lieutenant of Musa should execute the desperate and useless measure of burning his ships.

of the magnitude of the danger. At the royal summons, the dukes and counts, the bishops and nobles of the Gothic monarchy, assembled at the head of their followers; and the title of King of the Romans, which is employed by an Arabic historian, may be excused by the close affinity of language, religion, and manners, between the nations of Spain. His army consisted of ninety or a hundred thousand men; a formidable power, if their fidelity and discipline had been adequate to their numbers. The troops of Tarik had been augmented to twelve thousand Saracens; but the Christian malcontents were attracted by the influence of Julian, and a crowd of Africans most greedily tasted the temporal blessings of the Koran. In the neighbourhood of Cadiz, the town of Xeres [1] has been illustrated by the encounter which determined the fate of the kingdom; the stream of the Guadalete, which falls into the bay, divided the two camps, and marked the advancing and retreating skirmishes of three successive and bloody days. On the fourth day the two armies joined a more serious and decisive issue; but Alaric would have blushed at the sight of his unworthy successor, sustaining on his head a diadem of pearls, encumbered with a flowing robe of gold and silken embroidery, and reclining on a litter or car of ivory drawn by two white mules. Notwithstanding the valour of the Saracens, they fainted under the weight of multitudes, and the plain of Xeres was overspread with sixteen thousand of their dead bodies. " My brethren," said Tarik to his surviving companions, " the enemy is before you, the sea is behind; whither would ye fly? Follow your general: I am resolved either to lose my life or to trample on the prostrate king of the Romans." Besides the resource of despair, he confided in the secret correspondence and nocturnal interviews of Count Julian with the sons and the brother of Witiza. The two princes and the archbishop of Toledo occupied the most important post: their well-timed defection broke the ranks of the Christians; each warrior was prompted by fear or suspicion to consult his personal safety; and the remains of the Gothic army were scattered or destroyed in the flight and pursuit of the three following days. Amidst the general disorder Roderic started from his car, and mounted Orelia, the fleetest of his horses; but he escaped from a soldier's death to perish more ignobly in the waters of the Bætis or

---

[1] Xeres (the Roman colony of Asta Regia) is only two leagues from Cadiz. In the sixteenth century it was a granary of corn; and the wine of Xeres is familiar to the nations of Europe (Lud. Nonii Hispania, c. 13, p. 54-56, a work of correct and concise knowledge; D'Anville, Etats de l'Europe, etc. p. 154).

Guadalquivir. His diadem, his robes, and his courser were found on the bank; but as the body of the Gothic prince was lost in the waves, the pride and ignorance of the caliph must have been gratified with some meaner head, which was exposed in triumph before the palace of Damascus. " And such," continues a valiant historian of the Arabs, " is the fate of those kings who withdraw themselves from a field of battle." [1]

Count Julian had plunged so deep into guilt and infamy, that his only hope was in the ruin of his country. After the battle of Xeres he recommended the most effectual measures to the victorious Saracen. " The king of the Goths is slain; their princes have fled before you, the army is routed, the nation is astonished. Secure with sufficient detachments the cities of Bætica; but in person, and without delay, march to the royal city of Toledo, and allow not the distracted Christians either time or tranquillity for the election of a new monarch." Tarik listened to his advice. A Roman captive and proselyte, who had been enfranchised by the caliph himself, assaulted Cordova with seven hundred horse: he swam the river, surprised the town, and drove the Christians into the great church, where they defended themselves above three months. Another detachment reduced the sea-coast of Bætica, which in the last period of the Moorish power has comprised in a narrow space the populous kingdom of Granada. The march of Tarik from the Bætis to the Tagus [2] was directed through the Sierra Morena, that separates Andalusia and Castille, till he appeared in arms under the walls of Toledo.[3] The most zealous of the Catholics had escaped with the relics of their saints; and if the gates were shut, it was only till the victor had subscribed a fair and reasonable capitulation. The voluntary exiles were allowed

---

[1] Id sane infortunii regibus pedem ex acie referentibus sæpe contingit. Ben Hazil of Granada, in Biblioth. Arabico-Hispana, tom. ii. p. 327. Some credulous Spaniards believe that king Roderic, or Rodrigo, escaped to a hermit's cell; and others, that he was cast alive into a tub full of serpents, from whence he exclaimed, with a lamentable voice, " They devour the part with which I have so grievously sinned." (Don Quixote, part ii. l. iii. c. i.)

[2] The direct road from Corduba to Toledo was measured by Mr. Swinburne's mules in 72½ hours; but a larger computation must be adopted for the slow and devious marches of an army. The Arabs traversed the province of La Mancha, which the pen of Cervantes has transformed into classic ground to the readers of every nation.

[3] The antiquities of Toledo, *Urbs Parva* in the Punic wars, *Urbs Regia* in the sixth century, are briefly described by Nonius (Hispania, c. 59, p. 181-186). He borrows from Roderic the *fatale palatium* of Moorish portraits, but modestly insinuates that it was no more than a Roman amphitheatre.

to depart with their effects; seven churches were appropriated to the Christian worship; the archbishop and his clergy were at liberty to exercise their functions, the monks to practise or neglect their penance; and the Goths and Romans were left in all civil and criminal cases to the subordinate jurisdiction of their own laws and magistrates. But if the justice of Tarik protected the Christians, his gratitude and policy rewarded the Jews, to whose secret or open aid he was indebted for his most important acquisitions. Persecuted by the kings and synods of Spain, who had often pressed the alternative of banishment or baptism, that outcast nation embraced the moment of revenge: the comparison of their past and present state was the pledge of their fidelity; and the alliance between the disciples of Moses and of Mohammed was maintained till the final era of their common expulsion. From the royal seat of Toledo, the Arabian leader spread his conquests to the north, over the modern realms of Castille and Leon: but it is needless to enumerate the cities that yielded on his approach, or again to describe the table of emerald,[1] transported from the East by the Romans, acquired by the Goths among the spoils of Rome, and presented by the Arabs to the throne of Damascus. Beyond the Asturian mountains, the maritime town of Gijon was the term [2] of the lieutenant of Musa, who had performed, with the speed of a traveller, his victorious march, of seven hundred miles, from the rock of Gibraltar to the Bay of Biscay. The failure of land compelled him to retreat; and he was recalled to Toledo, to excuse his presumption of subduing a kingdom in the absence of his general. Spain, which, in a more savage and disorderly state, had resisted, two hundred years, the arms of the Romans, was overrun in a few months by those of the Saracens; and such was the eagerness of submission and treaty, that the governor of Cordova is recorded as the only chief who fell, without conditions,

---

[1] In the Historia Arabum (c. 9, p. 17, ad calcem Elmacin), Roderic of Toledo describes the emerald tables, and inserts the name of Medinat Almeyda, in Arabic words and letters. He appears to be conversant with the Mohammedan writers; but I cannot agree with M. de Guignes (Hist. des Huns, tom. i. p. 350), that he had read and transcribed Novairi; because he was dead a hundred years before Novairi composed his history. This mistake is founded on a still grosser error. M. de Guignes confounds the historian Roderic Ximenes archbishop of Toledo in the thirteenth century, with Cardinal Ximenes who governed Spain in the beginning of the sixteenth, and was the subject, not the author, of historical compositions.

[2] Tarik might have inscribed on the last rock the boast of Regnard and his companions in their Lapland journey:

" Hic tandem stetimus, nobis ubi defuit orbis."

a prisoner into their hands. The cause of the Goths had been irrevocably judged in the field of Xeres; and, in the national dismay, each part of the monarchy declined a contest with the antagonist who had vanquished the united strength of the whole.[1] That strength had been wasted by two successive seasons of famine and pestilence; and the governors, who were impatient to surrender, might exaggerate the difficulty of collecting the provisions of a siege. To disarm the Christians, superstition likewise contributed her terrors: and the subtle Arab encouraged the report of dreams, omens, and prophecies, and of the portraits of the destined conquerors of Spain, that were discovered on breaking open an apartment of the royal palace. Yet a spark of the vital flame was still alive: some invincible fugitives preferred a life of poverty and freedom in the Asturian valleys; the hardy mountaineers repulsed the slaves of the caliph; and the sword of Pelagius has been transformed into the sceptre of the Catholic kings.[2]

On the intelligence of this rapid success, the applause of Musa degenerated into envy, and he began, not to complain, but to fear, that Tarik would leave him nothing to subdue. At the head of ten thousand Arabs and eight thousand Africans, he passed over in person from Mauritania to Spain: the first of his companions were the noblest of the Koreish; his eldest son was left in the command of Africa; the three younger brethren were of an age and spirit to second the boldest enterprises of their father. At his landing in Algezire he was respectfully entertained by Count Julian, who stifled his inward remorse, and testified, both in words and actions, that the victory of the Arabs had not impaired his attachment to their cause. Some enemies yet remained for the sword of Musa. The tardy repentance of the Goths had compared their own numbers and those of the invaders; the cities from which the march of Tarik had declined considered themselves as impregnable; and the bravest patriots defended the fortifications of Seville and Merida. They were successively besieged and reduced by the labour of Musa, who transported his camp from the Bætis to the Anas, from the Guadalquivir to the Guadiana. When he beheld the works of

[1] Such was the argument of the traitor Oppas, and every chief to whom it was addressed did not answer with the spirit of Pelagius: Omnis Hispania dudum sub uno regimine Gothorum, omnis exercitus Hispaniæ in uno congregatus Ismaelitarum non valuit sustinere impetum. Chron. Alphonsi Regis, apud Pagi, tom. iii. p. 177.

[2] The revival of the Gothic kingdom in the Asturias is distinctly though concisely noticed by D'Anville (Etats de l'Europe, p. 159).

Roman magnificence, the bridge, the aqueducts, the triumphal arches, and the theatre of the ancient metropolis of Lusitania, " I should imagine," said he to his four companions, " that the human race must have united their art and power in the foundation of this city: happy is the man who shall become its master!" He aspired to that happiness, but the *Emeritans* sustained on this occasion the honour of their descent from the veteran legionaries of Augustus.[1] Disdaining the confinement of their walls, they gave battle to the Arabs on the plain; but an ambuscade rising from the shelter of a quarry, or a ruin, chastised their indiscretion, and intercepted their return. The wooden turrets of assault were rolled forwards to the foot of the rampart; but the defence of Merida was obstinate and long; and the *castle of the martyrs* was a perpetual testimony of the losses of the Moslems. The constancy of the besieged was at length subdued by famine and despair; and the prudent victor disguised his impatience under the names of clemency and esteem. The alternative of exile or tribute was allowed; the churches were divided between the two religions; and the wealth of those who had fallen in the siege, or retired to Gallicia, was confiscated as the reward of the faithful. In the midway between Merida and Toledo, the lieutenant of Musa saluted the vicegerent of the caliph, and conducted him to the palace of the Gothic kings. Their first interview was cold and formal; a rigid account was exacted of the treasures of Spain: the character of Tarik was exposed to suspicion and obloquy; and the hero was imprisoned, reviled, and ignominiously scourged by the hand, or the command, of Musa. Yet so strict was the discipline, so pure the zeal, or so tame the spirit, of the primitive Moslems, that after this public indignity Tarik could serve and be trusted in the reduction of the Tarragonese province. A mosch was erected at Saragossa by the liberality of the Koreish: the port of Barcelona was opened to the vessels of Syria; and the Goths were pursued beyond the Pyrenean mountains into their Gallic province of Septimania or Languedoc.[2] In the church of St. Mary, at

---

[1] The honourable relics of the Cantabrian war (Dion Cassius, l. liii. [c. 26] p. 720) were planted in this metropolis of Lusitania, perhaps of Spain (submittit cui tota suos Hispania fasces). Nonius (Hispania, c. 31, p. 106-110) enumerates the ancient structures, but concludes with a sigh: Urbs hæc olim nobilissima ad magnam incolarum infrequentiam delapsa est, et præter priscæ claritatis ruinas nihil ostendit.

[2] Both the interpreters of Novairi, De Guignes (Hist. des Huns, tom. i. p. 349) and Cardonne (Hist. de l'Afrique et de l'Espagne, tom. i. p. 93, 94, 104, 105), lead Musa into the Narbonnese Gaul. But I find no mention of this enterprise, either in Roderic of Toledo, or the MSS. of the Escurial,

Carcassonne, Musa found, but it is improbable that he left, seven equestrian statues of massy silver; and from his *term* or column of Narbonne, he returned on his footsteps to the Gallician and Lusitanian shores of the ocean. During the absence of the father, his son Abdelaziz chastised the insurgents of Seville, and reduced, from Malaga to Valentia, the sea-coast of the Mediterranean: his original treaty with the discreet and valiant Theodemir [1] will represent the manners and policy of the times. " *The conditions of peace agreed and sworn between Abdelaziz, the son of Musa, the son of Nassir, and Theodemir prince of the Goths.* In the name of the most merciful God, Abdelaziz makes peace on these conditions: *that* Theodemir shall not be disturbed in his principality, nor any injury be offered to the life or property, the wives and children, the religion and temples, of the Christians; *that* Theodemir shall freely deliver his seven cities, Orihuela, Valentola, Alicant, Mola, Vacasora, Bigerra (now Bejar), Ora (or Opta), and Lorca; *that* he shall not assist or entertain the enemies of the caliph, but shall faithfully communicate his knowledge of their hostile designs; *that* himself, and each of the Gothic nobles, shall annually pay one piece of gold, four measures of wheat, as many of barley, with a certain proportion of honey, oil, and vinegar; and that each of their vassals shall be taxed at one moiety of the said imposition. Given the fourth of Regeb, in the year of the Hegira ninety-four, and subscribed with the names of four Musulman witnesses." [2] Theodemir and his subjects were treated with uncommon lenity; but the rate of tribute appears to have fluctuated from a tenth to a fifth, according to the submission or obstinacy of the Christians.[3] In this revolution many partial calamities were inflicted

---

and the invasion of the Saracens is postponed by a French chronicle till the ninth year after the conquest of Spain, A.D. 721 (Pagi, Critica, tom. iii. p. 177, 195; Historians of France, tom. iii.). I much question whether Musa ever passed the Pyrenees.

[1] Four hundred years after Theodemir, his territories of Murcia and Carthagena retain in the Nubian geographer Edrisi (p. 154, 161) the name of Tadmir (D'Anville, Etats de l'Europe, p. 156; Pagi, tom. iii. p. 174). In the present decay of Spanish agriculture Mr. Swinburne (Travels into Spain, p. 119) surveyed with pleasure the delicious valley from Murcia to Orihuela, four leagues and a half of the finest corn, pulse, lucern, oranges, etc.

[2] See the treaty in Arabic and Latin, in the Bibliotheca Arabico-Hispana, tom. ii. p. 105, 106. It is signed the 4th of the month of Regeb, A.H. 94, the 5th of April, A.D. 713; a date which seems to prolong the resistance of Theodemir, and the government of Musa.

[3] From the history of Sandoval, p. 87. Fleury (Hist. Ecclés. tom. ix. p. 261) has given the substance of another treaty concluded A.Æ.C. 782, A.D. 734, between an Arabian chief and the Goths and Romans, of the

by the carnal or religious passions of the enthusiasts: some churches were profaned by the new worship: some relics or images were confounded with idols: the rebels were put to the sword, and one town (an obscure place between Cordova and Seville) was razed to its foundations. Yet if we compare the invasion of Spain by the Goths, or its recovery by the kings of Castille and Arragon, we must applaud the moderation and discipline of the Arabian conquerors.

The exploits of Musa were performed in the evening of life, though he affected to disguise his age by colouring with a red powder the whiteness of his beard. But in the love of action and glory his breast was still fired with the ardour of youth; and the possession of Spain was considered only as the first step to the monarchy of Europe. With a powerful armament by sea and land he was preparing to repass the Pyrenees, to extinguish in Gaul and Italy the declining kingdoms of the Franks and Lombards, and to preach the unity of God on the altar of the Vatican. From thence, subduing the barbarians of Germany, he proposed to follow the course of the Danube from its source to the Euxine Sea, to overthrow the Greek or Roman empire of Constantinople, and, returning from Europe to Asia, to unite his new acquisitions with Antioch and the provinces of Syria.[1] But his vast enterprise, perhaps of easy execution, must have seemed extravagant to vulgar minds; and the visionary conqueror was soon reminded of his dependence and servitude. The friends of Tarik had effectually stated his services and wrongs: at the court of Damascus the proceedings of Musa were blamed, his intentions were suspected, and his delay in complying with the first invitation was chastised by a harsher and more peremptory summons. An intrepid messenger of the caliph entered his camp at Lugo in Gallicia, and in the presence of the Saracens and Christians arrested the bridle of his horse. His own loyalty, or that of his troops, inculcated the duty of obedience: and his disgrace was alleviated by the recall of his

territory of Coimbra in Portugal. The tax of the churches is fixed at twenty-five pounds of gold; of the monasteries, fifty; of the cathedrals, one hundred: the Christians are judged by their count, but in capital cases he must consult the alcaide. The church doors must be shut, and they must respect the name of Mohammed. I have not the original before me; it would confirm or destroy a dark suspicion that the piece has been forged to introduce the immunity of a neighbouring convent.

[1] This design, which is attested by *several* Arabian historians (Cardonne, tom. i. p. 95, 96), may be compared with that of Mithridates, to march from the Crimea to Rome; or with that of Cæsar, to conquer the East and return home by the North; and all three are perhaps surpassed by the *real* and successful enterprise of Hannibal.

rival, and the permission of investing with his two governments his two sons, Abdallah and Abdelaziz. His long triumph from Ceuta to Damascus displayed the spoils of Africa and the treasures of Spain: four hundred Gothic nobles, with gold coronets and girdles, were distinguished in his train; and the number of male and female captives, selected for their birth or beauty, was computed at eighteen, or even at thirty, thousand persons. As soon as he reached Tiberias in Palestine, he was apprised of the sickness and danger of the caliph, by a private message from Soliman, his brother and presumptive heir, who wished to reserve for his own reign the spectacle of victory. Had Walid recovered, the delay of Musa would have been criminal: he pursued his march, and found an enemy on the throne. In his trial before a partial judge, against a popular antagonist, he was convicted of vanity and falsehood; and a fine of two hundred thousand pieces of gold either exhausted his poverty or proved his rapaciousness. The unworthy treatment of Tarik was revenged by a similar indignity; and the veteran commander, after a public whipping, stood a whole day in the sun before the palace gate, till he obtained a decent exile, under the pious name of a pilgrimage to Mecca. The resentment of the caliph might have been satiated with the ruin of Musa; but his fears demanded the extirpation of a potent and injured family. A sentence of death was intimated with secrecy and speed to the trusty servants of the throne both in Africa and Spain; and the forms, if not the substance, of justice were superseded in this bloody execution. In the mosch or palace of Cordova, Abdelaziz was slain by the swords of the conspirators; they accused their governor of claiming the honours of royalty; and his scandalous marriage with Egilona, the widow of Roderic, offended the prejudices both of the Christians and Moslems. By a refinement of cruelty, the head of the son was presented to the father, with an insulting question, whether he acknowledged the features of the rebel? "I know his features," he exclaimed with indignation: "I assert his innocence; and I imprecate the same, a juster fate, against the authors of his death." The age and despair of Musa raised him above the power of kings; and he expired at Mecca of the anguish of a broken heart. His rival was more favourably treated: his services were forgiven; and Tarik was permitted to mingle with the crowd of slaves.[1] I am ignorant whether Count Julian was

[1] I much regret our loss, or my ignorance, of two Arabic works of the eighth century, a Life of Musa, and a Poem on the exploits of Tarik. Of

rewarded with the death which he deserved indeed, though not from the hands of the Saracens; but the tale of their ingratitude to the sons of Witiza is disproved by the most unquestionable evidence. The two royal youths were reinstated in the private patrimony of their father; but on the decease of Eba, the elder, his daughter was unjustly despoiled of her portion by the violence of her uncle Sigebut. The Gothic maid pleaded her cause before the caliph Hashem, and obtained the restitution of her inheritance; but she was given in marriage to a noble Arabian, and their two sons, Isaac and Ibrahim, were received in Spain with the consideration that was due to their origin and riches.

A province is assimilated to the victorious state by the introduction of strangers and the imitative spirit of the natives; and Spain, which had been successively tinctured with Punic, and Roman, and Gothic blood, imbibed, in a few generations, the name and manners of the Arabs. The first conquerors, and the twenty successive lieutenants of the caliphs, were attended by a numerous train of civil and military followers, who preferred a distant fortune to a narrow home: the private and public interest was promoted by the establishment of faithful colonies; and the cities of Spain were proud to commemorate the tribe or country of their Eastern progenitors. The victorious though motley bands of Tarik and Musa asserted, by the name of *Spaniards*, their original claim of conquest; yet they allowed their brethren of Egypt to share their establishments of Murcia and Lisbon. The royal legion of Damascus was planted at Cordova; that of Emesa at Seville; that of Kinnisrin or Chalcis at Jaen; that of Palestine at Algezire and Medina Sidonia. The natives of Yemen and Persia were scattered round Toledo and the inland country, and the fertile seats of Granada were bestowed on ten thousand horsemen of Syria and Irak, the children of the purest and most noble of the Arabian tribes.[1] A spirit of emulation, sometimes beneficial, more

these authentic pieces, the former was composed by a grandson of Musa, who had escaped from the massacre of his kindred; the latter by the Vizir of the first Abdalrahman, caliph of Spain, who might have conversed with some of the veterans of the conqueror (Biblioth. Arabico-Hispana, tom. ii. p. 36, 139).

[1] Biblioth. Arab.-Hispana, tom. ii. p. 32, 252. The former of these quotations is taken from a *Biographia Hispanica*, by an Arabian of Valentia (see the copious Extracts of Casiri, tom. ii. p. 30-121); and the latter from a general Chronology of the Caliphs, and of the African and Spanish Dynasties, with a particular History of the kingdom of Granada, of which Casiri has given almost an entire version (Biblioth. Arabico-Hispana, tom.

frequently dangerous, was nourished by these hereditary factions. Ten years after the conquest, a map of the province was presented to the caliph: the seas, the rivers, and the harbours, the inhabitants and cities, the climate, the soil, and the mineral productions of the earth.[1] In the space of two centuries the gifts of nature were improved by the agriculture,[2] the manufactures, and the commerce of an industrious people; and the effects of their diligence have been magnified by the idleness of their fancy. The first of the Ommiades who reigned in Spain solicited the support of the Christians; and in his edict of peace and protection, he contents himself with a modest imposition of ten thousand ounces of gold, ten thousand pounds of silver, ten thousand horses, as many mules, one thousand cuirasses, with an equal number of helmets and lances.[3] The most powerful of his successors derived from the same kingdom the annual tribute of twelve millions and forty-five thousand dinars or pieces of gold, about six millions of sterling money;[4] a sum which, in the tenth century, most probably surpassed the united revenues of the Christian monarchs. His royal seat of Cordova contained six hundred moschs, nine hundred baths, and two hundred thousand houses; he gave laws to eighty cities of the first, to three hundred of the second and third order; and the fertile banks of the Guadalquivir were adorned with twelve thousand villages and hamlets. The Arabs might exaggerate the truth, but they created, and they describe, the

---

ii. p. 177-319). The author, Ebn Khateb, a native of Granada, and a contemporary of Novairi and Abulfeda (born A.D. 1313, died A.D. 1374), was an historian, geographer, physician, poet, etc. (tom. ii. p. 71, 72).

[1] Cardonne, Hist. de l'Afrique et de l'Espagne, tom. i. p. 116, 117.

[2] A copious treatise of husbandry, by an Arabian of Seville, in the twelfth century, is in the Escurial library, and Casiri had some thoughts of translating it. He gives a list of the authors quoted, Arabs as well as Greeks, Latins, etc.; but it is much if the Andalusian saw these strangers through the medium of his countryman Columella (Casiri, Biblioth. Arabico-Hispana, tom. i. p. 323-338).

[3] Biblioth. Arabico-Hispana, tom. ii. p. 104. Casiri translates the original testimony of the historian Rasis, as it is alleged in the Arabic Biographia Hispanica, pars ix. But I am most exceedingly surprised at the address, Principibus cæterisque Christianis Hispanis suis *Castellæ*. The name of Castellæ was unknown in the eighth century; the kingdom was not erected till the year 1022, an hundred years after the time of Rasis (Biblioth. tom. ii. p. 330), and the appellation was always expressive, not of a tributary province, but of a line of *castles* independent of the Moorish yoke (D'Anville, Etats de l'Europe, p. 166-170). Had Casiri been a critic, he would have cleared a difficulty, perhaps of his own making.

[4] Cardonne, tom. i. p. 337, 338. He computes the revenue at 130,000,000 of French livres. The entire picture of peace and prosperity relieves the bloody uniformity of the Moorish annals.

most prosperous era of the riches, the cultivation, and the populousness of Spain.[1]

The wars of the Moslems were sanctified by the prophet; but among the various precepts and examples of his life, the caliphs selected the lessons of toleration that might tend to disarm the resistance of the unbelievers. Arabia was the temple and patrimony of the God of Mohammed; but he beheld with less jealousy and affection the nations of the earth. The polytheists and idolaters, who were ignorant of his name, might be lawfully extirpated by his votaries;[2] but a wise policy supplied the obligation of justice; and after some acts of intolerant zeal, the Mohammedan conquerors of Hindostan have spared the pagodas of that devout and populous country. The disciples of Abraham, of Moses, and of Jesus were solemnly invited to accept the more *perfect* revelation of Mohammed; but if they preferred the payment of a moderate tribute, they were entitled to the freedom of conscience and religious worship.[3] In a field of battle, the forfeit lives of the prisoners were redeemed by the profession of *Islam ;* the females were bound to embrace the religion of their masters, and a race of sincere proselytes was gradually multiplied by the education of the infant captives. But the millions of African and Asiatic converts, who swelled the native band of the faithful Arabs, must have been allured, rather than constrained, to declare their belief in one God and the apostle of God. By the repetition of a sentence and the loss of a foreskin, the subject or the slave, the captive or the criminal, arose in a moment the free and equal companion of the victorious Moslems. Every sin was expiated, every engagement was dis-

[1] I am happy enough to possess a splendid and interesting work, which has only been distributed in presents by the court of Madrid: *Bibliotheca Arabico-Hispana Escurialensis, operâ et studio Michaelis Casiri, Syro Maronitæ. Matriti, in folio, tomus prior, 1760; tomus posterior, 1770.* The execution of this work does honour to the Spanish press; the MSS. to the number of MDCCCLI, are judiciously classed by the editor, and his copious extracts throw *some* light on the Mohammedan literature and history of Spain. These relics are now secure, but the task has been supinely delayed, till, in the year 1671, a fire consumed the greatest part of the Escurial library, rich in the spoils of Granada and Morocco.

[2] The *Harbii*, as they are styled, qui tolerari nequeunt, are, 1. Those who, *besides* God, worship the sun, moon, or idols. 2. Atheists. Utrique, quamdiu princeps aliquis inter Mohammedanos superest, oppugnari debent donec religionem amplectantur, nec requies iis concedenda est, nec pretium acceptandum pro obtinendâ conscientiæ libertate (Reland, Dissertat. x. de Jure Militari Mohammedan. tom. iii. p. 14): a rigid theory!

[3] The distinction between a proscribed and a tolerated sect, between the *Harbii* and the people of the Book, the believers in some divine revelation, is correctly defined in the conversation of the caliph Al Mamun with the idolaters or Sabæans of Charræ. Hottinger, Hist. Orient. p. 107, 108.

solved: the vow of celibacy was superseded by the indulgence
of nature; the active spirits who slept in the cloister were
awakened by the trumpet of the Saracens; and in the convul-
sion of the world, every member of a new society ascended to
the natural level of his capacity and courage. The minds of the
multitude were tempted by the invisible as well as temporal
blessings of the Arabian prophet; and charity will hope that
many of his proselytes entertained a serious conviction of the
truth and sanctity of his revelation. In the eyes of an inquisitive
polytheist, it must appear worthy of the human and the divine
nature. More pure than the system of Zoroaster, more liberal
than the law of Moses, the religion of Mohammed might seem less
inconsistent with reason than the creed of mystery and superstition which, in the seventh century, disgraced the simplicity
of the Gospel.

In the extensive provinces of Persia and Africa, the national
religion has been eradicated by the Mohammedan faith. The
ambiguous theology of the Magi stood alone among the sects of
the East: but the profane writings of Zoroaster [1] might, under
the reverend name of Abraham, be dexterously connected with
the chain of divine revelation. Their evil principle, the demon
Ahriman, might be represented as the rival, or as the creature,
of the God of light. The temples of Persia were devoid of images;
but the worship of the sun and of fire might be stigmatised as a
gross and criminal idolatry.[2] The milder sentiment was consecrated by the practice of Mohammed [3] and the prudence of the
caliphs: the Magians or Ghebers were ranked with the Jews
and Christians among the people of the written law;[4] and as

---

[1] The Zend or Pazend, the Bible of the Ghebers, is reckoned by themselves, or at least by the Mohammedans, among the ten books which
Abraham received from heaven; and their religion is honourably styled
the religion of Abraham (D'Herbelot, Biblioth. Orient. p. 701; Hyde, de
Religione veterum Persarum, c. iii. p. 27, 28, etc.). I much fear that we
do not possess any pure and *free* description of the system of Zoroaster.
Dr. Prideaux (Connection, vol. i. p. 300, octavo) adopts the opinion that
he had been the slave and scholar of some Jewish prophet in the captivity
of Babylon. Perhaps the Persians, who have been the masters of the
Jews, would assert the honour—a poor honour—of being *their* masters.
[2] The Arabian Nights, a faithful and amusing picture of the Oriental
world, represent in the most odious colours the Magians, or worshippers of
fire, to whom they attribute the annual sacrifice of a Musulman. The
religion of Zoroaster has not the least affinity with that of the Hindoos, yet
they are often confounded by the Mohammedans; and the sword of
Timour was sharpened by this mistake (Hist. de Timour Bec, par Chere-
feddin Ali Yezdi, l. v.).
[3] Vie de Mahomet, par Gagnier, tom. iii. p. 114, 115.
[4] Hæ tres sectæ, Judæi, Christiani, et qui inter Persas Magorum institutis
addicti sunt κατ' ἐξοχήν, *populi libri* dicuntur (Reland, Dissertat. tom. iii.

late as the third century of the Hegira, the city of Herat will
afford a lively contrast of private zeal and public toleration.[1]
Under the payment of an annual tribute, the Mohammedan law
secured to the Ghebers of Herat their civil and religious liberties:
but the recent and humble mosch was overshadowed by the
antique splendour of the adjoining temple of fire. A fanatic
Imam deplored, in his sermons, the scandalous neighbourhood,
and accused the weakness or indifference of the faithful. Excited by his voice, the people assembled in tumult; the two
houses of prayer were consumed by the flames, but the vacant
ground was immediately occupied by the foundations of a
new mosch. The injured Magi appealed to the sovereign of
Chorasan; he promised justice and relief; when, behold! four
thousand citizens of Herat, of a grave character and mature age,
unanimously swore that the idolatrous fane had *never* existed;
the inquisition was silenced, and their conscience was satisfied
(says the historian Mirchond [2]) with this holy and meritorious
perjury.[3] But the greatest part of the temples of Persia were
ruined by the insensible and general desertion of their votaries.
It was *insensible*, since it is not accompanied with any memorial
of time or place, of persecution or resistance. It was *general*,
since the whole realm, from Shiraz to Samarcand, imbibed the
faith of the Koran; and the preservation of the native tongue

p. 15). The caliph Al Mamun confirms this honourable distinction in
favour of the three sects, with the vague and equivocal religion of the
Sabæans, under which the ancient polytheists of Charræ were allowed to
shelter their idolatrous worship (Hottinger, Hist. Orient. p. 167, 168).

[1] This singular story is related by D'Herbelot (Biblioth. Orient. p. 448,
449) on the faith of Khondemir, and by Mirchond himself (Hist. priorum
Regum Persarum, etc., p. 9, 10, not. p. 88, 89).

[2] Mirchond (Mohammed Emir Khoondah Shah), a native of Herat, composed in the Persian language a general history of the East, from the
creation to the year of the Hegira 875 (A.D. 1471). In the year 904 (A.D.
1498) the historian obtained the command of a princely library, and his
applauded work, in seven or twelve parts, was abbreviated in three
volumes by his son Khondemir, A.H. 927 (A.D. 1520). The two writers,
most accurately distinguished by Petit de la Croix (Hist. de Genghizcan,
p. 537, 538, 544, 545), are loosely confounded by D'Herbelot (p. 358, 410,
994, 995); but his numerous extracts, under the improper name of Khondemir, belong to the father rather than the son. The historian of Genghizcan refers to a MS. of Mirchond, which he received from the hands of his
friend D'Herbelot himself. A curious fragment (the Taherian and Soffarian Dynasties) has been lately published in Persic and Latin (Viennæ,
1782, in 4to, cum notis Bernard de Jenisch); and the editor allows us to
hope for a continuation of Mirchond.

[3] Quo testimonio boni se quidpiam præstitisse opinabantur. Yet
Mirchond must have condemned their zeal, since he approved the legal
toleration of the Magi, cui (the fire temple) peracto singulis annis censû,
uti sacra Mohammedis lege cautum, ab omnibus molestiis ac oneribus
libero esse licuit.

reveals the descent of the Mohammedans of Persia.[1] In the mountains and deserts an obstinate race of unbelievers adhered to the superstition of their fathers; and a faint tradition of the Magian theology is kept alive in the province of Kirman, along the banks of the Indus, among the exiles of Surat, and in the colony which, in the last century, was planted by Shaw Abbas at the gates of Ispahan. The chief pontiff has retired to Mount Elbourz, eighteen leagues from the city of Yezd: the perpetual fire (if it continue to burn) is inaccessible to the profane: but his residence is the school, the oracle, and the pilgrimage of the Ghebers, whose hard and uniform features attest the unmingled purity of their blood. Under the jurisdiction of their elders, eighty thousand families maintain an innocent and industrious life; their subsistence is derived from some curious manufactures and mechanic trades; and they cultivate the earth with the fervour of a religious duty. Their ignorance withstood the despotism of Shaw Abbas, who demanded with threats and tortures the prophetic books of Zoroaster; and this obscure remnant of the Magians is spared by the moderation or contempt of their present sovereigns.[2]

The Northern coast of Africa is the only land in which the light of the Gospel, after a long and perfect establishment, has been totally extinguished. The arts, which had been taught by Carthage and Rome, were involved in a cloud of ignorance; the doctrine of Cyprian and Augustin was no longer studied. Five hundred episcopal churches were overturned by the hostile fury of the Donatists, the Vandals, and the Moors. The zeal and numbers of the clergy declined; and the people, without discipline, or knowledge, or hope, submissively sunk under the yoke of the Arabian prophet. Within fifty years after the expulsion of the Greeks, a lieutenant of Africa informed the caliph that the tribute of the infidels was abolished by their conversion;[3] and, though he sought to disguise his fraud and

---

[1] The last Magian of name and power appears to be Mardavige the Dilemite, who, in the beginning of the tenth century, reigned in the northern provinces of Persia, near the Caspian Sea (D'Herbelot, Biblioth. Orient. p. 355). But his soldiers and successors, the *Bowides*, either professed or embraced the Mohammedan faith; and under their dynasty (A.D. 933-1020) I should place the fall of the religion of Zoroaster.

[2] The present state of the Ghebers in Persia is taken from Sir John Chardin, not indeed the most learned, but the most judicious and inquisitive, of our modern travellers (Voyages en Perse, tom. ii. p. 109, 179-187, in 4to). His brethren, Pietro della Valle, Olearius, Thevenot, Tavernier, etc., whom I have fruitlessly searched, had neither eyes nor attention for this interesting people.

[3] The letter of Abdoulrahman, governor or tyrant of Africa, to the caliph

rebellion, his specious pretence was drawn from the rapid and extensive progress of the Mohammedan faith. In the next age an extraordinary mission of five bishops was detached from Alexandria to Cairoan. They were ordained by the Jacobite patriarch to cherish and revive the dying embers of Christianity:[1] but the interposition of a foreign prelate, a stranger to the Latins, an enemy to the Catholics, supposes the decay and dissolution of the African hierarchy. It was no longer the time when the successor of St. Cyprian, at the head of a numerous synod, could maintain an equal contest with the ambition of the Roman pontiff. In the eleventh century the unfortunate priest who was seated on the ruins of Carthage implored the arms and the protection of the Vatican; and he bitterly complains that his naked body had been scourged by the Saracens, and that his authority was disputed by the four suffragans, the tottering pillars of his throne. Two epistles of Gregory the Seventh[2] are destined to soothe the distress of the Catholics and the pride of a Moorish prince. The pope assures the sultan that they both worship the same God, and may hope to meet in the bosom of Abraham; but the complaint that three bishops could no longer be found to consecrate a brother, announces the speedy and inevitable ruin of the episcopal order. The Christians of Africa and Spain had long since submitted to the practice of circumcision and the legal abstinence from wine and pork; and the name of *Mozarabes*[3] (adoptive Arabs) was applied to their civil or religious conformity.[4] About the middle of the twelfth century the worship of Christ and the succession of

Aboul Abbas, the first of the Abbassides, is dated A.H. 132 (Cardonne, Hist. de l'Afrique et de l'Espagne, tom. i. p. 168).

[1] Bibliothèque Orientale, p. 66; Renaudot, Hist. Patriarch. Alex. p. 287, 288.

[2] Among the Epistles of the Popes, see Leo IX. Epist. 3; Gregor. VII. l. i. Epist. 22, 23, l. iii. Epist. 19, 20, 21; and the criticisms of Pagi (tom. iv. A.D. 1053, No. 14, A.D. 1073, No. 13), who investigates the name and family of the Moorish prince with whom the proudest of the Roman pontiffs so politely corresponds.

[3] Mozarabes, or Mostarabes, *adscititii*, as it is interpreted in Latin (Pocock, Specimen Hist. Arabum, p. 39, 40; Biblioth. Arabico-Hispana, tom. ii. p. 18). The Mozarabic liturgy, the ancient ritual of the church of Toledo, has been attacked by the popes, and exposed to the doubtful trials of the sword and of fire (Marian. Hist. Hispan. tom. i. l. ix. c. 18, p. 378). It was, or rather it is, in the Latin tongue; yet in the eleventh century it was found necessary (A.Æ.C. 1087—A.D. 1039) to transcribe an Arabic version of the canons of the councils of Spain (Biblioth. Arab. Hisp. tom. i. p. 547), for the use of the bishops and clergy in the Moorish kingdoms.

[4] About the middle of the tenth century the clergy of Cordova was reproached with this criminal compliance by the intrepid envoy of the emperor Otho I. (Vit. Johan. Gorz, in Secul. Benedict. V. No. 115, apud Fleury, Hist. Ecclés. tom. xii. p. 91).

pastors were abolished along the coast of Barbary, and in the
kingdoms of Cordova and Seville, of Valencia and Granada.[1]
The throne of the Almohades, or Unitarians, was founded on the
blindest fanaticism, and their extraordinary rigour might be
provoked or justified by the recent victories and intolerant zeal
of the princes of Sicily and Castille, of Arragon and Portugal.
The faith of the Mozarabes was occasionally revived by the
papal missionaries; and, on the landing of Charles the Fifth,
some families of Latin Christians were encouraged to rear their
heads at Tunis and Algiers.   But the seed of the Gospel was
quickly eradicated, and the long province from Tripoli to the
Atlantic has lost all memory of the language and religion of
Rome.[2]

After the revolution of eleven centuries the Jews and Christians of the Turkish empire enjoy the liberty of conscience
which was granted by the Arabian caliphs. During the first
age of the conquest they suspected the loyalty of the Catholics,
whose name of Melchites betrayed their secret attachment to
the Greek emperor, while the Nestorians and Jacobites, his
inveterate enemies, approved themselves the sincere and
voluntary friends of the Mohammedan government.[3] Yet this
partial jealousy was healed by time and submission; the churches
of Egypt were shared with the Catholics; [4] and all the Oriental
sects were included in the common benefits of toleration.   The
rank, the immunities, the domestic jurisdiction of the patriarchs,

[1] Pagi, Critica, tom. iv. A.D. 1149, No. 8, 9. He justly observes that,
when Seville, etc., were retaken by Ferdinand of Castille, no Christians,
except captives, were found in the place; and that the Mozarabic churches
of Africa and Spain, described by James à Vitriaco, A.D. 1218 (Hist.
Hierosol. c. 80, p. 1095, in Gest. Dei per Francos), are copied from some
older book. I shall add that the date of the Hegira 677 (A.D. 1278) must
apply to the copy, not the composition, of a treatise of jurisprudence,
which states the civil rights of the Christians of Cordova (Biblioth. Arab.
Hisp. tom. i. p. 471), and that the Jews were the only dissenters whom
Abul Waled, king of Granada (A.D. 1313), could either discountenance or
tolerate (tom. ii. p. 288).

[2] Renaudot, Hist. Patriarch. Alex. p. 288. Leo Africanus would have
flattered his Roman masters, could he have discovered any latent relics
of the Christianity of Africa.

[3] Absit (said the Catholic to the Vizir of Bagdad) ut pari loco habeas
Nestorianos, quorum præter Arabas nullus alius rex est, et Græcos quorum
reges amovendo Arabibus bello non desistunt, etc. See in the Collections
of Assemannus (Biblioth. Orient. tom. iv. p. 94-101) the state of the
Nestorians under the caliphs. That of the Jacobites is more concisely
exposed in the Preliminary Dissertation of the second volume of Assemannus.

[4] Eutych. Annal. tom. ii. p. 384, 387, 388. Renaudot, Hist. Patriarch.
Alex. p. 205, 206, 257, 332. A taint of the Monothelite heresy might
render the first of these Greek patriarchs less loyal to the emperors and
less obnoxious to the Arabs.

the bishops, and the clergy, were protected by the civil magistrate: the learning of individuals recommended them to the employments of secretaries and physicians: they were enriched by the lucrative collection of the revenue ; and their merit was sometimes raised to the command of cities and provinces. A caliph of the house of Abbas was heard to declare that the Christians were most worthy of trust in the administration of Persia. "The Moslems," said he, "will abuse their present fortune; the Magians regret their fallen greatness; and the Jews are impatient for their approaching deliverance." [1] But the slaves of despotism are exposed to the alternative of favour and disgrace. The captive churches of the East have been afflicted in every age by the avarice or bigotry of their rulers; and the ordinary and legal restraints must be offensive to the pride, or the zeal, of the Christians.[2] About two hundred years after Mohammed, they were separated from their fellow-subjects by a turban or girdle of a less honourable colour; instead of horses or mules, they were condemned to ride on asses, in the attitude of women. Their public and private buildings were measured by a diminutive standard; in the streets or the baths it is their duty to give way or bow down before the meanest of the people; and their testimony is rejected if it may tend to the prejudice of a true believer. The pomp of processions, the sound of bells or of psalmody, is interdicted in their worship; a decent reverence for the national faith is imposed on their sermons and conversations; and the sacrilegious attempt to enter a mosch, or to seduce a Musulman, will not be suffered to escape with impunity. In a time, however, of tranquillity and justice the Christians have never been compelled to renounce the Gospel, or to embrace the Koran; but the punishment of death is inflicted for the apostates who have professed and deserted the law of Mohammed. The martyrs of Cordova provoked the sentence of the cadhi by the public confession of their inconstancy, or their passionate invectives against the person and religion of the prophet.[3]

---

[1] Motadhed, who reigned from A.D. 892 to 902. The Magians still held their name and rank among the religions of the empire (Assemanni, Biblioth. Orient. tom. iv. p. 97).

[2] Reland explains the general restraints of the Mohammedan policy and jurisprudence (Dissertat. tom. iii. p. 16-20). The oppressive edicts of the caliph Motawakkel (A.D. 847-861), which are still in force, are noticed by Eutychius (Annal. tom. ii. p. 448) and D'Herbelot (Biblioth. Orient. p. 640). A persecution of the caliph Omar II. is related, and most probably magnified, by the Greek Theophanes (Chron. p. 334 [vol. i. p. 614, ed. Bonn]).

[3] The martyrs of Cordova (A.D. 850, etc.) are commemorated and justified by St. Eulogius, who at length fell a victim himself. A synod, convened by

At the end of the first century of the Hegira the caliphs were the most potent and absolute monarchs of the globe. Their prerogative was not circumscribed, either in right or in fact, by the power of the nobles, the freedom of the commons, the privileges of the church, the votes of a senate, or the memory of a free constitution. The authority of the companions of Mohammed expired with their lives; and the chiefs or emirs of the Arabian tribes left behind in the desert the spirit of equality and independence. The regal and sacerdotal characters were united in the successors of Mohammed; and if the Koran was the rule of their actions, they were the supreme judges and interpreters of that divine book. They reigned by the right of conquest over the nations of the East, to whom the name of liberty was unknown, and who were accustomed to applaud in their tyrants the acts of violence and severity that were exercised at their own expense. Under the last of the Ommiades the Arabian empire extended two hundred days' journey from east to west, from the confines of Tartary and India to the shores of the Atlantic Ocean. And if we retrench the sleeve of the robe, as it is styled by their writers, the long and narrow province of Africa, the solid and compact dominion from Fargana to Aden, from Tarsus to Surat, will spread on every side to the measure of four or five months of the march of a caravan.[1] We should vainly seek the indissoluble union and easy obedience that pervaded the government of Augustus and the Antonines; but the progress of the Mohammedan religion diffused over this ample space a general resemblance of manners and opinions. The language and laws of the Koran were studied with equal devotion at Samarcand and Seville: the Moor and the Indian embraced as countrymen and brothers in the pilgrimage of Mecca; and the Arabian language was adopted as the popular idiom in all the provinces to the westward of the Tigris.[2]

the caliph, ambiguously censured their rashness. The moderate Fleury cannot reconcile their conduct with the discipline of antiquity, toutefois l'autorité de l'église, etc. (Fleury, Hist. Ecclés. tom. x. p. 415-522, particularly p. 451, 508, 509). Their authentic acts throw a strong, though transient, light on the Spanish church in the ninth century.

[1] See the article *Eslamiah* (as we say Christendom), in the Bibliothèque Orientale (p. 325). This chart of the Mohammedan world is suited by the author, Ebn Alwardi, to the year of the Hegira 385 (A.D. 995). Since that time the losses in Spain have been overbalanced by the conquests in India, Tartary, and the European Turkey.

[2] The Arabic of the Koran is taught as a dead language in the college of Mecca. By the Danish traveller this ancient idiom is compared to the Latin; the vulgar tongue of Hejaz and Yemen to the Italian; and the Arabian dialects of Syria, Egypt, Africa, etc., to the Provençal, Spanish, and Portuguese (Niebuhr, Description de l'Arabie, p 74, etc.).

CHAPTER LII

The Two Sieges of Constantinople by the Arabs—Their Invasion of France, and Defeat by Charles Martel—Civil War of the Ommiades and Abbassides—Learning of the Arabs—Luxury of the Caliphs—Naval Enterprises on Crete, Sicily, and Rome—Decay and Division of the Empire of the Caliphs—Defeats and Victories of the Greek Emperors

WHEN the Arabs first issued from the desert they must have been surprised at the ease and rapidity of their own success. But when they advanced in the career of victory to the banks of the Indus and the summit of the Pyrenees, when they had repeatedly tried the edge of their scimitars and the energy of their faith, they might be equally astonished that any nation could resist their invincible arms, that any boundary should confine the dominion of the successor of the prophet. The confidence of soldiers and fanatics may indeed be excused, since the calm historian of the present hour, who strives to follow the rapid course of the Saracens, must study to explain by what means the church and state were saved from this impending, and, as it should seem, from this inevitable danger. The deserts of Scythia and Sarmatia might be guarded by their extent, their climate, their poverty, and the courage of the northern shepherds; China was remote and inaccessible; but the greatest part of the temperate zone was subject to the Mohammedan conquerors, the Greeks were exhausted by the calamities of war and the loss of their fairest provinces, and the barbarians of Europe might justly tremble at the precipitate fall of the Gothic monarchy. In this inquiry I shall unfold the events that rescued our ancestors of Britain, and our neighbours of Gaul, from the civil and religious yoke of the Koran; that protected the majesty of Rome, and delayed the servitude of Constantinople; that invigorated the defence of the Christians, and scattered among their enemies the seeds of division and decay.

Forty-six years after the flight of Mohammed from Mecca his disciples appeared in arms under the walls of Constantinople.[1] They were animated by a genuine or fictitious saying of the

[1] Theophanes places the *seven* years of the siege of Constantinople in the year of *our* Christian era 673 (of the Alexandrian 665, Sept. 1), and the peace of the Saracens four years afterwards; a glaring inconsistency! which Petavius, Goar, and Pagi (Critica, tom. iv. p. 63, 64) have struggled to remove. Of the Arabians, the Hegira 52 (A.D. 672, January 8) is assigned by Elmacin [p. 56], the year 48 (A.D. 668, Feb. 20) by Abulfeda, whose testimony I esteem the most convenient and creditable.

prophet, that, to the first army which besieged the city of the
Cæsars, their sins were forgiven: the long series of Roman
triumphs would be meritoriously transferred to the conquerors
of New Rome; and the wealth of nations was deposited in this
well-chosen seat of royalty and commerce. No sooner had the
caliph Moawiyah suppressed his rivals and established his throne,
than he aspired to expiate the guilt of civil blood by the success
and glory of this holy expedition; [1] his preparations by sea and
land were adequate to the importance of the object; his standard
was intrusted to Sophian, [2] a veteran warrior, but the troops
were encouraged by the example and presence of Yezid, the son
and presumptive heir of the commander of the faithful. The
Greeks had little to hope, nor had their enemies any reasons of
fear, from the courage and vigilance of the reigning emperor,
who disgraced the name of Constantine, and imitated only the
inglorious years of his grandfather Heraclius. Without delay or
opposition, the naval forces of the Saracens passed through the
unguarded channel of the Hellespont, which even now, under the
feeble and disorderly government of the Turks, is maintained as
the natural bulwark of the capital. [3] The Arabian fleet cast
anchor, and the troops were disembarked near the palace of
Hebdomon, seven miles from the city. During many days, from
the dawn of light to the evening, the line of assault was extended
from the golden gate to the eastern promontory, and the foremost warriors were impelled by the weight and effort of the
succeeding columns. But the besiegers had formed an insufficient estimate of the strength and resources of Constantinople.
The solid and lofty walls were guarded by numbers and discipline:
the spirit of the Romans was rekindled by the last danger of their
religion and empire: the fugitives from the conquered provinces

[1] For this first siege of Constantinople see Nicephorus (Breviar. p. 21, 22
[ed. Par.]); Theophanes (Chronograph. p. 294 [t. i. p. 541, ed. Bonn]);
Cedrenus (Compend. p. 437 [ed. Par.; tom. i. p. 764, ed. Bonn]); Zonaras
(Hist. tom. ii. l. xiv. [c. 20] p. 89); Elmacin (Hist. Saracen. p. 56, 57);
Abulfeda (Annal. Moslem. p. 107, 108, vers. Reiske); D'Herbelot (Biblioth.
Orient, Constantinah); Ockley's History of the Saracens, vol. ii. p. 127, 128.

[2] [The first leader of the Saracens in this expedition against Constanti-
nople was Abd Errahman, the son of the valiant Khaled—the Sword of
God—and after his death, which has been attributed to the envy of
Moawiyah, Sophian was the general.—O. S.]

[3] The state and defence of the Dardanelles is exposed in the Memoirs of
the Baron de Tott (tom. iii. p. 39-97), who was sent to fortify them against
the Russians. From a principal actor I should have expected more
accurate details; but he seems to write for the amusement, rather than
the instruction, of his reader. Perhaps, on the approach of the enemy,
the minister of Constantine was occupied, like that of Mustapha, in finding
two Canary-birds who should sing precisely the same note.

more successfully renewed the defence of Damascus and Alexandria; and the Saracens were dismayed by the strange and prodigious effects of artificial fire. This firm and effectual resistance diverted their arms to the more easy attempts of plundering the European and Asiatic coasts of the Propontis; and, after keeping the sea from the month of April to that of September, on the approach of winter they retreated fourscore miles from the capital, to the isle of Cyzicus, in which they had established their magazine of spoil and provisions. So patient was their perseverance, or so languid were their operations, that they repeated in the six following summers the same attack and retreat, with a gradual abatement of hope and vigour, till the mischances of shipwreck and disease, of the sword and of fire, compelled them to relinquish the fruitless enterprise. They might bewail the loss, or commemorate the martyrdom, of thirty thousand Moslems who fell in the siege of Constantinople; and the solemn funeral of Abu Ayub, or Job, excited the curiosity of the Christians themselves. That venerable Arab, one of the last of the companions of Mohammed, was numbered among the *ansars*, or auxiliaries, of Medina, who sheltered the head of the flying prophet. In his youth he fought, at Beder and Ohud, under the holy standard: in his mature age he was the friend and follower of Ali; and the last remnant of his strength and life was consumed in a distant and dangerous war against the enemies of the Koran. His memory was revered; but the place of his burial was neglected and unknown, during a period of seven hundred and eighty years, till the conquest of Constantinople by Mohammed the Second. A seasonable vision (for such are the manufacture of every religion) revealed the holy spot at the foot of the walls and the bottom of the harbour; and the mosch of Ayub has been deservedly chosen for the simple and martial inauguration of the Turkish sultans.[1]

The event of the siege revived, both in the East and West, the reputation of the Roman arms, and cast a momentary shade over the glories of the Saracens. The Greek ambassador was favourably received at Damascus, in a general council of the emirs or Koreish: a peace, or truce, of thirty years was ratified between the two empires; and the stipulation of an annual tribute, fifty horses of a noble breed, fifty slaves, and three

---

[1] Demetrius Cantemir's Hist. of the Othman Empire, p. 105, 106; Rycaut's State of the Ottoman Empire, p. 10, 11; Voyages de Thevenot, part i. p. 189. The Christians, who suppose that the martyr Abu Ayub is vulgarly confounded with the patriarch Job, betray their own ignorance rather than that of the Turks.

thousand pieces of gold, degraded the majesty of the commander of the faithful.[1] The aged caliph was desirous of possessing his dominions, and ending his days, in tranquillity and repose: while the Moors and Indians trembled at his name, his palace and city of Damascus was insulted by the Mardaites, or Maronites, of Mount Libanus, the firmest barrier of the empire, till they were disarmed and transplanted by the suspicious policy of the Greeks.[2] After the revolt of Arabia and Persia, the house of Ommiyah[3] was reduced to the kingdoms of Syria and Egypt: their distress and fear enforced their compliance with the pressing demands of the Christians; and the tribute was increased to a slave, a horse, and a thousand pieces of gold, for each of the three hundred and sixty-five days of the solar year. But as soon as the empire was again united by the arms and policy of Abdalmalek, he disclaimed a badge of servitude not less injurious to his conscience than to his pride; he discontinued the payment of the tribute; and the resentment of the Greeks was disabled from action by the mad tyranny of the second Justinian, the just rebellion of his subjects, and the frequent change of his antagonists and successors. Till the reign of Abdalmalek the Saracens had been content with the free possession of the Persian and Roman treasures in the coin of Chosroes and Cæsar. By the command of that caliph a national mint was established, both for silver and gold, and the inscription of the Dinar, though it might be censured by some timorous casuists, proclaimed the unity of the God of Mohammed.[4] Under the reign of the caliph Walid, the

---

[1] Theophanes, though a Greek, deserves credit for these tributes (Chronograph. p. 295, 296, 300, 301 [vol. i. p. 543, 552, ed. Bonn]), which are confirmed, with some variation, by the Arabic History of Abulpharagius (Dynast. p. 128, vers. Pocock).

[2] The censure of Theophanes is just and pointed, τὴν Ῥωμαϊκὴν δυναστείαν ἀκρωτηριάσας . . . πάνδεινα κακὰ πέπονθεν ἡ Ῥωμανία ὑπὸ τῶν Ἀράβων μεχρὶ τοῦ νῦν (Chronograph. p. 302, 303 [vol. i. p. 555, 556, ed. Bonn]). The series of these events may be traced in the Annals of Theophanes, and in the Abridgment of the Patriarch Nicephorus, p. 22, 24.

[3] These domestic revolutions are related in a clear and natural style, in the second volume of Ockley's History of the Saracens, p. 253-370. Besides our printed authors, he draws his materials from the Arabic MSS. of Oxford, which he would have more deeply searched had he been confined to the Bodleian library instead of the city jail; a fate how unworthy of the man and of his country!

[4] Elmacin, who dates the first coinage A.H. 76, A.D. 695, five or six years later than the Greek historians, has compared the weight of the best or common gold dinar to the drachm or dirhem of Egypt (p. 77), which may be equal to two pennies (48 grains) of our Troy weight (Hooper's Enquiry into Ancient Measures, p. 24-36), and equivalent to eight shillings of our sterling money. From the same Elmacin and the Arabian physicians some dinars as high as two dirhems, as low as half a dirhem, may be deduced.

Greek language and characters were excluded from the accounts of the public revenue.[1] If this change was productive of the invention or familiar use of our present numerals, the Arabic or Indian ciphers, as they are commonly styled, a regulation of office has promoted the most important discoveries of arithmetic, algebra, and the mathematical sciences.[2]

Whilst the caliph Walid sat idle on the throne of Damascus, while his lieutenants achieved the conquest of Transoxiana and Spain, a third army of Saracens overspread the provinces of Asia Minor, and approached the borders of the Byzantine capital. But the attempt and disgrace of the second siege was reserved for his brother Soliman, whose ambition appears to have been quickened by a more active and martial spirit. In the revolutions of the Greek empire, after the tyrant Justinian had been punished and avenged, a humble secretary, Anastasius or Artemius, was promoted by chance or merit to the vacant purple. He was alarmed by the sound of war; and his ambassador returned from Damascus with the tremendous news that the Saracens were preparing an armament by sea and land, such as would transcend the experience of the past, or the belief of the present, age. The precautions of Anastasius were not unworthy of his station, or of the impending danger. He issued a peremptory mandate, that all persons who were not provided with the means

The piece of silver was the dirhem, both in value and weight: but an old, though fair coin, struck at Waset, A.H. 88, and preserved in the Bodleian library, wants four grains of the Cairo standard (see the Modern Universal History, tom. i. p. 548, of the French translation).

[The following are the chief facts relating to the coinage of the Saracens, being based on Mr. S. Lane-Poole's *Coins and Medals* :—

At first the Arabs used the Byzantine coinage, until about A.H. 70, when the caliph Ali attempted to introduce a distinctively Muslim coinage. But it was very tentative, and it was not until six years later, A.H. 76, that the caliph Abd-El-Melik struck the first regular system. The two chief coins were the gold dinar (from Roman *denarius*) and the silver dirhem (from Greek *drachma*), the former weighing sixty-five grains and the latter forty-three. The dinar was worth about 11s. 6d. under the Ommiade caliphs, while the dirhem was worth about 1s. $1\frac{3}{16}d$.—O. S.]

[1] Καὶ ἐκώλυσε γράφεσθαι Ἑλληνιστὶ τοὺς δημοσίους τῶν λογοθεσίων κώδικας, ἀλλ' Ἀραβίοις αὐτὰ παρασημαίνεσθαι, χωρὶς τῶν ψήφων, ἐπειδὴ ἀδύνατον, τῇ ἐκείνων γλώσσῃ μονάδα, ἢ ὑάδα, ἢ τριάδα, ἢ ὀκτὼ ἥμισυ ἢ τρία γράφεσθαι. Theophan. Chronograph. p. 314 [t. i. p. 575, ed. Bonn]. This defect, if it really existed, must have stimulated the ingenuity of the Arabs to invent or borrow.

[2] According to a new, though probable, notion, maintained by M. de Villoison (Anecdota Græca, tom. ii. p. 152-157), our ciphers are not of Indian or Arabic invention. They were used by the Greek and Latin arithmeticians long before the age of Boethius. After the extinction of science in the West, they were adopted by the Arabic versions from the original MSS., and *restored* to the Latins about the eleventh century.

of subsistence for a three years' siege should evacuate the city: the public granaries and arsenals were abundantly replenished; the walls were restored and strengthened; and the engines for casting stones, or darts, or fire, were stationed along the ramparts, or in the brigantines of war, of which an additional number was hastily constructed. To prevent is safer, as well as more honourable, than to repel an attack; and a design was meditated, above the usual spirit of the Greeks, of burning the naval stores of the enemy, the cypress timber that had been hewn in Mount Libanus, and was piled along the sea-shore of Phœnicia, for the service of the Egyptian fleet. This generous enterprise was defeated by the cowardice or treachery of the troops, who, in the new language of the empire, were styled of the *Obsequian Theme*.[1] They murdered their chief, deserted their standard in the isle of Rhodes, dispersed themselves over the adjacent continent, and deserved pardon or reward by investing with the purple a simple officer of the revenue. The name of Theodosius might recommend him to the senate and people; but after some months he sunk into a cloister, and resigned, to the firmer hand of Leo the Isaurian, the urgent defence of the capital and empire. The most formidable of the Saracens, Moslemah the brother of the caliph, was advancing at the head of one hundred and twenty thousand Arabs and Persians, the greater part mounted on horses or camels; and the successful sieges of Tyana, Amorium, and Pergamus were of sufficient duration to exercise their skill and to elevate their hopes. At the well-known passage of Abydus, on the Hellespont, the Mohammedan arms were transported, for the first time, from Asia to Europe.[2] From thence, wheeling round the Thracian cities of the Propontis, Moslemah invested Constantinople on the land side, surrounded his camp with a ditch and rampart, prepared and planted his engines of assault, and declared, by words and actions, a patient resolution of expecting the return of seed-time and harvest, should the obstinacy of the besieged prove equal to his own. The Greeks would gladly have ransomed their religion and empire by a fine or assessment of a piece of gold on the head of each inhabitant of

---

[1] In the division of the *Themes*, or provinces described by Constantine Porphyrogenitus (de Thematibus, l. i. p. 9, 10 [ed. Par.; vol. iii. p. 24, *sqq.*, ed. Bonn]), the *Obsequium*, a Latin appellation of the army and palace, was the fourth in the public order. Nice was the metropolis, and its jurisdiction extended from the Hellespont over the adjacent parts of Bithynia and Phrygia (see the two maps prefixed by Delisle to the Imperium Orientale of Banduri).

[2] [This was the second attack on Constantinople; the first is recorded on page 386.—O. S.]

the city; but the liberal offer was rejected with disdain, and the presumption of Moslemah was exalted by the speedy approach and invincible force of the navies of Egypt and Syria. They are said to have amounted to eighteen hundred ships: the number betrays their inconsiderable size; and of the twenty stout and capacious vessels, whose magnitude impeded their progress, each was manned with no more than one hundred heavy-armed soldiers. This huge armada proceeded on a smooth sea, and with a gentle gale, towards the mouth of the Bosphorus; the surface of the strait was overshadowed, in the language of the Greeks, with a moving forest, and the same fatal night had been fixed by the Saracen chief for a general assault by sea and land. To allure the confidence of the enemy the emperor had thrown aside the chain that usually guarded the entrance of the harbour; but while they hesitated whether they should seize the opportunity or apprehend the snare, the ministers of destruction were at hand. The fire-ships of the Greeks were launched against them; the Arabs, their arms, and vessels were involved in the same flames; the disorderly fugitives were dashed against each other or overwhelmed in the waves; and I no longer find a vestige of the fleet that had threatened to extirpate the Roman name. A still more fatal and irreparable loss was that of the caliph Soliman, who died of an indigestion,[1] in his camp near Kinnisrin or Chalcis in Syria, as he was preparing to lead against Constantinople the remaining forces of the East. The brother of Moslemah was succeeded by a kinsman and an enemy; and the throne of an active and able prince was degraded by the useless and pernicious virtues of a bigot. While he started and satisfied the scruples of a blind conscience, the siege was continued through the winter by the neglect, rather than by the resolution of the caliph Omar.[2] The winter proved uncommonly rigorous: above a hundred days the ground was covered with deep snow,

[1] The caliph had emptied two baskets of eggs and of figs, which he swallowed alternately, and the repast was concluded with marrow and sugar. In one of his pilgrimages to Mecca, Soliman ate, at a single meal, seventy pomegranates, a kid, six fowls, and a huge quantity of the grapes of Tayef. If the bill of fare be correct, we must admire the appetite, rather than the luxury, of the sovereign of Asia (Abulfeda, Annal. Moslem. p. 126).

[2] See the article of Omar Ben Abdalaziz, in the Bibliothèque Orientale (p. 689, 690), præferens, says Elmacin (p. 91), religionem suam rebus suis mundanis. He was so desirous of being with God, that he would not have anointed his ear (his own saying) to obtain a perfect cure of his last malady. The caliph had only one shirt, and in an age of luxury his annual expense was no more than two drachms (Abulpharagius, p. 131). Haud diu gavisus eo principe fuit orbis Moslemus (Abulfeda, p. 127).

and the natives of the sultry climes of Egypt and Arabia lay
torpid and almost lifeless in their frozen camp. They revived on
the return of spring; a second effort had been made in their
favour, and their distress was relieved by the arrival of two
numerous fleets laden with corn, and arms, and soldiers; the first
from Alexandria, of four hundred transports and galleys; the
second, of three hundred and sixty vessels, from the ports of
Africa. But the Greek fires were again kindled, and, if the
destruction was less complete, it was owing to the experience
which had taught the Moslems to remain at a safe distance, or to
the perfidy of the Egyptian mariners, who deserted with their
ships to the emperor of the Christians. The trade and navigation of the capital were restored; and the produce of the fisheries
supplied the wants, and even the luxury, of the inhabitants. But
the calamities of famine and disease were soon felt by the troops
of Moslemah, and, as the former was miserably assuaged, so the
latter was dreadfully propagated, by the pernicious nutriment
which hunger compelled them to extract from the most unclean
or unnatural food. The spirit of conquest, and even of enthusiasm, was extinct: the Saracens could no longer straggle beyond
their lines, either single or in small parties, without exposing
themselves to the merciless retaliation of the Thracian peasants.
An army of Bulgarians was attracted from the Danube by the
gifts and promises of Leo; and these savage auxiliaries made
some atonement for the evils which they had inflicted on the
empire by the defeat and slaughter of twenty-two thousand
Asiatics. A report was dexterously scattered that the Franks,
the unknown nations of the Latin world, were arming by sea and
land in the defence of the Christian cause, and their formidable
aid was expected with far different sensations in the camp and
city. At length, after a siege of thirteen months,[1] the hopeless
Moslemah received from the caliph the welcome permission of
retreat. The march of the Arabian cavalry over the Hellespont
and through the provinces of Asia was executed without delay or
molestation; but an army of their brethren had been cut in
pieces on the side of Bithynia, and the remains of the fleet were
so repeatedly damaged by tempest and fire, that only five galleys

---

[1] Both Nicephorus [p. 36] and Theophanes agree that the siege of Constantinople was raised the 15th of August (A.D. 718); but as the former,
our best witness, affirms that it continued thirteen months [p. 35], the
latter must be mistaken in supposing that it began on the same day of the
preceding year. I do not find that Pagi has remarked this inconsistency.
[The siege of Constantinople was raised August 15, 718, having lasted
thirteen months.—O. S.]

entered the port of Alexandria to relate the tale of their various and almost incredible disasters.[1]

In the two sieges the deliverance of Constantinople may be chiefly ascribed to the novelty, the terrors, and the real efficacy of the *Greek fire*.[2] The important secret of compounding and directing this artificial flame was imparted by Callinicus, a native of Heliopolis in Syria, who deserted from the service of the caliph to that of the emperor.[3] The skill of a chemist and engineer was equivalent to the succour of fleets and armies; and this discovery or improvement of the military art was fortunately reserved for the distressful period when the degenerate Romans of the East were incapable of contending with the warlike enthusiasm and youthful vigour of the Saracens. The historian who presumes to analyse this extraordinary composition should suspect his own ignorance and that of his Byzantine guides, so prone to the marvellous, so careless, and, in this instance, so jealous of the truth. From their obscure, and perhaps fallacious hints, it should seem that the principal ingredient of the Greek fire was the *naphtha*,[4] or liquid bitumen, a light, tenacious, and inflammable oil,[5] which springs from the earth, and catches fire as

---

[1] In the second siege of Constantinople I have followed Nicephorus (Brev. p. 33-36), Theophanes (Chronograph. p. 324-334 [t. i. p. 593, *sqq*. ed. Bonn]), Cedrenus (Compend. p. 449-452 [p. 787-791, ed. Bonn]), Zonaras (tom. ii. [l. xiv. c. 27, l. xv. c. 3] p. 98-102), Elmacin (Hist. Saracen. p. 88), Abulfeda (Annal. Moslem. p. 126), and Abulpharagius (Dynast. p. 130), the most satisfactory of the Arabs.

[2] Our sure and indefatigable guide in the middle ages and Byzantine history, Charles du Fresne du Cange, has treated in several places of the Greek fire, and his collections leave few gleanings behind. See particularly Glossar. Med. et Infim. Græcitat. p. 1275, sub voce Πῦρ θαλάσσιον, ὑγρόν; Glossar. Med. et Infim. Latinitat. *Ignis Græcus ;* Observations sur Villehardouin, p. 305, 306; Observations sur Joinville, p. 71, 72.

[3] Theophanes styles him ἀρχιτεκτών (p. 295 [t. i. p. 542, ed. Bonn]). Cedrenus (p. 437 [tom. i. p. 765, ed. Bonn]) brings this artist from (the ruins of) Heliopolis in Egypt; and chemistry was indeed the peculiar science of the Egyptians.

[4] The naphtha, the oleum incendiarium of the history of Jerusalem (Gest. Dei per Francos, p. 1167), the Oriental fountain of James de Vitry (l. iii. c. 84 [p. 1098]), is introduced on slight evidence and strong probability. Cinnamus (l. vi. p. 165 [c. 10, p. 283, ed. Bonn]) calls the Greek fire πῦρ Μήδικον : and the naphtha is known to abound between the Tigris and the Caspian Sea. According to Pliny (Hist. Natur. ii. 109), it was subservient to the revenge of Medea, and in either etymology the ἔλαιον Μηδίας, or Μηδείας (Procop. de Bell. Gothic. l iv. c. 11 [t. ii. p. 512, ed. Bonn]), may fairly signify this liquid bitumen.

[5] On the different sorts of oils and bitumens see Dr. Watson's (the present Bishop of Llandaff's) Chemical Essays, vol. iii. essay i., a classic book, the best adapted to infuse the taste and knowledge of chemistry. The less perfect ideas of the ancients may be found in Strabo (Geograph. l. xvi. p. 1078 [p. 743, ed. Casaub.]) and Pliny (Hist. Natur. ii. 108, 109).

soon as it comes in contact with the air. The naphtha was mingled, I know not by what methods or in what proportions, with sulphur and with the pitch that is extracted from evergreen firs.[1] From this mixture, which produced a thick smoke and a loud explosion, proceeded a fierce and obstinate flame, which not only rose in perpendicular ascent, but likewise burnt with equal vehemence in descent or lateral progress; instead of being extinguished, it was nourished and quickened by the element of water; and sand, urine, or vinegar, were the only remedies that could damp the fury of this powerful agent, which was justly denominated by the Greeks the *liquid*, or the *maritime*, fire. For the annoyance of the enemy, it was employed with equal effect by sea and land, in battles or in sieges. It was either poured from the rampart in large boilers, or launched in red-hot balls of stone and iron, or darted in arrows and javelins, twisted round with flax and tow, which had deeply imbibed the inflammable oil; sometimes it was deposited in fireships, the victims and instruments of a more ample revenge, and was most commonly blown through long tubes of copper, which were planted on the prow of a galley, and fancifully shaped into the mouths of savage monsters, that seemed to vomit a stream of liquid and consuming fire. This important art was preserved at Constantinople, as the palladium of the state: the galleys and *artillery* might occasionally be lent to the allies of Rome; but the composition of the Greek fire was concealed with the most jealous scruple, and the terror of the enemies was increased and prolonged by their ignorance and surprise. In the treatise of the administration of the empire, the royal author [2] suggests the answers and excuses that might best elude the indiscreet curiosity and importunate

---

[1] Huic (*Naphthæ*) magna cognatio est ignium, transiliuntque protinus in eam undecunque visam. Of our travellers I am best pleased with Otter (tom. i. p. 153, 158).

[1] Anna Comnena has partly drawn aside the curtain. Ἀπὸ τῆς πεύκης, καὶ ἄλλων τινῶν τοιούτων δένδρων ἀειθάλων συνάγεται δάκρυον ἄκαυστον. Τοῦτο μετὰ θείου τριβόμενον ἐμβάλλεται εἰς αὐλίσκους καλάμων, καὶ ἐμφύσαται παρὰ τοῦ παίζοντος λάβρῳ καὶ συνεχεῖ πνεύματι (Alexiad. l. xiii. p. 383). Elsewhere (l. xi. p. 336) she mentions the property of burning, κατὰ τὸ πρανὲς καὶ ἐφ' ἑκάτερα. Leo, in the nineteenth chapter [§ 51] of his Tactics (Opera Meursii, tom. vi. p. 841, edit. Lami, Florent. 1745), speaks of the new invention of πῦρ μετὰ βροντῆς καὶ κάπνου. These are genuine and *Imperial* testimonies.

[There is little doubt that one kind of Greek fire was gunpowder, the recipe for its manufacture being preserved in a treatise of the ninth century. Its manufacture was certainly known before the time of Roger Bacon.— O. S.]

[2] Constantin. Porphyrogenit. de Administrat. Imperii, c. xiii. p. 64, 65 ed. Par.; tom. iii. p. 84, *sq.*, ed. Bonn].

demands of the barbarians. They should be told that the mystery of the Greek fire had been revealed by an angel to the first and greatest of the Constantines, with a sacred injunction that this gift of Heaven, this peculiar blessing of the Romans, should never be communicated to any foreign nation: that the prince and subject were alike bound to religious silence under the temporal and spiritual penalties of treason and sacrilege; and that the impious attempt would provoke the sudden and supernatural vengeance of the God of the Christians. By these precautions the secret was confined, above four hundred years, to the Romans of the East; and at the end of the eleventh century, the Pisans, to whom every sea and every art were familiar, suffered the effects, without understanding the composition, of the Greek fire. It was at length either discovered or stolen by the Mohammedans; and, in the holy wars of Syria and Egypt, they retorted an invention, contrived against themselves, on the heads of the Christians. A knight, who despised the swords and lances of the Saracens, relates with heartfelt sincerity his own fears, and those of his companions, at the sight and sound of the mischievous engine that discharged a torrent of the Greek fire, the *feu Gregeois*, as it is styled by the more early of the French writers. It came flying through the air, says Joinville,[1] like a winged long-tailed dragon, about the thickness of a hogshead, with the report of thunder and the velocity of lightning; and the darkness of the night was dispelled by this deadly illumination. The use of the Greek, or, as it might now be called, of the Saracen fire, was continued to the middle of the fourteenth century,[2] when the scientific or casual compound of nitre, sulphur, and charcoal effected a new revolution in the art of war and the history of mankind.[3]

[1] Histoire de St. Louis, p. 39; Paris, 1668, p. 44; Paris, de l'Imprimerie Royale, 1761. The former of these editions is precious for the observations of Ducange; the latter for the pure and original text of Joinville. We must have recourse to that text to discover that the feu Gregeois was shot with a pile or javelin from an engine that acted like a sling.

[2] The vanity, or envy, of shaking the established property of Fame, has tempted some moderns to carry gunpowder above the fourteenth (see Sir William Temple, Dutens, etc.), and the Greek fire above the seventh century (see the Saluste du Président des Brosses, tom. ii. p. 381). But their evidence, which precedes the vulgar era of the invention, is seldom clear or satisfactory, and subsequent writers may be suspected of fraud or credulity. In the earliest sieges some combustibles of oil and sulphur have been used, and the Greek fire has *some* affinities with gunpowder both in its nature and effects: for the antiquity of the first, a passage of Procopius (de Bell. Goth. l. iv. c. 11 [t. ii. p. 512, ed. Bonn]); for that of the second, some facts in the Arabic history of Spain (A.D. 1249, 1312, 1332; Biblioth. Arab. Hisp. tom. ii. p. 6, 7, 8) are the most difficult to elude.

[3] That extraordinary man, Friar Bacon, reveals two of the ingredients,

Constantinople and the Greek fire might exclude the Arabs from the eastern entrance of Europe; but in the West, on the side of the Pyrenees, the provinces of Gaul were threatened and invaded by the conquerors of Spain.[1] The decline of the French monarchy invited the attack of these insatiate fanatics. The descendants of Clovis had lost the inheritance of his martial and ferocious spirit; and their misfortune or demerit has affixed the epithet of *lazy* to the last kings of the Merovingian race.[2] They ascended the throne without power, and sunk into the grave without a name. A country palace, in the neighbourhood of Compiègne,[3] was allotted for their residence or prison: but each year, in the month of March or May, they were conducted in a waggon drawn by oxen to the assembly of the Franks, to give audience to foreign ambassadors and to ratify the acts of the mayor of the palace. That domestic officer was become the minister of the nation and the master of the prince. A public employment was converted into the patrimony of a private family: the elder Pepin left a king of mature years under the guardianship of his own widow and her child; and these feeble regents were forcibly dispossessed by the most active of his bastards. A government, half savage and half corrupt, was almost dissolved; and the tributary dukes, and provincial counts, and the territorial lords, were tempted to despise the weakness of

saltpetre and sulphur, and conceals the third in a sentence of mysterious gibberish, as if he dreaded the consequences of his own discovery (Biog. Brit. vol. i. p. 430, new edition).

[1] For the invasion of France, and the defeat of the Arabs by Charles Martel, see the Historia Arabum (c. 11, 12, 13, 14) of Roderic Ximenes, archbishop of Toledo, who had before him the Christian Chronicle of Isidore Pacensis, and the Mohammedan history of Novairi. The Moslems are silent or concise in the account of their losses, but M. Cardonne (tom. i. p. 129, 130, 131) has given a *pure* and simple account of all that he could collect from Ibn Halikan, Hidjazi, and an anonymous writer. The texts of the chronicles of France, and lives of saints, are inserted in the Collection of Bouquet (tom. iii.) and the Annals of Pagi, who (tom. iii. under the proper years) has restored the chronology, which is anticipated six years in the Annals of Baronius. The Dictionary of Bayle (*Abderame* and *Munuza*) has more merit for lively reflection than original research.

[2] Eginhart, de Vita Caroli Magni, c. ii. p. 13-18, edit. Schmink, Utrecht, 1711. Some modern critics accuse the minister of Charlemagne of exaggerating the weakness of the Merovingians; but the general outline is just, and the French reader will for ever repeat the beautiful lines of Boileau's Lutrin.

[3] *Mamaccæ*, on the Oise, between Compiègne and Noyon, which Eginhart calls preparvi reditûs villam (see the notes, and the map of ancient France for Dom. Bouquet's Collection). Compendium, or Compiègne, was a palace of more dignity (Hadrian. Valesii Notitia Galliarum, p. 152); and that laughing philosopher, the Abbé Galliani (Dialogues sur le Commerce des Bleds), may truly affirm that it was the residence of the rois très Chrétiens et très chevelûs.

the monarch, and to imitate the ambition of the mayor. Among these independent chiefs, one of the boldest and most successful was Eudes duke of Aquitain, who in the southern provinces of Gaul usurped the authority, and even the title, of king. The Goths, the Gascons, and the Franks assembled under the standard of this Christian hero: he repelled the first invasion of the Saracens; and Zama, lieutenant of the caliph, lost his army and his life under the walls of Toulouse. The ambition of his successors was stimulated by revenge; they repassed the Pyrenees with the means and the resolution of conquest. The advantageous situation which had recommended Narbonne [1] as the first Roman colony was again chosen by the Moslems: they claimed the province of Septimania or Languedoc as a just dependence of the Spanish monarchy: the vineyards of Gascony and the city of Bordeaux were possessed by the sovereign of Damascus and Samarcand; and the south of France, from the mouth of the Garonne to that of the Rhône, assumed the manners and religion of Arabia. [2]

But these narrow limits were scorned by the spirit of Abdalrahman, or Abderame, who had been restored by the caliph Hashem to the wishes of the soldiers and people of Spain. That veteran and daring commander adjudged to the obedience of the prophet whatever yet remained of France or of Europe; and prepared to execute the sentence, at the head of a formidable host, in the full confidence of surmounting all opposition either of nature or of man. His first care was to suppress a domestic rebel, who commanded the most important passes of the Pyrenees: Munuza, a Moorish chief, had accepted the alliance of the duke of Aquitain; and Eudes, from a motive of private or public interest, devoted his beauteous daughter to the embraces of the African misbeliever. But the strongest fortresses of Cerdagne were invested by a superior force; the rebel was over-

[1] Even before that colony, A.U.C. 630 (Velleius Patercul. i. 15), in the time of Polybius (Hist. l. iii. [c. 37] p. 265, edit. Gronov.) Narbonne was a Celtic town of the first eminence, and one of the most northern places of the known world (D'Anville, Notice de l'Ancienne Gaule, p. 473).

[2] [The first invasion of France by the Saracens was that conducted by Alhorr, A.D. 718; but it is probable that the city and province of Narbonne were not reduced by them until two or three years later under the leadership of Samah. That leader was slain in an unsuccessful attempt to take Toulouse, A.D. 721, and was succeeded by Abd Errahman for a short period, and then, after the death of Jezid II. and accession of Hashem, by Anabasa. The latter crossed the Pyrenees in 725, took Carcassonne and Nismes, and overran the whole of the south of France. After his death, which occurred in the following year, several other commanders followed, but nothing further of importance was done in France until Abd Errahman was again appointed in 731.—O. S.]

taken and slain in the mountains; and his widow was sent a captive to Damascus, to gratify the desires, or more probably the vanity, of the commander of the faithful. From the Pyrenees, Abderame proceeded without delay to the passage of the Rhône and the siege of Arles. An army of Christians attempted the relief of the city: the tombs of their leaders were yet visible in the thirteenth century; and many thousands of their dead bodies were carried down the rapid stream into the Mediterranean Sea. The arms of Abderame were not less successful on the side of the ocean. He passed without opposition the Garonne and Dordogne, which unite their waters in the gulf of Bordeaux; but he found, beyond those rivers, the camp of the intrepid Eudes, who had formed a second army and sustained a second defeat, so fatal to the Christians, that, according to their sad confession, God alone could reckon the number of the slain. The victorious Saracen overran the provinces of Aquitain, whose Gallic names are disguised, rather than lost, in the modern appellations of Perigord, Saintonge, and Poitou: his standards were planted on the walls, or at least before the gates, of Tours and of Sens; and his detachments overspread the kingdom of Burgundy as far as the well-known cities of Lyons and Besançon. The memory of these devastations, for Abderame did not spare the country or the people, was long preserved by tradition; and the invasion of France by the Moors or Mohammedans affords the groundwork of those fables which have been so wildly disfigured in the romances of chivalry, and so elegantly adorned by the Italian muse. In the decline of society and art, the deserted cities could supply a slender booty to the Saracens; their richest spoil was found in the churches and monasteries, which they stripped of their ornaments and delivered to the flames: and the tutelar saints, both Hilary of Poitiers and Martin of Tours, forgot their miraculous powers in the defence of their own sepulchres.[1] A victorious line of march had been prolonged above a thousand miles from the rock of Gibraltar to the banks of the Loire; the repetition of an equal space would have carried the Saracens to the confines of Poland and the Highlands of Scotland; the Rhine is not more impassable than the Nile or Euphrates, and the Arabian fleet might have sailed without a naval combat into the mouth of the

---

[1] With regard to the sanctuary of St. Martin of Tours, Roderic Ximenes accuses the Saracens of the *deed*. Turonis civitatem, ecclesiam et palatia vastatione et incendio simili diruit et consumpsit. The continuator of Fredegarius imputes to them no more than the *intention*. Ad domum beatissimi Martini evertendam destinant. At Carolus, etc. The French annalist was more jealous of the honour of the saint.

Thames. Perhaps the interpretation of the Koran would now be taught in the schools of Oxford, and her pulpits might demonstrate to a circumcised people the sanctity and truth of the revelation of Mohammed.[1]

From such calamities was Christendom delivered by the genius and fortune of one man. Charles, the illegitimate son of the elder Pepin, was content with the titles of mayor or duke of the Franks; but he deserved to become the father of a line of kings. In a laborious administration of twenty-four years he restored and supported the dignity of the throne, and the rebels of Germany and Gaul were successively crushed by the activity of a warrior who in the same campaign could display his banner on the Elbe, the Rhône, and the shores of the ocean. In the public danger he was summoned by the voice of his country; and his rival, the duke of Aquitain, was reduced to appear among the fugitives and suppliants. " Alas! " exclaimed the Franks, " what a misfortune! what an indignity! We have long heard of the name and conquests of the Arabs: we were apprehensive of their attack from the East; they have now conquered Spain, and invade our country on the side of the West. Yet their numbers and (since they have no buckler) their arms are inferior to our own." " If you follow my advice," replied the prudent mayor of the palace, " you will not interrupt their march, nor precipitate your attack. They are like a torrent, which it is dangerous to stem in its career. The thirst of riches, and the consciousness of success, redouble their valour, and valour is of more avail than arms or numbers. Be patient till they have loaded themselves with the incumbrance of wealth. The possession of wealth will divide their counsels and assure your victory." This subtle policy is perhaps a refinement of the Arabian writers; and the situation of Charles will suggest a more narrow and selfish motive of procrastination; the secret desire of humbling the pride and wasting the provinces of the rebel duke of Aquitain. It is yet more probable that the delays of Charles were inevitable and reluctant. A standing army was unknown under the first and second race; more than half the kingdom was now in the hands of the Saracens: according to their respective situation,

[1] Yet I sincerely doubt whether the Oxford mosch would have produced a volume of controversy so elegant and ingenious as the sermons lately preached by Mr. White, the Arabic professor, at Mr. Bampton's lecture. His observations on the character and religion of Mohammed are always adapted to his argument, and generally founded in truth and reason. He sustains the part of a lively and eloquent advocate, and sometimes rises to the merit of an historian and philosopher.

the Franks of Neustria and Austrasia were too conscious or too careless of the impending danger; and the voluntary aids of the Gepidæ and Germans were separated by a long interval from the standard of the Christian general. No sooner had he collected his forces than he sought and found the enemy in the centre of France, between Tours and Poitiers. His well-conducted march was covered by a range of hills, and Abderame appears to have been surprised by his unexpected presence. The nations of Asia, Africa, and Europe advanced with equal ardour to an encounter which would change the history of the world. In the six first days of desultory combat the horsemen and archers of the East maintained their advantage; but in the closer onset of the seventh day the Orientals were oppressed by the strength and stature of the Germans, who, with stout hearts and *iron* hands,[1] asserted the civil and religious freedom of their posterity. The epithet of *Martel*, the *hammer*, which has been added to the name of Charles, is expressive of his weighty and irresistible strokes: the valour of Eudes was excited by resentment and emulation; and their companions, in the eye of history, are the true Peers and Paladins of French chivalry. After a bloody field, in which Abderame was slain, the Saracens, in the close of the evening, retired to their camp. In the disorder and despair of the night the various tribes of Yemen and Damascus, of Africa and Spain, were provoked to turn their arms against each other: the remains of their host were suddenly dissolved, and each *emir* consulted his safety by a hasty and separate retreat. At the dawn of day the stillness of a hostile camp was suspected by the victorious Christians: on the report of their spies they ventured to explore the riches of the vacant tents; but if we except some celebrated relics, a small portion of the spoil was restored to the innocent and lawful owners. The joyful tidings were soon diffused over the Catholic world, and the monks of Italy could affirm and believe that three hundred and fifty, or three hundred and seventy-five, thousand of the Mohammedans had been crushed by the hammer of Charles,[2] while no more than fifteen

[1] Gens Austriæ membrorum pre-eminentiâ valida, et gens Germana corde et corpore præstantissima, quasi in ictû oculi, manû ferreâ, et pectore arduo, Arabes extinxerunt (Roderic. Toletan. c. xiv.).

[2] These numbers are stated by Paul Warnefrid, the deacon of Aquileia (de Gestis Langobard. l. vi. [c. 46] p. 921, edit. Grot.), and Anastasius, the librarian of the Roman church (in Vit. Gregorii II. [ap. Muratori Scrip. R. I. vol. iii. p. 155]), who tells a miraculous story of three consecrated sponges, which rendered invulnerable the French soldiers among whom they had been shared. It should seem that, in his letters to the pope, Eudes usurped the honour of the victory, for which he is chastised by the French annalists, who, with equal falsehood, accuse him of inviting the Saracens.

hundred Christians were slain in the field of Tours. But this incredible tale is sufficiently disproved by the caution of the French general, who apprehended the snares and accidents of a pursuit, and dismissed his German allies to their native forests. The inactivity of a conqueror betrays the loss of strength and blood, and the most cruel execution is inflicted, not in the ranks of battle, but on the backs of a flying enemy. Yet the victory of the Franks was complete and final; Aquitain was recovered by the arms of Eudes; the Arabs never resumed the conquest of Gaul, and they were soon driven beyond the Pyrenees by Charles Martel and his valiant race.[1] It might have been expected that the saviour of Christendom would have been canonised, or at least applauded, by the gratitude of the clergy, who are indebted to his sword for their present existence. But in the public distress the mayor of the palace had been compelled to apply the riches, or at least the revenues, of the bishops and abbots to the relief of the state and the reward of the soldiers. His merits were forgotten, his sacrilege alone was remembered, and, in an epistle to a Carlovingian prince, a Gallic synod presumes to declare that his ancestor was damned; that on the opening of his tomb the spectators were affrighted by a smell of fire and the aspect of a horrid dragon; and that a saint of the times was indulged with a pleasant vision of the soul and body of Charles Martel burning, to all eternity, in the abyss of hell.[2]

The loss of an army, or a province, in the Western world was less painful to the court of Damascus than the rise and progress of a domestic competitor. Except among the Syrians, the caliphs of the house of Ommiyah had never been the objects of

---

[1] Narbonne and the rest of Septimania was recovered by Pepin, the son of Charles Martel, A.D. 755 (Pagi, Critica, tom. iii. p. 300). Thirty-seven years afterwards it was pillaged by a sudden inroad of the Arabs, who employed the captives in the construction of the mosch of Cordova (De Guignes, Hist. des Huns, tom. i. p. 354).
[It is not strictly correct to say that the Arabs never resumed the conquest of Gaul. Maurontius, duke of Marseilles, had allied himself with the Arabs in place of an alliance with the Christian champion, and had given Arles, Avignon, and other places to the lords of Narbonne, who had also secured possession of Lyons and Valence. Accordingly, a few years after their defeat at Tours, the Saracens were again in force in France, besides garrisoning Valence and Lyon. They were once more beaten back by Charles Martel in two campaigns, A.D. 737 and A.D. 739.—O. S.]

[2] This pastoral letter, addressed to Lewis the Germanic, the grandson of Charlemagne, and most probably composed by the pen of the artful Hincmar, is dated in the year 858, and signed by the bishops of the provinces of Rheims and Rouen (Baronius, Annal. Eccles. A.D. 741; Fleury, Hist. Ecclés. tom. x. p. 514-516). Yet Baronius himself and the French critics reject with contempt this episcopal fiction.

the public favour. The life of Mohammed recorded their perseverance in idolatry and rebellion: their conversion had been
reluctant, their elevation irregular and factious, and their throne
was cemented with the most holy and noble blood of Arabia.
The best of their race, the pious Omar, was dissatisfied with his
own title: their personal virtues were insufficient to justify a
departure from the order of succession; and the eyes and wishes
of the faithful were turned towards the line of Hashem and the
kindred of the apostle of God. Of these the Fatimites were
either rash or pusillanimous; but the descendants of Abbas
cherished, with courage and discretion, the hopes of their rising
fortunes. From an obscure residence in Syria, they secretly
despatched their agents and missionaries, who preached in
the Eastern provinces their hereditary indefeasible right; and
Mohammed, the son of Ali, the son of Abdallah, the son of Abbas,
the uncle of the prophet, gave audience to the deputies of
Chorasan, and accepted their free gift of four hundred thousand
pieces of gold. After the death of Mohammed, the oath of
allegiance was administered in the name of his son Ibrahim to a
numerous band of votaries, who expected only a signal and a
leader; and the governor of Chorasan continued to deplore his
fruitless admonitions and the deadly slumber of the caliphs of
Damascus, till he himself, with all his adherents, was driven
from the city and palace of Meru by the rebellious arms of Abu
Moslem.[1] That maker of kings, the author, as he is named, of
the *call* of the Abbassides, was at length rewarded for his presumption of merit with the usual gratitude of courts. A mean,
perhaps a foreign, extraction could not repress the aspiring
energy of Abu Moslem. Jealous of his wives, liberal of his
wealth, prodigal of his own blood and of that of others, he could
boast with pleasure, and possibly with truth, that he had
destroyed six hundred thousand of his enemies; and such was the
intrepid gravity of his mind and countenance, that he was never
seen to smile except on a day of battle. In the visible separation
of parties, the *green* was consecrated to the Fatimites; the
Ommiades were distinguished by the *white ;* and the *black*, as the
most adverse, was naturally adopted by the Abbassides. Their
turbans and garments were stained with that gloomy colour:

---

[1] The steed and the saddle which had carried any of his wives were
instantly killed or burnt, lest they should be afterwards mounted by a
male. Twelve hundred mules or camels were required for his kitchen
furniture; and the daily consumption amounted to three thousand cakes,
a hundred sheep, besides oxen, poultry, etc. (Abulpharagius, Hist. Dynast.
p. 140).

two black standards, on pike-staves nine cubits long, were borne
aloft in the van of Abu Moslem; and their allegorical names of
the *night* and the *shadow* obscurely represented the indissoluble
union and perpetual succession of the line of Hashem. From the
Indus to the Euphrates, the East was convulsed by the quarrel
of the white and the black factions: the Abbassides were most
frequently victorious; but their public success was clouded by
the personal misfortune of their chief. The court of Damascus,
awakening from a long slumber, resolved to prevent the pilgrimage of Mecca, which Ibrahim had undertaken with a splendid
retinue, to recommend himself at once to the favour of the
prophet and of the people. A detachment of cavalry intercepted
his march and arrested his person; and the unhappy Ibrahim,
snatched away from the promise of untasted royalty, expired
in iron fetters in the dungeons of Haran. His two younger
brothers, Saffah [1] and Almansor, eluded the search of the tyrant,
and lay concealed at Cufa, till the zeal of the people and the
approach of his Eastern friends allowed them to expose their
persons to the impatient public. On Friday, in the dress of a
caliph, in the colours of the sect, Saffah proceeded with religious
and military pomp to the mosch: ascending the pulpit, he
prayed and preached as the lawful successor of Mohammed; and,
after his departure, his kinsmen bound a willing people by an
oath of fidelity. But it was on the banks of the Zab, and not in
the mosch of Cufa, that this important controversy was determined. Every advantage appeared to be on the side of the
white faction: the authority of established government; an
army of a hundred and twenty thousand soldiers, against a
sixth part of that number; and the presence and merit of the
caliph Mervan, the fourteenth and last of the house of Ommiyah.
Before his accession to the throne he had deserved, by his
Georgian warfare, the honourable epithet of the ass of Mesopotamia; [2] and he might have been ranked among the greatest

---

[1] [These two young men, brothers of the luckless Ibrahim, both occupied
the throne. Saffah or, to give him his full name, Abd Allah Abu'l Abbas,
viz., Abdallah=the father of Abbas. Saffah, which should be written
with the article Al Saffah—the Bloody—was a name which he acquired
after his reign (750-754). He was about ten years younger than his
brother, Al Mansur, who succeeded him (754-775), and was probably
elected first either on account of his determined and cruel character or
because his mother was an Arabian woman of noble family, while Al
Mansur's mother was a slave.—O. S.]

[2] *Al Hemar*. He had been governor of Mesopotamia, and the Arabic
proverb praises the courage of that warlike breed of asses who never fly
from an enemy. The surname of Mervan may justify the comparison of

princes, had not, says Abulfeda, the eternal order decreed that
moment for the ruin of his family; a decree against which all
human prudence and fortitude must struggle in vain. The
orders of Mervan were mistaken, or disobeyed: the return of his
horse, from which he had dismounted on a necessary occasion,
impressed the belief of his death; and the enthusiasm of the
black squadrons was ably conducted by Abdallah, the uncle
of his competitor.[1] After an irretrievable defeat, the caliph
escaped to Mosul; but the colours of the Abbassides were displayed from the rampart; he suddenly repassed the Tigris, cast
a melancholy look on his palace of Haran, crossed the Euphrates,
abandoned the fortifications of Damascus, and, without halting
in Palestine, pitched his last and fatal camp at Busir, on the
banks of the Nile.[2] His speed was urged by the incessant
diligence of Abdallah, who in every step of the pursuit acquired
strength and reputation: the remains of the white faction were
finally vanquished in Egypt; and the lance, which terminated
the life and anxiety of Mervan, was not less welcome perhaps
to the unfortunate than to the victorious chief. The merciless inquisition of the conqueror eradicated the most distant branches
of the hostile race: their bones were scattered, their memory
was accursed, and the martyrdom of Hossein was abundantly
revenged on the posterity of his tyrants. Fourscore of the
Ommiades, who had yielded to the faith or clemency of their

Homer (Iliad Λ, 557, etc.), and both will silence the moderns, who consider
the ass as a stupid and ignoble emblem (D'Herbelot, Biblioth. Orient.
p. 558).

[1] [According to another and more credible account, Merwan sent his son
Abd Allah, who had been fighting in the front of the battle, back to the
camp with some regiments in order to protect some treasure which had just
arrived, and which the soldiers were plundering. The army mistook the
movement for a flight, and immediately commenced a disorderly retreat.
The commander of the Abassides was Abu Aun, while the Abd Allah who
pursued Merwan was Al Saffah himself.—O. S.]

[2] Four several places, all in Egypt, bore the name of Busir, or Busiris, so
famous in Greek fable. The first, where Mervan was slain, was to the
west of the Nile, in the province of Fium, or Arsinoe; the second in the
Delta, in the Sebennytic nome; the third near the Pyramids; the fourth,
which was destroyed by Diocletian (see above, vol. i. p. 353), in the Thebais.
I shall here transcribe a note of the learned and orthodox Michaelis:
Videntur in pluribus Ægypti superioris urbibus Busiri, Copto [Esne],
arma sumpsisse Christiani, libertatemque de religione sentiendi defendisse,
sed succubuisse, quo in bello Coptus et Busiris diruta, et circa Esnam
magna strages edita. Bellum narrant sed causam belli ignorant scriptores
Byzantini, alioqui Coptum et Busirin non rebellasse dicturi, sed causam
Christianorum suscepturi (Not. 211, p. 100). For the geography of the
four Busirs, see Abulfeda (Descript. Ægypt. p. 9, vers. Michaelis, Gottingæ,
1776, in 4to), Michaelis (Not. 122-127, p. 58-63), and D'Anville (Mémoire
sur l'Egypte, p. 85, 147, 205).

foes, were invited to a banquet at Damascus. The laws of hospitality were violated by a promiscuous massacre: the board was spread over their fallen bodies; and the festivity of the guests was enlivened by the music of their dying groans. By the event of the civil war the dynasty of the Abbassides was firmly established; but the Christians only could triumph in the mutual hatred and common loss of the disciples of Mohammed.[1]

Yet the thousands who were swept away by the sword of war might have been speedily retrieved in the succeeding generation, if the consequences of the revolution had not tended to dissolve the power and unity of the empire of the Saracens. In the proscription of the Ommiades, a royal youth of the name of Abdalrahman alone escaped the rage of his enemies, who hunted the wandering exile from the banks of the Euphrates to the valleys of Mount Atlas. His presence in the neighbourhood of Spain revived the zeal of the white faction. The name and cause of the Abbassides had been first vindicated by the Persians: the West had been pure from civil arms; and the servants of the abdicated family still held, by a precarious tenure, the inheritance of their lands and the offices of government. Strongly prompted by gratitude, indignation, and fear, they invited the grandson of the caliph Hashem to ascend the throne of his ancestors; and, in his desperate condition, the extremes of rashness and prudence were almost the same. The acclamations of the people saluted his landing on the coast of Andalusia; and, after a successful struggle, Abdalrahman established the throne of Cordova, and was the father of the Ommiades of Spain, who reigned above two hundred and fifty years from the Atlantic to the Pyrenees.[2] He slew in battle a lieutenant of the Abbassides, who had invaded his dominions with a fleet and army: the head of Ala, in salt and camphire, was suspended by a daring messenger before the palace of Mecca; and the caliph Almansor

---

[1] See Abulfeda (Annal. Moslem. p. 136-145), Eutychius (Annal. tom. ii. p. 392, vers. Pocock), Elmacin (Hist. Saracen. p. 109-121), Abulpharagius (Hist. Dynast. p. 134-140), Roderic of Toledo (Hist. Arabum, c. xviii. p. 33), Theophanes (Chronograph. p. 356, 357 [vol. i. p. 654, ed. Bonn], who speaks of the Abbassides under the name of Χωρασάνιται and Μαυρο-φόροι), and the Bibliothèque of D'Herbelot, in the articles *Ommiades, Abbassides, Mærvan, Ibrahim, Saffah, Abou Moslem.*

[2] For the revolution of Spain, consult Roderic of Toledo (c. xviii. p. 34, etc.), the Bibliotheca Arabico-Hispana (tom. ii. p. 30, 198), and Cardonne (Hist. de l'Afrique et de l'Espagne, tom. i. p. 180-197, 205, 272, 323, etc.)

[The Ommiade rulers in Spain did not take the title of caliph until 929 A.D. They called themselves emirs or amirs. It is incorrect, therefore, to speak of a western caliphate until 929. The emirate of Cordova is the accurate designation.—O. S.]

rejoiced in his safety, that he was removed by seas and lands from such a formidable adversary. Their mutual designs or declarations of offensive war evaporated without effect; but instead of opening a door to the conquest of Europe, Spain was dissevered from the trunk of the monarchy, engaged in perpetual hostility with the East, and inclined to peace and friendship with the Christian sovereigns of Constantinople and France. The example of the Ommiades was imitated by the real or fictitious progeny of Ali, the Edrissites of Mauritania, and the more powerful Fatimites of Africa and Egypt. In the tenth century the chair of Mohammed was disputed by three caliphs or commanders of the faithful, who reigned at Bagdad, Cairoan, and Cordova, excommunicated each other, and agreed only in a principle of discord, that a sectary is more odious and criminal than an unbeliever.[1]

Mecca was the patrimony of the line of Hashem, yet the Abbassides were never tempted to reside either in the birthplace or the city of the prophet. Damascus was disgraced by the choice, and polluted with the blood, of the Ommiades; and, after some hesitation, Almansor, the brother and successor of Saffah, laid the foundations of Bagdad,[2] the Imperial seat of his posterity during a reign of five hundred years.[3] The chosen spot is on the eastern bank of the Tigris, about fifteen miles above the ruins of Modain: the double wall was of a circular form; and such was the rapid increase of a capital now dwindled to a provincial town, that the funeral of a popular saint might

---

[1] I shall not stop to refute the strange errors and fancies of Sir William Temple (his Works, vol. iii. p. 371-374, octavo edition) and Voltaire (Histoire Générale, c. xxviii. tom. ii. p. 124, 125, édition de Lausanne), concerning the division of the Saracen empire. The mistakes of Voltaire proceeded from the want of knowledge or reflection; but Sir William was deceived by a Spanish impostor, who has framed an apocryphal history of the conquest of Spain by the Arabs.

[2] The geographer D'Anville (l'Euphrate et le Tigre, p. 121-123), and the Orientalist D'Herbelot (Bibliothèque, p. 167, 168), may suffice for the knowledge of Bagdad. Our travellers, Pietro della Valle (tom. i. p. 688-698), Tavernier (tom. i. p. 230-238), Thevenot (part ii. p. 209-212), Otter (tom. i. p. 162-168), and Niebuhr (Voyage en Arabie, tom. ii. p. 239-271), have seen only its decay; and the Nubian geographer (p. 204), and the travelling Jew, Benjamin of Tudela (Itinerarium, p. 112-123, à Const. l'Empereur, apud Elzevir, 1633), are the only writers of my acquaintance who have known Bagdad under the reign of the Abbassides.
[Bagdad is divided into two parts by the Tigris. It was originally built on the western bank, but as the court removed to the eastern bank in the eleventh century, the original city became a kind of suburb, and the quarter on the eastern bank the more important.—O. S.]
[3] The foundations of Bagdad were laid A.H. 145, A.D. 762. Mostasem the last of the Abbassides, was taken and put to death by the Tartars, A.H. 656, A.D. 1258, the 20th of February.

be attended by eight hundred thousand men and sixty thousand women of Bagdad and the adjacent villages. In this *city of peace*,[1] amidst the riches of the East, the Abbassides soon disdained the abstinence and frugality of the first caliphs, and aspired to emulate the magnificence of the Persian kings. After his wars and buildings, Almansor left behind him in gold and silver about thirty millions sterling;[2] and this treasure was exhausted in a few years by the vices or virtues of his children. His son Mahadi, in a single pilgrimage to Mecca, expended six millions of dinars of gold. A pious and charitable motive may sanctify the foundation of cisterns and caravanseras, which he distributed along a measured road of seven hundred miles; but his train of camels, laden with snow, could serve only to astonish the natives of Arabia, and to refresh the fruits and liquors of the royal banquet.[3] The courtiers would surely praise the liberality of his grandson Almamon, who gave away four-fifths of the income of a province, a sum of two millions four hundred thousand gold dinars, before he drew his foot from the stirrup. At the nuptials of the same prince a thousand pearls of the largest size were showered on the head of the bride,[4] and a lottery of lands and houses displayed the capricious bounty of fortune. The glories of the court were brightened rather than impaired in the decline of the empire, and a Greek ambassador might admire, or pity, the magnificence of the feeble Moctader. "The caliph's whole army," says the historian Abulfeda, " both horse and foot, was under arms, which together made a body of one hundred and sixty thousand men. His state officers, the favourite slaves, stood near him in splendid apparel, their belts

---

[1] Medinat al Salem, Dar al Salem. Urbs pacis, or, as it is more neatly compounded by the Byzantine writers, Εἰρηνόπολις (Irenopolis). There is some dispute concerning the etymology of Bagdad, but the first syllable is allowed to signify a garden in the Persian tongue; the garden of Dad, a Christian hermit, whose cell had been the only habitation on the spot.

[2] Reliquit in ærario sexcenties millies mille stateres, et quater et vicies millies mille aureos aureos. Elmacin, Hist. Saracen. p. 126. I have reckoned the gold pieces at eight shillings, and the proportion to the silver as twelve to one. But I will never answer for the numbers of Erpenius; and the Latins are scarcely above the savages in the language of arithmetic.

[3] D'Herbelot, p. 530; Abulfeda, p. 154. Nivem Meccam apportavit, rem ibi aut nunquam aut rarissime visam.

[4] Abulfeda, p. 184, 189, describes the splendour and liberality of Almamon. Milton has alluded to this Oriental custom:

—Or where the gorgeous East, with richest hand,
Showers on her kings barbaric pearls and gold.

I have used the modern word *lottery* to express the *Missilia* of the Roman emperors, which entitled to some prize the person who caught them, as they were thrown among the crowd.

glittering with gold and gems. Near them were seven thousand eunuchs, four thousand of them white, the remainder black. The porters or doorkeepers were in number seven hundred. Barges and boats, with the most superb decorations, were seen swimming upon the Tigris. Nor was the palace itself less splendid, in which were hung up thirty-eight thousand pieces of tapestry, twelve thousand five hundred of which were of silk embroidered with gold. The carpets on the floor were twenty-two thousand. A hundred lions were brought out, with a keeper to each lion.[1] Among the other spectacles of rare and stupendous luxury was a tree of gold and silver spreading into eighteen large branches, on which, and on the lesser boughs, sat a variety of birds made of the same precious metals, as well as the leaves of the tree. While the machinery affected spontaneous motions, the several birds warbled their natural harmony. Through this scene of magnificence the Greek ambassador was led by the vizir to the foot of the caliph's throne." [2] In the West the Ommiades of Spain supported with equal pomp the title of commander of the faithful. Three miles from Cordova, in honour of his favourite sultana, the third and greatest of the Abdalrahmans constructed the city, palace, and gardens of Zehra. Twenty-five years, and above three millions sterling, were employed by the founder: his liberal taste invited the artists of Constantinople, the most skilful sculptors and architects of the age; and the buildings were sustained or adorned by twelve hundred columns of Spanish and African, of Greek and Italian marble. The hall of audience was encrusted with gold and pearls, and a great basin in the centre was surrounded with the curious and costly figures of birds and quadrupeds. In a lofty pavilion of the gardens one of these basins and fountains, so delightful in a sultry climate, was replenished not with water, but with the purest quicksilver. The seraglio of Abdalrahman, his wives, concubines, and black eunuchs, amounted to six thousand three hundred persons: and he was attended to the field by a guard of twelve thousand horse, whose belts and scimitars were studded with gold.[3]

[1] When Bell of Antermony (Travels, vol. i. p. 99) accompanied the Russian ambassador to the audience of the unfortunate Shah Hussein of Persia, *two* lions were introduced, to denote the power of the king over the fiercest animals.

[2] Abulfeda, p. 237; D'Herbelot, p. 590. This embassy was received at Bagdad, A.H. 305, A.D. 917. In the passage of Abulfeda, I have used, with some variations, the English translation of the learned and amiable Mr. Harris of Salisbury (Philological Enquiries, p. 363, 364).

[3] Cardonne, Histoire de l'Afrique et de l'Espagne, tom. i. p. 330-336. A

In a private condition our desires are perpetually repressed by poverty and subordination; but the lives and labours of millions are devoted to the service of a despotic prince, whose laws are blindly obeyed, and whose wishes are instantly gratified. Our imagination is dazzled by the splendid picture; and whatever may be the cool dictates of reason, there are few among us who would obstinately refuse a trial of the comforts and the cares of royalty. It may therefore be of some use to borrow the experience of the same Abdalrahman, whose magnificence has perhaps excited our admiration and envy, and to transcribe an authentic memorial which was found in the closet of the deceased caliph. " I have now reigned above fifty years in victory or peace; beloved by my subjects, dreaded by my enemies, and respected by my allies. Riches and honours, power and pleasure, have waited on my call, nor does any earthly blessing appear to have been wanting to my felicity. In this situation I have diligently numbered the days of pure and genuine happiness which have fallen to my lot: they amount to FOURTEEN:—O man! place not thy confidence in this present world!" [1] The luxury of the caliphs, so useless to their private happiness, relaxed the nerves, and terminated the progress, of the Arabian empire. Temporal and spiritual conquest had been the sole occupation of the first successors of Mohammed; and after supplying themselves with the necessaries of life, the whole revenue was scrupulously devoted to that salutary work. The Abbassides were impoverished by the multitude of their wants and their contempt of economy. Instead of pursuing the great object of ambition, their leisure, their affections, the powers of their mind, were diverted by pomp and pleasure: the rewards of valour were embezzled by women and eunuchs, and the royal camp was encumbered by the luxury of the palace. A similar temper was diffused among the subjects of the caliph. Their stern enthusiasm was softened by time and prosperity: they sought riches in the occupations of industry, fame in the pur-

just idea of the taste and architecture of the Arabians of Spain may be conceived from the description and plates of the Alhambra of Granada (Swinburne's Travels, p. 171-188).

[1] Cardonne, tom. i. p. 329, 330. This confession, the complaints of Solomon of the vanity of this world (read Prior's verbose but eloquent poem), and the happy ten days of the emperor Seghed (Rambler, No. 204, 205), will be triumphantly quoted by the detractors of human life. Their expectations are commonly immoderate, their estimates are seldom impartial. If I may speak of myself (the only person of whom I can speak with certainty), *my* happy hours have far exceeded, and far exceed, the scanty numbers of the caliph of Spain; and I shall not scruple to add, that many of them are due to the pleasing labour of the present composition.

suits of literature, and happiness in the tranquillity of domestic life. War was no longer the passion of the Saracens; and the increase of pay, the repetition of donatives, were insufficient to allure the posterity of those voluntary champions who had crowded to the standard of Abubeker and Omar for the hopes of spoil and of paradise.

Under the reign of the Ommiades the studies of the Moslems were confined to the interpretation of the Koran, and the eloquence and poetry of their native tongue. A people continually exposed to the dangers of the field must esteem the healing powers of medicine, or rather of surgery: but the starving physicians of Arabia murmured a complaint that exercise and temperance deprived them of the greatest part of their practice.[1] After their civil and domestic wars, the subjects of the Abassides, awakening from this mental lethargy, found leisure and felt curiosity for the acquisition of profane science. This spirit was first encouraged by the caliph Almansor, who, besides his knowledge of the Mohammedan law, had applied himself with success to the study of astronomy. But when the sceptre devolved to Almamon, the seventh of the Abbassides, he completed the designs of his grandfather, and invited the Muses from their ancient seats. His ambassadors at Constantinople, his agents in Armenia, Syria, and Egypt, collected the volumes of Grecian science: at his command they were translated by the most skilful interpreters into the Arabic language: his subjects were exhorted assiduously to peruse these instructive writings; and the successor of Mohammed assisted with pleasure and modesty at the assemblies and disputations of the learned. " He was not ignorant," says Abulpharagius, " that *they* are the elect of God, his best and most useful servants, whose lives are devoted to the improvement of their rational faculties. The mean ambition of the Chinese or the Turks may glory in the industry of their hands or the indulgence of their brutal appetites. Yet these dexterous artists must view, with hopeless emulation, the hexagons and pyramids of the cells of a beehive:[2] these fortitudinous heroes

---

[1] The Gulistan (p. 239) relates the conversation of Mohammed and a physician (Epistol. Renaudot. in Fabricius, Biblioth. Græc. tom. i. p. 814). The prophet himself was skilled in the art of medicine; and Gagnier (Vie de Mahomet, tom. iii. p. 394-405) has given an extract of the aphorisms which are extant under his name.

[2] See their curious architecture in Reaumur (Hist. des Insectes, tom. v. Mémoire viii.). These hexagons are closed by a pyramid; the angles of the three sides of a similar pyramid, such as would accomplish the given end with the smallest quantity possible of materials, were determined by a mathematician, at 109 degrees 26 minutes for the larger, 70 degrees 34

are awed by the superior fierceness of the lions and tigers; and in their amorous enjoyments they are much inferior to the vigour of the grossest and most sordid quadrupeds. The teachers of wisdom are the true luminaries and legislators of a world, which, without their aid, would again sink in ignorance and barbarism."[1] The zeal and curiosity of Almamon were imitated by succeeding princes of the line of Abbas: their rivals, the Fatimites of Africa and the Ommiades of Spain, were the patrons of the learned, as well as the commanders of the faithful; the same royal prerogative was claimed by their independent emirs of the provinces; and their emulation diffused the taste and the rewards of science from Samarcand and Bochara to Fez and Cordova. The vizir of a sultan consecrated a sum of two hundred thousand pieces of gold to the foundation of a college at Bagdad, which he endowed with an annual revenue of fifteen thousand dinars. The fruits of instruction were communicated, perhaps at different times, to six thousand disciples of every degree, from the son of the noble to that of the mechanic: a sufficient allowance was provided for the indigent scholars; and the merit or industry of the professors was repaid with adequate stipends. In every city the productions of Arabic literature were copied and collected by the curiosity of the studious and the vanity of the rich. A private doctor refused the invitation of the sultan of Bochara, because the carriage of his books would have required four hundred camels. The royal library of the Fatimites consisted of one hundred thousand manuscripts, elegantly transcribed and splendidly bound, which were lent, without jealousy or avarice, to the students of Cairo. Yet this collection must appear moderate, if we can believe that the Ommiades of Spain had formed a library of six hundred thousand volumes, forty-four of which were employed in the mere catalogue. Their capital, Cordova, with the adjacent towns of Malaga, Almeria, and Murcia, had given birth to more than three hundred writers, and above seventy public libraries were opened in the cities of the Andalusian kingdom. The age of Arabian learning continued about five hundred years, till the great eruption of the Moguls,

minutes for the smaller. The actual measure is 169 degrees 28 minutes, 70 degrees 32 minutes. Yet this perfect harmony raises the work at the expense of the artist: the bees are not masters of transcendent geometry.

[1] Said Ebn Ahmed, cadhi of Toledo, who died A.H. 462, A.D. 1069, has furnished Abulpharagius (Dynast. p. 160) with this curious passage, as well as with the text of Pocock's Specimen Historiæ Arabum. A number of literary anecdotes of philosophers, physicians, etc., who have flourished under each caliph, form the principal merit of the Dynasties of Abulpharagius.

and was coeval with the darkest and most slothful period of European annals; but since the sun of science has arisen in the West, it should seem that the Oriental studies have languished and declined.[1]

In the libraries of the Arabians, as in those of Europe, the far greater part of the innumerable volumes were possessed only of local value or imaginary merit.[2] The shelves were crowded with orators and poets, whose style was adapted to the taste and manners of their countrymen; with general and partial histories, which each revolving generation supplied with a new harvest of persons and events; with codes and commentaries of jurisprudence which derived their authority from the law of the prophet; with the interpreters of the Koran, and orthodox tradition: and with the whole theological tribe, polemics, mystics, scholastics, and moralists, the first or the last of writers, according to the different estimates of sceptics or believers. The works of speculation or science may be reduced to the four classes of philosophy, mathematics, astronomy, and physic. The sages of Greece were translated and illustrated in the Arabic language, and some treatises, now lost in the original, have been recovered in the versions of the East,[3] which possessed and studied the writings of Aristotle and Plato, of Euclid and Apollonius, of Ptolemy, Hippocrates, and Galen.[4] Among the ideal systems which have varied with the fashion of the times, the Arabians

[1] These literary anecdotes are borrowed from the Bibliotheca Arabico-Hispana (tom. ii. p. 38, 71, 201, 202), Leo Africanus (de Arab. Medicis et Philosophis, in Fabric. Biblioth. Græc. tom. xiii. p. 259-298, particularly p. 274), and Renaudot (Hist. Patriarch. Alex. p. 274, 275, 536, 537), besides the chronological remarks of Abulpharagius.

[2] The Arabic catalogue of the Escurial will give a just idea of the proportion of the classes. In the library of Cairo the MSS. of astronomy and medicine amounted to 6500, with two fair globes, the one of brass, the other of silver (Biblioth. Arab. Hisp. tom. i. p. 417).

[3] As for instance, the fifth, sixth, and seventh books (the eighth is still wanting) of the Conic Sections of Apollonius Pergæus, which were printed from the Florence MS. 1661 (Fabric. Biblioth. Græc. tom. ii. p. 559). Yet the fifth book had been previously restored by the mathematical divination of Viviani (see his Eloge in Fontenelle, tom. v. p. 59, etc.).

[4] The merit of these Arabic versions is freely discussed by Renaudot (Fabric. Biblioth. Græc. tom. i. p. 812-816), and piously defended by Casiri (Biblioth. Arab. Hispana, tom. i. p. 238-240). Most of the versions of Plato, Aristotle, Hippocrates, Galen, etc., are ascribed to Honain, a physician of the Nestorian sect, who flourished at Bagdad in the court of the caliphs, and died A.D. 876. He was at the head of a school or manufacture of translations, and the works of his sons and disciples were published under his name. See Abulpharagius (Dynast. p. 88, 115, 171-174, and apud Asseman. Biblioth. Orient. tom. ii. p. 438), D'Herbelot (Biblioth. Orientale, p. 456), Asseman. (Biblioth. Orient. tom. iii. p. 164), and Casiri (Biblioth. Arab. Hispana, tom. i. p. 238, etc. 251, 286-290, 302, 304, etc.).

adopted the philosophy of the Stagirite, alike intelligible or alike obscure for the readers of every age. Plato wrote for the Athenians, and his allegorical genius is too closely blended with the language and religion of Greece. After the fall of that religion, the Peripatetics, emerging from their obscurity, prevailed in the controversies of the Oriental sects, and their founder was long afterwards restored by the Mohammedans of Spain to the Latin schools.[1] The physics, both of the Academy and the Lycæum, as they are built, not on observation but on argument, have retarded the progress of real knowledge. The metaphysics of infinite, or finite, spirit, have too often been enlisted in the service of superstition. But the human faculties are fortified by the art and practice of dialectics; the ten predicaments of Aristotle collect and methodise our ideas,[2] and his syllogism is the keenest weapon of dispute. It was dexterously wielded in the schools of the Saracens, but, as it is more effectual for the detection of error than for the investigation of truth, it is not surprising that new generations of masters and disciples should still revolve in the same circle of logical argument. The mathematics are distinguished by a peculiar privilege, that, in the course of ages, they may always advance and can never recede. But the ancient geometry, if I am not misinformed, was resumed in the same state by the Italians of the fifteenth century; and whatever may be the origin of the name, the science of algebra is ascribed to the Grecian Diophantus by the modest testimony of the Arabs themselves.[3] They cultivated with more success the sublime science of astronomy, which elevates the mind of man to disdain his diminutive planet and momentary existence. The costly instruments of observation were supplied by the caliph Almamon, and the land of the Chaldeans still afforded the same spacious level, and the same unclouded horizon. In the plains of Sinaar, and a second time in those of Cufa, his mathematicians accurately measured a degree of the great circle of the earth, and determined at twenty-four thousand

---

[1] See Moshiem, Institut. Hist. Eccles. p. 181, 214, 236, 257, 315, 338, 396, 438, etc.

[2] The most elegant commentary on the Categories or Predicaments of Aristotle may be found in the Philosophical Arrangements of Mr. James Harris (London, 1775, in octavo), who laboured to revive the studies of Grecian literature and philosophy.

[3] Abulpharagius, Dynast. p. 81, 222; Biblioth. Arab. Hisp. tom. i. p. 370, 371. In quem (says the primate of the Jacobites) si immiserit se lector, oceanum hoc in genere (*Algebræ*) inveniet. The time of Diophantus of Alexandria is unknown; but his six books are still extant, and have been illustrated by the Greek Planudes and the Frenchman Meziriac (Fabric. Biblioth. Græc. tom. iv. p. 12-15).

miles the entire circumference of our globe.[1]   From the reign of
the Abbassides to that of the grand-children of Tamerlane, the
stars, without the aid of glasses, were diligently observed; and
the astronomical tables of Bagdad, Spain, and Samarcand [2]
correct some minute errors, without daring to renounce the
hypothesis of Ptolemy, without advancing a step towards the
discovery of the solar system.   In the Eastern courts, the truths
of science could be recommended only by ignorance and folly,
and the astronomer would have been disregarded, had he not
debased his wisdom or honesty by the vain predictions of
astrology.[3]   But in the science of medicine the Arabians have
been deservedly applauded.   The names of Mesua and Geber, of
Razis and Avicenna, are ranked with the Grecian masters; in
the city of Bagdad eight hundred and sixty physicians were
licensed to exercise their lucrative profession: [4] in Spain, the life
of the Catholic princes was intrusted to the skill of the Saracens,[5]
and the school of Salerno, their legitimate offspring, revived in
Italy and Europe the precepts of the healing art.[6]   The success
of each professor must have been influenced by personal and
accidental causes; but we may form a less fanciful estimate of
their general knowledge of anatomy,[7] botany,[8] and chemistry,[9]

   [1] Abulfeda (Annal. Moslem. p. 210, 211, vers. Reiske) describes this
operation according to Ibn Challecan and the best historians.   This
degree most accurately contains 200,000 royal or Hashemite cubits, which
Arabia had derived from the sacred and legal practice both of Palestine
and Egypt.   This ancient cubit is repeated 400 times in each basis of the
great pyramid, and seems to indicate the primitive and universal measures
of the East.   See the Métrologie of the laborious M. Paucton, p. 101-195.
   [2] See the Astronomical Tables of Ulugh Begh, with the preface of Dr.
Hyde, in the first volume of his Syntagma Dissertationum, Oxon. 1767.
   [3] The truth of astrology was allowed by Albumazar, and the best of the
Arabian astronomers, who drew their most certain predictions, not from
Venus and Mercury, but from Jupiter and the sun (Abulpharag. Dynast.
p. 161-163).   For the state and science of the Persian astronomers, see
Chardin (Voyages en Perse, tom. iii. p. 162-203).
   [4] Biblioth. Arabico-Hispana, tom. i. p. 438.   The original relates a
pleasant tale of an ignorant, but harmless, practitioner.
   [5] In the year 956 Sancho the Fat, king of Leon, was cured by the physicians of Cordova (Mariana, l. viii. c. 7, tom. i. p. 318).
   [6] The school of Salerno, and the introduction of the Arabian sciences
into Italy, are discussed with learning and judgment by Muratori (Antiquitat. Italiæ Medii Ævi, tom. iii. p. 932-940) and Giannone (Istoria Civile
di Napoli, tom. ii. p. 119-127).
   [7] See a good view of the progress of anatomy in Wotton (Reflections on
Ancient and Modern Learning, p. 208-256).   His reputation has been unworthily depreciated by the wits in the controversy of Boyle and Bentley.
   [8] Biblioth. Arab. Hispana, tom. i. p. 275.   Al Beithar, of Malaga, their
greatest botanist, had travelled into Africa, Persia, and India.
   [9] Dr. Watson (Elements of Chemistry, vol. i. p. 17, etc.) allows the
original merit of the Arabians.   Yet he quotes the modest confession of
the famous Geber of the ninth century (D'Herbelot, p. 387), that he had

the threefold basis of their theory and practice. A superstitious reverence for the dead confined both the Greeks and the Arabians to the dissection of apes and quadrupeds; the more solid and visible parts were known in the time of Galen, and the finer scrutiny of the human frame was reserved for the microscope and the injections of modern artists. Botany is an active science, and the discoveries of the torrid zone might enrich the herbal of Dioscorides with two thousand plants. Some traditionary knowledge might be secreted in the temples and monasteries of Egypt; much useful experience had been acquired in the practice of arts and manufactures; but the *science* of chemistry owes its origin and improvement to the industry of the Saracens. They first invented and named the alembic for the purposes of distillation, analysed the substances of the three kingdoms of nature, tried the distinction and affinities of alcalis and acids, and converted the poisonous minerals into soft and salutary medicines. But the most eager search of Arabian chemistry was the transmutation of metals, and the elixir of immortal health: the reason and the fortunes of thousands were evaporated in the crucibles of alchymy, and the consummation of the great work was promoted by the worthy aid of mystery, fable, and superstition.

But the Moslems deprived themselves of the principal benefits of a familiar intercourse with Greece and Rome, the knowledge of antiquity, the purity of taste, and the freedom of thought. Confident in the riches of their native tongue, the Arabians disdained the study of any foreign idiom. The Greek interpreters were chosen among their Christian subjects; they formed their translations sometimes on the original text, more frequently perhaps on a Syriac version: and in the crowd of astronomers and physicians there is no example of a poet, an orator, or even an historian, being taught to speak the language of the Saracens.[1] The mythology of Homer would have provoked the abhorrence of those stern fanatics: they possessed in lazy ignorance the colonies of the Macedonians, and the pro-

drawn most of his science, perhaps of the transmutation of metals, from the ancient sages. Whatever might be the origin or extent of their knowledge, the arts of chemistry and alchymy appear to have been known in Egypt at least three hundred years before Mohammed (Wotton's Reflections, p. 121-133; Pauw, Recherches sur les Egyptiens et les Chinois, tom. i. p. 376-429).

[1] Abulpharagius (Dynast. p. 26, 148) mentions a *Syriac* version of Homer's two poems, by Theophilus, a Christian Maronite of Mount Libanus, who professed astronomy at Roha or Edessa towards the end of the eighth century. His work would be a literary curiosity. I have read somewhere, but I do not believe, that Plutarch's Lives were translated into Turkish for the use of Mohammed the Second.

vinces of Carthage and Rome: the heroes of Plutarch and Livy were buried in oblivion; and the history of the world before Mohammed was reduced to a short legend of the patriarchs, the prophets, and the Persian kings. Our education in the Greek and Latin schools may have fixed in our minds a standard of exclusive taste; and I am not forward to condemn the literature and judgment of nations of whose language I am ignorant. Yet I *know* that the classics have much to teach, and I *believe* that the Orientals have much to learn: the temperate dignity of style, the graceful proportions of art, the forms of visible and intellectual beauty, the just delineation of character and passion, the rhetoric of narrative and argument, the regular fabric of epic and dramatic poetry.[1] The influence of truth and reason is of a less ambiguous complexion. The philosophers of Athens and Rome enjoyed the blessings, and asserted the rights, of civil and religious freedom. Their moral and political writings might have gradually unlocked the fetters of Eastern despotism, diffused a liberal spirit of inquiry and toleration, and encouraged the Arabian sages to suspect that their caliph was a tyrant, and their prophet an impostor.[2] The instinct of superstition was alarmed by the introduction even of the abstract sciences; and the more rigid doctors of the law condemned the rash and pernicious curiosity of Almamon.[3] To the thirst of martyrdom, the vision of paradise, and the belief of predestination, we must ascribe the invincible enthusiasm of the prince and people. And the sword of the Saracens became less formidable when their youth was drawn away from the camp to the college, when the armies of the faithful presumed to read and to reflect. Yet the foolish vanity of the Greeks was jealous of their studies, and reluctantly imparted the sacred fire to the barbarians of the East.[4]

[1] I have perused with much pleasure Sir William Jones's Latin Commentary on Asiatic Poetry (London, 1774, in octavo), which was composed in the youth of that wonderful linguist. At present, in the maturity of his taste and judgment, he would perhaps abate of the fervent and even partial praise which he has bestowed on the Orientals.

[2] Among the Arabian philosophers, Averroes has been accused of despising the religions of the Jews, the Christians, and the Mohammedans (see his article in Bayle's Dictionary). Each of these sects would agree that, in two instances out of three, his contempt was reasonable.

[3] D'Herbelot, Bibliothèque Orientale, p. 546.

[4] Θεόφιλος ἄτοπον κρίνας εἰ τὴν τῶν ὄντων γνῶσιν, δἰ ἣν τὸ Ῥωμαίων γένος θαυμάζεται, ἔκδοτον ποιήσει τοῖς ἔθνεσι, etc. Cedrenus, p. 548 [vol. ii. p. 169, ed. Bonn], who relates how manfully the emperor refused a mathematician to the instances and offers of the caliph Almamon. This absurd scruple is expressed almost in the same words by the continuator of Theophanes (Scriptores post Theophanem, p. 118 [ed. Par.; p. 190, ed. Bonn]).

In the bloody conflict of the Ommiades and Abbassides the Greeks had stolen the opportunity of avenging their wrongs and enlarging their limits. But a severe retribution was exacted by Mohadi, the third caliph of the new dynasty, who seized, in his turn, the favourable opportunity, while a woman and a child, Irene and Constantine, were seated on the Byzantine throne. An army of ninety-five thousand Persians and Arabs was sent from the Tigris to the Thracian Bosphorus, under the command of Harun,[1] or Aaron, the second son of the commander of the faithful. His encampment on the opposite heights of Chrysopolis, or Scutari, informed Irene, in her palace of Constantinople, of the loss of her troops and provinces. With the consent or connivance of their sovereign, her ministers subscribed an ignominious peace; and the exchange of some royal gifts could not disguise the annual tribute of seventy thousand dinars of gold, which was imposed on the Roman empire. The Saracens had too rashly advanced into the midst of a distant and hostile land; their retreat was solicited by the promise of faithful guides and plentiful markets; and not a Greek had courage to whisper that their weary forces might be surrounded and destroyed in their necessary passage between a slippery mountain and the river Sangarius. Five years after this expedition, Harun ascended the throne of his father and his elder brother; the most powerful and vigorous monarch of his race, illustrious in the West as the ally of Charlemagne, and familiar to the most childish readers as the perpetual hero of the Arabian tales. His title to the name of *Al Rashid* (the *Just*) is sullied by the extirpation of the generous, perhaps the innocent, Barmecides:[2] yet he could listen to the complaint of a poor

---

[1] See the reign and character of Harun al Rashid in the Bibliothèque Orientale, p. 431-433, under his proper title, and in the relative articles to which M. D'Herbelot refers. That learned collector has shown much taste in stripping the Oriental chronicles of their instructive and amusing anecdotes.

[2] [There seem to be grounds for believing that Haroun Al Raschid's cruelty towards the Barmecides was connected with his incestuous passion for his sister Abbasah. Haroun's fondness for Djafar (or Giafar), one of the Barmecide family, was so great that he not only made him his grand vizier, but loved him so extravagantly that he was never happy out of his company, and in order to reconcile his presence in the harem with Eastern notions of decorum, he made him contract a formal marriage with Abbasah, but under strict injunctions that he was not to exercise the rights of a husband. A mutual passion, however, caused the wedded pair to overstep these commands, a child was the fruit of their stolen interviews, and Haroun learned from a slave that he was deceived and disobeyed. After satisfying himself of the truth of this report by the likeness which the child bore its father, Haroun resolved on the destruction of

widow who had been pillaged by his troops, and who dared, in a passage of the Koran, to threaten the inattentive despot with the judgment of God and posterity. His court was adorned with luxury and science; but, in a reign of three-and-twenty years, Harun repeatedly visited his provinces from Chorasan to Egypt; nine times he performed the pilgrimage of Mecca; eight times he invaded the territories of the Romans; and as often as they declined the payment of the tribute, they were taught to feel that a month of depredation was more costly than a year of submission. But when the unnatural mother of Constantine was deposed and banished, her successor, Nicephorus, resolved to obliterate this badge of servitude and disgrace. The epistle of the emperor to the caliph was pointed with an allusion to the game of chess, which had already spread from Persia to Greece. "The queen (he spoke of Irene) considered you as a rook, and herself as a pawn. That pusillanimous female submitted to pay a tribute, the double of which she ought to have exacted from the barbarians. Restore therefore the fruits of your injustice, or abide the determination of the sword." At these words the ambassadors cast a bundle of swords before the foot of the throne. The caliph smiled at the menace, and, drawing his scimitar, *samsamah*, a weapon of historic or fabulous renown, he cut asunder the feeble arms of the Greeks, without turning the edge or endangering the temper of his blade. He then dictated an epistle of tremendous brevity: "In the name of the most merciful God, Harun al Rashid, commander of the faithful, to Nicephorus, the Roman dog. I have read thy letter, O thou son of an unbelieving mother. Thou shalt not hear, thou shalt behold, my reply." It was written in characters of blood and fire on the plains of Phrygia; and the warlike celerity of the Arabs could only be checked by the arts of deceit and the show of repentance. The triumphant caliph retired, after the fatigues of the campaign, to his favourite palace of Racca on the Euphrates:[1] but the distance of five hundred miles, and the inclemency of the season, encouraged his adversary to violate the peace. Nicephorus was astonished by the bold and rapid march of the commander of the faithful,

the whole family of the Barmecides. They were treacherously seized and murdered; Djafar was beheaded, and parts of his mutilated body were fixed to the gates and on the bridge at Bagdad.—O. S.]

[1] For the situation of Racca, the old Nicephorium, consult D'Anville (l'Euphrate et le Tigre, p. 24-27). The Arabian Nights represent Harun al Rashid as almost stationary in Bagdad. He respected the royal seat of the Abbassides; but the vices of the inhabitants had driven him from the city (Abulfed. Annal. p. 167).

who repassed, in the depth of winter, the snows of Mount Taurus: his stratagems of policy and war were exhausted; and the perfidious Greek escaped with three wounds from a field of battle overspread with forty thousand of his subjects.[1] Yet the emperor was ashamed of submission, and the caliph was resolved on victory. One hundred and thirty-five thousand regular soldiers received pay, and were inscribed in the military roll; and above three hundred thousand persons of every denomination marched under the black standard of the Abbassides. They swept the surface of Asia Minor far beyond Tyana and Ancyra, and invested the Pontic Heraclea,[2] once a flourishing state, now a paltry town; at that time capable of sustaining, in her antique walls, a month's siege against the forces of the East. The ruin was complete, the spoil was ample; but if Harun had been conversant with Grecian story, he would have regretted the statue of Hercules, whose attributes, the club, the bow, the quiver, and the lion's hide, were sculptured in massy gold. The progress of desolation by sea and land, from the Euxine to the isle of Cyprus, compelled the emperor Nicephorus to retract his haughty defiance. In the new treaty, the ruins of Heraclea were left for ever as a lesson and a trophy: and the coin of the tribute was marked with the image and superscription of Harun and his three sons.[3] Yet this plurality of lords might contribute to remove the dishonour of the Roman name. After the death of their father, the heirs of the caliph were involved in civil discord, and the conqueror, the liberal Almamon, was sufficiently engaged in the restoration of domestic peace and the introduction of foreign science.

Under the reign of Almamon at Bagdad, of Michael the Stammerer at Constantinople, the islands of Crete [4] and Sicily

[1] [Haroun invaded Asia Minor twice in A.D. 803. On the first occasion the promise of tribute induced him to retreat, but when the tribute was not paid he repassed the Taurus at the end of the year to demand it. The battle, in which 40,000 Greeks fell, was fought in 804, but the Arabs were led by Jabril, Haroun's general.—O. S.]

[2] M. de Tournefort, in his coasting voyage from Constantinople to Trebizond, passed a night at Heraclea or Eregri. His eye surveyed the present state, his reading collected the antiquities, of the city (Voyage du Levant, tom. iii. lettre xvi. p. 23-35). We have a separate history of Heraclea in the fragments of Memnon, which are preserved by Photius.

[3] The wars of Harun al Rashid against the Roman empire are related by Theophanes (p. 384, 385, 391, 396, 407, 408 [tom. i. p. 705, 717, 727, 748, sq., ed. Bonn]), Zonaras (tom. ii. l. xv. [c. 10-15], p. 115, 124), Cedrenus (p. 477, 478 [tom. ii. p. 34, sq., ed. Bonn]), Eutychius (Annal. tom. ii. p. 407), Elmacin (Hist. Saracen. p. 136, 151, 152), Abulpharagius (Dynast. p. 147, 151), and Abulfeda (p. 156, 166-168).

[4] The authors from whom I have learned the most of the ancient and modern state of Crete are Belon (Observations, etc., c. 3-20, Paris, 1555),

were subdued by the Arabs. The former of these conquests is disdained by their own writers, who were ignorant of the fame of Jupiter and Minos, but it has not been overlooked by the Byzantine historians, who now begin to cast a clearer light on the affairs of their own times.[1] A band of Andalusian volunteers, discontented with the climate or government of Spain, explored the adventures of the sea; but as they sailed in no more than ten or twenty galleys, their warfare must be branded with the name of piracy. As the subjects and sectaries of the *white* party, they might lawfully invade the dominions of the *black* caliphs. A rebellious faction introduced them into Alexandria;[2] they cut in pieces both friends and foes, pillaged the churches and the moschs, sold above six thousand Christian captives, and maintained their station in the capital of Egypt, till they were oppressed by the forces and the presence of Almamon himself. From the mouth of the Nile to the Hellespont, the islands and sea-coasts both of the Greeks and Moslems were exposed to their depredations; they saw, they envied, they tasted the fertility of Crete, and soon returned with forty galleys to a more serious attack. The Andalusians wandered over the land fearless and unmolested; but when they descended with their plunder to the sea-shore, their vessels were in flames, and their chief, Abu Caab, confessed himself the author of the mischief. Their clamours accused his madness or treachery. "Of what do you complain?" replied the crafty emir. "I have brought you to a land flowing with milk and honey. Here is your true country; repose from your toils, and forget the barren place of your nativity." "And our wives and children?" "Your beauteous captives will

---

Tournefort (Voyage du Levant, tom. i. lettre ii. et iii.), and Meursius (CRETA, in his works, tom. iii. p. 343-544). Although Crete is styled by Homer πίειρα, by Dionysius λιπάρη τε καὶ εὔβοτος, I cannot conceive that mountainous island to surpass, or even to equal, in fertility the greater part of Spain.

[1] The most authentic and circumstantial intelligence is obtained from the four books of the Continuation of Theophanes, compiled by the pen or the command of Constantine Porphyrogenitus, with the Life of his father Basil the Macedonian (Scriptores post Theophanem, p. 1-162, à Francisc. Combefis, Paris, 1685 [p. 4-260, ed. Bonn]). The loss of Crete and Sicily is related, l. ii. p. 46-52 [ed. Par.; p. 74-83, ed. Bonn]. To these we may add the secondary evidence of Joseph Genesius (l. ii. p. 21, Venet. 1733), George Cedrenus (Compend. p. 506-508 [p. 509-512, ed. Par.; p. 92-99, ed. Bonn]), and John Scylitzes Curopalata (apud Baron. Annal. Eccles. A.D. 827, No. 24, etc.). But the modern Greeks are such notorious plagiaries, that I should only quote a plurality of names.

[2] Renaudot (Hist. Patriarch. Alex. p. 251-256, 268-270) has described the ravages of the Andalusian Arabs in Egypt, but has forgot to connect them with the conquest of Crete.

supply the place of your wives, and in their embraces you will soon become the fathers of a new progeny." The first habitation was their camp, with a ditch and rampart in the bay of Suda; but an apostate monk led them to a more desirable position in the eastern parts; and the name of Candax, their fortress and colony, has been extended to the whole island, under the corrupt and modern appellation of *Candia*. The hundred cities of the age of Minos were diminished to thirty; and of these, only one, most probably Cydonia, had courage to retain the substance of freedom and the profession of Christianity. The Saracens of Crete soon repaired the loss of their navy; and the timbers of Mount Ida were launched into the main. During a hostile period, of one hundred and thirty-eight years, the princes of Constantinople attacked these licentious corsairs with fruitless curses and ineffectual arms.

The loss of Sicily [1] was occasioned by an act of superstitious rigour. An amorous youth, who had stolen a nun from her cloister, was sentenced by the emperor to the amputation of his tongue. Euphemius appealed to the reason and policy of the Saracens of Africa; and soon returned with the Imperial purple, a fleet of one hundred ships, and an army of seven hundred horse and ten thousand foot. They landed at Mazara, near the ruins of the ancient Selinus; but after some partial victories, Syracuse [2] was delivered by the Greeks, the apostate was slain before her walls, and his African friends were reduced to the necessity of feeding on the flesh of their own horses. In their turn they were relieved by a powerful reinforcement of their brethren of Andalusia; the largest and western part of the island was gradually reduced, and the commodious harbour of Palermo was chosen for the seat of the naval and military power of the Saracens. Syracuse preserved about fifty years the faith which she had sworn to Christ and to Cæsar. In the last and fatal siege her citizens displayed some remnant of the spirit which had formerly resisted the powers of Athens and Carthage. They stood above twenty days against the battering-rams and *cata-pultæ*, the mines and tortoises of the besiegers; and the place

---

[1] Δηλοῖ (says the continuator of Theophanes, l. ii. p. 51 [p. 82, ed. Bonn]), δὲ ταῦτα σαφέστατα καὶ πλατικώτερον ἡ τότε γραφεῖσα Θεογνώστῳ καὶ εἰς χεῖρας ἐλθοῦσα ἡμῶν. This history of the loss of Sicily is no longer extant. Muratori (Annali d'Italia, tom. vii. p. 719, 721, etc.) has added some circumstances from the Italian chronicles.

[2] The splendid and interesting tragedy of *Tancrede* would adapt itself much better to this epoch than to the date (A.D. 1005) which Voltaire himself has chosen. But I must gently reproach the poet for infusing into the Greek subjects the spirit of modern knights and ancient republicans.

might have been relieved, if the mariners of the Imperial fleet had not been detained at Constantinople in building a church to the Virgin Mary. The deacon Theodosius, with the bishop and clergy, was dragged in chains from the altar to Palermo, cast into a subterraneous dungeon, and exposed to the hourly peril of death or apostasy. His pathetic, and not inelegant complaint, may be read as the epitaph of his country.[1] From the Roman conquest to this final calamity, Syracuse, now dwindled to the primitive isle of Ortygea, had insensibly declined. Yet the relics were still precious; the plate of the cathedral weighed five thousand pounds of silver; the entire spoil was computed at one million of pieces of gold (about four hundred thousand pounds sterling), and the captives must outnumber the seventeen thousand Christians who were transported from the sack of Tauromenium into African servitude. In Sicily the religion and language of the Greeks were eradicated; and such was the docility of the rising generation, that fifteen thousand boys were circumcised and clothed on the same day with the son of the Fatimite caliph. The Arabian squadrons issued from the harbours of Palermo, Biserta, and Tunis; a hundred and fifty towns of Calabria and Campania were attacked and pillaged; nor could the suburbs of Rome be defended by the name of the Cæsars and apostles. Had the Mohammedans been united, Italy must have fallen an easy and glorious accession to the empire of the prophet. But the caliphs of Bagdad had lost their authority in the West; the Aglabites and Fatimites usurped the provinces of Africa, their emirs of Sicily aspired to independence; and the design of conquest and dominion was degraded to a repetition of predatory inroads.[2]

In the sufferings of prostrate Italy the name of Rome awakens a solemn and mournful recollection. A fleet of Saracens from the African coast presumed to enter the mouth of the Tiber, and to approach a city which even yet, in her fallen state, was revered as the metropolis of the Christian world. The gates and ramparts were guarded by a trembling people; but the tombs and temples of St. Peter and St. Paul were left exposed in the suburbs of the Vatican and of the Ostian way. Their invisible sanctity

[1] The narrative or lamentation of Theodosius is transcribed and illustrated by Pagi (Critica, tom. iii. p. 719, etc.). Constantine Porphyrogenitus (in Vit. Basil. c. 69, 70, p. 190-192 [Theoph. Cont. p. 309, sq., ed. Bonn]) mentions the loss of Syracuse and the triumph of the demons.

[2] The extracts from the Arabic histories of Sicily are given in Abulfeda (Annal. Moslem. p. 271-273), and in the first volume of Muratori's Scriptores Rerum Italicarum. M. de Guignes (Hist. des Huns, tom. i. p. 363, 364) has added some important facts.

had protected them against the Goths, the Vandals, and the Lombards; but the Arabs disdained both the Gospel and the legend; and their rapacious spirit was approved and animated by the precepts of the Koran. The Christian *idols* were stripped of their costly offerings; a silver altar was torn away from the shrine of St. Peter; and if the bodies or the buildings were left entire, their deliverance must be imputed to the haste rather than the scruples of the Saracens. In their course along the Appian way, they pillaged Fundi and besieged Gaëta; but they had turned aside from the walls of Rome, and, by their divisions, the Capitol was saved from the yoke of the prophet of Mecca. The same danger still impended on the heads of the Roman people; and their domestic force was unequal to the assault of an African emir. They claimed the protection of their Latin sovereign; but the Carlovingian standard was overthrown by a detachment of the barbarians: they meditated the restoration of the Greek emperors; but the attempt was treasonable, and the succour remote and precarious.[1] Their distress appeared to receive some aggravation from the death of their spiritual and temporal chief; but the pressing emergency superseded the forms and intrigues of an election; and the unanimous choice of Pope Leo the Fourth [2] was the safety of the church and city. This pontiff was born a Roman; the courage of the first ages of the republic glowed in his breast; and, amidst the ruins of his country, he stood erect, like one of the firm and lofty columns that rear their heads above the fragments of the Roman forum. The first days of his reign were consecrated to the purification and removal of relics, to prayers and processions, and to all the solemn offices of religion, which served at least to heal the imagination and restore the hopes of the multitude. The public defence had been long neglected, not from the presumption of peace, but from the distress and poverty of the times. As far as the scantiness of his means and the shortness of his leisure would allow, the ancient walls were repaired by the command of Leo;

---

[1] One of the most eminent Romans (Gratianus, magister militum et Romani palatii superista) was accused of declaring, Quia Franci nihil nobis boni faciunt, neque adjutorium præbent, sed magis quæ nostra sunt violenter tollunt. Quare non advocamus Græcos, et cum eis fœdus pacis componentes, Francorum regem et gentem de nostro regno et dominatione expellimus? Anastasius in Leone IV. p. 199 [ap. Muratori, Script. R. I. iii. p. 246].

[2] Voltaire (Hist. Générale, tom. ii. c. 38, p. 124) appears to be remarkably struck with the character of Pope Leo IV. I have borrowed his general expression, but the sight of the forum has furnished me with a more distinct and lively image.

fifteen towers, in the most accessible stations, were built or
renewed; two of these commanded on either side the Tiber; and
an iron chain was drawn across the stream to impede the ascent
of a hostile navy.   The Romans were assured of a short respite
by the welcome news that the siege of Gaëta had been raised, and
that a part of the enemy with their sacrilegious plunder had
perished in the waves.

But the storm which had been delayed soon burst upon them
with redoubled violence.   The Aglabite,[1] who reigned in Africa,
had inherited from his father a treasure and an army: a fleet of
Arabs and Moors, after a short refreshment in the harbours of
Sardinia, cast anchor before the mouth of the Tiber, sixteen
miles from the city; and their discipline and numbers appeared
to threaten, not a transient inroad, but a serious design of conquest and dominion.   But the vigilance of Leo had formed an
alliance with the vassals of the Greek empire, the free and maritime states of Gaëta, Naples, and Amalfi; and, in the hour of
danger, their galleys appeared in the port of Ostia under the
command of Cæsarius, the son of the Neapolitan duke, a noble
and valiant youth, who had already vanquished the fleets of the
Saracens.   With his principal companions, Cæsarius was invited
to the Lateran palace, and the dexterous pontiff affected to
inquire their errand, and to accept with joy and surprise their
providential succour.   The city bands, in arms, attended their
father to Ostia, where he reviewed and blessed his generous
deliverers.   They kissed his feet, received the communion with
martial devotion, and listened to the prayer of Leo, that the same
God who had supported St. Peter and St. Paul on the waves of
the sea would strengthen the hands of his champions against the
adversaries of his holy name.   After a similar prayer, and with
equal resolution, the Moslems advanced to the attack of the
Christian galleys, which preserved their advantageous station
along the coast.   The victory inclined to the side of the allies,
when it was less gloriously decided in their favour by a sudden
tempest, which confounded the skill and courage of the stoutest
mariners.   The Christians were sheltered in a friendly harbour,
while the Africans were scattered and dashed in pieces among
the rocks and islands of a hostile shore.   Those who escaped
from shipwreck and hunger neither found not deserved mercy

---

[1] De Guignes, Hist. Générale des Huns, tom. i. p. 363, 364; Cardonne,
Hist. de l'Afrique et de l'Espagne sous la Domination des Arabes, tom. ii.
p. 24, 25.   I observe, and cannot reconcile, the difference of these writers
in the succession of the Aglabites.

at the hands of their implacable pursuers. The sword and the gibbet reduced the dangerous multitude of captives; and the remainder was more usefully employed to restore the sacred edifices which they had attempted to subvert. The pontiff, at the head of the citizens and allies, paid his grateful devotion at the shrines of the apostles; and, among the spoils of this naval victory, thirteen Arabian bows of pure and massy silver were suspended round the altar of the fisherman of Galilee. The reign of Leo the Fourth was employed in the defence and ornament of the Roman state. The churches were renewed and embellished: near four thousand pounds of silver were consecrated to repair the losses of St. Peter; and his sanctuary was decorated with a plate of gold of the weight of two hundred and sixteen pounds, embossed with the portraits of the pope and emperor, and encircled with a string of pearls. Yet this vain magnificence reflects less glory on the character of Leo than the paternal care with which he rebuilt the walls of Horta and Ameria; and transported the wandering inhabitants of Centumcellæ to his new foundation of Leopolis, twelve miles from the sea-shore.[1] By his liberality a colony of Corsicans, with their wives and children, was planted in the station of Porto at the mouth of the Tiber: the falling city was restored for their use, the fields and vineyards were divided among the new settlers: their first efforts were assisted by a gift of horses and cattle; and the hardy exiles, who breathed revenge against the Saracens, swore to live and die under the standard of St. Peter. The nations of the West and North who visited the threshold of the apostles had gradually formed the large and populous suburb of the Vatican, and their various habitations were distinguished, in the language of the times, as the *schools* of the Greeks and Goths, of the Lombards and Saxons. But this venerable spot was still open to sacrilegious insult: the design of enclosing it with walls and towers exhausted all that authority could command, or charity would supply: and the pious labour of four years was animated in every season and at every hour by the presence of the indefatigable pontiff. The love of fame, a generous but worldly passion, may be detected in the name of the *Leonine city*, which he bestowed on the Vatican; yet the pride of the dedication was tempered with Christian penance and humility. The boundary was trod by the bishop and his clergy, barefoot, in

---

[1] Beretti (Chorographia Italiæ Medii Ævi, p. 106, 108) has illustrated Centumcellæ, Leopolis, Civitas Leonina, and the other places of the Roman duchy.

sackcloth and ashes; the songs of triumph were modulated to psalms and litanies; the walls were besprinkled with holy water; and the ceremony was concluded with a prayer, that, under the guardian care of the apostles and the angelic host, both the old and the new Rome might ever be preserved pure, prosperous, and impregnable.[1]

The emperor Theophilus, son of Michael the Stammerer, was one of the most active and high-spirited princes who reigned at Constantinople during the middle age. In offensive or defensive war he marched in person five times against the Saracens, formidable in his attack, esteemed by the enemy in his losses and defeats. In the last of these expeditions he penetrated into Syria, and besieged the obscure town of Sozopetra; the casual birthplace of the caliph Motassem, whose father Harun was attended in peace or war by the most favoured of his wives and concubines. The revolt of a Persian impostor employed at that moment the arms of the Saracen, and he could only intercede in favour of a place for which he felt and acknowledged some degree of filial affection. These solicitations determined the emperor to wound his pride in so sensible a part. Sozopetra was levelled with the ground, the Syrian prisoners were marked or mutilated with ignominious cruelty, and a thousand female captives were forced away from the adjacent territory. Among these a matron of the house of Abbas invoked, in an agony of despair, the name of Motassem; and the insults of the Greeks engaged the honour of her kinsman to avenge his indignity, and to answer her appeal. Under the reign of the two elder brothers, the inheritance of the youngest had been confined to Anatolia, Armenia, Georgia, and Circassia; this frontier station had exercised his military talents; and among his accidental claims to the name of *Octonary*,[2] the most meritorious are the *eight* battles which he gained or fought against the enemies of the Koran. In this personal quarrel, the troops of Irak, Syria, and Egypt were recruited from the tribes of Arabia and the Turkish hordes:

[1] The Arabs and the Greeks are alike silent concerning the invasion of Rome by the Africans. The Latin chronicles do not afford much instruction (see the Annals of Baronius and Pagi). Our authentic and contemporary guide for the Popes of the ninth century is Anastasius, librarian of the Roman church. His Life of Leo IV. contains twenty-four pages (p. 175-199, edit. Paris); and if a great part consists of superstitious trifles, we must blame or commend his hero, who was much oftener in a church than in a camp.

[2] The same number was applied to the following circumstance in the life of Motassem: he was the *eighth* of the Abbassides; he reigned *eight* years, *eight* months, and *eight* days; left *eight* sons, *eight* daughters, *eight* thousand slaves, *eight* millions of gold.

his cavalry might be numerous, though we should deduct some myriads from the hundred and thirty thousand horses of the royal stables; and the expense of the armament was computed at four millions sterling, or one hundred thousand pounds of gold. From Tarsus, the place of assembly, the Saracens advanced in three divisions along the high road of Constantinople: Motassem himself commanded the centre, and the vanguard was given to his son Abbas, who, in the trial of the first adventures, might succeed with the more glory, or fail with the least reproach. In the revenge of his injury the caliph prepared to retaliate a similar affront. The father of Theophilus was a native of Amorium [1] in Phrygia: the original seat of the Imperial house had been adorned with privileges and monuments; and, whatever might be the indifference of the people, Constantinople itself was scarcely of more value in the eyes of the sovereign and his court. The name of AMORIUM was inscribed on the shields of the Saracens; and their three armies were again united under the walls of the devoted city. It had been proposed by the wisest counsellors to evacuate Amorium, to remove the inhabitants, and to abandon the empty structures to the vain resentment of the barbarians. The emperor embraced the more generous resolution of defending, in a siege and battle, the country of his ancestors. When the armies drew near, the front of the Mohammedan line appeared to a Roman eye more closely planted with spears and javelins; but the event of the action was not glorious on either side to the national troops. The Arabs were broken, but it was by the swords of thirty thousand Persians, who had obtained service and settlement in the Byzantine empire. The Greeks were repulsed and vanquished, but it was by the arrows of the Turkish cavalry; and had not their bowstrings been damped and relaxed by the evening rain, very few of the Christians could have escaped with the emperor from the field of battle. They breathed at Dorylæum, at the distance of three days; and Theophilus, reviewing his trembling squadrons, forgave the common flight both of the prince and people. After this discovery of his weakness, he vainly hoped to deprecate the fate of Amorium: the inexorable caliph rejected with contempt his prayers and promises, and detained the Roman

---

[1] Amorium is seldom mentioned by the old geographers, and totally forgotten in the Roman Itineraries. After the sixth century it became an episcopal see, and at length the metropolis of the new Galatia (Carol. Scto. Paulo, Geograph. Sacra. p. 234). The city rose again from its ruins, if we should read *Ammuria*, not *Anguria*, in the text of the Nubian geographer (p. 236).

ambassadors to be the witnesses of his great revenge. They had nearly been the witnesses of his shame. The vigorous assaults of fifty-five days were encountered by a faithful governor, a veteran garrison, and a desperate people; and the Saracens must have raised the siege, if a domestic traitor had not pointed to the weakest part of the wall, a place which was decorated with the statues of a lion and a bull. The vow of Motassem was accomplished with unrelenting rigour: tired, rather than satiated, with destruction, he returned to his new palace of Samara, in the neighbourhood of Bagdad, while the *unfortunate* [1] Theophilus implored the tardy and doubtful aid of his Western rival the emperor of the Franks. Yet in the siege of Amorium about seventy thousand Moslems had perished; their loss had been revenged by the slaughter of thirty thousand Christians, and the sufferings of an equal number of captives, who were treated as the most atrocious criminals. Mutual necessity could sometimes extort the exchange or ransom of prisoners; [2] but in the national and religious conflict of the two empires, peace was without confidence, and war without mercy. Quarter was seldom given in the field; those who escaped the edge of the sword were condemned to hopeless servitude or exquisite torture; and a Catholic emperor relates, with visible satisfaction, the execution of the Saracens of Crete, who were flayed alive, or plunged into caldrons of boiling oil. [3] To a point of honour Motassem had sacrificed a flourishing city, two hundred thousand lives, and the property of millions. The same caliph descended from his horse, and dirtied his robe, to relieve the distress of a decrepit old man, who, with his laden ass, had tumbled into a

---

[1] In the East he was styled Δυστυχὴς (Continuator Theophan. l. iii. p. 84 [p. 135, ed. Bonn]): but such was the ignorance of the West, that his ambassadors, in public discourse, might boldly narrate, de victoriis, quas adversus exteras bellando gentes cœlitus fuerat assecutus (Annalist. Bertinian. apud Pagi, tom. iii. p. 720).

[2] Abulpharagius (Dynast. p. 167, 168) relates one of these singular transactions on the bridge of the river Lamus in Cilicia, the limit of the two empires, and one day's journey westward of Tarsus (D'Anville, Géographie Ancienne, tom. ii. p. 91). Four thousand four hundred and sixty Moslems, eight hundred women and children, one hundred confederates, were exchanged for an equal number of Greeks. They passed each other in the middle of the bridge, and when they reached their respective friends they shouted *Allah Acbar*, and *Kyrie Eleison*. Many of the prisoners of Amorium were probably among them, but in the same year (A.H. 231) the most illustrious of them, the forty-two martyrs, were beheaded by the caliph's order.

[3] Constantin. Porphyrogenitus, in Vit. Basil. c. 61, p. 186 [p. 301, ed. Bonn]. These Saracens were indeed treated with peculiar severity as pirates and renegadoes.

ditch. On which of these actions did he reflect with the most pleasure when he was summoned by the angel of death? [1]

With Motassem, the eighth of the Abbassides, the glory of his family and nation expired. When the Arabian conquerors had spread themselves over the East, and were mingled with the servile crowds of Persia, Syria, and Egypt, they insensibly lost the freeborn and martial virtues of the desert. The courage of the South is the artificial fruit of discipline and prejudice; the active power of enthusiasm had decayed, and the mercenary forces of the caliphs were recruited in those climates of the North, of which valour is the hardy and spontaneous production. Of the Turks [2] who dwelt beyond the Oxus and Jaxartes, the robust youths, either taken in war, or purchased in trade, were educated in the exercises of the field and the profession of the Mohammedan faith. The Turkish guards stood in arms round the throne of their benefactor, and their chiefs usurped the dominion of the palace and the provinces. Motassem, the first author of this dangerous example, introduced into the capital above fifty thousand Turks: their licentious conduct provoked the public indignation, and the quarrels of the soldiers and people induced the caliph to retire from Bagdad, and establish his own residence and the camp of his barbarian favourites at Samara on the Tigris, about twelve leagues above the city of Peace.[3] His son Motawakkel was a jealous and cruel tyrant: odious to his subjects, he cast himself on the fidelity of the strangers, and these strangers, ambitious and apprehensive, were tempted by the rich promise of a revolution. At the instigation, or at least in the cause of his son, they burst into his apartment at the hour of supper, and the caliph was cut into seven pieces by the same swords which he had recently distributed among the guards of his life and throne. To this throne, yet streaming with a father's blood, Montasser was triumphantly led; but in a reign of six months he found only the pangs of a guilty conscience. If he

[1] For Theophilus, Motassem, and the Amorian war, see the Continuator of Theophanes (l. iii. p. 77-84 [p. 124-135, ed. Bonn]), Genesius (l. iii. p. 24-34), Cedrenus (p. 528-532 [tom. ii. p. 129-137, ed. Bonn]), Elmacin (Hist. Saracen. p. 180), Abulpharagius (Dynast. p. 165, 166), Abulfeda (Annal. Moslem. p. 191), D'Herbelot (Biblioth. Orientale, p. 639, 640).

[2] M. de Guignes, who sometimes leaps, and sometimes stumbles, in the gulf between Chinese and Mohammedan story, thinks he can see that these Turks are the *Hoei-ke*, alias the *Kao-tche*, or *high-waggons* ; that they were divided into fifteen hordes, from China and Siberia to the dominions of the caliphs and Samanides, etc. (Hist. des Huns, tom. iii. p. 1-33, 124-131).

[3] He changed the old name of Sumere, or Samara, into the fanciful title of *Ser-mênraï*, that which gives pleasure at first sight (D'Herbelot, Bibliothèque Orientale, p. 808; D'Anville, l'Euphrate et le Tigre, p. 97, 98).

wept at the sight of an old tapestry which represented the crime and punishment of the son of Chosroes; if his days were abridged by grief and remorse, we may allow some pity to a parricide, who exclaimed, in the bitterness of death, that he had lost both this world and the world to come. After this act of treason, the ensigns of royalty, the garment and walking staff of Mohammed, were given and torn away by the foreign mercenaries, who in four years created, deposed, and murdered three commanders of the faithful. As often as the Turks were inflamed by fear, or rage, or avarice, these caliphs were dragged by the feet, exposed naked to the scorching sun, beaten with iron clubs, and compelled to purchase, by the abdication of their dignity, a short reprieve of inevitable fate.[1] At length, however, the fury of the tempest was spent or diverted: the Abbassides returned to the less turbulent residence of Bagdad; the insolence of the Turks was curbed with a firmer and more skilful hand, and their numbers were divided and destroyed in foreign warfare. But the nations of the East had been taught to trample on the successors of the prophet; and the blessings of domestic peace were obtained by the relaxation of strength and discipline. So uniform are the mischiefs of military despotism, that I seem to repeat the story of the Prætorians of Rome.[2]

While the flame of enthusiasm was damped by the business, the pleasure, and the knowledge of the age, it burnt with concentrated heat in the breasts of the chosen few, the congenial spirits, who were ambitious of reigning either in this world or in the next. How carefully soever the book of prophecy had been sealed by the apostle of Mecca, the wishes, and (if we may profane the word) even the reason of fanaticism, might believe that, after the successive missions of Adam, Noah, Abraham, Moses, Jesus, and Mohammed, the same God, in the fulness of time, would reveal a still more perfect and permanent law. In the two hundred and seventy-seventh year of the Hegira, and in the neighbourhood of Cufa, an Arabian preacher of the name of

---

[1] Take a specimen, the death of the caliph Motaz: Correptum pedibus pertrahunt, et sudibus probe permulcant, et spoliatum laceris vestibus in sole collocant, præ cujus acerrimo æstû pedes alternos attollebat et demittebat. Adstantium aliquis misero colaphos continuo ingerebat, quos ille objectis manibus avertere studebat. . . . Quo facto traditus tortori fuit, totoque triduo cibo potuque prohibitus. . . . Suffocatus, etc. (Abulfeda, p. 206). Of the caliph Mohtadi, he says, cervices ipsi perpetuis ictibus contundebant, testiculosque pedibus conculcabant (p. 208).

[2] See under the reigns of Motassem, Motawakkel, Montasser, Mostain, Motaz, Mohtadi, and Motamed, in the Bibliothèque of D'Herbelot, and the now familiar Annals of Elmacin, Abulpharagius, and Abulfeda.

Carmath assumed the lofty and incomprehensible style of the Guide, the Director, the Demonstration, the Word, the Holy Ghost, the Camel, the Herald of the Messiah, who had conversed with him in a human shape, and the representative of Mohammed the son of Ali, of St. John the Baptist, and of the angel Gabriel. In his mystic volume the precepts of the Koran were refined to a more spiritual sense; he relaxed the duties of ablution, fasting, and pilgrimage; allowed the indiscriminate use of wine and forbidden food; and nourished the fervour of his disciples by the daily repetition of fifty prayers. The idleness and ferment of the rustic crowd awakened the attention of the magistrates of Cufa; a timid persecution assisted the progress of the new sect; and the name of the prophet became more revered after his person had been withdrawn from the world. His twelve apostles dispersed themselves among the Bedoweens, "a race of men," says Abulfeda, "equally devoid of reason and of religion;" and the success of their preaching seemed to threaten Arabia with a new revolution. The Carmathians were ripe for rebellion, since they disclaimed the title of the house of Abbas, and abhorred the worldly pomp of the caliphs of Bagdad. They were susceptible of discipline, since they vowed a blind and absolute submission to their Imam, who was called to the prophetic office by the voice of God and the people. Instead of the legal tithes he claimed the fifth of their substance and spoil; the most flagitious sins were no more than the type of disobedience; and the brethren were united and concealed by an oath of secrecy.

After a bloody conflict they prevailed in the province of Bahrein, along the Persian Gulf: far and wide the tribes of the desert were subject to the sceptre, or rather to the sword, of Abu Said and his son Abu Taher; and these rebellious imams could muster in the field a hundred and seven thousand fanatics. The mercenaries of the caliph were displayed at the approach of an enemy who neither asked nor accepted quarter; and the difference between them in fortitude and patience is expressive of the change which three centuries of prosperity had effected in the character of the Arabians. Such troops were discomfited in every action; the cities of Racca and Baalbec, of Cufa and Bassora, were taken and pillaged; Bagdad was filled with consternation; and the caliph trembled behind the veils of his palace. In a daring inroad beyond the Tigris, Abu Taher advanced to the gates of the capital with no more than five hundred horse. By the special order of Moctader the bridges had been broken down, and the person or head of the rebel was expected every hour by the commander of the faithful. His lieutenant, from a motive of fear or pity, apprised Abu Taher of his danger, and recommended a speedy escape. " Your master," said the intrepid Carmathian to the messenger, " is at the head of thirty thousand soldiers: three such men as these are wanting in his host: " at the same instant, turning to three of his companions, he commanded the first to plunge a dagger into his breast, the second to leap into the Tigris, and the third to cast himself headlong down a precipice. They obeyed without a murmur. " Relate," continued the imam, " what you have seen: before the evening your general shall be chained among my dogs." Before the evening the camp was surprised, and the menace was executed. The rapine of the Carmathians was sanctified by their aversion to the worship of Mecca: they robbed a caravan of pilgrims, and twenty thousand devout Moslems were abandoned on the burning sands to a death of hunger and thirst. Another year they suffered the pilgrims to proceed without interruption; but, in the festival of devotion, Abu Taher stormed the holy city, and trampled on the most venerable relics of the Mohammedan faith. Thirty thousand citizens and strangers were put to the sword; the sacred precincts were polluted by the burial of three thousand dead bodies; the well of Zemzem overflowed with blood; the golden spout was forced from its place; the veil of the Caaba was divided among these impious sectaries; and the black stone, the first monument of the nation, was borne away in triumph to their capital. After this deed of sacrilege and cruelty they continued to infest the confines of Irak, Syria, and Egypt: but the vital principle of enthusiasm had withered at the root. Their scruples or their avarice again opened the pilgrimage of Mecca, and restored the black stone of the Caaba; and it is needless to inquire into what factions they were broken, or by whose swords they were finally extirpated. The sect of the Carmathians may be considered as the second visible cause of the decline and fall of the empire of the caliphs.[1]

The third and most obvious cause was the weight and magnitude of the empire itself. The caliph Almamon might proudly assert that it was easier for him to rule the East and the West

---

[1] For the sect of the Carmathians, consult Elmacin (Hist. Saracen. p. 219, 224, 229, 231, 238, 241, 243), Abulpharagius (Dynast. p. 179-182), Abulfeda (Annal. Moslem. p. 218, 219, etc. 245, 265, 274), and D'Herbelot (Bibliothèque Orientale, p. 256-258, 635). I find some inconsistencies of theology and chronology, which it would not be easy nor of much import- ance to reconcile.

than to manage a chess-board of two feet square: [1] yet I suspect that in both those games he was guilty of many fatal mistakes; and I perceive that in the distant provinces the authority of the first and most powerful of the Abbassides was already impaired. The analogy of despotism invests the representative with the full majesty of the prince; the division and balance of powers might relax the habits of obedience, might encourage the passive subject to inquire into the origin and administration of civil government. He who is born in the purple is seldom worthy to reign; but the elevation of a private man, of a peasant perhaps, or a slave, affords a strong presumption of his courage and capacity. The viceroy of a remote kingdom aspires to secure the property and inheritance of his precarious trust; the nations must rejoice in the presence of their sovereign; and the command of armies and treasures are at once the object and the instrument of his ambition. A change was scarcely visible as long as the lieutenants of the caliph were content with their vicarious title; while they solicited for themselves or their sons a renewal of the Imperial grant, and still maintained on the coin and in the public prayers the name and prerogative of the commander of the faithful. But in the long and hereditary exercise of power they assumed the pride and attributes of royalty; the alternative of peace or war, of reward or punishment, depended solely on their will; and the revenues of their government were reserved for local services or private magnificence. Instead of a regular supply of men and money, the successors of the prophet were flattered with the ostentatious gift of an elephant, or a cast of hawks, a suit of silk hangings, or some pounds of musk and amber.[2]

After the revolt of Spain from the temporal and spiritual supremacy of the Abbassides, the first symptoms of disobedience broke forth in the province of Africa. Ibrahim, the son of Aglab, the lieutenant of the vigilant and rigid Harun, bequeathed to the dynasty of the *Aglabites* the inheritance of his name and power. The indolence or policy of the caliphs dissembled the injury and loss, and pursued only with poison the founder of the *Edrisites*,[3]

[1] Hyde, Syntagma Dissertat. tom. ii. p. 57, in Hist. Shahiludii.
[2] The dynasties of the Arabian empire may be studied in the Annals of Elmacin, Abulpharagius, and Abulfeda, under the *proper* years; in the dictionary of D'Herbelot, under the *proper* names. The tables of M. de Guignes (Hist. des Huns, tom. i.) exhibit a general chronology of the East, interspersed with some historical anecdotes; but his attachment to national blood has sometimes confounded the order of time and place.
[3] The Aglabites and Edrisites are the professed subject of M. de Cardonne (Hist. de l'Afrique et de l'Espagne sous la Domination des Arabes, tom. ii. p. 1-63).

who erected the kingdom and city of Fez on the shores of the Western ocean.[1] In the East the first dynasty was that of the *Taherites* [2]—the posterity of the valiant Taher, who, in the civil wars of the sons of Harun, had served with too much zeal and success the cause of Almamon, the younger brother. He was sent into honourable exile, to command on the banks of the Oxus; and the independence of his successors, who reigned in Chorasan till the fourth generation, was palliated by their modest and respectful demeanour, the happiness of their subjects, and the security of their frontier. They were supplanted by one of those adventurers so frequent in the annals of the East, who left his trade of a brazier (from whence the name of *Soffarides*) for the profession of a robber. In a nocturnal visit to the treasure of the prince of Sistan, Jacob, the son of Leith, stumbled over a lump of salt, which he unwarily tasted with his tongue. Salt, among the Orientals, is the symbol of hospitality, and the pious robber immediately retired without spoil or damage. The discovery of this honourable behaviour recommended Jacob to pardon and trust; he led an army at first for his benefactor, at last for himself, subdued Persia, and threatened the residence of the Abassides. On his march towards Bagdad the conqueror was arrested by a fever. He gave audience in bed to the ambassador of the caliph; and beside him on a table were exposed a naked scimitar, a crust of brown bread, and a bunch of onions. " If I die," said he, " your master is delivered from his fears. If I live, *this* must determine between us. If I am vanquished, I can return without reluctance to the homely fare of my youth." From the height where he stood, the descent would not have been so soft or harmless: a timely death secured his own repose and that of the caliph, who paid with the most lavish concessions the retreat of his brother Amrou to the palaces of Shiraz and Ispahan. The Abbassides were too feeble to contend, too proud to forgive: they invited the powerful dynasty of the *Samanides*, who passed

---

[1] To escape the reproach of error, I must criticise the inaccuracies of M. de Guignes (tom. i. p. 359) concerning the Edrisites. 1. The dynasty and city of Fez could not be founded in the year of the Hegira 173, since the founder was a *posthumous* child of a descendant of Ali, who fled from Mecca in the year 168. 2. This founder, Edris, the son of Edris, instead of living to the improbable age of 120 years, A.H. 313, died A.H. 214, in the prime of manhood. 3. The dynasty ended A.H. 307, twenty-three years sooner than it is fixed by the historian of the Huns. See the accurate Annals of Abulfeda, p. 158, 159, 185, 238.

[2] The dynasties of the Taherites and Soffarides, with the rise of that of the Samanides, are described in the original history and Latin version of Mirchond: yet the most interesting facts had already been drained by the diligence of M. D'Herbelot.

the Oxus with ten thousand horse, so poor that their stirrups were of wood; so brave, that they vanquished the Soffarian army, eight times more numerous than their own. The captive Amrou was sent in chains, a grateful offering, to the court of Bagdad; and as the victor was content with the inheritance of Transoxiana and Chorasan, the realms of Persia returned for a while to the allegiance of the caliphs. The provinces of Syria and Egypt were twice dismembered by their Turkish slaves of the race of *Toulun* and *Ikshid*.[1] These barbarians, in religion and manners the countrymen of Mohammed, emerged from the bloody factions of the palace to a provincial command and an independent throne: their names became famous and formidable in their time; but the founders of these two potent dynasties confessed, either in words or actions, the vanity of ambition. The first on his deathbed implored the mercy of God to a sinner, ignorant of the limits of his own power: the second, in the midst of four hundred thousand soldiers and eight thousand slaves, concealed from every human eye the chamber where he attempted to sleep. Their sons were educated in the vices of kings; and both Egypt and Syria were recovered and possessed by the Abbassides during an interval of thirty years. In the decline of their empire, Mesopotamia, with the important cities of Mosul and Aleppo, was occupied by the Arabian princes of the tribe of *Hamadan*. The poets of their court could repeat, without a blush, that nature had formed their countenances for beauty, their tongues for eloquence, and their hands for liberality and valour: but the genuine tale of the elevation and reign of the *Hamadanites* exhibits a scene of treachery, murder, and parricide. At the same fatal period the Persian kingdom was again usurped by the dynasty of the *Bowides*, by the sword of three brothers, who, under various names, were styled the support and columns of the state, and who, from the Caspian sea to the ocean, would suffer no tyrants but themselves. Under their reign the language and genius of Persia revived, and the Arabs, three hundred and four years after the death of Mohammed, were deprived of the sceptre of the East.

Rahdi, the twentieth of the Abbassides, and the thirty-ninth of the successors of Mohammed, was the last who deserved the title of commander of the faithful;[2] the last (says Abulfeda)

---

[1] M. de Guignes (Hist. des Huns, tom. iii. p. 124-154) has exhausted the Toulunides and Ikshidites of Egypt, and thrown some light on the Carmathians and Hamadanites.

[2] Hic est ultimus chalifah qui multum atque sæpius pro concione peroraret. . . . Fuit etiam ultimus qui otium cum eruditis et facetis homini-

who spoke to the people or conversed with the learned; the last who, in the expense of his household, represented the wealth and magnificence of the ancient caliphs. After him, the lords of the Eastern world were reduced to the most abject misery, and exposed to the blows and insults of a servile condition. The revolt of the provinces circumscribed their dominions within the walls of Bagdad: but that capital still contained an innumerable multitude, vain of their past fortune, discontented with their present state, and oppressed by the demands of a treasury which had formerly been replenished by the spoil and tribute of nations. Their idleness was exercised by faction and controversy. Under the mask of piety, the rigid followers of Hanbal[1] invaded the pleasures of domestic life, burst into the houses of plebeians and princes, spilt the wine, broke the instruments, beat the musicians, and dishonoured, with infamous suspicions, the associates of every handsome youth. In each profession which allowed room for two persons, the one was a votary, the other an antagonist, of Ali; and the Abbassides were awakened by the clamorous grief of the sectaries, who denied their title, and cursed their progenitors. A turbulent people could only be repressed by a military force; but who could satisfy the avarice or assert the discipline of the mercenaries themselves? The African and the Turkish guards drew their swords against each other, and the chief commanders, the emirs al Omra,[2] imprisoned or deposed their sovereigns, and violated the sanctuary of the mosch and haram. If the caliphs escaped to the camp or court of any neighbouring prince, their deliverance was a change of servitude, till they were prompted by despair to invite the Bowides, the

bus fallere hilariterque agere soleret. Ultimus tandem chalifarum cui sumtus, stipendia, reditus, et thesauri, culinæ, cæteraque omnis aulica pompa priorum chalifarum ad instar comparata fuerint. Videbimus enim paullo post quam indignis et servilibus ludibriis exagitati, quam ad humilem fortunam altimumque contemptum abjecti fuerint hi quondam potentissimi totius terrarum Orientalium orbis domini.   Abulfed. Annal. Moslem. p. 261. I have given this passage as the manner and tone of Abulfeda, but the cast of Latin eloquence belongs more properly to Reiske. The Arabian historian (p. 255, 257, 261-269, 283, etc.) has supplied me with the most interesting facts of this paragraph.

[1] Their master, on a similar occasion, showed himself of a more indulgent and tolerating spirit. Ahmed Ebn Hanbal, the head of one of the four orthodox sects, was born at Bagdad A.H. 164, and died there A.H. 241. He fought and suffered in the dispute concerning the creation of the Koran.

[2] The office of vizir was superseded by the emir al Omra, Imperator Imperatorum, a title first instituted by Rahdi, and which merged at length in the Bowides and Seljukides: vectigalibus, et tributis, et curiis per omnes regiones præfecit, jussitque in omnibus suggestis nominis ejus in concionibus mentionem fieri (Abulpharagius, Dynast. p. 199). It is likewise mentioned by Elmacin (p. 254, 255).

sultans of Persia, who silenced the factions of Bagdad by their irresistible arms. The civil and military powers were assumed by Moezaldowlat, the second of the three brothers, and a stipend of sixty thousand pounds sterling was assigned by his generosity for the private expense of the commander of the faithful. But on the fortieth day, at the audience of the ambassadors of Chorasan, and in the presence of a trembling multitude, the caliph was dragged from his throne to a dungeon, by the command of the stranger, and the rude hands of his Dilemites. His palace was pillaged, his eyes were put out, and the mean ambition of the Abbassides aspired to the vacant station of danger and disgrace. In the school of adversity the luxurious caliphs resumed the grave and abstemious virtues of the primitive times. Despoiled of their armour and silken robes, they fasted, they prayed, they studied the Koran and the tradition of the Sonnites: they performed, with zeal and knowledge, the functions of their ecclesiastical character. The respect of nations still waited on the successors of the apostle, the oracles of the law and conscience of the faithful; and the weakness or division of their tyrants sometimes restored the Abbassides to the sovereignty of Bagdad. But their misfortunes had been embittered by the triumph of the Fatimites, the real or spurious progeny of Ali. Arising from the extremity of Africa, these successful rivals extinguished, in Egypt and Syria, both the spiritual and temporal authority of the Abbassides; and the monarch of the Nile insulted the humble pontiff on the banks of the Tigris.

In the declining age of the caliphs, in the century which elapsed after the war of Theophilus and Motassem, the hostile transactions of the two nations were confined to some inroads by sea and land, the fruits of their close vicinity and indelible hatred. But when the Eastern world was convulsed and broken, the Greeks were roused from their lethargy by the hopes of conquest and revenge. The Byzantine empire, since the accession of the Basilian race, had reposed in peace and dignity; and they might encounter with their entire strength the front of some petty emir, whose rear was assaulted and threatened by his national foes of the Mohammedan faith. The lofty titles of the morning-star, and the death of the Saracens,[1] were applied in the public acclamations to Nicephorus Phocas, a prince as renowned in the

---

[1] Liutprand, whose choleric temper was embittered by his uneasy situation, suggests the names of reproach and contempt more applicable to Nicephorus than the vain titles of the Greeks, Ecce venit stella matutina, surgit Eous, reverberat obtutû solis radios, pallida Saracenorum mors, Nicephorus μεδων.

camp as he was unpopular in the city. In the subordinate station of great domestic, or general of the East, he reduced the island of Crete, and extirpated the nest of pirates who had so long defied, with impunity, the majesty of the empire.[1] His military genius was displayed in the conduct and success of the enterprise, which had so often failed with loss and dishonour. The Saracens were confounded by the landing of his troops on safe and level bridges, which he cast from the vessels to the shore. Seven months were consumed in the siege of Candia; the despair of the native Cretans was stimulated by the frequent aid of their brethren of Africa and Spain; and, after the massy wall and double ditch had been stormed by the Greeks, a hopeless conflict was still maintained in the streets and houses of the city. The whole island was subdued in the capital, and a submissive people accepted, without resistance, the baptism of the conqueror.[2] Constantinople applauded the long-forgotten pomp of a triumph; but the Imperial diadem was the sole reward that could repay the service, or satisfy the ambition, of Nicephorus.

After the death of the younger Romanus, the fourth in lineal descent of the Basilian race, his widow Theophania successively married Nicephorus Phocas and his assassin John Zimisces, the two heroes of the age. They reigned as the guardians and colleagues of her infant sons; and the twelve years of their military command form the most splendid period of the Byzantine annals. The subjects and confederates whom they led to war appeared, at least in the eyes of an enemy, two hundred thousand strong; and of these about thirty thousand were armed with cuirasses:[3] a train of four thousand mules attended their march; and their evening camp was regularly fortified with an enclosure of iron spikes. A series of bloody and undecisive combats is nothing more than an anticipation of what would have been

---

[1] Notwithstanding the insinuation of Zonaras, καὶ εἰ μὴ, etc. (tom. ii. l. xvi. [c. 23] p. 197), it is an undoubted fact that Crete was completely and finally subdued by Nicephorus Phocas (Pagi, Critica, tom. iii. p. 873-875; Meursius, Creta, l. iii. c. 7, tom. iii. p. 464, 465).

[2] A Greek Life of St. Nicon the Armenian was found in the Sforza library, and translated into Latin by the Jesuit Sirmond, for the use of Cardinal Baronius. This contemporary legend casts a ray of light on Crete and Peloponnesus in the tenth century. He found the newly-recovered island, fœdis detestandæ Agarenorum superstitionis vestigiis adhuc plenam ac refertam . . . but the victorious missionary, perhaps with some carnal aid, ad baptismum omnes veræque fidei disciplinam pepulit. Ecclesiis per totam insulam ædificatis, etc. (Annal. Eccles. A.D. 961).

[3] Elmacin, Hist. Saracen. p. 278, 279. Liutprand was disposed to depreciate the Greek power, yet he owns that Nicephorus led against Assyria an army of eighty thousand men.

effected in a few years by the course of nature: but I shall briefly prosecute the conquests of the two emperors from the hills of Cappadocia to the desert of Bagdad. The sieges of Mopsuestia and Tarsus, in Cilicia, first exercised the skill and perseverance of their troops, on whom, at this moment, I shall not hesitate to bestow the name of Romans. In the double city of Mopsuestia, which is divided by the river Sarus, two hundred thousand Moslems were predestined to death or slavery,[1] a surprising degree of population, which must at least include the inhabitants of the dependent districts. They were surrounded and taken by assault; but Tarsus was reduced by the slow progress of famine; and no sooner had the Saracens yielded on honourable terms than they were mortified by the distant and unprofitable view of the naval succours of Egypt. They were dismissed with a safe-conduct to the confines of Syria: a part of the old Christians had quietly lived under their dominion; and the vacant habitations were replenished by a new colony. But the mosch was converted into a stable; the pulpit was delivered to the flames; many rich crosses of gold and gems, the spoil of Asiatic churches, were made a grateful offering to the piety or avarice of the emperor; and he transported the gates of Mopsuestia and Tarsus, which were fixed in the wall of Constantinople, an eternal monument of his victory. After they had forced and secured the narrow passes of Mount Amanus, the two Roman princes repeatedly carried their arms into the heart of Syria. Yet, instead of assaulting the walls of Antioch, the humanity or superstition of Nicephorus appeared to respect the ancient metropolis of the East: he contented himself with drawing round the city a line of circumvallation; left a stationary army; and instructed his lieutenant to expect, without impatience, the return of spring. But in the depth of winter, in a dark and rainy night, an adventurous subaltern, with three hundred soldiers, approached the rampart, applied his scaling-ladders, occupied two adjacent towers, stood firm against the pressure of multitudes, and bravely maintained his post till he was relieved by the tardy, though effectual, support of his reluctant chief. The first tumult of slaughter and rapine subsided; the reign of Cæsar and

---

[1] Ducenta fere millia hominum numerabat urbs (Abulfeda, Annal. Moslem. p. 281) of Mopsuestia, or Masifa, Mampsysta, Mansista, Mamista, as it is corruptly, or perhaps more correctly, styled in the middle ages (Wesseling, Itinerar. p. 580). Yet I cannot credit this extreme populousness a few years after the testimony of the emperor Leo, οὐ γὰρ πολυπληθία στρατοῦ τοῖς Κίλιξι βαρβάροις ἐστὶν (Tactica, c. xviii. [§ 139] in Meursii Oper. tom. vi. p. 817).

of Christ was restored; and the efforts of a hundred thousand
Saracens, of the armies of Syria and the fleets of Afric, were consumed without effect before the walls of Antioch. The royal
city of Aleppo was subject to Seifeddowlat, of the dynasty of
Hamadan, who clouded his past glory by the precipitate retreat
which abandoned his kingdom and capital to the Roman invaders. In his stately palace, that stood without the walls of
Aleppo, they joyfully seized a well-furnished magazine of arms,
a stable of fourteen hundred mules, and three hundred bags of
silver and gold. But the walls of the city withstood the strokes
of their battering-rams; and the besiegers pitched their tents
on the neighbouring mountain of Jaushan. Their retreat exasperated the quarrel of the townsmen and mercenaries; the
guard of the gates and ramparts was deserted; and, while they
furiously charged each other in the market-place, they were
surprised and destroyed by the sword of a common enemy. The
male sex was exterminated by the sword; ten thousand youths
were led into captivity; the weight of the precious spoil exceeded
the strength and number of the beasts of burthen; the superfluous
remainder was burnt; and, after a licentious possession of ten
days, the Romans marched away from the naked and bleeding
city. In their Syrian inroads they commanded the husbandmen
to cultivate their lands, that they themselves, in the ensuing
season, might reap the benefit: more than a hundred cities
were reduced to obedience; and eighteen pulpits of the principal
moschs were committed to the flames to expiate the sacrilege of
the disciples of Mohammed. The classic names of Hierapolis,
Apamea, and Emesa revive for a moment in the list of conquest:
the emperor Zimisces encamped in the paradise of Damascus, and
accepted the ransom of a submissive people; and the torrent was
only stopped by the impregnable fortress of Tripoli, on the sea-
coast of Phœnicia. Since the days of Heraclius, the Euphrates,
below the passage of Mount Taurus, had been impervious, and
almost invisible, to the Greeks. The river yielded a free passage
to the victorious Zimisces: and the historian may imitate the
speed with which he overran the once famous cities of Samosata,
Edessa, Martyropolis, Amida,[1] and Nisibis, the ancient limit of
the empire in the neighbourhood of the Tigris. His ardour was
quickened by the desire of grasping the virgin treasures of

---

[1] The text of Leo the Deacon, in the corrupt names of Emeta and
Myctarsim, reveals the cities of Amida and Martyropolis (Miafarekin; see
Abulfeda, Geograph. p. 245, vers. Reiske). Of the former, Leo observes,
urbs munita et illustris; of the latter, clara atque conspicua opibusque et
pecore, reliquis ejus provinciis urbibus atque oppidis longe præstans.

Ecbatana,[1] a well-known name, under which the Byzantine writer has concealed the capital of the Abbassides. The consternation of the fugitives had already diffused the terror of his name; but the fancied riches of Bagdad had already been dissipated by the avarice and prodigality of domestic tyrants. The prayers of the people, and the stern demands of the lieutenant of the Bowides, required the caliph to provide for the defence of the city. The helpless Mothi replied, that his arms, his revenues, and his provinces had been torn from his hands, and that he was ready to abdicate a dignity which he was unable to support. The emir was inexorable; the furniture of the palace was sold; and the paltry price of forty thousand pieces of gold was instantly consumed in private luxury. But the apprehensions of Bagdad were relieved by the retreat of the Greeks: thirst and hunger guarded the desert of Mesopotamia; and the emperor, satiated with glory, and laden with Oriental spoils, returned to Constantinople, and displayed, in his triumph, the silk, the aromatics, and three hundred myriads of gold and silver. Yet the powers of the East had been bent, not broken, by this transient hurricane. After the departure of the Greeks, the fugitive princes returned to their capitals; the subjects disclaimed their involuntary oaths of allegiance; the Moslems again purified their temples, and overturned the idols of the saints and martyrs; the Nestorians and Jacobites preferred a Saracen to an orthodox master; and the numbers and spirit of the Melchites were inadequate to the support of the church and state. Of these extensive conquests, Antioch, with the cities of Cilicia and the isle of Cyprus, was alone restored, a permanent and useful accession to the Roman empire.[2]

---

[1] Ut et Ecbatana pergeret Agarenorumque regiam everteret . . . aiunt enim urbium quæ usquam sunt ac toto orbe existunt felicissimam esse auroque ditissimam (Leo Diacon. apud Pagium, tom. iv. p. 34). This splendid description suits only with Bagdad, and cannot possibly apply either to Hamadan, the true Ecbatana (D'Anville, Géog. Ancienne, tom. ii. p. 237), or Tauris, which has been commonly mistaken for that city. The name of Ecbatana, in the same indefinite sense, is transferred by a more classic authority (Cicero pro Lege Maniliâ, c. 4) to the royal seat of Mithridates, king of Pontus.

[2] See the Annals of Elmacin, Abulpharagius, and Abulfeda, from A.H. 351 to A.H. 361; and the reigns of Nicephorus Phocas and John Zimisces, in the Chronicles of Zonaras (tom. ii. l. xvi. [c. 24] p. 199; l. xvii. [c. 4] 215) and Cedrenus (Compend. p. 649-684 [tom. ii. p. 351-415, ed. Bonn]). Their manifold defects are partly supplied by the MS. history of Leo the Deacon, which Pagi obtained from the Benedictines, and has inserted almost entire, in a Latin version (Critica, tom. iii. p. 873; tom. iv. p. 37).

CHAPTER LIII

State of the Eastern Empire in the Tenth Century—Extent and Division —Wealth and Revenue—Palace of Constantinople—Titles and Offices—Pride and Power of the Emperors—Tactics of the Greeks, Arabs, and Franks—Loss of the Latin Tongue—Studies and Solitude of the Greeks

A RAY of historic light seems to beam from the darkness of the tenth century. We open with curiosity and respect the royal volumes of Constantine Porphyrogenitus,[1] which he composed at a mature age for the instruction of his son, and which promise to unfold the state of the Eastern empire, both in peace and war, both at home and abroad. In the first of these works he minutely describes the pompous ceremonies of the church and palace of Constantinople, according to his own practice and that of his predecessors.[2] In the second he attempts an accurate survey of the provinces, the *themes*, as they were then denominated, both of Europe and Asia.[3] The system of Roman tactics, the discipline and order of the troops, and the military operations by land and sea, are explained in the third of these didactic collections, which

---

[1] The epithet of Πορφυρογέννητος, Porphyrogenitus, born in the purple, is elegantly defined by Claudian:—

> Ardua privatos nescit fortuna Penates;
> Et regnum cum luce dedit. Cognata potestas
> Excepit Tyrio venerabile pignus in ostro.

And Ducange, in his Greek and Latin Glossaries, produces many passages expressive of the same idea.

[2] A splendid MS. of Constantine, de Cæremoniis Aulæ et Ecclesiæ Byzantinæ, wandered from Constantinople to Buda, Frankfort, and Leipsic, where it was published in a splendid edition by Leich and Reiske (A.D. 1751, in folio), with such lavish praise as editors never fail to bestow on the worthy or worthless object of their toil.

[3] See, in the first volume of Banduri's Imperium Orientale, Constantinus de Thematibus, p. 1-24 [tom. iii. p. 11-64, ed. Bonn]; de Administrando Imperio, p. 45-127, edit. Venet. [t. iii. p. 65-270, ed. Bonn]. The text of the old edition of Meursius is corrected from a MS. of the royal library of Paris, which Isaac Casaubon had formerly seen (Epist. ad Polybium, p. 10), and the sense is illustrated by two maps of William Deslisle, the prince of geographers till the appearance of the greater D'Anville.

[In the tenth century the empire was divided into a number of *themes* (θέμα—a company) or provinces, over each of which presided a strategos or commander. They took their origin in the seventh century, and lasted down through the eighth and ninth centuries. Finlay, in his *Byzantine Empire*, gives the list of these themes or military provinces:—

1. The Armeniacs	4. The Marines	7. Italy
2. The Anatolics	5. Thrace	8. Sicily
3. The Opsikion	6. The Helladics	9. Africa

Cf. Diehl, *L'Origine des Thèmes*.—O. S.]

may be ascribed to Constantine or his father Leo.[1] In the fourth, of the administration of the empire, he reveals the secrets of the Byzantine policy, in friendly or hostile intercourse with the nations of the earth. The literary labours of the age, the practical systems of law, agriculture, and history, might redound to the benefit of the subject, and the honour of the Macedonian princes. The sixty books of the *Basilics*,[2] the code and pandects of civil jurisprudence, were gradually framed in the three first reigns of

[1] The Tactics of Leo and Constantine are published with the aid of some new MSS. in the great edition of the works of Meursius, by the learned John Lami (tom. vi. p. 531-920, 1211-1417, Florent. 1745), yet the text is still corrupt and mutilated, the version is still obscure and faulty. The Imperial library of Vienna would afford some valuable materials to a new editor (Fabric. Biblioth. Græc. tom. vi. p. 369, 370).

[2] On the subject of the *Basilics*, Fabricius (Biblioth. Græc. tom. xii. p. 425-514), and Heineccius (Hist. Juris Romani, p. 396-399), and Giannone (Istoria Civile di Napoli, tom. i. p. 450-458), as historical civilians, may be usefully consulted. Forty-one books of this Greek code have been published, with a Latin version, by Charles Annibal Fabrottus (Paris, 1647), in seven tomes in folio; four other books have been since discovered, and are inserted in Gerard Meerman's Novus Thesaurus Juris Civ. et Canon. tom. v. Of the whole work, the sixty books, John Leunclavius has printed (Basil, 1575) an *eclogue* or synopsis. The 113 novels, or new laws, of Leo, may be found in the Corpus Juris Civilis.

[The question of Byzantine law may be fittingly discussed now, inasmuch as the recent labours of well-known scholars have thrown new light on the subject. Although the compilation of Justinian was mainly intended for people who spoke Greek, the emperor restricted its use by promulgating it in the Latin language, which was unintelligible to the greater part of his subjects. This defect was remedied to a great extent by a Greek school of jurists, which had flourished even before his reign, and who translated the Corpus Juris into the Greek language. The consequence was that the original was soon disused throughout the Eastern empire, and that Greek translations of the Institutions, the Pandects, and the Code usurped their place. These translations, however, were not stamped by any official authority; and in the times of confusion which followed the reign of Heraclius even the translations were neglected, and their place was supplied by the writings of commentators who had published abridgments of the laws. Leo III., the Isaurian, attempted to remedy this evil by publishing a Greek Manual of Law, which became the primary authority in all the courts in the empire. This Manual, which was revised by Constantine Copronymus, the son of Leo, bore the title of *Ecloga* ('Εκλογή τῶν νόμων), and is still extant in many MSS. which, until a recent time, were erroneously supposed to be *Prochiron*, or Manual of Basil, Constantine, and Leo, of which we shall speak presently. The *Ecloga* of Leo and Constantine Copronymus contains eighteen titles, and adopts an order entirely different from that of the Institutes of Justinian. It omits entirely some very important matters, such as servitudes and the different modes of acquiring property. Its authority was abrogated by Basil I., who severely censured it on account of its imperfections, and declares it to be an insult to the earlier legislators.

A more complete reform in the Byzantine law was effected by Basil I. His legislation was comprised in three works: 1. *Prochiron* (πρόχειρος νόμος), a manual intended to serve as an introduction to the science. 2. *Basilica* (τὰ βασιλικά), a revision of the ancient laws. 3. *Epanogog*

that prosperous dynasty. The art of agriculture had amused the leisure, and exercised the pens, of the best and wisest of the ancients; and their chosen precepts are comprised in the twenty books of the *Geoponics* [1] of Constantine. At his command the historical examples of vice and virtue were methodised in fifty-

(Ἐπαναγωγὴ τῶν νόμων), a second edition of the Prochiron Manual published after the Basilica.

The *Prochiron* is issued in the names of Basil and of his two sons, Constantine and Leo, and was probably issued about A.D. 870. It contains forty titles. The former half of the work is executed in an entirely different manner from the latter. In the first twenty titles the same plan has been followed as in the Basilica; the extracts from the Institutions are first given, and these are followed successively by extracts from the Pandects, Code, Novellæ of Justinian, and then from the Novellæ of succeeding emperors, but in the last twenty titles this well-arranged plan is abandoned, from a determination to hurry the work to a conclusion. The Ecloga of Leo, which Basil so strongly condemns, now becomes the basis of his work; the extracts from the Institutions and the Novellæ are very numerous, while the Pandects and the Code are almost entirely neglected.

The *Basilica* contains a complete code of Byzantine law. It was originally published by Basil about 884, under the title " The Revision of the Old Laws " (Ἀνακάθαρσις τῶν παλαιῶν νόμων). It was divided into forty books, though Basil in the Prochiron had announced that the new Code would consist of sixty books. This Code, however, was again revised and enlarged by Leo the Philosopher, and was published in his own name and that of his son, Constantine Porphyrogenitus, between 905 and 911. It is this new and revised Code which we now possess under the title of *Basilica* or Imperial laws. The earlier Code of Basil has entirely disappeared. The *Basilica*, like the Pandects of Justinian, is a collection of all the authorities of Byzantine law. It is compiled from the Greek translations of Justinian's laws, and from the Greek commentaries on them which had received the sanction of the Byzantine legal schools. It was not a new translation of the Latin text of Justinian, but it embodied the Greek texts which had been in existence more than three centuries. Each of the sixty books is distributed into titles, which are again subdivided into chapters and paragraphs. Each title contains, with more or less accuracy, all the laws relating to this subject in the Institutions, Pandects, Code, and Novellæ, and thus presents in one place the enactments upon a subject previously dispersed in four collections. The *Basilica* does not contain everything that is found in the Corpus Juris, but it contains numerous fragments of the opinions of the ancient jurists, and of imperial constitutions, which are not contained in the compilation of Justinian. The publication of the *Basilica* led to the gradual disuse of the original compilations of Justinian in the East. But the Roman law was thus more firmly established in Eastern Europe and Western Asia. The *Basilica* continued to be the law of the Byzantine empire until its conquest by the Turks, and is the basis of the jurisprudence of Greece to-day. Cf. Finlay, *Byzantine Empire*, also Bury, *Later Roman Empire*, and Constantine Porphyrogenitus on *The Administration of the Roman Empire.*— O. S.]

[1] I have used the last and best edition of the Geoponics (by Nicolas Niclas, Lipsiæ, 1781, 2 vols. in octavo). I read in the preface that the same emperor restored the long-forgotten systems of rhetoric and philosophy; and his two books of *Hippiatrica,* or Horse-physic, were published at Paris, 1530, in folio (Fabric. Biblioth. Græc. tom. vi. p. 493-500).

three books,[1] and every citizen might apply to his contemporaries or himself the lesson or the warning of past times. From the august character of a legislator, the sovereign of the East descends to the more humble office of a teacher and a scribe; and if his successors and subjects were regardless of his paternal cares, *we* may inherit and enjoy the everlasting legacy.

A closer survey will indeed reduce the value of the gift and the gratitude of posterity: in the possession of these Imperial treasures we may still deplore our poverty and ignorance; and the fading glories of their authors will be obliterated by indifference or contempt. The Basilics will sink to a broken copy, a partial and mutilated version in the Greek language, of the laws of Justinian; but the sense of the old civilians is often superseded by the influence of bigotry: and the absolute prohibition of divorce, concubinage, and interest for money, enslaves the freedom of trade and the happiness of private life. In the historical book a subject of Constantine might admire the inimitable virtues of Greece and Rome: he might learn to what a pitch of energy and elevation the human character had formerly aspired. But a contrary effect must have been produced by a new edition of the lives of the saints, which the great logothete, or chancellor of the empire, was directed to prepare; and the dark fund of superstition was enriched by the fabulous and florid legends of Simon the *Metaphrast*.[2] The merits and miracles of the whole calendar are of less account in the eyes of a sage than the toil of a single husbandman, who multiplies the gifts of the Creator and supplies the food of his brethren. Yet the royal authors of the *Geoponics* were more seriously employed in expounding the precepts of the destroying art, which has been taught since the days of Xenophon[3] as the art of heroes and kings. But the *Tactics* of Leo and Constantine are mingled

---

[1] Of these fifty-three books, or titles, only two have been preserved and printed—de Legationibus (by Fulvius Ursinus, Antwerp, 1582, and Daniel Hœschelius, August. Vindel. 1603) and de Virtutibus et Vitiis (by Henry Valesius, or de Valois, Paris, 1634).

[2] The life and writings of Simeon Metaphrastes are described by Hankius (de Scriptoribus Byzant. p. 418-460). This biographer of the saints indulged himself in a loose paraphrase of the sense or nonsense of more ancient acts. His Greek rhetoric is again paraphrased in the Latin version of Surius, and scarcely a thread can be now visible of the original texture.

[3] According to the first book of the Cyropædia, professors of tactics, a small part of the science of war, were already instituted in Persia, by which Greece must be understood. A good edition of all the Scriptores Tactici would be a task not unworthy of a scholar. His industry might discover some new MSS., and his learning might illustrate the military history of the ancients. But this scholar should be likewise a soldier; and, alas! Quintus Icilius is no more.

with the baser alloy of the age in which they lived. It was destitute of original genius; they implicitly transcribe the rules and maxims which had been confirmed by victories. It was unskilled in the propriety of style and method; they blindly confound the most distant and discordant institutions, the phalanx of Sparta and that of Macedon, the legions of Cato and Trajan, of Augustus and Theodosius. Even the use, or at least the importance, of these military rudiments may be fairly questioned: their general theory is dictated by reason; but the merit, as well as difficulty, consists in the application. The discipline of a soldier is formed by exercise rather than by study: the talents of a commander are appropriated to those calm, though rapid, minds, which nature produces to decide the fate of armies and nations: the former is the habit of a life, the latter the glance of a moment; and the battles won by lessons of tactics may be numbered with the epic poems created from the rules of criticism. The book of ceremonies is a recital, tedious yet imperfect, of the despicable pageantry which had infected the church and state since the gradual decay of the purity of the one and the power of the other. A review of the themes or provinces might promise such authentic and useful information as the curiosity of government only can obtain, instead of traditionary fables on the origin of the cities, and malicious epigrams on the vices of their inhabitants.[1] Such information the historian would have been pleased to record; nor should his silence be condemned if the most interesting objects, the population of the capital and provinces, the amount of the taxes and revenues, the numbers of subjects and strangers who served under the Imperial standard, have been unnoticed by Leo the Philosopher and his son Constantine. His treatise of the public administration is stained with the same blemishes; yet it is discriminated by peculiar merit: the antiquities of the nations may be doubtful or fabulous; but the geography and manners of the barbaric world are delineated with curious accuracy. Of these nations the

---

[1] After observing that the demerit of the Cappadocians rose in proportion to their rank and riches, he inserts a more pointed epigram, which is ascribed to Demodocus:—

Καππαδόκην ποτ᾽ ἔχιδνα κακὴ δάκεν, ἀλλὰ καὶ αὐτὴ
Κάτθανε, γευσαμένη αἵματος ἰοβόλου.

The sting is precisely the same with the French epigram against Fréron: Un serpent mordit Jean Fréron—Eh bien? Le serpent en mourut. But, as the Paris wits are seldom read in the Anthology, I should be curious to learn through what channel it was conveyed for their imitation (Constantin. Porphyrogen. de Themat. c. ii. [tom. iii. p. 21, ed. Bonn]; Brunck, Analect. Græc. tom. ii. p. 56; Brodæi Anthologia, l. ii. p. 244).

Franks alone were qualified to observe in their turn, and to describe, the metropolis of the East. The ambassador of the great Otho, a bishop of Cremona, has painted the state of Constantinople about the middle of the tenth century: his style is glowing, his narrative lively, his observation keen; and even the prejudices and passions of Liutprand are stamped with an original character of freedom and genius.[1] From this scanty fund of foreign and domestic materials I shall investigate the form and substance of the Byzantine empire; the provinces and wealth, the civil government and military force, the character and literature, of the Greeks in a period of six hundred years, from the reign of Heraclius to the successful invasion of the Franks or Latins.

After the final division between the sons of Theodosius, the swarms of barbarians from Scythia and Germany overspread the provinces and extinguished the empire of ancient Rome. The weakness of Constantinople was concealed by extent of dominion; her limits were inviolate, or at least entire; and the kingdom of Justinian was enlarged by the splendid acquisition of Africa and Italy. But the possession of these new conquests was transient and precarious, and almost a moiety of the Eastern empire was torn away by the arms of the Saracens. Syria and Egypt were oppressed by the Arabian caliphs, and, after the reduction of Africa, their lieutenants invaded and subdued the Roman province which had been changed into the Gothic monarchy of Spain. The islands of the Mediterranean were not inaccessible to their naval powers; and it was from their extreme stations, the harbours of Crete and the fortresses of Cilicia, that the faithful or rebel emirs insulted the majesty of the throne and capital. The remaining provinces, under the obedience of the emperors, were cast into a new mould; and the jurisdiction of the presidents, the consulars, and the counts was superseded by the institution of the *themes*,[2] or military governments, which prevailed under the successors of Heraclius, and are described by the pen of the royal author. Of the twenty-nine themes, twelve in Europe and seventeen in Asia, the origin is obscure, the etymology doubtful or capricious, the limits were arbitrary and fluctuating;

---

[1] The Legatio Liutprandi Episcopi Cremonensis ad Nicephorum Phocam is inserted in Muratori, Scriptores Rerum Italicarum, tom. ii. pars. i.

[2] See Constantine de Thematibus, in Banduri, tom. i. p. 1-30, who owns that the word is οὐκ παλαιά. Θέμα is used by Maurice (Stratagem. l. ii. c. 2) for a legion, from whence the name was easily transferred to its post or province (Ducange, Gloss. Græc. tom. i. p. 487, 488). Some etymologies are attempted for the Opsician, Optimatian, Thracesian, themes.

but some particular names that sound the most strangely to our ear were derived from the character and attributes of the troops that were maintained at the expense and for the guard of the respective divisions. The vanity of the Greek princes most eagerly grasped the shadow of conquest and the memory of lost dominion. A new Mesopotamia was created on the western side of the Euphrates; the appellation and prætor of Sicily were transferred to a narrow slip of Calabria; and a fragment of the duchy of Beneventum was promoted to the style and title of the theme of Lombardy. In the decline of the Arabian empire the successors of Constantine might indulge their pride in more solid advantages. The victories of Nicephorus, John Zimisces, and Basil the Second, revived the fame, and enlarged the boundaries, of the Roman name; the province of Cilicia, the metropolis of Antioch, the islands of Crete and Cyprus were restored to the allegiance of Christ and Cæsar; one-third of Italy was annexed to the throne of Constantinople, the kingdom of Bulgaria was destroyed, and the last sovereigns of the Macedonian dynasty extended their sway from the sources of the Tigris to the neighbourhood of Rome. In the eleventh century the prospect was again clouded by new enemies and new misfortunes; the relics of Italy were swept away by the Norman adventurers, and almost all the Asiatic branches were dissevered from the Roman trunk by the Turkish conquerors. After these losses the emperors of the Comnenian family continued to reign from the Danube to Peloponnesus, and from Belgrade to Nice, Trebizond, and the winding stream of the Meander. The spacious provinces of Thrace, Macedonia, and Greece were obedient to their sceptre; the possession of Cyprus, Rhodes, and Crete was accompanied by the fifty islands of the Ægean or Holy Sea,[1] and the remnant of their empire transcends the measure of the largest of the European kingdoms.

The same princes might assert, with dignity and truth, that of all the monarchs of Christendom they possessed the greatest

---

[1] Ἅγιος πελαγὸς, as it is styled by the modern Greeks, from which the corrupt names of Archipelago, l'Archipel, and the Arches have been transformed by geographers and seamen (D'Anville, Géographie Ancienne, tom. i. p. 281; Analyse de la Carte de la Grèce, p. 60). The numbers of monks or caloyers in all the islands and the adjacent mountain of Athos (Observations de Belon, fol. 32, verso), Monte Santo, might justify the epithet of holy, ἅγιος, a slight alteration from the original αἰγαιος, imposed by the Dorians, who, in their dialect, gave the figurative name of αἶγες, or goats, to the bounding waves (Vossius, apud Cellarium. Geograph. Antiq. tom. i. p. 829).

city,[1] the most ample revenue, the most flourishing and populous state. With the decline and fall of the empire the cities of the West had decayed and fallen; nor could the ruins of Rome, or the mud walls, wooden hovels, and narrow precincts of Paris and London, prepare the Latin stranger to contemplate the situation and extent of Constantinople, her stately palaces and churches, and the arts and luxury of an innumerable people. Her treasures might attract, but her virgin strength had repelled, and still promised to repel, the audacious invasion of the Persian and Bulgarian, the Arab and the Russian. The provinces were less fortunate and impregnable, and few districts, few cities, could be discovered which had not been violated by some fierce barbarian, impatient to despoil, because he was hopeless to possess. From the age of Justinian the Eastern empire was sinking below its former level; the powers of destruction were more active than those of improvement; and the calamities of war were embittered by the more permanent evils of civil and ecclesiastical tyranny. The captive who had escaped from the barbarians was often stripped and imprisoned by the ministers of his sovereign; the Greek superstition relaxed the mind by prayer, and emaciated the body by fasting; and the multitude of convents and festivals diverted many hands and many days from the temporal service of mankind. Yet the subjects of the Byzantine empire were still the most dexterous and diligent of nations; their country was blessed by nature with every advantage of soil, climate, and situation; and, in the support and restoration of the arts, their patient and peaceful temper was more useful than the warlike spirit and feudal anarchy of Europe. The provinces that still adhered to the empire were repeopled and enriched by the misfortunes of those which were irrecoverably lost. From the yoke of the caliphs, the Catholics of Syria, Egypt, and Africa retired to the allegiance of their prince, to the society of their brethren; the movable wealth, which eludes the search of oppression, accompanied and alleviated their exile, and Constantinople received into her bosom the fugitive trade of Alexandria and Tyre. The chiefs of Armenia and Scythia, who fled from hostile or religious persecution, were hospitably entertained; their followers were encouraged to build new cities and to cultivate waste lands; and many spots, both in Europe and Asia, preserved the name, the manners, or at least the memory, of these

---

[1] According to the Jewish traveller who had visited Europe and Asia, Constantinople was equalled only by Bagdad, the great city of the Ismaelites (Voyage de Benjamin de Tudèle, par Baratier, tom. i. c. 5, p. 46).

national colonies. Even the tribes of barbarians who had seated themselves in arms on the territory of the empire were gradually reclaimed to the laws of the church and state, and, as long as they were separated from the Greeks, their posterity supplied a race of faithful and obedient soldiers. Did we possess sufficient materials to survey the twenty-nine themes of the Byzantine monarchy, our curiosity might be satisfied with a chosen example: it is fortunate enough that the clearest light should be thrown on the most interesting province, and the name of PELOPONNESUS will awaken the attention of the classic reader.

As early as the eighth century, in the troubled reign of the Iconoclasts, Greece, and even Peloponnesus,[1] were overrun by

---

[1] Ἐσθλαβώθη δὲ πᾶσα ἡ χώρα καὶ γέγονε βάρβαρος, says Constantine (Thematibus, l. ii. c. 6, p. 25 [tom. iii. p. 53, ed. Bonn]), in a style as barbarous as the idea, which he confirms, as usual, by a foolish epigram. The epitomiser of Strabo likewise observes, καὶ νῦν δὲ πᾶσαν Ἤπειρον, καὶ Ἑλλάδα σχεδὸν, καὶ Πελοπόννησον, καὶ Μακεδονίαν, Σκύθαι Σκλάβοι νέμονται (l. vii. p. 98, edit. Hudson.; p. 1251, edit. Casaub. [Almel.]): a passage which leads Dodwell a weary dance (Geograph. Minor. tom. ii. dissert. vi. p. 170-191), to enumerate the inroads of the Sclavi, and to fix the date (A.D. 980) of this petty geographer.

[The question of the Slavs in Greece is a very obscure one, and has engaged the attention of many of our best scholars. Prof. Fallmerayer, for instance, maintains that the Hellenic race in Europe was exterminated by the Slavonians, and that the present inhabitants of Greece are Byzantinised Slavonians. There can be no doubt that the Slavonians formed the bulk of the population of Greece for several centuries. This is expressly stated by the Emperor Constantine Porphyrogenitus, who refers the completion of the Slavonic colonisation of Greece to the time of the great pestilence, which depopulated the East in A.D. 746. In the same century the European navigators spoke of the Peloponnesus as "Slavonian land." But of the history of the Slavonian conquests in Greece we have only the scantiest account. Their invasion of the country in the reign of Justinian has been already mentioned, and their permanent settlement in the Peloponnesus appears to have been made under the shelter of the Avar power towards the end of the sixth century. Under the feeble sway of the successors of Justinian the Slavonians in the Peloponnesus became independent of the Byzantine empire, and no attempt was made to check their growing power till the reign of Leo III., the Isaurian, who breathed new life into the decaying empire. The Slavonians in their turn made a vigorous effort to maintain their independence, and to become masters of the whole of the Peloponnesus. For this purpose, in the year 807, they made the unsuccessful attempt upon Patras mentioned by Gibbon. From this time the Greeks gradually regained the ascendency; but in the reign of Theophilus, the Slavonians again rose in arms and were masters of the open country for several years. They were, however, subdued by Theodora, who governed the empire during the minority of her son Michael III., A.D. 842, and it was on this occasion that the Ezeritæ and Milengi, two Slavonian tribes, the former in the neighbourhood of Helos and the latter in that of Sparta, became tributary to the Byzantine government. They, however, rebelled in the reign of Romanus I., and upon being re-conquered, their tribute was fixed at 1200 pieces of gold. When the Franks invaded the Peloponnesus at the beginning of the thirteenth century the Melingi were masters of Mount Taÿgetus; and in Elis, Slavonians were in possession of a district

some Sclavonian bands who outstripped the royal standard of
Bulgaria. The strangers of old, Cadmus, and Danaus, and
Pelops, had planted in that fruitful soil the seeds of policy and
learning; but the savages of the north eradicated what yet
remained of their sickly and withered roots. In this irruption
the country and the inhabitants were transformed; the Grecian
blood was contaminated; and the proudest nobles of Peloponnesus were branded with the names of foreigners and *slaves*. By
the diligence of succeeding princes, the land was in some measure
purified from the barbarians; and the humble remnant was
bound by an oath of obedience, tribute, and military service,
which they often renewed and often violated. The siege of
Patras was formed by a singular concurrence of the Sclavonians
of Peloponnesus and the Saracens of Africa. In their last distress
a pious fiction of the approach of the prætor of Corinth revived
the courage of the citizens. Their sally was bold and successful;
the strangers embarked, the rebels submitted, and the glory of
the day was ascribed to a phantom or a stranger, who fought
in the foremost ranks under the character of St. Andrew the
Apostle. The shrine which contained his relics was decorated
with the trophies of victory, and the captive race was for ever
devoted to the service and vassalage of the metropolitan church
of Patras. By the revolt of two Sclavonian tribes in the neighbourhood of Helos and Lacedæmon, the peace of the peninsula
was often disturbed. They sometimes insulted the weakness,
and sometimes resisted the oppression, of the Byzantine government, till at length the approach of their hostile brethren
extorted a golden bull to define the rights and obligations of
the Ezzerites and Milengi, whose annual tribute was defined at
twelve hundred pieces of gold. From these strangers the Imperial geographer has accurately distinguished a domestic and
perhaps original race, who, in some degree, might derive their
blood from the much-injured Helots. The liberality of the
Romans, and especially of Augustus, had enfranchised the maritime cities from the dominion of Sparta; and the continuance of
the same benefit ennobled them with the title of *Eleuthero*, or
Free-Laconians.[1] In the time of Constantine Porphyrogenitus

called Skorta, extending from the ruins of Olympia to the sources of the
Ladon. The Slav language has long ceased to be spoken in Greece, and
the only dialectical remains are the names they gave.—O. S.]

[1] Strabon. Geograph. l. viii. p. 562 [p. 366, ed. Casaub.]; Pausanias,
Græc. Descriptio, l. iii. c. 21, p. 264, 265; Plin. Hist. Natur. l. iv. c. 8.

[There is another people which deserve mention even more than the
Mainotes as the genuine descendants of the ancient Hellenes. These are
the *Tzakones*, the inhabitants of Tzakonia, which is only another form of

they had acquired the name of *Mainotes*, under which they dishonour the claim of liberty by the inhuman pillage of all that is
shipwrecked on their rocky shores.   Their territory, barren of
corn but fruitful of olives, extended to the Cape of Malea: they
accepted a chief or prince from the Byzantine prætor; and a
light tribute of four hundred pieces of gold was the badge of their
immunity rather than of their dependence.   The freemen of
Laconia assumed the character of Romans, and long adhered to
the religion of the Greeks.   By the zeal of the emperor Basil,
they were baptised in the faith of Christ: but the altars of Venus
and Neptune had been crowned by these rustic votaries five
hundred years after they were proscribed in the Roman world.
In the theme of Peloponnesus [1] forty cities were still numbered,
and the declining state of Sparta, Argos, and Corinth may be
suspended in the tenth century, at an equal distance, perhaps,
between their antique splendour and their present desolation.
The duty of military service, either in person or by substitute,
was imposed on the lands or benefices of the province; a sum of
five pieces of gold was assessed on each of the substantial tenants;
and the same capitation was shared among several heads of
inferior value.   On the proclamation of an Italian war, the
Peloponnesians excused themselves by a voluntary oblation of
one hundred pounds of gold (four thousand pounds sterling), and
a thousand horses with their arms and trappings.   The churches
and monasteries furnished their contingent; a sacrilegious profit
was extorted from the sale of ecclesiastical honours; and the
indigent bishop of Leucadia [2] was made responsible for a pension
of one hundred pieces of gold.[3]

But the wealth of the province, and the trust of the revenue,
were founded on the fair and plentiful produce of trade and
manufactures; and some symptoms of liberal policy may be
traced in a law which exempts from all personal taxes the mariners
of Peloponnesus, and the workmen in parchment and purple.
This denomination may be fairly applied or extended to the

Laconia.   The dialect of the Tzakones differs materially from modern
Greek, and bears a much closer resemblance to ancient Greek.—O. S.]
  [1] Constantin. de Administrando Imperio [de Thematibus], l. ii. c. 50, 51,
52 [tom. iii. p. 52, ed. Bonn].
  [2] The rock of Leucate was the southern promontory of his island and
diocese.   Had he been the exclusive guardian of the Lover's Leap, so well
known to the readers of Ovid (Epist. Sappho) and the Spectator, he might
have been the richest prelate of the Greek church.
  [3] Leucatensis mihi juravit episcopus, quotannis ecclesiam suam debere
Nicephoro aureos centum persolvere, similiter et ceteras plus minusve
secundum vires suas.   (Liutprand in Legat. p. 489 [Murat. Scrip. R. I.
tom. ii.]).

manufactures of linen, woollen, and more especially of silk: the two former of which had flourished in Greece since the days of Homer; and the last was introduced perhaps as early as the reign of Justinian. These arts, which were exercised at Corinth, Thebes, and Argos, afforded food and occupation to a numerous people: the men, women, and children were distributed according to their age and strength; and if many of these were domestic slaves, their masters, who directed the work and enjoyed the profit, were of a free and honourable condition. The gifts which a rich and generous matron of Peloponnesus presented to the emperor Basil, her adopted son, were doubtless fabricated in the Grecian looms. Danielis bestowed a carpet of fine wool, of a pattern which imitated the spots of a peacock's tail, of a magnitude to overspread the floor of a new church, erected in the triple name of Christ, of Michael the archangel, and of the prophet Elijah. She gave six hundred pieces of silk and linen, of various use and denomination: the silk was painted with the Tyrian dye, and adorned by the labours of the needle; and the linen was so exquisitely fine, that an entire piece might be rolled in the hollow of a cane.[1] In his description of the Greek manufactures, an historian of Sicily discriminates their price, according to the weight and quality of the silk, the closeness of the texture, the beauty of the colours, and the taste and materials of the embroidery. A single, or even a double or treble thread was thought sufficient for ordinary sale; but the union of six threads composed a piece of stronger and more costly workmanship. Among the colours, he celebrates, with affectation of eloquence, the fiery blaze of the scarlet, and the softer lustre of the green. The embroidery was raised either in silk or gold: the more simple ornament of stripes or circles was surpassed by the nicer imitation of flowers: the vestments that were fabricated for the palace or the altar often glittered with precious stones; and the figures were delineated in strings of Oriental pearls.[2] Till the twelfth century, Greece alone, of all the countries of Christendom, was

---

[1] See Constantine (in Vit. Basil. c. 74, 75, 76, p. 195, 197 [p. 317-320, ed. Bonn], in Script. post Theophanem), who allows himself to use many technical or barbarous words: barbarous, says he, τῇ τῶν πολλῶν ἀμαθίᾳ, καλὸν γὰρ ἐπὶ τούτοις κοινολεκτεῖν. Ducange labours on some; but he was not a weaver.

[2] The manufactures of Palermo, as they are described by Hugo Falcandus (Hist. Sicula in proem. In Muratori Script. Rerum Italicarum, tom. vii. p. 256), are a copy of those of Greece. Without transcribing his declamatory sentences, which I have softened in the text, I shall observe that in this passage the strange word *exarentasmata* is very properly changed for *exanthemata* by Carusius, the first editor. Falcandus lived about the year 1190.

possessed of the insect who is taught by nature, and of the workmen who are instructed by art, to prepare this elegant luxury. But the secret had been stolen by the dexterity and diligence of the Arabs: the caliphs of the East and West scorned to borrow from the unbelievers their furniture and apparel; and two cities of Spain, Almeria and Lisbon, were famous for the manufacture, the use, and perhaps the exportation of silk. It was first introduced into Sicily by the Normans; and this emigration of trade distinguishes the victory of Roger from the uniform and fruitless hostilities of every age. After the sack of Corinth, Athens, and Thebes, his lieutenant embarked with a captive train of weavers and artificers of both sexes, a trophy glorious to their master and disgraceful to the Greek emperor.[1] The king of Sicily was not insensible of the value of the present; and, in the restitution of the prisoners, he excepted only the male and female manufacturers of Thebes and Corinth, who labour, says the Byzantine historian, under a barbarous lord, like the old Eretrians in the service of Darius.[2] A stately edifice, in the palace of Palermo, was erected for the use of this industrious colony;[3] and the art was propagated by their children and disciples to satisfy the increasing demand of the western world. The decay of the looms of Sicily may be ascribed to the troubles of the island and the competition of the Italian cities. In the year thirteen hundred and fourteen, Lucca alone, among her sister republics, enjoyed the lucrative monopoly.[4] A domestic revolution dispersed the manufacturers to Florence, Bologna, Venice, Milan, and even the countries beyond the Alps; and thirteen years after this event,

[1] Inde ad interiora Graeciae progressi, Corinthum, Thebas, Athenas, antiquâ nobilitate celebres, expugnant; et, maximâ ibidem praedâ direptâ, opifices etiam, qui Sericos pannos texere solent, ob ignominiam Imperatoris illius, suique principis gloriam, captivos deducunt. Quos Rogerius, in Palermo Siciliae metropoli collocans, artem texendi suos edocere praecepit; et exhinc praedicta ars illa, prius à Graecis tantum inter Christianos habita, Romanis patere coepit ingeniis. (Otho Frisingen. de Gestis Frederici I. l. i. c. 33, in Muratori Script. Ital. tom. vi. p. 668.) This exception allows the bishop to celebrate Lisbon and Almeria in sericorum pannorum opificio praenobilissimae (in Chron. apud Muratori, Annali d'Italia, tom. ix. p. 415).

[2] Nicetas in Manuel, l. ii. c. 8, p. 65 [p. 129, 130, ed. Bonn]. He describes these Greeks as skilled εὐητρίους ὀθόνας ὑφαίνειν, as ἱστῷ προσανέχοντας τῶν ἐξαμίτων καὶ χρισοπάστων στολῶν.

[3] Hugo Falcandus styles them nobiles officinas. The Arabs had not introduced silk, though they had planted canes and made sugar in the plain of Palermo.

[4] See the Life of Castruccio Castricani, not by Machiavel, but by his more authentic biographer Nicholas Tegrimi. Muratori, who has inserted it in the eleventh volume of his Scriptores, quotes this curious passage in his Italian Antiquities (tom. i. dissert. xxv. p. 378).

the statutes of Modena enjoin the planting of mulberry-trees and regulate the duties on raw silk.[1] The northern climates are less propitious to the education of the silkworm; but the industry of France and England[2] is supplied and enriched by the productions of Italy and China.

I must repeat the complaint that the vague and scanty memorials of the times will not afford any just estimate of the taxes, the revenue, and the resources of the Greek empire. From every province of Europe and Asia the rivulets of gold and silver discharged into the Imperial reservoir a copious and perennial stream. The separation of the branches from the trunk increased the relative magnitude of Constantinople; and the maxims of despotism contracted the state to the capital, the capital to the palace, and the palace to the royal person. A Jewish traveller, who visited the East in the twelfth century, is lost in his admiration of the Byzantine riches. " It is here," says Benjamin of Tudela, " in the queen of cities, that the tributes of the Greek empire are annually deposited, and the lofty towers are filled with precious magazines of silk, purple, and gold. It is said that Constantinople pays each day to her sovereign twenty thousand pieces of gold, which are levied on the shops, taverns, and markets, on the merchants of Persia and Egypt, of Russia and Hungary, of Italy and Spain, who frequent the capital by sea and land."[3] In all pecuniary matters the authority of a Jew is doubtless respectable; but as the three hundred and sixty-five days would produce a yearly income exceeding seven millions sterling, I am tempted to retrench at least the numerous festivals of the Greek calendar. The mass of treasure that was saved by Theodora and Basil the Second will suggest a splendid, though indefinite, idea of their supplies and resources. The mother of Michael, before she retired to a cloister, attempted to check or expose the prodigality of her ungrateful son by a free and faithful account of the wealth which he inherited; one hundred and nine

[1] From the MS. statutes, as they are quoted by Muratori in his Italian Antiquities (tom. ii. dissert. xxx. p. 46-48).
[2] The broad silk manufacture was established in England in the year 1620 (Anderson's Chronological Deduction, vol. ii. p. 4): but it is to the revocation of the Edict of Nantes that we owe the Spitafields colony.
[The palace of Theophilus was called the Trekonchon from its three apses. In the under story was a " whispering gallery "—Μυστήριον—which gave great delight to Theophilus. See Continuator of Theophanes. —O. S.]
[3] Voyage de Benjamin de Tudèle, tom. i. c. 5, p. 44-52. The Hebrew text has been translated into French by that marvellous child Baratier, who has added a volume of crude learning. The errors and fictions of the Jewish rabbi are not a sufficient ground to deny the reality of his travels.

thousand pounds of gold and three hundred thousand of silver, the fruits of her own economy and that of her deceased husband.[1] The avarice of Basil is not less renowned than his valour and fortune: his victorious armies were paid and rewarded without breaking into the mass of two hundred thousand pounds of gold (about eight millions sterling), which he had buried in the subterraneous vaults of the palace.[2] Such accumulation of treasure is rejected by the theory and practice of modern policy; and we are more apt to compute the national riches by the use and abuse of the public credit. Yet the maxims of antiquity are still embraced by a monarch formidable to his enemies; by a republic respectable to her allies; and both have attained their respective ends of military power and domestic tranquillity.

Whatever might be consumed for the present wants or reserved for the future use of the state, the first and most sacred demand was for the pomp and pleasure of the emperor; and his discretion only could define the measure of his private expense. The princes of Constantinople were far removed from the simplicity of nature; yet, with the revolving seasons, they were led by taste or fashion to withdraw to a purer air from the smoke and tumult of the capital. They enjoyed, or affected to enjoy, the rustic festival of the vintage: their leisure was amused by the exercise of the chase and the calmer occupation of fishing; and in the summer heats they were shaded from the sun, and refreshed by the cooling breezes from the sea. The coasts and islands of Asia and Europe were covered with their magnificent villas; but instead of the modest art which secretly strives to hide itself and to decorate the scenery of nature, the marble structure of their gardens served only to expose the riches of the lord and the labours of the architect. The successive casualties of inheritance and forfeiture had rendered the sovereign proprietor of many stately houses in the city and suburbs, of which twelve were appropriated to the ministers of state; but the great palace,[3] the centre of the Imperial residence, was fixed

---

[1] See the continuator of Theophanes (l. iv. p. 107 [ed. Par.; p. 172, ed. Bonn]), Cedrenus (p. 544 [tom. ii. p. 158, ed. Bonn]), and Zonaras (tom. ii. l. xvi. [c. 2] p. 157).

[2] Zonaras (tom. ii. l. xvii. [c. 8] p. 225), instead of pounds, uses the more classic appellation of talents, which, in a literal sense and strict computation, would multiply sixty-fold the treasure of Basil.

[3] For a copious and minute description of the Imperial palace, see the Constantinop. Christiana (l. ii. c. 4, p. 113-123) of Ducange, the Tillemont of the middle ages. Never has laborious Germany produced two antiquarians more laborious and accurate than these two natives of lively France.

during eleven centuries to the same position, between the hippo-drome, the cathedral of St. Sophia, and the gardens, which descended by many a terrace to the shores of the Propontis. The primitive edifice of the first Constantine was a copy, or rival, of ancient Rome; the gradual improvements of his successors aspired to emulate the wonders of the old world,[1] and in the tenth century the Byzantine palace excited the admiration, at least of the Latins, by an unquestionable pre-eminence of strength, size, and magnificence.[2] But the toil and treasure of so many ages had produced a vast and irregular pile: each separate building was marked with the character of the times and of the founder; and the want of space might excuse the reigning monarch who demolished, perhaps with secret satisfaction, the works of his predecessors. The economy of the emperor Theophilus allowed a more free and ample scope for his domestic luxury and splendour. A favourite ambassador, who had astonished the Abbassides themselves by his pride and liberality, presented on his return the model of a palace which the caliph of Bagdad had recently constructed on the banks of the Tigris. The model was instantly copied and surpassed: the new buildings of Theophilus[3] were accompanied with gardens and with five churches, one of which was conspicuous for size and beauty: it was crowned with three domes, the roof of gilt brass reposed on columns of Italian marble, and the walls were incrusted with marbles of various colours. In the face of the church a semi-circular portico, of the figure and name of the Greek *sigma*, was

---

[1] The Byzantine palace surpasses the Capitol, the palace of Pergamus, the Rufinian wood ($\phi\alpha\iota\delta\rho\grave{o}\nu$ $\mathring{\alpha}\gamma\alpha\lambda\mu\alpha$), the temple of Hadrian at Cyzicus, the Pyramids, the Pharus, etc., according to an epigram (Antholog. Græc. l. iv. p. 498, 499; Brodæi, apud Wechel) ascribed to Julian, ex-præfect of Egypt. Seventy-one of his epigrams, some lively, are collected in Brunck (Analect. Græc. tom. ii. p. 493-510); but this is wanting.

[2] Constantinopolitanum Palatium non pulchritudine solum, verum etiam fortitudine, omnibus quas unquam viderim munitionibus præstat (Liut-prand, Hist. l. v. c. 9, p. 465).

[3] See the anonymous continuator of Theophanes (p. 59, 61, 86 [p. 94, 98, 139, ed. Bonn]), whom I have followed in the neat and concise abstract of Le Beau (Hist. du Bas Empire, tom. xiv. p. 436, 438).

[There is one fact with regard to the Byzantine finance which deserves to be mentioned. From the fall of the Western Roman empire in 476 to the conquest of Constantinople by the Crusaders in 1204, the gold coinage of the empire was maintained constantly of the same weight and standard. The concave gold byzants (bezants) of Isaac II. were precisely of the same weight and value as the solidus of Leo the Great and Zeno the Isaurian. Gold was the circulating medium of the empire, and the purity of the Byzantine coinage rendered it for many centuries the only gold currency that circulated in Europe. In England, Sweden, and Russia the byzant of Constantinople long enjoyed the same superiority as is now conceded to the British coinage.—O. S.]

supported by fifteen columns of Phrygian marble, and the subterraneous vaults were of a similar construction. The square
before the sigma was decorated with a fountain, and the margin
of the basin was lined and encompassed with plates of silver. In
the beginning of each season the basin, instead of water, was
replenished with the most exquisite fruits, which were abandoned
to the populace for the entertainment of the prince. He enjoyed
this tumultuous spectacle from a throne resplendent with gold
and gems, which was raised by a marble staircase to the height of
a lofty terrace. Below the throne were seated the officers of his
guards, the magistrates, the chiefs of the factions of the circus;
the inferior steps were occupied by the people, and the place
below was covered with troops of dancers, singers, and panto-
mimes. The square was surrounded by the hall of justice, the
arsenal, and the various offices of business and pleasure; and the
purple chamber was named from the annual distribution of robes
of scarlet and purple by the hand of the empress herself. The
long series of the apartments was adapted to the seasons, and
decorated with marble and porphyry, with painting, sculpture,
and mosaics, with a profusion of gold, silver, and precious stones.
His fanciful magnificence employed the skill and patience of such
artists as the times could afford; but the taste of Athens would
have despised their frivolous and costly labours; a golden tree,
with its leaves and branches, which sheltered a multitude of birds
warbling their artificial notes, and two lions of massy gold, and
of the natural size, who looked and roared like their brethren of
the forest. The successors of Theophilus, of the Basilian and
Comnenian dynasties, were not less ambitious of leaving some
memorial of their residence; and the portion of the palace most
splendid and august was dignified with the title of the golden
triclinium.[1] With becoming modesty the rich and noble Greeks
aspired to imitate their sovereign, and when they passed through
the streets on horseback, in their robes of silk and embroidery,
they were mistaken by the children for kings.[2] A matron of
Peloponnesus,[3] who had cherished the infant fortunes of Basil

---

[1] In aureo triclinio quæ præstantior est pars potentissime degens (*the
usurper Romanus*), cæteras partes (*filiis*) distribuerat (Liutprand. Hist. l.
v. c. 9, p. 465). For this lax signification of Triclinium (ædificium tria vel
plura κλίνη scilicet στέγη complectens), see Ducange (Gloss. Græc. et
Observations sur Joinville, p. 240) and Reiske (ad Constantinum de
Ceremoniis, p. 7).

[2] In equis vecti (says Benjamin of Tudela) regum filiis videntur per-
similes. I prefer the Latin version of Constantine l'Empereur (p. 46) to
the French of Baratier (tom. i. p. 49).

[3] See the account of her journey, munificence, and testament, in the

the Macedonian, was excited by tenderness or vanity to visit the
greatness of her adopted son. In a journey of five hundred miles
from Patras to Constantinople, her age or indolence declined the
fatigue of a horse or carriage; the soft litter or bed of Danielis
was transported on the shoulders of ten robust slaves, and, as
they were relieved at easy distances, a band of three hundred was
selected for the performance of this service. She was entertained in the Byzantine palace with filial reverence and the
honours of a queen; and whatever might be the origin of her
wealth, her gifts were not unworthy of the regal dignity. I have
already described the fine and curious manufactures of Peloponnesus, of linen, silk, and woollen; but the most acceptable of her
presents consisted in three hundred beautiful youths, of whom
one hundred were eunuchs;[1] " for she was not ignorant," says
the historian, " that the air of the palace is more congenial to
such insects, than a shepherd's dairy to the flies of the summer."
During her lifetime she bestowed the greater part of her estates
in Peloponnesus, and her testament instituted Leo, the son of
Basil, her universal heir. After the payment of the legacies,
fourscore villas or farms were added to the Imperial domain, and
three thousand slaves of Danielis were enfranchised by their new
lord, and transplanted as a colony to the Italian coast. From
this example of a private matron we may estimate the wealth
and magnificence of the emperors. Yet our enjoyments are
confined by a narrow circle, and, whatsoever may be its value,
the luxury of life is possessed with more innocence and safety by
the master of his own, than by the steward of the public, fortune.

In an absolute government, which levels the distinctions of
noble and plebeian birth, the sovereign is the sole fountain of
honour; and the rank, both in the palace and the empire,
depends on the titles and offices which are bestowed and resumed
by his arbitrary will. Above a thousand years, from Vespasian
to Alexius Comnenus,[2] the *Cæsar* was the second person, or at

---

Life of Basil, by his grandson Constantine (c. 74, 75, 76, p. 195-197 [Theo-
phan. Contin. p. 227, *sqq.*, 317, *sqq.*, ed. Bonn]).

[1] *Carsamatium* (καρξιμαδες, Ducange, Gloss.) Græci vocant, amputatis
virilibus et virgâ, puerum eunuchum: quos Verdunenses mercatores ob
immensum lucrum facere solent et in Hispaniam ducere (Liutprand, l. vi.
c. 3, p. 470). The last abomination of the abominable slave-trade! Yet I
am surprised to find in the tenth century such active speculations of commerce in Lorraine.

[2] See the Alexiad (l. iii. p. 78, 79 [ed. Par.; tom. i. p. 147, *sq.*, ed. Bonn])
of Anna Comnena, who, except in filial piety, may be compared to Made-
moiselle de Montpensier. In her awful reverence for titles and forms, she
styles her father Ἐπιστημονάρχης, the inventor of this royal art, the
τέχνη τεχνῶν, and ἐπιστήμη ἐπιστημῶν.

least the second degree, after the supreme title of *Augustus* was more freely communicated to the sons and brothers of the reigning monarch. To elude without violating his promise to a powerful associate, the husband of his sister, and, without giving himself an equal, to reward the piety of his brother Isaac, the crafty Alexius interposed a new and supereminent dignity. The happy flexibility of the Greek tongue allowed him to compound the names of Augustus and Emperor (Sebastos and Autocrator), and the union produced the sonorous title of *Sebastocrator*. He was exalted above the Cæsar on the first step of the throne: the public acclamations repeated his name; and he was only distinguished from the sovereign by some peculiar ornaments of the head and feet. The emperor alone could assume the purple or red buskins, and the close diadem or tiara, which imitated the fashion of the Persian kings.[1] It was a high pyramidal cap of cloth or silk, almost concealed by a profusion of pearls and jewels: the crown was formed by a horizontal circle and two arches of gold: at the summit, the point of their intersection, was placed a globe or cross, and two strings or lappets of pearl depended on either cheek. Instead of red, the buskins of the Sebastocrator and Cæsar were green; and on their *open* coronets, or crowns, the precious gems were more sparingly distributed. Beside and below the Cæsar the fancy of Alexius created the *Panhypersebastos* and the *Protosebastos*, whose sound and signification will satisfy a Grecian ear. They imply a superiority and a priority above the simple name of Augustus; and this sacred and primitive title of the Roman prince was degraded to the kinsmen and servants of the Byzantine court. The daughter of Alexius applauds with fond complacency this artful gradation of hopes and honours; but the science of words is accessible to the meanest capacity; and this vain dictionary was easily enriched by the pride of his successors. To their favourite sons or brothers they imparted the more lofty appellation of Lord or *Despot*, which was illustrated with new ornaments and prerogatives, and placed immediately after the person of the emperor himself. The five titles of, 1. *Despot ;* 2. *Sebastocrator ;* 3. *Cæsar ;* 4. *Panhypersebastos ;* and, 5. *Protosebastos ;* were usually confined to the princes of his blood: they were the emanations of his majesty; but as they exercised

---

[1] Στέμμα, στέφανος, διάδημα ; see Reiske, ad Ceremoniale, p. 14, 15. Ducange has given a learned dissertation on the crowns of Constantinople, Rome, France, etc. (sur Joinville, xxv. p. 289-303); but of his thirty-four models none exactly tally with Anna's description.

no regular functions, their existence was useless, and their authority precarious.

But in every monarchy the substantial powers of government must be divided and exercised by the ministers of the palace and treasury, the fleet and army. The titles alone can differ; and in the revolution of ages, the counts and præfects, the prætor and quæstor, insensibly descended, while their servants rose above their heads to the first honours of the state. 1. In a monarchy, which refers every object to the person of the prince, the care and ceremonies of the palace form the most respectable department. The *Curopalata*,[1] so illustrious in the age of Justinian, was supplanted by the *Protovestiare*, whose primitive functions were limited to the custody of the wardrobe. From thence his jurisdiction was extended over the numerous menials of pomp and luxury; and he presided with his silver wand at the public and private audience. 2. In the ancient system of Constantine, the name of *Logothete*, or accountant, was applied to the receivers of the finances: the principal officers were distinguished as the Logothetes of the domain, of the posts, the army, the private and public treasure; and the *great Logothete*, the supreme guardian of the laws and revenues, is compared with the chancellor of the Latin monarchies.[2] His discerning eye pervaded the civil administration; and he was assisted, in due subordination, by the eparch or præfect of the city, the first secretary, and the keepers of the privy seal, the archives, and the red and purple ink which was reserved for the sacred signature of the emperor alone.[3] The introductor and interpreter of foreign ambassadors

---

[1] Par exstans curis, solo diademate dispar,
Ordine pro rerum vocitatus *Cura-Palati*;

says the African Corippus (de Laudibus Justini, l. i. 136); and in the same century (the sixth) Cassiodorus represents him, who, aureâ virgâ decoratus. inter obsequia numerosa, ante pedes Regios primus incederet (Variar. vii. 5). But this great officer (unknown) ἀνεπίγνωστος, exercising no function, νῦν δὲ οὐδεμίαν, was cast down by the modern Greeks to the fifteenth rank (Codin. c. 5, p. 65 [ed. Par.; p. 35, ed. Bonn]).

[2] Nicetas (in Manuel, l. vii. c. i. [p. 262, ed. Bonn]) defines him ὡς ἡ Λατίνων [βούλεται] φωνὴ Καγκελλάριον, ὡς δ' Ἕλληνες εἴποιεν Λογοθέτην. Yet the epithet of μέγας was added by the elder Andronicus (Ducange, tom. i. p. 822, 823).

[3] From Leo I. (A.D. 470) the Imperial ink, which is still visible on some original acts, was a mixture of vermilion and cinnabar, or purple. The emperor's guardians, who shared in this prerogative, always marked in green ink the indiction and the month. See the Dictionnaire Diplomatique (tom. i. p. 511-513), a valuable abridgment.

were the great *Chiauss*[1] and the *Dragoman*,[2] two names of
Turkish origin, and which are still familiar to the Sublime Porte.
3. From the humble style and service of guards, the *Domestics*
insensibly rose to the station of generals; the military themes
of the East and West, the legions of Europe and Asia, were often
divided, till the *great Domestic* was finally invested with the
universal and absolute command of the land forces. The
Protostrator, in his original functions, was the assistant of the
emperor when he mounted on horseback: he gradually became
the lieutenant of the great Domestic in the field; and his jurisdiction extended over the stables, the cavalry, and the royal train of
hunting and hawking. The *Stratopedarch* was the great judge
of the camp: the *Protospathaire* commanded the guards; the
Constable,[3] the *great Æteriarch*, and the *Acolyth*, were the
separate chiefs of the Franks, the barbarians, and the Varangi,
or English, the mercenary strangers, who, in the decay of the
national spirit, formed the nerve of the Byzantine armies.
4. The naval powers were under the command of the *great Duke;*
in his absence they obeyed the *great Drungaire* of the fleet; and,
in *his* place, the *Emir*, or *Admiral*, a name of Saracen extraction,[4]
but which has been naturalised in all the modern languages of
Europe. Of these officers, and of many more whom it would
be useless to enumerate, the civil and military hierarchy was
framed. Their honours and emoluments, their dress and titles,
their mutual salutations and respective pre-eminence, were
balanced with more exquisite labour than would have fixed the
constitution of a free people; and the code was almost perfect
when this baseless fabric, the monument of pride and servitude,
was for ever buried in the ruins of the empire.[5]

[1] The sultan sent a Σιαούς to Alexius (Anna Comnena, l. vi. p. 170 [tom.
i. p. 301, ed. Bonn]; Ducange ad loc.); and Pachymer often speaks of the
μέγας τζαούς (l. vii. c. 1, l. xii. c. 30, l. xiii. c. 22). The Chiaoush basha is
now at the head of 700 officers (Rycaut's Ottoman Empire, p. 349, octavo
edition).

[2] *Tagerman* is the Arabic name of an interpreter (D'Herbelot, p. 854,
855); πρῶτος τῶν ἑρμηνέων, οὓς κοινῶς ὀνομάζουσι δραγομάνους, says Codinus
(c. v. No. 70, p. 67 [p. 40, ed. Bonn]). See Villehardouin (No. 96), Busbe-
quius (Epist. iv. p. 338), and Ducange (Observations sur Villehardouin,
and Gloss. Græc. et Latin.).

[3] Κοντόσταυλος, or κοντόσταυλος, a corruption from the Latin Comes
stabuli, or the French Connétable. In a military sense it was used by the
Greeks in the eleventh century, at least as early as in France.

[4] It was directly borrowed from the Normans. In the twelfth century
Giannone reckons the admiral of Sicily among the great officers.

[5] This sketch of honours and offices is drawn from George Codinus Curopalata, who survived the taking of Constantinople by the Turks: his
elaborate, though trifling, work de Officiis Ecclesiæ et Aulæ C. P.) has been

The most lofty titles, and the most humble postures, which devotion has applied to the Supreme Being, have been prostituted by flattery and fear to creatures of the same nature with ourselves. The mode of *adoration*,[1] of falling prostrate on the ground and kissing the feet of the emperor, was borrowed by Diocletian from Persian servitude; but it was continued and aggravated till the last age of the Greek monarchy. Excepting only on Sundays, when it was waived, from a motive of religious pride, this humiliating reverence was exacted from all who entered the royal presence, from the princes invested with the diadem and purple, and from the ambassadors who represented their independent sovereigns, the caliphs of Asia, Egypt, or Spain, the kings of France and Italy, and the Latin emperors of ancient Rome. In his transactions of business, Liutprand, bishop of Cremona,[2] asserted the free spirit of a Frank and the dignity of his master Otho. Yet his sincerity cannot disguise the abasement of his first audience. When he approached the throne, the birds of the golden tree began to warble their notes, which were accompanied by the roarings of the two lions of gold. With his two companions Liutprand was compelled to bow and to fall prostrate; and thrice he touched the ground with his forehead. He arose; but in the short interval the throne had been hoisted by an engine from the floor to the ceiling, the Imperial figure appeared in new and more gorgeous apparel, and the interview was concluded in haughty and majestic silence. In this honest and curious narrative the bishop of Cremona represents the ceremonies of the Byzantine court, which are still practised in the Sublime Porte, and which were preserved in the last age by the dukes of Muscovy or Russia. After a long journey by the sea and land, from Venice to Constantinople, the ambassador halted at the golden gate, till he was conducted by the formal officers to the hospitable palace prepared for his reception; but this palace was a prison, and his jealous keepers prohibited all social intercourse either with strangers or natives. At his first audience he offered the gifts of his master—slaves, and golden vases, and costly armour. The ostentatious pay-

illustrated by the notes of Goar, and the three books of Gretser, a learned Jesuit.

[1] The respectful salutation of carrying the hand to the mouth, *ad os*, is the root of the Latin word *adoro, adorare*. See our learned Selden (vol. iii. p. 143-145, 942), in his Titles of Honour. It seems, from the first book of Herodotus, to be of Persian origin.

[2] The two embassies of Liutprand to Constantinople, all that he saw or suffered in the Greek capital, are pleasantly described by himself (Hist. l. vi. c. 1-4, p. 469-471; Legatio ad Nicephorum Phocam, p. 479-489).

ment of the officers and troops displayed before his eyes the
riches of the empire: he was entertained at a royal banquet,[1]
in which the ambassadors of the nations were marshalled by the
esteem or contempt of the Greeks: from his own table, the
emperor, as the most signal favour, sent the plates which he had
tasted; and his favourites were dismissed with a robe of honour.[2]
In the morning and evening of each day his civil and military
servants attended their duty in the palace; their labour was
repaid by the sight, perhaps by the smile, of their lord; his
commands were signified by a nod or a sign: but all earthly
greatness *stood* silent and submissive in his presence.   In his
regular or extraordinary processions through the capital, he un-
veiled his person to the public view: the rites of policy were
connected with those of religion, and his visits to the principal
churches were regulated by the festivals of the Greek calendar.
On the eve of these processions the gracious or devout intention
of the monarch was proclaimed by the heralds.   The streets
were cleared and purified; the pavement was strewed with flowers;
the most precious furniture, the gold and silver plate and silken
hangings, were displayed from the windows and balconies; and
a severe discipline restrained and silenced the tumult of the
populace.   The march was opened by the military officers at
the head of their troops: they were followed in long order by the
magistrates and ministers of the civil government: the person
of the emperor was guarded by his eunuchs and domestics, and
at the church door he was solemnly received by the patriarch
and his clergy.   The task of applause was not abandoned to the
rude and spontaneous voices of the crowd.   The most convenient
stations were occupied by the bands of the blue and green
factions of the circus; and their furious conflicts, which had
shaken the capital, were insensibly sunk to an emulation of
servitude.   From either side they echoed in responsive melody
the praises of the emperor; their poets and musicians directed
the choir, and long life [3] and victory were the burden of every

---

[1] Among the amusements of the feast, a boy balanced, on his forehead,
a pike or pole, twenty-four feet long, with a cross bar of two cubits a little
below the top.   Two boys, naked, though cinctured (*campestrati*), together,
and singly, climbed, stood, played, descended, etc., ita me stupidum red-
didit: utrum mirabilius nescio (p. 470 [Liutpr. Hist. vi. c. 4]).   At another
repast an homily of Chrysostom on the Acts of the Apostles was read elatâ
voce non Latine (p. 483 [Murat. S. I. t. ii.]).

[2] *Gala* is not improbably derived from Cala, or Caloat, in Arabic a robe
of honour (Reiske, Not. in Ceremon. p. 84).

[3] Πολυχρονίζειν is explained by εὐφημίζειν (Codin. c. 7 [c. 6, p. 53, ed.
Bonn]; Ducange, Gloss. Græc. tom. i. p. 1199).

song. The same acclamations were performed at the audience, the banquet, and the church; and as an evidence of boundless sway, they were repeated in the Latin,[1] Gothic, Persian, French, and even English language,[2] by the mercenaries who sustained the real or fictitious character of those nations. By the pen of Constantine Porphyrogenitus this science of form and flattery has been reduced into a pompous and trifling volume,[3] which the vanity of succeeding times might enrich with an ample supplement. Yet the calmer reflection of a prince would surely suggest that the same acclamations were applied to every character and every reign: and if he had risen from a private rank, he might remember that his own voice had been the loudest and most eager in applause, at the very moment when he envied the fortune, or conspired against the life, of his predecessor.[4]

The princes of the North, of the nations, says Constantine, without faith or fame, were ambitious of mingling their blood with the blood of the Cæsars, by their marriage with a royal virgin, or by the nuptials of their daughters with a Roman prince.[5] The aged monarch, in his instructions to his son, reveals the secret maxims of policy and pride, and suggests the most decent reasons for refusing these insolent and unreasonable demands. Every animal, says the discreet emperor, is prompted by nature to seek a mate among the animals of his own species; and the human species is divided into various tribes, by the distinction of language, religion, and manners. A just regard to the purity of descent preserves the harmony of public and private

---

[1] Κονσέρβετ Δέους ἡμπέριουμ βέστρουμ — βίκτωρ σῆς σέμπερ — βήβητε Δόμηνι Ἡμπεράτορες, ἦν μούλτος ἄννος (Ceremon. c. 75, p. 215 [tom. i. p. 370, ed. Bonn]). The want of the Latin V obliged the Greeks to employ their β; nor do they regard quantity. Till he recollected the true language, these strange sentences might puzzle a professor.

[2] Πολυχρονίζουσι Βάραγγοι, κατὰ τὴν πάτριον καὶ οὗτοι γλῶσσαν αὐτῶν, ἤγουν Ἰγκλινιστὶ (Codin. p. 90 [p. 57, ed. Bonn]). I wish he had preserved the words, however corrupt, of their English acclamation.

[3] For all these ceremonies see the professed work of Constantine Porphyrogenitus, with the notes, or rather dissertations, of his German editors, Leich and Reiske. For the rank of the *standing* courtiers, p. 80 [ed. Lips.; tom. i. p. 136, ed. Bonn], not. 23, 62; for the adoration, except on Sundays, p. 95, 240 [p. 162, 414, ed. Bonn], not. 131; the processions, p. 2 [p. 5, ed. Bonn], etc., not. p. 3, etc.; the acclamations passim, not. 25, etc.; the factions and Hippodrome, p. 177-214 [c. 68-73, p. 303-369, ed. Bonn], not. 9, 93, etc.; the Gothic games, p. 221 [p. 381, ed. Bonn], not. 111; vintage, p. 217 [c. 78, p. 373, ed. Bonn], not. 109: much more information is scattered over the work.

[4] Et privato Othoni nuper atque eadem dicenti nota adulatio (Tacit. Hist. i. 85).

[5] The thirteenth chapter, de Administratione Imperii, may be explained and rectified by the Familiæ Byzantinæ of Ducange.

life; but the mixture of foreign blood is the fruitful source of
disorder and discord. Such had ever been the opinion and
practice of the sage Romans: their jurisprudence proscribed
the marriage of a citizen and a stranger: in the days of freedom
and virtue a senator would have scorned to match his daughter
with a king: the glory of Mark Antony was sullied by an
Egyptian wife: [1] and the emperor Titus was compelled, by
popular censure, to dismiss with reluctance the reluctant
Berenice.[2] This perpetual interdict was ratified by the fabulous
sanction of the great Constantine. The ambassadors of the
nations, more especially of the unbelieving nations, were solemnly
admonished that such strange alliances had been condemned by
the founder of the church and city. The irrevocable law was
inscribed on the altar of St. Sophia; and the impious prince who
should stain the majesty of the purple was excluded from the
civil and ecclesiastical communion of the Romans. If the ambassadors were instructed by any false brethren in the Byzantine
history, they might produce three memorable examples of the
violation of this imaginary law: the marriage of Leo, or rather of
his father Constantine the Fourth, with the daughter of the king
of the Chazars, the nuptials of the grand-daughter of Romanus
with a Bulgarian prince, and the union of Bertha of France or
Italy with young Romanus, the son of Constantine Porphyrogenitus himself. To these objections three answers were prepared, which solved the difficulty and established the law.   I.
The deed and the guilt of Constantine Copronymus were acknowledged. The Isaurian heretic, who sullied the baptismal font
and declared war against the holy images, had indeed embraced
a barbarian wife. By this impious alliance he accomplished the
measure of his crimes, and was devoted to the just censure of the
church and of posterity.   II. Romanus could not be alleged as
a legitimate emperor; he was a plebeian usurper, ignorant of the
laws, and regardless of the honour of the monarchy. His son
Christopher, the father of the bride, was the third in rank in the
college of princes, at once the subject and the accomplice of a

---

[1] Sequiturque nefas! Ægyptia conjunx (Virgil, Æneid viii. 686). Yet
this Egyptian wife was the daughter of a long line of kings. Quid te
mutavit? (says Antony in a private letter to Augustus) an quod reginam
ineo? Uxor mea est (Sueton. in August. c. 69). Yet I much question
(for I cannot stay to inquire) whether the triumvir ever dared to celebrate
his marriage either with Roman or Egyptian rites.

[2] Berenicem invitus invitam dimisit (Suetonius in Tito, c. 7). Have I
observed elsewhere that this Jewish beauty was at this time above fifty
years of age? The judicious Racine has most discreetly suppressed both
her age and her country.

rebellious parent. The Bulgarians were sincere and devout Christians; and the safety of the empire, with the redemption of many thousand captives, depended on this preposterous alliance. Yet no consideration could dispense from the law of Constantine: the clergy, the senate, and the people disapproved the conduct of Romanus; and he was reproached, both in his life and death, as the author of the public disgrace. III. For the marriage of his own son with the daughter of Hugo, king of Italy, a more honourable defence is contrived by the wise Porphyrogenitus. Constantine, the great and holy, esteemed the fidelity and valour of the Franks;[1] and his prophetic spirit beheld the vision of their future greatness. They alone were excepted from the general prohibition: Hugo, king of France, was the lineal descendant of Charlemagne;[2] and his daughter, Bertha, inherited the prerogatives of her family and nation. The voice of truth and malice insensibly betrayed the fraud or error of the Imperial court. The patrimonial estate of Hugo was reduced from the monarchy of France to the simple county of Arles; though it was not denied that, in the confusion of the times, he had usurped the sovereignty of Provence, and invaded the kingdom of Italy. His father was a private noble; and if Bertha derived her female descent from the Carlovingian line, every step was polluted with illegitimacy or vice. The grandmother of Hugo was the famous Valdrada, the concubine, rather than the wife, of the second Lothair; whose adultery, divorce, and second nuptials had provoked against him the thunders of the Vatican. His mother, as she was styled, the great Bertha, was successively the wife of the Count of Arles and of the Marquis of Tuscany: France and Italy were scandalised by her gallantries; and, till the age of threescore, her lovers, of every degree, were the zealous servants of her ambition. The example of maternal incontinence was copied by the king of Italy; and the three favourite concubines of Hugo were decorated with the classic names of Venus, Juno, and Semele.[3] The daughter of Venus

---

[1] Constantine was made to praise the εὐγένεια and περιφάνεια of the Franks, with whom he claimed a private and public alliance. The French writers (Isaac Casaubon in Dedicat. Polybii) are highly delighted with these compliments.

[2] Constantine Porphyrogenitus (de Administrat. Imp. c. 26) exhibits a pedigree and Life of the illustrious king Hugo (περιβλέπτου ῥηγὸς Οὔγωνος). A more correct idea may be formed from the Criticism of Pagi, the Annals of Muratori, and the Abridgment of St. Marc. A.D. 925-946.

[3] After the mention of the three goddesses, Liutprand very naturally adds, et quoniam non rex solus iis abutebatur, earum nati ex incertis patribus originem ducunt (Hist. l. iv. c. 6): for the marriage of the younger Bertha, see Hist. l. v. c. 5; for the incontinence of the elder, dulcis exer-

was granted to the solicitations of the Byzantine court: her
name of Bertha was changed to that of Eudoxia; and she was
wedded, or rather betrothed, to young Romanus, the future
heir of the empire of the East. The consummation of this
foreign alliance was suspended by the tender age of the two
parties; and, at the end of five years, the union was dissolved by
the death of the virgin spouse. The second wife of the emperor
Romanus was a maiden of plebeian, but of Roman, birth; and
their two daughters, Theophano and Anne, were given in
marriage to the princes of the earth. The eldest was bestowed,
as the pledge of peace, on the eldest son of the great Otho, who
had solicited this alliance with arms and embassies. It might
legally be questioned how far a Saxon was entitled to the
privilege of the French nation; but every scruple was silenced
by the fame and piety of a hero who had restored the empire of
the West. After the death of her father-in-law and husband,
Theophano governed Rome, Italy, and Germany, during the
minority of her son, the third Otho; and the Latins have
praised the virtues of an empress who sacrificed to a superior
duty the remembrance of her country.[1] In the nuptials of her
sister Anne, every prejudice was lost, and every consideration of
dignity was superseded, by the stronger argument of necessity
and fear. A Pagan of the North, Wolodomir, great prince of
Russia, aspired to a daughter of the Roman purple; and his
claim was enforced by the threats of war, the promise of conversion, and the offer of a powerful succour against a domestic rebel.
A victim of her religion and country, the Grecian princess was
torn from the palace of her fathers, and condemned to a savage
reign and a hopeless exile on the banks of the Borysthenes, or
in the neighbourhood of the Polar circle.[2] Yet the marriage
of Anne was fortunate and fruitful: the daughter of her grandson
Jeroslaus was recommended by her Imperial descent; and the
king of France, Henry I., sought a wife on the last borders of
Europe and Christendom.[3]

citio Hymenæi, l. ii. c. 15; for the virtues and vices of Hugo, l. iii. c. 5.
Yet it must not be forgot that the bishop of Cremona was a lover of scandal.

[1] Licet illa Imperatrix Græca sibi et aliis fuisset satis utilis et optima, etc.,
is the preamble of an inimical writer, apud Pagi, tom. iv. A.D. 989, No. 3.
Her marriage and principal actions may be found in Muratori, Pagi, and
St. Marc, under the proper years.

[2] Cedrenus, tom. ii. p. 699 [p. 444, ed. Bonn]; Zonaras, tom. ii. p. 221
[l. xvii. c. 7]; Elmacin, Hist. Saracenica, l. iii. c. 6; Nestor apud Levesque.
tom. ii. p. 112; Pagi, Critica, A.D. 987, No. 6: a singular concourse! Wolodomir and Anne are ranked among the saints of the Russian church. Yet
we know his vices, and are ignorant of her virtues.

[3] Henricus Primus duxit uxorem Scythicam [et] Russam, filiam regis

In the Byzantine palace the emperor was the first slave of the ceremonies which he imposed, of the rigid forms which regulated each word and gesture, besieged him in the palace, and violated the leisure of his rural solitude. But the lives and fortunes of millions hung on his arbitrary will; and the firmest minds, superior to the allurements of pomp and luxury, may be seduced by the more active pleasure of commanding their equals. The legislative and executive powers were centred in the person of the monarch, and the last remains of the authority of the senate were finally eradicated by Leo the Philosopher.[1] A lethargy of servitude had benumbed the minds of the Greeks: in the wildest tumults of rebellion they never aspired to the idea of a free constitution; and the private character of the prince was the only source and measure of their public happiness. Superstition riveted their chains; in the church of St. Sophia he was solemnly crowned by the patriarch; at the foot of the altar they pledged their passive and unconditional obedience to his government and family. On his side he engaged to abstain as much as possible from the capital punishments of death and mutilation; his orthodox creed was subscribed with his own hand, and he promised to obey the decrees of the seven synods and the canons of the holy church.[2] But the assurance of mercy was loose and indefinite: he swore, not to his people, but to an invisible judge; and except in the inexpiable guilt of heresy, the ministers of heaven were always prepared to preach the indefeasible right, and to absolve the venial transgressions, of their sovereign. The Greek ecclesiastics were themselves the subjects of the civil magistrate: at the nod of a tyrant the bishops were created, or transferred, or deposed, or punished with an ignominious death; whatever might be their wealth or influence, they could never succeed like the Latin clergy in the establish-

Jeroslai. An embassy of bishops was sent into Russia, and the father gratanter filiam cum multis donis misit. This event happened in the year 1051. See the passages of the original chronicles in Bouquet's Historians of France (tom. xi. p. 29, 159, 161, 319, 384, 481). Voltaire might wonder at this alliance; but he should not have owned his ignorance of the country, religion, etc., of Jeroslaus—a name so conspicuous in the Russian annals.

[1] A constitution of Leo the Philosopher (lxxviii.) ne senatus-consulta amplius fiant, speaks the language of naked despotism, ἐξ οὗ τὸ μόναρχον κράτος τὴν τουῶτν ἀνήπται διοίκησιν, καὶ ἄκαιρον καὶ μάταιον τὸ ἄχρηστον μετὰ τῶν χρείαν παρεχομένων συνάπτεσθαι.

[2] Codinus (de Officiis, c. xvii. p. 120, 121 [p. 87, ed. Bonn] gives an idea of this oath, so strong to the church, πιστὸς καὶ γνήσιος δοῦλος καὶ υἱὸς τῆς ἁγίας ἐκκλησίας, so weak to the people, καὶ ἀπέχεσθαι φόνων καὶ ἀκρωτηριασμῶν καὶ τῶν ὁμοίων τούτοις κατὰ τὸ δυνατόν.

ment of an independent republic; and the patriarch of Constantinople condemned, what he secretly envied, the temporal greatness of his Roman brother. Yet the exercise of boundless despotism is happily checked by the laws of nature and necessity. In proportion to his wisdom and virtue, the master of an empire is confined to the path of his sacred and laborious duty. In proportion to his vice and folly, he drops the sceptre too weighty for his hands; and the motions of the royal image are ruled by the imperceptible thread of some minister or favourite, who undertakes for his private interest to exercise the task of the public oppression. In some fatal moment the most absolute monarch may dread the reason or the caprice of a nation of slaves; and experience has proved that whatever is gained in the extent is lost in the safety and solidity of regal power.

Whatever titles a despot may assume, whatever claims he may assert, it is on the sword that he must ultimately depend to guard him against his foreign and domestic enemies. From the age of Charlemagne to that of the Crusades the world (for I overlook the remote monarchy of China) was occupied and disputed by the three great empires or nations of the Greeks, the Saracens, and the Franks. Their military strength may be ascertained by a comparison of their courage, their arts and riches, and their obedience to a supreme head, who might call into action all the energies of the state. The Greeks, far inferior to their rivals in the first, were superior to the Franks, and at least equal to the Saracens, in the second and third of these warlike qualifications.

The wealth of the Greeks enabled them to purchase the service of the poorer nations, and to maintain a naval power for the protection of their coasts and the annoyance of their enemies.[1] A commerce of mutual benefit exchanged the gold of Constantinople for the blood of the Sclavonians and Turks, the Bulgarians and Russians: their valour contributed to the victories of Nicephorus and Zimisces; and if a hostile people pressed too closely on the frontier, they were recalled to the defence of their country, and the desire of peace, by the well-managed attack of a more distant tribe.[2] The command of the Mediterranean,

---

[1] If we listen to the threats of Nicephorus to the ambassador of Otho, Nec est in mari domino tuo classium numerus. Navigantium fortitudo mihi soli inest, qui eum classibus aggrediar, bello maritimas ejus civitates demoliar; et quæ fluminibus sunt vicina redigam in favillam. (Liutprand in Legat. ad Nicephorum Phocam, in Muratori Scriptores Rerum Italicarum, tom. ii. pars. i. p. 481.) He observes, in another place, qui cæteris præstant Venetici sunt et Amalphitani.

[2] Nec ipsa ( )iet eum (the emperor Otho) in quâ ortus est pauper et

from the mouth of the Tanais to the Columns of Hercules, was always claimed, and often possessed, by the successors of Constantine. Their capital was filled with naval stores and dexterous artificers: the situation of Greece and Asia, the long coasts, deep gulfs, and numerous islands, accustomed their subjects to the exercise of navigation; and the trade of Venice and Amalfi supplied a nursery of seamen to the Imperial fleet.[1] Since the time of the Peloponnesian and Punic wars, the sphere of action had not been enlarged; and the science of naval architecture appears to have declined. The art of constructing those stupendous machines which displayed three, or six, or ten ranges of oars, rising above, or falling behind, each other, was unknown to the shipbuilders of Constantinople, as well as to the mechanicians of modern days.[2] The *Dromones*,[3] or light galleys of the Byzantine empire, were content with two tier of oars; each tier was composed of five-and-twenty benches; and two rowers were seated on each bench, who plied their oars on either side of the vessel. To these we must add the captain or centurion, who, in time of action, stood erect with his armour-bearer on the poop, two steersmen at the helm, and two officers at the prow, the one to manage the anchor, the other to point and play against the enemy the tube of liquid fire. The whole crew, as in the infancy of the art, performed the double service of mariners and soldiers; they were provided with defensive and offensive arms— with bows and arrows, which they used from the upper deck; with long pikes, which they pushed through the port-holes of the lower tier. Sometimes, indeed, the ships of war were of a larger and more solid construction; and the labours of combat and navigation were more regularly divided between seventy soldiers and two hundred and thirty mariners. But for the most part

pellicea Saxonia: pecuniâ quâ pollemus omnes nationes super eum invitabimus; et quasi Keramicum [id est, vas fictile] confringemus (Liutprand in Legat. p. 487). The two books, de Administrando Imperio, perpetually inculcate the same policy.

[1] The nineteenth chapter of the Tactics of Leo (Meurs. Opera, tom. vi. p. 825-848), which is given more correct from a manuscript of Gudius, by the laborious Fabricius (Biblioth. Græc. tom. vi. p. 372-379), relates to the *Naumachia* or naval war.

[2] Even of fifteen and sixteen rows of oars, in the navy of Demetrius Poliorcetes. These were for real use: the forty rows of Ptolemy Philadelphus were applied to a floating palace, whose tonnage, according to Dr. Arbuthnot (Tables of Ancient Coins, etc. p. 231-236), is compared as 4½ to 1, with an English 100-gun ship.

[3] The Dromones of Leo, etc., are so clearly described with two tier of oars, that I must censure the version of Meursius and Fabricius, who pervert the sense by a blind attachment to the classic appellation of *Triremes*. The Byzantine historians are sometimes guilty of the same inaccuracy.

they were of the light and manageable size; and as the cape of Malea in Peloponnesus was still clothed with its ancient terrors, an Imperial fleet was transported five miles over land across the Isthmus of Corinth.[1] The principles of maritime tactics had not undergone any change since the time of Thucydides: a squadron of galleys still advanced in a crescent, charged to the front, and strove to impel their sharp beaks against the feeble sides of their antagonists. A machine for casting stones and darts was built of strong timbers in the midst of the deck; and the operation of boarding was effected by a crane that hoisted baskets of armed men. The language of signals, so clear and copious in the naval grammar of the moderns, was imperfectly expressed by the various positions and colours of a commanding flag. In the darkness of the night the same orders to chase, to attack, to halt, to retreat, to break, to form, were conveyed by the lights of the leading galley. By land, the fire-signals were repeated from one mountain to another; a chain of eight stations commanded a space of five hundred miles; and Constantinople in a few hours was apprised of the hostile motions of the Saracens of Tarsus.[2] Some estimate may be formed of the power of the Greek emperors by the curious and minute detail of the armament which was prepared for the reduction of Crete. A fleet of one hundred and twelve galleys, and seventy-five vessels of the Pamphylian style, was equipped in the capital, the islands of the Ægean Sea, and the seaports of Asia, Macedonia, and Greece. It carried thirty-four thousand mariners, seven thousand three hundred and forty soldiers, seven hundred Russians, and five thousand and eighty-seven Mardaites, whose fathers had been transplanted from the mountains of Libanus. Their pay, most probably of a month, was computed at thirty-four centenaries of gold, about one hundred and thirty-six thousand pounds sterling. Our fancy is bewildered by the endless recapitulation of arms and engines, of clothes and linen, of bread for the men and forage

---

[1] Constantin. Porphyrogen. in Vit. Basil. c. lxi. p. 185. He calmly praises the stratagem as a βουλὴν συνετὴν καὶ σοφήν; but the sailing round Peloponnesus is described by his terrified fancy as a circumnavigation of a thousand miles.

[2] The Continuator of Theophanes (l. iv. p. 122, 123 [p. 197, ed. Bonn]) names the successive stations, the castle of Lulum near Tarsus, Mount Argæus, Isamus, Ægilus, the hill of Mamas, Cyrisus, Mocilus, the hill of Auxentius, the sun-dial of the Pharus of the great palace. He affirms that the news were transmitted ἐν ἀκάρει, in an indivisible moment of time. Miserable amplification, which, by saying too much, says nothing. How much more forcible and instructive would have been the definition of three, or six, or twelve hours!

for the horses, and of stores and utensils of every description, inadequate to the conquest of a petty island, but amply sufficient for the establishment of a flourishing colony.[1]

The invention of the Greek fire did not, like that of gunpowder, produce a total revolution in the art of war. To these liquid combustibles the city and empire of Constantine owed their deliverance; and they were employed in sieges and sea-fights with terrible effect. But they were either less improved, or less susceptible of improvement: the engines of antiquity, the catapultæ, balistæ, and battering-rams, were still of most frequent and powerful use in the attack and defence of fortifications; nor was the decision of battles reduced to the quick and heavy *fire* of a line of infantry, whom it were fruitless to protect with armour against a similar fire of their enemies. Steel and iron were still the common instruments of destruction and safety; and the helmets, cuirasses, and shields of the tenth century did not, either in form or substance, essentially differ from those which had covered the companions of Alexander or Achilles.[2] But instead of accustoming the modern Greeks, like the legionaries of old, to the constant and easy use of this salutary weight, their armour was laid aside in light chariots, which followed the march, till, on the approach of an enemy, they resumed with haste and reluctance the unusual encumbrance. Their offensive weapons consisted of swords, battle-axes, and spears; but the Macedonian pike was shortened a fourth of its length, and reduced to the more convenient measure of twelve cubits or feet. The sharpness of the Scythian and Arabian arrows had been severely felt; and the emperors lament the decay of archery as a cause of the public misfortunes, and recommend, as an advice and a command, that the military youth, till the age of forty, should assiduously practise the exercise of the bow.[3] The *bands*, or regiments, were usually three hundred strong;

---

[1] See the Ceremoniale of Constantine Porphyrogenitus, l. ii. c. 44, p. 376-392 [tom. i. p. 651, *sqq.*, ed. Bonn]. A critical reader will discern some inconsistencies in different parts of this account; but they are not more obscure or more stubborn than the establishment and effectives, the present and fit for duty, the rank and file and the private, of a modern return, which retain in proper hands the knowledge of these profitable mysteries.

[2] See the fifth, sixth, and seventh chapters, περὶ ὅπλων, περὶ ὁπλίσεως, and περὶ γυμνασίας, in the Tactics of Leo, with the corresponding passages in those of Constantine.

[3] They observe τῆς γὰρ τοξείας παντελῶς ἀμεληθείσης . . . ἐν τοῖς Ρωμαίοις τὰ πολλὰ νῦν εἴωθε σφάλματα γένεσθαι. (Leo, Tactic. p. 581 [c. vi. § 5]; Constantin. p. 1216). Yet such were not the maxims of the Greeks and Romans, who despised the loose and distant practice of archery.

and, as a medium between the extremes of four and sixteen, the
foot-soldiers of Leo and Constantine were formed eight deep;
but the cavalry charged in four ranks, from the reasonable consideration that the weight of the front could not be increased
by any pressure of the hindmost horses. If the ranks of the
infantry or cavalry were sometimes doubled, this cautious array
betrayed a secret distrust of the courage of the troops, whose
numbers might swell the appearance of the line, but of whom
only a chosen band would dare to encounter the spears and
swords of the barbarians. The order of battle must have varied
according to the ground, the object, and the adversary; but their
ordinary disposition, in two lines and a reserve, presented a succession of hopes and resources most agreeable to the temper as
well as the judgment of the Greeks.[1] In case of a repulse, the
first line fell back into the intervals of the second; and the
reserve, breaking into two divisions, wheeled round the flanks to
improve the victory or cover the retreat. Whatever authority
could enact was accomplished, at least in theory, by the camps
and marches, the exercises and evolutions, the edicts and books,
of the Byzantine monarch.[2] Whatever art could produce from
the forge, the loom, or the laboratory, was abundantly supplied
by the riches of the prince and the industry of his numerous
workmen. But neither authority nor art could frame the most
important machine, the soldier himself; and if the *ceremonies*
of Constantine always suppose the safe and triumphal return
of the emperor,[3] his *tactics* seldom soar above the means of
escaping a defeat and procrastinating the war.[4] Notwithstanding some transient success, the Greeks were sunk in their own
esteem and that of their neighbours. A cold hand and a
loquacious tongue was the vulgar description of the nation; the
author of the Tactics was besieged in his capital; and the last

---

[1] Compare the passages of the Tactics, p. 669 and 721, and the twelfth
with the eighteenth chapter.

[2] In the preface to his Tactics, Leo very freely deplores the loss of discipline and the calamities of the times, and repeats, without scruple (Proem.
p. 357), the reproaches of ἀμέλεια, ἀταξία, ἀγυμνασία, δειλία etc.,
nor does it appear that the same censures were less deserved in the next
generation by the disciples of Constantine.

[3] See in the Ceremonial (l. ii. c. 19, p. 353 [tom. i. p. 610, *sq.*, ed. Bonn])
the form of the emperor's trampling on the necks of the captive Saracens,
while the singers chanted " Thou hast made my enemies my footstool! "
and the people shouted forty times the kyrie eleison.

[4] Leo observes (Tactic. p. 668) that a fair open battle against any nation
whatsoever is ἐπισφαλὲς and ἐπικίνδυνόν: the words are strong, and the
remark is true; yet if such had been the opinion of the old Romans, Leo
had never reigned on the shores of the Thracian Bosphorus.

of the barbarians, who trembled at the name of the Saracens
or Franks, could proudly exhibit the medals of gold and silver
which they had extorted from the feeble sovereign of Constantinople. What spirit their government and character denied
might have been inspired, in some degree, by the influence of
religion; but the religion of the Greeks could only teach them
to suffer and to yield. The emperor Nicephorus, who restored
for a moment the discipline and glory of the Roman name, was
desirous of bestowing the honours of martyrdom on the Christians who lost their lives in a holy war against the infidels. But
this political law was defeated by the opposition of the patriarch,
the bishops, and the principal senators; and they strenuously
urged the canons of St. Basil, that all who were polluted by the
bloody trade of a soldier should be separated, during three
years, from the communion of the faithful.[1]

These scruples of the Greeks have been compared with the
tears of the primitive Moslems when they were held back from
battle; and this contrast of base superstition and high-spirited
enthusiasm unfolds to a philosophic eye the history of the rival
nations. The subjects of the last caliphs [2] had undoubtedly
degenerated from the zeal and faith of the companions of the
prophet. Yet their martial creed still represented the Deity as
the author of war; [3] the vital though latent spark of fanaticism
still glowed in the heart of their religion, and among the Saracens
who dwelt on the Christian borders it was frequently rekindled
to a lively and active flame. Their regular force was formed of
the valiant slaves who had been educated to guard the person
and accompany the standard of their lord; but the Musulman
people of Syria and Cilicia, of Africa and Spain, was awakened
by the trumpet which proclaimed a holy war against the infidels.
The rich were ambitious of death or victory in the cause of God;
the poor were allured by the hopes of plunder; and the old, the
infirm, and the women assumed their share of meritorious service

---

[1] Zonaras (tom. ii. l. xvi. [c. 25] p. 202, 203) and Cedrenus (Compend.
p. 668 [p. 658, ed. Par.; tom. ii. p. 369, ed. Bonn]), who relate the design
of Nicephorus, most unfortunately apply the epithet of γενναίως to the
opposition of the patriarch.

[2] The eighth chapter of the tactics of the different nations is the most
historical and useful of the whole collection of Leo. The manners and
arms of the Saracens (Tactic. p. 809-817, and a fragment from the Medicean
MS. in the preface of the sixth volume of Meursius) the Roman emperor
was too frequently called upon to study.

[3] Παντὸς δὲ καὶ κακοῦ ἔργου τὸν Θεὸν εἶναι αἴτιον ὑποτίθενται, καὶ πολέμοις
χαίρειν λέγουσι τὸν Θεόν, τὸν διασκορπίζοντα ἔθνη τὰ τοὺς πολέμους θέλοντα.
Leon. Tactic. p. 809 [c. 18, § 111].

by sending their substitutes, with arms and horses, into the field. These offensive and defensive arms were similar in strength and temper to those of the Romans, whom they far excelled in the management of the horse and the bow; the massy silver of their belts, their bridles, and their swords displayed the magnificence of a prosperous nation; and, except some black archers of the South, the Arabs disdained the naked bravery of their ancestors. Instead of waggons they were attended by a long train of camels, mules, and asses; the multitude of these animals, whom they bedecked with flags and streamers, appeared to swell the pomp and magnitude of their host, and the horses of the enemy were often disordered by the uncouth figure and odious smell of the camels of the East.   Invincible by their patience of thirst and heat, their spirits were frozen by a winter's cold, and the consciousness of their propensity to sleep exacted the most rigorous precautions against the surprises of the night.   Their order of battle was a long square of two deep and solid lines; the first of archers, the second of cavalry.   In their engagements by sea and land they sustained with patient firmness the fury of the attack, and seldom advanced to the charge till they could discern and oppress the lassitude of their foes.   But if they were repulsed and broken, they knew not how to rally or renew the combat, and their dismay was heightened by the superstitious prejudice that God had declared himself on the side of their enemies.   The decline and fall of the caliphs countenanced this fearful opinion, nor were there wanting, among the Mohammedans and Christians, some obscure prophecies [1] which prognosticated their alternate defeats.   The unity of the Arabian empire was dissolved, but the independent fragments were equal to populous and powerful kingdoms, and in their naval and military armaments an emir of Aleppo or Tunis might command no despicable fund of skill, and industry, and treasure.   In their transactions of peace and war with the Saracens, the princes of Constantinople too often felt that these barbarians had nothing barbarous in their discipline, and that, if they were destitute of original genius, they had been endowed with a quick spirit of curiosity and imitation.   The model was indeed more perfect than the copy; their ships, and engines, and fortifications were of a less skilful construction; and they confess, without shame, that the same God who has

---

[1] Liutprand (p. 484, 485) relates and interprets the oracles of the Greeks and Saracens, in which, after the fashion of prophecy, the past is clear and historical, the future is dark, enigmatical, and erroneous.   From this boundary of light and shade an impartial critic may commonly determine the date of the composition.

given a tongue to the Arabians had more nicely fashioned the hands of the Chinese and the heads of the Greeks.[1]

A name of some German tribes between the Rhine and the Weser had spread its victorious influence over the greatest part of Gaul, Germany, and Italy; and the common appellation of FRANKS[2] was applied by the Greeks and Arabians to the Christians of the Latin church, the nations of the West, who stretched beyond *their* knowledge to the shores of the Atlantic Ocean. The vast body had been inspired and united by the soul of Charlemagne; but the division and degeneracy of his race soon annihilated the Imperial power, which would have rivalled the Cæsars of Byzantium, and revenged the indignities of the Christian name. The enemies no longer feared, nor could the subjects any longer trust, the application of a public revenue, the labours of trade and manufactures in the military service, the mutual aid of provinces and armies, and the naval squadrons which were regularly stationed from the mouth of the Elbe to that of the Tiber. In the beginning of the tenth century the family of Charlemagne had almost disappeared; his monarchy was broken into many hostile and independent states; the regal title was assumed by the most ambitious chiefs; their revolt was imitated in a long subordination of anarchy and discord; and the nobles of every province disobeyed their sovereign, oppressed their vassals, and exercised perpetual hostilities against their equals and neighbours. Their private wars, which overturned the fabric of government, fomented the martial spirit of the nation. In the system of modern Europe the power of the sword is possessed, at least in fact, by five or six mighty potentates; their operations are conducted on a distant frontier by an order of men who devote their lives to the study and practice of the military art: the rest of the country and community enjoys in the midst of war the tranquillity of peace, and is only made sensible of the change by the aggravation or decrease of the public taxes. In the disorders of the tenth and eleventh centuries every peasant was a soldier, and every village a fortification; each wood or valley was a scene of murder and

---

[1] The sense of this distinction is expressed by Abulpharagius (Dynast. p. 2, 62, 101); but I cannot recollect the passage in which it is conveyed by this lively apophthegm.

[2] Ex Francis, quo nomine tam Latinos quam Teutones comprehendit, ludum habuit (Liutprand in Legat. ad Imp. Nicephorum, p. 483, 484). This extension of the name may be confirmed from Constantine (de Administrando Imperio, l. ii. c. 27, 28) and Eutychius (Annal. tom. i. p. 55, 56), who both lived before the Crusades. The testimonies of Abulpharagius (Dynast. p. 69) and Abulfeda (Præfat. ad Geograph.) are more recent.

rapine; and the lords of each castle were compelled to assume the character of princes and warriors. To their own courage and policy they boldly trusted for the safety of their family, the protection of their lands, and the revenge of their injuries; and, like the conquerors of a larger size, they were too apt to transgress the privilege of defensive war. The powers of the mind and body were hardened by the presence of danger and necessity of resolution: the same spirit refused to desert a friend and to forgive an enemy; and, instead of sleeping under the guardian care of the magistrate, they proudly disdained the authority of the laws. In the days of feudal anarchy the instruments of agriculture and art were converted into the weapons of bloodshed; the peaceful occupations of civil and ecclesiastical society were abolished or corrupted; and the bishop who exchanged his mitre for a helmet was more forcibly urged by the manners of the times than by the obligation of his tenure.[1]

The love of freedom and of arms was felt with conscious pride by the Franks themselves, and is observed by the Greeks with some degree of amazement and terror. " The Franks," says the emperor Constantine, " are bold and valiant to the verge of temerity; and their dauntless spirit is supported by the contempt of danger and death. In the field, and in close onset, they press to the front and rush headlong against the enemy, without deigning to compute either his numbers or their own. Their ranks are formed by the firm connections of consanguinity and friendship; and their martial deeds are prompted by the desire of saving or revenging their dearest companions. In their eyes a retreat is a shameful flight, and flight is indelible infamy." [2] A nation endowed with such high and intrepid spirit must have been secure of victory if these advantages had not been counterbalanced by many weighty defects. The decay of their naval power left the Greeks and Saracens in possession of the sea for every purpose of annoyance and supply. In the age which preceded the institution of knighthood the Franks were

---

[1] On this subject of ecclesiastical and beneficiary discipline, Father Thomassin (tom. iii. l. i. c. 40, 45, 46, 47) may be usefully consulted. A general law of Charlemagne exempted the bishops from personal service; but the opposite practice, which prevailed from the ninth to the fifteenth century, is countenanced by the example or silence of saints and doctors. . . . You justify your cowardice by the holy canons, says Ratherius of Verona; the canons likewise forbid you to whore, and yet——

[2] In the eighteenth chapter of his Tactics, the emperor Leo has fairly stated the military vices and virtues of the Franks (whom Meursius ridiculously translates by *Galli*) and the Lombards or Langobards. See likewise the twenty-sixth Dissertation of Muratori de Antiquitatibus Italiæ medii Ævi.

rude and unskilful in the service of cavalry; [1] and in all perilous emergencies their warriors were so conscious of their ignorance, that they chose to dismount from their horses and fight on foot. Unpractised in the use of pikes or of missile weapons, they were encumbered by the length of their swords, the weight of their armour, the magnitude of their shields, and, if I may repeat the satire of the meagre Greeks, by their unwieldy intemperance. Their independent spirit disdained the yoke of subordination, and abandoned the standard of their chief if he attempted to keep the field beyond the term of their stipulation or service. On all sides they were open to the snares of an enemy less brave but more artful than themselves. They might be bribed, for the barbarians were venal; or surprised in the night, for they neglected the precautions of a close encampment or vigilant sentinels. The fatigues of a summer's campaign exhausted their strength and patience, and they sunk in despair if their voracious appetite was disappointed of a plentiful supply of wine and of food. This general character of the Franks was marked with some national and local shades, which I should ascribe to accident rather than to climate, but which were visible both to natives and to foreigners. An ambassador of the great Otho declared, in the palace of Constantinople, that the Saxons could dispute with swords better than with pens, and that they preferred inevitable death to the dishonour of turning their backs to an enemy.[2] It was the glory of the nobles of France that, in their humble dwellings, war and rapine were the only pleasure, the sole occupation, of their lives. They affected to deride the palaces, the banquets, the polished manners of the Italians, who in the estimate of the Greeks themselves had degenerated from the liberty and valour of the ancient Lombards.[3]

By the well-known edict of Caracalla, his subjects, from Britain to Egypt, were entitled to the name and privileges of Romans, and their national sovereign might fix his occasional or permanent residence in any province of their common country. In the division of the East and West an ideal unity was

---

[1] Domini tui milites (says the proud Nicephorus) equitandi ignari, pedestris pugnæ sunt inscii: scutorum magnitudo, loricarum gravitudo, ensium longitudo, galearumque pondus neutrâ parte pugnare eos sinit; ac subridens, impedit, inquit, et eos gastrimargia, hoc est ventris ingluvies, etc. Liutprand in Legat. p. 480, 481.

[2] In Saxonia certo scio . . . decentius ensibus pugnare quam calamis,

[3] Φράγγοι τοίνυν καὶ Λογίβαρδοι λόγον ἐλευθερίας περὶ πολλοῦ ποιοῦνται, ἀλλ᾽ οἱ μὲν Λογίβαρδοι τὸ πλέον τῆς τοιαύτης ἀρετῆς νῦν ἀπώλεσαν. Leonis et prius mortem obire quam hostibus terga dare (Liutprand, p. 482). Tactica, c. 18, p. 804. The emperor Leo died A.D. 911: an historical poem,

scrupulously preserved, and in their titles, laws, and statutes the successors of Arcadius and Honorius announced themselves as the inseparable colleagues of the same office, as the joint sovereigns of the Roman world and city, which were bounded by the same limits. After the fall of the Western monarchy the majesty of the purple resided solely in the princes of Constantinople, and of these Justinian was the first who, after a divorce of sixty years, regained the dominion of ancient Rome, and asserted, by the right of conquest, the august title of Emperor of the Romans.[1] A motive of vanity or discontent solicited one of his successors, Constans the Second, to abandon the Thracian Bosphorus and to restore the pristine honours of the Tiber: an extravagant project (exclaims the malicious Byzantine), as if he had despoiled a beautiful and blooming virgin, to enrich, or rather to expose, the deformity of a wrinkled and decrepit matron.[2] But the sword of the Lombards opposed his settlement in Italy; he entered Rome not as a conqueror, but as a fugitive, and, after a visit of twelve days, he pillaged and for ever deserted the ancient capital of the world.[3] The final revolt and separation of Italy was accomplished about two centuries

which ends in 916, and appears to have been composed in 940, by a native of Venetia, discriminates in these verses the manners of Italy and France:

—— Quid inertia bello
Pectora (Ubertus ait) duris prætenditis armis,
O Itali?   Potius vobis sacra pocula cordi;
Sæpius et stomachum nitidis laxare saginis
Elatasque domos rutilo fulcire metallo.
Non eadem Gallos similis vel cura remordet;
Vicinas quibus est studium devincere terras,
Depressumque larem spoliis hinc inde coactis
Sustentare ——

(Anonym. Carmen Panegyricum de Laudibus Berengarii Augusti, l. ii. in Muratori Script. Rerum Italic. tom. ii. pars i. p. 395).

[1] Justinian, says the historian Agathias (l. v. p. 157 [ed. Par.; p. 306, ed. Bonn]), πρῶτος 'Ρωμαίων αὐτοκράτωρ ὀνόματί τε καὶ πράγματι. Yet the specific title of Emperor of the Romans was not used at Constantinople till it had been claimed by the French and German emperors of old Rome.

[2] Constantine Manasses reprobates this design in his barbarous verse:

Τὴν πόλιν τὴν βασίλειαν ἀποκοσμῆσαι θέλων,
Καὶ τὴν ἀρχὴν χαρίσασθαι τῇ τριπεμπέλῳ 'Ρώμῃ,
Ὡς εἴτις ἀβροστόλιστον ἀποκοσμήσει νύμφην,
Καὶ γραῦν τινὰ τρικόρωνον ὡς κόρην ὡραΐσει·
[v. 3836, p. 165, ed. Bonn.]

and it is confirmed by Theophanes, Zonaras, Cedrenus, and the Historia Miscella: voluit in urbem Romam Imperium transferre (l. xix. p. 137, in tom. i. pars i. of the Scriptores Rer. Ital. of Muratori).

[3] Paul. Diacon. l. v. c. 11, p. 480; Anastasius in Vitis Pontificum, in Muratori's Collection, tom. iii. pars i. p. 141.

after the conquests of Justinian, and from his reign we may date the gradual oblivion of the Latin tongue. That legislator had composed his Institutes, his Code, and his Pandects in a language which he celebrates as the proper and public style of the Roman government, the consecrated idiom of the palace and senate of Constantinople, of the camps and tribunals of the East.[1] But this foreign dialect was unknown to the people and soldiers of the Asiatic provinces, it was imperfectly understood by the greater part of the interpreters of the laws and the ministers of the state. After a short conflict, nature and habit prevailed over the obsolete institutions of human power: for the general benefit of his subjects Justinian promulgated his novels in the two languages, the several parts of his voluminous jurisprudence were successively translated,[2] the original was forgotten, the version was studied, and the Greek, whose intrinsic merit deserved indeed the preference, obtained a legal as well as popular establishment in the Byzantine monarchy. The birth and residence of succeeding princes estranged them from the Roman idiom; Tiberius by the Arabs,[3] and Maurice by the Italians,[4] are distinguished as the first of the Greek Cæsars, as the founders of a new dynasty and empire; the silent revolution was accomplished before the death of Heraclius, and the ruins of the Latin speech were darkly preserved in the terms of jurisprudence and the acclamations of the palace. After the restoration of the Western empire by Charlemagne and the

[1] Consult the preface of Ducange (ad Gloss. Græc. medii Ævi) and the Novels of Justinian (vii. lxvi.). The Greek language was κοινός, the Latin was πάτριος to himself, κυριώτατος to the πολιτείας σχῆμα, the system of government.

[2] Οὐ μὴν ἀλλὰ καὶ Λατινικὴ λέξις καὶ φράσις εἰσέτι τοὺς νόμους κρύπτουσα τοὺς συνεῖναι ταύτην μὴ δυναμένους ἰσχυρῶς ἀπετείχιζε (Matth. Blastares, Hist. Juris, apud Fabric. Biblioth. Græc. tom. xii. p. 369 [ed. Hamb. 1724]). The Code and Pandects (the latter by Thalelæus) were translated in the time of Justinian (p. 358, 366). Theophilus, one of the original triumvirs, has left an elegant, though diffuse, paraphrase of the Institutes. On the other hand, Julian, antecessor of Constantinople (A.D. 570), 120 Novellas Græcas eleganti Latinitate donavit (Heineccius, Hist. J. R. p. 396) for the use of Italy and Africa.

[3] Abulpharagius assigns the seventh Dynasty to the Franks or Romans, the eighth to the Greeks, the ninth to the Arabs. A tempore Augusti Cæsaris donec imperaret Tiberius Cæsar spatio circiter annorum 600 fuerunt Imperatores C. P. Patricii, et præcipua pars exercitûs Roman [i.e. Franci]: extra quod, consiliarii, scribæ et populus, omnes Græci fuerunt: deinde regnum etiam Græcanicum factum est (p. 95, vers. Pocock). The Christian and ecclesiastical studies of Abulpharagius gave him some advantage over the more ignorant *Moslems.*

[4] Primus ex Græcorum genere in Imperio confirmatus est; or, according to another MS. of Paulus Diaconus (l. iii. c. 15, p. 443), in Græcorum Imperio.

Othos, the names of Franks and Latins acquired an equal signification and extent, and these haughty barbarians asserted, with
some justice, their superior claim to the language and dominion
of Rome. They insulted the aliens of the East who had renounced the dress and idiom of Romans, and their reasonable
practice will justify the frequent appellation of Greeks.[1] But
this contemptuous appellation was indignantly rejected by the
prince and people to whom it is applied. Whatsoever changes
had been introduced by the lapse of ages, they alleged a lineal
and unbroken succession from Augustus and Constantine; and,
in the lowest period of degeneracy and decay, the name of
Romans adhered to the last fragments of the empire of Constantinople.[2]

While the government of the East was transacted in Latin,
the Greek was the language of literature and philosophy, nor
could the masters of this rich and perfect idiom be tempted to
envy the borrowed learning and imitative taste of their Roman
disciples. After the fall of Paganism, the loss of Syria and
Egypt, and the extinction of the schools of Alexandria and
Athens, the studies of the Greeks insensibly retired to some
regular monasteries, and, above all, to the royal college of
Constantinople, which was burnt in the reign of Leo the
Isaurian.[3] In the pompous style of the age, the president of that
foundation was named the Sun of Science; his twelve associates,
the professors in the different arts and faculties, were the twelve
signs of the zodiac; a library of thirty-six thousand five
hundred volumes was open to their inquiries; and they could
show an ancient manuscript of Homer, on a roll of parchment one
hundred and twenty feet in length, the intestines, as it was

---

[1] Quia linguam, mores, vestesque mutâstis, putavit Sanctissimus Papa
(an audacious irony), ita vobis displicere Romanorum nomen. His
nuncios, rogabant Nicephorum Imperatorem Græcorum, ut cum Othone
Imperatore Romanorum amicitiam faceret (Liutprand in Legatione, p. 486).

[2] By Laonicus Chalcocondyles, who survived the last siege of Constantinople, the account is thus stated (l. i. p. 3 [p. 6, ed. Bonn]). Constantine
transplanted his Latins of Italy to a Greek city of Thrace: they adopted
the language and manners of the natives, who were confounded with them
under the name of Romans. The kings of Constantinople, says the
historian, ἐπὶ τῷ σφᾶς αὐτοὺς Ῥωμαίων βασιλεῖς τε καὶ αὐτοκράτορας σεμ-
νύνεσθαι ἀποκαλεῖν, Ἑλλήνων δὲ βασιλεῖς οὐκέτι οὐδαμῇ ἀξιοῦν.

[3] See Ducange (C. P. Christiana, l. ii. p. 150, 151), who collects the
testimonies, not of Theophanes, but at least of Zonaras (tom. ii. l. xv. [c. 3]
p. 104), Cedrenus (p. 454 [tom. i. p. 795, sq., ed. Bonn]), Michael Glycas
(p. 281 [p. 522, ed. Bonn]), Constantine Manasses (p. 87 [v. 4257, p. 182,
ed. Bonn]). After refuting the absurd charge against the emperor, Spanheim (Hist. Imaginum, p. 99-111), like a true advocate, proceeds to doubt
or deny the reality of the fire, and almost of the library.

fabled, of a prodigious serpent.[1] But the seventh and eighth
centuries were a period of discord and darkness; the library was
burnt, the college was abolished, the Iconoclasts are represented
as the foes of antiquity, and a savage ignorance and contempt of
letters has disgraced the princes of the Heraclean and Isaurian
dynasties.[2]

In the ninth century we trace the first dawnings of the restoration of science.[3] After the fanaticism of the Arabs had subsided,
the caliphs aspired to conquer the arts, rather than the provinces,
of the empire: their liberal curiosity rekindled the emulation of
the Greeks, brushed away the dust from their ancient libraries,
and taught them to know and reward the philosophers, whose
labours had been hitherto repaid by the pleasure of study and
the pursuit of truth. The Cæsar Bardas, the uncle of Michael
the Third, was the generous protector of letters, a title which
alone has preserved his memory and excused his ambition. A
particle of the treasures of his nephew was sometimes diverted
from the indulgence of vice and folly; a school was opened in the
palace of Magnaura, and the presence of Bardas excited the
emulation of the masters and students. At their head was the
philosopher Leo, archbishop of Thessalonica; his profound skill
in astronomy and the mathematics was admired by the strangers
of the East, and this occult science was magnified by vulgar
credulity, which modestly supposes that all knowledge superior
to its own must be the effect of inspiration or magic. At the
pressing entreaty of the Cæsar, his friend, the celebrated Photius,[4]
renounced the freedom of a secular and studious life, ascended
the patriarchal throne, and was alternately excommunicated
and absolved by the synods of the East and West. By the confession even of priestly hatred, no art or science, except poetry,
was foreign to this universal scholar, who was deep in thought,
indefatigable in reading, and eloquent in diction. Whilst he
exercised the office of protospathaire, or captain of the guards,

---

[1] According to Malchus (apud Zonar. l. xiv. p. 53), this Homer was burnt
in the time of Basiliscus. The MS. might be renewed—but on a serpent's
skin? Most strange and incredible!

[2] The ἀλογία of Zonaras, the ἀγρία καὶ ἀμαθία of Cedrenus, are strong
words, perhaps not ill-suited to these reigns.

[3] See Zonaras (l. xvi. [c. 4] p. 160, 161) and Cedrenus (p. 549, 550 [tom.
ii. p. 168, sqq., ed. Bonn]). Like Friar Bacon, the philosopher Leo has
been transformed by ignorance into a conjurer; yet not so undeservedly,
if he be the author of the oracles more commonly ascribed to the emperor
of the same name. The physics of Leo in MS. are in the library of Vienna
(Fabricius, Biblioth. Græc. tom. vi. p. 366; tom. xii. p. 781). Quiescant!

[4] The ecclesiastical and literary character of Photius is copiously discussed by Hanckius (de Scriptoribus Byzant. p. 269-396) and Fabricius.

Photius was sent ambassador to the caliph of Bagdad.[1] The tedious hours of exile, perhaps of confinement, were beguiled by the hasty composition of his *Library*, a living monument of erudition and criticism. Two hundred and fourscore writers, historians, orators, philosophers, theologians, are reviewed without any regular method; he abridges their narrative or doctrine, appreciates their style and character, and judges even the fathers of the church with a discreet freedom which often breaks through the superstition of the times. The emperor Basil, who lamented the defects of his own education, intrusted to the care of Photius his son and successor Leo the Philosopher, and the reign of that prince and of his son Constantine Porphyrogenitus forms one of the most prosperous eras of the Byzantine literature. By their munificence the treasures of antiquity were deposited in the Imperial library; by their pens, or those of their associates, they were imparted in such extracts and abridgments as might amuse the curiosity, without oppressing the indolence, of the public. Besides the *Basilics*, or code of laws, the arts of husbandry and war, of feeding or destroying the human species, were propagated with equal diligence; and the history of Greece and Rome was digested into fifty-three heads or titles, of which two only (of embassies, and of virtues and vices) have escaped the injuries of time. In every station the reader might contemplate the image of the past world, apply the lesson or warning of each page, and learn to admire, perhaps to imitate, the examples of a brighter period. I shall not expatiate on the works of the Byzantine Greeks, who, by the assiduous study of the ancients, have deserved, in some measure, the remembrance and gratitude of the moderns. The scholars of the present age may still enjoy the benefit of the philosophical commonplace-book of Stobæus, the grammatical and historic lexicon of Suidas, the Chiliads of Tzetzes, which comprise six hundred narratives in twelve thousand verses, and the commentaries on Homer of Eustathius archbishop of Thessalonica, who, from his horn of plenty, has poured the names and authorities of four hundred writers. From these originals, and

---

[1] Εἰς Ἀσσυρίους can only mean Bagdad, the seat of the caliph; and the relation of his embassy might have been curious and instructive. But how did he procure his books? A library so numerous could neither be found at Bagdad, nor transported with his baggage, nor preserved in his memory. Yet the last, however incredible, seems to be affirmed by Photius himself, ὅσας αὐτῶν ἡ μνήμη διέσωζε. Camusat (Hist. Critique des Journaux, p. 87-94) gives a good account of the Myriobiblon.

from the numerous tribe of scholiasts and critics,[1] some estimate
may be formed of the literary wealth of the twelfth century.
Constantinople was enlightened by the genius of Homer and
Demosthenes, of Aristotle and Plato; and in the enjoyment or
neglect of our present riches we must envy the generation that
could still peruse the history of Theopompus, the orations of
Hyperides, the comedies of Menander,[2] and the odes of Alcæus
and Sappho. The frequent labour of illustration attests not
only the existence but the popularity of the Grecian classics; the
general knowledge of the age may be deduced from the example
of two learned females, the empress Eudocia and the princess
Anna Comnena, who cultivated, in the purple, the arts of
rhetoric and philosophy.[3] The vulgar dialect of the city was
gross and barbarous: a more correct and elaborate style distinguished the discourse, or at least the compositions, of the church
and palace, which sometimes affected to copy the purity of the
Attic models.

In our modern education, the painful though necessary attain-
ment of two languages which are no longer living may consume
the time and damp the ardour of the youthful student. The
poets and orators were long imprisoned in the barbarous dialects
of our Western ancestors, devoid of harmony or grace; and their
genius, without precept or example, was abandoned to the rude
and native powers of their judgment and fancy. But the Greeks
of Constantinople, after purging away the impurities of their

---

[1] Of these modern Greeks, see the respective articles in the Bibliotheca
Græca of Fabricius; a laborious work, yet susceptible of a better method
and many improvements: of Eustathius (tom. i. p. 289-292, 306-329), of
the Pselli (a diatribe of Leo Allatius, ad calcem tom. v.), of Constantine
Porphyrogenitus (tom. vi. p. 486-509), of John Stobæus (tom. viii. 665-
728), of Suidas (tom. ix. p. 620-827), John Tzetzes (tom. xii. p. 245-273).
Mr. Harris, in his Philological Arrangements, opus senile, has given a
sketch of this Byzantine learning (p. 287-300).

[2] From obscure and hearsay evidence, Gerard Vossius (de Poetis Græcis,
c. 6) and Le Clerc (Bibliothèque Choisie, tom. xix. p. 285) mention a commentary of Michael Psellus on twenty-four plays of Menander, still extant
in MS. at Constantinople. Yet such classic studies seem incompatible
with the gravity or dulness of a schoolman who pored over the categories
(de Psellis, p. 42); and Michael has probably been confounded with
Homerus *Sellius*, who wrote arguments to the comedies of Menander. In
the tenth century Suidas quotes fifty plays, but he often transcribes the
old scholiast of Aristophanes.

[3] Anna Comnena may boast of her Greek style (τὸ Ἑλληνίζειν ἐς ἄκρον
ἐσπουδακυῖα), and Zonaras, her contemporary, but not her flatterer, may
add with truth, γλῶτταν εἶχεν ἀκριβῶς Ἀττικίζουσαν. The princess
was conversant with the artful dialogues of Plato, and had studied the
τετρακτὺς, or *quadrivium* of astrology, geometry, arithmetic, and music
(see her preface to the Alexiad, with Ducange's notes).

vulgar speech, acquired the free use of their ancient language, the most happy composition of human art, and a familiar knowledge of the sublime masters who had pleased or instructed the first of nations. But these advantages only tend to aggravate the reproach and shame of a degenerate people. They held in their lifeless hands the riches of their fathers, without inheriting the spirit which had created and improved that sacred patrimony : they read, they praised, they compiled, but their languid souls seemed alike incapable of thought and action. In the revolution of ten centuries, not a single discovery was made to exalt the dignity or promote the happiness of mankind. Not a single idea has been added to the speculative systems of antiquity, and a succession of patient disciples became in their turn the dogmatic teachers of the next servile generation. Not a single composition of history, philosophy, or literature, has been saved from oblivion by the intrinsic beauties of style or sentiment, of original fancy, or even of successful imitation. In prose, the least offensive of the Byzantine writers are absolved from censure by their naked and unpresuming simplicity : but the orators, most eloquent [1] in their own conceit, are the farthest removed from the models whom they affect to emulate. In every page our taste and reason are wounded by the choice of gigantic and obsolete words, a stiff and intricate phraseology, the discord of images, the childish play of false or unseasonable ornament, and the painful attempt to elevate themselves, to astonish the reader, and to involve a trivial meaning in the smoke of obscurity and exaggeration. Their prose is soaring to the vicious affectation of poetry : their poetry is sinking below the flatness and insipidity of prose. The tragic, epic, and lyric muses were silent and inglorious : the bards of Constantinople seldom rose above a riddle or epigram, a panegyric or tale ; they forgot even the rules of prosody ; and with the melody of Homer yet sounding in their ears, they confound all measure of feet and syllables in the impotent strains which have received the name of *political* or city verses.[2] The minds of the Greeks were bound in the fetters of a base and imperious superstition, which extends her dominion round the circle of profane science.

---

[1] To censure the Byzantine taste, Ducange (Prefat. Gloss. Græc. p. 17) strings the authorities of Aulus Gellius, Jerom, Petronius, George Hamartolus, Longinus, who give at once the precept and the example.

[2] The *versus politici*, those common prostitutes, as, from their easiness, they are styled by Leo Allatius, usually consist of fifteen syllables. They are used by Constantine Manasses, John Tzetzes, etc. (Ducange, Gloss. Latin. tom. iii. p. i. p. 345, 346, edit. Basil. 1762).

Their understandings were bewildered in metaphysical controversy: in the belief of visions and miracles they had lost all principles of moral evidence, and their taste was vitiated by the homilies of the monks, an absurd medley of declamation and Scripture. Even these contemptible studies were no longer dignified by the abuse of superior talents: the leaders of the Greek church were humbly content to admire and copy the oracles of antiquity, nor did the schools or pulpit produce any rivals of the fame of Athanasius and Chrysostom.[1]

In all the pursuits of active and speculative life, the emulation of states and individuals is the most powerful spring of the efforts and improvements of mankind. The cities of ancient Greece were cast in the happy mixture of union and independence, which is repeated on a larger scale, but in a looser form, by the nations of modern Europe: the union of language, religion, and manners, which renders them the spectators and judges of each other's merit:[2] the independence of government and interest, which asserts their separate freedom, and excites them to strive for pre-eminence in the career of glory. The situation of the Romans was less favourable; yet in the early ages of the republic, which fixed the national character, a similar emulation was kindled among the states of Latium and Italy; and in the arts and sciences they aspired to equal or surpass their Grecian masters. The empire of the Cæsars undoubtedly checked the activity and progress of the human mind: its magnitude might indeed allow some scope for domestic competition; but when it was gradually reduced, at first to the East, and at last to Greece and Constantinople, the Byzantine subjects were degraded to an abject and languid temper, the natural effect of their solitary and insulated state. From the North they were oppressed by nameless tribes of barbarians, to whom they scarcely imparted the appellation of men. The language and religion of the more polished Arabs were an insurmountable bar to all social intercourse. The conquerors of Europe were their brethren in the Christian faith; but the speech of the Franks or Latins was unknown, their manners were rude, and they were rarely connected, in peace or war, with the successors of Heraclius. Alone in the universe, the self-satisfied pride of the Greeks was not disturbed by the comparison of foreign merit; and it is no wonder if they fainted in the race, since they had neither com-

---

[1] As St. Bernard of the Latin, so St. John Damascenus, in the eighth century, is revered as the last father of the Greek, church.

[2] Hume's Essays, vol. i. p. 125.

petitors to urge their speed, nor judges to crown their victory. The nations of Europe and Asia were mingled by the expeditions to the Holy Land; and it is under the Comnenian dynasty that a faint emulation of knowledge and military virtue was rekindled in the Byzantine empire.

CHAPTER LIV

Origin and Doctrine of the Paulicians—Their Persecution by the Greek Emperors—Revolt in Armenia, etc.—Transplantation into Thrace—Propagation in the West—The Seeds, Character, and Consequences of the Reformation

IN the profession of Christianity the variety of national characters may be clearly distinguished. The natives of Syria and Egypt abandoned their lives to lazy and contemplative devotion: Rome again aspired to the dominion of the world; and the wit of the lively and loquacious Greeks was consumed in the disputes of metaphysical theology. The incomprehensible mysteries of the Trinity and Incarnation, instead of commanding their silent submission, were agitated in vehement and subtle controversies, which enlarged their faith at the expense, perhaps, of their charity and reason. From the council of Nice to the end of the seventh century, the peace and unity of the church was invaded by these spiritual wars; and so deeply did they affect the decline and fall of the empire, that the historian has too often been compelled to attend the synods, to explore the creeds, and to enumerate the sects, of this busy period of ecclesiastical annals. From the beginning of the eighth century to the last ages of the Byzantine empire the sound of controversy was seldom heard: curiosity was exhausted, zeal was fatigued, and in the decrees of six councils the articles of the Catholic faith had been irrevocably defined. The spirit of dispute, however vain and pernicious, requires some energy and exercise of the mental faculties; and the prostrate Greeks were content to fast, to pray, and to believe in blind obedience to the patriarch and his clergy. During a long dream of superstition the Virgin and the saints, their visions and miracles, their relics and images, were preached by the monks, and worshipped by the people; and the appellation of people might be extended, without injustice, to the first ranks of civil society. At an unseasonable moment the Isaurian emperors attempted somewhat rudely to awaken their subjects: under their influence reason might obtain some proselytes, a far greater number was swayed by interest or fear; but the Eastern world embraced or deplored their visible deities, and the restoration of images was celebrated as the feast of orthodoxy. In this passive and unanimous state the ecclesiastical rulers were relieved from the toil, or deprived of the pleasure, of persecution. The Pagans had disappeared; the Jews were silent and obscure; the disputes with the Latins were rare and remote hostilities against a national enemy; and the sects of Egypt and Syria enjoyed a free toleration under the shadow of the Arabian caliphs. About the middle of the seventh century a branch of Manichæans was selected as the victims of spiritual tyranny: their patience was at length exasperated to despair and rebellion; and their exile has scattered over the West the seeds of reformation. These important events will justify some inquiry into the doctrine and story of the PAULICIANS;[1] and, as they cannot plead for themselves, our candid criticism will magnify the *good*, and abate or suspect the *evil*, that is reported by their adversaries.

The Gnostics, who had distracted the infancy, were oppressed by the greatness and authority of the church. Instead of emulating or surpassing the wealth, learning, and numbers of the Catholics, their obscure remnant was driven from the capitals of the East and West, and confined to the villages and mountains along the borders of the Euphrates. Some vestige of the Marcionites may be detected in the fifth century;[2] but the numerous sects were finally lost in the odious name of the Manichæans: and these heretics, who presumed to reconcile the doctrines of Zoroaster and Christ, were pursued by the two religions with equal and unrelenting hatred. Under the grandson of Heraclius, in the neighbourhood of Samosata, more famous for the birth of Lucian than for the title of a Syrian kingdom, a reformer arose, esteemed by the *Paulicians* as the

---

[1] The errors and virtues of the Paulicians are weighed, with his usual judgment and candour, by the learned Mosheim (Hist. Ecclesiast. seculum ix. p. 311, etc.). He draws his original intelligence from Photius (contra Manichæos, l. i.) and Peter Siculus (Hist. Manichæorum). The first of these accounts has not fallen into my hands; the second, which Mosheim prefers, I have read in a Latin version inserted in the Maxima Bibliotheca Patrum (tom. xvi. p. 754-764) from the edition of the Jesuit Raderus (Ingolstadii, 1604, in 4to).

[2] In the time of Theodoret, the diocese of Cyrrhus, in Syria, contained eight hundred villages. Of these, two were inhabited by Arians and Eunomians, and eight by *Marcionites*, whom the laborious bishop reconciled to the Catholic church (Dupin, Biblioth. Ecclésiastique, tom. iv. p. 81, 82).

chosen messenger of truth. In his humble dwelling of Mana-
nalis, Constantine entertained a deacon who returned from
Syrian captivity, and received the inestimable gift of the New
Testament, which was already concealed from the vulgar by the
prudence of the Greek, and perhaps of the Gnostic, clergy.[1]
These books became the measure of his studies and the rule of his
faith; and the Catholics, who dispute his interpretation, acknowledge that his text was genuine and sincere. But he attached
himself with peculiar devotion to the writings and character of
St. Paul: the name of the Paulicians is derived by their enemies
from some unknown and domestic teacher; but I am confident
that they gloried in their affinity to the apostle of the Gentiles.
His disciples, Titus, Timothy, Sylvanus, Tychichus, were represented by Constantine, and his fellow-labourers: the names of
the apostolic churches were applied to the congregations which
they assembled in Armenia and Cappadocia; and this innocent
allegory revived the example and memory of the first ages. In
the Gospel and the Epistles of St. Paul his faithful follower
investigated the creed of primitive Christianity; and, whatever
might be the success, a Protestant reader will applaud the spirit
of the inquiry. But if the Scriptures of the Paulicians were pure,
they were not perfect. Their founders rejected the two Epistles
of St. Peter,[2] the apostle of the circumcision, whose dispute with
their favourite for the observance of the law could not easily be
forgiven.[3] They agreed with their Gnostic brethren in the
universal contempt for the Old Testament, the books of Moses
and the prophets, which have been consecrated by the decrees of
the Catholic church. With equal boldness, and doubtless with
more reason, Constantine, the new Sylvanus, disclaimed the
visions which in so many bulky and splendid volumes had been
published by the Oriental sects;[4] the fabulous productions of

[1] Nobis profanis ista (*sacra Evangelia*) legere non licet sacerdotibus dun-
taxat, was the first scruple of a Catholic when he was advised to read the
Bible (Petr. Sicul. p. 761).

[2] In rejecting the *second* Epistle of St. Peter, the Paulicians are justified
by some of the most respectable of the ancients and moderns (see Wetstein
ad loc., Simon, Hist. Critique du Nouveau Testament, c. 17). They likewise overlooked the Apocalypse (Petr. Sicul. p. 756); but as such neglect is
not imputed as a crime, the Greeks of the ninth century must have been
careless of the credit and honour of the Revelations.

[3] This contention, which has not escaped the malice of Porphyry,
supposes some error and passion in one or both of the apostles. By
Chrysostom, Jerome, and Erasmus, it is represented as a sham quarrel, a
pious fraud, for the benefit of the Gentiles and the correction of the Jews
(Middleton's Works, vol. ii. p. 1-20).

[4] Those who are curious of this heterodox library may consult the researches of Beausobre (Hist. Critique du Manichéisme, tom. i. p. 305-437).

the Hebrew patriarchs and the sages of the East; the spurious gospels, epistles, and acts, which in the first age had overwhelmed the orthodox code; the theology of Manes, and the authors of the kindred heresies; and the thirty generations, or æons, which had been created by the fruitful fancy of Valentine. The Paulicians sincerely condemned the memory and opinions of the Manichæan sect, and complained of the injustice which impressed that invidious name on the simple votaries of St. Paul and of Christ.

Of the ecclesiastical chain, many links had been broken by the Paulician reformers; and their liberty was enlarged, as they reduced the number of masters at whose voice profane reason must bow to mystery and miracle. The early separation of the Gnostics had preceded the establishment of the Catholic worship; and against the gradual innovations of discipline and doctrine they were as strongly guarded by habit and aversion as by the silence of St. Paul and the evangelists. The objects which had been transformed by the magic of superstition appeared to the eyes of the Paulicians in their genuine and naked colours. An image made without hands was the common workmanship of a mortal artist, to whose skill alone the wood and canvas must be indebted for their merit or value. The miraculous relics were a heap of bones and ashes, destitute of life or virtue, or of any relation, perhaps, with the person to whom they were ascribed. The true and vivifying cross was a piece of sound or rotten timber; the body and blood of Christ, a loaf of bread and a cup of wine, the gifts of nature and the symbols of grace. The mother of God was degraded from her celestial honours and immaculate virginity; and the saints and angels were no longer solicited to exercise the laborious office of mediation in heaven and ministry upon earth. In the practice, or at least in the theory, of the sacraments, the Paulicians were inclined to abolish all visible objects of worship, and the words of the Gospel were, in their judgment, the baptism and communion of the faithful. They indulged a convenient latitude for the interpretation of Scripture: and as often as they were pressed by the literal sense, they could escape to the intricate mazes of figure and allegory. Their utmost diligence must have been employed to dissolve the connection between the Old and the New Testament; since they

---

Even in Africa, St. Austin could describe the Manichæan books, tam multi, tam grandes, tam pretiosi codices (contra Faust. xiii. 14); but he adds, without pity, Incendite omnes illas membranas: and his advice has been rigorously followed.

adored the latter as the oracles of God, and abhorred the former as the fabulous and absurd invention of men or demons. We cannot be surprised that they should have found in the Gospel the orthodox mystery of the Trinity: but instead of confessing the human nature and substantial sufferings of Christ, they amused their fancy with a celestial body that passed through the virgin like water through a pipe; with a fantastic crucifixion, that eluded the vain and impotent malice of the Jews. A creed thus simple and spiritual was not adapted to the genius of the times;[1] and the rational Christian, who might have been contented with the light yoke and easy burden of Jesus and his apostles, was justly offended that the Paulicians should dare to violate the unity of God, the first article of natural and revealed religion. Their belief and their trust was in the Father, of Christ, of the human soul, and of the invisible world. But they likewise held the eternity of matter; a stubborn and rebellious substance, the origin of a second principle, of an active being, who has created this visible world, and exercises his temporal reign till the final consummation of death and sin.[2] The appearances of moral and physical evil had established the two principles in the ancient philosophy and religion of the East, from whence this doctrine was transfused to the various swarms of the Gnostics. A thousand shades may be devised in the nature and character of *Ahriman*, from a rival god to a subordinate demon, from passion and frailty to pure and perfect malevolence: but, in spite of our efforts, the goodness and the power of Ormusd are placed at the opposite extremities of the line; and every step that approaches the one must recede in equal proportion from the other.[3]

The apostolic labours of Constantine-Sylvanus soon multiplied the number of his disciples, the secret recompense of spiritual ambition. The remnant of the Gnostic sects, and especially the Manichæans of Armenia, were united under his standard; many Catholics were converted or seduced by his arguments; and he preached with success in the regions of Pontus[4] and Cappadocia,

[1] The six capital errors of the Paulicians are defined by Peter Siculus (p. 756) with much prejudice and passion.

[2] Primum illorum axioma est, duo rerum esse principia; Deum malum et Deum bonum, aliumque hujus mundi conditorem et principem, et alium futuri ævi (Petr. Sicul. p. 756).

[3] Two learned critics, Beausobre (Hist. Critique du Manichéisme, l. i. iv. v. vi.) and Mosheim (Institut. Hist. Eccles. and de Rebus Christianis ante Constantinum, sec. i. ii. iii.), have laboured to explore and discriminate the various systems of the Gnostics on the subject of the two principles.

[4] The countries between the Euphrates and the Halys were possessed above 350 years by the Medes (Herodot. l. i. c. 103) and Persians; and the kings of Pontus were of the royal race of the Achæmenides (Sallust. Frag-

which had long since imbibed the religion of Zoroaster. The
Paulician teachers were distinguished only by their Scriptural
names, by the modest title of Fellow-pilgrims, by the austerity of
their lives, their zeal or knowledge, and the credit of some extraordinary gifts of the Holy Spirit. But they were incapable of
desiring, or at least of obtaining, the wealth and honours of the
Catholic prelacy: such anti-Christian pride they bitterly censured: and even the rank of elders or presbyters was condemned
as an institution of the Jewish synagogue. The new sect was
loosely spread over the provinces of Asia Minor to the westward
of the Euphrates; six of their principal congregations represented the churches to which St. Paul had addressed his epistles;
and their founder chose his residence in the neighbourhood of
Colonia,[1] in the same district of Pontus which had been celebrated by the altars of Bellona [2] and the miracles of Gregory.[3]
After a mission of twenty-seven years, Sylvanus, who had retired
from the tolerating government of the Arabs, fell a sacrifice to
Roman persecution. The laws of the pious emperors, which
seldom touched the lives of less odious heretics, proscribed without mercy or disguise the tenets, the books, and the persons of
the Montanists and Manichæans: the books were delivered to the
flames; and all who should presume to secrete such writings, or
to profess such opinions, were devoted to an ignominious death.[4]
A Greek minister, armed with legal and military powers, appeared
at Colonia to strike the shepherd, and to reclaim, if possible, the

ment. l. iii. with the French supplement and notes of the President de
Brosses).

[1] Most probably founded by Pompey after the conquest of Pontus.
This Colonia, on the Lycus above Neo-Cæsarea, is named by the Turks
Coulei-hisar, or Chonac, a populous town in a strong country (D'Anville,
Géographie Ancienne, tom. ii. p. 34; Tournefort, Voyage du Levant, tom.
iii. lettre xxi. p. 293).

[2] The temple of Bellona, at Comana in Pontus, was a powerful and
wealthy foundation, and the high priest was respected as the second person
in the kingdom. As the sacerdotal office had been occupied by his mother's
family, Strabo (l. xii. p. 809, 835, 836, 837 [p. 535, 557, *sqq.*, ed. Casaub.])
dwells with peculiar complacency on the temple, the worship, and festival,
which was twice celebrated every year. But the Bellona of Pontus had
the features and character of the goddess, not of war, but of love.

[3] Gregory, bishop of Neo-Cæsarea (A.D. 240-265), surnamed Thauma-
turgus, or the Wonder-worker. A hundred years afterwards, the history
or romance of his life was composed by Gregory of Nyssa, his namesake
and countryman, the brother of the great St. Basil.

[4] Hoc cæterum ad sua egregia facinora, divini atque orthodoxi Imperatores addiderunt, ut Manichæos Montanosque capitali puniri sententiâ
juberent, eorumque libros, quocunque in loco inventi essent, flammis tradi;
quod siquis uspiam eosdem occultasse deprehenderetur, hunc eundem
mortis pœnæ addici, ejusque bona in fiscum inferri (Petr. Sicul. p. 759).
What more could bigotry and persecution desire?

lost sheep. By a refinement of cruelty, Simeon placed the unfortunate Sylvanus before a line of his disciples, who were commanded, as the price of their pardon and the proof of their repentance, to massacre their spiritual father. They turned aside from the impious office; the stones dropped from their filial hands; and of the whole number only one executioner could be found, a new David, as he is styled by the Catholics, who boldly overthrew the giant of heresy. This apostate, Justus was his name, again deceived and betrayed his unsuspecting brethren, and a new conformity to the acts of St. Paul may be found in the conversion of Simeon: like the apostle, he embraced the doctrine which he had been sent to persecute, renounced his honours and fortunes, and acquired among the Paulicians the fame of a missionary and a martyr. They were not ambitious of martyrdom,[1] but in a calamitous period of one hundred and fifty years their patience sustained whatever zeal could inflict; and power was insufficient to eradicate the obstinate vegetation of fanaticism and reason. From the blood and ashes of the first victims a succession of teachers and congregations repeatedly arose: amidst their foreign hostilities they found leisure for domestic quarrels: they preached, they disputed, they suffered; and the virtues, the apparent virtues, of Sergius, in a pilgrimage of thirty-three years, are reluctantly confessed by the orthodox historians.[2] The native cruelty of Justinian the Second was stimulated by a pious cause; and he vainly hoped to extinguish, in a single conflagration, the name and memory of the Paulicians. By their primitive simplicity, their abhorrence of popular superstition, the Iconoclast princes might have been reconciled to some erroneous doctrines; but they themselves were exposed to the calumnies of the monks, and they chose to be the tyrants, lest they should be accused as the accomplices, of the Manichæans. Such a reproach has sullied the clemency of Nicephorus, who relaxed in their favour the severity of the penal statutes, nor will his character sustain the honour of a more liberal motive. The feeble Michael the First, the rigid Leo the Armenian, were foremost in the race of persecution; but the prize must doubtless be

[1] It should seem that the Paulicians allowed themselves some latitude of equivocation and mental reservation, till the Catholics discovered the pressing questions which reduced them to the alternative of apostasy or martyrdom (Petr. Sicul. p. 760).

[2] The persecution is told by Petrus Siculus (p. 579-763) with satisfaction and pleasantry. Justus *justa* persolvit. Simeon was not τιτος but κῆτος (the pronunciation of the two vowels must have been nearly the same), a great whale that drowned the mariners who mistook him for an island. See likewise Cedrenus (p. 432-435 [tom. i. p. 756-761, ed. Bonn]).

adjudged to the sanguinary devotion of Theodora, who restored the images to the Oriental church. Her inquisitors explored the cities and mountains of the lesser Asia, and the flatterers of the empress have affirmed that, in a short reign, one hundred thousand Paulicians were extirpated by the sword, the gibbet, or the flames. Her guilt or merit has perhaps been stretched beyond the measure of truth: but if the account be allowed, it must be presumed that many simple Iconoclasts were punished under a more odious name; and that some who were driven from the church, unwillingly took refuge in the bosom of heresy.

The most furious and desperate of rebels are the sectaries of a religion long persecuted, and at length provoked. In a holy cause they are no longer susceptible of fear or remorse: the justice of their arms hardens them against the feelings of humanity; and they revenge their fathers' wrongs on the children of their tyrants. Such have been the Hussites of Bohemia and the Calvinists of France, and such, in the ninth century, were the Paulicians of Armenia and the adjacent provinces.[1] They were first awakened to the massacre of a governor and bishop, who exercised the Imperial mandate of converting or destroying the heretics; and the deepest recesses of Mount Argæus protected their independence and revenge. A more dangerous and consuming flame was kindled by the persecution of Theodora, and the revolt of Carbeas, a valiant Paulician, who commanded the guards of the general of the East. His father had been impaled by the Catholic inquisitors; and religion, or at least nature, might justify his desertion and revenge. Five thousand of his brethren were united by the same motives; they renounced the allegiance of anti-Christian Rome; a Saracen emir introduced Carbeas to the caliph; and the commander of the faithful extended his sceptre to the implacable enemy of the Greeks. In the mountains between Siwas and Trebizond he founded or fortified the city of Tephrice,[2] which is still occupied by a fierce and licentious people, and the neighbouring hills were covered with the Paulician fugitives, who now reconciled the use of the Bible and the sword. During more than thirty years Asia

---

[1] Petrus Siculus (p. 763, 764), the continuator of Theophanes (l. iv. c. 4 [c. 16], p. 103, 104 [p. 165-167, ed. Bonn]), Cedrenus (p. 541, 542, 545 [tom. ii. p. 153 sqq.]), and Zonaras (tom. ii. l. xvi. [c. 2] p. 156), describe the revolt and exploits of Carbeas and his Paulicians.

[2] Otter (Voyage en Turquie et en Perse, tom. ii.) is probably the only Frank who has visited the independent barbarians of Tephrice, now Divrigni, from whom he fortunately escaped in the train of a Turkish officer.

was afflicted by the calamities of foreign and domestic war: in their hostile inroads the disciples of St. Paul were joined with those of Mohammed; and the peaceful Christians, the aged parent and tender virgin, who were delivered into barbarous servitude, might justly accuse the intolerant spirit of their sovereign. So urgent was the mischief, so intolerable the shame, that even the dissolute Michael, the son of Theodora, was compelled to march in person against the Paulicians: he was defeated under the walls of Samosata; and the Roman emperor fled before the heretics whom his mother had condemned to the flames. The Saracens fought under the same banners, but the victory was ascribed to Carbeas; and the captive generals, with more than a hundred tribunes, were either released by his avarice or tortured by his fanaticism. The valour and ambition of Chrysocheir,[1] his successor, embraced a wider circle of rapine and revenge. In alliance with his faithful Moslems, he boldly penetrated into the heart of Asia; the troops of the frontier and the palace were repeatedly overthrown; the edicts of persecution were answered by the pillage of Nice and Nicomedia, of Ancyra and Ephesus; nor could the apostle St. John protect from violation his city and sepulchre. The cathedral of Ephesus was turned into a stable for mules and horses; and the Paulicians vied with the Saracens in their contempt and abhorrence of images and relics. It is not unpleasing to observe the triumph of rebellion over the same despotism which has disdained the prayers of an injured people. The emperor Basil, the Macedonian, was reduced to sue for peace, to offer a ransom for the captives, and to request, in the language of moderation and charity, that Chrysocheir would spare his fellow-Christians, and content himself with a royal donative of gold and silver and silk garments. "If the emperor," replied the insolent fanatic, "be desirous of peace, let him abdicate the East, and reign without molestation in the West. If he refuse, the servants of the Lord will precipitate him from the throne." The reluctant Basil suspended the treaty, accepted the defiance, and led his army into the land of heresy, which he wasted with fire and sword. The open country of the Paulicians was exposed to the same calamities which they had inflicted; but when he had explored the strength of Tephrice, the multitude of the barbarians, and

---

[1] In the history of Chrysocheir, Genesius (Chron. p. 67-70, edit. Venet.) has exposed the nakedness of the empire. Constantine Porphyrogenitus (in Vit. Basil. c. 37-43, p. 166-171 [p. 266-276, ed. Bonn]) has displayed the glory of his grandfather. Cedrenus (p. 570-573 [tom. ii. p. 209-212, ed. Bonn]) is without their passions or their knowledge.

the ample magazines of arms and provisions, he desisted with a sigh from the hopeless siege.   On his return to Constantinople he laboured, by the foundation of convents and churches, to secure the aid of his celestial patrons, of Michael the archangel and the prophet Elijah; and it was his daily prayer that he might live to transpierce, with three arrows, the head of his impious adversary. Beyond his expectations, the wish was accomplished: after a successful inroad Chrysocheir was surprised and slain in his retreat; and the rebel's head was triumphantly presented at the foot of the throne.   On the reception of this welcome trophy, Basil instantly called for his bow, discharged three arrows with unerring aim, and accepted the applause of the court, who hailed the victory of the royal archer.   With Chrysocheir, the glory of the Paulicians faded and withered: [1] on the second expedition of the emperor, the impregnable Tephrice was deserted by the heretics, who sued for mercy or escaped to the borders.   The city was ruined, but the spirit of independence survived in the mountains: the Paulicians defended, above a century, their religion and liberty, infested the Roman limits, and maintained their perpetual alliance with the enemies of the empire and the Gospel.

About the middle of the eighth century, Constantine, surnamed Copronymus by the worshippers of images, had made an expedition into Armenia, and found, in the cities of Melitene and Theodosiopolis, a great number of Paulicians, his kindred heretics. As a favour, or punishment, he transplanted them from the banks of the Euphrates to Constantinople and Thrace; and by this emigration their doctrine was introduced and diffused in Europe.[2]   If the sectaries of the metropolis were soon mingled with the promiscuous mass, those of the country struck a deep root in a foreign soil.   The Paulicians of Thrace resisted the storms of persecution, maintained a secret correspondence with their Armenian brethren, and gave aid and comfort to their preachers, who solicited, not without success, the infant faith of the Bulgarians.[3]   In the tenth century they were restored and

---

[1] Συναπεμαράνθη πᾶσα ἡ ἀνθοῦσα τῆς Τεφρικῆς εὐανδρία [p. 212].   How elegant is the Greek tongue, even in the mouth of Cedrenus!

[2] Copronymus transported his συγγενεῖς, heretics; and thus ἐπλατύνθη ἡ αἵρεσις τῶν Παυλικιανῶν, says Cedrenus (p. 463 [tom. ii. p. 10, ed. Bonn]), who has copied the annals of Theophanes.

[3] Petrus Siculus, who resided nine months at Tephrice (A.D. 870) for the ransom of captives (p. 764), was informed of their intended mission, and addressed his preservative, the Historia Manichæorum, to the new archbishop of the Bulgarians (p. 754).

multiplied by a more powerful colony which John Zimisces [1] transported from the Chalybian hills to the valleys of Mount Hæmus. The Oriental clergy, who would have preferred the destruction, impatiently sighed for the absence, of the Manichæans: the warlike emperor had felt and esteemed their valour: their attachment to the Saracens was pregnant with mischief; but, on the side of the Danube, against the barbarians of Scythia, their service might be useful, and their loss would be desirable. Their exile in a distant land was softened by a free toleration: the Paulicians held the city of Philippopolis and the keys of Thrace; the Catholics were their subjects; the Jacobite emigrants their associates: they occupied a line of villages and castles in Macedonia and Epirus; and many native Bulgarians were associated to the communion of arms and heresy. As long as they were awed by power and treated with moderation, their voluntary bands were distinguished in the armies of the empire; and the courage of these *dogs*, ever greedy of war, ever thirsty of human blood, is noticed with astonishment, and almost with reproach, by the pusillanimous Greeks. The same spirit rendered them arrogant and contumacious: they were easily provoked by caprice or injury; and their privileges were often violated by the faithless bigotry of the government and clergy. In the midst of the Norman war, two thousand five hundred Manichæans deserted the standard of Alexius Comnenus,[2] and retired to their native homes. He dissembled till the moment of revenge; invited the chiefs to a friendly conference; and punished the innocent and guilty by imprisonment, confiscation, and baptism. In an interval of peace the emperor undertook the pious office of reconciling them to the church and state: his winter quarters were fixed at Philippopolis; and the thirteenth apostle, as he is styled by his pious daughter, consumed whole days and nights in theological controversy. His arguments were fortified, their obstinacy was melted, by the honours and rewards which he bestowed on the most eminent proselytes; and a new city, surrounded with gardens, enriched with immunities, and dignified with his own name, was founded by Alexius, for the residence of his vulgar converts. The important station of

[1] The colony of Paulicians and Jacobites transplanted by John Zimisces (A.D. 970) from Armenia to Thrace is mentioned by Zonaras (tom. ii. l. xvii. [c. 1] p. 209) and Anna Comnena (Alexiad, l. xiv. p. 450, etc. [ed. Pars 1651]).

[2] The Alexiad of Anna Comnena (l. v. p. 131 [t. i. p. 232, ed. Bonn], l. vi. p. 154, 155 [p. 272 *sq.*, ed. Bonn], l. xiv. p. 450-457 [ed. Par. 1651], with the Annotations of Ducange) records the transactions of her apostolic father with the Manichæans whose abominable heresy she was desirous of refuting.

Philippopolis was wrested from their hands; the contumacious leaders were secured in a dungeon, or banished from their country; and their lives were spared by the prudence, rather than the mercy, of an emperor, at whose command a poor and solitary heretic was burnt alive before the church of St. Sophia.[1] But the proud hope of eradicating the prejudices of a nation was speedily overturned by the invincible zeal of the Paulicians, who ceased to dissemble or refused to obey. After the departure and death of Alexius they soon resumed their civil and religious laws. In the beginning of the thirteenth century their pope or primate (a manifest corruption) resided on the confines of Bulgaria, Croatia, and Dalmatia, and governed by his vicars the filial congregations of Italy and France.[2] From that era a minute scrutiny might prolong and perpetuate the chain of tradition. At the end of the last age the sect or colony still inhabited the valleys of Mount Hæmus, where their ignorance and poverty were more frequently tormented by the Greek clergy than by the Turkish government. The modern Paulicians have lost all memory of their origin; and their religion is disgraced by the worship of the cross, and the practice of bloody sacrifice, which some captives have imported from the wilds of Tartary.[3]

In the West the first teachers of the Manichæan theology had been repulsed by the people or suppressed by the prince. The favour and success of the Paulicians in the eleventh and twelfth centuries must be imputed to the strong, though secret, discontent which armed the most pious Christians against the church of Rome. Her avarice was oppressive, her despotism odious: less degenerate perhaps than the Greeks in the worship of saints and images, her innovations were more rapid and scandalous: she had rigorously defined and imposed the doctrine of transubstantiation: the lives of the Latin clergy were more corrupt, and the Eastern bishops might pass for the successors of the apostles if they were compared with the lordly prelates who wielded by turns the crosier, the sceptre, and the sword. Three different roads might introduce the Paulicians into the heart of Europe. After the conversion of Hungary the pilgrims who visited Jerusalem might safely follow the course of the Danube: in their

---

[1] Basil, a monk, and the author of the Bogomiles, a sect of Gnostics who soon vanished (Anna Comnena, Alexiad, l. xv. p. 486-494 [ed. Par.]; Mosheim, Hist. Ecclesiastica, p. 420).

[2] Matt. Paris, Hist. Major, p. 267. This passage of our English historian is alleged by Ducange in an excellent note on Villehardouin (No. 208), who found the Paulicians at Philippopolis the friends of the Bulgarians.

[3] See Marsigli, Stato Militare dell' Imperio Ottomano, p. 24.

journey and return they passed through Philippopolis; and the sectaries, disguising their name and heresy, might accompany the French or German caravans to their respective countries. The trade and dominion of Venice pervaded the coast of the Adriatic, and the hospitable republic opened her bosom to foreigners of every climate and religion. Under the Byzantine standard the Paulicians were often transported to the Greek provinces of Italy and Sicily: in peace and war they freely conversed with strangers and natives, and their opinions were silently propagated in Rome, Milan, and the kingdoms beyond the Alps.[1] It was soon discovered that many thousand Catholics of every rank, and of either sex, had embraced the Manichæan heresy; and the flames which consumed twelve canons of Orleans was the first act and signal of persecution. The Bulgarians,[2] a name so innocent in its origin, so odious in its application, spread their branches over the face of Europe. United in common hatred of idolatry and Rome, they were connected by a form of episcopal and presbyterian government; their various sects were discriminated by some fainter or darker shades of theology; but they generally agreed in the two principles—the contempt of the Old Testament, and the denial of the body of Christ either on the cross or in the eucharist. A confession of simple worship and blameless manners is extorted from their enemies; and so high was their standard of perfection, that the increasing congregations were divided into two classes of disciples, of those who practised and of those who aspired. It was in the country of the Albigeois,[3] in the southern provinces of France, that the Pauli-

---

[1] The introduction of the Paulicians into Italy and France is amply discussed by Muratori (Antiquitat. Italiæ medii Ævi, tom. v. dissert. lx. p. 81-152) and Mosheim (p. 379-382, 419-422). Yet both have overlooked a curious passage of William the Apulian, who clearly describes them in a battle between the Greeks and Normans, A.D. 1040 (in Muratori, Script. Rerum Ital. tom. v. p. 256):

  Cum Græcis aderant quidam, quos pessimus error
  Fecerat amentes, et ab ipso nomen habebant.

But he is so ignorant of their doctrine as to make them a kind of Sabellians or Patripassians.

[2] *Bulgari, Boulgres, Bougres,* a national appellation, has been applied by the French as a term of reproach to usurers and unnatural sinners. The *Paterini,* or *Patelini,* has been made to signify a smooth and flattering hypocrite, such as *l'Avocat Patelin* of that original and pleasant farce (Ducange, Gloss. Latinitat. medii et infimi Ævi). The Manichæans were likewise named *Cathari,* or the pure, by corruption, *Gazari,* etc.

[3] Of the laws, crusade, and persecution against the Albigeois, a just, though general, idea is expressed by Mosheim (p. 477-481). The detail may be found in the ecclesiastical historians, ancient and modern, Catholics and Protestants; and among these Fleury is the most impartial and moderate.

cians were most deeply implanted; and the same vicissitudes of martyrdom and revenge which had been displayed in the neighbourhood of the Euphrates were repeated in the thirteenth century on the banks of the Rhône. The laws of the Eastern emperors were revived by Frederic the Second. The insurgents of Tephrice were represented by the barons and cities of Languedoc: Pope Innocent III. surpassed the sanguinary fame of Theodora. It was in cruelty alone that her soldiers could equal the heroes of the Crusades, and the cruelty of her priests was far excelled by the founders of the Inquisition [1]—an office more adapted to confirm than to refute the belief of an evil principle. The visible assemblies of the Paulicians, or Albigeois, were extirpated by fire and sword; and the bleeding remnant escaped by flight, concealment, or Catholic conformity. But the invincible spirit which they had kindled still lived and breathed in the Western world. In the state, in the church, and even in the cloister, a latent succession was preserved of the disciples of St. Paul, who protested against the tyranny of Rome, embraced the Bible as the rule of faith, and purified their creed from all the visions of the Gnostic theology. The struggles of Wickliff in England, of Huss in Bohemia, were premature and ineffectual; but the names of Zuinglius, Luther, and Calvin are pronounced with gratitude as the deliverers of nations.

A philosopher, who calculates the degree of their merit and the value of their reformation, will prudently ask from what articles of faith, *above* or *against* our reason, they have enfranchised the Christians; for such enfranchisement is doubtless a benefit so far as it may be compatible with truth and piety. After a fair discussion we shall rather be surprised by the timidity than scandalised by the freedom of our first reformers.[2] With the Jews, they adopted the belief and defence of all the Hebrew Scriptures, with all their prodigies, from the garden of Eden to the visions of the prophet Daniel; and they were bound, like the Catholics, to justify against the Jews the abolition of a divine

---

[1] The Acts (Liber Sententiarum) of the Inquisition of Toulouse (A.D. 1307-1323) have been published by Limborch (Amstelodami, 1692), with a previous History of the Inquisition in general. They deserved a more learned and critical editor. As we must not calumniate even Satan, or the Holy Office, I will observe that, of a list of criminals which fills nineteen folio pages, only fifteen men and four women were delivered to the secular arm.

[2] The opinions and proceedings of the reformers are exposed in the second part of the general history of Mosheim; but the balance, which he has held with so clear an eye and so steady a hand, begins to incline in favour of his Lutheran brethren.

law. In the great mysteries of the Trinity and Incarnation the reformers were severely orthodox: they freely adopted the theology of the four or the six first councils; and with the Athanasian creed they pronounced the eternal damnation of all who did not believe the Catholic faith. Transubstantiation, the invisible change of the bread and wine into the body and blood of Christ, is a tenet that may defy the power of argument and pleasantry; but instead of consulting the evidence of their senses, of their sight, their feeling, and their taste, the first Protestants were entangled in their own scruples, and awed by the words of Jesus in the institution of the sacrament. Luther maintained a *corporeal*, and Calvin a *real*, presence of Christ in the eucharist; and the opinion of Zuinglius, that it is no more than a spiritual communion, a simple memorial, has slowly prevailed in the reformed churches.[1] But the loss of one mystery was amply compensated by the stupendous doctrines of original sin, redemption, faith, grace, and predestination, which have been strained from the epistles of St. Paul. These subtle questions had most assuredly been prepared by the fathers and schoolmen; but the final improvement and popular use may be attributed to the first reformers, who enforced them as the absolute and essential terms of salvation. Hitherto the weight of supernatural belief inclines against the Protestants; and many a sober Christian would rather admit that a wafer is God than that God is a cruel and capricious tyrant.

Yet the services of Luther and his rivals are solid and important; and the philosopher must own his obligations to these fearless enthusiasts.[2] I. By their hands the lofty fabric of superstition, from the abuse of indulgences to the intercession of the Virgin, has been levelled with the ground. Myriads of both sexes of the monastic profession were restored to the liberty and labours of social life. A hierarchy of saints and angels, of imperfect and subordinate deities, were stripped of their temporal power, and reduced to the enjoyment of celestial happiness: their images and relics were banished from the church; and the credulity of the people was no longer nourished with the daily repetition of miracles and visions. The imitation of paganism

---

[1] Under Edward VI. our reformation was more bold and perfect: but in the fundamental articles of the church of England, a strong and explicit declaration against the real presence was obliterated in the original copy, to please the people, or the Lutherans, or Queen Elizabeth (Burnet's History of the Reformation, vol. ii. p. 82, 128, 302).

[2] "Had it not been for such men as Luther and myself," said the fanatic Whiston to Halley the philosopher, "you would now be kneeling before an image of St. Winifred."

was supplied by a pure and spiritual worship of prayer and thanksgiving, the most worthy of man, the least unworthy of the Deity. It only remains to observe whether such sublime simplicity be consistent with popular devotion; whether the vulgar, in the absence of all visible objects, will not be inflamed by enthusiasm or insensibly subside in languor and indifference. II. The chain of authority was broken, which restrains the bigot from thinking as he pleases, and the slave from speaking as he thinks: the popes, fathers, and councils were no longer the supreme and infallible judges of the world; and each Christian was taught to acknowledge no law but the Scriptures, no interpreter but his own conscience. This freedom, however, was the consequence rather than the design of the Reformation. The patriot reformers were ambitious of succeeding the tyrants whom they had dethroned. They imposed with equal rigour their creeds and confessions; they asserted the right of the magistrate to punish heretics with death. The pious or personal animosity of Calvin proscribed in Servetus [1] the guilt of his own rebellion; [2] and the flames of Smithfield, in which he was afterwards consumed, had been kindled for the Anabaptists by the zeal of Cranmer. [3] The nature of the tiger was the same, but he was gradually deprived of his teeth and fangs. A spiritual and temporal kingdom was possessed by the Roman pontiff: the Protestant doctors were subjects of a humble rank, without revenue or jurisdiction. *His* decrees were consecrated by the antiquity of the Catholic church; *their* arguments and disputes were submitted to the people; and their appeal to private judgment was accepted, beyond their wishes, by curiosity and enthusiasm. Since the days of Luther

---

[1] The article of *Servet* in the Dictionnaire Critique of Chauffepié is the best account which I have seen of this shameful transaction. See likewise the Abbé d'Artigny, Nouveaux Mémoires d'Histoire, etc., tom. ii. p. 55-154.

[2] I am more deeply scandalised at the single execution of Servetus than at the hecatombs which have blazed in the Auto da Fès of Spain and Portugal. 1. The zeal of Calvin seems to have been envenomed by personal malice, and perhaps envy. He accused his adversary before their common enemies, the judges of Vienne, and betrayed, for his destruction, the sacred trust of a private correspondence. 2. The deed of cruelty was not varnished by the pretence of danger to the church or state. In his passage through Geneva Servetus was a harmless stranger, who neither preached, nor printed, nor made proselytes. 3. A Catholic inquisitor yields the same obedience which he requires, but Calvin violated the golden rule of doing as he would be done by; a rule which I read in a moral treatise of Isocrates (in Nicocle, tom. i. p. 93, edit. Battie), four hundred years before the publication of the Gospel. Ἁ πάσχοντες ὑφ' ἑτέρων ὀργίζεσθε, ταῦτα τοῖς ἄλλοις μὴ ποιεῖτε.

[3] See Burnet, vol. ii. p. 84-86. The sense and humanity of the young king were oppressed by the authority of the primate.

and Calvin a secret reformation has been silently working in the bosom of the reformed churches; many weeds of prejudice were eradicated; and the disciples of Erasmus [1] diffused a spirit of freedom and moderation. The liberty of conscience has been claimed as a common benefit, an inalienable right: [2] the free governments of Holland [3] and England [4] introduced the practice of toleration; and the narrow allowance of the laws has been enlarged by the prudence and humanity of the times. In the exercise the mind has understood the limits of its powers, and the words and shadows that might amuse the child can no longer satisfy his manly reason. The volumes of controversy are overspread with cobwebs: the doctrine of a Protestant church is far removed from the knowledge or belief of its private members; and the forms of orthodoxy, the articles of faith, are subscribed with a sigh, or a smile, by the modern clergy. Yet the friends of Christianity are alarmed at the boundless impulse of inquiry and scepticism. The predictions of the Catholics are accomplished: the web of mystery is unravelled by the Arminians, Arians, and Socinians, whose numbers must not be computed from their separate congregations; and the pillars of Revelation are shaken by those men who preserve the name without the substance of religion, who indulge the licence without the temper of philosophy.[5]

[1] Erasmus may be considered as the father of rational theology. After a slumber of a hundred years, it was revived by the Arminians of Holland, Grotius, Limborch, and Le Clerc: in England by Chillingworth, the latitudinarians of Cambridge (Burnet, Hist. of own Times, vol. i. p. 261-268, octavo edition), Tillotson, Clarke, Hoadley, etc.

[2] I am sorry to observe that the three writers of the last age, by whom the rights of toleration have been so nobly defended, Bayle, Leibnitz, and Locke, are all laymen and philosophers.

[3] See the excellent chapter of Sir William Temple on the Religion of the United Provinces. I am not satisfied with Grotius (de Rebus Belgicis, Annal. l. i. p. 13, 14, edit. in 12mo), who approves the Imperial laws of persecution, and only condemns the bloody tribunal of the Inquisition.

[4] Sir William Blackstone (Commentaries, vol. iv. p. 53, 54) explains the law of England as it was fixed at the Revolution. The exceptions of Papists, and of those who deny the Trinity, would still leave a tolerable scope for persecution, if the national spirit were not more effectual than a hundred statutes.

[5] I shall recommend to public animadversion two passages in Dr. Priestley which betray the ultimate tendency of his opinions. At the first of these (Hist. of the Corruptions of Christianity, vol. i. p. 275, 276) the priest, at the second (vol. ii. p. 484) the magistrate, may tremble!

CHAPTER LV

The Bulgarians—Origin, Migrations, and Settlement of the Hungarians—
Their Inroads in the East and West—The Monarchy of Russia—
Geography and Trade—Wars of the Russians against the Greek
Empire—Conversion of the Barbarians

UNDER the reign of Constantine, the grandson of Heraclius, the
ancient barrier of the Danube, so often violated and so often
restored, was irretrievably swept away by a new deluge of barbarians. Their progress was favoured by the caliphs, their
unknown and accidental auxiliaries: the Roman legions were
occupied in Asia; and after the loss of Syria, Egypt, and Africa,
the Cæsars were twice reduced to the danger and disgrace of
defending their capital against the Saracens. If, in the account
of this interesting people, I have deviated from the strict and
original line of my undertaking, the merit of the subject will hide
my transgression, or solicit my excuse. In the East, in the West,
in war, in religion, in science, in their prosperity, and in their
decay, the Arabians press themselves on our curiosity: the first
overthrow of the church and empire of the Greeks may be imputed
to their arms; and the disciples of Mohammed still hold the civil
and religious sceptre of the Oriental world. But the same labour
would be unworthily bestowed on the swarms of savages who,
between the seventh and the twelfth century, descended from the
plains of Scythia, in transient inroad or perpetual emigration.[1]
Their names are uncouth, their origins doubtful, their actions
obscure, their superstition was blind, their valour brutal, and the
uniformity of their public and private lives was neither softened
by innocence nor refined by policy. The majesty of the Byzantine throne repelled and survived their disorderly attacks; the
greater part of these barbarians has disappeared without leaving
any memorial of their existence, and the despicable remnant
continues, and may long continue, to groan under the dominion
of a foreign tyrant. From the antiquities of, I. *Bulgarians*,
II. *Hungarians*, and, III. *Russians*, I shall content myself with
selecting such facts as yet deserve to be remembered. The con-

---

[1] *All* the passages of the Byzantine history which relate to the barbarians
are compiled, methodised, and transcribed, in a Latin version, by the
laborious John Gotthelf Stritter, in his "Memoriæ Populorum, ad Danu-
bium, Pontum Euxinum, Paludem Mæotidem, Caucasum, Mare Caspium,
et inde magis ad Septemtriones incolentium." Petropoli, 1771-1779; in
four tomes, or six volumes, in 4to. But the fashion has not enhanced the
price of these raw materials.

quests of the, IV. NORMANS, and the monarchy of the, V. TURKS, will naturally terminate in the memorable Crusades to the Holy Land and the double fall of the city and empire of Constantine.

I. In his march to Italy, Theodoric,[1] the Ostrogoth, had trampled on the arms of the Bulgarians. After this defeat the name and the nation are lost during a century and a half; and it may be suspected that the same or a similar appellation was revived by strange colonies from the Borysthenes, the Tanais, or the Volga. A king of the ancient Bulgaria [2] bequeathed to his five sons a last lesson of moderation and concord. It was received as youth has ever received the counsels of age and experience: the five princes buried their father; divided his subjects and cattle; forgot his advice; separated from each other; and wandered in quest of fortune, till we find the most adventurous in the heart of Italy, under the protection of the exarch of Ravenna.[3] But the stream of emigration was directed or impelled towards the capital. The modern Bulgaria, along the southern banks of the Danube, was stamped with the name and image which it has retained to the present hour: the new conquerors successively acquired, by war or treaty, the Roman provinces of Dardania, Thessaly, and the two Epirus'; [4] the ecclesiastical supremacy was translated from the native city of Justinian; and, in their prosperous age, the obscure town of Lychnidus, or Achrida, was honoured with the throne of a king and a patriarch.[5] The unquestionable evidence of language

---

[1] Hist. vol. v. p. 8.

[2] Theophanes, p. 296-299 [tom. i. p. 544-550, ed. Bonn]; Anastasius, p. 113; Nicephorus, C. P. p. 22, 23. Theophanes places the old Bulgaria on the banks of the Atell or Volga; but he deprives himself of all geographical credit by discharging that river into the Euxine Sea.

[3] Paul. Diacon. de Gestis Langobard. l. v. c. 29, p. 881, 882. The apparent difference between the Lombard historian and the abovementioned Greeks is easily reconciled by Camillo Pellegrino (de Ducatû Beneventano, dissert. vii. in the Scriptores Rerum Ital. tom. v. p. 186, 187) and Beretti (Chorograph. Italiæ medii Ævi. p. 273, etc.). This Bulgarian colony was planted in a vacant district of Samnium, and learned the Latin without forgetting their native language.

[4] These provinces of the Greek idiom and empire are assigned to the Bulgarian kingdom in the dispute of ecclesiastical jurisdiction between the patriarchs of Rome and Constantinople (Baronius, Annal. Eccles. A.D. 869, No. 75).

[5] The situation and royalty of Lychnidus, or Achrida, are clearly expressed in Cedrenus (p. 713 [tom. ii. p. 468, ed. Bonn]). The removal of an archbishop or patriarch from Justinianea prima to Lychnidus, and at length to Ternovo, has produced some perplexity in the ideas or language of the Greeks (Nicephorus Gregoras, l. ii. c. 2, p. 14, 15 [tom. i. p. 27, ed. Bonn]; Thomassin, Discipline de l'Eglise, tom. i. l. i. c. 19, 23); and a Frenchman (D'Anville) is more accurately skilled in the geography of their own country (Hist. de l'Académie des Inscriptions, tom. xxxi.).

attests the descent of the Bulgarians from the original stock of the Sclavonian, or more properly Slavonian, race;[1] and the kindred bands of Servians, Bosnians, Rascians, Croatians, Wallachians,[2] etc., followed either the standard or the example of the leading tribe. From the Euxine to the Adriatic, in the state of captives, or subjects, or allies, or enemies, of the Greek empire, they overspread the land; and the national appellation of the SLAVES [3] has been degraded by chance or malice from the signi-

---

[1] Chalcocondyles, a competent judge, affirms the identity of the language of the Dalmatians, Bosnians, Servians, *Bulgarians*, Poles (de Rebus Turcicis, l. x. p. 283 [ed. Par.; p. 530, ed. Bonn]), and elsewhere of the Bohemians (l. ii. p. 38 [p. 73, ed. Bonn]). The same author has marked the separate idiom of the Hungarians.

[The statement by Gibbon that the Bulgarians are Slavonic in origin is both incorrect and contradicts his own statement in chapter xlii., where he had correctly identified the Bulgarians and the Huns, as already proved by Zeuss, who has shown that they consequently belonged to the Turkish and not to the Slavonic race. In the sixth century several tribes of the Bulgarians were subject to the Avars, but in 634, Cubrat, a friend of the Romans, threw off the yoke of the Avars. A few years later (c. 670) the Bulgarians appear as enemies of the Romans, and to the great terror of Constantinople they crossed the Danube and, uniting themselves with the Slavonic inhabitants, founded the Bulgarian kingdom between the Danube and the Hæmus. The name of the conquerors still remains, but their language has long given way to that of the Slavonians. A portion of the Bulgarians remained in their earlier abodes to the eastward; and Theophanes, in a passage quoted by Gibbon, correctly places Old Bulgaria on the Etel or Atal or the Volga, the former being the name of this river in the Tartar language, while the latter probably comes from the Bulgarians. The Bulgarian kingdom on the Volga was called by the Russian historians "Great or Black Bulgaria," and the Danubian Bulgaria often took the name "Little or White Bulgaria." Great Bulgaria extended from the confluence of the Kama and the Volga to the shores of the Euxine and the Caspian. The ruins of its capital city, Bolgari, have been discovered in the province of Kasan on the banks of the Danube. In the tenth century the Bulgarians were Mohammedans, and attempted to convert the Czar Vladimir of Russia with his people to the religion of the prophet. The Bulgarians were frequently visited commercially by the Arabs, and they continued a powerful people until they were overwhelmed by the invasion of the Mongols. Cf. Zeuss, *Die Deutchen und die Nachbarstämme.*—O. S.]

[2] See the work of John Christopher de Jordan, de Originibus Sclavicis, Vindobonæ, 1745, in four parts, or two volumes in folio. His collections and researches are useful to elucidate the antiquities of Bohemia and the adjacent countries; but his plan is narrow, his style barbarous, his criticism shallow, and the Aulic counsellor is not free from the prejudices of a Bohemian.

[It is a mistake for Gibbon to assert that the Wallachians were of Slavonic origin, nor were they akin to the Servians, Bosnians, and other Slavonic tribes. They are a Romance people, of Illyrian origin, speaking a language derived from the Latin, like French, Italian, Spanish. They still call themselves Rumunjè—Roumanians.—O. S.]

[3] Jordan subscribes to the well-known and probable derivation from *Slava, laus, gloria*, a word of familiar use in the different dialects and parts of speech, and which forms the termination of the most illustrious names (de Originibus Sclavicis, pars i. p. 40, pars iv. p. 101, 102).

fication of glory to that of servitude.[1] Among these colonies, the Chrobatians,[2] or Croats, who now attend the motions of an Austrian army, are the descendants of a mighty people, the conquerors and sovereigns of Dalmatia. The maritime cities, and of these the infant republic of Ragusa, implored the aid and instructions of the Byzantine court: they were advised by the magnanimous Basil to reserve a small acknowledgment of their fidelity to the Roman empire, and to appease, by an annual tribute, the wrath of these irresistible barbarians. The kingdom of Croatia was shared by eleven *Zoupans*, or feudatory lords; and their united forces were numbered at sixty thousand horse and one hundred thousand foot. A long sea-coast, indented with capacious harbours, covered with a string of islands, and almost in sight of the Italian shores, disposed both the natives and strangers to the practice of navigation. The boats or brigantines of the Croats were constructed after the fashion of the old Liburnians: one hundred and eighty vessels may excite the idea of a respectable navy; but our seamen will smile at the allowance of ten, or twenty, or forty men, for each of these ships of war. They were gradually converted to the more honourable service of commerce; yet the Sclavonian pirates were still frequent and dangerous; and it was not before the close of the tenth century that the freedom and sovereignty of the Gulf were effectually vindicated by the Venetian republic.[3] The ancestors of these Dalmatian kings were equally removed from the use and abuse of navigation: they dwelt in the White Croatia, in the inland regions of Silesia and Little Poland, thirty days' journey, according to the Greek computation, from the sea of darkness.

The glory of the Bulgarians [4] was confined to a narrow scope

[1] This conversion of a national into an appellative name appears to have arisen in the eighth century, in the Oriental France, where the princes and bishops were rich in Sclavonian captives, not of the Bohemian (exclaims Jordan), but of Sorabian race. From thence the word was extended to general use, to the modern languages, and even to the style of the last Byzantines (see the Greek and Latin Glossaries of Ducange). The confusion of the Σερβλοι or Servians, with the Latin *Servi*, was still more fortunate and familiar (Constant. Porphyr. de Administrando Imperio, c. 32, p. 99 [tom. iii. p. 152, ed. Bonn]).

[2] The emperor Constantine Porphyrogenitus, most accurate for his own times, most fabulous for preceding ages, describes the Sclavonians of Dalmatia ([de Admin. Imp.] c. 29-36).

[3] See the anonymous Chronicle of the eleventh century, ascribed to John Sagorninus (p. 94-102), and that composed in the fourteenth by the Doge Andrew Dandolo (Script. Rerum Ital. tom. xii. p. 227-230)—the two oldest monuments of the history of Venice.

[4] The first kingdom of the Bulgarians may be found, under the proper dates, in the Annals of Cedrenus and Zonaras. The Byzantine materials

both of time and place. In the ninth and tenth centuries they reigned to the south of the Danube, but the more powerful nations that had followed their emigration repelled all return to the north and all progress to the west. Yet in the obscure catalogue of their exploits they might boast an honour which had hitherto been appropriated to the Goths, that of slaying in battle one of the successors of Augustus and Constantine. The emperor Nicephorus had lost his fame in the Arabian, he lost his life in the Sclavonian, war. In his first operations he advanced with boldness and success into the centre of Bulgaria, and burnt the *royal court*, which was probably no more than an edifice and village of timber. But while he searched the spoil and refused all offers of treaty, his enemies collected their spirits and their forces; the passes of retreat were insuperably barred, and the trembling Nicephorus was heard to exclaim, " Alas, alas! unless we could assume the wings of birds, we cannot hope to escape." Two days he waited his fate in the inactivity of despair, but, on the morning of the third, the Bulgarians surprised the camp, and the Roman prince, with the great officers of the empire, were slaughtered in their tents. The body of Valens had been saved from insult, but the head of Nicephorus was exposed on a spear, and his skull, enchased with gold, was often replenished in the feasts of victory. The Greeks bewailed the dishonour of the throne, but they acknowledged the just punishment of avarice and cruelty. This savage cup was deeply tinctured with the manners of the Scythian wilderness, but they were softened before the end of the same century by a peaceful intercourse with the Greeks, the possession of a cultivated region, and the introduction of the Christian worship. The nobles of Bulgaria were educated in the schools and palace of Constantinople, and Simeon,[1] a youth of the royal line, was instructed in the rhetoric of Demosthenes and the logic of Aristotle. He relinquished the profession of a monk for that of a king and warrior, and in his reign of more than forty years Bulgaria assumed a rank among the civilised powers of the earth. The Greeks, whom he repeatedly attacked, derived a faint consolation from indulging themselves in the reproaches of perfidy and sacrilege. They

are collected by Stritter (Memoriæ Populorum, tom. ii. pars. ii. p. 441-647); and the series of their kings is disposed and settled by Ducange (Fam. Byzant. p. 305-318).

[1] Simeonem semi-Græcum esse aiebant, eo quod à pueritiâ Byzantii Demosthenis rhetoricam et Aristotelis syllogismos didicerat. Liutprand, l. iii. c. 8. He says, in another place, Simeon, fortis bellator, Bulgariæ [Bulgaris] præerat; Christianus, sed vicinis Græcis valde inimicus (l. i. c. 2).

purchased the aid of the pagan Turks, but Simeon, in a second
battle, redeemed the loss of the first, at a time when it was
esteemed a victory to elude the arms of that formidable nation.
The Servians were overthrown, made captive, and dispersed;
and those who visited the country before their restoration could
discover no more than fifty vagrants, without women or children,
who extorted a precarious subsistence from the chase. On
classic ground, on the banks of the Achelöus, the Greeks were
defeated: their horn was broken by the strength of the barbaric
Hercules.[1] He formed the siege of Constantinople, and, in a
personal conference with the emperor, Simeon imposed the conditions of peace. They met with the most jealous precautions
the royal galley was drawn close to an artificial and well-fortified
platform, and the majesty of the purple was emulated by the
pomp of the Bulgarian. "Are you a Christian?" said the
humble Romanus; "it is your duty to abstain from the blood of
your fellow-Christians. Has the thirst of riches seduced you
from the blessings of peace? Sheathe your sword, open your
hand, and I will satiate the utmost measure of your desires."
The reconciliation was sealed by a domestic alliance; the freedom of trade was granted or restored; the first honours of the
court were secured to the friends of Bulgaria, above the ambassadors of enemies or strangers;[2] and her princes were dignified
with the high and invidious title of *Basileus*, or emperor. But
this friendship was soon disturbed: after the death of Simeon the
nations were again in arms, his feeble successors were divided and
extinguished, and, in the beginning of the eleventh century, the

[1]   —— Rigidum fera dextera cornu
    Dum tenet infregit, truncâque à fronte revellit.

Ovid (Metamorph. ix. 1-100) has boldly painted the combat of the river-
god and the hero—the native and the stranger.
[The place where the Greeks were overthrown by the Servians was not
on the banks of the Achelous in Greece, but at a place of the same name in
Bulgaria. Finlay, in his *Byzantine Empire*, says, "The name Achelous
seems to have misled Gibbon into a singular complication of errors."—O. S.]

[2] The ambassador of Otho was provoked by the Greek excuses, cum
Christophori filiam Petrus Bulgarorum *Vasileus* conjugem duceret, *Sym-
phona*, id est consonantia, scripto juramento firmata sunt, ut omnium
gentium *Apostolis*, id est nunciis, penes nos Bulgarorum Apostoli præ-
ponantur, honorentur, diligantur (Liutprand in Legatione, p. 482). See
the Ceremoniale of Constantine Porphyrogenitus, tom. i. p. 82 [p. 139, ed.
Bonn], tom. ii. p. 429, 430, 434, 435, 443, 444, 446, 447 [tom. i. p. 740-743,
749-752, 767, *sqq.*, ed. Bonn], with the annotations of Reiske.
[Before the time of Simeon, Bulgarian rulers were content with the title
"Knez." Simeon first assumed the title tsar (from tsesar—Cæsar). It
may be remembered that Terbel had been made a Cæsar by Justinian II.
The archbishopric of Bulgaria had been raised to the dignity of a patri-
archate. Simeon's residence was Great Peristhlava.—O. S.]

second Basil, who was born in the purple, deserved the appellation of conqueror of the Bulgarians. His avarice was in some measure gratified by a treasure of four hundred thousand pounds sterling (ten thousand pounds weight of gold), which he found in the palace of Lychnidus. His cruelty inflicted a cool and exquisite vengeance on fifteen thousand captives who had been guilty of the defence of their country. They were deprived of sight, but to one of each hundred a single eye was left, that he might conduct his blind century to the presence of their king. Their king is said to have expired of grief and horror; the nation was awed by this terrible example; the Bulgarians were swept away from their settlements, and circumscribed within a narrow province; the surviving chiefs bequeathed to their children the advice of patience and the duty of revenge.

II. When the black swarm of Hungarians first hung over Europe, about nine hundred years after the Christian era, they were mistaken by fear and superstition for the Gog and Magog of the Scriptures, the signs and forerunners of the end of the world.[1] Since the introduction of letters they have explored their own antiquities with a strong and laudable impulse of patriotic curiosity.[2] Their rational criticism can no longer be amused with a vain pedigree of Attila and the Huns: but they complain that their primitive records have perished in the Tartar war; that the truth or fiction of their rustic songs is long since forgotten; and that the fragments of a rude chronicle[3] must be painfully reconciled with the contemporary though foreign

[1] A bishop of Wurtzburg submitted this opinion to a reverend abbot; but *he* more gravely decided that Gog and Magog were the spiritual persecutors of the church; since Gog signifies the roof, the pride of the heresiarchs, and Magog what comes from, the roof, the propagation of their sects. Yet these men once commanded the respect of mankind (Fleury, Hist. Eccles. tom. xi. p. 594, etc.).

[2] The two national authors from whom I have derived the most assistance are George Pray (Dissertationes ad Annales veterum Hungarorum, etc., Vindobonæ, 1775, in folio) and Stephen Katona (Hist. Critica Ducum et Regum Hungariæ stirpis Arpadianæ, Pæstini, 1778-1781, 5 vols. in octavo). The first embraces a large and often conjectural space; the latter, by his learning, judgment, and perspicuity, deserves the name of a critical historian.

[3] The author of this Chronicle is styled the notary of king Bela. Katona has assigned him to the twelfth century, and defends his character against the hypercriticism of Pray. This rude annalist must have transcribed some historical records, since he could affirm with dignity, rejectis falsis fabulis rusticorum, et garrulo cantû joculatorum. In the fifteenth century these fables were collected by Thurotzius, and embellished by the Italian Bonfinius. See the Preliminary Discourse in the Hist. Critica Ducum, p. 7-33.

intelligence of the Imperial geographer.[1] *Magyar* is the national and oriental denomination of the Hungarians; but, among the tribes of Scythia, they are distinguished by the Greeks under the proper and peculiar name of *Turks*, as the descendants of that mighty people who had conquered and reigned from China to the Volga. The Pannonian colony preserved a correspondence of trade and amity with the eastern Turks on the confines of Persia; and after a separation of three hundred and fifty years the missionaries of the king of Hungary discovered and visited their ancient country near the banks of the Volga. They were hospitably entertained by a people of pagans and savages who still bore the name of Hungarians; conversed in their native tongue, recollected a tradition of their long-lost brethren, and listened with amazement to the marvellous tale of their new kingdom and religion. The zeal of conversion was animated by the interest of consanguinity, and one of the greatest of their princes had formed the generous, though fruitless, design of replenishing the solitude of Pannonia by this domestic colony from the heart of Tartary.[2] From this primitive country they were driven to the West by the tide of war and emigration, by the weight of the more distant tribes, who at the same time were fugitives and conquerors. Reason or fortune directed their course towards the frontiers of the Roman empire; they halted in the usual stations along the banks of the great rivers; and in the territories of Moscow, Kiow, and Moldavia, some vestiges have been discovered of their temporary residence. In this long and various peregrination they could not always escape the dominion of the stronger, and the purity of their blood was improved or sullied by the mixture of a foreign race; from a motive of compulsion or choice, several tribes of the Chazars were associated to the standard of their ancient vassals, introduced the use of a second language, and obtained by their superior renown the most honourable place in the front of battle. The military force of the Turks and their allies marched in seven equal and artificial divisions: each division was formed of thirty thousand eight hundred and fifty-seven warriors, and the proportion of women, children, and servants supposes and requires at least a million of emigrants.

---

[1] See Constantine de Administrando Imperio, c. 3, 4, 13, 38-42. Katona has nicely fixed the composition of this work to the years 949, 950, 951 (p. 4-7). The critical historian (p. 34-107) endeavours to prove the existence, and to relate the actions, of a first duke *Almus*, the father of Arpad, who is tacitly rejected by Constantine.

[2] Pray (Dissert. p. 37-39, etc.) produces and illustrates the original passages of the Hungarian missionaries, Bonfinius and Æneas Sylvius.

Their public counsels were directed by seven *vayvods*, or hereditary chiefs; but the experience of discord and weakness recommended the more simple and vigorous administration of a single
person. The sceptre, which had been declined by the modest
Lebedias, was granted to the birth or merit of Almus and his son
Arpad, and the authority of the supreme khan of the Chazars
confirmed the engagement of the prince and people; of the
people to obey his commands, of the prince to consult their
happiness and glory.

With this narrative we might be reasonably content, if the
penetration of modern learning had not opened a new and larger
prospect of the antiquities of nations. The Hungarian language
stands alone, and as it were insulated, among the Sclavonian
dialects; but it bears a close and clear affinity to the idioms of
the Fennic race,[1] of an obsolete and savage race, which formerly
occupied the northern regions of Asia and Europe. The genuine
appellation of *Ugri* or *Igours* is found on the western confines of
China;[2] their migration to the banks of the Irtish is attested by
Tartar evidence;[3] a similar name and language are detected in

---

[1] Fischer, in the Quæstiones Petropolitanæ, de Origine Ungrorum, and
Pray, Dissertat. i. ii. iii., etc., have drawn up several comparative tables of
the Hungarian with the Fennic dialects. The affinity is indeed striking,
but the lists are short; the words are purposely chosen; and I read in the
learned Bayer (Comment. Academ. Petropol. tom. x. p. 374) that, although
the Hungarian has adopted many Fennic words (innumeras voces), it
essentially differs toto genio et naturâ.

[The question which Gibbon discusses is whether—Are the Hungarians
Turkish or Finnic? Their language manifests the elements of both
tongues. Those who advocate a Turkish origin explain the presence of
the Finnic element in the vocabulary by a prolonged residence in the
vicinity of the Voguls and the Ostiaks; while those who support the
Finnic hypothesis explain the Turkish element by local borrowing by the
way during their migrations. It is unquestionable that Hungarian has
many points of affinity with Vogul, Ostiak, and kindred tongues. The
Magyar at one time lived in Jugria near the Irtish, where they were the
neighbours of the Voguls. In the eighth century they migrated southward, and early in the ninth were living with the empire of the Chazars,
where they absorbed a tribe named the Kabars, who became part of the
Hungarians. These Kabars (says Constantine Porphyrogenitus) taught
the Hungarians the Chazaric tongue. Hence the upholders of a Finnic
origin of the Turks can explain the Turkish element in Hungary by a
known cause, the coalition with the Kabars.

The original Magyars seem to have been, like the Kabars, a Turkish tribe
which coalesced with the Finnic Ugrians or Hungarians. Ugria is called
Great Hungary by the Franciscan monk Piano Carpini, who travelled in
1426 to the court of the Great Khan.—O. S.]

[2] In the region of Turfan, which is clearly and minutely described by
the Chinese Geographers (Gaubil, Hist. du Grand Gengiscan, p. 13; De
Guignes, Hist. des Huns, tom. ii. p. 31, etc.).

[3] Hist. Généalogique des Tartars, par Abulghazi Bahadur Khan, partie
ii. p. 90-98.

the southern parts of Siberia;[1] and the remains of the Fennic tribes are widely, though thinly, scattered from the sources of the Oby to the shores of Lapland.[2] The consanguinity of the Hungarians and Laplanders would display the powerful energy of climate on the children of a common parent; the lively contrast between the bold adventurers who are intoxicated with the wines of the Danube, and the wretched fugitives who are immersed beneath the snows of the polar circle. Arms and freedom have ever been the ruling, though too often the unsuccessful, passion of the Hungarians, who are endowed by nature with a vigorous constitution of soul and body.[3] Extreme cold has diminished the stature and congealed the faculties of the Laplanders; and the Arctic tribes, alone among the sons of men, are ignorant of war and unconscious of human blood: a happy ignorance, if reason and virtue were the guardians of their peace![4]

It is the observation of the Imperial author of the Tactics,[5] that all the Scythian hordes resembled each other in their pastoral and military life, that they all practised the same means of subsistence, and employed the same instruments of destruction. But he adds that the two nations of Bulgarians and Hungarians were superior to their brethren, and similar to each other, in the improvements, however rude, of their discipline and government: their visible likeness determines Leo to confound

---

[1] In their journey to Pekin, both Isbrand Ives (Harris's Collection of Voyages and Travels, vol. ii. p. 920, 921) and Bell (Travels, vol. i. p. 174) found the Vogulitz in the neighbourhood of Tobolsky. By the tortures of the etymological art, *Ugur* and *Vogul* are reduced to the same name; the circumjacent mountains really bear the appellation of *Ugrian ;* and of all the Fennic dialects, the Vogulian is the nearest to the Hungarian (Fischer, Dissert. i. p. 20-30; Pray, Dissert. ii. p. 31-34).

[2] The eight tribes of the Fennic race are described in the curious work of M. Levêque (Hist. des Peuples soumis à la Domination de la Russie, tom. i. p. 361-561).

[3] This picture of the Hungarians and Bulgarians is chiefly drawn from the Tactics of Leo, p. 796-801, and the Latin Annals, which are alleged by Baronius, Pagi, and Muratori, A.D. 889, etc.

[4] Buffon, Hist. Naturelle, tom. v. p. 6, in 12mo. Gustavus Adolphus attempted, without success, to form a regiment of Laplanders. Grotius says of these Arctic tribes, arma arcus et pharetra, sed adversus feras (Annal. l. iv. p. 236); and attempts, after the manner of Tacitus, to varnish with philosophy their brutal ignorance.

[5] Leo has observed that the government of the Turks was monarchical, and that their punishments were rigorous. (Tactic. p. 796 [c. xviii. § 46] ἀπεινεῖς καὶ βαρείας). Rhegino (in Chron. A.D. 889) mentions theft as a capital crime, and his jurisprudence is confirmed by the original code of St. Stephen (A.D. 1016). If a slave were guilty, he was chastised, for the first time, with the loss of his nose, or a fine of five heifers; for the second, with the loss of his ears, or a similar fine; for the third, with death; which the freeman did not incur till the fourth offence, as his first penalty was the loss of liberty (Katona, Hist. Regum Hungar. tom. i. p. 231, 232).

his friends and enemies in one common description; and the picture may be heightened by some strokes from their contemporaries of the tenth century. Except the merit and fame of military prowess, all that is valued by mankind appeared vile and contemptible to these barbarians, whose native fierceness was stimulated by the consciousness of numbers and freedom. The tents of the Hungarians were of leather, their garments of fur; they shaved their hair and scarified their faces: in speech they were slow, in action prompt, in treaty perfidious; and they shared the common reproach of barbarians, too ignorant to conceive the importance of truth, too proud to deny or palliate the breach of their most solemn engagements. Their simplicity has been praised; yet they abstained only from the luxury they had never known: whatever they saw they coveted; their desires were insatiate, and their sole industry was the hand of violence and rapine. By the definition of a pastoral nation I have recalled a long description of the economy, the warfare, and the government that prevail in that state of society; I may add, that to fishing as well as to the chase the Hungarians were indebted for a part of their subsistence; and since they *seldom* cultivated the ground, they must, at least in their new settlements, have sometimes practised a slight and unskilful husbandry. In their emigrations, perhaps in their expeditions, the host was accompanied by thousands of sheep and oxen, which increased the cloud of formidable dust, and afforded a constant and wholesome supply of milk and animal food. A plentiful command of forage was the first care of the general; and if the flocks and herds were secure of their pastures, the hardy warrior was alike insensible of danger and fatigue. The confusion of men and cattle that overspread the country exposed their camp to a nocturnal surprise, had not a still wider circuit been occupied by their light cavalry, perpetually in motion to discover and delay the approach of the enemy. After some experience of the Roman tactics, they adopted the use of the sword and spear, the helmet of the soldier, and the iron breastplate of his steed: but their native and deadly weapon was the Tartar bow: from the earliest infancy their children and servants were exercised in the double science of archery and horsemanship; their arm was strong; their aim was sure; and in the most rapid career they were taught to throw themselves backwards, and to shoot a volley of arrows into the air. In open combat, in secret ambush, in flight, or pursuit, they were equally formidable: an appearance of order was maintained in the foremost ranks, but their charge was driven forwards by the impatient pressure of succeeding crowds. They pursued, headlong and rash, with loosened reins and horrific outcries; but, if they fled, with real or dissembled fear, the ardour of a pursuing foe was checked and chastised by the same habits of irregular speed and sudden evolution. In the abuse of victory they astonished Europe, yet smarting from the wounds of the Saracen and the Dane: mercy they rarely asked, and more rarely bestowed: both sexes were accused as equally inaccessible to pity; and their appetite for raw flesh might countenance the popular tale that they drank the blood and feasted on the hearts of the slain. Yet the Hungarians were not devoid of those principles of justice and humanity which nature has implanted in every bosom. The licence of public and private injuries was restrained by laws and punishments; and in the security of an open camp, theft is the most tempting and most dangerous offence. Among the barbarians there were many whose spontaneous virtue supplied their laws and corrected their manners, who performed the duties, and sympathised with the affections, of social life.

After a long pilgrimage of flight or victory, the Turkish hordes approached the common limits of the French and Byzantine empires. Their first conquests and final settlements extended on either side of the Danube above Vienna, below Belgrade, and beyond the measure of the Roman province of Pannonia, or the modern kingdom of Hungary.[1] That ample and fertile land was loosely occupied by the Moravians, a Sclavonian name and tribe, which were driven by the invaders into the compass of a narrow province. Charlemagne had stretched a vague and nominal empire as far as the edge of Transylvania; but, after the failure of his legitimate line, the dukes of Moravia forgot their obedience and tribute to the monarchs of Oriental France. The bastard Arnulph was provoked to invite the arms of the Turks: they rushed through the real or figurative wall which his indiscretion had thrown open; and the king of Germany has been justly reproached as a traitor to the civil and ecclesiastical society of the Christians. During the life of Arnulph the Hungarians were checked by gratitude or fear; but in the infancy of his son Lewis they discovered and invaded Bavaria; and such was their Scythian speed, that in a single day a circuit of fifty miles was stripped and consumed. In the battle of Augsburg the Christians maintained their advantage till the seventh hour

---

[1] See Katona, Hist. Ducum Hungar. p. 321-352.

of the day: they were deceived and vanquished by the flying stratagems of the Turkish cavalry. The conflagration spread over the provinces of Bavaria, Swabia, and Franconia; and the Hungarians[1] promoted the reign of anarchy by forcing the stoutest barons to discipline their vassals and fortify their castles.

The origin of walled towns is ascribed to this calamitous period; nor could any distance be secure against an enemy who, almost at the same instant, laid in ashes the Helvetian monastery of St. Gall, and the city of Bremen on the shores of the northern ocean. Above thirty years the Germanic empire, or kingdom, was subject to the ignominy of tribute; and resistance was disarmed by the menace, the serious and effectual menace, of dragging the women and children into captivity, and of slaughtering the males above the age of ten years. I have neither power nor inclination to follow the Hungarians beyond the Rhine; but I must observe with surprise that the southern provinces of France were blasted by the tempest, and that Spain, behind her Pyrenees, was astonished at the approach of these formidable strangers.[2] The vicinity of Italy had tempted their early inroads; but from their camp on the Brenta they beheld with some terror the apparent strength and populousness of the new-discovered country. They requested leave to retire; their request was proudly rejected by the Italian king; and the lives of twenty thousand Christians paid the forfeit of his obstinacy and rashness. Among the cities of the West the royal Pavia was conspicuous in fame and splendour; and the pre-eminence of Rome itself was only derived from the relics of the apostles. The Hungarians appeared; Pavia was in flames; forty-three churches were consumed; and, after the massacre of the people, they spared about two hundred wretches who had gathered some bushels of gold and silver (a vague exaggeration) from the smoking ruins of their country. In these annual excursions from the Alps to the neighbourhood of Rome and Capua, the churches that yet escaped resounded with a fearful litany: " Oh! save and deliver us from the arrows of

---

[1] Hungarorum gens, cujus omnes fere nationes expertæ sævitiam, etc., is the preface of Liutprand (l. i. c. 2), who frequently expatiates on the calamities of his own times. See l. i. c. 5, l. ii. c. 1, 2, 4, 5, 6, 7, l. iii. c. 1, etc., l. v. c. 8, 15, in Legat. p. 485. His colours are glaring, but his chronology must be rectified by Pagi and Muratori.

[2] The three bloody reigns of Arpad, Zoltan, and Toxus are critically illustrated by Katona (Hist. Ducum, etc., p. 107-499). His diligence has searched both natives and foreigners; yet to the deeds of mischief, or glory, I have been able to add the destruction of Bremen (Adam Bremensis, i. 43).

the Hungarians!" But the saints were deaf or inexorable; and the torrent rolled forwards, till it was stopped by the extreme land of Calabria.[1] A composition was offered and accepted for the head of each Italian subject; and ten bushels of silver were poured forth in the Turkish camp. But falsehood is the natural antagonist of violence; and the robbers were defrauded both in the numbers of the assessment and the standard of the metal. On the side of the East the Hungarians were opposed in doubtful conflict by the equal arms of the Bulgarians, whose faith forbade an alliance with the pagans, and whose situation formed the barrier of the Byzantine empire. The barrier was overturned; the emperor of Constantinople beheld the waving banners of the Turks; and one of their boldest warriors presumed to strike a battle-axe into the golden gate. The arts and treasures of the Greeks diverted the assault; but the Hungarians might boast in their retreat that they had imposed a tribute on the spirit of Bulgaria and the majesty of the Cæsars.[2] The remote and rapid operations of the same campaign appear to magnify the power and numbers of the Turks; but their courage is most deserving of praise, since a light troop of three or four hundred horse would often attempt and execute the most daring inroads to the gates of Thessalonica and Constantinople. At this disastrous era of the ninth and tenth centuries, Europe was afflicted by a triple scourge from the North, the East, and the South: the Norman, the Hungarian, and the Saracen sometimes trod the same ground of desolation; and these savage foes might have been compared

---

[1] Muratori has considered with patriotic care the danger and resources of Modena. The citizens besought St. Germinianus, their patron, to avert, by his intercession, the *rabies, flagellum*, etc.

> Nunc te rogamus, licet servi pessimi,
> Ab Ungerorum nos defendas jaculis.

The bishop erected walls for the public defence, not contra dominos serenos (Antiquitat. Ital. med. Ævi, tom. i. dissertat. i. p. 21, 22), and the song of the nightly watch is not without elegance or use (tom. iii. diss. xl. p. 709). The Italian annalist has accurately traced the series of their inroads (Annali d'Italia, tom. vii. p. 365, 367, 393, 401, 437, 440; tom. viii. p. 19, 41, 52, etc.).

[2] Both the Hungarian and Russian annals suppose that they besieged, or attacked, or insulted Constantinople (Pray, dissertat. x. p. 239; Katona, Hist. Ducum, p. 354-360); and the fact is *almost* confessed by the Byzantine historians (Leo Grammaticus, p. 506 [ed. Par.; p. 322, ed. Bonn]; Cedrenus, tom. ii. p. 629 [tom. ii. p. 316, ed. Bonn]); yet, however glorious to the nation, it is denied or doubted by the critical historian, and even by the notary of Bela. Their scepticism is meritorius; they could not safely transcribe or believe the rusticorum fabulas; but Katona might have given due attention to the evidence of Liutprand, Bulgarorum gentem atque *Græcorum* tributariam fecerant (Hist. l. ii. c. 4, p. 435).

by Homer to the two lions growling over the carcase of a mangled stag.[1]

The deliverance of Germany and Christendom was achieved by the Saxon princes Henry the Fowler and Otho the Great, who, in two memorable battles, for ever broke the power of the Hungarians.[2] The valiant Henry was roused from a bed of sickness by the invasion of his country, but his mind was vigorous and his prudence successful. " My companions," said he, on the morning of the combat, "maintain your ranks, receive on your bucklers the first arrows of the pagans, and prevent their second discharge by the equal and rapid career of your lances." They obeyed and conquered; and the historical picture of the castle of Merseburgh expressed the features, or at least the character, of Henry, who, in an age of ignorance, intrusted to the finer arts the perpetuity of his name.[3] At the end of twenty years the children of the Turks who had fallen by his sword invaded the empire of his son, and their force is defined, in the lowest estimate, at one hundred thousand horse. They were invited by domestic faction; the gates of Germany were treacherously unlocked, and they spread, far beyond the Rhine and the Meuse, into the heart of Flanders. But the vigour and prudence of Otho dispelled the conspiracy; the princes were made sensible that, unless they were true to each other, their religion and country were irrecoverably lost, and the national powers were reviewed in the plains of Augsburg. They marched and fought in eight legions, according to the division of provinces and tribes: the first, second, and

---

[1] ———— λέονθ' ὡς, δηρινθήτην,

 Ὥτ' ὄρεος κορυφῇσι περὶ κταμένης ἐλάφοιο,

 Ἄμφω πεινάοντε, μέγα φρονέοντε μάχεσθον.—Iliad. xvi. 756.

[2] They are amply and critically discussed by Katona (Hist. Ducum, p. 360-368, 427-470). Liutprand (l. ii. c. 8, 9) is the best evidence for the former, and Witichind (Annal. Saxon. l. iii.) of the latter; but the critical historian will not even overlook the horn of a warrior, which is said to be preserved at Jaz-berin.

[3] Hunc vero triumphum, tam laude quam memoriâ dignum, ad Meresburgum rex in superiori cœnaculo domûs per ζωγραφίαν, id est, picturam, notari præcepit, adeo ut rem veram potius quam verisimilem videas: a high encomium (Liutprand, l. ii. c. 9). Another palace in Germany had been painted with holy subjects by the order of Charlemagne; and Muratori may justly affirm, nulla sæcula fuere in quibus pictores desiderati fuerint (Antiquitat. Ital. medii Ævi, tom. ii. dissert. xxiv. p. 360, 361). Our domestic claims to antiquity of ignorance and original imperfection (Mr. Walpole's lively words) are of a much more recent date (Anecdotes of Painting, vol. i. p. 2, etc.).

[The battle is usually named the battle of Merseburg, but it took place at Riada, and Riada, in all likelihood, corresponds to Rietteburg at the confluence of the rivers Unstrut and Helme.—O. S.]

third were composed of Bavarians, the fourth of Franconians, the fifth of Saxons under the immediate command of the monarch, the sixth and seventh consisted of Swabians, and the eighth legion, of a thousand Bohemians, closed the rear of the host. The resources of discipline and valour were fortified by the arts of superstition, which, on this occasion, may deserve the epithets of generous and salutary. The soldiers were purified with a fast, the camp was blessed with the relics of saints and martyrs, and the Christian hero girded on his side the sword of Constantine, grasped the invincible spear of Charlemagne, and waved the banner of St. Maurice, the præfect of the Thebæan legion. But his firmest confidence was placed in the holy lance,[1] whose point was fashioned of the nails of the cross, and which his father had extorted from the king of Burgundy by the threats of war and the gift of a province. The Hungarians were expected in the front; they secretly passed the Lech, a river of Bavaria that falls into the Danube, turned the rear of the Christian army, plundered the baggage, and disordered the legions of Bohemia and Swabia. The battle was restored by the Franconians, whose duke, the valiant Conrad, was pierced with an arrow as he rested from his fatigues; the Saxons fought under the eyes of their king, and his victory surpassed, in merit and importance, the triumphs of the last two hundred years. The loss of the Hungarians was still greater in the flight than in the action; they were encompassed by the rivers of Bavaria, and their past cruelties excluded them from the hope of mercy. Three captive princes were hanged at Ratisbon, the multitude of prisoners was slain or mutilated, and the fugitives who presumed to appear in the face of their country were condemned to everlasting poverty and disgrace.[2] Yet the spirit of the nation was humbled, and the most accessible passes of Hungary were fortified with a ditch and rampart. Adversity suggested the counsels of moderation and peace: the robbers of the West acquiesced in a sedentary life; and the next generation was taught, by a discerning prince, that far more might be gained by multiplying and exchanging the produce of a fruitful soil. The native race, the Turkish or Fennic blood, was mingled with new colonies of Scythian or Sclavonian origin:[3] many thousands of robust and industrious

---

[1] See Baronius, Annal. Eccles., A.D. 929, No. 2-5. The lance of Christ is taken from the best evidence—Liutprand (l. iv. c. 12), Sigebert, and the Acts of St. Gerard; but the other military relics depend on the faith of the Gesta Anglorum post Bedam, l. ii. c. 8.

[2] Katona, Hist. Ducum Hungariæ, p. 500, etc.

[3] Among these colonies we may distinguish—1. The Chazars, or Cabari,

captives had been imported from all the countries of Europe;[1] and after the marriage of Geisa with a Bavarian princess, he bestowed honours and estates on the nobles of Germany.[2] The son of Geisa was invested with the regal title, and the house of Arpad reigned three hundred years in the kingdom of Hungary. But the freeborn barbarians were not dazzled by the lustre of the diadem, and the people asserted their indefeasible right of choosing, deposing, and punishing the hereditary servant of the state.

III. The name of RUSSIANS[3] was first divulged, in the ninth century, by an embassy from Theophilus, emperor of the East, to

who joined the Hungarians on their march (Constant. de Admin. Imp. c. 39, 40, p. 108, 109 [tom. iii. p. 171, *seqq.*, ed. Bonn]). 2. The Jazyges, Moravians, and Siculi, whom they found in the land; the last were *perhaps* a remnant of the Huns of Attila, and were intrusted with the guard of the borders. 3. The Russians, who, like the Swiss in France, imparted a general name to the royal porters. 4. The Bulgarians, whose chiefs (A.D. 956) were invited, cum magnâ multitudine *Hismahelitarum*. Had any of these Sclavonians embraced the Mohammedan religion? 5. The Bisseni and Cumans, a mixed multitude of Patzinacites, Uzi, Chazars, etc., who had spread to the lower Danube. The last colony of 40,000 Cumans, A.D. 1239, was received and converted by the kings of Hungary, who derived from that tribe a new regal appellation (Pray, dissert. vi. vii. p. 109-173; Katona, Hist. Ducum, p. 95-99, 259-264, 476, 479-483, etc.).

[The Jazyges, Moravians, and Siculi. The first named must not be confounded with the earlier Sarmatian people of this name. They were a division of the Cumanians called by the Hungarian Jaszok (from singular *jasz*, archers, whence their name Jazyges): they dwelt on the right bank of the Theiss. The Siculi were probably the remnant of the Huns of Attila. The Hismahelitæ must have been Mohammedans, as Gibbon conjectures. They were probably Baschkirs who had settled in Bulgaria. The Bisseni is the name given by the Hungarian chroniclers to the Turkish tribe of the Petcheneges, called Πατζινακῖται by Constantine Porphyrogenitus, and Peczenjezi by the Slavonians. The Cumani, afterwards called Kiptschahs, were the people named Uzi by Constan. Porphyr. They are called Gusses, or Goss, by Arabian writers. The Uzi or Cumani were also Turks and spoke the same language as the Petcheneges. At a later period these two peoples were found in possession of the whole country to the northward of the Euxine.—O. S.]

[1] Christiani autem, quorum pars major populi est, qui ex omni parte mundi illuc tracti sunt captivi, etc. Such was the language of Piligrinus, the first missionary who entered Hungary, A.D. 973. Pars major is strong. Hist. Ducum, p. 517.

[2] The fideles Teutonici of Geisa are authenticated in old charters; and Katona, with his usual industry, has made a fair estimate of these colonies, which had been so loosely magnified by the Italian Ranzanus (Hist. Critic Ducum, p. 667-681).

[3] Among the Greeks, this national appellation has a singular form, ῾Ρῶς, as an undeclinable word, of which many fanciful etymologies have been suggested. I have perused, with pleasure and profit, a dissertation de Origine Russorum (Comment. Academ. Petropolitanæ, tom. viii. p. 388-436) by Theophilus Sigefrid Bayer, a learned German, who spent his life and labours in the service of Russia. A geographical tract of D'Anville, de l'Empire de Russie, son Origine, et ses Accroissemens (Paris, 1772, in 12mo), has likewise been of use.

the emperor of the West, Lewis, the son of Charlemagne. The Greeks were accompanied by the envoys of the great duke, or chagan, or *czar*, of the Russians. In their journey to Constantinople they had traversed many hostile nations, and they hoped to escape the dangers of their return by requesting the French monarch to transport them by sea to their native country. A closer examination detected their origin: they were the brethren of the Swedes and Normans, whose name was already odious and formidable in France; and it might justly be apprehended that these Russian strangers were not the messengers of peace, but the emissaries of war. They were detained, while the Greeks were dismissed; and Lewis expected a more satisfactory account, that he might obey the laws of hospitality or prudence according to the interest of both empires.[1] This Scandinavian origin of the people, or at least the princes, of Russia, may be confirmed and illustrated by the national annals [2] and the general history of the North. The Normans, who had so long been concealed by a veil of impenetrable darkness, suddenly burst forth in the spirit of naval and military enterprise. The vast, and, as it is said, the populous, regions of Denmark, Sweden, and Norway were crowded with independent chieftains and desperate adventurers, who sighed in the laziness of peace, and smiled in the agonies of death. Piracy was the exercise, the trade, the glory, and the virtue of the Scandinavian youth. Impatient of a bleak climate and narrow limits, they started from the banquet, grasped their arms, sounded their horn, ascended their vessels, and explored every coast that promised either spoil or settlement. The Baltic was the first scene of their naval achievements; they visited the eastern shores, the silent residence of Fennic and Sclavonian tribes; and the primitive Russians of the lake Ladoga paid a tribute, the skins of white squirrels, to these strangers, whom they saluted with the title of *Varangians* [3] or Corsairs. Their superiority in arms, discipline, and renown commanded the fear and reverence of the natives. In their wars against the

---

[1] See the entire passage (dignum, says Bayer, ut aureis in tabulis figatur) in the Annales Bertiniani Francorum (in Script. Ital. Muratori. tom. ii. pars i. p. 525), A.D. 839, twenty-two years before the era of Ruric. In the tenth century Liutprand (Hist. l. v. c. 6) speaks of the Russians and Normans as the same Aquilonares homines of a red complexion.

[2] My knowledge of these annals is drawn from M. Levêque, Histoire de Russie. Nestor, the first and best of these ancient annalists, was a monk of Kiow, who died in the beginning of the twelfth century; but his Chronicle was obscure till it was published at Petersburgh, 1767, in 4to; Levêque, Hist. de Russie, tom. i. p. xvi.; Coxe's Travels, vol. ii. p. 184.

[3] Theophil. Sig. Bayer de Varagis (for the name is differently spelt), in Comment. Academ. Petropolitanæ, tom. iv. p. 275-311.

more inland savages the Varangians condescended to serve as friends and auxiliaries, and gradually, by choice or conquest, obtained the dominion of a people whom they were qualified to protect. Their tyranny was expelled, their valour was again recalled, till at length Ruric, a Scandinavian chief, became the father of a dynasty which reigned above seven hundred years. His brothers extended his influence; the example of service and usurpation was imitated by his companions in the southern provinces of Russia; and their establishments, by the usual methods of war and assassination, were cemented into the fabric of a powerful monarchy.

As long as the descendants of Ruric were considered as aliens and conquerors, they ruled by the sword of the Varangians, distributed estates and subjects to their faithful captains, and supplied their numbers with fresh streams of adventurers from the Baltic coast.[1] But when the Scandinavian chiefs had struck a deep and permanent root into the soil, they mingled with the Russians in blood, religion, and language, and the first Waladimir had the merit of delivering his country from these foreign mercenaries. They had seated him on the throne; his riches were insufficient to satisfy their demands; but they listened to his pleasing advice, that they should seek, not a more grateful, but a more wealthy, master; that they should embark for Greece, where, instead of the skins of squirrels, silk and gold would be the recompense of their service. At the same time the Russian prince admonished his Byzantine ally to disperse and employ, to recompense and restrain, these impetuous children of the North. Contemporary writers have recorded the introduction, name, and character of the *Varangians :* each day they rose in confidence and esteem; the whole body was assembled at Constantinople to perform the duty of guards; and their strength was recruited by a numerous band of their countrymen from the island of Thule. On this occasion the vague appellation of Thule is applied to England; and the new Varangians were a colony of English and Danes who fled from the yoke of the Norman conqueror. The habits of pilgrimage and piracy had approximated the countries of the earth; these exiles were entertained in the Byzantine court; and they preserved, till the last age of the empire, the inheritance of spotless loyalty, and the use

---

[1] Yet, as late as the year 1018, Kiow and Russia were still guarded ex fugitivorum servorum robore, confluentium et maxime Danorum. Bayer, who quotes (p. 292) the Chronicle of Ditmar of Merseburg, observes that it was unusual for the Germans to enlist in a foreign service.

of the Danish or English tongue. With their broad and double-edged battle-axes on their shoulders, they attended the Greek emperor to the temple, the senate, and the hippodrome; he slept and feasted under their trusty guard; and the keys of the palace, the treasury, and the capital, were held by the firm and faithful hands of the Varangians.[1]

In the tenth century the geography of Scythia was extended far beyond the limits of ancient knowledge; and the monarchy of the Russians obtains a vast and conspicuous place in the map of Constantine.[2] The sons of Ruric were masters of the spacious province of Wolodomir, or Moscow; and, if they were confined on that side by the hordes of the East, their Western frontier in those early days was enlarged to the Baltic Sea and the country of the Prussians. Their northern reign ascended above the sixtieth degree of latitude, over the Hyperborean regions, which fancy had peopled with monsters, or clouded with eternal darkness. To the south they followed the course of the Borysthenes, and approached with that river the neighbourhood of the Euxine Sea. The tribes that dwelt, or wandered, in this ample circuit were obedient to the same conqueror, and insensibly blended into the same nation. The language of Russia is a dialect of the Sclavonian; but in the tenth century these two modes of speech were different from each other; and, as the Sclavonian prevailed in the South, it may be presumed that the original Russians of the North, the primitive subjects of the Varangian chief, were a portion of the Fennic race. With the emigration, union, or dissolution of the wandering tribes, the loose and indefinite picture of the Scythian desert has continually shifted. But the most ancient map of Russia affords some places which still retain their

---

[1] Ducange has collected from the original authors the state and history of the Varangi at Constantinople (Glossar. Med. et Infimæ Græcitatis, sub voce Βάραγγοι ; Med. et Infimæ Latinitatis, sub voce *Vagri ;* Not. ad Alexiad. Annæ Comnenæ, p. 256, 257, 258; Notes sur Villehardouin, p. 296-299). See likewise the annotations of Reiske to the Ceremoniale Aulæ Byzant. of Contantine, tom. ii. p. 149, 150. Saxo Grammaticus affirms that they spoke Danish; but Codinus maintains them till the fifteenth century in the use of their native English: Πολυχρονίζουσι οἱ Βάραγγοι κατὰ τὴν πάτριον γλῶσσαν αὐτῶν, ἤγουν Ἰγκλινιστί [p. 57, ed. Bonn].

[2] The original record of the geography and trade of Russia is produced by the emperor Constantine Porphyrogenitus (de Administrat. Imperii, c. 2, p. 55, 56, c. 9, p. 59-61, c. 13, p. 63-67, c. 37, p. 106, c. 42, p. 112, 113 [tom. iii. p. 59, *sq.,* p. 74-79, p. 82-90, p. 165, p. 177, *sqq.,* ed. Bonn]), and illustrated by the diligence of Bayer (de Geographiâ Russiæ vicinarumque Regionum circiter A.C. 948, in Comment. Academ. Petropol. tom. ix. p. 367-422, tom. x. p. 371-421), with the aid of the chronicles and traditions of Russia, Scandinavia, etc.

name and position; and the two capitals, Novogorod [1] and Kiow, [2] are coeval with the first age of the monarchy. Novogorod had not yet deserved the epithet of great, nor the alliance of the Hanseatic League, which diffused the streams of opulence and the principles of freedom. Kiow could not yet boast of three hundred churches, an innumerable people, and a degree of greatness and splendour which was compared with Constantinople by those who had never seen the residence of the Cæsars. In their origin the two cities were no more than camps or fairs, the most convenient stations in which the barbarians might assemble for the occasional business of war or trade. Yet even these assemblies announce some progress in the arts of society; a new breed of cattle was imported from the southern provinces; and the spirit of commercial enterprise pervaded the sea and land, from the Baltic to the Euxine, from the mouth of the Oder to the port of Constantinople. In the days of idolatry and barbarism the Sclavonic city of Julin was frequented and enriched by the Normans, who had prudently secured a free mart of purchase and exchange. [3] From this harbour, at the entrance of the Oder, the corsair, or merchant, sailed in forty-three days to the eastern shores of the Baltic, the most distant nations were intermingled, and the holy groves of Curland *are said* to have been decorated with *Grecian* and Spanish gold. [4] Between the sea and

---

[1] The haughty proverb, " Who can resist God and the great Novogorod?" is applied by M. Levêque (Hist. de Russie, tom. i. p. 60) even to the times that preceded the reign of Ruric. In the course of his history he frequently celebrates this republic, which was suppressed A.D. 1475 (tom. ii. p. 252-266). That accurate traveller, Adam Olearius, describes (in 1635) the remains of Novogorod, and the route by sea and land of the Holstein ambassadors, tom. i. p. 123-129.

[2] In hac magnâ civitate, quæ est caput regni, plus trecentæ ecclesiæ habentur et nundinæ octo, populi etiam ignota manus (Eggehardus ad A.D. 1018, apud Bayer, tom. ix. p. 412). He likewise quotes (tom. x. p. 397) the words of the Saxon annalist, Cujus (*Russiæ*) metropolis est Chive, æmula sceptri Constantinopolitani, quæ est clarissimum decus Græciæ. The fame of Kiow, especially in the eleventh century, had reached the German and the Arabian geographers.

[3] In Odoræ ostio quâ Scythicas alluit paludes, nobilissima civitas Julinum, celeberrimam Barbaris et Græcis, qui sunt in circuitû, præstans stationem. Est sane maxima omnium quas Europa claudit civitatum (Adam Bremensis, Hist. Eccles. p. 19 [l. ii. c. 12]). A strange exaggeration even in the eleventh century. The trade of the Baltic, and the Hanseatic League, are carefully treated in Anderson's Historical Deduction of Commerce; at least, in *our* language, I am not acquainted with any book so satisfactory.

[4] According to Adam of Bremen (de Sitû Daniæ, p. 58 [c. 223, p. 146, ed. Maderi]), the old Curland extended eight days' journey along the coast; and by Peter Teutoburgicus (p. 68, A.D. 1326) Memel is defined as the common frontier of Russia, Curland, and Prussia. Aurum ibi plurimum (says Adam), divinis, auguribus, atque necromanticis omnes domus sunt

Novogorod an easy intercourse was discovered; in the summer, through a gulf, a lake, and a navigable river; in the winter season, over the hard and level surface of boundless snows. From the neighbourhood of that city the Russians descended the streams that fall into the Borysthenes; their canoes, of a single tree, were laden with slaves of every age, furs of every species, the spoil of their beehives, and the hides of their cattle; and the whole produce of the North was collected and discharged in the magazines of Kiow. The month of June was the ordinary season of the departure of the fleet: the timber of the canoes was framed into the oars and benches of more solid and capacious boats; and they proceeded without obstacle down the Borysthenes, as far as the seven or thirteen ridges of rocks, which traverse the bed, and precipitate the waters, of the river. At the more shallow falls it was sufficient to lighten the vessels; but the deeper cataracts were impassable; and the mariners, who dragged their vessels and their slaves six miles over land, were exposed in this toilsome journey to the robbers of the desert.[1] At the first island below the falls, the Russians celebrated the festival of their escape: at a second, near the mouth of the river, they repaired their shattered vessels for the longer and more perilous voyage of the Black Sea. If they steered along the coast, the Danube was accessible; with a fair wind they could reach in thirty-six or forty hours the opposite shores of Anatolia; and Constantinople admitted the annual visit of the strangers of the North. They returned at the stated season with a rich cargo of corn, wine, and oil, the manufactures of Greece, and the spices of India. Some of their countrymen resided in the capital and provinces; and the national treaties protected the persons, effects, and privileges of the Russian merchant.[2]

plenæ . . . a toto orbe ibi responsa petuntur, maxime ab Hispanis (forsan *Zupanis*, id est regulis Lettoviæ) et Græcis. The name of Greeks was applied to the Russians even before their conversion; an imperfect conversion, if they still consulted the wizards of Curland (Bayer, tom. x. p. 378, 402, etc.; Grotius, Prolegomen. ad Hist. Goth. p. 99).

[1] Constantine only reckons seven cataracts, of which he gives the Russian and Sclavonic names; but thirteen are enumerated by the Sieur de Beauplan, a French engineer, who had surveyed the course and navigation of the Dnieper or Borysthenes (Description de l'Ukraine, Rouen, 1660, a thin quarto); but the map is unluckily wanting in my copy.

[2] Nestor, apud Levêque, Hist. de Russie, tom. i. p. 78-80. From the Dnieper or Borysthenes, the Russians went to Black Bulgaria, Chazaria, and *Syria*. To Syria, how? where? when? May we not, instead of Συρία, read Συανία (de Administrat. Imp. c. 42, p. 113)? The alteration is slight; the position of Suania, between Chazaria and Lazica, is perfectly suitable; and the name was still used in the eleventh century (Cedren. tom. ii. p. 770 [p. 573, ed. Bonn]).

But the same communication which had been opened for the benefit, was soon abused for the injury, of mankind. In a period of one hundred and ninety years the Russians made four attempts to plunder the treasures of Constantinople: the event was various, but the motive, the means, and the object were the same in these naval expeditions.[1] The Russian traders had seen the magnificence, and tasted the luxury, of the city of the Cæsars. A marvellous tale, and a scanty supply, excited the desires of their savage countrymen: they envied the gifts of nature which their climate denied; they coveted the works of art, which they were too lazy to imitate and too indigent to purchase; the Varangian princes unfurled the banners of piratical adventure, and their bravest soldiers were drawn from the nations that dwelt in the northern isles of the ocean.[2] The image of their naval armaments was revived in the last century in the fleets of the Cosacks, which issued from the Borysthenes to navigate the same seas for a similar purpose.[3] The Greek appellation of *monoxyla*, or single canoes, might be justly applied to the bottom of their vessels. It was scooped out of the long stem of a beech or willow, but the slight and narrow foundation was raised and continued on either side with planks, till it attained the length of sixty and the height of about twelve feet. These boats were built without a deck, but with two rudders and a mast; to move with sails and oars; and to contain from forty to seventy men, with their arms, and provisions of fresh water and salt fish. The first trial of the Russians was made with two hundred boats; but when the national force was exerted they might arm against Constantinople a thousand or twelve hundred vessels. Their fleet was not much inferior to the royal navy of Agamemnon, but it was magnified in the eyes of fear to ten or fifteen times the real proportion of its strength and numbers. Had the Greek emperors been endowed with foresight to discern, and vigour to prevent, perhaps they might have sealed with a maritime force the mouth of the Borysthenes. Their indolence abandoned the coast of Anatolia to the calamities of a piratical

---

[1] The wars of the Russians and Greeks in the ninth, tenth, and eleventh centuries, are related in the Byzantine annals, especially those of Zonaras and Cedrenus; and all their testimonies are collected in the *Russica* of Stritter, tom. ii. pars ii. p. 939-1044.

[2] Προσεταιρισάμενος δὲ καὶ συμμαχικὸν οὐκ ὀλίγον ἀπὸ τῶν κατοικούντων ἐν ταῖς προσαρκτίοις τοῦ Ὠκεανοῦ νήσοις ἐθνῶν. Cedrenus in Compend. p. 758 [tom. ii. p. 551, ed. Bonn].

[3] See Beauplan (Description de l'Ukraine, p. 54-61): his descriptions are lively, his plans accurate, and, except the circumstance of fire-arms, we may read old Russians for modern Cosacks.

war, which, after an interval of six hundred years, again infested
the Euxine; but as long as the capital was respected, the sufferings of a distant province escaped the notice both of the prince
and the historian. The storm, which had swept along from the
Phasis and Trebizond, at length burst on the Bosphorus of
Thrace; a strait of fifteen miles, in which the rude vessels of the
Russian might have been stopped and destroyed by a more skilful
adversary. In their first enterprise [1] under the princes of Kiow,
they passed without opposition, and occupied the port of Constantinople in the absence of the emperor Michael, the son of
Theophilus. Through a crowd of perils he landed at the palace
stairs, and immediately repaired to a church of the Virgin Mary.[2]
By the advice of the patriarch, her garment, a precious relic, was
drawn from the sanctuary and dipped in the sea; and a seasonable tempest, which determined the retreat of the Russians, was
devoutly ascribed to the mother of God.[3] The silence of the
Greeks may inspire some doubt of the truth, or at least of the
importance, of the second attempt by Oleg, the guardian of the
sons of Ruric.[4] A strong barrier of arms and fortifications defended the Bosphorus: they were eluded by the usual expedient
of drawing the boats over the isthmus; and this simple operation
is described in the national chronicles as if the Russian fleet had
sailed over dry land with a brisk and favourable gale. The
leader of the third armament, Igor, the son of Ruric, had chosen
a moment of weakness and decay, when the naval powers of the
empire were employed against the Saracens. But if courage be
not wanting, the instruments of defence are seldom deficient.
Fifteen broken and decayed galleys were boldly launched against
the enemy; but instead of the single tube of Greek fire usually
planted on the prow, the sides and stern of each vessel were

[1] It is to be lamented that Bayer has only given a Dissertation de Russorum *primâ* Expeditione Constantinopolitanâ (Comment. Academ.
Petropol. tom. vi. p. 365-391). After disentangling some chronological
intricacies, he fixes it in the years 864 or 865, a date which might have
smoothed some doubts and difficulties in the beginning of M. Levêque's
history.

[2] When Photius wrote his encyclic epistle on the conversion of the
Russians, the miracle was not yet sufficiently ripe; he reproaches the
nation as εἰς ὠμότητα καὶ μιαιφονίαν πάντας δευτέρους ταττόμενον.

[3] Leo Grammaticus, p. 463, 464 [p. 241, ed. Bonn]; Constantini Continuator, in Script. post Theophanem, p. 121, 122 [p. 196, 197, ed. Bonn];
Symeon Logothet. p. 445, 446 [p. 674, 675, ed. Bonn]; Georg. Monach.
p. 535, 536 [p. 826, 827, ed. Bonn]; Cedrenus, tom. ii. p. 551 [p. 173, ed.
Bonn]; Zonaras, tom. ii. p. 162 [l. xvi. c. 5].

[4] See Nestor and Nicon, in Levêque's Hist. de Russie, tom. i. p. 74-80.
Katona (Hist. Ducum, p. 75-79) uses his advantage to disprove this
Russian victory, which would cloud the siege of Kiow by the Hungarians.

abundantly supplied with that liquid combustible. The engineers were dexterous; the weather was propitious; many thousand Russians, who chose rather to be drowned than burnt, leaped into the sea; and those who escaped to the Thracian shore were inhumanly slaughtered by the peasants and soldiers. Yet one third of the canoes escaped into shallow water; and the next spring Igor was again prepared to retrieve his disgrace and claim his revenge.[1] After a long peace, Jaroslaus, the great-grandson of Igor, resumed the same project of a naval invasion. A fleet, under the command of his son, was repulsed at the entrance of the Bosphorus, by the same artificial flames. But in the rashness of pursuit the vanguard of the Greeks was encompassed by an irresistible multitude of boats and men; their provision of fire was probably exhausted; and twenty-four galleys were either taken, sunk, or destroyed.[2]

Yet the threats or calamities of a Russian war were more frequently diverted by treaty than by arms. In these naval hostilities every disadvantage was on the side of the Greeks; their savage enemy afforded no mercy: his poverty promised no spoil; his impenetrable retreat deprived the conqueror of the hopes of revenge; and the pride or weakness of empire indulged an opinion that no honour could be gained or lost in the intercourse with barbarians. At first their demands were high and inadmissible, three pounds of gold for each soldier or mariner of the fleet: the Russian youth adhered to the design of conquest and glory; but the counsels of moderation were recommended by the hoary sages. " Be content," they said, " with the liberal offers of Cæsar; is it not far better to obtain without a combat the possession of gold, silver, silks, and all the objects of our desires? Are we sure of victory? Can we conclude a treaty with the sea? We do not tread on the land; we float on the abyss of water, and a common death hangs over our heads." [3] The memory of these Arctic fleets, that seemed to descend from the polar circle, left a deep impression of terror on the Imperial city. By the vulgar of every rank it was asserted and believed

---

[1] Leo Grammaticus, p. 506, 507 [p. 323, 324, ed. Bonn]; Incert. Contin. p. 263, 264 [p. 424, sqq., ed. Bonn]; Symeon Logothet. p. 490, 491; Georg. Monach. p. 588, 589 [p. 914, 915, ed. Bonn]; Cedren. tom. ii. p. 629 [p. 316, ed. Bonn]; Zonaras, tom. ii. p. 190, 191 [l. xvi. c. 19]; and Liutprand, l. v. c. 6, who writes from the narratives of his father-in-law, then ambassador at Constantinople, and corrects the vain exaggeration of the Greeks.

[2] I can only appeal to Cedrenus (tom. ii. p. 758, 759 [p. 551, sq., ed Bonn]) and Zonaras (tom. ii. p. 253, 254 [l. xvii. c. 24]); but they grow more weighty and credible as they draw near to their own times.

[3] Nestor, apud Levêque, Hist. de Russie, tom. i. p. 87.

that an equestrian statue in the square of Taurus was secretly inscribed with a prophecy, how the Russians, in the last days, should become masters of Constantinople.[1]   In our own time, a Russian armament, instead of sailing from the Borysthenes, has circumnavigated the continent of Europe; and the Turkish capital has been threatened by a squadron of strong and lofty ships of war, each of which, with its naval science and thundering artillery, could have sunk or scattered a hundred canoes, such as those of their ancestors.   Perhaps the present generation may yet behold the accomplishment of the prediction, of a rare prediction, of which the style is unambiguous and the date unquestionable.

By land the Russians were less formidable than by sea; and as they fought for the most part on foot, their irregular legions must often have been broken and overthrown by the cavalry of the Scythian hordes.   Yet their growing towns, however slight and imperfect, presented a shelter to the subject, and a barrier to the enemy: the monarchy of Kiow, till a fatal partition, assumed the dominion of the North; and the nations from the Volga to the Danube were subdued or repelled by the arms of Swatoslaus,[2] the son of Igor, the son of Oleg, the son of Ruric.   The vigour of his mind and body was fortified by the hardships of a military and savage life.   Wrapped in a bear-skin, Swatoslaus usually slept on the ground, his head reclining on a saddle; his diet was coarse and frugal, and, like the heroes of Homer,[3] his meat (it was often horse-flesh) was broiled or roasted on the coals.   The exercise of war gave stability and discipline to his army; and it may be presumed that no soldier was permitted to transcend the luxury of his chief.   By an embassy from Nicephorus, the Greek emperor, he was moved to undertake the conquest of Bulgaria; and a gift of fifteen hundred pounds of gold was laid at his feet to

[1] This brazen statue, which had been brought from Antioch, and was melted down by the Latins, was supposed to represent either Joshua or Bellerophon—an odd dilemma.   See Nicetas Choniates (p. 413, 414 [ed. Par.; p. 848, 849, ed. Bonn]), Codinus (de Originibus, C. P. p. 24), and the anonymous writer de Antiquitat. C. P. (Banduri, Imp. Orient. tom. i. p. 17, 18), who lived about the year 1100.   They witness the belief of the prophecy; the rest is immaterial.

[2] The life of Swatoslaus, or Sviatoslaf, or Sphendosthlabus, is extracted from the Russian Chronicles by M. Levêque (Hist. de Russie, tom. i. p. 94-107).

[3] This resemblance may be clearly seen in the ninth book of the Iliad (205-221) in the minute detail of the cookery of Achilles.   By such a picture a modern epic poet would disgrace his work and disgust his reader; but the Greek verses are harmonious—a dead language can seldom appear low or familiar; and, at the distance of two thousand seven hundred years, we are amused with the primitive manners of antiquity.

defray the expense, or reward the toils, of the expedition. An army of sixty thousand men was assembled and embarked; they sailed from the Borysthenes to the Danube; their landing was effected on the Mæsian shore; and, after a sharp encounter, the swords of the Russians prevailed against the arrows of the Bulgarian horse. The vanquished king sunk into the grave; his children were made captive; and his dominions, as far as Mount Hæmus, were subdued or ravaged by the northern invaders. But instead of relinquishing his prey, and performing his engagements, the Varangian prince was more disposed to advance than to retire, and, had his ambition been crowned with success, the seat of empire in that early period might have been transferred to a more temperate and fruitful climate. Swatoslaus enjoyed and acknowledged the advantages of his new position, in which he could unite, by exchange or rapine, the various productions of the earth. By an easy navigation he might draw from Russia the native commodities of furs, wax, and hydromel: Hungary supplied him with a breed of horses and the spoils of the West; and Greece abounded with gold, silver, and the foreign luxuries which his poverty had affected to disdain. The bands of Patzinacites, Chazars, and Turks repaired to the standard of victory; and the ambassador of Nicephorus betrayed his trust, assumed the purple, and promised to share with his new allies the treasures of the Eastern world. From the banks of the Danube the Russian prince pursued his march as far as Adrianople; a formal summons to evacuate the Roman province was dismissed with contempt; and Swatoslaus fiercely replied that Constantinople might soon expect the presence of an enemy and a master.

Nicephorus could no longer expel the mischief which he had introduced; but his throne and wife were inherited by John Zimisces,[1] who, in a diminutive body, possessed the spirit and abilities of a hero. The first victory of his lieutenants deprived the Russians of their foreign allies, twenty thousand of whom were either destroyed by the sword, or provoked to revolt, or tempted to desert. Thrace was delivered, but seventy thousand barbarians were still in arms; and the legions that had been recalled from the new conquests of Syria prepared, with the return of the spring, to march under the banners of a warlike prince,

---

[1] This singular epithet is derived from the Armenian language, and Τζιμισκῆς is interpreted in Greek by μουζακίτζης or μοιρακίτζης. As I profess myself equally ignorant of *these* words, I may be indulged in the question in the play, " Pray, which of you is the interpreter? " From the context, they seem to signify *Adolescentulus* (Leo Diacon. l. iv. MS. apud Ducange, Glossar. Græc. p. 1570).

who declared himself the friend and avenger of the injured
Bulgaria. The passes of Mount Hæmus had been left unguarded;
they were instantly occupied; the Roman vanguard was formed
of the *immortals* (a proud imitation of the Persian style); the
emperor led the main body of ten thousand five hundred foot;
and the rest of his forces followed in slow and cautious array,
with the baggage and military engines. The first exploit of
Zimisces was the reduction of Marcianopolis, or Peristhlaba,[1] in
two days; the trumpets sounded; the walls were scaled; eight
thousand five hundred Russians were put to the sword; and the
sons of the Bulgarian king were rescued from an ignominious
prison, and invested with a nominal diadem. After these repeated losses Swatoslaus retired to the strong post of Dristra, on
the banks of the Danube, and was pursued by an enemy who
alternately employed the arms of celerity and delay. The
Byzantine galleys ascended the river; the legions completed a
line of circumvallation; and the Russian prince was encompassed, assaulted, and famished in the fortifications of the camp
and city. Many deeds of valour were performed; several
desperate sallies were attempted; nor was it till after a siege of
sixty-five days that Swatoslaus yielded to his adverse fortune.
The liberal terms which he obtained announce the prudence of
the victor, who respected the valour and apprehended the despair
of an unconquered mind. The great duke of Russia bound himself, by solemn imprecations, to relinquish all hostile designs; a
safe passage was opened for his return; the liberty of trade and
navigation was restored; a measure of corn was distributed to
each of his soldiers; and the allowance of twenty-two thousand
measures attests the loss and the remnant of the barbarians.
After a painful voyage they again reached the mouth of the
Borysthenes; but their provisions were exhausted; the season
was unfavourable; they passed the winter on the ice; and,
before they could prosecute their march, Swatoslaus was surprised and oppressed by the neighbouring tribes, with whom the
Greeks entertained a perpetual and useful correspondence.[2]   Far

---

[1] In the Sclavonic tongue the name of Peristhlaba implied the great
or illustrious city, μεγάλη καὶ οὖσα καὶ λεγομένη, says Anna Comnena
(Alexiad, l. vii. p. 194). From its position between Mount Hæmus and
the Lower Danube, it appears to fill the ground, or at least the station, of
Marcianopolis. The situation of Durostolus, or Dristra, is well known and
conspicuous (Comment. Academ. Petropol. tom. ix. p. 415, 416; D'Anville,
Géographie Ancienne, tom. i. p. 307, 311).

[2] The political management of the Greeks, more especially with the
Patzinacites, is explained in the seven first chapters, de Administratione
Imperii.

different was the return of Zimisces, who was received in his capital like Camillus or Marius, the saviours of ancient Rome. But the merit of the victory was attributed by the pious emperor to the mother of God: and the image of the Virgin Mary, with the divine infant in her arms, was placed on a triumphal car, adorned with the spoils of war and the ensigns of Bulgarian royalty. Zimisces made his public entry on horseback; the diadem on his head, a crown of laurel in his hand; and Constantinople was astonished to applaud the martial virtues of her sovereign.[1]

Photius of Constantinople, a patriarch whose ambition was equal to his curiosity, congratulates himself and the Greek church on the conversion of the Russians.[2] Those fierce and bloody barbarians had been persuaded, by the voice of reason and religion, to acknowledge Jesus for their God, the Christian missionaries for their teachers, and the Romans for their friends and brethren. His triumph was transient and premature. In the various fortune of their piratical adventures, some Russian chiefs might allow themselves to be sprinkled with the waters of baptism; and a Greek bishop, with the name of metropolitan, might administer the sacraments in the church of Kiow to a congregation of slaves and natives. But the seed of the Gospel was sown on a barren soil: many were the apostates, the converts were few, and the baptism of Olga may be fixed as the era of Russian Christianity.[3] A female, perhaps of the basest origin, who could revenge the death and assume the sceptre of her husband Igor, must have been endowed with those active virtues which command the fear and obedience of barbarians. In a moment of foreign and domestic peace she sailed from Kiow to Constantinople, and the emperor Constantine Porphyrogenitus has described, with minute diligence, the ceremonial of her reception in his capital and palace. The steps, the titles, the salutations,

---

[1] In the narrative of this war Leo the Deacon (apud Pagi, Critica, tom. iv. A.D. 968-973) is more authentic and circumstantial than Cedrenus (tom. ii. p. 660-683) and Zonaras (tom. ii. p. 205-214). These declaimers have multiplied to 308,000 and 330,000 men those Russian forces of which the contemporary had given a moderate and consistent account.

[2] Phot. Epistol. ii. No. 35, p. 58, edit. Montacut. It was unworthy of the learning of the editor to mistake the Russian nation, τὸ Ῥῶς, for a war-cry of the Bulgarians; nor did it become the enlightened patriarch to accuse the Sclavonian idolaters τῆς Ἑλληνικῆς καὶ ἀθέου δόξης. They were neither Greeks nor atheists.

[3] M. Levêque has extracted, from old chronicles and modern researches, the most satisfactory account of the religion of the *Slavi* and the conversion of Russia (Hist. de Russie, tom. i. p. 35-54, 59, 92, 93, 113-121, 124-129, 148, 149, etc.).

the banquet, the presents, were exquisitely adjusted to gratify the vanity of the stranger, with due reverence to the superior majesty of the purple.[1]   In the sacrament of baptism she received the venerable name of the empress Helena; and her conversion might be preceded or followed by her uncle, two interpreters, sixteen damsels of a higher, and eighteen of a lower rank, twenty-two domestics or ministers, and forty-four Russian merchants, who composed the retinue of the great princess Olga. After her return to Kiow and Novogorod, she firmly persisted in her new religion; but her labours in the propagation of the Gospel were not crowned with success; and both her family and nation adhered with obstinacy or indifference to the gods of their fathers. Her son Swatoslaus was apprehensive of the scorn and ridicule of his companions; and her grandson Wolodomir devoted his youthful zeal to multiply and decorate the monuments of ancient worship.   The savage deities of the North were still propitiated with human sacrifices: in the choice of the victim a citizen was preferred to a stranger, a Christian to an idolater; and the father who defended his son from the sacerdotal knife was involved in the same doom by the rage of a fanatic tumult. Yet the lessons and example of the pious Olga had made a deep, though secret, impression on the minds of the prince and people: the Greek missionaries continued to preach, to dispute, and to baptise; and the ambassadors or merchants of Russia compared the idolatry of the woods with the elegant superstition of Constantinople. They had gazed with admiration on the dome of St. Sophia: the lively pictures of saints and martyrs, the riches of the altar, the number and vestments of the priests, the pomp and order of the ceremonies; they were edified by the alternate succession of devout silence and harmonious song; nor was it difficult to persuade them that a choir of angels descended each day from heaven to join in the devotion of the Christians.[2]   But the conversion of Wolodomir was determined, or hastened, by his desire of a Roman bride.   At the same time, and in the city of Cherson, the rites of baptism and marriage were celebrated by the Christian pontiff: the city he restored to the emperor Basil, the brother of his spouse; but the brazen gates were transported, as it is said, to Novogorod, and erected before the first church as a trophy of

[1] See the Ceremoniale Aulæ Byzant. tom. ii. c. 15, p. 343-345: the style of Olga, or Elga, is Ἀρχόντισσα Ῥωσίας.   For the chief of barbarians the Greeks whimsically borrowed the title of an Athenian magistrate, with a female termination, which would have astonished the ear of Demosthenes.
[2] See an anonymous fragment, published by Banduri (Imperium Orientale, tom. ii. p. 112, 113), de Conversione Russorum.

his victory and faith.[1] At his despotic command Peroun, the god of thunder, whom he had so long adored, was dragged through the streets of Kiow, and twelve sturdy barbarians battered with clubs the misshapen image, which was indignantly cast into the waters of the Borysthenes. The edict of Wolodomir had proclaimed that all who should refuse the rites of baptism would be treated as the enemies of God and their prince; and the rivers were constantly filled with many thousands of obedient Russians, who acquiesced in the truth and excellence of a doctrine which had been embraced by the great duke and his boyars. In the next generation the relics of paganism were finally extirpated; but as the two brothers of Wolodomir had died without baptism, their bones were taken from the grave and sanctified by an irregular and posthumous sacrament.

In the ninth, tenth, and eleventh centuries of the Christian era the reign of the Gospel and of the church was extended over Bulgaria, Hungary, Bohemia, Saxony, Denmark, Norway, Sweden, Poland, and Russia.[2] The triumphs of apostolic zeal were repeated in the iron age of Christianity; and the northern and eastern regions of Europe submitted to a religion more different in theory than in practice from the worship of their native idols. A laudable ambition excited the monks both of Germany and Greece to visit the tents and huts of the barbarians: poverty, hardships, and dangers were the lot of the first missionaries; their courage was active and patient; their motive pure and meritorious; their present reward consisted in the testimony of their conscience and the respect of a grateful people; but the fruitful harvest of their toils was inherited and enjoyed by the proud and wealthy prelates of succeeding times. The first conversions were free and spontaneous: a holy life and an eloquent tongue were the only arms of the missionaries; but the domestic fables of the pagans were silenced by the miracles and visions of the strangers; and the favourable temper of the

---

[1] Cherson, or Corsun, is mentioned by Herberstein (apud Pagi, tom. iv. p. 56) as the place of Wolodomir's baptism and marriage; and both the tradition and the gates are still preserved at Novogorod. Yet an observing traveller transports the brazen gates from Magdeburg in Germany (Coxe's Travels into Russia, etc., vol. i. p. 452), and quotes an inscription which seems to justify his opinion. The modern reader must not confound this old Cherson of the Tauric or Crimæan peninsula with a new city of the same name which has arisen near the mouth of the Borysthenes, and was lately honoured by the memorable interview of the empress of Russia with the emperor of the West.

[2] Consult the Latin text, or English version, of Mosheim's excellent History of the Church, under the first head or section of each of these centuries.

chiefs was accelerated by the dictates of vanity and interest.
The leaders of nations, who were saluted with the titles of kings
and saints,[1] held it lawful and pious to impose the Catholic faith
on their subjects and neighbours: the coast of the Baltic, from
Holstein to the gulf of Finland, was invaded under the standard
of the cross; and the reign of idolatry was closed by the conversion of Lithuania in the fourteenth century.   Yet truth
and candour must acknowledge that the conversion of the
North imparted many temporal benefits both to the old and the
new Christians.   The rage of war, inherent to the human species,
could not be healed by the evangelic precepts of charity and peace;
and the ambition of Catholic princes has renewed in every age
the calamities of hostile contention.   But the admission of the
barbarians into the pale of civil and ecclesiastical society delivered Europe from the depredations, by sea and land, of the
Normans, the Hungarians, and the Russians, who learned to
spare their brethren and cultivate their possessions.[2]   The
establishment of law and order was promoted by the influence of
the clergy; and the rudiments of art and science were introduced
into the savage countries of the globe.   The liberal piety of the
Russian princes engaged in their service the most skilful of the
Greeks to decorate the cities and instruct the inhabitants: the
dome and the paintings of St. Sophia were rudely copied in the
churches of Kiow and Novogorod: the writings of the fathers
were translated into the Sclavonic idiom; and three hundred
noble youths were invited or compelled to attend the lessons of
the college of Jaroslaus.   It should appear that Russia might
have derived an early and rapid improvement from her peculiar
connection with the church and state of Constantinople, which
in that age so justly despised the ignorance of the Latins.   But
the Byzantine nation was servile, solitary, and verging to a
hasty decline: after the fall of Kiow the navigation of the

[1] In the year 1000 the ambassadors of St. Stephen received from Pope
Silvester the title of King of Hungary, with a diadem of Greek workmanship.   It had been designed for the duke of Poland; but the Poles, by
their own confession, were yet too barbarous to deserve an *angelical* and
apostolical crown. (Katona, Hist. Critic. Regum Stirpis Arpadianæ, tom.
i. p. 1-20.)

[2] Listen to the exultations of Adam of Bremen (A.D. 1080), of which the
substance is agreeable to truth: Ecce illa ferocissima Danorum, etc.,
natio . . . jamdudum novit in Dei laudibus Alleluia resonare.   Ecce
populus ille piraticus . . . suis nunc finibus contentus est. . . .   Ecce
patria horribilis semper inaccessa propter cultum idolorum . . . prædica-
tores veritatis ubique certatim admittit, etc. etc. (de Sitû Daniæ, etc.,
p. 40, 41, edit. Elzevir [c. 251, p. 161, ed. Maderi]: a curious and original
prospect of the north of Europe, and the introduction of Christianity).

Borysthenes was forgotten; the great princes of Wolodomir and Moscow were separated from the sea and Christendom; and the divided monarchy was oppressed by the ignominy and blindness of Tartar servitude.[1] The Sclavonic and Scandinavian kingdoms, which had been converted by the Latin missionaries, were exposed, it is true, to the spiritual jurisdiction and temporal claims of the popes;[2] but they were united, in language and religious worship, with each other and with Rome; they imbibed the free and generous spirit of the European republic, and gradually shared the light of knowledge which arose on the western world.

CHAPTER LVI

The Saracens, Franks, and Greeks, in Italy—First Adventures and Settlement of the Normans—Character and Conquests of Robert Guiscard, Duke of Apulia—Deliverance of Sicily by his Brother Roger—Victories of Robert over the Emperors of the East and West—Roger, King of Sicily, invades Africa and Greece—The Emperor Manuel Comnenus—Wars of the Greeks and Normans—Extinction of the Normans

THE three great nations of the world, the Greeks, the Saracens, and the Franks, encountered each other on the theatre of Italy.[3] The southern provinces, which now compose the kingdom of Naples, were subject, for the most part, to the Lombard dukes

---

[1] The great princes removed in 1156 from Kiow, which was ruined by the Tartars in 1240. Moscow became the seat of empire in the fourteenth century. See the first and second volumes of Levêque's History, and Mr. Coxe's Travels into the North, tom. i. p. 241, etc.

[2] The ambassadors of St. Stephen had used the reverential expressions of *regnum oblatum, debitam obedientiam,* etc., which were most rigorously interpreted by Gregory VII.; and the Hungarian Catholics are distressed between the sanctity of the pope and the independence of the crown (Katona, Hist. Critica, tom. i. p. 20-25; tom. ii. p. 304, 346, 360, etc.).

[3] For the general history of Italy in the ninth and tenth centuries I may properly refer to the fifth, sixth, and seventh books of Sigonius de Regno Italiæ (in the second volume of his works, Milan, 1732); the Annals of Baronius, with the Criticism of Pagi; the seventh and eighth books of the Istoria Civile del Regno di Napoli of Giannone; the seventh and eighth volumes (the octavo edition) of the Annali d'Italia of Muratori, and the second volume of the Abrégé Chronologique of M. de St. Marc, a work which, under a superficial title, contains much genuine learning and industry. But my long-accustomed reader will give me credit for saying that I myself have ascended to the fountain-head as often as such ascent could be either profitable or possible; and that I have diligently turned over the originals in the first volumes of Muratori's great collection of the *Scriptores Rerum Italicarum.*

and princes of Beneventum [1]—so powerful in war, that they checked for a moment the genius of Charlemagne—so liberal in peace, that they maintained in their capital an academy of thirty-two philosophers and grammarians. The division of this flourishing state produced the rival principalities of Benevento, Salerno, and Capua; and the thoughtless ambition or revenge of the competitors invited the Saracens to the ruin of their common inheritance. During a calamitous period of two hundred years Italy was exposed to a repetition of wounds, which the invaders were not capable of healing by the union and tranquillity of a perfect conquest. Their frequent and almost annual squadrons issued from the port of Palermo, and were entertained with too much indulgence by the Christians of Naples: the more formidable fleets were prepared on the African coast; and even the Arabs of Andalusia were sometimes tempted to assist or oppose the Moslems of an adverse sect. In the revolution of human events a new ambuscade was concealed in the Caudine forks, the fields of Cannæ were bedewed a second time with the blood of the Africans, and the sovereign of Rome again attacked or defended the walls of Capua and Tarentum. A colony of Saracens had been planted at Bari, which commands the entrance of the Adriatic Gulf; and their impartial depredations provoked the resentment and conciliated the union of the two emperors. An offensive alliance was concluded between Basil the Macedonian, the first of his race, and Lewis the great-grandson of Charlemagne; [2] and each party supplied the deficiencies of his associate. It would have been imprudent in the Byzantine monarch to transport his stationary troops of Asia to an Italian campaign; and the Latin arms would have been insufficient if *his* superior navy had not occupied the mouth of the Gulf. The fortress of Bari was invested by the infantry of the Franks, and by the cavalry and galleys of the Greeks; and, after a defence of four years, the Arabian emir submitted to the clemency of Lewis, who commanded in person the operations of the siege. This important conquest had been achieved by the concord of the East and West; but their recent amity was soon embittered by the mutual complaints of jealousy and pride. The Greeks assumed as their own the merit of the

[1] Camillo Pellegrino, a learned Capuan of the last century, has illustrated the history of the duchy of Beneventum, in his two books, Historia Principum Longobardorum, in the Scriptores of Muratori, tom. ii. pars. i. p. 221-345, and tom. v. p. 159-245.
[2] See Constantin. Porphyrogen. de Thematibus, l. ii. c. xi. [tom. iii. p. 62, ed. Bonn] in Vit. Basil. c. 55, p. 181.

conquest and the pomp of the triumph, extolled the greatness of their powers, and affected to deride the intemperance and sloth of the handful of barbarians who appeared under the banners of the Carlovingian prince. His reply is expressed with the eloquence of indignation and truth: " We confess the magnitude of your preparations," says the great-grandson of Charlemagne. " Your armies were indeed as numerous as a cloud of summer locusts, who darken the day, flap their wings, and, after a short flight, tumble weary and breathless to the ground. Like them, ye sunk after a feeble effort; ye were vanquished by your own cowardice, and withdrew from the scene of action to injure and despoil our Christian subjects of the Sclavonian coast. We were few in number, and why were we few? because, after a tedious expectation of your arrival, I had dismissed my host, and retained only a chosen band of warriors to continue the blockade of the city. If they indulged their hospitable feasts in the face of danger and death, did these feasts abate the vigour of their enterprise? Is it by your fasting that the walls of Bari have been overturned? Did not these valiant Franks, diminished as they were by languor and fatigue, intercept and vanquish the three most powerful emirs of the Saracens? and did not their defeat precipitate the fall of the city? Bari is now fallen; Tarentum trembles; Calabria will be delivered; and, if we command the sea, the island of Sicily may be rescued from the hands of the infidels. My brother " (a name most offensive to the vanity of the Greek), " accelerate your naval succours, respect your allies, and distrust your flatterers." [1]

These lofty hopes were soon extinguished by the death of Lewis, and the decay of the Carlovingian house; and whoever might deserve the honour, the Greek emperors, Basil and his son Leo, secured the advantage, of the reduction of Bari. The Italians of Apulia and Calabria were persuaded or compelled to acknowledge their supremacy, and an ideal line from Mount Garganus to the bay of Salerno leaves the far greater part of the kingdom of Naples under the dominion of the Eastern empire. Beyond that line the dukes or republics of Amalfi [2] and Naples, who had never forfeited their voluntary allegiance, rejoiced in

---

[1] The original epistle of the emperor Lewis II. to the emperor Basil, a curious record of the age, was first published by Baronius (Annal. Eccles. A.D. 871, No. 51-71), from the Vatican MS. of Erchempert, or rather of the anonymous historian of Salerno.

[2] See an excellent Dissertation de Republicâ Amalphitanâ, in the Appendix (p. 1-42) of Henry Brenckmann's Historia Pandectarum (Trajecti ad Rhenum, 1722, in 4to).

the neighbourhood of their lawful sovereign; and Amalfi was
enriched by supplying Europe with the produce and manufactures of Asia. But the Lombard princes of Benevento,
Salerno, and Capua [1] were reluctantly torn from the communion
of the Latin world, and too often violated their oaths of servitude
and tribute. The city of Bari rose to dignity and wealth as the
metropolis of the new theme or province of Lombardy; the title
of patrician, and afterwards the singular name of *Catapan*,[2]
was assigned to the supreme governor; and the policy both of
the church and state was modelled in exact subordination to
the throne of Constantinople. As long as the sceptre was disputed by the princes of Italy, their efforts were feeble and
adverse; and the Greeks resisted or eluded the forces of Germany
which descended from the Alps under the Imperial standard of
the Othos. The first and greatest of those Saxon princes was
compelled to relinquish the siege of Bari: the second, after the
loss of his stoutest bishops and barons, escaped with honour
from the bloody field of Crotona. On that day the scale of war
was turned against the Franks by the valour of the Saracens.[3]
These corsairs had indeed been driven by the Byzantine fleets
from the fortresses and coasts of Italy; but a sense of interest
was more prevalent than superstition or resentment, and the

---

[1] Your master, says Nicephorus, has given aid and protection principibus
Capuano et Beneventano, servis meis, quos oppugnare dispono. . . . Nova
(potius *nota*) res est quòd eorum patres et avi nostro Imperio tributa
dederunt (Liutprand, in Legat. p. 484). Salerno is not mentioned, yet the
prince changed his party about the same time, and Camillo Pellegrino
(Script. Rer. Ital. tom. ii. pars i. p. 285) has nicely discerned this change in
the style of the anonymous Chronicle. On the rational ground of history
and language, Liutprand (p. 480) had asserted the Latin claim to Apulia
and Calabria.

[The Theme of Italy extended from the Ofanto on the north and the
Bradano on the west to the southern point of Apulia, and included the
south of Calabria, the old Bruttii. It was about the year 1000 that the
governor of the Theme of Italy conquered the land on the north side of
their province, between the Ofanto and Fortore.—O. S.]

[2] See the Greek and Latin Glossaries of Ducange (Κατεπανω, *cata-
panus*), and his notes on the Alexias (p. 275). Against the contemporary
notion, which derives it from Κατὰ πᾶν, *juxta omne*, he treats it as a corruption of the Latin *capitaneus*. Yet M. de St. Marc has accurately observed
(Abrégé Chronologique, tom. ii. p. 924) that in this age the capitanei were
not *captains*, but only nobles of the first rank, the great valvassors of Italy.

[3] Οὐ μόνον διὰ πολέμων ἀκριβῶς τεταγμένων τὸ τοιοῦτον ὑπήγαγε τὸ ἔθνος
(the Lombards) ἀλλὰ καὶ ἀγχινοίᾳ χρησάμενος, καὶ δικαιοσύνῃ καὶ χρηστότητι
ἐπιεικῶς τε τοῖς προσερχομένοις προσφερόμενος (Leon. Tactic. c. xv. [§ 38]
p. 741). The little Chronicle of Beneventum (tom. ii. pars i. p. 280) gives
a far different character of the Greeks during the five years (A.D. 891-896)
that Leo was master of the city.

caliph of Egypt had transported forty thousand Moslems to the aid of his Christian ally. The successors of Basil amused themselves with the belief that the conquest of Lombardy had been achieved, and was still preserved, by the justice of their laws, the virtues of their ministers, and the gratitude of a people whom they had rescued from anarchy and oppression. A series of rebellions might dart a ray of truth into the palace of Constantinople; and the illusions of flattery were dispelled by the easy and rapid success of the Norman adventurers.

The revolution of human affairs had produced in Apulia and Calabria a melancholy contrast between the age of Pythagoras and the tenth century of the Christian era. At the former period the coast of Great Greece (as it was then styled) was planted with free and opulent cities: these cities were peopled with soldiers, artists, and philosophers; and the military strength of Tarentum, Sybaris, or Crotona was not inferior to that of a powerful kingdom. At the second era these once flourishing provinces were clouded with ignorance, impoverished by tyranny, and depopulated by barbarian war: nor can we severely accuse the exaggeration of a contemporary, that a fair and ample district was reduced to the same desolation which had covered the earth after the general deluge.[1] Among the hostilities of the Arabs, the Franks, and the Greeks in the southern Italy, I shall select two or three anecdotes expressive of their national manners. 1. It was the amusement of the Saracens to profane, as well as to pillage, the monasteries and churches. At the siege of Salerno a Musulman chief spread his couch on the communion table, and on that altar sacrificed each night the virginity of a Christian nun. As he wrestled with a reluctant maid, a beam in the roof was accidentally or dexterously thrown down on his head; and the death of the lustful emir was imputed to the wrath of Christ, which was at length awakened to the defence of his faithful spouse.[2] 2. The Saracens besieged the cities of

---

[1] Calabriam adeunt, eamque inter se divisam reperientes funditus depopulati sunt (or depopularunt), ita ut deserta sit velut in diluvio. Such is the text of Herempert, or Erchempert, according to the two editions of Carraccioli (Rer. Italic. Script. tom. v. p. 23) and of Camillo Pellegrino (tom. ii. pars i. p. 246). Both were extremely scarce when they were reprinted by Muratori.

[2] Baronius (Annal. Eccles. A.D. 874, No. 2) has drawn this story from a MS. of Erchempert, who died at Capua only fifteen years after the event. But the Cardinal was deceived by a false title, and we can only quote the anonymous Chronicle of Salerno (Paralipomena, c. 110), composed towards the end of the tenth century, and published in the second volume of Muratori's Collection. See the Dissertations of Camillo Pellegrino, tom. ii. pars i. p. 231-281, etc.

Beneventum and Capua: after a vain appeal to the successors of
Charlemagne, the Lombards implored the clemency and aid of
the Greek emperor.[1] A fearless citizen dropped from the walls,
passed the intrenchments, accomplished his commission, and
fell into the hands of the barbarians as he was returning with
the welcome news. They commanded him to assist their enterprise, and deceive his countrymen, with the assurance that wealth
and honours should be the reward of his falsehood, and that his
sincerity would be punished with immediate death. He affected
to yield, but as soon as he was conducted within hearing of the
Christians on the rampart, " Friends and brethren," he cried
with a loud voice, " be bold and patient; maintain the city;
your sovereign is informed of your distress, and your deliverers
are at hand. I know my doom, and commit my wife and
children to your gratitude." The rage of the Arabs confirmed
his evidence; and the self-devoted patriot was transpierced with
a hundred spears. He deserves to live in the memory of the
virtuous, but the repetition of the same story in ancient and
modern times may sprinkle some doubts on the reality of this
generous deed.[2] 3. The recital of the third incident may
provoke a smile amidst the horrors of war. Theobald, marquis
of Camerino and Spoleto,[3] supported the rebels of Beneventum;
and his wanton cruelty was not incompatible in that age with
the character of a hero. His captives of the Greek nation or
party were castrated without mercy, and the outrage was
aggravated by a cruel jest, that he wished to present the emperor
with a supply of eunuchs, the most precious ornaments of the
Byzantine court. The garrison of a castle had been defeated
in a sally, and the prisoners were sentenced to the customary

<hr/>

[1] Constantine Porphyrogenitus (in Vit. Basil. c. 58, p. 183 [p. 296, ed.
Bonn]) is the original author of this story. He places it under the reigns of
Basil and Lewis II.; yet the reduction of Beneventum by the Greeks is
dated A.D. 891, after the decease of both of those princes.

[2] In the year 663 the same tragedy is described by Paul the Deacon (de
Gestis Langobard. l. v. c. 7, 8, p. 870, 871, edit. Grot.), under the walls of
the same city of Beneventum. But the actors are different, and the guilt
is imputed to the Greeks themselves, which in the Byzantine edition is
applied to the Saracens. In the late war in Germany, M. d'Assas, a French
officer of the regiment of Auvergne, is said to have devoted himself in a
similar manner. His behaviour is the more heroic, as mere silence was
required by the enemy who had made him prisoner (Voltaire, Siècle de
Louis XV. c. 33, tom. ix. p. 172).

[3] Theobald, who is styled Heros by Liutprand, was properly duke of
Spoleto and marquis of Camerino, from the year 926 to 935. The title and
office of marquis (commander of the march or frontier) was introduced
into Italy by the French emperors (Abrégé Chronologique, tom. ii. p. 645-
732, etc.).

operation. But the sacrifice was disturbed by the intrusion of a frantic female, who, with bleeding cheeks, dishevelled hair, and importunate clamours, compelled the marquis to listen to her complaint. "Is it thus," she cried, "ye magnanimous heroes, that ye wage war against women, against women who have never injured ye, and whose only arms are the distaff and the loom?" Theobald denied the charge, and protested that, since the Amazons, he had never heard of a female war. "And how," she furiously exclaimed, "can you attack us more directly, how can you wound us in a more vital part, than by robbing our husbands of what we most dearly cherish, the source of our joys, and the hope of our posterity? The plunder of our flocks and herds I have endured without a murmur, but this fatal injury, this irreparable loss, subdues my patience, and calls aloud on the justice of heaven and earth." A general laugh applauded her eloquence; the savage Franks, inaccessible to pity, were moved by her ridiculous, yet rational, despair; and with the deliverance of the captives she obtained the restitution of her effects. As she returned in triumph to the castle she was overtaken by a messenger, to inquire, in the name of Theobald, what punishment should be inflicted on her husband, were he again taken in arms? "Should such," she answered without hesitation, "be his guilt and misfortune, he has eyes, and a nose, and hands, and feet. These are his own, and these he may deserve to forfeit by his personal offences. But let my lord be pleased to spare what his little handmaid presumes to claim as her peculiar and lawful property." [1]

The establishment of the Normans in the kingdoms of Naples and Sicily [2] is an event most romantic in its origin, and in its consequences most important both to Italy and the Eastern empire. The broken provinces of the Greeks, Lombards, and Saracens were exposed to every invader, and every sea and

---

[1] Liutprand, Hist. l. iv. c. 4, in the Rerum Italic. Script. tom. ii. pars i. p. 453, 454. Should the licentiousness of the tale be questioned, I may exclaim, with poor Sterne, that it is hard if I may not transcribe with caution what a bishop could write without scruple. What if I had translated, ut viris certetis testiculos amputare, in quibus nostri corporis refocillatio, etc.?

[2] The original monuments of the Normans in Italy are collected in the fifth volume of Muratori; and among these we may distinguish the poem of William Appulus (p. 245-278) and the history of Galfridus (*Jeffrey*) Malaterra (p. 537-607). Both were natives of France, but they wrote on the spot, in the age of the first conquerors (before A.D. 1100), and with the spirit of freemen. It is needless to recapitulate the compilers and critics of Italian history, Sigonius, Baronius, Pagi, Giannone, Muratori, St. Marc, etc., whom I have always consulted, and never copied.

land were invaded by the adventurous spirit of the Scandinavian
pirates. After a long indulgence of rapine and slaughter, a fair
and ample territory was accepted, occupied, and named, by the
Normans of France: they renounced their gods for the God of
the Christians; [1] and the dukes of Normandy acknowledged
themselves the vassals of the successors of Charlemagne and
Capet. The savage fierceness which they had brought from
the snowy mountains of Norway was refined, without being
corrupted, in a warmer climate; the companions of Rollo
insensibly mingled with the natives; they imbibed the manners,
language, [2] and gallantry of the French nation; and, in a martial
age, the Normans might claim the palm of valour and glorious
achievements. Of the fashionable superstitions, they embraced
with ardour the pilgrimages of Rome, Italy, and the Holy Land.
In this active devotion their minds and bodies were invigorated
by exercise: danger was the incentive, novelty the recompense;
and the prospect of the world was decorated by wonder, credulity,
and ambitious hope. They confederated for their mutual defence; and the robbers of the Alps, who had been allured by
the garb of a pilgrim, were often chastised by the arm of a
warrior. In one of these pious visits to the cavern of Mount
Garganus in Apulia, which had been sanctified by the apparition
of the archangel Michael, [3] they were accosted by a stranger in
the Greek habit, but who soon revealed himself as a rebel, a

[1] Some of the first converts were baptised ten or twelve times, for the
sake of the white garment usually given at this ceremony. At the funeral
of Rollo, the gifts to monasteries for the repose of his soul were accompanied
by a sacrifice of one hundred captives. But in a generation or two the
national change was pure and general.

[2] The Danish language was still spoken by the Normans of Bayeux on
the sea-coast, at a time (A.D. 940) when it was already forgotten at Rouen,
in the court and capital. Quem (Richard I.) confestim pater Baiocas
mittens Botoni militiæ suæ principi nutriendum tradidit, ut, ibi *linguâ*
eruditus *Danicâ*, suis exterisque hominibus sciret aperte dare responsa
(Wilhelm. Gemeticensis de Ducibus Normannis, l. iii. c. 8, p. 623, edit.
Camden). Of the vernacular and favourite idiom of William the Conqueror (A.D. 1035), Selden (Opera, tom. ii. p. 1640-1656) has given a specimen, obsolete and obscure even to antiquarians and lawyers.
[A band of forty Normans returning in 1016 from the Holy Land had
rescued the city of Salerno from the attack of a numerous fleet of Saracens.
Gaimar, the Lombard prince of Salerno, wished to retain them in his
service, and to take them into his pay. They said, " We fight for our
religion, and not for pay." Gaimar entreated them to send some Norman
knights to his court, which they did, and they seem to have been the
beginning of the connection of the Normans with Italy.—O. S.]

[3] See Leandro Alberti (Descrizione d'Italia, p. 250) and Baronius (A.D.
493, No. 43). If the archangel inherited the temple and oracle, perhaps
the cavern, of old Calchas the soothsayer (Strab. Geograph. l. vi. p. 435,
436 [p. 284, ed. Casaub.]), the Catholics (on this occasion) have surpassed
the Greeks in the elegance of their superstition.

fugitive, and a mortal foe of the Greek empire. His name was Melo; a noble citizen of Bari, who, after an unsuccessful revolt, was compelled to seek new allies and avengers of his country. The bold appearance of the Normans revived his hopes and solicited his confidence: they listened to the complaints, and still more to the promises, of the patriot. The assurance of wealth demonstrated the justice of his cause; and they viewed, as the inheritance of the brave, the fruitful land which was oppressed by effeminate tyrants. On their return to Normandy they kindled a spark of enterprise, and a small but intrepid band was freely associated for the deliverance of Apulia. They passed the Alps by separate roads, and in the disguise of pilgrims; but in the neighbourhood of Rome they were saluted by the chief of Bari, who supplied the more indigent with arms and horses, and instantly led them to the field of action. In the first conflict their valour prevailed; but in the second engagement they were overwhelmed by the numbers and military engines of the Greeks, and indignantly retreated with their faces to the enemy. The unfortunate Melo ended his life a suppliant at the court of Germany: his Norman followers, excluded from their native and their promised land, wandered among the hills and valleys of Italy, and earned their daily subsistence by the sword. To that formidable sword the princes of Capua, Beneventum, Salerno, and Naples alternately appealed in their domestic quarrels; the superior spirit and discipline of the Normans gave victory to the side which they espoused; and their cautious policy observed the balance of power, lest the preponderance of any rival state should render their aid less important and their service less profitable. Their first asylum was a strong camp in the depth of the marshes of Campania; but they were soon endowed by the liberality of the duke of Naples with a more plentiful and permanent seat. Eight miles from his residence, as a bulwark against Capua, the town of Aversa was built and fortified for their use; and they enjoyed as their own the corn and fruits, the meadows and groves, of that fertile district. The report of their success attracted every year new swarms of pilgrims and soldiers: the poor were urged by necessity; the rich were excited by hope; and the brave and active spirits of Normandy were impatient of ease and ambitious of renown. The independent standard of Aversa afforded shelter and encouragement to the outlaws of the province, to every fugitive who had escaped from the injustice or justice of his superiors; and these foreign associates were quickly assimilated in manners and language to the Gallic colony. The first leader of the Normans was Count Rainulf; and, in the origin of society, pre-eminence of rank is the reward and the proof of superior merit.[1]

Since the conquest of Sicily by the Arabs, the Grecian emperors had been anxious to regain that valuable possession; but their efforts, however strenuous, had been opposed by the distance and the sea. Their costly armaments, after a gleam of success, added new pages of calamity and disgrace to the Byzantine annals: twenty thousand of their best troops were lost in a single expedition; and the victorious Moslems derided the policy of a nation which intrusted eunuchs not only with the custody of their women, but with the command of their men.[2] After a reign of two hundred years, the Saracens were ruined by their divisions.[3] The emir disclaimed the authority of the king of Tunis; the people rose against the emir; the cities were usurped by the chiefs; each meaner rebel was independent in his village or castle; and the weaker of two rival brothers implored the friendship of the Christians. In every service of danger the Normans were prompt and useful; and five hundred *knights*, or warriors on horseback, were enrolled by Arduin, the agent and interpreter of the Greeks, under the standard of Maniaces, governor of Lom-

---

[1] See the first book of William Appulus. His words are applicable to every swarm of barbarians and freebooters:—

> Si vicinorum quis *pernitiosus* ad illos
> Confugiebat, eum gratanter suscipiebant:
> Moribus et linguâ quoscumque venire videbant
> Informant propriâ; gens efficiatur ut una. [p 255.]

And elsewhere, of the native adventurers of Normandy:—

> Pars parat, exiguæ vel opes aderant quia nullæ;
> Pars, quia de magnis majora subire volebant. [p. 254.]

[This account is not accurate. After the retreat of the emperor Henry II., the Normans, united under the command of Rainulf, had taken possession of Aversa, then a small castle in the duchy of Naples. They had been masters of it a few years when Pandulf the Fourth, prince of Capua, found means to take Naples by surprise. Sergius, master of the soldiers, and head of the republic, with the principal citizens, abandoned a city in which he could not behold without horror the establishment of a foreign dominion. He retired to Aversa, and when, with the assistance of the Greeks and of the citizens faithful to their country, he had collected money enough to satisfy the rapacity of the Normans, he advanced at their head to attack the garrison of the prince of Capua, defeated it, and re-entered Naples. It was then that he confirmed the Normans in the possession of Aversa and its territory, which he raised into a count's fief, and granted the investiture thereof to Rainulf.—O. S.]

[2] Liutprand in Legatione, p. 485. Pagi has illustrated this event from the MS. history of the deacon Leo (tom. iv. A.D. 965, No. 17-19).

[3] See the Arabian Chronicle of Sicily, apud Muratori, Script. Rerum Ital. tom. i. p. 253.

bardy. Before their landing the brothers were reconciled; the union of Sicily and Africa was restored; and the island was guarded to the water's edge. The Normans led the van, and the Arabs of Messina felt the valour of an untried foe. In a second action the emir of Syracuse was unhorsed and transpierced by the *iron arm* of William of Hauteville. In a third engagement his intrepid companions discomfited the host of sixty thousand Saracens, and left the Greeks no more than the labour of the pursuit: a splendid victory; but of which the pen of the historian may divide the merit with the lance of the Normans. It is, however, true, that they essentially promoted the success of Maniaces, who reduced thirteen cities, and the greater part of Sicily, under the obedience of the emperor. But his military fame was sullied by ingratitude and tyranny. In the division of the spoil the deserts of his brave auxiliaries were forgotten; and neither their avarice nor their pride could brook this injurious treatment. They complained by the mouth of their interpreter: their complaint was disregarded; their interpreter was scourged; the sufferings were *his;* the insult and resentment belonged to *those* whose sentiments he had delivered. Yet they dissembled till they had obtained, or stolen, a safe passage to the Italian continent: their brethren of Aversa sympathised in their indignation, and the province of Apulia was invaded as the forfeit of the debt.[1] Above twenty years after the first emigration, the Normans took the field with no more than seven hundred horse and five hundred foot; and after the recall of the Byzantine legions[2] from the Sicilian war, their numbers are magnified to the amount of threescore thousand men. Their herald proposed the option of battle or retreat; "Of battle," was the unanimous cry of the Normans; and one of their stoutest warriors, with a stroke of his fist, felled to the ground the horse of the Greek messenger. He was dismissed with a fresh horse; the insult was concealed from the Imperial troops; but in two successive battles they were more fatally instructed of the prowess of their adversaries. In the plains of Cannæ the Asiatics fled before the adventurers of France; the duke of

---

[1] Jeffrey Malaterra, who relates the Sicilian war and the conquest of Apulia (l. i. c. 7, 8, 9, 19). The same events are described by Cedrenus (tom. ii. p. 741-743, 755, 756) and Zonaras (tom. ii. p. 237, 238 [l. xvii. c. 15]); and the Greeks are so hardened to disgrace, that their narratives are impartial enough.

[2] Cedrenus specifies the τάγμα of the Obsequium (Phrygia), and the μέρος of the Thracesians (Lydia: consult Constantine de Thematibus, i. 3, 4 [tom. iii. p. 22 sqq., ed. Bonn], with Delisle's map); and afterwards names the Pisidians and Lycaonians with the fœderati.

Lombardy was made prisoner; the Apulians acquiesced in a new dominion; and the four places of Bari, Otranto, Brundusium, and Tarentum were alone saved in the shipwreck of the Grecian fortunes. From this era we may date the establishment of the Norman power, which soon eclipsed the infant colony of Aversa. Twelve counts [1] were chosen by the popular suffrage; and age, birth, and merit were the motives of their choice. The tributes of their peculiar districts were appropriated to their use; and each count erected a fortress in the midst of his lands, and at the head of his vassals. In the centre of the province the common habitation of Melphi was reserved as the metropolis and citadel of the republic; a house and separate quarter was allotted to each of the twelve counts; and the national concerns were regulated by this military senate. The first of his peers, their president and general, was entitled Count of Apulia; and this dignity was conferred on William of the iron arm, who, in the language of the age, is styled a lion in battle, a lamb in society, and an angel in council.[2] The manners of his countrymen are fairly delineated by a contemporary and national historian.[3] " The Normans," says Malaterra, " are a cunning and revengeful people; eloquence and dissimulation appear to be their hereditary qualities: they can stoop to flatter; but, unless they are curbed by the restraint of law, they indulge the licentious-

----

[1] Omnes conveniunt; et bis sex nobiliores,
　　Quos genus et gravitas morum decorabat et ætas,
　　Elegere duces.　Provectis ad comitatum
　　His alii parent; comitatus nomen honoris
　　Quo donantur, erat.　Hi totas undique terras
　　Divisere sibi, ni sors inimica repugnet;
　　Singula proponunt loca quæ contingere sorte
　　Cuique duci debent, et quæque tributa locorum. [p. 255.]

And after speaking of Melphi, William Appulus adds,

　　Pro numero comitum bis sex statuere plateas,
　　Atque domus comitum totidem fabricantur in urbe. [p. 256.]

Leo Ostiensis (l. ii. c. 67) enumerates the divisions of the Apulian cities, which it is needless to repeat.

[2] Gulielm. Appulus, l. ii. c. 12, according to the reference of Giannone (Istoria Civile di Napoli, tom. ii. p. 31), which I cannot verify in the original. The Apulian praises indeed his *validas vires, probitas animi,* and *vivida virtus ;* and declares that, had he lived, no poet could have equalled his merits (l. i. p. 258, l. ii. p. 259). He was bewailed by the Normans, quippe qui tanti consilii virum (says Malaterra, l. i. c. 12, p. 552), tam armis strenuum, tam sibi munificum, affabilem, morigeratum ulterius se habere diffidebant.

[3] The gens astutissima, injuriarum ultrix . . . adulari sciens . . . eloquentiis inserviens, of Malaterra (l. i. c. 3, p. 550), are expressive of the popular and proverbial character of the Normans.

ness of nature and passion. Their princes affect the praise of popular munificence; the people observe the medium, or rather blend the extremes, of avarice and prodigality; and in their eager thirst of wealth and dominion, they despise whatever they possess, and hope whatever they desire. Arms and horses, the luxury of dress, the exercises of hunting and hawking [1] are the delight of the Normans; but, on pressing occasions, they can endure with incredible patience the inclemency of every climate, and the toil and abstinence of a military life." [2]

The Normans of Apulia were seated on the verge of the two empires, and, according to the policy of the hour, they accepted the investiture of their lands from the sovereigns of Germany or Constantinople. But the firmest title of these adventurers was the right of conquest: they neither loved nor trusted; they were neither trusted nor beloved; the contempt of the princes was mixed with fear, and the fear of the natives was mingled with hatred and resentment. Every object of desire, a horse, a woman, a garden, tempted and gratified the rapaciousness of the strangers,[3] and the avarice of their chiefs was only coloured by the more specious names of ambition and glory. The twelve counts were sometimes joined in a league of injustice; in their domestic quarrels they disputed the spoils of the people; the virtues of William were buried in his grave; and Drogo, his brother and successor, was better qualified to lead the valour, than to restrain the violence, of his peers. Under the reign of Constantine Monomachus, the policy, rather than benevolence, of the Byzantine court attempted to relieve Italy from this adherent mischief, more grievous than a flight of barbarians;[4] and Argyrus, the son of Melo, was invested for this purpose with

---

[1] The hunting and hawking more properly belong to the *descendants* of the Norwegian sailors; though they might import from Norway and Iceland the finest casts of falcons.

[2] We may compare this portrait with that of William of Malmesbury (de Gestis Anglorum, l. iii. p. 101, 102), who appreciates, like a philosophic historian, the vices and virtues of the Saxons and Normans. England was assuredly a gainer by the conquest.

[3] The biographer of St. Leo IX. pours his holy venom on the Normans. Videns indisciplinatam et alienam gentem Normannorum, crudeli et inauditâ rabie et plusquam Paganâ impietate adversus ecclesias Dei insurgere, passim Christianos trucidare, etc. (Wibert, c. 6). The honest Apulian (l. ii. p. 259) says calmly of their accuser, Veris commiscens fallacia.

[4] The policy of the Greeks, revolt of Maniaces, etc., must be collected from Cedrenus (tom. ii. p. 757, 758 [p. 548, *sq.*, ed. Bonn]), William Appulus (l. i. p. 257, 258, l. ii. p. 259), and the two Chronicles of Bari, by Lupus Protospata (Muratori, Script. Ital. tom. v. p. 42, 43, 44), and an anonymous writer (Antiquitat. Italiæ medii Ævi, tom. i. p. 31-35). This last is a fragment of some value.

the most lofty titles [1] and the most ample commission. The memory of his father might recommend him to the Normans, and he had already engaged their voluntary service to quell the revolt of Maniaces, and to avenge their own and the public injury. It was the design of Constantine to transplant this war-like colony from the Italian provinces to the Persian war, and the son of Melo distributed among the chiefs the gold and manu-factures of Greece as the first-fruits of the Imperial bounty. But his arts were baffled by the sense and spirit of the conquerors of Apulia: his gifts, or at least his proposals, were rejected, and they unanimously refused to relinquish their possessions and their hopes for the distant prospect of Asiatic fortune. After the means of persuasion had failed, Argyrus resolved to compel or to destroy: the Latin powers were solicited against the common enemy, and an offensive alliance was formed of the pope and the two emperors of the East and West. The throne of St. Peter was occupied by Leo the Ninth, a simple saint, [2] of a temper most apt to deceive himself and the world, and whose venerable character would consecrate with the name of piety the measures least compatible with the practice of religion. His humanity was affected by the complaints, perhaps the calumnies, of an injured people; the impious Normans had interrupted the pay-ment of tithes, and the temporal sword might be lawfully un-sheathed against the sacrilegious robbers who were deaf to the censures of the church. As a German of noble birth and royal kindred, Leo had free access to the court and confidence of the emperor Henry the Third, and in search of arms and allies his ardent zeal transported him from Apulia to Saxony, from the Elbe to the Tiber. During these hostile preparations, Argyrus indulged himself in the use of secret and guilty weapons: a crowd of Normans became the victims of public or private revenge, and the valiant Drogo was murdered in a church. But his spirit survived in his brother Humphrey, the third count of Apulia. The assassins were chastised, and the son of

---

[1] Argyrus received, says the anonymous Chronicle of Bari, imperial letters, Fœderatûs et Patriciatûs, et Catapani et Vestatûs. In his Annals Muratori (tom. viii. p. 426) very properly reads, or interprets, *Sevestatus*, the title of Sebastos or Augustus. But in his Antiquities he was taught by Ducange to make it a palatine office, master of the wardrobe.

[2] A Life of St. Leo IX., deeply tinged with the passions and prejudices of the age, has been composed by Wibert, printed at Paris, 1615, in octavo, and since inserted in the Collections of the Bollandists, of Mabillon, and of Muratori. The public and private history of that pope is diligently treated by M. de St. Marc. (Abrégé, tom. ii. p. 140-210, and p. 25-95, second column.)

Melo, overthrown and wounded, was driven from the field to hide his shame behind the walls of Bari, and to await the tardy succour of his allies.

But the power of Constantine was distracted by a Turkish war, the mind of Henry was feeble and irresolute, and the pope, instead of repassing the Alps with a German army, was accompanied only by a guard of seven hundred Swabians and some volunteers of Lorraine. In his long progress from Mantua to Beneventum a vile and promiscuous multitude of Italians was enlisted under the holy standard;[1] the priest and the robber slept in the same tent, the pikes and crosses were intermingled in the front, and the martial saint repeated the lessons of his youth in the order of march, of encampment, and of combat. The Normans of Apulia could muster in the field no more than three thousand horse, with a handful of infantry; the defection of the natives intercepted their provisions and retreat; and their spirit, incapable of fear, was chilled for a moment by superstitious awe. On the hostile approach of Leo, they knelt, without disgrace or reluctance, before their spiritual father. But the pope was inexorable; his lofty Germans affected to deride the diminutive stature of their adversaries; and the Normans were informed that death or exile was their only alternative. Flight they disdained, and, as many of them had been three days without tasting food, they embraced the assurance of a more easy and honourable death. They climbed the hill of Civitella, descended into the plain, and charged in three divisions the army of the pope. On the left, and in the centre, Richard count of Aversa, and Robert the famous Guiscard, attacked, broke, routed, and pursued the Italian multitudes, who fought without discipline and fled without shame. A harder trial was reserved for the valour of Count Humphrey, who led the cavalry of the right wing. The Germans[2] have been described as unskilful in the management of the horse and lance, but on foot they formed a strong and impenetrable phalanx, and neither man, nor steed, nor armour could resist the

---

[1] See the expedition of Leo IX. against the Normans. See William Appulus (l. ii. p. 259-261) and Jeffrey Malaterra (l. i. c. 13, 14, 15, p. 253). They are impartial, as the national is counterbalanced by the clerical prejudice.

[2] Teutonici, quia cæsaries et forma decoros
Fecerat egregie proceri corporis illos,
Corpora derident Normannica, quæ breviora
Esse videbantur. [p. 259.]

The verses of the Apulian are commonly in this strain, though he heats himself a little in the battle. Two of his similes from hawking and sorcery are descriptive of manners.

weight of their long and two-handed swords. After a severe conflict they were encompassed by the squadrons returning from the pursuit, and died in their ranks with the esteem of their foes and the satisfaction of revenge. The gates of Civitella were shut against the flying pope, and he was overtaken by the pious conquerors, who kissed his feet to implore his blessing and the absolution of their sinful victory. The soldiers beheld in their enemy and captive the vicar of Christ; and, though we may suppose the policy of the chiefs, it is probable that they were infected by the popular superstition. In the calm of retirement the well-meaning pope deplored the effusion of Christian blood which must be imputed to his account; he felt that he had been the author of sin and scandal; and, as his undertaking had failed, the indecency of his military character was universally condemned.[1] With these dispositions he listened to the offers of a beneficial treaty, deserted an alliance which he had preached as the cause of God, and ratified the past and future conquests of the Normans. By whatever hands they had been usurped, the provinces of Apulia and Calabria were a part of the donation of Constantine and the patrimony of St. Peter: the grant and the acceptance confirmed the mutual claims of the pontiff and the adventurers. They promised to support each other with spiritual and temporal arms; a tribute or quit-rent of twelve pence was afterwards stipulated for every plough-land, and since this memorable transaction the kingdom of Naples has remained above seven hundred years a fief of the Holy See.[2]

The pedigree of Robert Guiscard[3] is variously deduced from the peasants and the dukes of Normandy: from the peasants, by the pride and ignorance of a Grecian princess;[4] from the

[1] Several respectable censures or complaints are produced by M. de St. Marc (tom. ii. p. 200-204). As Peter Damianus, the oracle of the times, had denied the popes the right of making war, the hermit (lugens eremi incola) is arraigned by the cardinal, and Baronius (Annal. Eccles. A.D. 1053, No. 10-17) most strenuously asserts the two swords of St. Peter.

[2] The origin and nature of the papal investitures are ably discussed by Giannone (Istoria Civile di Napoli, tom. ii. p. 37-49, 57-66) as a lawyer and antiquarian. Yet he vainly strives to reconcile the duties of patriot and Catholic, adopts an empty distinction of " Ecclesia Romana non dedit sed accepit," and shrinks from an honest but dangerous confession of the truth.

[3] The birth, character, and first actions of Robert Guiscard may be found in Jeffrey Malaterra (l. i. c. 3, 4, 11, 16, 17, 18, 38, 39, 40), William Appulus (l. ii. p. 260-262), William Gemeticensis or of Jumieges (l. xi. c. 30, p. 663, 664, edit. Camden), and Anna Comnena (Alexiad, l. i. p. 23-27, l. vi. p. 165, 166 [tom. i. p. 49-56, 293-295, ed. Bonn]), with the annotations of Ducange (Not. in Alexiad. p. 230-232, 320), who has swept all the French and Latin Chronicles for supplemental intelligence.

[4] Ὁ δὲ Ῥομπέρτος (a Greek corruption) οὗτος Νορμάννος τὸ γένος, τὴν τύχην

dukes, by the ignorance and flattery of the Italian subjects.[1]
His genuine descent may be ascribed to the second or middle
order of private nobility.[2] He sprang from a race of *valvassors*
or *bannerets*, of the diocese of Coutances, in the Lower Normandy;
the castle of Hauteville was their honourable seat; his father
Tancred was conspicuous in the court and army of the duke,
and his military service was furnished by ten soldiers or knights.
Two marriages, of a rank not unworthy of his own, made him the
father of twelve sons, who were educated at home by the impartial tenderness of his second wife. But a narrow patrimony
was insufficient for this numerous and daring progeny; they saw
around the neighbourhood the mischiefs of poverty and discord,
and resolved to seek in foreign wars a more glorious inheritance.
Two only remained to perpetuate the race and cherish their
father's age; their ten brothers, as they successively attained the
vigour of manhood, departed from the castle, passed the Alps,
and joined the Apulian camp of the Normans. The elder were
prompted by native spirit: their success encouraged their
younger brethren; and the three first in seniority, William,
Drogo, and Humphrey, deserved to be the chiefs of their nation
and the founders of the new republic. Robert was the eldest of
the seven sons of the second marriage, and even the reluctant
praise of his foes has endowed him with the heroic qualities of
a soldier and a statesman. His lofty stature surpassed the
tallest of his army; his limbs were cast in the true proportion of
strength and gracefulness; and to the decline of life he maintained the patient vigour of health and the commanding dignity
of his form. His complexion was ruddy, his shoulders were
broad, his hair and beard were long and of a flaxen colour, his

---

ἄσημος [tom. i. p. 50]. . . . Again, ἐξ ἀφανοῦς πανὺ τύχης περιφάνης. And
elsewhere (l. iv. p. 84 [ed. Ven.; p. 104, ed. Par.; tom. i. p. 190, ed. Bonn]),
ἀπὸ ἐσχάτης πενίας καὶ τύχης ἀφανοῦς. Anna Comnena was born in the
purple; yet her father was no more than a private though illustrious
subject, who raised himself to the empire.

[1] Giannone (tom. ii. p. 2) forgets all his original authors, and rests this
princely descent on the credit of Inveges, an Augustine monk of Palermo
in the last century. They continue the succession of dukes from Rollo to
William II. the Bastard or Conqueror, whom they hold (communemente
si tiene) to be the father of Tancred of Hauteville: a most strange and
stupendous blunder! The sons of Tancred fought in Apulia before William
II. was three years old (A.D. 1037).

[2] The judgment of Ducange is just and moderate: Certè humilis fuit ac
tenuis Roberti familia, si ducalem et regium spectemus apicem, ad quem
postea pervenit; quæ honesta tamen et præter nobilium vulgarium statum
et conditionem illustris habita est, " quæ nec humi reperet nec altum quid
tumeret." (Wilhelm. Malmsbur. de Gestis Anglorum, l. iii. p. 107; Not.
ad Alexiad. p. 230.)

eyes sparkled with fire, and his voice, like that of Achilles, could impress obedience and terror amidst the tumult of battle. In the ruder ages of chivalry such qualifications are not below the notice of the poet or historian; they may observe that Robert, at once, and with equal dexterity, could wield in the right hand his sword, his lance in the left; that in the battle of Civitella he was thrice unhorsed, and that in the close of that memorable day he was adjudged to have borne away the prize of valour from the warriors of the two armies.[1] His boundless ambition was founded on the consciousness of superior worth; in the pursuit of greatness he was never arrested by the scruples of justice, and seldom moved by the feelings of humanity; though not insensible of fame, the choice of open or clandestine means was determined only by his present advantage. The surname of *Guiscard*[2] was applied to this master of political wisdom, which is too often confounded with the practice of dissimulation and deceit, and Robert is praised by the Apulian poet for excelling the cunning of Ulysses and the eloquence of Cicero. Yet these arts were disguised by an appearance of military frankness; in his highest fortune he was accessible and courteous to his fellow-soldiers; and while he indulged the prejudices of his new subjects, he affected in his dress and manners to maintain the ancient fashion of his country. He grasped with a rapacious, that he might distribute with a liberal, hand; his primitive indigence had taught the habits of frugality; the gain of a merchant was not below his attention; and his prisoners were tortured with slow and unfeeling cruelty to force a discovery of their secret treasure. According to the Greeks, he departed from Normandy with only five followers on horseback and thirty on foot; yet even this allowance appears too bountiful; the sixth son of Tancred of Hauteville passed the Alps as a pilgrim, and his first military

---

[1] I shall quote with pleasure some of the best lines of the Apulian (l. ii. p. 260).

> Pugnat utrâque manû, nec lancea cassa, nec ensis
> Cassus erat, quocunque manû deducere vellet.
> Ter dejectus equo, ter viribus ipse resumptis
> Major in arma redit: stimulos furor ipse ministrat.
> Ut Leo cum frendens, etc.
>
> . . . . .
> Nullus in hoc bello sicuti post bella probatum est
> Victor vel victus, tam magnos edidit ictus.

[2] The Norman writers and editors most conversant with their own idiom interpret *Guiscard* or *Wiscard* by *Callidus*, a cunning man. The root (*wise*) is familiar to our ear; and in the old word *Wiseacre* I can discern something of a similar sense and termination. Τὴν ψύχην πανουργότατος is no bad translation of the surname and character of Robert.

band was levied among the adventurers of Italy. His brothers and countrymen had divided the fertile lands of Apulia, but they guarded their shares with the jealousy of avarice; the aspiring youth was driven forwards to the mountains of Calabria, and in his first exploits against the Greeks and the natives it is not easy to discriminate the hero from the robber. To surprise a castle or a convent, to ensnare a wealthy citizen, to plunder the adjacent villages for necessary food, were the obscure labours which formed and exercised the powers of his mind and body. The volunteers of Normandy adhered to his standard, and, under his command, the peasants of Calabria assumed the name and character of Normans.

As the genius of Robert expanded with his fortune, he awakened the jealousy of his elder brother, by whom, in a transient quarrel, his life was threatened and his liberty restrained. After the death of Humphrey the tender age of his sons excluded them from the command; they were reduced to a private estate by the ambition of their guardian and uncle; and Guiscard was exalted on a buckler, and saluted count of Apulia and general of the republic. With an increase of authority and of force, he resumed the conquest of Calabria, and soon aspired to a rank that should raise him for ever above the heads of his equals. By some acts of rapine or sacrilege he had incurred a papal excommunication: but Nicholas the Second was easily persuaded that the divisions of friends could terminate only in their mutual prejudice; that the Normans were the faithful champions of the Holy See; and it was safer to trust the alliance of a prince than the caprice of an aristocracy. A synod of one hundred bishops was convened at Melphi; and the count interrupted an important enterprise to guard the person and execute the decrees of the Roman pontiff. His gratitude and policy conferred on Robert and his posterity the ducal title,[1] with the investiture of Apulia, Calabria, and all the lands, both in Italy and Sicily, which his sword could rescue from the schismatic Greeks and the unbelieving Saracens.[2] This apostolic sanction might justify his arms: but the obedi-

---

[1] The acquisition of the ducal title by Robert Guiscard is a nice and obscure business. With the good advice of Giannone, Muratori, and St. Marc, I have endeavoured to form a consistent and probable narrative.

[2] Baronius (Annal. Eccles. A.D. 1059, No. 69) has published the original act. He professes to have copied it from the *Liber Censuum*, a Vatican MS. Yet a Liber Censuum of the twelfth century has been printed by Muratori (Antiquit. medii Ævi, tom. v. p. 851-908); and the names of Vatican and Cardinal awaken the suspicions of a Protestant, and even of a philosopher.

ence of a free and victorious people could not be transferred
without their consent; and Guiscard dissembled his elevation
till the ensuing campaign had been illustrated by the conquest
of Consenza and Reggio. In the hour of triumph he assembled
his troops and solicited the Normans to confirm by their suffrage
the judgment of the vicar of Christ: the soldiers hailed with
joyful acclamations their valiant duke; and the counts, his
former equals, pronounced the oath of fidelity with hollow
smiles and secret indignation. After this inauguration, Robert
styled himself, " By the grace of God and St. Peter, duke of
Apulia, Calabria, and hereafter of Sicily; " and it was the labour
of twenty years to deserve and realise these lofty appellations.
Such tardy progress, in a narrow space, may seem unworthy of
the abilities of the chief and the spirit of the nation: but the
Normans were few in number; their resources were scanty;
their service was voluntary and precarious. The bravest designs
of the duke were sometimes opposed by the free voice of his
parliament of barons: the twelve counts of popular election
conspired against his authority; and against their perfidious
uncle the sons of Humphrey demanded justice and revenge.
By his policy and vigour Guiscard discovered their plots, suppressed their rebellions, and punished the guilty with death or
exile; but in these domestic feuds his years, and the national
strength, were unprofitably consumed. After the defeat of his
foreign enemies, the Greeks, Lombards, and Saracens, their
broken forces retreated to the strong and populous cities of the
sea-coast. They excelled in the arts of fortification and defence;
the Normans were accustomed to serve on horseback in the field,
and their rude attempts could only succeed by the efforts of
persevering courage. The resistance of Salerno was maintained
above eight months: the siege or blockade of Bari lasted near
four years. In these actions the Norman duke was the foremost in every danger, in every fatigue the last and most patient.
As he pressed the citadel of Salerno a huge stone from the rampart shattered one of his military engines, and by a splinter he
was wounded in the breast. Before the gates of Bari he lodged
in a miserable hut or barrack, composed of dry branches, and
thatched with straw—a perilous station, on all sides open to the
inclemency of the winter and the spears of the enemy.[1]

The Italian conquests of Robert correspond with the limits of

[1] Read the Life of Guiscard in the second and third books of the Apulian,
the first and second books of Malaterra.

the present kingdom of Naples; and the countries united by his arms have not been dissevered by the revolutions of seven hundred years.[1] The monarchy has been composed of the Greek provinces of Calabria and Apulia, of the Lombard principality of Salerno, the republic of Amalphi, and the inland dependencies of the large and ancient duchy of Beneventum. Three districts only were exempted from the common law of subjection—the first for ever, and the two last till the middle of the succeeding century. The city and immediate territory of Benevento had been transferred, by gift or exchange, from the German emperor to the Roman pontiff; and although this holy land was sometimes invaded, the name of St. Peter was finally more potent than the sword of the Normans. Their first colony of Aversa subdued and held the state of Capua, and her princes were reduced to beg their bread before the palace of their fathers. The dukes of Naples, the present metropolis, maintained the popular freedom under the shadow of the Byzantine empire. Among the new acquisitions of Guiscard the science of Salerno [2] and the trade of Amalphi [3] may detain for a moment the curiosity of the reader. I. Of the learned faculties jurisprudence implies the previous establishment of laws and property; and theology may perhaps be superseded by the full light of religion and reason. But the savage and the sage must alike implore the assistance of physic; and if *our* diseases are inflamed by luxury, the mischiefs of blows and wounds would be more frequent in the ruder ages of society. The treasures of Grecian medicine had been communicated to the Arabian colonies of Africa, Spain, and Sicily; and in the intercourse of peace and war a spark of knowledge had been kindled and cherished at Salerno, an illustrious city, in which the men were

---

[1] The conquests of Robert Guiscard and Roger I., the exemption of Benevento and the twelve provinces of the kingdom, are fairly exposed by Giannone in the second volume of his Istoria Civile, l. ix. x. xi., and l. xvii. p. 460-470. This modern division was not established before the time of Frederick II.

[2] Giannone (tom. ii. p. 119-127), Muratori (Antiquitat. medii Ævi, tom. iii. dissert. xliv. p. 935, 936), and Tiraboschi (Istoria della Letteratura Italiana), have given an historical account of these physicians; their medical knowledge and practice must be left to our physicians.

[3] At the end of the Historia Pandectarum of Henry Brenckmann (Trajecti ad Rhenum, 1722, in 4to) the indefatigable author has inserted two dissertations—de Republicâ Amalphitanâ, and de Amalphi à Pisanis direptâ, which are built on the testimonies of one hundred and forty writers. Yet he has forgotten two most important passages of the embassy of Liutprand (A.D. 969), which compare the trade and navigation of Amalphi with that of Venice.

honest and the women beautiful.[1]   A school, the first that arose in the darkness of Europe, was consecrated to the healing art: the conscience of monks and bishops was reconciled to that salutary and lucrative profession; and a crowd of patients of the most eminent rank and most distant climates invited or visited the physicians of Salerno.[2]   They were protected by the Norman conquerors; and Guiscard, though bred in arms, could discern the merit and value of a philosopher.   After a pilgrimage of thirty-nine years, Constantine, an African Christian, returned from Bagdad, a master of the language and learning of the Arabians; and Salerno was enriched by the practice, the lessons, and the writings of the pupil of Avicenna.   The school of medicine has long slept in the name of a university; but her precepts are abridged in a string of aphorisms, bound together in the Leonine verses, or Latin rhymes, of the twelfth century.[3]   II. Seven miles to the west of Salerno, and thirty to the south of Naples, the obscure town of Amalphi displayed the power and rewards of industry.   The land, however fertile, was of narrow extent; but the sea was accessible and open: the inhabitants first assumed the office of supplying the western world with the manufactures and productions of the East; and this useful traffic was the source of their opulence and freedom.   The government was popular, under the administration of a duke and the supremacy of the Greek emperor.   Fifty thousand citizens were numbered in the walls of Amalphi; nor was any city more abundantly provided with gold, silver, and the objects of precious luxury.   The mariners who swarmed in her port excelled in the theory and practice of navigation and astronomy;

---

[1] Urbs Latii non est hâc delitiosior urbe,
    Frugibus, arboribus, vinoque redundat; et unde
    Non tibi poma, nuces, non pulchra palatia desunt,
    Non species muliebris abest probitasque virorum.
                                Gulielmus Appulus, l. iii. p. 267.

[2] [With regard to the position of Salerno as a university, Rashdall, in his *Universities in the Middle Ages*, says, " Salerno remains a completely isolated factor in the academic polity of the Middle Ages.   While its position as a school of medicine was for two centuries at least as unique as that of Paris in theology and Bologna in law, while throughout the Middle Ages no school of medicine except Montpellier rivalled its fame, it remained without influence in the development of academic institutions."—O. S.]

[3] Muratori carries their antiquity above the year (1066) of the death of Edward the Confessor, the *rex Anglorum* to whom they are addressed. Nor is this date affected by the opinion, or rather mistake, of Pasquier (Recherches de la France, l. vii. c. 2) and Ducange (Glossar. Latin.).   The practice of rhyming, as early as the seventh century, was borrowed from the languages of the North and East (Muratori, Antiquat. tom. iii. dissert. xl. p. 686-708).

and the discovery of the compass, which has opened the globe, is due to their ingenuity or good fortune. Their trade was extended to the coasts, or at least to the commodities, of Africa, Arabia, and India; and their settlements in Constantinople, Antioch, Jerusalem, and Alexandria acquired the privileges of independent colonies.[1] After three hundred years of prosperity Amalphi was oppressed by the arms of the Normans, and sacked by the jealousy of Pisa; but the poverty of one thousand fishermen is yet dignified by the remains of an arsenal, a cathedral, and the palaces of royal merchants.

Roger, the twelfth and last of the sons of Tancred, had been long detained in Normandy by his own and his father's age. He accepted the welcome summons; hastened to the Apulian camp; and deserved at first the esteem, and afterwards the envy, of his elder brother. Their valour and ambition were equal; but the youth, the beauty, the elegant manners, of Roger, engaged the disinterested love of the soldiers and people. So scanty was his allowance, for himself and forty followers, that he descended from conquest to robbery, and from robbery to domestic theft; and so loose were the notions of property, that, by his own historian, at his special command, he is accused of stealing horses from a stable at Melphi.[2] His spirit emerged from poverty and disgrace: from these base practices he rose to the merit and glory of a holy war; and the invasion of Sicily was seconded by the zeal and policy of his brother Guiscard. After the retreat of the Greeks, the *idolaters*, a most audacious reproach of the Catholics, had retrieved their losses and possessions; but the deliverance of the island, so vainly undertaken by the forces

---

[1] The description of Amalphi, by William the Apulian (l. iii. p. 267), contains much truth and some poetry, and the third line may be applied to the sailor's compass:—

> Nulla magis locuples argento, vestibus, auro
> Partibus innumeris: hâc [ac] plurimus urbe moratur
> Nauta *maris cœlique vias aperire peritus.*
> Huc et Alexandri diversa feruntur ab urbe
> Regis, et Antiochi. Gens hæc freta plurima transit.
> His [Huic] Arabes, Indi, Siculi noscuntur et Afri.
> Hæc gens est totum prope nobilitata per orbem,
> Et mercando ferens, et amans mercata referre.

[2] Latrocinio armigerorum suorum in multis sustentabatur, quod quidem ad ejus ignominiam non dicimus; sed ipso ita præcipiente adhuc viliora et reprehensibiliora dicturi sumus [de ipso scripturi sumus] ut pluribus patescat, quam laboriose et cum quantâ angustiâ a profundâ paupertate ad summum culmen divitiarum vel honoris attigerit. Such is the preface of Malaterra (l. i. c. 25) to the horse-stealing. From the moment (l. i. c. 19) that he has mentioned his patron Roger, the elder brother sinks into the second character. Something similar in Velleius Paterculus may be observed of Augustus and Tiberius.

of the Eastern empire, was achieved by a small and private band of adventurers.[1]   In the first attempt Roger braved, in an open boat, the real and fabulous dangers of Scylla and Charybdis; landed with only sixty soldiers on a hostile shore; drove the Saracens to the gates of Messina; and safely returned with the spoils of the adjacent country.   In the fortress of Trani his active and patient courage were equally conspicuous.   In his old age he related with pleasure that, by the distress of the siege, himself, and the countess his wife, had been reduced to a single cloak or mantle, which they wore alternately: that in a sally his horse had been slain, and he was dragged away by the Saracens; but that he owed his rescue to his good sword, and had retreated with his saddle on his back, lest the meanest trophy might be left in the hands of the miscreants.   In the siege of Trani, three hundred Normans withstood and repulsed the forces of the island.   In the field of Ceramio fifty thousand horse and foot were overthrown by one hundred and thirty-six Christian soldiers, without reckoning St. George, who fought on horseback in the foremost ranks.   The captive banners, with four camels, were reserved for the successor of St. Peter; and had these barbaric spoils been exposed not in the Vatican, but in the Capitol, they might have revived the memory of the Punic triumphs.   These insufficient numbers of the Normans most probably denote their knights, the soldiers of honourable and equestrian rank, each of whom was attended by five or six followers in the field;[2] yet, with the aid of this interpretation, and after every fair allowance on the side of valour, arms, and reputation, the discomfiture of so many myriads will reduce the prudent reader to the alternative of a miracle or a fable.   The Arabs of Sicily derived a frequent and powerful succour from their countrymen of Africa: in the siege of Palermo the Norman cavalry was assisted by the galleys of Pisa; and, in the hour of action, the envy of the two brothers was sublimed to a generous and invincible emulation.   After a war of thirty years,[3] Roger,

---

[1] Duo sibi proficua deputans, animæ scilicet et corporis, si terram idolis deditam ad cultum divinum revocaret (Galfrid Malaterra, l. ii. c. 1).   The conquest of Sicily is related in the three last books, and he himself has given an accurate summary of the chapters (p. 544-546).

[2] See the word *Milites* in the Latin Glossary of Ducange.

[3] Of odd particulars, I learn from Malaterra that the Arabs had introduced into Sicily the use of camels (l. ii., c. 33) and of carrier-pigeons (c. 42); and that the bite of the tarantula provokes a windy disposition, quæ per anum inhoneste crepitando emergit—a symptom most ridiculously felt by the whole Norman army in their camp near Palermo (c. 36).   I shall add an etymology not unworthy of the eleventh century: *Messana* is derived from *Messis*, the place from whence the harvests of the isle were sent in tribute to Rome (l. ii. c. 1).

with the title of great count, obtained the sovereignty of the largest and most fruitful island of the Mediterranean; and his administration displays a liberal and enlightened mind above the limits of his age and education. The Moslems were maintained in the free enjoyment of their religion and property:[1] a philosopher and physician of Mazara, of the race of Mohammed, harangued the conqueror, and was invited to court; his geography of the seven climates was translated into Latin; and Roger, after a diligent perusal, preferred the work of the Arabian to the writings of the Grecian Ptolemy.[2] A remnant of Christian natives had promoted the success of the Normans: they were rewarded by the triumph of the cross. The island was restored to the jurisdiction of the Roman pontiff; new bishops were planted in the principal cities; and the clergy was satisfied by a liberal endowment of churches and monasteries. Yet the Catholic hero asserted the rights of the civil magistrate. Instead of resigning the investiture of benefices, he dexterously applied to his own profit the papal claims: the supremacy of the crown was secured and enlarged by the singular bull which declares the princes of Sicily hereditary and perpetual legates of the Holy See.[3]

To Robert Guiscard the conquest of Sicily was more glorious than beneficial: the possession of Apulia and Calabria was inadequate to his ambition; and he resolved to embrace or create the first occasion of invading, perhaps of subduing, the Roman empire of the East.[4] From his first wife, the partner of his humble fortunes, he had been divorced under the pretence of

---

[1] See the capitulation of Palermo in Malaterra, l. ii. c. 45, and Giannone, who remarks the general toleration of the Saracens (tom. ii. p. 72).

[2] John Leo Afer, de Medicis et Philosophis Arabibus, c. 14, apud Fabric. Biblioth. Græc. tom. xiii. p. 278, 279. This philosopher is named Esseriph Essachalli, and he died in Africa, A.H. 516—A.D. 1122. Yet this story bears a strange resemblance to the Sherif al Edrissi, who presented his book (Geographia Nubiensis, see preface, p. 88, 90, 170) to Roger king of Sicily, A.H. 548—A.D. 1153 (D'Herbelot, Bibliothèque Orientale, p. 786; Prideaux's Life of Mahomet, p. 188; Petit de la Croix, Hist. de Gengiscan, p. 535, 536; Casiri, Biblioth. Arab. Hispan. tom. ii. p. 9-13); and I am afraid of some mistake.

[3] Malaterra remarks the foundation of the bishoprics (l. iv. c. 7), and produces the original of the bull (l. iv. c. 29). Giannone gives a rational idea of this privilege, and the tribunal of the monarchy of Sicily (tom. ii. p. 95-102); and St. Marc (Abrégé, tom. iii. p. 217-301, first column) labours the case with the diligence of a Sicilian lawyer.

[4] In the first expedition of Robert against the Greeks, I follow Anna Comnena (the first, third, fourth, and fifth books of the Alexiad), William Appulus (l. iv. and v., p. 270-275), and Jeffrey Malaterra (l. iii. c. 13, 14, 24-29, 39). Their information is contemporary and authentic, but none of them were eye-witnesses of the war.

consanguinity; and her son Bohemond was destined to imitate,
rather than to succeed, his illustrious father. The second wife of
Guiscard was the daughter of the princes of Salerno; the Lombards acquiesced in the lineal succession of their son Roger; their
five daughters were given in honourable nuptials,[1] and one of
them was betrothed, in a tender age, to Constantine, a beautiful
youth, the son and heir of the emperor Michael.[2] But the throne
of Constantinople was shaken by a revolution: the Imperial
family of Ducas was confined to the palace or the cloister; and
Robert deplored and resented the disgrace of his daughter and
the expulsion of his ally. A Greek, who styled himself the father
of Constantine, soon appeared at Salerno, and related the adventures of his fall and flight. That unfortunate friend was
acknowledged by the duke, and adorned with the pomp and titles
of Imperial dignity: in his triumphal progress through Apulia
and Calabria, Michael [3] was saluted with the tears and acclamations of the people; and pope Gregory the Seventh exhorted the
bishops to preach, and the Catholics to fight, in the pious work of
his restoration. His conversations with Robert were frequent
and familiar; and their mutual promises were justified by the
valour of the Normans and the treasures of the East. Yet this
Michael, by the confession of the Greeks and Latins, was a
pageant and an impostor; a monk who had fled from his convent,
or a domestic who had served in the palace. The fraud had been
contrived by the subtle Guiscard; and he trusted that, after this
pretender had given a decent colour to his arms, he would sink,
at the nod of the conqueror, into his primitive obscurity. But
victory was the only argument that could determine the belief of

[1] One of them was married to Hugh, the son of Azzo, or Axo, a marquis
of Lombardy, rich, powerful, and *noble* (Gulielm. Appul. l. iii. p. 267) in
the eleventh century, and whose ancestors in the tenth and ninth are explored by the critical industry of Leibnitz and Muratori. From the two
elder sons of the marquis Azzo are derived the illustrious lines of Bruns-
wick and Este. See Muratori, Antichità Estense.

[2] Anna Comnena somewhat too wantonly praises and bewails that
handsome boy, who, after the rupture of his barbaric nuptials (l. i. p. 23
[tom. i. p. 49, ed. Bonn]), was betrothed as her husband; he was ἄγαλμα
φύσεως . . . Θεοῦ χειρῶν φιλοτίμημα . . . χρυσοῦ γένους ἀπορρον, etc.
(p. 27 [tom. i. p. 57, ed. Bonn]). Elsewhere she describes the red and
white of his skin, his hawk's eyes, etc., l. iii. p. 71 [tom. i. p. 135, ed. Bonn].

[3] Anna Comnena, l. i. p. 28, 29 [tom. i. p. 58, *sq.*, ed. Bonn]; Gulielm.
Appul. l. iv. p. 271; Galfrid Malaterra, l. iii. c. 13, p. 579, 580. Malaterra
is more cautious in his style; but the Apulian is bold and positive.

—— Mentitus se Michaelem
Venerat a Danais quidam seductor ad illum.

As Gregory VII. had believed, Baronius, almost alone, recognises the
emperor Michael (A.D. 1080, No. 44).

the Greeks; and the ardour of the Latins was much inferior to their credulity: the Norman veterans wished to enjoy the harvest of their toils, and the unwarlike Italians trembled at the known and unknown dangers of a transmarine expedition. In his new levies Robert exerted the influence of gifts and promises, the terrors of civil and ecclesiastical authority; and some acts of violence might justify the reproach that age and infancy were pressed without distinction into the service of their unrelenting prince. After two years' incessant preparations the land and naval forces were assembled at Otranto, at the heel, or extreme promontory, of Italy; and Robert was accompanied by his wife, who fought by his side, his son Bohemond, and the representative of the emperor Michael. Thirteen hundred knights [1] of Norman race or discipline formed the sinews of the army, which might be swelled to thirty thousand [2] followers of every denomination. The men, the horses, the arms, the engines, the wooden towers covered with raw hides, were embarked on board one hundred and fifty vessels: the transports had been built in the ports of Italy, and the galleys were supplied by the alliance of the republic of Ragusa.

At the mouth of the Adriatic Gulf the shores of Italy and Epirus incline towards each other. The space between Brundusium and Durazzo, the Roman passage, is no more than one hundred miles; [3] at the last station of Otranto it is contracted to fifty; [4] and this narrow distance had suggested to Pyrrhus and Pompey the sublime or extravagant idea of a bridge. Before the general embarkation the Norman duke despatched Bohemond with fifteen galleys to seize or threaten the isle of Corfu, to survey the opposite coast, and to secure a harbour in the neighbourhood

[1] Ipse armatæ militiæ non plusquam MCCC milites secum habuisse, ab eis qui eidem negotio interfuerunt attestatur (Malaterra, l. iii. c. 24, p. 583). These are the same whom the Apulian (l. iv. p. 273) styles the equestris gens ducis, equites de gente ducis.

[2] Εἰς τριάκοντα χιλιάδας, says Anna Comnena (Alexias, l. i. p. 37 [tom. i. p. 75, ed. Bonn]) ; and her account tallies with the number and lading of the ships. Ivit in [contra] Dyrrachium cum xv millibus hominum, says the Chronicon Breve Normannicum (Muratori, Scriptores, tom. v. p. 278). I have endeavoured to reconcile these reckonings.

[3] The Itinerary of Jerusalem (p. 609, edit. Wesseling) gives a true and reasonable space of a thousand stadia, or one hundred miles, which is strangely doubled by Strabo (l. vi. p. 433 [p. 283, ed. Casaub.]) and Pliny (Hist. Natur. iii. 16).

[4] Pliny (Hist. Nat. iii. 6, 16) allows *quinquaginta* millia for this brevissimus cursus, and agrees with the real distance from Otranto to La Vallona, or Aulon (D'Anville, Analyse de la Carte des Côtes de la Grèce, etc., p. 3-6). Hermolaus Barbarus, who substitutes *centum* (Harduin, Not. lxvi. in Plin. l. iii.), might have been corrected by every Venetian pilot who had sailed out of the gulf.

of Vallona for the landing of the troops. They passed and landed without perceiving an enemy; and this successful experiment displayed the neglect and decay of the naval power of the Greeks. The islands of Epirus and the maritime towns were subdued by the arms or the name of Robert, who led his fleet and army from Corfu (I use the modern appellation) to the siege of Durazzo. That city, the western key of the empire, was guarded by ancient renown and recent fortifications, by George Palæologus, a patrician, victorious in the Oriental wars, and a numerous garrison of Albanians and Macedonians, who, in every age, have maintained the character of soldiers. In the prosecution of his enterprise the courage of Guiscard was assailed by every form of danger and mischance. In the most propitious season of the year, as his fleet passed along the coast, a storm of wind and snow unexpectedly arose: the Adriatic was swelled by the raging blast of the south, and a new shipwreck confirmed the old infamy of the Acroceraunian rocks.[1] The sails, the masts, and the oars were shattered or torn away; the sea and shore were covered with the fragments of vessels, with arms and dead bodies; and the greatest part of the provisions were either drowned or damaged. The ducal galley was laboriously rescued from the waves, and Robert halted seven days on the adjacent cape to collect the relics of his loss and revive the drooping spirits of his soldiers. The Normans were no longer the bold and experienced mariners who had explored the ocean from Greenland to Mount Atlas, and who smiled at the petty dangers of the Mediterranean. They had wept during the tempest; they were alarmed by the hostile approach of the Venetians, who had been solicited by the prayers and promises of the Byzantine court. The first day's action was not disadvantageous to Bohemond, a beardless youth,[2] who led the naval powers of his father. All night the galleys of the republic lay on their anchors in the form of a crescent; and the victory of the second day was decided by the dexterity of their evolutions, the station of their archers, the weight of their javelins, and the borrowed aid of the Greek fire.

---

[1] Infames scopulos Acroceraunia, Horat. carm. i. 3. The præcipitem Africum decertantem Aquilonibus et rabiem Noti, and the monstra natantia of the Adriatic, are somewhat enlarged; but Horace trembling for the life of Virgil is an interesting moment in the history of poetry and friendship.

[2] Τῶν δὲ εἰς τὸν πώγωνα αὐτοῦ ἐφυβρισάντων (Alexias, l. iv. p. 106 [tom. i. p. 193, ed. Born]). Yet the Normans shaved, and the Venetians wore their beards: they must have derided the *no* beard of Bohemond; a harsh interpretation! (Ducange, Not. ad Alexiad. p. 283.)

The Apulian and Ragusian vessels fled to the shore, several were cut from their cables and dragged away by the conqueror; and a sally from the town carried slaughter and dismay to the tents of the Norman duke. A seasonable relief was poured into Durazzo, and, as soon as the besiegers had lost the command of the sea, the islands and maritime towns withdrew from the camp the supply of tribute and provision. That camp was soon afflicted with a pestilential disease; five hundred knights perished by an inglorious death; and the list of burials (if all could obtain a decent burial) amounted to ten thousand persons. Under these calamities the mind of Guiscard alone was firm and invincible; and while he collected new forces from Apulia and Sicily, he battered, or scaled, or sapped, the walls of Durazzo. But his industry and valour were encountered by equal valour and more perfect industry. A movable turret, of a size and capacity to contain five hundred soldiers, had been rolled forwards to the foot of the rampart: but the descent of the door or drawbridge was checked by an enormous beam, and the wooden structure was instantly consumed by artificial flames.

While the Roman empire was attacked by the Turks in the East, and the Normans in the West, the aged successor of Michael surrendered the sceptre to the hands of Alexius, an illustrious captain, and the founder of the Comnenian dynasty. The princess Anne, his daughter and historian, observes, in her affected style, that even Hercules was unequal to a double combat; and, on this principle, she approves a hasty peace with the Turks, which allowed her father to undertake in person the relief of Durazzo. On his accession, Alexius found the camp without soldiers, and the treasury without money; yet such were the vigour and activity of his measures, that in six months he assembled an army of seventy thousand men,[1] and performed a march of five hundred miles. His troops were levied in Europe and Asia, from Peloponnesus to the Black Sea; his majesty was displayed in the silver arms and rich trappings of the companies of horse-guards; and the emperor was attended by a train of nobles and princes, some of whom, in rapid succession, had been

---

[1] Muratori (Annali d'Italia, tom. ix. p. 136, 137) observes that some authors (Petrus Diacon. Chron. Casinen. l. iii. c. 49) compose the Greek army of 170,000 men, but that the *hundred* may be struck off, and that Malaterra reckons only 70,000: a slight inattention. The passage to which he alludes is in the Chronicle of Lupus Protospata (Script. Ital. tom. v. p. 45). Malaterra (l. iii. c. 27) speaks in high but indefinite terms of the emperor, cum copiis innumerabilibus: like the Apulian poet (l. iv. p. 272):—

More locustarum montes et plana teguntur.

clothed with the purple, and were indulged by the lenity of the
times in a life of affluence and dignity. Their youthful ardour
might animate the multitude; but their love of pleasure and contempt of subordination were pregnant with disorder and mischief;
and their importunate clamours for speedy and decisive action
disconcerted the prudence of Alexius, who might have surrounded
and starved the besieging army. The enumeration of provinces
recalls a sad comparison of the past and present limits of the
Roman world: the raw levies were drawn together in haste and
terror; and the garrisons of Anatolia, or Asia Minor, had been
purchased by the evacuation of the cities which were immediately
occupied by the Turks. The strength of the Greek army consisted in the Varangians, the Scandinavian guards, whose
numbers were recently augmented by a colony of exiles and
volunteers from the British island of Thule. Under the yoke of
the Norman conqueror, the Danes and English were oppressed
and united; a band of adventurous youths resolved to desert a
land of slavery; the sea was open to their escape; and, in their
long pilgrimage, they visited every coast that afforded any hope
of liberty and revenge. They were entertained in the service of
the Greek emperor; and their first station was in a new city on
the Asiatic shore: but Alexius soon recalled them to the defence
of his person and palace; and bequeathed to his successors the
inheritance of their faith and valour.[1] The name of a Norman
invader revived the memory of their wrongs: they marched
with alacrity against the national foe, and panted to regain in
Epirus the glory which they had lost in the battle of Hastings.
The Varangians were supported by some companies of Franks or
Latins; and the rebels who had fled to Constantinople from the
tyranny of Guiscard were eager to signalise their zeal and gratify
their revenge. In this emergency the emperor had not disdained
the impure aid of the Paulicians or Manichæans of Thrace and
Bulgaria; and these heretics united with the patience of martyrdom the spirit and discipline of active valour.[2] The treaty with
the sultan had procured a supply of some thousand Turks; and
the arrows of the Scythian horse were opposed to the lances of
the Norman cavalry. On the report and distant prospect of

---

[1] See William of Malmesbury de Gestis Anglorum, l. ii. p. 92. Alexius
fidem Anglorum suspiciens præcipuis familiaritatibus suis eos applicabat,
amorem eorum filio transcribens. Ordericus Vitalis (Hist. Eccles. l. iv.
p. 508, l. vii. p. 641) relates their emigration from England and their
service in Greece.

[2] See the Apulian (l. i. p. 256). The character and story of these Manichæans has been the subject of the fifty-fourth chapter.

these formidable numbers, Robert assembled a council of his principal officers. " You behold," said he, " your danger: it is urgent and inevitable. 'The hills are covered with arms and standards; and the emperor of the Greeks is accustomed to wars and triumphs. Obedience and union are our only safety; and I am ready to yield the command to a more worthy leader." The vote and acclamation, even of his secret enemies, assured him, in that perilous moment, of their esteem and confidence; and the duke thus continued: " Let us trust in the rewards of victory, and deprive cowardice of the means of escape. Let us burn our vessels and our baggage, and give battle on this spot, as if it were the place of our nativity and our burial." The resolution was unanimously approved; and, without confining himself to his lines, Guiscard awaited in battle-array the nearer approach of the enemy. His rear was covered by a small river; his right wing extended to the sea; his left to the hills: nor was he conscious, perhaps, that on the same ground Cæsar and Pompey had formerly disputed the empire of the world.[1]

Against the advice of his wisest captains, Alexius resolved to risk the event of a general action, and exhorted the garrison of Durazzo to assist their own deliverance by a well-timed sally from the town. He marched in two columns to surprise the Normans before daybreak on two different sides: his light cavalry was scattered over the plain; the archers formed the second line; and the Varangians claimed the honours of the vanguard. In the first onset the battle-axes of the strangers made a deep and bloody impression on the army of Guiscard, which was now reduced to fifteen thousand men. The Lombards and Calabrians ignominiously turned their backs; they fled towards the river and the sea; but the bridge had been broken down to check the sally of the garrison, and the coast was lined with the Venetian galleys, who played their engines among the disorderly throng. On the verge of ruin, they were saved by the spirit and conduct of their chiefs. Gaita, the wife of Robert, is painted by the Greeks as a warlike Amazon, a second Pallas; less skilful in arts, but not less terrible in arms, than the Athenian goddess:[2] though

---

[1] See the simple and masterly narrative of Cæsar himself (Comment. de Bell. Civil. iii. 41-75). It is a pity that Quintus Icilius (M. Guischard) did not live to analyse these operations, as he has done the campaigns of Africa and Spain.

[2] Παλλὰς ἄλλη κἂν μὴ 'Αθήνη, which is very properly translated by the President Cousin (Hist. de Constantinople, tom. iv. p. 131, in 12mo), qui combattoit comme une Pallas, quoiqu'elle ne fût pas aussi savante que celle d'Athènes. The Grecian goddess was composed of two discordant

wounded by an arrow, she stood her ground, and strove, by her exhortation and example, to rally the flying troops.[1] Her female voice was seconded by the more powerful voice and arm of the Norman duke, as calm in action as he was magnanimous in council: "Whither," he cried aloud, "whither do ye fly? Your enemy is implacable; and death is less grievous than servitude." The moment was decisive: as the Varangians advanced before the line, they discovered the nakedness of their flanks: the main battle of the duke, of eight hundred knights, stood firm and entire; they couched their lances, and the Greeks deplore the furious and irresistible shock of the French cavalry.[2] Alexius was not deficient in the duties of a soldier or a general; but he no sooner beheld the slaughter of the Varangians, and the flight of the Turks, than he despised his subjects, and despaired of his fortune. The princess Anne, who drops a tear on this melancholy event, is reduced to praise the strength and swiftness of her father's horse, and his vigorous struggle when he was almost overthrown by the stroke of a lance which had shivered the Imperial helmet. His desperate valour broke through a squadron of Franks who opposed his flight; and after wandering two days and as many nights in the mountains, he found some repose, of body, though not of mind, in the walls of Lychnidus. The victorious Robert reproached the tardy and feeble pursuit which had suffered the escape of so illustrious a prize: but he consoled his disappointment by the trophies and standards of the field, the wealth and luxury of the Byzantine camp, and the glory of defeating an army five times more numerous than his own. A multitude of Italians had been the victims of their own fears; but only thirty of his knights were slain in this memorable

characters—of Neith, the workwoman of Sais in Egypt, and of a virgin Amazon of the Tritonian lake in Libya (Banier, Mythologie, tom. iv. p. 1-31, in 12mo).

[1] Anna Comnena (l. iv. p. 116 [tom. i. p. 210, ed. Bonn]) admires, with some degree of terror, her masculine virtues. They were more familiar to the Latins; and though the Apulian (l. iv. p. 273) mentions her presence and her wound, he represents her as far less intrepid.

> Uxor in hoc bello Roberti forte sagittâ
> Quâdam læsa fuit: quo vulnere *territa*, nullam
> Dum sperabat opem, se pœne *subegerat* hosti.

The last is an unlucky word for a female prisoner.

[2] 'Aπὸ τῆς τοῦ 'Pομπερτοῦ προηγησαμένης μάχης γινώσκων τὴν πρώτην κατὰ τῶν ἐναντίων ἱππασίαν τῶν Κελτῶν ἀνύποιστον (Anna, l. v. p. 133 [tom. i. p. 137, ed. Bonn]); and elsewhere καὶ γὰρ Κελτὸς ἀνὴρ πᾶς ἐποχούμενος μὲν ἀνύποιστος τὴν ὁρμὴν καὶ τὴν δέαν ἐστίν (p. 140 [tom. i. p. 251, ed. Bonn]). The pedantry of the princess in the choice of classic appellations encouraged Ducange to apply to his countrymen the characters of the ancient Gauls.

day. In the Roman host, the loss of Greeks, Turks, and English amounted to five or six thousand:[1] the plain of Durazzo was stained with noble and róyal blood; and the end of the impostor Michael was more honourable than his life.

It is more than probable that Guiscard was not afflicted by the loss of a costly pageant, which had merited only the contempt and derision of the Greeks. After their defeat they still persevered in the defence of Durazzo; and a Venetian commander supplied the place of George Palæologus, who had been imprudently called away from his station. The tents of the besiegers were converted into barracks, to sustain the inclemency of the winter; and in answer to the defiance of the garrison, Robert insinuated that his patience was at least equal to their obstinacy.[2] Perhaps he already trusted to his secret correspondence with a Venetian noble, who sold the city for a rich and honourable marriage. At the dead of night several rope-ladders were dropped from the walls; the light Calabrians ascended in silence; and the Greeks were awakened by the name and trumpets of the conqueror. Yet they defended the streets three days against an enemy already master of the rampart; and near seven months elapsed between the first investment and the final surrender of the place. From Durazzo the Norman duke advanced into the heart of Epirus or Albania; traversed the first mountains of Thessaly; surprised three hundred English in the city of Castoria; approached Thessalonica; and made Constantinople tremble. A more pressing duty suspended the prosecution of his ambitious designs. By shipwreck, pestilence, and the sword, his army was reduced to a third of the original numbers; and instead of being recruited from Italy, he was informed, by plaintive epistles, of the mischiefs and dangers which had been produced by his absence: the revolt of the cities and barons of Apulia; the distress of the pope; and the approach or invasion of Henry king of Germany. Highly presuming that his person was sufficient for the public safety, he repassed the sea in a single brigantine, and left the remains of the army under the command of his son and the Norman counts, exhorting Bohemond

---

[1] Lupus Protospata (tom. v. p. 45) says 6000; William the Apulian more than 5000 (l. iv. p. 273). Their modesty is singular and laudable: they might with so little trouble have slain two or three myriads of schismatics and infidels!

[2] The Romans had changed the inauspicious name of *Epi-damnus* to Dyrrachium (Plin. iii. 26); and the vulgar corruption of Duracium (see Malaterra) bore some affinity to *hardness*. One of Robert's names was Durand, *à durando*: poor wit! (Alberic. Monach. in Chron. apud Muratori, Annali d'Italia, tom. ix. p. 137.)

to respect the freedom of his peers, and the counts to obey the authority of their leader. The son of Guiscard trod in the footsteps of his father; and the two destroyers are compared by the Greeks to the caterpillar and the locust, the last of whom devours whatever has escaped the teeth of the former.[1] After winning two battles against the emperor, he descended into the plain of Thessaly, and besieged Larissa, the fabulous realm of Achilles,[2] which contained the treasure and magazines of the Byzantine camp. Yet a just praise must not be refused to the fortitude and prudence of Alexius, who bravely struggled with the calamities of the times. In the poverty of the state, he presumed to borrow the superfluous ornaments of the churches: the desertion of the Manichæans was supplied by some tribes of Moldavia: a reinforcement of seven thousand Turks replaced and revenged the loss of their brethren; and the Greek soldiers were exercised to ride, to draw the bow, and to the daily practice of ambuscades and evolutions. Alexius had been taught by experience that the formidable cavalry of the Franks on foot was unfit for action, and almost incapable of motion;[3] his archers were directed to aim their arrows at the horse rather than the man; and a variety of spikes and snares were scattered over the ground on which he might expect an attack. In the neighbourhood of Larissa the events of war were protracted and balanced. The courage of Bohemond was always conspicuous, and often successful; but his camp was pillaged by a stratagem of the Greeks; the city was impregnable; and the venal or discontented counts deserted his standard, betrayed their trusts, and enlisted in the service of the emperor. Alexius returned to Constantinople with the advantage, rather than the honour, of victory. After evacuating the conquests which he could no longer defend, the son of Guis-

---

[1] Βρούχους καὶ ἀκρίδας εἶπεν ἄν τις αὐτούς, [τὸν] πατέρα καὶ [τὸν] υἱὸν (Anna, l. i. p. 35 [tom. i. p. 70, ed. Bonn]). By these similes, so different from those of Homer, she wishes to inspire contempt as well as horror for the little noxious animal, a conqueror. Most unfortunately, the common sense, or common nonsense, of mankind, resists her laudable design.

[2] Prodiit hâc auctor Trojanæ cladis Achilles.

The supposition of the Apulian (l. v. p. 275) may be excused by the more classic poetry of Virgil (Æneid II. 197), Larissæus Achilles, but it is not justified by the geography of Homer.

[3] The τῶν πεδίλων προάλματα, which encumbered the knights on foot, have been ignorantly translated spurs (Anna Comnena, Alexias, l. v. p. 140 [tom. i. p. 251, ed. Bonn]). Ducange has explained the true sense by a ridiculous and inconvenient fashion, which lasted from the eleventh to the fifteenth century. These peaks, in the form of a scorpion, were sometimes two feet, and fastened to the knee with a silver chain.

card embarked for Italy, and was embraced by a father who esteemed his merit, and sympathised in his misfortune.

Of the Latin princes, the allies of Alexius and enemies of Robert, the most prompt and powerful was Henry the Third or Fourth, king of Germany and Italy, and future emperor of the West. The epistle of the Greek monarch [1] to his brother is filled with the warmest professions of friendship, and the most lively desire of strengthening their alliance by every public and private tie. He congratulates Henry on his success in a just and pious war, and complains that the prosperity of his own empire is disturbed by the audacious enterprises of the Norman Robert. The list of his presents expresses the manners of the age—a radiated crown of gold, a cross set with pearls to hang on the breast, a case of relics with the names and titles of the saints, a vase of crystal, a vase of sardonyx, some balm, most probably of Mecca, and one hundred pieces of purple. To these he added a more solid present, of one hundred and forty-four thousand Byzantines of gold, with a farther assurance of two hundred and sixteen thousand, so soon as Henry should have entered in arms the Apulian territories, and confirmed by an oath the league against the common enemy. The German,[2] who was already in Lombardy at the head of an army and a faction, accepted these liberal offers, and marched towards the south: his speed was checked by the sound of the battle of Durazzo; but the influence of his arms, or name, in the hasty return of Robert, was a full equivalent for the Grecian bribe. Henry was the sincere adversary of the Normans, the allies and vassals of Gregory the Seventh, his implacable foe. The long quarrel of the throne and mitre had been recently kindled by the zeal and ambition of that haughty priest: [3] the king and the pope had degraded each other; and each had seated a rival on the temporal or spiritual throne of his

---

[1] The epistle itself (Alexias, l. iii. p. 93, 94, 95 [tom. i. p. 174-177, ed. Bonn]) well deserves to be read. There is one expression, ἀστροπέλεκυν δεδεμένον μετὰ χρυσαφίου [p. 177], which Ducange does not understand. I have endeavoured to grope out a tolerable meaning: χρυσάφιον is a golden crown; ἀστροπέλεκυς is explained by Simon Portius (in Lexico Græco-Barbar.), by κεραυνὸς, πρηστὴρ, a flash of lightning.

[2] For these general events I must refer to the general historians Sigonius, Baronius, Muratori, Mosheim, St. Marc, etc.

[3] The lives of Gregory VII. are either legends or invectives (St. Marc, Abrégé, tom. iii. p. 235, etc.); and his miraculous or magical performances are alike incredible to a modern reader. He will, as usual, find some instruction in Le Clerc (Vie de Hildebrand, Biblioth. ancienne et moderne, tom. viii.), and much amusement in Bayle (Dictionnaire Critique, Grégoire VII.). That pope was undoubtedly a great man, a second Athanasius, in a more fortunate age of the church. May I presume to add that the

antagonist. After the defeat and death of his Swabian rebel, Henry descended into Italy, to assume the Imperial crown, and to drive from the Vatican the tyrant of the church.[1] But the Roman people adhered to the cause of Gregory: their resolution was fortified by supplies of men and money from Apulia; and the city was thrice ineffectually besieged by the king of Germany. In the fourth year he corrupted, as it is said, with Byzantine gold, the nobles of Rome, whose estates and castles had been ruined by the war. The gates, the bridges, and fifty hostages were delivered into his hands: the anti-pope, Clement the Third, was consecrated in the Lateran: the grateful pontiff crowned his protector in the Vatican; and the emperor Henry fixed his residence in the Capitol, as the lawful successor of Augustus and Charlemagne. The ruins of the Septizonium were still defended by the nephew of Gregory: the pope himself was invested in the castle of St. Angelo; and his last hope was in the courage and fidelity of his Norman vassal. Their friendship had been interrupted by some reciprocal injuries and complaints; but, on this pressing occasion, Guiscard was urged by the obligation of his oath, by his interest, more potent than oaths, by the love of fame, and his enmity to the two emperors. Unfurling the holy banner, he resolved to fly to the relief of the prince of the apostles: the most numerous of his armies, six thousand horse and thirty thousand foot, was instantly assembled; and his march from Salerno to Rome was animated by the public applause and the promise of the divine favour. Henry, invincible in sixty-six battles, trembled at his approach; recollected some indispensable affairs that required his presence in Lombardy; exhorted the Romans to persevere in their allegiance; and hastily retreated three days before the entrance of the Normans. In less than three years the son of Tancred of Hauteville enjoyed the glory of delivering the pope, and of compelling the two emperors, of the

portrait of Athanasius is one of the passages of my history (vol. ii. p. 290, seq.) with which I am the least dissatisfied?

[There is a good work by Johannes Voigt, *Hildebrand als Papst Gregor VII. und sein Zeitalter* (Weimar, 1815), and this gave rise to a work in English by J. W. Bowden, *The Life and Pontificate of Gregory VII.* (1840). Cf. also Stenzel, *Geschichte Deutschlands unter den Fränkischen Kaisern*, and Spörer, *Papst Gregorius VII. und sein Zeitalter* (1859-61).—O. S.]

[1] Anna, with the rancour of a Greek schismatic, calls him κατάπτυστος οὗτος Πάπας (l. i. p. 32 [tom. i. p. 66, ed. Bonn]), a pope, or priest, worthy to be spit upon; and accuses him of scourging, shaving, and perhaps of castrating, the ambassadors of Henry (p. 31, 33). But this outrage is improbable and doubtful (see the sensible preface of Cousin).

East and West, to fly before his victorious arms.[1] But the triumph of Robert was clouded by the calamities of Rome. By the aid of the friends of Gregory the walls had been perforated or scaled; but the Imperial faction was still powerful and active; on the third day the people rose in a furious tumult; and a hasty word of the conqueror, in his defence or revenge, was the signal of fire and pillage.[2] The Saracens of Sicily, the subjects of Roger, and auxiliaries of his brother, embraced this fair occasion of rifling and profaning the holy city of the Christians; many thousands of the citizens, in the sight and by the allies of their spiritual father, were exposed to violation, captivity, or death; and a spacious quarter of the city, from the Lateran to the Coliseum, was consumed by the flames, and devoted to perpetual solitude.[3] From a city where he was now hated, and might be no longer feared, Gregory retired to end his days in the palace of Salerno. The artful pontiff might flatter the vanity of Guiscard with the hope of a Roman or Imperial crown; but this dangerous measure, which would have inflamed the ambition of the Norman, must for ever have alienated the most faithful princes of Germany.

The deliverer and scourge of Rome might have indulged himself in a season of repose; but in the same year of the flight of the German emperor the indefatigable Robert resumed the design of his Eastern conquests. The zeal or gratitude of Gregory had promised to his valour the kingdoms of Greece and Asia;[4] his

---

[1]   Sic uno tempore victi
Sunt terræ Domini duo: rex Alemannicus iste,
Imperii rector Romani maximus ille.
Alter ad arma ruens armis superatur; et alter
Nominis auditi solâ formidine cessit.

It is singular enough, that the Apulian, a Latin, should distinguish the Greek as the ruler of the Roman empire (l. iv. p. 274).

[2] The narrative of Malaterra (l. iii. c. 37, p. 587, 588) is authentic, circumstantial, and fair. Dux ignem exclamans urbe incensa, etc. The Apulian softens the mischief (inde quibusdam ædibus exustis), which is again exaggerated in some partial chronicles (Muratori Annali, tom. ix. p. 147).

[3] After mentioning this devastation, the Jesuit Donatus (de Româ veteri et novâ, l. iv. c. 8, p. 489) prettily adds, Duraret hodieque in Cœlio monte, interque ipsum et capitolium, miserabilis facies prostratæ urbis, nisi in hortorum vinetorumque amœnitatem Roma resurrexisset, ut perpetuâ viriditate contegeret vulnera et ruinas suas.

[4] The royalty of Robert, either promised or bestowed by the pope (Anna, l. i. p. 32 [tom. i. p. 65, ed. Bonn]), is sufficiently confirmed by the Apulian (l. iv. p. 270).

          Romani regni sibi promisisse coronam
          Papa ferebatur.

Nor can I understand why Gretser and the other papal advocates should be displeased with this new instance of apostolic jurisdiction.

troops were assembled in arms, flushed with success, and eager
for action. Their numbers, in the language of Homer, are compared by Anna to a swarm of bees;[1] yet the utmost and moderate
limits of the powers of Guiscard have been already defined: they
were contained in this second occasion in one hundred and
twenty vessels, and, as the season was far advanced, the harbour
of Brundusium[2] was preferred to the open road of Otranto.
Alexius, apprehensive of a second attack, had assiduously
laboured to restore the naval forces of the empire, and obtained
from the republic of Venice an important succour of thirty-six
transports, fourteen galleys, and nine galeots or ships of extraordinary strength and magnitude.   Their services were liberally
paid by the licence or monopoly of trade, a profitable gift of
many shops and houses in the port of Constantinople, and a
tribute to St. Mark, the more acceptable, as it was the produce of
a tax on their rivals of Amalphi.   By the union of the Greeks and
Venetians the Adriatic was covered with a hostile fleet; but
their own neglect, or the vigilance of Robert, the change of a
wind, or the shelter of a mist, opened a free passage, and the
Norman troops were safely disembarked on the coast of Epirus.
With twenty strong and well-appointed galleys their intrepid
duke immediately sought the enemy, and, though more accustomed to fight on horseback, he trusted his own life, and the
lives of his brother and two sons, to the event of a naval combat.
The dominion of the sea was disputed in three engagements, in
sight of the isle of Corfu; in the two former the skill and numbers
of the allies were superior; but in the third the Normans obtained
a final and complete victory.[3]   The light brigantines of the
Greeks were scattered in ignominious flight; the nine castles of

[1] See Homer, Iliad B (I hate this pedantic mode of quotation by the
letters of the Greek alphabet), 87, etc.   His bees are the image of a disorderly crowd; their discipline and public works seem to be the ideas of a
later age (Virgil. Æneid. l. i. [v. 430, *sqq.*]).

[2] Gulielm. Appulus, l. v. p. 276.   The admirable port of Brundusium
was double; the outward harbour was a gulf covered by an island, and
narrowing by degrees, till it communicated by a small gullet with the inner
harbour, which embraced the city on both sides.   Cæsar and nature have
laboured for its ruin; and against such agents what are the feeble efforts of
the Neapolitan government? (Swinburne's Travels in the Two Sicilies,
vol. i. p. 384-390.)

[3] William of Apulia (l. v. p. 276) describes the victory of the Normans,
and forgets the two previous defeats, which are diligently recorded by
Anna Comnena (l. vi. p. 159, 160, 161 [p. 282-285, ed. Bonn]).   In her
turn, she invents or magnifies a fourth action, to give the Venetians revenge
and rewards.   Their own feelings were far different, since they deposed
their doge, propter excidium stoli (Dandulus in Chron. in Muratori, Script.
Rerum Italicarum, tom. xii. p. 249).

the Venetians maintained a more obstinate conflict: seven were sunk, two were taken; two thousand five hundred captives implored in vain the mercy of the victor; and the daughter of Alexius deplores the loss of thirteen thousand of his subjects or allies. The want of experience had been supplied by the genius of Guiscard; and each evening, when he had sounded a retreat, he calmly explored the causes of his repulse, and invented new methods how to remedy his own defects and to baffle the advantages of the enemy. The winter season suspended his progress; with the return of spring he again aspired to the conquest of Constantinople; but, instead of traversing the hills of Epirus, he turned his arms against Greece and the islands, where the spoils would repay the labour, and where the land and sea forces might pursue their joint operations with vigour and effect. But in the isle of Cephalonia his projects were fatally blasted by an epidemical disease: Robert himself, in the seventieth year of his age, expired in his tent, and a suspicion of poison was imputed, by public rumour, to his wife, or to the Greek emperor.[1] This premature death might allow a boundless scope for the imagination of his future exploits, and the event sufficiently declares that the Norman greatness was founded on his life.[2] Without the appearance of an enemy a victorious army dispersed or retreated in disorder and consternation, and Alexius, who had trembled for his empire, rejoiced in his deliverance. The galley which transported the remains of Guiscard was shipwrecked on the Italian shore, but the duke's body was recovered from the sea, and deposited in the sepulchre of Venusia,[3] a place more illustrious for

[1] The most authentic writers, William of Apulia (l. v. 277), Jeffrey Malaterra (l. iii. c. 41, p. 589), and Romuald of Salerno (Chron. in Muratori, Script. Rerum Ital. tom. vii.), are ignorant of this crime, so apparent to our countrymen William of Malmesbury (l. iii. p. 107) and Roger de Hoveden (p. 710, in Script. post Bedam); and the latter can tell how the just Alexius married, crowned, and burnt alive, his female accomplice. The English historian is indeed so blind, that he ranks Robert Guiscard, or Wiscard, among the knights of Henry I., who ascended the throne fifteen years after the duke of Apulia's death.
[Robert Guiscard when he died was just on the eve of sailing to Cephalonia. He died in his winter quarters at Bundicia near the mouth of the river Glykys, on the shores of Epirus.—O. S.]

[2] The joyful Anna Comnena scatters some flowers over the grave of an enemy (Alexiad, l. v. [vi.] p. 162-166 [tom. i. p. 288-295, ed. Bonn]; and his best praise is the esteem and envy of William the Conqueror, the sovereign of his family. Græcia (says Malaterra) hostibus recedentibus libera læta quievit: Apulia tota sive Calabria turbatur.

[3]   Urbs Venusina nitet tantis decorata sepulchris,

is one of the last lines of the Apulian's poem (l. v. p. 278). William of Malmesbury (l. iii. p. 107) inserts an epitaph on Guiscard, which is not worth transcribing.

the birth of Horace [1] than for the burial of the Norman heroes.
Roger, his second son and successor, immediately sunk to the
humble station of a duke of Apulia; the esteem or partiality of
his father left the valiant Bohemond to the inheritance of his
sword. The national tranquillity was disturbed by his claims,
till the first crusade against the infidels of the East opened a
more splendid field of glory and conquest.[2]

Of human life the most glorious or humble prospects are alike
and soon bounded by the sepulchre. The male line of Robert
Guiscard was extinguished, both in Apulia and at Antioch, in the
second generation; but his younger brother became the father of
a line of kings; and the son of the great count was endowed with
the name, the conquests, and the spirit of the first Roger.[3] The
heir of that Norman adventurer was born in Sicily, and at the age
of only four years he succeeded to the sovereignty of the island, a
lot which reason might envy could she indulge for a moment the
visionary, though virtuous, wish of dominion. Had Roger been
content with his fruitful patrimony, a happy and grateful
people might have blessed their benefactor; and if a wise administration could have restored the prosperous times of the
Greek colonies,[4] the opulence and power of Sicily alone might
have equalled the widest scope that could be acquired and
desolated by the sword of war. But the ambition of the great
count was ignorant of these noble pursuits; it was gratified by
the vulgar means of violence and artifice. He sought to obtain
the undivided possession of Palermo, of which one moiety had
been ceded to the elder branch; struggled to enlarge his Calabrian limits beyond the measure of former treaties; and impatiently watched the declining health of his cousin William of
Apulia, the grandson of Robert. On the first intelligence of his

[1] Yet Horace had few obligations to Venusia: he was carried to Rome
in his childhood (Serm. i. 6 [v. 76]); and his repeated allusions to the
doubtful limit of Apulia and Lucania (Carm. iii. 4; Serm. ii. 1 [v. 34,
sqq.]) are unworthy of his age and genius.

[2] See Giannone (tom. ii. p. 88-93) and the historians of the first crusade.

[3] The reign of Roger and the Norman kings of Sicily fills four books of
the Istoria Civile of Giannone (tom. ii. l. xi.-xiv. p. 136-340), and is spread
over the ninth and tenth volumes of the Italian Annals of Muratori. In
the Bibliothèque Italique (tom. i. p. 175-222) I find a useful abstract of
Capecelatro, a modern Neapolitan, who has composed, in two volumes,
the history of his country from Roger I. to Frederic II. inclusive.

[4] According to the testimony of Philistus and Diodorus, the tyrant
Dionysius of Syracuse could maintain a standing force of 10,000 horse,
100,000 foot, and 400 galleys. Compare Hume (Essays, vol. i. p. 268, 435)
and his adversary Wallace (Numbers of Mankind, p. 306, 307). The ruins
of Agrigentum are the theme of every traveller, D'Orville, Reidesel,
Swinburne, etc.

premature death, Roger sailed from Palermo with seven galleys, cast anchor in the bay of Salerno, received, after ten days' negotiation, an oath of fidelity from the Norman capital, commanded the submission of the barons, and extorted a legal investiture from the reluctant popes, who could not long endure either the friendship or enmity of a powerful vassal. The sacred spot of Benevento was respectfully spared, as the patrimony of St. Peter; but the reduction of Capua and Naples completed the design of his uncle Guiscard; and the sole inheritance of the Norman conquests was possessed by the victorious Roger. A conscious superiority of power and merit prompted him to disdain the titles of duke and of count; and the isle of Sicily, with a third perhaps of the continent of Italy, might form the basis of a kingdom [1] which would only yield to the monarchies of France and England. The chiefs of the nation who attended his coronation at Palermo might doubtless pronounce under what name he should reign over them; but the example of a Greek tyrant or a Saracen emir were insufficient to justify his regal character; and the nine kings of the Latin world [2] might disclaim their new associate unless he were consecrated by the authority of the supreme pontiff. The pride of Anacletus was pleased to confer a title which the pride of the Norman had stooped to solicit; [3] but his own legitimacy was attacked by the adverse election of Innocent the Second; and while Anacletus sat in the Vatican, the successful fugitive was acknowledged by the nations of Europe. The infant monarchy of Roger was shaken, and almost overthrown, by the unlucky choice of an ecclesiastical patron; and the sword of Lothaire the Second of Germany, the excommunications of Innocent, the fleets of Pisa, and the zeal of St. Bernard, were united for the ruin of the Sicilian robber. After a gallant resistance the Norman prince was driven from the continent of Italy: a new duke of Apulia was invested by the pope

[1] A contemporary historian of the acts of Roger from the year 1127 to 1135 founds his title on merit and power, the consent of the barons, and the ancient royalty of Sicily and Palermo, without introducing pope Anacletus (Alexand. Cœnobii Telesini Abbatis de Rebus Gestis Regis Rogerii, lib. iv. in Muratori, Script. Rerum Ital. tom. v. p. 607-645).

[2] The kings of France, England, Scotland, Castille, Arragon, Navarre, Sweden, Denmark, and Hungary. The three first were more ancient than Charlemagne; the three next were created by their sword; the three last by their baptism; and of these the king of Hungary alone was honoured or debased by a papal crown.

[3] Fazellus and a crowd of Sicilians had imagined a more early and independent coronation (A.D. 1130, May 1), which Giannone unwillingly rejects (tom. ii. p. 137-144). This fiction is disproved by the silence of contemporaries; nor can it be restored by a spurious charter of Messina (Muratori, Annali d'Italia, tom. ix. p. 340; Pagi, Critica, tom. iv. p. 467, 468).

and the emperor, each of whom held one end of the *gonfanon*, or flagstaff, as a token that they asserted their right, and suspended their quarrel. But such jealous friendship was of short and precarious duration: the German armies soon vanished in disease and desertion:[1] the Apulian duke, with all his adherents, was exterminated by a conqueror who seldom forgave either the dead or the living; like his predecessor Leo the Ninth, the feeble though haughty pontiff became the captive and friend of the Normans; and their reconciliation was celebrated by the eloquence of Bernard, who now revered the title and virtues of the king of Sicily.

As a penance for his impious war against the successor of St. Peter, that monarch might have promised to display the banner of the cross, and he accomplished with ardour a vow so propitious to his interest and revenge. The recent injuries of Sicily might provoke a just retaliation on the heads of the Saracens: the Normans, whose blood had been mingled with so many subject streams, were encouraged to remember and emulate the naval trophies of their fathers, and in the maturity of their strength they contended with the decline of an African power. When the Fatimite caliph departed for the conquest of Egypt, he rewarded the real merit and apparent fidelity of his servant Joseph with a gift of his royal mantle, and forty Arabian horses, his palace, with its sumptuous furniture, and the government of the kingdoms of Tunis and Algiers. The Zeirides,[2] the descendants of Joseph, forgot their allegiance and gratitude to a distant benefactor, grasped and abused the fruits of prosperity; and after running the little course of an Oriental dynasty, were now fainting in their own weakness. On the side of the land they were oppressed by the Almohades, the fanatic princes of Morocco, while the sea-coast was open to the enterprises of the Greeks and Franks, who, before the close of the eleventh century, had extorted a ransom of two hundred thousand pieces of gold. By the first arms of Roger, the island or rock of Malta, which has been since ennobled by a military and religious colony, was inseparably annexed to the crown of Sicily. Tripoli,[3] a strong and maritime city, was

---

[1] Roger corrupted the second person of Lothaire's army, who sounded, or rather cried, a retreat; for the Germans (says Cinnamus, l. iii. c. i. p. 52 [ed. Par.; p. 90, ed. Bonn]) are ignorant of the use of trumpets. Most ignorant himself!

[2] See De Guignes, Hist. Générale des Huns, tom. i. p. 369-373, and Cardonne, Hist. de l'Afrique, etc., sous la Domination des Arabes, tom. ii. p. 70-144. Their common original appears to be Novairi.

[3] Tripoli (says the Nubian geographer, or, more properly, the Sherif al Edrisi) urbs fortis, saxeo muro vallata, sita prope litus maris. Hanc expugnavit Rogerius, qui mulieribus captivis ductis, viros peremit.

the next object of his attack; and the slaughter of the males, the captivity of the females, might be justified by the frequent practice of the Moslems themselves.   The capital of the Zeirides was named Africa from the country, and Mahadia [1] from the Arabian founder: it is strongly built on a neck of land, but the imperfection of the harbour is not compensated by the fertility of the adjacent plain.   Mahadia was besieged by George the Sicilian admiral, with a fleet of one hundred and fifty galleys, amply provided with men and the instruments of mischief: the sovereign had fled, the Moorish governor refused to capitulate, declined the last and irresistible assault, and, secretly escaping with the Moslem inhabitants, abandoned the place and its treasures to the rapacious Franks.   In successive expeditions the king of Sicily or his lieutenants reduced the cities of Tunis, Safax, Capsia, Bona, and a long tract of the sea-coast; [2] the fortresses were garrisoned, the country was tributary, and a boast that it held Africa in subjection might be inscribed with some flattery on the sword of Roger. [3]   After his death that sword was broken; and these transmarine possessions were neglected, evacuated, or lost, under the troubled reign of his successor. [4]   The triumphs of Scipio and Belisarius have proved that the African continent is neither inaccessible nor invincible; yet the great princes and powers of Christendom have repeatedly failed in their armaments against the Moors, who may still glory in the easy conquest and long servitude of Spain.

Since the decease of Robert Guiscard the Normans had relinquished, above sixty years, their hostile designs against the empire of the East.   The policy of Roger solicited a public and private union with the Greek princes, whose alliance would dignify his regal character: he demanded in marriage a daughter of the Comnenian family, and the first steps of the treaty seemed to promise a favourable event.   But the contemptuous treatment of his ambassadors exasperated the vanity of the new

[1] See the geography of Leo Africanus (in Ramusio, tom. i. fol. 74 verso, fol. 75 recto) and Shaw's Travels(p. 110), the seventh book of Thuanus, and the eleventh of the Abbé de Vertot.   The possession and defence of the place was offered by Charles V. and wisely declined by the knights of Malta.

[2] Pagi has accurately marked the African conquests of Roger; and his criticism was supplied by his friend the Abbé de Longuerue, with some Arabic memorials (A.D. 1147, No. 26, 27; A.D. 1148, No. 16; A.D. 1153, No. 16).

[3] Appulus et Calaber, Siculus mihi servit et Afer.

A proud inscription, which denotes that the Norman conquerors were still discriminated from their Christian and Moslem subjects.

[4] Hugo Falcandus (Hist. Sicula, in Muratori Script. tom. vii. p. 270, 271) ascribes these losses to the neglect or treachery of the admiral Majo.

monarch; and the insolence of the Byzantine court was expiated, according to the laws of nations, by the sufferings of a guiltless people.[1] With a fleet of seventy galleys George the admiral of Sicily appeared before Corfu; and both the island and city were delivered into his hands by the disaffected inhabitants, who had yet to learn that a siege is still more calamitous than a tribute. In this invasion, of some moment in the annals of commerce, the Normans spread themselves by sea, and over the provinces of Greece; and the venerable age of Athens, Thebes, and Corinth, was violated by rapine and cruelty. Of the wrongs of Athens no memorial remains. The ancient walls which encompassed, without guarding, the opulence of Thebes, were scaled by the Latin Christians; but their sole use of the Gospel was to sanctify an oath that the lawful owners had not secreted any relic of their inheritance or industry. On the approach of the Normans the lower town of Corinth was evacuated: the Greeks retired to the citadel, which was seated on a lofty eminence, abundantly watered by the classic fountain of Pirene; an impregnable fortress, if the want of courage could be balanced by any advantages of art or nature. As soon as the besiegers had surmounted the labour (their sole labour) of climbing the hill, their general, from the commanding eminence, admired his own victory, and testified his gratitude to Heaven by tearing from the altar the precious image of Theodore the tutelary saint. The silk-weavers of both sexes, whom George transported to Sicily, composed the most valuable part of the spoil; and in comparing the skilful industry of the mechanic with the sloth and cowardice of the soldier, he was heard to exclaim that the distaff and loom were the only weapons which the Greeks were capable of using. The progress of this naval armament was marked by two conspicuous events, the rescue of the king of France and the insult of the Byzantine capital. In his return by sea from an unfortunate crusade, Louis the Seventh was intercepted by the Greeks, who basely violated the laws of honour and religion. The fortunate encounter of the Norman fleet delivered the royal captive; and after a free and honourable entertainment in the court of Sicily, Louis continued his journey to Rome and Paris.[2] In the absence

---

[1] The silence of the Sicilian historians, who end too soon or begin too late, must be supplied by Otho of Frisingen, a German (de Gestis Frederici I. l. i. c. 33, in Muratori Script. tom. vi. p. 668), the Venetian Andrew Dandulus (Id. tom. xii. p. 282, 283), and the Greek writers Cinnamus (l. iii. c. 2-5) and Nicetas (in Manuel. l. iii. c. 1-6 [p. 131, *sqq.*, ed. Bonn]).

[2] To this imperfect capture and speedy rescue I apply the παρ᾽ ὀλίγον ἦλθε τοῦ ἀλῶναι of Cinnamus, l. ii. c. 19, p. 49 [p. 87, ed. Bonn]. Muratori, on tolerable evidence (Annali d'Italia, tom. ix. p. 420, 421), laughs at the

of the emperor, Constantinople and the Hellespont were left without defence and without the suspicion of danger. The clergy and people, for the soldiers had followed the standard of Manuel, were astonished and dismayed at the hostile appearance of a line of galleys, which boldly cast anchor in the front of the Imperial city. The forces of the Sicilian admiral were inadequate to the siege or assault of an immense and populous metropolis; but George enjoyed the glory of humbling the Greek arrogance, and of marking the path of conquest to the navies of the West. He landed some soldiers to rifle the fruits of the royal gardens, and pointed with silver, or more probably with fire, the arrows which he discharged against the palace of the Cæsars.[1] This playful outrage of the pirates of Sicily, who had surprised an unguarded moment, Manuel affected to despise, while his martial spirit and the forces of the empire were awakened to revenge. The Archipelago and Ionian Sea were covered with his squadrons and those of Venice; but I know not by what favourable allowance of transports, victuallers, and pinnaces, our reason, or even our fancy, can be reconciled to the stupendous account of fifteen hundred vessels, which is proposed by a Byzantine historian. These operations were directed with prudence and energy: in his homeward voyage George lost nineteen of his galleys, which were separated and taken: after an obstinate defence Corfu implored the clemency of her lawful sovereign; nor could a ship, a soldier, of the Norman prince, be found, unless as a captive, within the limits of the Eastern empire. The prosperity and the health of Roger were already in a declining state: while he listened in his palace of Palermo to the messengers of victory or defeat, the invincible Manuel, the foremost in every assault, was celebrated by the Greeks and Latins as the Alexander or Hercules of the age.

A prince of such a temper could not be satisfied with having repelled the insolence of a barbarian. It was the right and duty, it might be the interest and glory, of Manuel to restore the ancient majesty of the empire, to recover the provinces of Italy and Sicily, and to chastise this pretended king, the grand-

---

delicacy of the French, who maintain, marisque nullo impediente periculo ad regnum proprium reversum esse; yet I observe that their advocate, Ducange, is less positive as the commentator on Cinnamus than as the editor of Joinville.

[1] In palatium regium sagittas igneas injecti, says Dandulus; but Nicetas, l. ii. c. 8, p. 66 [p. 130, ed. Bonn], transforms them into βέλη ἀργυρέους ἔχοντα ἀτράκτους, and adds that Manuel styled this insult παίγνιον and γέλωτα . . . ληστεύοντα. These arrows, by the compiler, Vincent de Beauvais, are again transmuted into gold.

son of a Norman vassal.[1] The natives of Calabria were still attached to the Greek language and worship, which had been inexorably proscribed by the Latin clergy: after the loss of her dukes Apulia was chained as a servile appendage to the crown of Sicily: the founder of the monarchy had ruled by the sword; and his death had abated the fear, without healing the discontent, of his subjects: the feudal government was always pregnant with the seeds of rebellion; and a nephew of Roger himself invited the enemies of his family and nation. The majesty of the purple, and a series of Hungarian and Turkish wars, prevented Manuel from embarking his person in the Italian expedition. To the brave and noble Palæologus, his lieutenant, the Greek monarch intrusted a fleet and army: the siege of Bari was his first exploit; and, in every operation, gold as well as steel was the instrument of victory. Salerno, and some places along the western coast, maintained their fidelity to the Norman king; but he lost in two campaigns the greater part of his continental possessions; and the modest emperor, disdaining all flattery and falsehood, was content with the reduction of three hundred cities or villages of Apulia and Calabria, whose names and titles were inscribed on all the walls of the palace. The prejudices of the Latins were gratified by a genuine or fictitious donation under the seal of the German Cæsars;[2] but the successor of Constantine soon renounced this ignominious pretence, claimed the indefeasible dominion of Italy, and professed his design of chasing the barbarians beyond the Alps. By the artful speeches, liberal gifts, and unbounded promises of their Eastern ally, the free cities were encouraged to persevere in their generous struggle against the despotism of Frederic Barbarossa: the walls of Milan were rebuilt by the contributions of Manuel; and he poured, says the historian, a river of gold into the bosom of Ancona, whose attachment to the Greeks was fortified by the jealous enmity of the Venetians.[3] The situation and trade of

---

[1] For the invasion of Italy, which is almost overlooked by Nicetas, see the more polite history of Cinnamus (l. iv. c. 1-15, p. 78-101 [p. 134-175, ed. Bonn]), who introduces a diffuse narrative by a lofty profession, περὶ τε Σικελίας, καὶ τῆς Ἰταλῶν ἐσκέπτετο γῆς, ὡς καὶ ταύτας Ῥωμαίοις ἀνασώσαιτο, iii. 5 [p. 101, ed. Bonn].

[2] The Latin, Otho (de Gestis Frederici I. l. ii. c. 30, p. 734), attests the forgery; the Greek, Cinnamus (l. iv. c. 1, p. 78 [p. 135, ed. Bonn]), claims a promise of restitution from Conrad and Frederic. An act of fraud is always credible when it is told of the Greeks.

[3] Quod Anconitani Græcum imperium nimis diligerent . . . Veneti speciali odio Anconam oderunt. The cause of love, perhaps of envy, were the beneficia, flumen aureum of the emperor; and the Latin narrative is confirmed by Cinnamus (l. iv. c. 14, p. 98 [p. 170, ed. Bonn]).

Ancona rendered it an important garrison in the heart of Italy: it was twice besieged by the arms of Frederic; the Imperial forces were twice repulsed by the spirit of freedom; that spirit was animated by the ambassador of Constantinople; and the most intrepid patriots, the most faithful servants, were rewarded by the wealth and honours of the Byzantine court.[1]   The pride of Manuel disdained and rejected a barbarian colleague; his ambition was excited by the hope of stripping the purple from the German usurpers, and of establishing in the West as in the East his lawful title of sole emperor of the Romans.   With this view he solicited the alliance of the people and the bishop of Rome. Several of the nobles embraced the cause of the Greek monarch; the splendid nuptials of his niece with Odo Frangipani secured the support of that powerful family,[2] and his royal standard or image was entertained with due reverence in the ancient metropolis.[3]   During the quarrel between Frederic and Alexander the Third, the pope twice received in the Vatican the ambassadors of Constantinople.   They flattered his piety by the long-promised union of the two churches, tempted the avarice of his venal court, and exhorted the Roman pontiff to seize the just provocation, the favourable moment, to humble the savage insolence of the Alemanni and to acknowledge the true representative of Constantine and Augustus.[4]

But these Italian conquests, this universal reign, soon escaped from the hand of the Greek emperor.   His first demands were eluded by the prudence of Alexander the Third, who paused on this deep and momentous revolution;[5] nor could the pope be seduced by a personal dispute to renounce the perpetual inheritance of the Latin name.   After his re-union with Frederic, he

[1] Muratori mentions the two sieges of Ancona; the first, in 1167, against Frederic I. in person (Annali, tom. x. p. 39, etc.); the second, in 1173, against his lieutenant Christian, Archbishop of Mentz, a man unworthy of his name and office (p. 76, etc.).   It is of the second siege that we possess an original narrative, which he has published in his great collection (tom. vi. p. 921-946).

[2] We derive this anecdote from an anonymous chronicle of Fossa Nova, published by Muratori (Script. Ital. tom. vii. p. 874).

The Βασίλειον σημεῖον of Cinnamus (l. iv. c. 14, p. 99 [p. 171, ed. Bonn]) is susceptible of this double sense.   A standard is more Latin, an image more Greek.

[4] Nihilominus quoque petebat, ut quia occasio justa et tempus opportunum et acceptabile se obtulerant, Romani corona imperii a sancto apostolo sibi redderetur; quoniam non ad Frederici Alamanni, sed ad suum jus asseruit pertinere (Vit. Alexandri III. a Cardinal. Arragoniæ, in Script. Rerum Ital. tom. iii. par. i. p. 458).   His second embassy was accompanied cum immensa multitudine pecuniarum.

[5] Nimis alta et perplexa sunt (Vit. Alexandri III. p. 460, 461) says the cautious pope.

spoke a more peremptory language, confirmed the acts of his predecessors, excommunicated the adherents of Manuel, and pronounced the final separation of the churches, or at least the empires, of Constantinople and Rome.[1] The free cities of Lombardy no longer remembered their foreign benefactor, and, without preserving the friendship of Ancona, he soon incurred the enmity of Venice.[2] By his own avarice, or the complaints of his subjects, the Greek emperor was provoked to arrest the persons, and confiscate the effects, of the Venetian merchants. This violation of the public faith exasperated a free and commercial people: one hundred galleys were launched and armed in as many days; they swept the coasts of Dalmatia and Greece: but after some mutual wounds, the war was terminated by an agreement, inglorious to the empire, insufficient for the republic; and a complete vengeance of these and of fresh injuries was reserved for the succeeding generation. The lieutenant of Manuel had informed his sovereign that he was strong enough to quell any domestic revolt of Apulia and Calabria; but that his forces were inadequate to resist the impending attack of the king of Sicily. His prophecy was soon verified: the death of Palæologus devolved the command on several chiefs, alike eminent in rank, alike defective in military talents; the Greeks were oppressed by land and sea; and a captive remnant that escaped the swords of the Normans and Saracens abjured all future hostility against the person or dominions of their conqueror.[3] Yet the king of Sicily esteemed the courage and constancy of Manuel, who had landed a second army on the Italian shore: he respectfully addressed the new Justinian; solicited a peace or truce of thirty years; accepted as a gift the regal title; and acknowledged himself the military vassal of the Roman empire.[4] The Byzantine Cæsars acquiesced in this shadow

---

[1] Μηδὲν μετὸν εἶναι λέγων Ῥώμῃ τῇ νεωτέρᾳ πρὸς τὴν πρεσβυτέραν, πάλαι ἀπορραγεισῶν (Cinnamus, l. iv. c. 14, p. 99 [p. 171, ed. Bonn]).

[2] In his sixth book, Cinnamus describes the Venetian war, which Nicetas has not thought worthy of his attention. The Italian accounts, which do not satisfy our curiosity, are reported by the annalist Muratori, under the years 1171, etc.

[3] This victory is mentioned by Romuald of Salerno (in Muratori, Script. Ital. tom. vii. p. 198). It is whimsical enough that, in the praise of the king of Sicily, Cinnamus (l. iv. c. 13, p. 97, 98 [p. 168, ed. Bonn]) is much warmer and more copious than Falcandus (p. 268, 270). But the Greek is fond of description, and the Latin historian is not fond of William the Bad.

[4] For the epistle of William I. see Cinnamus (l. iv. c. 15, p. 101, 102 [p. 173-175, ed. Bonn]) and Nicetas (l. ii. c. 8 [p. 128, ed. Bonn]). It is difficult to affirm whether these Greeks deceived themselves or the public in these flattering portraits of the grandeur of the empire.

of dominion, without expecting, perhaps without desiring, the service of a Norman army; and the truce of thirty years was not disturbed by any hostilities between Sicily and Constantinople. About the end of that period, the throne of Manuel was usurped by an inhuman tyrant, who had deserved the abhorrence of his country and mankind: the sword of William the Second, the grandson of Roger, was drawn by a fugitive of the Comnenian race; and the subjects of Andronicus might salute the strangers as friends, since they detested their sovereign as the worst of enemies. The Latin historians[1] expatiate on the rapid progress of the four counts who invaded Romania with a fleet and army, and reduced many castles and cities to the obedience of the king of Sicily. The Greeks[2] accuse and magnify the wanton and sacrilegious cruelties that were perpetrated in the sack of Thessalonica, the second city of the empire. The former deplore the fate of those invincible but unsuspecting warriors who were destroyed by the arts of a vanquished foe. The latter applaud, in songs of triumph, the repeated victories of their countrymen on the sea of Marmora or Propontis, on the banks of the Strymon, and under the walls of Durazzo. A revolution which punished the crimes of Andronicus had united against the Franks the zeal and courage of the successful insurgents: ten thousand were slain in battle; and Isaac Angelus, the new emperor, might indulge his vanity or vengeance in the treatment of four thousand captives. Such was the event of the last contest between the Greeks and Normans: before the expiration of twenty years the rival nations were lost or degraded in foreign servitude; and the successors of Constantine did not long survive to insult the fall of the Sicilian monarchy.

The sceptre of Roger successively devolved to his son and grandson: they might be confounded under the name of William: they are strongly discriminated by the epithets of the *bad* and the *good*; but these epithets, which appear to describe

---

[1] I can only quote of original evidence the poor chronicles of Sicard of Cremona (p. 603), and of Fossa Nova (p. 875), as they are published in the seventh tome of Muratori's historians. The king of Sicily sent his troops contra nequitiam Andronici . . . ad acquirendum imperium C. P. They were capti aut confusi . . . decepti captique, by Isaac.

[2] By the failure of Cinnamus, we are now reduced to Nicetas (in Andronico, l. i. c. 7, 8, 9, l. ii. c. 1, in Isaac Angelo, l. i. c. 1-4), who now becomes a respectable contemporary. As he survived the emperor and the empire, he is above flattery: but the fall of Constantinople exasperated his prejudices against the Latins. For the honour of learning I shall observe that Homer's great commentator, Eustathius, archbishop of Thessalonica, refused to desert his flock.

the perfection of vice and virtue, cannot strictly be applied to
either of the Norman princes. When he was roused to arms by
danger and shame, the first William did not degenerate from the
valour of his race; but his temper was slothful; his manners
were dissolute; his passions headstrong and mischievous; and
the monarch is responsible, not only for his personal vices, but
for those of Majo, the great admiral, who abused the confidence,
and conspired against the life, of his benefactor. From the
Arabian conquest, Sicily had imbibed a deep tincture of Oriental
manners; the despotism, the pomp, and even the harem, of a
sultan; and a Christian people was oppressed and insulted by
the ascendant of the eunuchs, who openly professed, or secretly
cherished, the religion of Mohammed. An eloquent historian
of the times [1] has delineated the misfortunes of his country: [2]
the ambition and fall of the ungrateful Majo; the revolt and
punishment of his assassins; the imprisonment and deliverance
of the king himself; the private feuds that arose from the public
confusion; and the various forms of calamity and discord which
afflicted Palermo, the island, and the continent, during the reign
of William the First, and the minority of his son. The youth,
innocence, and beauty of William the Second, [3] endeared him to
the nation: the factions were reconciled; the laws were revived;
and from the manhood to the premature death of that amiable
prince, Sicily enjoyed a short season of peace, justice, and happiness, whose value was enhanced by the remembrance of the past

---

[1] The Historia Sicula of Hugo Falcandus, which properly extends from
1154 to 1169, is inserted in the seventh volume of Muratori's Collection
(tom. vii. p. 259-344), and preceded by an eloquent preface or epistle
(p. 251-258, de Calamitatibus Siciliæ). Falcandus has been styled the
Tacitus of Sicily; and, after a just, but immense, abatement, from the
first to the twelfth century, from a senator to a monk, I would not strip
him of his title: his narrative is rapid and perspicuous, his style bold and
elegant, his observation keen; he had studied mankind, and feels like a
man. I can only regret the narrow and barren field on which his labours
have been cast.

[2] The laborious Benedictines (l'Art de vérifier les Dates, p. 896) are of
opinion that the true name of Falcandus is Fulcandus or Foucault. According to them, Hugues Foucault, a Frenchman by birth, and at length
Abbot of St. Denys, had followed into Sicily his patron Stephen de la
Perche, uncle to the mother of William II., archbishop of Palermo, and
great chancellor of the kingdom. Yet Falcandus has all the feelings of a
Sicilian; and the title of *Alumnus* (which he bestows on himself) appears to
indicate that he was born, or at least educated, in the island.

[3] Falcand. p. 303. Richard de St. Germano begins his history from the
death and praises of William II. After some unmeaning epithets, he thus
continues: Legis et justitiæ cultus tempore suo vigebat in regno; suâ erat
quilibet sorte contentus; (were they mortals?) ubique pax, ubique
securitas, nec latronum metuebat viator insidias, nec maris nauta offendi-
cula piratarum (Script. Rerum Ital. tom. vii. p. 969).

and the dread of futurity. The legitimate male posterity of Tancred of Hauteville was extinct in the person of the second William; but his aunt, the daughter of Roger, had married the most powerful prince of the age; and Henry the Sixth, the son of Frederic Barbarossa, descended from the Alps, to claim the Imperial crown and the inheritance of his wife. Against the unanimous wish of a free people, this inheritance could only be acquired by arms; and I am pleased to transcribe the style and sense of the historian Falcandus, who writes at the moment, and on the spot, with the feelings of a patriot, and the prophetic eye of a statesman. "Constantia, the daughter of Sicily, nursed from her cradle in the pleasures and plenty, and educated in the arts and manners, of this fortunate isle, departed long since to enrich the barbarians with our treasures, and now returns, with her savage allies, to contaminate the beauties of her venerable parent. Already I behold the swarms of angry barbarians: our opulent cities, the places flourishing in a long peace, are shaken with fear, desolated by slaughter, consumed by rapine, and polluted by intemperance and lust. I see the massacre or captivity of our citizens, the rapes of our virgins and matrons.[1] In this extremity (he interrogates a friend) how must the Sicilians act? By the unanimous election of a king of valour and experience, Sicily and Calabria might yet be preserved;[2] for in the levity of the Apulians, ever eager for new revolutions, I can repose neither confidence nor hope.[3] Should Calabria be lost, the lofty towers, the numerous youth, and the naval strength of Messina,[4] might guard the passage against a foreign invader. If the savage Germans coalesce with the pirates of Messina; if they destroy with fire the fruitful region, so often

---

[1] Constantia, primis a cunabulis in deliciarum tuarum affluentiâ diutius educata, tuisque institutis, doctrinis et moribus informata, tandem opibus tuis Barbaros delatura discessit: et nunc cum ingentibus copiis revertitur, ut pulcherrimæ nutricis ornamenta barbaricâ fœditate contaminet. . . . Intueri mihi jam videor turbulentas barbarorum acies . . . civitates opulentas et loca diuturnâ pace florentia metû concutere, cæde vastare, rapinis atterere, et fœdare luxuriâ: [occurrunt] hinc cives aut gladiis intercepti, aut servitute depressi, virgines constupratæ, matronæ, etc. [p. 253 and 254.]

[2] Certe si regem [sibi] non dubiæ virtutis elegerint, nec a Saracenis Christiani dissentiant, poterit rex creatus rebus licet quasi desperatis et perditis subvenire, et incursus hostium, si prudenter egerit, propulsare. [p. 253 and 254.]

[3] In Apulis, qui, semper novitate gaudentes, novarum rerum studiis aguntur, nihil arbitror spei aut fiduciæ reponendum. [ib.]

[4] Si civium tuorum virtutem et audaciam attendas, . . . murorum etiam ambitum densis turribus circumseptum. [ib.]

wasted by the fires of Mount Ætna,[1] what resource will be left for the interior parts of the island, these noble cities which should never be violated by the hostile footsteps of a barbarian?[2] Catana has again been overwhelmed by an earthquake: the ancient virtue of Syracuse expires in poverty and solitude;[3] but Palermo is still crowned with a diadem, and her triple walls enclose the active multitudes of Christians and Saracens. If the two nations, under one king, can unite for their common safety, they may rush on the barbarians with invincible arms. But if the Saracens, fatigued by a repetition of injuries, should now retire and rebel; if they should occupy the castles of the mountains and sea-coast, the unfortunate Christians, exposed to a double attack, and placed as it were between the hammer and the anvil, must resign themselves to hopeless and inevitable servitude."[4] We must not forget that a priest here prefers his country to his religion: and that the Moslems, whose alliance he seeks, were still numerous and powerful in the state of Sicily.

The hopes, or at least the wishes, of Falcandus were at first gratified by the free and unanimous election of Tancred, the grandson of the first king, whose birth was illegitimate, but whose civil and military virtues shone without a blemish. During four years, the term of his life and reign, he stood in arms on the farthest verge of the Apulian frontier against the powers of Germany; and the restitution of a royal captive, of Constantia herself, without injury or ransom, may appear to surpass the most liberal measure of policy or reason. After his decease the kingdom of his widow and infant son fell without a struggle, and Henry pursued his victorious march from Capua to Palermo.

[1] Cum crudelitate piraticâ Theutonum confligat atrocitas, et inter ambustos lapides, et Ethnæ flagrantis incendia, etc. [ib.]

[2] Eam partem, quam nobilissimarum civitatum fulgor illustrat, quæ et toti regno singulari meruit privilegio præminere, nefarium esset . . . vel barbarorum ingressû pollui. I wish to transcribe his florid, but curious, description of the palace, city, and luxuriant plain of Palermo. [ib.]

[3] Vires non suppetunt, et conatus tuos tam inopia civium, quam paucitas bellatorum elidunt. [ib.]

[4] At vero, quia difficile est Christianos in tanto rerum turbine, sublato regis timore Saracenos non opprimere, si Saraceni injuriis fatigati ab eis cœperint dissidere, et castella forte maritima vel montanas munitiones occupaverint; ut hinc cum Theutonicis summâ [sit] virtute pugnandum, illinc Saracenis crebris insultibus occurrendum, quid putas acturi sunt Siculi inter has depressi augustias, et velut inter malleum et incudem multo cum discrimine constituti? hoc utique agent quod poterunt, ut se Barbaris miserabili conditione dedentes, in eorum se conferant potestatem. O utinam plebis et procerum Christianorum et Saracenorum vota conveniant; ut regem sibi concorditer eligentes, [irruentes] barbaros totis viribus, toto conamine, totisque desideriis proturbare contendant [p. 254]. The Normans and Sicilians appear to be confounded.

The political balance of Italy was destroyed by his success; and if the pope and the free cities had consulted their obvious and real interest, they would have combined the powers of earth and heaven to prevent the dangerous union of the German empire with the kingdom of Sicily. But the subtle policy, for which the Vatican has so often been praised or arraigned, was on this occasion blind and inactive; and if it were true that Celestine the Third had kicked away the Imperial crown from the head of the prostrate Henry,[1] such an act of impotent pride could serve only to cancel an obligation and provoke an enemy. The Genoese, who enjoyed a beneficial trade and establishment in Sicily, listened to the promise of his boundless gratitude and speedy departure:[2] their fleet commanded the straits of Messina, and opened the harbour of Palermo; and the first act of his government was to abolish the privileges and to seize the property of these imprudent allies. The last hope of Falcandus was defeated by the discord of the Christians and Mahommedans: they fought in the capital; several thousands of the latter were slain, but their surviving brethren fortified the mountains, and disturbed above thirty years the peace of the island. By the policy of Frederic the Second, sixty thousand Saracens were transplanted to Nocera in Apulia. In their wars against the Roman church, the emperor and his son Mainfroy were strengthened and disgraced by the service of the enemies of Christ; and this national colony maintained their religion and manners in the heart of Italy till they were extirpated, at the end of the thirteenth century, by the zeal and revenge of the house of Anjou.[3] All the calamities which the prophetic orator had deplored were surpassed by the cruelty and avarice of the German conqueror. He violated the royal sepulchres, and explored the secret treasures of the palace, Palermo, and the whole kingdom; the pearls and jewels, however precious, might be easily removed, but one hundred and sixty horses were laden

---

[1] The testimony of an Englishman, of Roger de Hoveden (p. 689), will lightly weigh against the silence of German and Italian history (Muratori, Annali d'Italia, tom. x. p. 156). The priests and pilgrims, who returned from Rome, exalted, by every tale, the omnipotence of the holy father.

[2] Ego enim in eo cum Teutonicis manere non debeo (Caffari, Annal. Genuenses, in Muratori, Script. Rerum Italicarum, tom. vi. p. 367, 368).

[3] For the Saracens of Sicily and Nocera, see the Annals of Muratori (tom. x. p. 149, and A.D. 1223, 1247), Giannone (tom. ii. p. 385), and of the originals, in Muratori's Collection, Richard de St. Germano (tom. vii. p. 996), Matteo Spinelli de Giovenazzo (tom. vii. p. 1064), Nicholas de Jamsilla (tom. x. 494), and Matteo Villani (tom. xiv. l. vii. p. 103). The last of these insinuates that, in reducing the Saracens of Nocera, Charles II. of Anjou employed rather artifice than violence.

with the gold and silver of Sicily.[1]   The young king, his mother and sisters, and the nobles of both sexes, were separately confined in the fortresses of the Alps, and, on the slightest rumour of rebellion, the captives were deprived of life, of their eyes, or of the hope of posterity.   Constantia herself was touched with sympathy for the miseries of her country, and the heiress of the Norman line might struggle to check her despotic husband, and to save the patrimony of her new-born son, of an emperor so famous in the next age under the name of Frederic the Second. Ten years after this revolution, the French monarchs annexed to their crown the duchy of Normandy: the sceptre of her ancient dukes had been transmitted, by a grand-daughter of William the Conqueror, to the house of Plantagenet; and the adventurous Normans, who had raised so many trophies in France, England, and Ireland, in Apulia, Sicily, and the East, were lost, either in victory or servitude, among the vanquished nations.

[1] Muratori quotes a passage from Arnold of Lubec (l. iv. c. 20):   Reperit thesauros absconditos, et omnem lapidum pretiosorum et gemmarum gloriam, ita ut oneratis 160 somariis, gloriose ad terram suam redierit. Roger de Hoveden, who mentions the violation of the royal tombs and corpses, computes the spoil of Salerno at 200,000 ounces of gold (p. 746). On these occasions I am almost tempted to exclaim with the listening maid in La Fontaine, " Je voudrois bien avoir ce qui manque."
   [It is remarkable that at this very time the tombs of the Roman emperors were violated and ransacked by their degenerate successor Alexius Comnenus to enable him to pay the German tribute exacted by the menaces of the emperor Henry.—O. S.]

Everyman
A selection of titles

* indicates volumes available in paperback

Complete lists of Everyman's Library and Everyman Paperbacks are available from the Sales Department, J.M. Dent and Sons Ltd, Aldine House, 33 Welbeck Street, London W1M 8LX.

BIOGRAPHY

Autobiography of Richard Baxter
Bligh, William. *A Book of the 'Bounty'*
* Chesterfield, Lord. *Letters to His Son and Others*
Cibber, Colley. *An Apology for the Life of Colley Cibber*
* Dana, Richard Henry. *Two Years Before the Mast*
* De Quincey, Thomas. *Confessions of an English Opium-Eater*
Forster, John. *Life of Charles Dickens* (2 vols)
* Gaskell, Elizabeth. *The Life of Charlotte Brontë*
* Gilchrist, Alexander. *The Life of William Blake*
* Hudson, W.H. *Far Away and Long Ago*
* Johnson, Samuel. *Lives of the English Poets: a selection*
Pepys, Samuel. *Diary* (3 vols)
Thomas, Dylan
    Adventures in the Skin Trade
    Portrait of the Artist as a Young Dog
Tolstoy, Leo. *Childhood, Boyhood and Youth*
Vasari, Giorgio. *Lives of the Painters, Sculptors, and Architects*
    (4 vols)

ESSAYS AND CRITICISM

Arnold, Matthew. *On the Study of Celtic Literature*
* Bacon, Francis. *Essays*
* Coleridge, Samuel Taylor. *Biographia Literaria*
* Jerome, Jerome K. *Idle Thoughts of an Idle Fellow*
* Emerson, Ralph. *Essays*

* Milton, John. *Prose Writings*
  Montaigne, Michael Eyquem de. *Essays* (3 vols)
  Spencer, Herbert. *Essays on Education and Kindred Subjects*
* Swift, Jonathan. *Tale of a Tub and other satires*

FICTION

Alcott, Louisa May. *Little Women*
* *American Short Stories of the Nineteenth Century*
  Austen, Jane.
  * *Emma*
  * *Mansfield Park*
  * *Northanger Abbey*
  * *Persuasion*
  * *Pride and Prejudice*
  * *Sense and Sensibility*
* *Australian Short Stories*
  Bennett, Arnold
  * *The Card*
  * *The Old Wives' Tale*
  Boccaccio, Giovanni. *The Decameron*
  Brontë, Anne
  * *Agnes Grey*
  * *The Tenant of Wildfell Hall*
  Brontë, Charlotte
  * *Jane Eyre*
  * *The Professor* and *Emma* (a fragment)
  * *Shirley*
  * *Villette*
* Brontë, Emily. *Wuthering Heights* and *Poems*
* Bunyan, John. *Pilgrim's Progress*
* Carroll, Lewis. *Alice in Wonderland*
  Collins, Wilkie
  * *The Moonstone*
  * *The Woman in White*
  Conrad, Joseph
  * *The Nigger of the 'Narcissus', Typhoon, Falk and other
    stories*
  * *Youth, Heart of Darkness* and *The End of the Tether*

Somerville and Ross. *Some Experiences of an Irish R.M.*
    and *Further Experiences of an Irish R.M.*
Sterne, Lawrence. *Tristram Shandy*
Stevenson, R.L.
    *Dr Jekyll and Mr Hyde, The Merry Men and other tales
    *Kidnapped
    *The Master of Ballantrae and *Weir of Hermiston*
    *Treasure Island
Stowe, Harriet Beecher. *Uncle Tom's Cabin*
*Swift, Jonathan. *Gulliver's Travels*
*Thackeray, W.M. *Vanity Fair*
Thirteen Famous Ghost Stories
*Thomas, Dylan. *The Collected Stories*
*Tolstoy, Leo. *Master and Man and other parables and tales*
Trollope, Anthony
    Barchester Towers
    Dr Thorne
    Last Chronicle of Barset
    Small House at Allington
    *The Warden
*Twain, Mark. *Tom Sawyer* and *Huckleberry Finn*
*Voltaire. *Candide and other tales*
Wells, H.G.
    *The Time Machine
    *The Wheels of Chance
*Victorian Short Stories
*Wilde, Oscar. *The Picture of Dorian Gray*
*Wood, Mrs Henry. *East Lynne*
Woolf, Virginia. *To the Lighthouse*

HISTORY

---

*The Anglo-Saxon Chronicle
*Burnet, Gilbert. *History of His Own Time*
Gibbon, Edward. *The Decline and Fall of the Roman Empire*
    (6 vols)
*Hollingshead, John. *Ragged London in 1861*
*Stow, John. *The Survey of London*
*Woodhouse, A.S.P. *Puritanism and Liberty*

LEGENDS AND SAGAS

* *Beowulf and Its Analogues*
* Chrétien de Troyes. *Arthurian Romances*
* *Egils saga*
* *Kudrun*
* Wace and Layamon. *Arthurian Chronicles*
* *The Mabinogion*
* *The Saga of Gisli*
* *The Saga of Grettir the Strong*
* Snorri Sturluson. *Edda*
* *The Story of Burnt Njal*

POETRY AND DRAMA

* *Anglo-Saxon Poetry*
* Arnold, Matthew. *Selected Poems and Prose*
* Blake, William. *Selected Poems*
* Brontës, The. *Selected Poems*
* Browning, Robert. *Men and Women and other poems*
* Burns, Robert. *The Kilmarnock Poems*
* Chaucer, Geoffrey. *Canterbury Tales*
* Clare, John. *Selected Poems*
* Coleridge, Samuel Taylor. *Poems*
* Donne, John. *The Complete English Poems*
* *Elizabethan Sonnets*
* *English Moral Interludes*
* *Everyman and Medieval Miracle Plays*
* *Everyman's Book of Evergreen Verse*
* *Everyman's Book of Victorian Verse*
* Gay, John. *The Beggar's Opera and other eighteenth-century plays*
* *The Golden Treasury of Longer Poems*
* Hardy, Thomas. *Selected Poems*
* Herbert, George. *The English Poems*
* Hopkins, Gerard Manley. *The Major Poems*
  Ibsen, Henrik
  * *A Doll's House; The Wild Duck; The Lady from the Sea*
  * *Hedda Gabler; The Master Builder; John Gabriel Borkman*

* Keats, John. *Poems*
* Langland, William. *The Vision of Piers Plowman*
* Marlowe, Christopher. *Complete Plays and Poems*
* Marvell, Andrew. *Complete Poetry*
* Middleton, Thomas. *Three Plays*
* Milton, John. *Complete Poems*
* *Palgrave's Golden Treasury*
* *Pearl, Cleanness, Patience* and *Sir Gawain and the Green Knight*
* *Poems of the Second World War*
* Pope, Alexander. *Collected Poems*
* *Restoration Plays*
* *The Rubáiyát of Omar Khayyám and other Persian poems*
* Shelley, Percy Bysshe. *Selected Poems*
* Spencer, Edmund. *The Faerie Queene: Books I to III*
* *The Stuffed Owl*
* Synge, J.M. *Plays, Poems and Prose*
* Tennyson, Alfred. *In Memoriam, Maud and other poems*
  Thomas, Dylan
    * *Collected Poems, 1934–1952*
    * *The Poems*
    * *Under Milk Wood*
* Wilde, Oscar. *Plays, Prose Writings and Poems*
* Wordsworth, William. *Selected Poems*

RELIGION AND PHILOSOPHY

* Bacon, Francis. *The Advancement of Learning*
* Berkeley, George. *Philosophical Works*
* *The Buddha's Philosophy of Man*
* Carlyle, Thomas. *Sartor Resartus*
* *Chinese Philosophy in Classical Times*
* Descartes, René. *A Discourse on Method*
* *Hindu Scriptures*
* Kant, Immanuel. *A Critique of Pure Reason*
* *The Koran*
* Leibniz, Gottfried Wilhelm. *Philosophical Writings*
* Locke, John. *An Essay Concerning Human Understanding (abridgment)*
* More, Thomas. *Utopia*

Pascal, Blaise. *Pensées*
Plato. *The Trial and Death of Socrates*
* *The Ramayana and Mahábhárata*
* Spinoza, Benedictus de. *Ethics*

SCIENCES: POLITICAL AND GENERAL

Aristotle. *Ethics*
Coleridge, Samuel Taylor. *On the Constitution of the Church
    and State*
* Darwin, Charles. *The Origin of Species*
Derry, John. *English Politics & the American Revolution*
Harvey, William. *The Circulation of the Blood and other
    writings*
* Hobbes, Thomas. *Leviathan*
* Locke, John. *Two Treatises of Government*
* Machiavelli, Niccolò. *The Prince and other political writings*
* Malthus, Thomas. *An Essay on the Principle of Population*
* Mill, J.S. *Utilitarianism; On Liberty; Representative
    Government*
* Plato. *The Republic*
* Ricardo, David. *Principles of Political Economy and
    Taxation*
Rousseau, J.-J.
    * *Emile*
    * *The Social Contract* and *Discourses*
* Wollstonecraft, Mary. *A Vindication of the Rights of Woman*

TRAVEL AND TOPOGRAPHY

Boswell, James. *The Journal of a Tour to the Hebrides*
* Darwin, Charles. *The Voyage of the 'Beagle'*
* Hudson, W.H. *Idle Days in Patagonia*
* Kingsley, Mary. *Travels in West Africa*
* Stevenson, R.L. *An Inland Voyage; Travels with a Donkey; The
    Silverado Squatters*
* Thomas, Edward. *The South Country*
* *Travels of Marco Polo*
* White, Gilbert. *The Natural History of Selborne*